The Jews in the Soviet Union since 1917

Paradox of Survival

Volume I

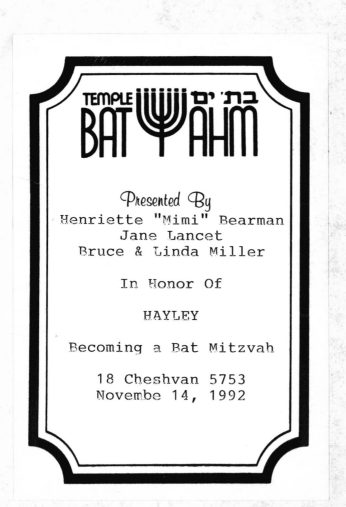

The Jews in the
Soviet Union since 1917

Paradox of Survival

Volume I

Nora Levin

NEW YORK UNIVERSITY PRESS
New York and London

First published in paperback in 1990

Library of Congress Cataloging-in-Publication Data
Levin, Nora.
  The Jews in the Soviet Union since 1917
  Bibliography: p.
  includes index.
    1. Jews — Soviet Union — History — 1917-
  2. Soviet Union — Ethnic relations.   I. Title.
  DS135.R92L48   1987   947'.004924   87-21951
  ISBN 0-8147-5018-4 (set)   ISBN 0-8147-5050-8 pbk. (set)
  ISBN 0-8147-5034-6 (v. 1)   ISBN 0-8147-5051-6 pbk. (v. 1)
  ISBN 0-8147-5035-4 (v. 2)   ISBN 0-8147-5052-4 pbk. (v. 2)

Book design by Ken Venezio

New York University Press books are printed on acid-free paper,
and their binding materials are chosen for strength and durability.

Dedicated to the many thousands of men and women in the Soviet Union who have suffered and perished struggling to maintain personal honor, integrity, and freedom for the sake of Jewish survival, despite terror, wasting exile, and the breakdown of trust.

Contents

Volume II

Photographs

Volume II

Maps

Tables

Preface

In writing this book, I have had in mind nonspecialist readers and undergraduate students who may be interested in some of the major experiences of Soviet Jews since 1917. I have tried to utilize all of the reliable secondary sources and certain primary sources as well in composing a history of a Jewish minority that is generally little known except for the emergence of the refusenik-emigration movement of the last fifteen years. The work is written in a fairly traditional style inasmuch as I find no rapport or much sympathy with certain of the modern strained efforts to find "inner structures" in the history of human communities, or quantitative techniques, involving the construction of models, uniformities, coded factors, and hypotheses, that presumably create a scientific cast to the writing of history, but more often a disturbing dogmatism. Roads to understanding the past are obviously varied, and one must choose the one that seems to yield this understanding best.

The past I have tried to describe has been one of hope, great suffering, achievement, illusion, opportunity, despair, submission, and struggle. Together with millions of other Soviet peoples, Soviet Jews have had to endure destructive purges, war, terror, unpredictable and sudden changes in party policy, long isolation from the West, and periods of great material want. But beyond those common experiences, Soviet Jews have also been victims of old and new forms of anti-Semitism, the Nazi decimation of over a million of their number, and official inability or unwillingness to understand Jewish history except in rigid class-struggle terms, or the Jewish Diaspora except in the image of an international conspiracy. Moreover, Soviet Jews constitute a very small minority about which there has been much theoretical ambiguity and inconsistency, yet disproportionately great attention in practice.

The fate of Jewish culture under Soviet rule has been entangled in many contradictory elements I have tried to analyze: the antinationalist and antireligious ideology of Marxism-Leninism and doctrinaire predictions of the ultimate disappearance of Jews; Lenin's vehement opposition to the Jewish Labor Bund and its view of national-cultural autonomy; Soviet industrial and agricultural upheavals; political and economic expediency; domestic and foreign policy needs; the anti-Semitism of key Soviet leaders, especially Stalin; and victimization of Jews during political power struggles. Jews have the legal status of a "nationality" and are required to carry internal passports identifying themselves as "Evrei"—Jews, but their cultural rights and forms of expression, except in the early years of the Bolshevik regime, the temporary experiment of Birobidzhan, and Stalin's opportunistic creation of the Jewish Antifascist Committee during the war, have been virtually nonexistent. Yet, despite official repression and destruction, some Jews in the Soviet Union struggled to keep alive vestiges of tradition, memories, and study, many years before the emergence of a Jewish national movement after the Six-Day War in 1967.

Interest in Soviet Jewry has been aroused in recent years as the story of the struggle of activists has burst upon the contemporary scene. A Jewish national movement has come into being in a society that had been abandoned as a place where Jewish culture could survive. The repercussions cannot yet be fully assessed, but they will be deep and long-lasting. Important as this movement is, however, it cannot be understood without a deeper knowledge of the past out of which it rose.

Long before the recent movement arose, some Jews in the Soviet Union were secretly celebrating holidays, studying Hebrew, reciting prayers, recalling *their* past, wondering about a much longer history that had been sealed up, and about Jews in other lands whom they could not know. The furtive springs of these earlier times have helped to nourish today's activism. Moreover, the experience of World War II, the evidence of European and Soviet anti-Semitism and the murder of over one million Soviet Jews, which brought grievous losses to every Jewish family, aroused intense feelings even among the most assimilated. The singular victimization of Jews during the Holocaust and the struggle for a Jewish national home in Palestine drew many Soviet Jews into a sense of community and shared fate that Soviet communism had not been able to dissolve.

The regime itself briefly and cynically raised Jewish national consciousness to a new, hopeful pitch when it created the Jewish Antifascist Committee in 1942 and spoke openly of the Nazis as the deadly foe of the *Jewish people,* a phrase that had long been condemned. But as suddenly as the policy was switched on it was switched off, with murderous consequences. Yet new generations of Soviet Jews know the names of Mikhoels, Bergelson, and Markish and something of their achievements. The light shed by the great writers who were murdered in 1952 has been inextinguishable.

However, for Soviet Jews who wanted to retain links with pre-Bolshevik Jewish cultural traditions, light has been very dim since 1917. The early Bolshevik period offered some hope for a sovietized brand of Jewish culture, and there have been a few cycles of official concessions, but the general Jewish landscape has been bleak. By comparison, despite its grinding poverty and oppression, Jewish life in the Pale of Settlement seems variegated, animated, and vivid. One wonders if new generations of Russian Jews will ever know the story of those earlier Russian Jews. Some threads have been traced and transmitted by old-generation Zionists, lovers of Jewish books, and through books that have been brought into the Soviet Union by visitors and by exhibitors during the recent Moscow book fairs. Nor was everything obliterated by the purges, terror, prison camps, and wasting exile. But the struggle to salvage and give meaning to an old culture in a hostile society has been painful and dangerous.

Much still remains hidden in the history of Soviet Jewry, but we have learned more in recent years as some of the seals have been broken. Large segments of this Jewry now live in Israel and the United States, bringing with them buried memories and release from decades of fear. They have a genuine interest as well as curiosity about their past, and misconceptions that the gritty facts of history may be able to set aside.

This history is complex and sometimes impenetrable because of the nature of Soviet society and the complicated adaptations needed to survive. Assimilation has been widespread, but a specifically Jewish history can be traced, not only because the "Jewish problem" has never been resolved, but also because some Soviet Jews have always insisted on wanting to maintain and transmit some aspects of their Jewishness, despite crushing official pressures and punishment. Moreover, these needs were at times tantalizingly encouraged by the regime, and the opportunities, though severely limited, were eagerly grasped.

The inconsistencies and contradictions of Soviet Jewish policy have battered Jews since 1917, making a steady adjustment to each change a very difficult one, reminding one at times of similar wildly fluctuating policies of tsarist Russia. Yet there are great differences. Tsarist Russia was harsh and oppressive, but compared to Soviet totalitarian power, it was slack. Moreover, Jews of tsarist Russia had the security and support of autonomous communities, a rich and diverse religious and cultural life and leadership, and the continuity of certain traditions. Shtetl life may have been declining in the late nineteenth century, but secular ideologies such as Zionism and Jewish socialism were offering new solutions to the Jewish predicament. The March Revolution brought a burst of new hope and energy to Jews, but the Bolshevik Revolution changed everything. "New men" were to be created, not excluding Jews.

In my account of these transformations, I have emphasized experiences that have been generally overlooked: for example, the struggle of most Jews to resist sovietization in the early years of the Revolution, despite the leading roles some Jews played in establishing the communist regime. Readers may be familiar with the *Evsektsiya* and their zealous attacks on traditional Jewish life, but not with the persistent opposition and resistance to them. That Jews were eventually forced to succumb to the Leninist version of Jewish "nationality" does not detract from their struggle.

Lenin's polemic against the Bund is also described in considerable detail because it forms the bedrock Soviet doctrine against "Jewish nationalism" and a differentiated culture. This formulation still prevails despite Soviet rhetoric about the rights of national minorities. There was, of course, more scope for creative Jewish activity within the Soviet frame under Lenin than during the Stalin dictatorship and later, but the mold was set by Lenin. I have also focused attention on the uprooting of one-tenth of the Jewish population and their resettlement on the land in the 1920s—a massive restructuring of Jewish life which was traumatic but interesting and successful. However, Stalin suddenly aborted it and plunged the country into punishing collectivization and industrialization plans. For Jews, the new panacea was to be Birobidzhan.

The regime's "Jewish policy" has been full of such jolts and stop-start decisions, leading one to conclude that there never has been a Jewish policy, but that a deeply rooted Russian anti-Semitism, possibly dating back to the fear of a so-called "Judaizing heresy" and, even earlier, to the conversion of the Khazars to Judaism, lies under the tortured renderings of Soviet nationality policy vis-à-vis Jews and the brief, unsuccessful efforts to curb anti-Semitism. This persistent residue thus links Soviet with tsarist Russia, but the Soviet Union has added the disguises of crafty statecraft. Every important decision affecting Jews has been a function of some internal or global policy—as in the case of the Jewish Antifascist Committee—or a way of camouflaging an inside power struggle. In 1949–53, the destruction of whatever existed of Jewish culture was a Soviet reflex against the Cold War and Israel's slippage toward the West. Emigration relaxation and sudden stoppage have been linked to a brief easing of East-West tensions in the 1970s and hardening after 1980. More recently, the policy has softened somewhat.

Hopes have been expressed for a general loosening and liberalization of Soviet life under Mikhail Gorbachev, but an earlier thaw under Khrushchev did nothing to liberalize Jewish cultural expression. The Soviet-produced anti-Semitic and anti-Zionist propaganda has now penetrated much of the globe; its baleful effects cannot be undone. However, they may be stanched if relations between Israel and the Soviet Union are resumed, and if the Soviet Union is given some role in future Middle East peace talks. The possibilities of transmitting and creating a Jewish culture in Yiddish and Russian also exist and ought not to be written off.

From the very beginning of its existence, the Soviet Union has been plagued by a persisting nationality problem. All minority nationals, as well as Jews, have suffered under Soviet domination, especially those such as the Germans and Armenians, who, like the Jews, have diasporas. The Soviet fear of outside contact and "otherness" borders on the pathological. Jews are the pre-eminent "other," and, although their fate has been unique, their history offers a rough paradigm of the struggle of non-Russians to be and to remain different. The future of these peoples is grim, especially so for Jews, but past history has shown surprising eruptions of spirit and will, none more so than in the story of Soviet Jewry

Acknowledgments

Many influences have helped to shape this book: the pre-Bolshevik culture of my parents; my friendship with many Soviet Jews in this country, in Israel, and in the Soviet Union; my deep interest in Russian literature; the challenges of my students at Gratz College as I developed courses in Soviet Jewish history in the past ten years; and the scholarship of Solomon M. Schwarz, Leonard Schapiro, Salo W. Baron, Yehoshua A. Gilboa, Chone Shmeruk, Benjamin Pinkus, Shimon Redlich, Zvi Y. Gitelman, Alfred A. Greenbaum, Martin Gilbert, and Lukasz Hirszowicz.

These are somewhat general acknowledgments. More specifically I am indebted to the YIVO Institute for Jewish Research for permission to use its valuable Joseph Rosen Archive and to Fruma Mohrer for her personal help in securing materials; to Dina Abramowicz, librarian of YIVO, for her unfailing interest in and quick response to queries; to Bessy L. Pupko, administrative assistant in the New York office of the Institute of Jewish Affairs, World Jewish Congress, for her help in making available materials dealing with the Jewish Antifascist Committee; and to the Gratz College Holocaust Oral History Archive for access to taped interviews with Soviet Jews.

I also wish to acknowledge the interesting and informative correspondence from Shlomo Tzirulnikov, Dr. Benjamin Fain, Dina Beilina, Paul Novick, Hayim Sheynin, the late Nahum Goldmann, Minna Shore, Rabbi Dr. Moses Rosen, Itche Goldberg, Dr. Michael Zand, Dr. Aron Katsenelinboigen, Morris U. Schappes, and Rakhmiel Peltz.

Several friends have been very generous in sharing sources and in lending me materials for exceedingly long periods. For this help and their patience, I am especially grateful to Nelly Vortmann, Max Rosenfeld, Shimon Kipnis, Connie Smukler, and the late Ben Shamus.

Bernard Stehle and Dr. Nathaniel Entin have done their professional utmost to bring old photographs to new clarity and have invested much time in this effort, for which I am very grateful. Special thanks are also due Judith Stehle for her care in drawing the maps I sketched.

I also wish to thank my old friends Joseph Yenish, Nechama Glick, Eleanor Vorobyevskaya, Dr. Leon Friedman, and Renee Campbell for their help in providing translations of several sources. To my friend Edith Finch, I owe an immense debt for her painstaking, critical help in reading the galleys. To another friend of many years Elsie Levitan, a special thanks for her support, encouragement, and helpful suggestions after reading the entire manuscript.

I also wish to acknowledge the initial and sustained interest and confidence in the manuscript of Kitty Moore, senior editor of New York University Press; and the patient care and technical help of Despina P. Gimbel, managing editor, and editorial assistants Placida Grace Hernández and Jason W. Renker. My gratitude to Dr. Ann Hirst, a very gifted copy editor, is boundless. For the ultimate work, of course, I am fully responsible.

For permission to quote selections from copyrighted works, the author is indebted to:

American Heritage Press, a division of McGraw-Hill Book Co., New York: Peter Reddaway, ed., *Uncensored Russia*, © 1972.

American Jewish Committee, New York: Solomon M. Schwarz, *The Jews in the Soviet Union*, © 1951, reprinted 1972.

Amnesty International Publications, London: *A Chronicle of Current Events*, No. 47, © 1978; No. 50, © 1979.

Associated University Presses, London: Yehoshua A. Gilboa, *A Language Silenced: The Suppression of Hebrew Literature and Culture in the Soviet Union*, © 1982.

Ballatine Books, a division of Random House, Inc., New York: Esther Markish, *The Long Return*, tr. by David Goldstein, © 1974, Opera Mundi.

Beacon Press, Boston: Joshua Rubenstein, *Soviet Dissidents: Their Struggle for Human Rights*, © 1980.

Cambridge University Press, Cambridge: Benjamin Pinkus, *The Soviet Government and the Jews: A Documented Study, 1948–1967*, © 1984.

Center for Research and Documentation of East European Jewry, Jerusalem: Alfred A. Greenbaum, *Jewish Scholarship and Scholarly Institutions in Soviet Russia, 1918–1953*, © 1977, by the author.

Conference on Jewish Social Studies, New York: Shimon Redlich, "The

Jewish Antifascist Committee in the Soviet Union," *Jewish Social Studies*, Vol. 31 (1969); Isaac London, "Days of Anxiety," *Jewish Social Studies*, Vol. 15 (1953).

Crown Publishers, New York: B. Z. Goldberg, *The Jewish Problem in the Soviet Union*, © 1961. Used by permission of Crown Publishers, Inc.

Current Digest of the Soviet Press, Columbus, Ohio: Evgeny Evtushenko, "The Heirs of Stalin," translation copyright by the *Current Digest*. Reprinted by permission of the *Digest*.

Doubleday and Co., Inc., New York: Gunther Lawrence, Three Million More, © 1970.

East European Quarterly, Boulder, Colo. Shimon Redlich, *Propaganda and Nationalism in Wartime Russia: The Jewish Antifascist Committee in the USSR, 1941–1948*, © 1982.

Harcourt Brace Jovanovich, Orlando, Fla.: Evgenia Ginzburg, *Within the Whirlwind*, © 1979 by Arnold Mondadori Editore S.p.A., Milano; English translation © 1981 by Harcourt Brace Jovanovich, Inc., and William Collins and Co., Ltd. Reprinted by permission of Harcourt Brace Jovanovich.

Holocaust Library, New York: Ilya Ehrenburg and Vasily Grossman, eds., *The Black Book*, © 1981 by Holocaust Publications, Inc.

Henry Holt and Co., New York: Irving Howe, ed., *A Treasury of Yiddish Poetry*, © 1969 by Irving Howe and Eliazer Greenberg.

Institute of Jewish Affairs, London: Benjamin Pinkus, "Yiddish Language Courts and Nationalities Policy in the Soviet Union," *Soviet Jewish Affairs*, No. 2 (1971); Aryeh Y. Yodfat, "The Closure of the Synagogues in the Soviet Union," *Soviet Jewish Affairs*, Vol. 3, no. 1 (1973); David Garber, "Choir and Drama in Riga," *Soviet Jewish Affairs*, Vol. 4, no. 1 (1974); Mikhail Agursky, "My Father and the Great Terror," *Soviet Jewish Affairs*, Vol. 5, no. 2 (1975); Zvi Halevy, "Jewish Students in the Soviet Universities in the 1920s," *Soviet Jewish Affairs*, Vol. 6, no. 1 (1976); Dov Levin, "The Jews and the Inception of Soviet Rule in Bukovina"; and Willa Orbach, "The Destruction of the Jews in the Nazi-Occupied Territories of the USSR," *Soviet Jewish Affairs*, Vol. 6, no. 2 (1976); "Documents: The Soviet Union and the Jews during World War II," Introduced and annotated by Lukasz Hirszowicz; Y. Ro'i, "Soviet Policies and Attitudes toward Israel, 1948–1978," *Soviet Jewish Affairs*, Vol 8, no. 1 (1978); Z. Alexander, "Jewish Emigration from the USSR in 1980," *Soviet Jewish Affairs*, Vol. 11, no. 2 (1981); Z. Nezer, "Jewish Emigration from the USSR in 1981–82,"

Soviet Jewish Affairs, Vol. 12, no. 3 (1982); Robert J. Brym, "Soviet Emigration Policy: Internal Determinants," *Soviet Jewish Affairs*, Vol. 15, no. 2 (1985); and L. Hirszowicz, "The 27th Soviet Party Congress," *Soviet Jewish Affairs*, Vol. 16, no. 2 (1986). All issues © by the Institute of Jewish Affairs.

Jewish Publication Society of America, Philadelphia: Yosef Hayim Yerushalmi, *Haggadah and History*, © 1975 by the Jewish Publication Society.

Ktav Publishing House, New York: Zosa Szajkowski, *Jews, Wars, and Communism*, Vol. I, © 1972; Elias Schulman, *A History of Jewish Education in the Soviet Union*, © 1971.

Little, Brown and Co., Boston: Yehoshua A. Gilboa, *The Black Years of Soviet Jewry, 1939–1953*, © 1971.

Macmillan Publishing Co., New York: Salo W. Baron, *The Russian Jew under Tsars and Soviets*, 2d ed., © 1976; Robert Conquest, *The Great Terror*, © 1968; Basil Dmytryshyn, *USSR: A Concise History*, 3d ed., © 1978.

Oxford University Press, Oxford: L. Kochan, ed., *The Jews in Soviet Russia Since 1917*, 3d ed., © 1978.

Pantheon Books, New York: Boris Pasternak, *Doctor Zhivago*, tr. by Max Hayward and Marya Harari, © 1958.

Popular Library, New York: Richard Cohen, *Let My People Go*, © 1971.

Princeton University Press, Princeton: Zvi Y. Gitelman, *Jewish Nationality and Soviet Politics: The Jewish Section of the CPSU*, © 1972; by Princeton University Press.

Quadrangle Press, Chicago: Ronald I. Rubin, ed., *The Unredeemed: Anti-Semitism in the Soviet Union*, © 1968.

Transaction Inc., New Brunswick, N.J.: Yaacov Ro'i, *From Encroachment to Involvement*, pp. 38–39, © 1974 by the Shiloah Center for Middle Eastern and African Studies, Tel Aviv University, Israel.

Universe Books, New York: Leonard Schroeter, *The Last Exodus*, © 1974.

Viking Press, New York: William Korey, *The Soviet Cage*, © 1973.

Westview Press, Boulder, Colo.: Thomas E. Sawyer, *The Jewish Minority in the Soviet Union*, © 1979.

Thomas Yoseloff, New York: Gregory Aaronson, et al., eds., *Russian Jewry, 1917–1967*, © 1969; Joseph B. Schechtman, *Star in Eclipse*, © 1961.

Chronology of Events
Related to the Text

1897 Meeting of the First Zionist Congress in Basel, Switzerland, and the founding of the Jewish Labor Bund (General League of Jewish Workers in Lithuania, Poland, and Russia).

1898 Founding of the Russian Social Democratic Workers Party (RSDWP).

1903 Pogrom in Kishinev.

1905 Failure of 1905 Revolution in Russia.

1905–06 Pogroms in Minsk, Bialystok, Kovno, Lodz, Zhitomir, Brest-Litovsk, Melitopol, and Simferopol.

1911–13 Case against and Trial of Mendel Beilis.

1912 Complete breakaway of Bolsheviks from other RSDWP factions.

1913 Publication of Stalin's essay, "Marxism and the National and Colonial Question."

1914–17 German occupation of Polish provinces and western Russia, including important Jewish centers such as Vilna, Kovno, Grodno, and Bialystok.

March 12, 1917 (Gregorian calendar; February 27, according to Julian calendar). Fall of tsarist regime. Provisional Government established March 16. Pale of Settlement abolished; Jews granted full equality.

April 3, 1917 Lenin returns to Petrograd from exile.

May 24, 1917 All-Russian Zionist Congress meeting in Petrograd.

November 7, 1917 (October 25, according to Julian calendar) Seizure of power by the Bolsheviks.

(All subsequent dates according to Gregorian calendar)

January 1918 Constituent Assembly dissolved by Central Executive Committee of Bolshevik Party.

March 3, 1918 Trotsky signs Brest-Litovsk Treaty. Soviet Russia temporarily loses Georgia and the Ukraine; Lithuania, Latvia, Estonia and Bessarabia until 1940; Finland and Poland become independent.

1918 Creation of Commissariat for Jewish National Affairs *(Evkom)* and

Jewish Sections of the Communist Party *(Evreiskie Sektsii,* or *Evsektsii,* popularly known as the *Evsektsiya).*

1918–21 Pogroms in the Ukraine and White Russia.

March 1919 Adoption of War Communism by Eighth Party Congress.

1919–22 Civil war and foreign interventions in Russia.

1921–22 Purges of Bundists, Mensheviks, and other non-Bolsheviks from Communist Party.

March 1921–27 Period of New Economic Policy (NEP).

December 1922 Soviet republics federated under Union of Soviet Socialist Republics (USSR).

January 21, 1924 Death of Lenin.

January 31, 1924 Ratification of Constitution of USSR, consisting of Russian Soviet Federated Socialist Republic (RSFSR), Ukrainian SSR, Belorussian SSR, and Transcaucasian SFSR.

August 1924 Creation of Commission for Settlement of Jewish Workers on the Land (KOMZET in Russian, KOMERD in Yiddish).

November 1924 Formal creation of American Jewish Agricultural Corporation (Agro-Joint) to help settle Jews on the land.

1924–28 Precollectivization resettlement of Jews on the land.

January 1925 Creation of Society to Settle Jewish Workers on the Land (OZET in Russian, GEZERD in Yiddish).

1926–27 Struggle of "United Opposition" against Stalin; beginning of Stalin's drive for absolute power over party and state.

1928 Shakhty Trial; Birobidzhan allocated to KOMZET for Jewish settlement.

1928–33 First Five Year Plan; collectivization of agriculture; consolidation of Stalin's power.

1929 Trotsky exiled.

1930 Dissolution of *Evsektsiya.*

November 1933 Official recognition of USSR by United States.

May 1934 Creation of Birobidzhan as Jewish Autonomous Region (JAR).

August 1934 Meeting of First All-Union Congress of Soviet Writers and endorsement of "socialist realism" in literature.

December 1, 1934 Assassination of Sergei Kirov, party leader in Leningrad.

1935–37 Soviet "Popular Front" policy.

1936–38 Purge trials of old Bolsheviks, expulsions and arrests of party members and military leadership; arrest, exile, and execution of many Jewish cultural and political leaders; destruction of many Jewish institutions, journals, newspapers, theaters; closing down of Agro-Joint.

September 29, 1938 Surrender of Sudetanland, Czechoslovakia, to Germany at Munich.

August 23, 1939 Nazi-Soviet Non-Aggression Pact.

September 1, 1939 German invasion of Poland.

1939–40 Soviet absorption of eastern Poland, western Ukraine, western Belorussia, Latvia, Estonia, Lithuania, Bessarabia, and northern Bukovina.

June 22, 1941 German invasion of Soviet Union.

1941–42 Mass murder of Jews by *Einsatzgruppen* and in mass executions at Babi Yar, Ponary, and other killing sites in the Soviet Union.

April 1942 Creation of Jewish Antifascist Committee.

January 30, 1943 Soviet victory at Stalingrad, considered critical turning point of war.

May 22, 1943 Dissolution of Comintern.

June–December 1943 Visit of Mikhoels and Feffer to Jewish communities in the United States, Mexico, Canada, and England.

February 1945 Yalta Conference, recognition of dominant Soviet influence in Romania, Hungary, and Bulgaria, absorption of Baltic states, and Curzon Line in Poland; division of Germany into four occupation zones; trials of war criminals.

May 7, 1945 Unconditional surrender of Germany, ending the war.

1946 Stepped up anti-American Cold War rhetoric; Zhdanov's attacks against "rootless cosmopolitans," Western influences in art and literature, and general retreat to Russian nationalism.

1947 Establishment of Cominform (September); Truman Doctrine, granting American aid to Greece and Turkey, attacked by Soviet Union; Soviet support for Jewish State at U.N.

January 13, 1948 Death of Mikhoels, famous Yiddish actor and director of Moscow State Yiddish Theater.

May 14, 1948 Creation of State of Israel; recognition by Soviet Union on May 16.

August 31, 1948 Death of Zhdanov.

September 21, 1948 Publication of Ehrenburg's article, "About a Certain Letter" in *Pravda*.

October 1948 Arrival of Golda Myerson (Meir), first Israeli envoy to the Soviet Union.

November 1948–49 Dissolution of Jewish Antifascist Committee, Yiddish theaters, Yiddish newspapers, choirs and drama groups; Emes Publishing House closed down; arrests of Jewish cultural leaders and writers; purges in Birobidzhan; beginning of Black Years (1948–53).

August 12, 1952 Execution of twenty-four leading Soviet Jewish writers, intellectuals, and artists.

November 1952 Trial of Rudolph Slansky and ten other Jewish Communists in Prague.

January 1953 Arrests of nine Soviet physicians, including six Jews, allegedly involved in "Doctors' Plot."

March 5, 1953 Death of Stalin.

September 13, 1953 Khrushchev becomes First Secretary of Communist Party.

1953–57 Various amnesty decrees freeing millions of Soviet prisoners.

1954 Publication of Ehrenburg's *The Thaw*, marking the beginning of a brief liberalization of literature and the arts.

February 14–26, 1956 Khrushchev's denunciation of Stalin's crimes at Twentieth Congress of the Communist Party; de-Stalinization followed.

October–November 1956 Soviet occupation of Hungary.

November 1957 Appearance of Pasternak's *Doctor Zhivago* in Italy.

1958–70 Publication of liberal journal *Novy Mir (New World)*, ed. by Alexander Tvardovsky.

August 1961 Appearance of Yiddish journal *Sovetish Heymland*.

November 1962 Publication of Solzhenitsyn's *One Day in the Life of Ivan Denisovich* in *Novy Mir*.

1963 Publication of Trofim Kichko's *Judaism Without Embellishment*, an openly anti-Semitic book.

1963 Publication of Hebrew-Russian Dictionary, edited by F. Shapiro, in Moscow.

October 1964–March 1971 Samizdat publication of *Political Diary*, ed. by Roy Medvedev.

October 15, 1964 Removal of Khrushchev and designation of Leonid Brezhnev as First Secretary of the Central Committee of the Communist Party of the Soviet Union.

February 1966 Trial of Andrei Sinyavsky and Yuri Daniel.

March–April 1966 Brezhnev named Secretary General of the Communist Party by the Twenty-third Party Congress.

December 3, 1966 Announcement by Kosygin that Jews may be permitted to emigrate in order to reunite families.

June 5–11, 1967 Six-Day War; Israeli victory results in Soviet decision to break diplomatic relations with Israel.

1968–71 Growth of independent Jewish national movement and dissident Democratic Movement.

1968 Publication of Sakharov's *Thoughts on Progress, Peaceful Coexistence and Intellectual Freedom* in samizdat and abroad.

April 1968 First appearance of *Chronicle of Current Events*, organ of Soviet Human Rights Movement.

August 1968 Invasion of Czechoslovakia by Warsaw Pact armies.

August 6, 1969 Letter of 18 Georgian Jewish families to U.N. requesting right to emigrate to Israel.

April 1970 First issue of *Iskhod* (Exodus), samizdat journal of Jewish emigration movement.

December 15–24, 1970 First Leningrad Trial.

February 23–25, 1971 First World Conference of Jewish Communities on Soviet Jewry, Brussels, Belgium.

March 1971 Beginning of substantial Jewish emigration.

May 11–20, 1971 Second Leningrad Trial.

1971 Trials of Jewish activists in Riga, Sverdlovsk, Odessa, Kishinev, Samarkand, and Leningrad.

December 1972 First issue of *Evrei v SSSR (Jews in the USSR),* devoted to Jewish history and culture and social and personal problems of Jews.

October 6–22, 1973 Yom Kippur War; Soviet support of Arab states.

December 1973 First volume of Solzhenitsyn's *Gulag Archipelago* published in Paris.

February 1974 Arrest and involuntary exile of Solzhenitsyn.

June 27–July 3, 1974 Nixon-Brezhnev summit in Moscow.

December 1974 Passage of Jackson-Vanik Amendment to U.S. Trade Act of 1972, linking most-favored nation treatment in trade to liberalized emigration from communist countries; passage of Stevenson Amendment to Export-Import Bank Act of 1974, limiting credits to Soviet Union.

August 1975 USSR signs Helsinki Agreement on European Security and Cooperation.

1976 Formation of Helsinki Watch Groups in various Soviet cities.

February 1976 Second Conference of Jewish Communities on Soviet Jewry in Brussels.

December 21–23, 1976 Scheduled Moscow symposium on Jewish culture blocked by Soviet authorities.

1977–79 Arrests and trials of many Jewish activists and members of Helsinki Watch Groups.

September 6–14, 1977 First Moscow International Book Fair.

July 10–14, 1978 Trial of Shcharansky, sentenced to three years' imprisonment and ten years in strict regime camp.

September 4–10, 1979 Second Moscow International Book Fair.

December 1979 Soviet invasion of Afghanistan, foreshadowing end of so-called détente (1972–80).

January 1980 Arrest and banishment of Sakharov to Gorky.

1980 Wave of strikes in Poland; formation of independent trade union movement, Solidarity.

November 1980–September 1983 Review of Helsinki Accords in Madrid.

September 2–8, 1981 Third Moscow International Book Fair.

March 1982 Release of Ida Nudel from exile; lived in Bendery, Moldavian SSR until October 1987 when she was permitted to emigrate.

November 12, 1982 Yuri Andropov succeeds Brezhnev who died on November 10, as Secretary General of the Communist Party.

April 21, 1983 Creation of "Soviet Public Anti-Zionist Committee."

May 1983 Visit of Soviet delegation to Israel, commemorating anniversary of VE Day in Forest of the Red Army, near Jerusalem.

September 6–12, 1983 Fourth Moscow International Book Fair.

1984 Publication of new Russian-Yiddish Dictionary in Moscow.

February 9, 1984 Andropov dies, is succeeded by Konstantin Chernenko.

March 10, 1985 Chernenko dies, is succeeded by Mikhail Gorbachev.

September 10–16, 1985 Fifth Moscow International Book Fair.

November 19–21, 1985 First summit meeting between President Ronald Reagan and Gorbachev.

February 11, 1986 Release of Shcharansky in a prisoner-spy exchange.

February 25–March 6, 1986 Twenty-seventh Congress of the Communist Party of the Soviet Union.

October 11–12, 1986 Reagan-Gorbachev meeting in Reykjavik, Iceland.

November 4–December 19, 1986 Helsinki Accords Review Conference, Vienna.

December 1986 Release of Sakharov and Elena Bonner from exile in Gorky. Death in prison camp of Anatoly Marchenko, non-Jewish dissident and long-time champion of Soviet political prisoners.

January 1, 1987 Announcement of new emigration regulations, restricting reunification rights to first-degree relatives.

September–October 1987 Release of all "Prisoners of Zion" and exit visas given to a number of long-term refuseniks, including Brailovsky, Begun, Nudel, and Slepak.

1

Pre-Bolshevik Jewish Parties and Lenin's View of Jewish Nationality

March 1917: Spring is in the air. The sun shines, but it does not warm. Nothing seems to warm any more. Everything is chaos and confusion. No Mirabeau among the conservatives, no Danton among the radicals. What will be the end? But wait! Someone has just burst in with great news. The Provisional Government has swept away all inequalities with one stroke . . . our suffering, Jewish suffering, is at an end. The dream, the hope of a lifetime, is fulfilled.

December 1917: The capital is freezing. No coal, no wood anywhere. . . . My wife went for wood . . . my heart sank when I saw her coming with an empty basket. . . . Now the last kopek is spent, and no food, no wood, no lighting material. . . . We moved into the kitchen, where, by shutting off the other rooms, we might keep from freezing. . . . We are all there and I am trying to work . . . Cold and hunger. . . .

SIMON DUBNOW, *Kniga Zhizni* (Book of Life)

He realized that he was a pigmy before the monstrous machine of the future; he was anxious about this future, and loved it and was secretly proud of it, and as though for the last time, as if in farewell, he avidly looked at the trees and clouds and the people walking in the streets, the great Russian city struggling through misfortune—and was ready to sacrifice himself for the general good, and could do nothing.

BORIS PASTERNAK, *Dr. Zhivago*

THE Bolshevik Revolution, which radically changed the lives of Russian Jews, had its origin in the crisis which swept away tsarism in March 1917. The collapse came toward the end of Russia's involvement in World War I, by which time the Russian army had lost its will to fight and the Russian people, their capacity to absorb more suffering. Mutinies by soldiers and police multiplied; food shortages led to strikes and riots; and talk of an imminent revolution was widespread. But the government was inert. Tsar Nicholas II and the tsarina, autocratic and stubborn by habit, were locked away from the real conditions of Russian life, by inclination, by the hypnotic monk Rasputin, and, then, after his murder, by a dazed fatalism and unapproachability. On January 12, when the British ambassador went to the tsar to express the anxiety of the Allies, he was scolded with the celebrated remark: "Do you mean that *I* am to regain the confidence of my people, Ambassador, or that they are to regain *my* confidence?"

A movement for change inspired by liberals in the Duma, by British diplomacy, and by certain court circles ran parallel to the slow, elemental mass discontent, while Bolsheviks and Mensheviks in the Social Democratic party burrowed underground within factories and the armed forces. Plots to kill or kidnap the tsar abounded. In increasing numbers, soldiers joined workers as massive demonstrations shook the capital Petrograd. Revolution was in the air, but no party or man seemed able to give it expression. Disturbances rumbled in early March but none was exceptional in itself or charged with the drama proclaiming the end of an age. Striking workers poured into the streets demanding bread and looting bakeries. Crowds attacked police stations, jails, and law courts. Random fires broke out. The tsar suddenly left the capital and went to his military headquarters in Mogilev. By March 12 (February 27 old style calendar), many police and army regiments had disintegrated. The Duma, which the tsar had ordered disbanded, now became the real center of events.

Excited mobs swarmed toward the Tauride Palace where the Duma was meeting and previously hesitant deputies decided to take power themselves. Liberals, who formed the Progressive bloc, three right-wing deputies, and one socialist, Alexander Kerensky, formed a Provisional Government to govern until a Constituent Assembly could be elected by the people. On March 15 (March 2) the tsar abdicated. A Provisional Government, headed by Prince George Lvov, was established, creating a democratic republic and abolishing all national and religious disabilities. Jews, together with large masses of Russians and subject nationalities, greeted the March revolution with great joy and hope. Jews spoke of it as "the deliverance of a people," "a great tidal wave of democracy," and "a miracle . . . that will be recorded as one of the greatest events in the history of Israel." A magazine for Jewish children compared it to the Passover liberation of Jews from Egypt.[1]

Jews had little reason to lament the downfall of a regime that had confined them to a huge ghetto—the Pale of Settlement—and had, with few exceptions, barred them from the normal course of Russian life.

An important commitment of the new government, given the ethnic diversity of Russia, was its promise to grant cultural-national autonomy to all national minorities, including Jews. One of the first acts of the new government was a decree removing all disabilities and restrictive laws Jews had suffered in the Pale of Settlement, and eliminating the Pale itself. Theoretically, Jews were now equal citizens of Russia and could move about freely. Despite the horrors of World War I, which had made the Pale a bloody battlefield and left hundreds of thousands uprooted, and despite the loss of great Jewish centers such as Warsaw, Vilna, Bialystok, Kovno and Grodno, which were occupied by the Germans, there was a quite remarkable blossoming of Jewish political and cultural activity. Yiddish publications, extinguished in 1915 by the military censorship, reappeared and many new ones were started. *Kehillas* (Jewish communal bodies) revived and began to organize themselves democratically. Conferences of Jewish teachers, cooperatives, and mutual aid societies sprang to life. From relief for refugees to the reorganization of Jewish schools, a fever of activity, contentious as well as cooperative, gripped Jews, newly released from tsarist oppression. This new freedom also excited political activity, which had remained largely underground since the failure of the Revolution of 1905 and reached an unprecedented pitch of intensity in 1917. The revival and growth of Jewish cultural and political life, however, meant institutions and parties that opposed Bolshevik assumptions and doctrines. Moreover, Jewish religious beliefs and practices were at variance with Bolshevism. Yet these forces formed the spirit and substance of Jewish life. Because they resisted Bolshevik ideas and organizations as long as possible, a brief summary of their pre-Bolshevik positions will be helpful in grasping the vigor of that resistance and in understanding subsequent events.

There were approximately five and a half million Jews in the Russian Empire in 1914, 4.1 percent of the total population, reduced by 1917 to three and a half million through war, pogroms, and the loss of large chunks of pre-1914 Russian territory. A large majority of these Jews—religiously observant and opposed to political action—had been fearful, submissive, and powerless in tsarist times. But the upheavals of the

March Revolution led to the formation of the first religious political parties. In the summer of 1917, fifty local religious-political groups met and called for an eight hour working day, the right to strike, land redistribution, and the promotion of religious education.[2] A united religious front group call *Akhdus* (unity) also emerged.

However, the impetus for political action came chiefly from secular movements in Jewish life—Zionism and the Jewish labor and socialist movement. Both were movements of reaction against religious orthodoxy and against the intensified oppression and powerlessness of Jews in tsarist Russia, which had reached an intolerable pitch after the pogroms of 1881–82 and 1903–6. But they had worked out irreconcilably different philosophies and programs as they analyzed the Jewish predicament. The Zionists, in general, were convinced that Russia—at least up to the March Revolution—would never give Jews the political, social, and economic rights that would ensure their security and agitated for a free Jewish life in a restored Palestine. The Diaspora was given up as hopelessly anti-Semitic, and Diaspora Jewish life, as cruelly stunted and deformed. Zionists believed that Jewish life could be normalized only under wholly new terms of existence. The Zionist party had over 300,000 members in 1,200 local groups, but since their hopes were fastened on Palestine, except for the socialist Zionists, their interest in Russian politics was slight—until the March Revolution.

In sharp contrast and opposition were Jewish socialists who had organized the General League of Jewish Workingmen in Russia and Poland (popularly known as the Bund) in 1897, and had evolved over two decades as a well-organized, disciplined movement of the Jewish proletariat and socialist intellectuals struggling to change life in Russia. It was a Marxist party, which, for a time, was an integral part of the Russian Social Democratic Workers party (RSDWP), but it clashed fatefully with Lenin over questions of party organization and Jewish cultural-national autonomy.[3] The growing number of Jewish workers and artisans, whose interests were in conflict with *kahal* authorities and Jewish employers, sharpened class conflict and class consciousness. The Bund believed that a revolution was necessary to solve the Jewish problem, that anti-Jewish discrimination as well as "delusions" about Jewish nationhood would vanish with the overthrow of tsarism and the evils of capitalism. In time, however, as the Bund confronted anti-Semitism among Russian socialists and workers and began to understand the particular economic and social vulnerabilities of Jews, it, too, concluded that certain problems were unique to Jewish workers. During the political reaction that set in after the abortive Revolution of 1905, the Bund worked its tortuous way to a formulation of national-cultural autonomy for all national minorities in a projected federated Russian socialist state, and extraterritorial cultural autonomy for scattered minorities, including Jews.

The Bund was enthusiastically backed not only by Jewish workers, but by modernist elements in Russian Jewry, including middle-class intellectuals. It was the first movement in the Pale to introduce modern Western economic and political ideas and the notion that even Jews could resist the oppression of the regime and improve immediate working conditions through organized agitation and strikes. The Bund could justifiably claim to have more worker cohesiveness, unity, and class support than any other Social Democratic organization in Russia up to the Bolshevik Revolution. It had 33,700 members in December 1917. The other major components of the RSDWP—the Bolsheviks and Mensheviks—were torn by inner conflicts and unable to build a mass worker base.

In May 1917, another Jewish movement emerged, combining two formerly separate parties: Socialist-Zionist territorialists, who believed that a Palestine solution was utopian and advocated Jewish colonization in any autonomous Jewish territory; and SERP (Jewish Socialist Labor party), after the abbreviation of its Russian name. SERP originally opposed both Palestinian and territorialist solutions and had favored Jewish national autonomy in Russia, based on an elected Jewish national assembly. The merged party was called the *Faraynigte* (United Jewish Socialist Workers' party). It temporarily put aside the territorial question, maintained ties with the Social Revolutionary party and the Mensheviks in the trade unions, and became particularly effective in the Ukraine, where it drew support from secularist defenders of Yiddish. The membership of the *Faraynigte* stood at 13,000 in the spring of 1917.[4]

Another Jewish party *Poale Tsion* (Workers of Zion) was also a socialist party with a genuinely proletarian membership which tried to make a synthesis of Marxism and Zionism based on the theories of Ber Borokhov.[5] Borokhov maintained that Jews must correct the economic and social abnormalities of Diaspora life by going to Palestine and engaging in a class struggle there which would lead to the "normalization" of Jewish life. By 1906, Borokhov succeeded in mobilizing most of the pro-Palestine groups into the Jewish Social Democratic party Poale Tsion and in hammering out a platform, based on his important theoretical essay "On the Question: Zion and Territory." In this Borokhov applied a materialist analysis to the Jewish problem and established Zionism as an elemental force created by the anomalies and insecurities of Jewish experience.

Borokhov's ideas strongly appealed to radically minded Jews who could not accept prevailing socialist views on Jewish problems and socialist indifference to the uniqueness of the Jewish predicament, including the intractability of anti-Semitism. Moreover, they understood that, contrary to Marx, industrialization was not turning Jewish artisans and petty traders into a proletariat, but, instead, into a rootless mass of petty traders, *luftmenshen* (literally, people living on air with no skills or earning capacity), and laborers in declining parts of the economy. Jewish tailors, glaziers, tinsmiths, and water-carriers were being wedged into narrowing crevices of the Russian economy because of the imposed restrictions which choked off a more normal and wholesome economic life.

The Bundists conceded the unusual nature of impoverished Jewish artisans, but believed they had a revolutionary potential and would eventually be absorbed in factories. Borokhov, however, was certain that this class was doomed to extinction, that they were the symptom of the abnormal position of Jews in the Diaspora which no social revolution would change. In time, Poale Tsion also fought for causes within Russia: the battle for Jewish political and civic rights, the formation of Jewish trade unions, strikes, the creation of Jewish secular schools, and support for Hebrew and Yiddish culture.

This new approach, differing sharply from the quasi-mystical and messianic Zionism of an earlier period, created a materialist, secular Zionism which challenged the Bund on its own terms and drove the two movements into fierce rivalry and polemics. At heart, each movement was passionately convinced of the truth of its analysis and struggled bitterly against the other in intense personal and ideological confrontations that blazed across Jewish life until the Bolshevik conquest of power crushed the power of both. Yet, ironically, this hostility lived on in a new guise. When the new regime set up the Jewish Sections of the Communist party, known as the *Evsektsiya*, to persuade and then coerce Jews to move into the Soviet mainstream, the *Evsektsiya* exploited the vehemently anti-Zionist animus of some Bundists who had become Communists and denounced "the counter-revolutionary essence" of Zionism.

In tsarist Russia, Zionism had been an illegal movement, but after the March Revolution, all segments of the movement experienced unprecedented growth, and following the Balfour Declaration, Zionism became the clearly dominant movement in Russian Jewry. Aside from Poale Tsion and Faraynigte, which ran separate slates, religious and secular Zionists showed conspicuous strength in a number of elections held in 1917–18. In reports of 193 kehillas in nine provinces of the Ukraine, for example, Zionists had 36 percent of the delegates—the largest of any party, while in the elections to the All-Russian Jewish Congress, the Zionists were far ahead with approximately 60 percent of the vote.[6] Zionists also controlled a conference of 149 representatives from forty Jewish communities in central Russia held in Moscow in July 1918. The Zionist-sponsored cultural and educational society called *Tarbut* maintained over 250 Hebrew schools and societies throughout the country and sponsored over fifty journals in Yiddish, Hebrew, and Russian. By October 1917, there were 1,200 local Zionist groups with a total membership of 300,000.[7] Almost from the first, however, there was anti-Zionist hostility, spearheaded by the Jews in the pre-Bolshevik anti-Zionist parties who ultimately moved into the Bolshevik orbit and anticipated the regime's ideological opposition.

Besides Jewish socialist and Zionist activity after the March Revolution, there occurred intense Jewish communal activity, elections to town councils, a variety of open conferences, and the organization of the Soviet of Workers' and Soldiers' Deputies, first in Petrograd, and then in other cities, involving the participation of Bundists and other Jewish and non-Jewish socialists. At the first All-Russian Congress of Soviets in June–July 1917, a resolution was adopted acknowledging the right of all national minorities to cultural self-determination. Virtually unanimously, articulate Jewish opinion endorsed extra-territorial cultural-national autonomy on the basis of voluntary affiliation to a Jewish body. Preparations were made for an All-Russian Congress of Jewish Communities to lay the foundation for a national organization of the Jewish minority within the future democratic state.

The war, meanwhile, had intensified national aspirations and separatist tendencies among the Poles, Ukrainians, Lithuanians, Latvians, Estonians, and Armenians. The Bund's program of cultural autonomy now acquired great popularity among non-Jewish socialists who sought to save the unity of the Russian state through concessions to national minorities, and was soon adopted by all of the major political parties except the Bolsheviks. As early as May 1917, the principle was adopted by the Social Revolutionary party (which won an overwhelming popular majority in the elections for the Constituent Assembly in November 1917), and the Menshevik Social Democrats in August. When the Assembly convened in January 1918, Viktor M. Chernov, the chairman, said: "The Jewish people, which has no continuous territory of its own, shall be entitled, equally with the other peoples, to fashion on the territory of the Russian Republic organs of national self-government, and to express in these the will of its active elements."[8] But the Assembly, which enjoyed only a few hours' existence, was forcibly dissolved by the Bolsheviks.

Enthusiasm for the All-Russian Jewish Congress had also been high, although the voting in the autumn of 1917 was limited because of serious internal disturbances in Russia and the inroads of the German army in the summer of 1917. Representatives of thirteen cities with 50,000 Jews or more, as well as local political parties and their central committees, came to a preliminary conference to plan the projected Congress. The Bund feared Zionist predominance at the Congress and insisted that the resolutions be in the form of recommendations; the Zionists wanted them to be binding. A compromise was finally hammered out, eliminating "the Palestine question" and concentrating on the issue of Jewish rights both within and outside of Russia and the precise framework of Jewish national autonomy within the anticipated Russian federal union. The call to the Congress was dramatic:

Citizens, Jews! The Jewish people in Russia now faces an event which has no parallel in Jewish history for two thousand years. Not only has the Jew as an individual, as a citizen, acquired equality of rights—which has also happened in other countries—but the Jewish national looks forward to the possibility of securing national rights. Never and nowhere have the Jews lived through such a serious, responsible moment as the present—responsible to the present and the future generations.[9]

Elections to the kehillas also sent new political juices coursing through the Jewish communities. The elections were vigorously—even bitterly—but democratically waged, as Jews in little towns and big cities voted their convictions. In most areas of the former empire, Zionists won, with various combined socialist parties trailing some distance behind. The elections to the Jewish Congress and those for the Constituent Assembly showed a similar configuration.[10] The Zionist victories reflected the increasing popularity of Zionism surfacing after its illegal status in tsarist Russia, but even more, the electrifying effect of the Balfour Declaration.[11] In a brief letter sent by British Foreign Secretary Arthur James Balfour to Lord Rothschild, President of the British Zionist Federation, the British government declared its sympathy with Zionist aspirations and "view[ed] with favor the establishment in Palestine of a national home for the Jewish people." With this pledge, the British Prime Minister Lloyd George was undoubtedly hoping to win a British protectorate over Palestine and bolster the sagging Allied cause by mobilizing world Jewish opinion behind the Allied war effort. He also hoped to bring Russian Jewry over to the cause of the Entente and outmaneuver the Germans who, in their desire to establish a foothold in Palestine, were actively courting the favor of the Zionist movement. For Jews the world over, the declaration promised a miraculous deliverance from homelessness and suffering.

The Jewish parties, as they were described, clearly dominated Jewish political activity in Russia after the March Revolution, but some Jews among the assimilated intelligentsia supported the non-Jewish parties: Cadets (Constitutional Democrats), Mensheviks, Bolsheviks, and the Social Revolutionary party. Some Jews had been drawn to the Russian revolutionary parties as a way of escaping from the narrow, provincial, often squalid life of the *shtetlach* (small market towns) with their rigid religious practices, into the new, modern, freer life of exciting social ideas and political activism. The wretchedness of the Russian masses smote the consciences of many of these idealistic Jews and they read and discussed populist and Marxist literature with burning intensity. Some also yearned to escape the problems and dilemmas of being a Jew and to find acceptance in the larger non-Jewish world.

In tsarist Russia, membership in any of the revolutionary movements was exhilarating but very risky and exacted a great personal price. Few who joined escaped the punitive bureaucracy, the vast police apparatus, censorship, arrest, prison, and exile. Years of underground life with its dangers, secrecy, illegality, and camouflages often damaged personal identities and relationships which could not be normalized in the brief period of Russian democracy under the Provisional Government. Jews who broke with their communities searching for a larger, broader, more Russian or internationalist commitment, were considered deserters or betrayers. In their eagerness to create new lives for themselves, they changed their names and severed all ties with their old relationships and communities. The large intellectual and psychic space left was filled with a fiery secular messianism. These Jews were not only burdened by the exaction and strains of an illegal political life, but also by the complex psychological adjustments needed to take on a new identity and dissolve out the old.

This identity transformation was conspicuous among Jewish Bolsheviks, who were Jews by family origin only and felt no special ties to other Jews or any interest in specific Jewish problems. They denied the exceptional character of anti-Semitism, believing that it was a disease of capitalism which would disappear with the destruction of capitalism. Leon Trotsky, born Lev Davidovich Bronstein, a central figure in the early years of the Bolshevik Revolution, was typical of the russified, Bolshevik Jew. In his autobiography, he speaks about "sailing away" from his petit bourgeois environment with its "instinct of acquisition," and his brief, meaningless contact with Hebrew, the Bible, and religious tradition. He was aware of national inequalities, the restrictions on Jews and other minorities, and the violent anti-Semitism of the Black Hundreds, but these "were lost among all the other phases of social injustice" and "intense hatred of the existing order, of injustice, of tyranny." The national question, "so important in the life of Russia, had practically no personal significance for me. Even in my early youth, the national bias and national prejudices had only bewildered my sense of reason, in some cases stirring in me nothing but disdain and even a moral nausea." In a debate with Vladimir Medem, a Bundist leader, in 1903, when Medem asked him, "You consider yourself either a Russian or a Jew?" Trotsky answered, "No, you are wrong. I am a Social Democrat and only that."[12]

Trotsky's reactions were similar to those of other Jewish Bolsheviks: Zinoviev, Sverdlov, Kamenev, Radek, Litvinov, Kaganovich, and others—all russified, cosmopolitan, hostile to the point of vindictiveness in their attitudes toward Jewish national culture, Zionism, and religious tradition. Lenin seems to have fully and wholeheartedly accepted these non-Jewish Jews for what they felt themselves to be—international socialists. However, they were always identified as Jews by anti-Bolsheviks everywhere, by the masses of people in the Soviet Union, and by the Communist parties inside and outside of the Soviet Union.

They have sometimes been described as "marginal men," "doubly alienated" and "self-hating," creating their own world of revolutionary agitation and formulas for a socialist utopia. These Jews had no Jewish support or following in any segment of organized Jewish life in Russia. Nor did Jews as a whole support Bolshevik ideas or the Revolution when it came. However, individual Jews loomed prominently in the Sixth Bolshevik Congress (July 26–August 3, 1917), in the Central Committee elected by the Congress, and in the top and secondary leadership of the party in the early years of the Soviet regime.[13] It was they who stamped Bolshevism as "Jewish" in the prevailing view both of supporters and opponents of Bolshevism.

Zionist parties gained the support of a majority of Jews, but they were to play a far less important role in the future of Soviet Jews than the socialists. Except for a small fraction of left-wing Poale Zionists, which was allowed to function for a time, all Zionists in Russia became the targets of Bolshevik attack and persecution and formed an opposition which eventually was declared illegal and was destroyed. The Jewish socialists, on the other hand, struggled for a short time to compete, co-exist, and adjust to the realities of Bolshevik power. But the struggle was foredoomed, not only because of Lenin's ruthless, single-minded determination to establish a strong, centralized party and government, but because of the long-standing antagonisms between the Jewish Labor Bund and Lenin, which were to have a fateful effect on Jewish life under Soviet communism.

The Bund was created in 1897—a year before the Russian Social Democratic party—as a Jewish workers' Marxist party whose aim was to become part of the Russian party and serve the revolutionary cause. However, in its efforts to organize Jewish workers—mostly wretchedly poor artisans in the Pale of Settlement, not the industrial proletariat envisioned by Marx—the early Bund leaders discovered that there were economic and cultural-religious problems unique to the Jewish workers, as well as popular and government-inspired anti-Semitism, which infected even Russian socialist comrades. The class struggle, worker solidarity, and other Marxist axioms simply could not solve the problems of Jewish workers or the stubborn intractability of anti-Semitism. Thus, the Bund evolved a multi-layered program that combined agitation in behalf of the Russian proletariat, defense of the specific interests and rights of Jewish workers, and the fight against anti-Jewish laws. Stunned by the ferocity of the Kishinev pogrom of 1903 and the pogroms of 1905–6, the Bund had to reassess its original Marxist position to make room for the peculiar vulnerability of the Jewish working masses. It was the first Jewish movement to organize armed self-defense units to protect Jewish communities. This responsibility, the need to use Yiddish in organizing Jewish workers and developing cultural as well as political activities, and the growing appeal of Zionism brought the Bund to a more flexible position. By 1905 it had adopted the concept of cultural-national autonomy for all national minorities in Russia, including Jews, within a federated Russia.

Lenin raged against these ideas[14] as bourgeois nationalism, while envying the Bund's excellent organizational skills, inner discipline, and cohesiveness, as well as the unusual balance of workers and intellectuals in the Bund's membership, in contrast to the factionalism, weak organization, and top-heavy intellectual weight in the Russian party. He harangued the Bund almost from the start of their contacts on a number of issues: because the Bund wanted to be sole representative of the Jewish proletariat in organizational matters, then, because it wanted a federated party structure and state—against his vehement desire and intention to create strong centralized power in both—and, finally, over the question of national-cultural autonomy. The Bund left the parent party in 1903, but was readmitted in 1906. However, their relationship became increasingly antagonistic, and among the many elements in the party that eventually broke with Lenin and formed the Menshevik bloc were former Bundists. The Mensheviks wanted to develop a grass-roots workers' movement in the factories and among the embryonic trade unions; Lenin, instead, wanted a small, secret, conspiratorial party of professionals. There were bitter differences over how to channel the revolutionary mood of the workers in 1905, a temporary mending of the rift, and then new conflict when nonpartisan "workers' clubs" and "political unions" initiated mainly by the Mensheviks, began to appear in St. Petersburg (changed to Petrograd in 1914), in addition to workers' committees, trade unions, and numerous socialist parties that were coalescing in the St. Petersburg Soviet. Lenin at first feared that the soviet might become the nucleus of a provisional government; then he began to regard it as a rival to the party. Later, he changed his mind again, but by then the soviet had been crushed and by January 1906, the momentum of revolution as well.

Increasingly, Bundists and Mensheviks were repelled by Lenin's splitting tactics, conspiratorial intrigues, rejection of all who disagreed with him, and questionable fund-raising methods—often verging on terrorism. Differences over the nature of the coming revolution also became vehement.

Before the split within the RSDWP, Jews were concentrated in the Bund and Menshevik faction. For example, at the Party Congress in London in 1907, there were almost one hundred Jewish delegates, one-third of the total. Approximately fifty-seven were Bundists, while one-fifth of the pro-Menshevik delegates were Jews. In June 1917, eight of the seventeen members of the Menshevik Central Committee were Jews.[15] Over a considerable period, the Bund and the Mensheviks shared the same outlook in many respects, but the Bund was clearly and vigorously a *Jewish* movement of and for the Jewish proletariat while the Mensheviks mainly attracted Western-oriented, assimilated Jewish intellectuals.

Mensheviks still held to the basic Marxist notion that only the development of a strong proletariat could produce the socialist revolution, but that this would happen only after Russian capitalism matured, that is, after the so-called bourgeois revolution. The Bolsheviks argued that the Russian bourgeoisie were not only too weak to complete the bourgeois-democratic revolution but were already becoming counterrevolutionary. Only the proletariat, Lenin insisted, would complete the bourgeois revolution. There were also bitter arguments over participation in the Duma and the involvement of socialists in trade unions. Okhrana agents were infesting Bolshevik ranks, and the bizarre dénouement in the case of double agent Roman Malinovsky, whom Lenin liked and admired, split the two camps irrevocably, with the final break coming in 1912. (With the aid of the police and Bolsheviks, Malinovsky was elected to the Fourth Duma where he attacked Mensheviks under Lenin's orders and simultaneously sent transcripts of Lenin's decisions and secret plans to the police. Lenin blocked Menshevik efforts to have him investigated; subsequent recriminations destroyed personal relations and any possibility of RSDWP unity.)

The Mensheviks, by this time, had begun to look more favorably on the principle of national-cultural autonomy, and at an August 1912 conference of right-wing Mensheviks asserted that "national-cultural autonomy was not contrary to the party's program guaranteeing national self-determination." By 1917, the entire Menshevik party, which included many Jewish members and which, by then, was politically linked with the Jewish Labor Bund, incorporated the principle into its official party program. Mark Liber, Raphael Abramovich, Isaiah Izen-shtat, Tsvia Hurvich, and Vladimir Kosovky were among the leading Bundists who became actively involved in Menshevik politics as the two movements drew closer together. However, in the historically decisive crisis that ensued, Menshevik leadership under Yuli Martov was no match for Lenin. The Mensheviks drifted uncertainly, unable to chart a clear program for Russian workers and make the necessary alliances and political decisions that would have set Russia on a non-Bolshevik course. It was Lenin who seized the whirlwind in November 1917. It was also Lenin who sketchily formulated Soviet ideas regarding national cultures and forms of cultural expression in a socialist state. These, however, were somewhat vague and loosely framed.

Jews constituted a small minority in the pre-Bolshevik and Bolshevik state, and although Lenin and other early Bolshevik leaders were genuinely interested in freeing them from tsarist oppression, there was and is no well-developed body of theory regarding the meaning of Jewish nationality in the projected or actual Soviet state, in terms of cultural rights and forms of expression. Yet the question has been argued continuously if fruitlessly because of the absence of a firmly grounded principle and the inconsistent interpretations of scattered phrases and statements. Both Lenin and Stalin themselves were inconsistent and their own inconsistent statements have been invoked, stretched, or ignored, depending upon larger considerations. There have also been occasional party resolutions dealing with the Jewish minority, described as a "nationality," but these have been interpreted in wildly fluctuating ways. Soviet officials have both condemned and encouraged the concept of Jewish nationality, depending on domestic and foreign policy considerations. The question of Jewish nationality rights still hangs very much in the air and the absence of a sturdy theoretical framework has undoubtedly contributed to the ambiguities, contradictions, and controversies that have afflicted Soviet Jewish life. Lenin himself did not share Marx's repugnant views about Jews, but undoubtedly they crept into the thinking of other Bolsheviks.

Lenin's views on Jewish national existence were partly shaped by his approach to the whole question of the future of national cultures in the coming socialist state, but most uncompromisingly by his polemic with the Bund. His approach to the general question of nationalism has been divided by one historian[16] into four periods, suggesting an evolution: the first, from 1897 to 1913, corresponding to the formation of the Bolshevik Party; the second, from 1913 to 1918, the years of World War I and the Bolshevik Revolution; third, from 1918 to 1923, the years of the consolidation of the new state; and the brief period from 1923 to his death in 1924, when his ideas showed some rethinking on the nationality problem out of fear of Great Russian chauvinism.

Before World War I, Lenin and Russian Social Democrats generally paid relatively little attention to the national question, viewing the solution to the Russian national problem not in *national* equality, but in the civil and political equality of all citizens and proletarian unity among all nationalities. In 1903, in dealing with Armenian Social Democrats, who wanted national self-determination and full political autonomy for all the nations of the Russian Empire, Lenin argued that while the workers of Russia's national minorities were perfectly entitled to demand national independence, the Social Democrats could not make such demands in a general program. While the movement would always protest against national oppression, it would also oppose attempts to divide workers of different nationalities. The right of self-determination for every nation had been recognized in the Party Manifesto of 1898, but was merely taken over as a formula from the Second International and not digested or analytically debated by the Russian Social Democrats, as was being done by the Germans and Austrians. In these early years, Lenin chided or attacked Armenians, Poles, Caucasians, as well as Jewish Bundists for their "nationalist" ideas. After 1903, his approach to the national question went through various shifts of emphasis and a detectable fuzziness. It seems obvious that at the time he had not regarded the national questions sufficiently serious to be thought through.[17] Moreover, he was preoccupied with party organization and with making the Bolsheviks the central force in the entire party. The Menshevik Conference of 1912, the Balkan Wars, and then World War I forced him to give the whole matter much more serious attention.

Lenin's opposition to the principle of national-cultural autonomy and a federalized party focused on his polemics against the Bund until 1912. But he went to Cracow in Austrian Poland in that year, and in the midst of the nationalisms erupting out of the Balkan War, the hostilities of the various Polish socialist parties, and the unconventional views of the Austrian Marxists on the national question, Lenin expanded his targets.[18] To his amazement, the Austrian Marxists, influenced by Karl

Renner and Otto Bauer, advocated precisely those ideas he excoriated. Anticipating the Austrian Empire's federalization rather than its liquidation, with equal national, cultural, and administrative rights for all the nationalities within it, and eager to appease the disruptive nationalisms within the Dual Monarchy, the Austrians favored national-cultural autonomy and federalism—both Bundist positions, although Bauer and Karl Kautsky opposed it for Jews.

A Georgian Bolshevik, Koba Djugashvili (Stalin), who had carried out expropriations in the Caucasus, arrived in Cracow at this time and was known to have opposed local nationalism in the Transcaucasian revolutionary movement.[19] His visit was welcomed by Lenin, who later wrote to Maxim Gorky, the Russian writer: "About nationalism, I fully agree with you that we have to bear down harder. We have here a wonderful Georgian [Stalin] who had undertaken to write a long article . . . after gathering *all* the Austrian and other materials. We will take care of this matter."[20]

To help him prepare materials for his critical essays on the national question (1913–14), Lenin sent Stalin to Vienna. The result was Stalin's "Marxism and the National and Colonial Question," published in a party journal in the spring of 1913, an essay which repeated Lenin's attacks on cultural autonomy and which remains the basic statement in Communist party literature on the Jewish national question, but subject to revision. Stalin defines the nation as a "historically evolved stable community of language, territory, economic life and psychological make-up manifested in a community of culture."[21] Only when all these characteristics are present do we have a nation. By definition, Jews were thus excluded. The Austrian definitions of a nation as a "cultural community no longer tied to the soil," or "an aggregate of people bound into a community of character by a community of fate" (Bauer), were sharply criticized for blocking the right of self-determination by maintaining the multinational state, substituting equality of cultural rights for sovereign political rights, and for perpetuating national prejudices.

When Stalin deals specifically with Jews, he does not analyze the linguistically homogeneous population in the Pale that the Bund was concerned with, but with disparate Jewries:

What . . . national cohesion can there be . . . between the Georgian, Daghestanian, Russian and American Jew? . . . If there is anything common to them left it is their religion, their common origin and certain relics of national character. How can it be seriously maintained that petrified religious rites and fading psychological relics affect the "fate" of these Jews more powerfully than the living . . . environment that surrounds them?[22]

Moreover, Stalin added, few Jews live on the soil; nor do Jews constitute a majority in any province in Russia. Interspersed as national minorities in areas inhabited by other nationalities, they serve "foreign" nations as manufacturers and traders and professionals, adapting themselves to the "foreign nations." All this, taken together with the increasing reshuffling of nationalities in developed forms of capitalism, will inevitably lead to the assimilation of Jews.[23] The abolition of the Pale of Settlement will hasten this process. Like Lenin, Stalin harshly criticized the Bundist program of extra-territorial autonomy as "a refined species of nationalism," claiming autonomy for "a nation whose future is denied and whose present existence remains to be proved."

Stalin acknowledged that Jews rejected inevitable assimilation by demanding an autonomous status and protection of minority rights. But, he argued, autonomy for Jews would mean guarding the "harmful" as well as the "useful" traits; it would also foster "national narrowmindedness and the spread of prejudice" and would disorganize and demoralize the labor movement."[24]

Stalin, in fact, was echoing Lenin's views, and it seems likely that Lenin edited Stalin's essay.[25] Lenin himself did not deal with the Jewish question systematically but in numerous, scattered references. His first detailed statement appeared soon after the Bund's withdrawal from the RSDWP in 1903, in the October 22, 1903 issue of *Iskra*, the party paper which Lenin edited. In an article entitled "The Bund's Position Within the Party," Lenin called the Bundist idea of Jewish national autonomy a

Zionist idea . . . false and reactionary in its essence . . . The idea of a separate Jewish people, which is utterly untenable scientifically is reactionary in its political implications . . . Everywhere in Europe the downfall of medievalism and the development of political freedom went hand in hand with the political emancipation of the Jews . . . and their . . . progressive assimilation by the surrounding population . . . The Jewish question is this exactly: assimilation or separateness? And the idea of a Jewish "nationality" is manifestly reactionary . . . [It] is in conflict with the interests of the Jewish proletariat, for, directly or indirectly, it engenders in its ranks a mood hostile to assimilation, a "ghetto" mood.[26]

This thesis approximated the Bolshevik position, and when discussing Jewish issues, the Bolshevik press frequently quoted from Lenin's views.[27] Those views remained unchanged in 1913. In the spring of that year, in two articles in *Pravda*, he condemned the Czech Social Democrats in Austria as separatists "clinging to the coattails of liquidators and Bundists," and wrote a draft platform for Latvian Bolsheviks (to bolster them in their struggle against the dominant Menshevik Latvian movement), in which he attacked cultural-national autonomy and federation.[28] His "Theses on the National Question" delivered in July 1913 propounded the right of self-determination (even including secession) for all nationalities, yet at the same time urging the proletariat to ally only with workers of all nations in *their* struggle—a double harness which later caused great confusion in socialist ranks. The "cultural-national autonomy slogan" is described as "erroneous and harmful," "a complete failure in Austria," leading to the secession of Czech Social Democrats, "advocated only by Jewish bourgeois parties" and "uncritically followed by the Bund."[29] In the autumn of 1913, at a conference of the party's central committee, all of the foregoing ideas were adopted.

After the conference, Lenin started work on "Critical Remarks on the National Question." Using a Marxist class analysis, Lenin opposed bourgeois national culture to proletarian internationalist culture, creating an abstraction which became dogma to Communists, and which has served as the text from which the standard Bolshevik formulations on the nature of Jewish culture have been derived. The elements of democratic and socialist culture, Lenin declared, are present in every national culture, but every nation also possesses a dominant culture— the culture of the landlords, the clergy, and the bourgeoisie. Those who wish to serve the proletariat must unite the workers of all nations and fight bourgeois nationalism, both domestic and foreign. The same struggle applies to the

most oppressed and persecuted nation, the Jews. Jewish national culture is the slogan of rabbis and bourgeoisie, the slogan of our enemies. But there are other elements in Jewish culture and . . . history as a whole. Out of ten and a half million Jews throughout the world, somewhat over a half live in Galicia and Russia, backward and semi-barbarous countries, where the Jews are *forcibly* kept in the status of a caste. The other lives in the civilised world, and there the Jews do not live as a segregated caste. There the great world-progressive features of Jewish culture stand clearly revealed . . . Whoever, directly or indirectly puts forward the slogan of Jewish "national culture" is (whatever his good intentions may be) an enemy of the proletariat, a supporter of all that is *outmoded* and connected with *caste* among the Jewish people; he is an accomplice of the rabbis and the bourgeoisie . . . In advocating the slogan of national culture and building upon it an entire plan . . . of what they call "cultural-national autonomy," the Bundists are *in effect* instruments of bourgeois nationalism among the workers.[30]

Thus, argued Lenin, who knew little of Jewish history, literature, or religious tradition, Jewish reactionaries and Bundists who oppose assimilation are "turning back the wheel of history." Bourgeois nationalism and proletarian internationalism are "irreconcilably hostile," and those, like the Bund, who advance the idea of national culture are guilty of "the most refined, most absolute and most extreme nationalism." However,

. . . those Jewish Marxists who merge with the Russian, Lithuanian, Ukrainian, and other workers in international Marxist organizations, contributing their share (in both Russian and Yiddish) to the creation of an international culture of the labor movement—those Jews carry on (in defiance of the separatism of the Bund) the best Jewish tradition when they combat the slogan of "national culture."[31]

In the Bund struggle against Lenin, no one quoted from Marx's essay "Zur Judenfrage,"[32] very possibly because of its shocking and vulgar anti-Semitism, but Marxists generally, including Lenin and Stalin, accepted the Marxist dogma that Jews would ultimately disappear as a definable group, and that, as individual and class exploitation ends, national differences and antagonisms would disappear as well.

Stalin had ridiculed the Bund for proposing autonomy for a nation that had no future and whose status was as yet unproven. Lenin attacked national cultural autonomy as divisive, yet he insisted that the rights of national minorities be guaranteed although it was "inappropriate and impossible to define particulars in a program."[33] He also maintained that "in every national culture there are elements of a democratic and Socialist culture" which Marxists must take from the dominant national culture of the landowners, priests, and bourgeoisie,[34] but warned that only what is "progressive" is permissible to use, "in order that this recognition may not lead to bourgeois ideology obscuring proletarian consciousness."[35] A murky zone is then described, which subsequently caused great bewilderment among the party faithful, in which the Marxist struggle against national oppression may betray proletarian unity, a "higher unity," if "bourgeois nationalism" is assisted. Specific content is sacrificed to rigid formula and the spell of the Marxist dialectic:

To throw off the feudal yoke, all national oppression, and all privileges enjoyed by any particular nation or language, is the imperative duty of the proletariat . . . Combat all national oppression? Yes, of course! Fight *for* any kind of national development, *for* "national culture" in general?—Of course not . . .[36]

Many questions were left in limbo by this dialectic which Bundists, among others, challenged: Would the right of self-determination and secession be forfeited if Russia were to become ripe for a socialist revolution? How could workers know when the struggle against national oppression shaded into a struggle for national development? What guideposts could resolve the dilemma of the Polish and Ukrainian proletariat, indoctrinated in the goal of the "fusion of nations," suffering under Russian oppression, struggling to break out of the yoke, and confronting secession and the creation of yet another nationalism? Was not a certain measure of national development necessary to awaken the masses to the "struggle against national oppression of any kind?" Tragically, it was only at the end of his life that Lenin began to accept the strength of national feeling—too late to redirect party policy.

One of the last direct exchanges between Lenin and the Bund on these questions took place in the fall of 1913. The Bundist Peisakh Liebman (Liebman Hersh) published an article in *Tsayt* charging that "self-determination" was too vague to have any real political meaning: "When the Jewish working class . . . began to work out the specific content of this concept, the master theoreticians of Russian Social-Democracy cried out, 'Nationalism'. . . . Every attempt to give clear and concrete expression was attacked as a petit bourgeois heresy against Marxist doctrine." He further argued that:

Anyone in the least familiar with the national question knows that international culture is not non-national . . . ; non-national culture, which must not be Russian, Jewish or Polish, but only pure culture, is nonsense. International ideas can appeal to the working class only when they are adapted to the language spoken by the worker, and to the concrete national conditions under which he lives. The worker should not be indifferent to the condition and development of his national culture, because it is . . . only through it that he is able to participate in the "international culture of democracy and of the world working-class movement." This is well known, but V.I. turns a deaf ear to it all . . .[37]

Lenin denounced these views with contempt and accused the Bund of "spreading faith in a non-class national culture" and "bourgeois culture in the workers' ranks." When he shifted to "concrete examples," his meaning became obscured:

. . . Our task is to fight the dominant Black-Hundred and bourgeois national culture of the Great Russians and to develop . . . the rudiments also existing in the history of our democratic and working class movement. Fight your own Great-Russian landlords and bourgeoisie, fight their "culture" in the name of internationalism, and in so fighting, "adapt" yourself to the special features of the Purishkeviches [A reference to Vladimir Purishkevich, a notorious advocate of violent anti-Semitism in pre-Revolutionary Russia.] . . . that is your task, not preaching or tolerating the slogan of national culture.[38]

What precisely does it mean for the proletariat to "adapt" to anti-Semites while fighting bourgeois culture? It sounds ominously as if some of the techniques will have to be borrowed from them. Yet Lenin vehemently opposed all manifestations of anti-Semitism. His attacks on the Bund must not be construed as anti-Semitism. He was shocked by the Beilis Case, the pogroms in tsarist Russia, and continuing Russian anti-Semitism, which he condemned vigorously and addressed specifically in March 1914 in a bill he wrote for the Bolshevik bloc in the Fourth Duma. Lenin described it as a bill abolishing all national restrictions against all nations," but said that it dealt "in particular detail with restrictions against the Jews. The reason is obvious: no nationality in Russia is so oppressed and persecuted as the Jewish. Anti-Semitism is striking ever deeper root among the propertied classes. . . . During the past few years, the persecution of the Jews has assumed incredible dimensions."[39] At this time he also seems to have accepted the idea of Jews as a nationality from the title of the bill: "A Bill for the Abolition of all Disabilities of the Jews and of all Restrictions on the Grounds of Origin of Nationality." Moreover, the first provision of the bill read: "Citizens of all nationalities inhabiting Russia are equal before the law." Their nationality would thus be constitutionally affirmed; immediate, practical questions were those of language and schools.

A paradox is suggested immediately: Lenin believed that his bill would eliminate the barbarous conditions under which Jews were forced to live and would lead to assimilation. Yet equality of rights meant employment of teachers of Yiddish and Jewish history in areas where Jews wanted such cultural expression. This freedom would or could conceivably sustain Jewish identity, however, and defeat assimilationist trends.[40]

In dealing with the language problem, Lenin seems to have had the Swiss model in mind, recognizing the equality of all national languages within a politically indivisible country. In April 1914, he wrote, "A democratic state is bound to grant *complete freedom* for the various languages and annul *all* privileges for any one language. A democratic state will not permit the oppression . . . of any one nationality by another, either in any particular region or in any branch of public affairs. . . . The workers of all nations have but one educational policy: freedom for the native language, and democratic and *secular* education."[41] In an essay (September 1913) called "Liberals and Democrats on the Language Questions," Lenin had expressed his policy of equality for national languages, thus granting Jews the right to use Yiddish, Hebrew, or any other language of their choice. In May 1914, he wrote a proposal for a bill which guaranteed the rights of nationalities to have their national culture taught in their schools, a position which was foreshadowed in his essay, "The Nationalization of Jewish Schools," in which he came out against school segregation of any kind, but for the preservation of national culture inside public schools.[42]

This formulation was much easier to theorize about than apply realistically, the more so since the only nationalism Lenin accepted was "proletarian nationalism," which meant to him "the acceptance of the state as standing above nationalities, while at the same time granting equality of the law to them. Lenin firmly believed that national inequalities could only be resolved within the proletarian state."[43] Proletarian nationalism was opposed to separatism of all kinds, especially to school and language segregation. Yet Lenin was not hostile to the preservation of national language and culture. Each national culture would be treated equally before the state, and presumably the linguistic, historical, and cultural traditions of each national group would be maintained, "at least until the economic development had eroded the social and psychological need for national loyalties."[44] Lenin thus was awaiting the economic development of human society to "eliminate the social basis of nationalism"—a phenomenon yet to be realized—if ever.

When the Bolsheviks seized power in 1917, there is another acknowledgment in their party program of the Jews as a distinct "nationality," indeed, as a "nation," despite Stalin's earlier disclaimer:

On the part of the workers of those nations, who in the capitalist era, were oppressors, special consideration is called for in attitudes toward the national spirit of oppressed nations [natsii] (for example, on the part of Byelorussians, Ukrainians, Poles toward Jews . . .)[45]

References to Jews in these terms appear quite frequently and in many different contexts throughout Soviet history, as will be seen, but never firmly or unequivocally defined so as to be universally understood by Soviet Jews. Most often, Soviet perceptions of Jews shade toward frustration because Jews haven't completely assimilated or disappeared. There is confusion and impatience over their survival in spite of Marxist predictions and ideological assumptions, and, most insistently, hostility. Lenin was never hostile toward Jews qua Jews, but like other early Bolshevik leaders, he understood their persistence throughout history solely as the result of anti-Semitism, in turn caused by capitalist exploitation. Socialism, it was maintained, would eliminate capitalism, and, thus, anti-Semitism. The Jews whom Lenin knew best—Grigori Zinoviev, Leon Trotsky, Yuli Martov, and Lev Kamenev—were wholly russified, and represented proto-types of the Jew-to-be.

Lenin never departed from the Marxist idea of national differences and antagonisms as "vanishing ever more and more" with the approach of socialism, but his conditional acceptance of self-determination and tantalizingly ambiguous formulations created a storm of polemical counter-blasts within the party. The outbreak of war provoked further controversy and complicated positions. The blurred lines between the "bourgeois" and "socialist" revolutions were now to be crisscrossed by inflamed nationalisms, confusing loyalties, and opposing interpretations of nebulous formulations. By March 1919, after the Bolsheviks had seized power, the nation's "will to secede" in Russia became the right of the "toiling masses"—that is, the prerogative of the Communist party. And by an ironical turnabout, Stalin eventually adopted the concept of cultural autonomy as a proud achievement of the Soviet Union but shriveled it to mean little more than the right to disseminate centrally issued directives in many languages, later euphemistically phrased by Stalin: "national in form, but socialist in content." Yet any enforced assimilation seemed precluded by Lenin's strictures against oppression by a national (Great Russian) culture, and the Declaration of the Rights of Nationalities, issued by the Council of People's Commissars on November 15, 1917. This declaration, which was signed by Lenin and Stalin, as Commissar of Nationalities, gave broad guarantees for the "removal of every and any national and national-religious privilege and restriction" and the "free development of the national minorities and ethnographic groups living within the confines of Russia."[46]

There was another specific reference at the Tenth Party Congress in 1921 to minorities within the Soviet Union without a territorial base— Letts, Estonians, Poles, and Jews, described as "fluid" national minorities. The tsarist policy of "destroying these minorities by every means, even pogroms," is contrasted with "the right of national minorities to free development" under the Soviet system.[47] Russian Jews thus had reason to hope that they would be able to enjoy cultural and even religious rights. Such hope was reinforced by an interview Lenin gave to a Jewish correspondent of the *Manchester Guardian* in 1922, and reproduced in *Pravda*, in which Lenin declared that on the basis of Soviet experience during the past five years, the government was convinced that "the only way to eliminate nationalist strife was to offer maximum satisfaction to the aspirations of all nationalities." Moreover, Lenin himself recognized that "for the forseeable future, nationalism would remain a real historical force to be accommodated." In the translation of these generalities, however, lay a thorny way for Jews, as for others. There were palpable contradictions between guarantees and Marxist doctrine, improvisations to meet immediate situations, and the zeal of Jewish Communists to seem to be upholding the purest essence of doctrine. In the near term, Jewish cultural fate hung on the translation of Lenin's vague ideas against the background of his ideological war against the Bund. This implementation first fell to the zealous *Evsektsiya*—the Jewish Sections of the Bolshevik party, then to Stalin and his successors.

Toward the end of Lenin's life, we see a mellowing of earlier harsh and strident dogmas. For example, he condemned Stalin's fierce campaign in 1922 against the Georgian communists, who wanted independence from the Soviet state. He deplored the fact that the Georgian action was justified out of the need for unity in the *apparat*—in the very same all-Russian apparat inherited from tsarism and "only barely touched up by Soviet experience." Moreover, he was at last beginning to understand the tenacious power of national feeling and possible abuses by a Russian-dominated party. In December 1922, he wrote:

Without doubt . . . given our present administration, a host of typically Russian abuses may arise. Special care is needed to combat these abuses, regardless of the sincerity of those who engage in the combat. We need a detailed code, which only the nationals living in a given republic are capable of drawing up properly. And we should not rule out in advance the possibility of reversing our present approach at the next congress of Soviets, i.e., to leave the union of socialist republics in being only as regards military and diplomatic relations, but in all others to reinstate the full independence of the separate republican governments.

Bear in mind that incompatability between them and Moscow . . . can be . . . paralyzed by party authority.[48]

We are left with many nagging questions. In 1921, Lenin had switched his thinking about the Russian peasant and, much to the embarrassment of orthodox Bolsheviks, re-introduced private enterprise. "Learn to trade," he later told his comrades. He backtracked on other formulas earlier preached as Communist gospel. In the last article he wrote, he said that the greatest attention should be directed toward instilling culture among the masses. "We could do for a start with some genuine bourgeois culture," he told astounded readers.[49] Would he have given range to minority cultures, to Jews, had he lived to see the tenacious struggle many of them were making to preserve or at least salvage what the Bolsheviks were destroying wholesale? In the greater reflectiveness that came with the convalescence after a succession of strokes and distancing from the hectic political arena, would he have understood the power, the meaning, the immense hold of *their* culture in the lives of Russian Jewry? Would he have dispensed with the instruments of suppression and terror, the police, and the centralized party apparatus he had created? Would he have removed Stalin, general secretary of the party, from whom he broke "all personal and comradely relations" in March 1923?

The questions are irresistible, but futile, of course, for control over these and other fundamental issues was soon to pass to Stalin—a very different man from Lenin—whose "Great Russian chauvinism and brutal domination of the party apparatus" Lenin warned against in January 1923. Already in 1922 a power struggle was developing between Zinoviev, president of the Communist International and of the Petrograd Soviet; Trotsky, chairman of the Military Revolutionary Council and Commissar of War; and Stalin. Eventually Stalin gained complete control of the party machine and the state. The fate of Russian Jews would henceforth be in his hands, ironically foreshadowed by his appointment as People's Commissar for the Affairs of Nationalities (Narkomnats)—"the first act of the Bolshevik Revolution in the national question."[50]

This commissariat and specific national commissariats or departments under it were to deal with the special affairs and needs of any nation or nationality. The first of these was the Polish Commissariat established in 1917; by the end of 1918, others were created for Armenians, Belorussians, Latvians, Lithuanians, Muslims, and Jews.[51] There were also departments for Estonians, Germans, Czechs, and Ukrainians. In May 1920, all commissariats were transformed into departments. On the party level, responsibility was given to national sections, the first of which was established for the Latvians. These vast changes, however, could apply only to Jews and others who were under Bolshevik control at the time. Between 1914 and 1921 much of the old Russian Empire was being torn away by German victories and by civil war. Jewish lives were lost, saved, and broken by these upheavals.

2

Jews in the Cross Fire of War and the Bolshevik Struggle for Power, 1914–21

The Bolshevik Revolution was neither made by the Jews, nor for the Jews, nor against the Jews. Our people in Russia were simply caught between the mill-stones of history and were confronted by a dilemma—either to be crushed and turned into historical dust, or to extricate themselves by a determined effort of readjustment . . . to the changed conditions, no matter how painful and tortuous this process should prove to be.

DR. JOSEPH ROSEN

The worst thing that can befall the leader of an extreme party is to be compelled to take over a government in an epoch when the movement is not yet ripe for the domination of the class which he represents, and for the realization of the measures which that domination implies. . . . Thus he necessarily finds himself in an unsolvable dilemma.

ENGELS, *The Peasant War in Germany*

W E have seen that some Jews participated in political parties and movements in Russia before and after the end of tsarism, but most were powerless bystanders or victims of the forces that churned events beginning in 1914. First were the convulsions of war; then the unsteady drift of the Provisional Government; Lenin's sudden seizure of power; and civil war, involving Bolshevik, German, Ukrainian, Polish, and tsarist armies struggling for control of contested territories until 1921. Russian Jews were caught in the cross fire of these events.

During World War I, the horrors of the campaigns on the Eastern front fell with particular fury upon the Pale of Settlement and the area became a huge bloodied battlefield. Jews in hundreds of communities were killed, maimed, put to flight, or made homeless. In characteristic fashion, the tsarist government both used and punished Jews at the same time. While some 500,000 Jews—10 percent of the Jewish population—served in the Russian army, military and civil officials were treating Jews as if they were the enemy. Not only were none of the disabilities imposed in the Pale lifted, but Jews were branded as spies, cowards, and deserters, despite the large numbers fighting in the battlefields and Jewish support of the war for the defense of Russia.[1] Many Jews hoped that the Russian alliance with England and France would liberalize their legal status, but their hopes were soon shattered. The Russian press began printing slanders, and unfounded stories circulated that Jews were giving aid and comfort to Germans. The public use of Yiddish was forbidden and Jewish mothers were not permitted to visit their wounded sons outside the Pale. The shocking incongruity of Jewish soldiers fighting for a country that was menacing their families was embarrassing to the Russian government and Allies, who were petitioned to denounce the expulsions and anti-Jewish barbarities committed by the military. But there was no improvement.

Another shattering blow came during the first German invasion of Russian territory late in 1914 and early 1915, when Russian authorities ordered massive expulsions of Jews in the Pale of Settlement from the provinces of Kurland, Kovno, Grodno, and the Polish provinces, on the grounds that they were a disloyal element. Over a half million Jews were expelled, often with less than a day's notice. Maxim Gorky was later to write:

In 1915, the most shameful anti-Jewish propaganda was started in the army. . . . It has been established that this Jew-baiting originated at headquarters, and, of course, could not but contribute to the disintegration of the army, in which there were about half a million Jews. The people, enraged and blinded by want, were unable to detect their true enemy. If the authorities sanctioned the killing and robbery of Jews—why not kill and rob them?[2]

A non-Jewish deputy in the Duma witnessed the expulsion of the whole Jewish population of Radom. At eleven o'clock at night

the people were informed that they had to leave, with a threat that anyone found at daybreak would be hanged . . . Old men, invalids, and paralytics had to be carried on people's arms because there were no vehicles. The police and gendarmes treated the Jewish refugees precisely like criminals. . . . In one case a train . . . was completely sealed and when finally opened, most of the inmates were found half dead.[3]

It is estimated that 100,000 Jews died of starvation and exposure during these forced expulsions, while for many who survived, there was a desperate struggle for life in the widespread upheavals. By August 1915, the terrible overcrowding within the Pale caused by these expulsions forced the government to open up the interior. About one-third of the refugees were given residence permits outside the Pale, but they were allowed only in the towns and cities, not the villages, and were not allowed to work in munitions. Younger Jews, however, were admitted into Russian schools. Many Russians were thus to have their first contact with Jews as a result of these grudging government concessions, concessions, in effect, which abolished the Pale and had far-reaching consequences later on.[4]

Very early in the war, Germany occupied Congress Poland, Lithuania, the Baltic states, and part of Belorussia, and aggravated the hostility of the Russian government by professing friendship for the oppressed Jews in the German-occupied territory. The German press meanwhile played up Germany's role as liberator of the East. General Ludendorff did indeed repeal tsarist and anti-Jewish legislation and issue proclamations of friendship—"An Meine Libe Yiden in Poylen"— in choice Yiddish, but the ravages of war in the German areas drove Jews to desperation. German commanders seized food, gold, silver, and other metals to help fight off the shortages cause by the British blockade. Some aid came through from the American Jewish Joint Distribution Committee, but many Jews subsisted on weeds and grass.

Lenin's determination to take Russia out of the war catapulted him to power, but other Russian socialists were divided on the issue. Many feared that a German victory would mean a continuation of tsarism. Even Bolsheviks were split on the war question and a number volunteered to serve in the Russian army. Lenin disagreed violently, arguing that world revolution would follow Russia's defeat. At first most Bundists supported a majority of Mensheviks, who took an antiwar internationalist position; the Social Democratic deputies in the Duma voted against military appropriations. This was the prevailing attitude of the Bund until after the Revolution of March 1917, when the tsar abdicated. By April 1917, many leading Bundists had moved to the "revolutionary defensist" position advocated by leading Mensheviks.[5] The "revolutionary defensists" argued that the war had to be prosecuted, not for simply patriotic reasons, but in order to preserve the revolution from destruction at the hand of imperialist Germany.[6] They also feared the dismemberment of the Russian Empire if the Revolution was premature. The Menshevik "defensists" favored socialist participation in the Provisional Government but at the April 1917 conference in Petrograd, the Bund voted against such participation[7]—a decision that almost caused a split between the Bund and the Mensheviks. A leading Bundist, Raphael Abramovich, expressed the dangers of such a split: "We knew that were we to leave Menshevism, we would have to unite with the Bolsheviks. Are we ready to do that? No, because a great abyss separates us! Therefore, a split in the Menshevik party would mean only a weakening of the working class because we would have to build a third party."[8]

The stresses and strains in the Bund, cautiously alluded to by its leaders, at times threatened its own unity. Workers, uprooted and scarcely surviving, were sick of war. Their needs were stark and practical—on quite a different level from the principles established by the Bund leadership. Moreover, the organizational structure of the Bund was greatly disrupted by the war, and the composition of its membership changed substantially after the March 1917 Revolution.[9] Large numbers of Jewish workers, in fact, were now outside the Pale and in need of basic relief. In White Russia, as well as in the Ukraine, major centers of Jewish life were in abject poverty and traumatized by pogroms and invading Polish armies, though loss of life was less severe in White Russia than in the Ukraine.[10]

The terrible slaughter of the war in 1914–16 shocked the revolutionaries, but did not cause them to lose their taste for disputation. Often in exile and far from the fighting fronts, they conducted war strategy at a high pitch. Some defensists now feared a Russian defeat or a separate peace with Germany and the destruction of the revolutionary movement. Lenin, in Switzerland, hostile to all the European socialist parties because of their patriotic lines, wanted the spread of civil war, chaos, and world revolution. Later, he was prepared to deal with Germany to hasten the Revolution.

The winter of 1916, one of the hardest in Russian history, spread gloom and despair over the country. Thousands of soldiers were deserting every day, as the lack of food, arms, medical supplies, and the prospect of defeat dried up the will to carry on. The German government, which had been mulling over the possibility of fomenting revolution elsewhere, now began to focus with special intensity on Russia. A two-pronged tactic emerged: to promote independence movements in the Caucasus, the Ukraine, Poland, and Finland; and to strike at the heart of Russia itself through the Russian revolutionary movement. An Estonian socialist, Alexander Keskuela, who hated Russia and yearned to secure the liberation of Estonia from Russia, suggested enlisting the Bolshevik leader Lenin in the German plan.[11] With funds from Germany and the Bund for the Liberation of the Ukraine, Lenin financed Bolshevik publications, printed mainly on the presses of the German Admiralty. By September 1915, he had conveyed to Keskuela concrete terms for making peace with Germany in the event that Bolsheviks gained power in Russia. These negotiations formed the first steps in his single-minded determination to take Russia out of the war and bring about a Communist revolution. Such a revolution, in turn, would irrevocably transform Jewish life in Russia. Everything turned upon Lenin.

Meanwhile, events in Russia itself were staggering toward the downfall of tsarism and the creation of a Provisional Government, committed to keeping Russia in the war. Yet there was no clear direction, no forceful leadership. A Siberian peasant put it well: "We feel that we have escaped from a dark cave into the bright sunlight. And here we stand not knowing where to go or what to do." The man who *would* know what to do and where to go—Lenin—finally stopped his wandering. He was crossing Europe with German connivance in a sealed German train, and arrived at the Finland Station in Petrograd the night of April 16, 1917.

A vast crowd blocked the square in front of the stations and red banners and Bolshevik slogans decked the railroad platforms. A thunderous "La Marseillaise" boomed forth amid shouts of welcome as Lenin's train drew to a stop. He electrified the crowd, greeting them as the

vanguard of the world-wide proletarian army . . . The piratical imperialist war is the beginning of civil war throughout Europe . . . World-wide socialism has already dawned . . . The Russian revolution accomplished by you has prepared the way and opened a new epoch. Long live the world-wide socialist revolution.[12]

"Suddenly, before the eyes of all of us," the Menshevik Sukhanov recalled, "completely swallowed up by the routine drudgery of the revolution, there was presented a bright, blinding, exotic beacon. . . .

There has broken in upon us in the revolution a note that was . . . novel, harsh and somewhat deafening."[13]

Contrary to the ideas of his Bolshevik colleagues, Lenin was determined to bring down the Provisional Government and sue for peace. He attacked the Petrograd Soviet, a council of workers, soldiers, and socialists of all kinds, and urged peasants to seize the land, and workers, the factories. Capitalism was to be overthrown and in its place there would be state control of all production and the nationalization of land. Conditions in Russia, Lenin said, justified the transition to the second stage of the revolution. But the soviet must be extricated from its involvement in the Provisional Government and become the weapon of the proletariat.

Lenin's new perception of the soviet now became very significant.[14] In earlier years and as late as January 1917 he had been contemptuous of the soviets, but by March, he had hailed the Petrograd[15] Soviet as a "new unofficial, undeveloped, still comparatively weak *workers' government* expressing the interests of the proletariat and of all the poorest part of the town and country population."[16] Later, this view was strengthened and became celebrated as the "April Theses," in which Lenin argued that all power must be handed over to the soviets which had been set up in Petrograd, Moscow, and other large cities.

There were few Jews in the Provisional Government, provincial, or city administrations, but the proportion of Jews in the Petrograd Soviet was quite high. In April 1917, 20 percent of the 124 members of the Executive Committee of the Petrograd Soviet were Jews, all but two representing non-Bolshevik parties. Members of the Bund played an especially active role in numerous local soviets, often serving on soviet executive committees. In the Berdichev Soviet, for example, there were seventy-one Bundists, and its chairman was the Bundist David Lipets.[17] Mark Liber and Raphael Abramovich, Bundist leaders, were outstanding figures at the Congress of Soviets in June 1917. Bundists were also active in trade union congresses, artisan conventions, and teachers' congresses and won many seats in city dumas, giving some of them political and administrative experience that translated into government positions after the Bolshevik takeover.

On May 8, the Executive Committee of the Petrograd Soviet voted to summon an International Socialist Conference representing all parties and factions of the working class that accepted their proposal to compel belligerent governments to negotiate for peace without annexations or indemnities. For a time, several socialists in the Petrograd Soviet joined the Provisional Government, but their desire for peace could not be reconciled with Russia's obligations to its wartime allies. Lenin demanded that the soviet take power at once from the floundering government. However, the time was not yet ripe.

Bundists and other moderate socialists heard Lenin's vituperative attack on the Provisional Government and its Minister of War Alexander Kerensky at the Congress of Soviets. The restless and discontented soldiers and sailors in the soviets would eventually respond to Lenin's call for violence, but Lenin disaffected many of his own comrades as well as non-Bolshevik socialists by his hard line. At the congress, moreover, the Bolsheviks were a very small minority. When the Menshevik Minister of Posts said, "At the present moment, there is no political party which would say, 'Give the power into our hands, go away, we will take your place!' There is no such party in Russia." Lenin replied, "There is."[18] The Congress voted to support the Provisional Government and rejected the Bolshevik resolution demanding the transfer of power to the soviets. Moreover, Lenin was under attack for having accepted German help and having worked with the double agent Roman Malinovsky. In July, an abortive Bolshevik-led uprising forced him to flee to Finland. Until the fall of 1917, Bolshevik influence declined, and the Provisional Government hung on, vacillating between a policy of resolute action and fear of offending the non-Bolshevik socialists. The drift of events thereafter played into Lenin's hands and seemed to justify his boldest calculations. They were especially strengthened by the Kornilov affair.

In July, Kerensky became Prime Minister and appointed General Lavr Kornilov as Commander-in-Chief of the Russian armies. Both men wanted to stop the demoralization of soldiers at the front and plan a victorious offensive. In addition, Kornilov wanted to eliminate the influence of the soviets and "Bolshevik Petrograd." By September, he attempted a coup d'état by provoking disturbances in Petrograd and seizing the capital, but most of the soldiers and the Petrograd Soviet opposed him. The Bolsheviks now saw their opportunity. They were not willing to fight for Kerensky, but were perfectly willing to fight against and expose Kornilov. They secured arms from government arsenals and became the prime political force in the swirling confusion of the time, drawing the workers and peasants to identify a new enemy: not the unpatriotic Bolsheviks who wanted "peace, bread, and land" for the people, but the tsarist generals who wanted to make war on the Russian people. The Bolsheviks increased their strength in the soviets, winning majorities in the Petrograd and Moscow soviets, and among the soldiers, while Kerensky wavered uncertainly. The number of party members increased ten-fold to 200,000 between January and August 1917. Moreover, Trotsky, released from prison in the middle of September, was elected president of the Petrograd Soviet and became the driving force in its "military-revolutionary committee," which made the military preparations for the Revolution.

Jews, among others, had been appearing in soldiers' committees that had emerged, especially in Petrograd. In the field, the old tsarist anti-Semitism was still rife and despite the great shortage of officers, even Jews with university degrees were barred from officer class. Western press sources reported that "the Russian military authorities instigated the propagation of anti-Semitism on a broad scale in the Russian army and pointed out the serious consequences of this . . . ,"[19] but nothing could be done by the Provisional Government to remedy this problem in the turbulent days of its short life. Continuing persecutions, expulsions, and imprisonment of Jewish soldiers, however, caused a number of them to ultimately shift their allegiance to the Bolshevik side.[20]

The shift of loyalty of the Petrograd garrison in October 1917 from the Provisional Government to the Bolsheviks was crucial to the ultimate Bolshevik victory.[21] The garrison of several hundred thousand men was vital to the control of the city, and the city, to ultimate power in Russia. By the fall of 1917, many soldiers in the garrison had been moved to the front, creating seething discontent among men heartily sick of the war. All of the Russian socialist parties competed for influence among the soldiers in the garrison, as well as in the Petrograd Soviet, which vied with the Provisional Government as an authoritative force, but the Bolsheviks alone aimed at absolute control of both. Party cells were established in a number of garrison units and antiwar propaganda penetrated deeply. Discipline was disintegrating, especially so after word came of a massive German breakthrough at the front that further discredited the war effort. Moreover, soldier and sailor committees within the soviet became more susceptible to Bolshevik arguments, even if wary of the commands of the party. By October there were almost no troops upon whom the government could rely. "The soldiers of the Petrograd garrison supported the Bolsheviks in the struggle for transfer of all power to the soviets because only the Bol-

sheviks were untainted by support for the war effort and only the overthrow of the Provisional Government seemed to offer them hope of
avoiding the injustices of the tsarist military system and death at the
front."[22] Moreover, the crisis over the garrison ended the earlier disarray within the Bolshevik party and gave Lenin the opportune moment
to seize power.

From his hiding place in Helsingfors, Lenin bombarded the Bolshevik Central Committee with instructions to plan for an armed rising
and the seizure of Petrograd. "Delay means death," he thundered. On
October 9 (22 new style), he returned secretly and in disguise to Petrograd and in a virtually bloodless coup on October 25 (November 7 new
style), after stormy internal disputes over whether the time was ripe
for a forcible seizure of power, the tiny Bolshevik party took power in
Russia—one of many upheavals that had swept the capital, but the one
that ultimately consolidated Bolshevik power. Just eight years earlier,
Lenin's wife Krupskaya had lamented, "we have no people at all," and
Zinoviev had to admit, "at this unhappy period the party as a whole
ceased to exist."[23]

The hurtling events following the Bolshevik coup on October 25th
(November 7) could scarcely be grasped. Trotsky, who played a key
role in the coup, called it a "revolution by telegraph." Scarcely a shot
had been fired. By no means secure, however, the Bolsheviks had
aroused fierce antagonisms within the socialist movement and division
within its own ranks as to whether to regard the Revolution as bourgeois-democratic or proletarian-socialist.[24] However, Lenin soon crushed
all varieties of opposition.

Yet much of Russia was unsubdued and remained hostile to the Bolsheviks. An anti-Bolshevik volunteer army was being raised with good
prospects of getting Allied support. Peasant support was also proble-
matical. Lenin, however, acting as if support already existed, was also
counting on European revolutions to preserve his regime. Under his
chairmanship, the Soviet Council of People's Commissars established
on November 8, met at the Smolny Institute and churned out a fantastic stream of decrees uprooting every institution and tradition in Russian and Jewish life. "People's commissars" ordered the partition of
land and distribution to the peasants, nationalization of businesses and
industry, and confiscation of private wealth.

The Bolsheviks had solid support in Petrograd and Moscow but fell
far behind the other parties elsewhere, as was evident in the elections

to the Constituent Assembly on November 25. When the results were tallied, the Bolsheviks had less than a quarter of the votes—29 percent counting the support of the Left Social Revolutionaries. The Bolshevik party had been committed to the Assembly, and had pledged to convene it, but Lenin knew his party could not win a majority and quickly neutralized, then dissolved the Assembly. In a speech of December 14, 1917, he said:

> We are asked to call the Constituent Assembly as originally conceived. No, thank you! It was conceived against the people and we carried out the rising to make certain that it will not be used against the people . . . When a revolutionary class is struggling against the propertied classes which offer resistance, that resistance has to be suppressed, and we shall suppress it. . . .[25]

He discredited the deputies as well as the concept of the Assembly and tried to sabotage the meeting itself. However, deputies to the Constituent Assembly decided to meet on November 28, only to find the gates to the Tauride Palace closed and guarded by heavily armed Bolshevik Lettish soldiers.

The Bolshevik party debated the question, but for Lenin the Assembly was a spent bourgeois force. The March Revolution had created a new reality—"revolutionary social democracy"—a higher form of the democratic principle than the Constituent Assembly. His *Theses on the Constituent Assembly*, published anonymously in *Pravda* in December 1917 soon became Bolshevik party doctrine, making support for the Assembly treason to the proletariat. It also created an irrevocable breach between the Bolsheviks and other socialist parties, who were now viewed as counterrevolutionaries because they believed the revolution was still in its democratic-bourgeois stage. The Assembly, nevertheless, met on January 5, 1918, amid catcalls and jeers from the Bolsheviks. It even passed resolutions approving an armistice with Germany, redistributing land, and declaring Russia a republic, but on the following day the Executive Committee of the Congress of Soviets, which was summoned to torpedo the Assembly, passed a resolution dissolving it. Guards were posted at the doors of the palace to prevent the deputies from returning. The Assembly, which represented Russia's last brief hope for democracy, never met again. The All-Russian Central Committee of the All-Russian Congress of Soviets had already adopted resolutions declaring Russia a "republic of Soviets of workers', soldiers' and peasants' deputies," and establishing the Russian Soviet Republic "on the basis of a free union of free nations, as a federation of national

Soviet republics." The leap to a new Bolshevik-controlled order had been made, disposing once and for all the old dilemma of power which many Marxist revolutionaries had struggled with since the 1880s[26] and which inhibited them in the critical days of the battered Provisional Government.

However, in January 1918, this new power faced serious military threats. All over western Russia, the German armies had been advancing toward the Ukraine and Estonia, to the very approaches to Petrograd. In swift stages, Russia now faced the nightmare of enemy occupation, famine, and fratricidal warfare. Peace had to be made with the Germans and the movement for an independent Ukraine had to be crushed. The events in the Ukraine were to play a fateful role for Jews in Soviet Russia.

For Jews, the Ukraine was the crucible of their suffering, the same area which had witnessed intense anti-Jewish feeling and murderous pogroms in the past. The Ukraine, nevertheless, was also the main center of Jewish life in Russia, containing more than one and a half million Jews and vital cultural and communal institutions. The Jewish population in the Ukraine was largely urban, with major Jewish centers in Odessa, Ekaterinoslav, Berdichev, and Kiev; in a few cities, Jews constituted an absolute majority or very large proportion. Odessa, for example, had a Jewish population of 150,000 before the Revolution; Kiev, over 50,000. But there were also many small shtetlach in the Ukraine, sunk in poverty. A largely illiterate Ukrainian peasantry in the region had been oppressed for many years by Polish and Russian overlords, and the Jews, also considered non-Ukrainian, played important but unpopular economic roles in the Ukrainian economy as merchants, managers of landed estates, factory owners, artisans, and workers. Indeed, almost the whole of the urban population was non-Ukrainian, and in the cities, Ukrainian was seldom heard. The dominant languages there were Russian, Polish, and Yiddish. A smouldering peasant nationalism was fueled by a vehement hostility toward Russians, Poles, and especially Jews.

The Ukrainian nationalist movement was slow in building. It had been sharply repressed by the tsarist regime, but was vigorously encouraged by the Germans, and even earlier, by the Provisional Government. On July 1, 1917 the Ukrainian Central Council, called *Rada*, appointed three vice-secretaries in charge of Russian, Polish, and Jewish affairs and resolved to guarantee minority rights under a vaguely defined Ukrainian autonomy. The vice-secretary in charge of Jewish affairs, Dr. Moishe Silberfarb, soon set up a secretariat for education and community affairs and a commission to draft the legal text for Jewish national autonomy.[27] The Ukrainian People's Republic was established on November 20, 1917, and on January 22, 1918, the Rada declared its independence from Russia.

Jews were caught in an insoluble quandary. Many had viewed the prospect of a Ukrainian state federated with other Russian republics sympathetically, and all Jewish members of the Rada voted for the November 20 measure. However, in an atmosphere of growing suspicion and nationalist fever, there were some doubts and reservations expressed, which clearly annoyed the Ukrainians and provoked their mounting distrust. In their own hunger for freedom, many Ukrainian peasants seized upon Jews as the cause of their wretchedness. Moreover, the Russian minority in the Ukraine, in a familiar role, diverted popular discontent to the perennial Jewish scapegoat. In September 1917, pro-tsarist groups issued a proclamation declaring: "Russian people, awake from your sleep! A short time ago the sun shone and the Russian tsar used to visit Kiev. Now you find Jews everywhere! Let us throw off the yoke; we can no longer bear it! They will destroy the Fatherland. Down with the Jews! Russian people, unity! Bring the tsar back to us."[28]

A wave of anti-Jewish riots broke out in the autumn of 1917. The Ukrainian General Secretary for Army Affairs, Simeon Petlyura, promised to take emergency measures to stop them, but no practical steps were taken. Despairing of any help from the armed forces, Zionists and Jewish soldiers began to form Jewish self-defense units to protect Jewish communities. Abusive anti-Jewish speeches and insults within the Rada also filled Jews with alarm over their vulnerability to official as well as popular anti-Semitism.[29] The accumulating tensions broke into open conflict when complete separation from Russia was voted. Before the vote was taken, Jewish speakers were mocked and jeered when they discussed Jewish autonomy. Consequently, they feared that the Ukrainian government would soon be captured by anti-Semitic elements and that an independent Ukraine would break up the Jewish community of the old Russian Empire. The Jewish socialist parties voted against independence, while the other Jewish parties abstained. Jewish hesitancy in accepting Ukrainian independence undoubtedly contributed to the spread of pogroms, but Jewish fear and suspicion of Ukrainian hostility were based on hard facts of history, a history of pogroms, expulsions, blood libels, and the horrors of the Khmielnitsky massacres.

A new complication, endangering Jews even more than the vote in the Rada, developed in the last weeks of 1917. A Bolshevik force was being organized and consolidated by reinforcements from the outside. A Bolshevik-led mutiny broke out in the Kiev arsenal and two Ukrainian regiments joined the workers. Some Jews identified with Bolshevism, especially in Kiev, Ekaterinoslav, and Odessa, giving rise to talk about "Jew-Bolsheviks" and "Yid-traitors." Yet, in the Rada's struggle against the first Bolshevik invasion of the Ukraine in January 1918, Jewish political parties took a pro-Ukrainian position. The Bolsheviks were looked upon as a foreign power, an army of occupation destroying the possibility of a democratic future in the Ukraine. At the time, even Jewish socialist parties refused to recognize or collaborate with the Bolsheviks.[30]

The Bolshevik "invasion," however, was very brief, owing to German intervention and military help. On February 9, 1918, the Ukrainian government signed a separate peace treaty with Germany and Austria and the Bolsheviks were pushed back. On March 1, the government of the Ukrainian People's Republic was proclaimed in accordance with the Treaty of Brest-Litovsk, signed by Germany and Trotsky, and the Ukrainian government returned to Kiev under the protection of Austro-German bayonets. There followed another wave of anti-Jewish riots, some instigated by starving deserters from the front, others by Petlyura's units and Ukrainian bands of rebellious peasants called Haidamaks. The main center of the pogroms was on the right bank of the Dnieper in the provinces of Kiev, Podolia, and Volhynia, where civil war and nationalist passions raged in full fury. The Petlyura movement, generally held responsible for the largest number of Jewish victims, had its roots in this area; here, too, Cossack chiefs called atamans and partisan leaders stirred up peasants against the Jewish population for alleged pro-Bolshevik support.[31]

The presence of Jewish deputies in the Rada, as well as their nominal participation in the Ukrainian Cabinet of Ministers did not clear the air of intense Judeophobia outside the Rada. On April 28 the German Army Command dissolved the Rada and elevated a former tsarist, General

Pavlo Skoropadsky, to the ephemeral throne of hetman—the old Za-
porog Cossack title of leader—of the Ukrainian state.[32] The extremely
tense political situation was hardly conducive to thoughtful planning
about a permanent national organization of Ukrainian Jewry, but some
rudimentary work was started, only to be shattered by new political
upheavals.

For Jewish Bund workers, the horror of the pogroms had obscured the
old theoretical differences between the Bund and the Bolsheviks. The
most important consideration was the Red Army's protection against
the forces of Petlyura and White Army General Anton Denikin. The
leadership did not lose sight of those differences but saw the German
Revolution of 1918 in a new light: It seemed to confirm the Bolshevik
analysis of the propelling effect of the Russian Revolution and the ability of the world proletariat to seize power.[33] Some Bundist leaders in
the Ukraine became more receptive to the Bolshevik view. Cut off from
the rest of the party, they were not only physically separated but experienced a difficult local political struggle. In the fall of 1918, three
factions began to emerge in the Ukrainian Bund: left, center, and right.
Then in November, the Germans surrendered to the Allies, and the
Hetman regime, deprived of the support of German troops, collapsed.
A Bolshevik government installed itself in Kharkov, and a five-man
Directorate, with Petlyura at the head, assumed power in Kiev. As late
as December, the Bund (including the left wing) favored a pact with
the Directory so long as it concluded a military alliance with the Soviet
regime and so long as the Soviet base of power was broadened.[34]

The German withdrawal plunged the Ukraine into unparalleled an-
archy; mass killings of Jews started as soon as Ukrainian and Soviet
forces clashed. Petlyura's poorly disciplined units organized pogroms
which increased in violence month after month and assumed the character of frightful massacres. The massacre at Proskurov in February
1919 was in itself so devastating that it was responsible for the "Great
Fear" that swept through every Jewish shtetl in Russia that spring. A
nurse who worked in the Danish Red Cross later charged that Ataman
Semosenko, who was under Petlyura's command, was responsible for
the destruction of the whole community: "There was a girl of nineteen
whose breast wounds were so severe the doctors considered amputa-
tion . . . a girl of fourteen whose fingers had been slashed away . . .

a baby pierced on a sabre . . . the paralyzed son of a rabbi slain in his bed . . . two children cast alive in a fire. . . . Corpses lay rotting in the street as peasants rifled clothes and cut away fingers and ears for rings and earrings."[35] In March 1919, soldiers of the Petlyura regime carried out the most violent anti-Jewish atrocities in Eastern Europe since the Khmielnitsky massacres of 1648; again, in May, another pitch of horror was reached when a Soviet military commander, Grigoriev, rebelled against the Bolshevik government. One hundred and twenty pogroms were organized by Grigoriev that month.[36]

Meanwhile, leftist Bund groups, unable to find an alternative, and believing the unfolding social revolution required a re-orientation, tried to differentiate the Bund position from that of the Communist party. ("Communist" replaced "Bolshevik" after March 1918.) Nevertheless, they began joining the Communist party, "completely losing their political independence and forgetting the special national tasks which the Jewish working class had even today," according to Benjamin Kheifetz, leader of the right-wing Bundists.[37] When Red Army troops attacked the forces of the Directory, the provisional bureau of the main committee of the Ukrainian Bund voted 3–2 to support Soviet power and concluded a military alliance with the Bolsheviks, though it had serious reservations about Bolshevik terror and nationality policies.

The splits and soul-searching of the Bund were also reflected in the Ukrainian Social Democratic Workers' party, the left wing of which argued that only a Soviet Ukraine could prevent the Bolsheviks from annexing the Ukraine.[38] Eventually the left wing in the Kiev Bund led by Moishe Rafes believed it could save the Bund's national program and guarantee Jewish national autonomy by forming a separate Jewish Communist party (Kombund) and split away from the rest of the Kiev Bund. A similar split took place in Ekaterinaslav, Kharkov, and Poltava in the Ukraine. In Belorussia (White Russia) where the Bund had a firmer base, a longer tradition, and worker-artisan membership and where there were no pogroms, the split came later in 1920.

"The split in the Ukrainian Bund came about not so much on the national question but on the broader political question of the nature and future of the revolution. Furthermore, the left Bundists were very careful to assert both their organizational independence of the Communist Party and the right to formulate their own nationality policy."[39] The dilemma was painfully described by one Bundist who had joined the Bolsheviks: "To whom can we turn? . . . . To civilized Europe which signs treaties with the anti-Semitic Directory? The armed carriers of socialism, the Bolsheviks, are the only force which can oppose the pogroms. . . . For us there is no other way. . . . This is the best and only way to combat the pogroms."[40] The pogroms, meanwhile, showed no signs of abating in the Ukraine.

Petlyura apparently had no desire to curb the excesses of his units and is reliably quoted as having said: "It is a pity that pogroms take place, but they uphold the discipline in the army."[41] Even worse atrocities were perpetrated by the well-organized White, anti-Bolshevik Volunteer Army of General Anton Denikin,[42] which penetrated the Ukraine in June 1919. Denikin's troops were charged with at least 213 pogroms between May and November, 1919[43] in the course of their war against the Ukrainian nationalists. These atrocities have been documented in a number of places, including an authoritative report prepared by the Ukrainian Jewish leader Dr. Vladimir Tiomkin in 1921, in which he accuses Denikin's army of the most horrible massacres in the Ukraine. "We have come," one of the generals said, "not to fight the Bolsheviks, but to make war on the Jews." Jews "were flayed or burned alive by units of the Volunteer Army."[44] Their sadism has been recorded in the following letter, written by one of the officers:

My dear Kostia,
   Come to our rooms this evening at seven to have a cup of tea with us. We intend to show you something very interesting. Denis has picked up a small Jewish boy who[m] he calls "the Commissar" and with whom he intends to have great fun this evening. He has prepared something in the nature of a crown and a bamboo stick. He will place the crown on the head of the little Jew and will press it down with the stick until the skull of the Jew bursts. Is this not entertaining?[45]

There are also gruesome accounts of men being buried alive, children's bodies smashed against walls and their parents butchered, women raped, others left insane.

Ironically, many Jews had awaited the coming of the Volunteer Army with high hopes; as artisans, tradesmen, and petty bourgeoisie, they had suffered from Soviet economic policies and hoped to resume their customary lives after a White victory.[46] Like Soviet policy between 1939 and 1941, when Soviet Jews were denied information about Nazi anti-Jewish atrocities, so those of the White Army were not revealed in Soviet publications. Every Jewish community had to learn from bitter experience.[47] Self-defense against the Petlyurists had sometimes been successful,[48] but against the Volunteer Army it was hopeless. For their part, White Army officers were obsessed with a delusional anti-Semitism bordering on the pathological, using images and language reminiscent of Nazi propaganda. Under pressure from such officers, Denikin dismissed a number of Jews who had joined the White Army. Finally, in December 1919, after many requests, he relented and denounced pogroms, but his soldiers and officers assumed that he was merely appeasing foreign public opinion; his statement was followed by the bloodiest pogroms in the history of Kiev.[49]

Between 1918 and the early months of 1921, when Soviet control was established in the Ukraine, it is estimated that pogroms took place in 700 communities. Between 50,000 and 60,000 Jews were killed. Another 100,000 were maimed or died of wounds; 200,000 were orphaned.[50] In later years, Israel Zangwill, the Jewish writer, graphically described the Jewish tragedy in the Ukraine in a few compressed words: "It is as Bolsheviks that the Jews of South Russia have been massacred by the armies of Petlyura, though the armies of Sokolow have massacred them as partisans of Petlyura, the armies of Makhno as bourgeois capitalists, the armies of Grigoriev as Communists, and the armies of Denikin at once as Bolsheviks, capitalists and Ukrainian nationalists. It is Aesop's old fable."[51]

In 1920, a number of Red Army pogroms were instigated by Semyon Budenny's First Cavalry, most of whose soldiers had previously served under Denikin. In Kremenchug, for example, Jews recognized them from the pogroms of a year before.[52] The Red Army Command, however, vigorously condemned these pogroms and disarmed the guilty regiments. In October 1920, Mikhail Kalinin, President of the Soviet Union, attended a military parade in the Ukraine and made a speech condemning Red Army pogroms and demanding that the Red Army fight a class war, not a national one.[53] Bolshevik advances further inflamed anti-Semitism and set new cycles of massacres into motion, but as the Soviet forces progressively consolidated their power, the Ukraine was reoccupied and a certain measure of security for Jews was achieved.

The frightfulness of the pogroms more than anything else forced Jews to look to the Bolsheviks, and especially to the Red Army, as their only refuge. On one occasion, the entire Jewish population of a town of 4,000 Jews trooped after a retiring Bolshevik regiment. Obviously, this had important political implications, although many Jews mentally divorced the Red Army from the Communist party and government. A special recruitment section of the Red Army was set up to enlist Jewish youth. They were welcomed, but it was realized that "many enter the Red Army partially out of hatred for the White pogromists" and a desire for revenge.[54] Even those who opposed bolshevism on ideological grounds supported the Red Army. According to an eyewitness, "Jewish youth leave the shtetlach and run to Kiev—to enter the Red Army. They are not Bolsheviks at all . . . but they go into the Red Army because one can die with rifle in hand."[55]

The terrible consequences of the pogroms were felt for many years in the Ukraine, when thousands of homeless children wandered the streets, begging or stealing, often subsisting on grass. A pall of grief and stunned disbelief hung over many Ukrainian Jews throughout the 1920s. Jewish economic life did not start to recover until the 1930s. In later years, all of the major Soviet Yiddish writers were haunted by the memory of direct experience of the pogroms; their poems and novels are filled with pogrom scenes.

The pacification of the Ukraine was only one of many overwhelming crises that beset the new regime. Besides counterrevolutionary White armies and independence movements in the Ukraine, Finland, and Poland, there was an Allied intervention aimed at getting Russia back into the war after Russia had signed the separate peace treaty of Brest-Litovsk with Germany (March 1918).[56] Famine, mutinies, social chaos and economic turmoil also plagued the land.

The struggle of Poland at the time to wrench herself free from Russia also trapped Jews in the violence of war, pogroms,[57] and disfigured loyalties. Poland was reconstituted as a state in 1918, but was attacked by the Red Army in 1920. Jewish soldiers who had volunteered to fight with the Poles were detained as potential traitors and Jews generally were treated as Bolshevik supporters. The Bolshevik offensive was quickly smashed and the Poles then invaded the Ukraine, setting fire to Jewish homes and shops, attacking areas already laid waste by Petlyura and Denikin, killing 30,000 additional Jews.

Altogether two million Jews of tsarist Russia passed to Polish control in the new territorial settlement, representing a great loss to Russian Jewry, for those Jews lived within the great centers of Jewish life: Warsaw, Vilna, Kovno, Bialystok, and Grodno—the heart of East European Jewry—which were wrenched away from Russian Jewry, leaving it much weakened and less able to resist the subsequent sovietization of Jewish life. Moreover, the web of relationships, individual as well as institutional, between both Jewries was broken and then destroyed in the physical severance. Twenty years later, when they touched briefly (see Chapter 15), they met as strangers.

During the four years, 1917 to 1921, in which the Bolsheviks consolidated their power, Jews experienced their control in diverse ways. Those who were protected by Soviet arms during the civil war and pogroms were grateful, but also ambivalent if not apprehensive about the future. The poet Chaim Grade has told the story of a Red Army commissar who shot a soldier for having taken a watch from a Jew during the Soviet occupation of Vilna—a totally new, bracing experience for Jews. For the first time, somebody was defending them.[58] Many young Jews, too, and refugees who survived in the large cities outside the Pale, found new opportunities for education and work under the new regime (see Chapter 11). Others rushed to fill new jobs in government agencies but felt new stings of anti-Semitism in places where Jews had never been. The large masses of Jews were shocked and bewildered by the swift and brutal Bolshevik measures which destroyed their property, their religious and national culture, and often their livelihood. The freedom and cultural and political efflorescence of the brief March Revolution was extinguished—an immense loss especially for Jews— and replaced by the sudden, harsh crudities of "war communism" and the destructive actions of the Evsektsiya—the Jewish Sections of the Communist party—organized to bring bolshevism to *di idishe gass*—"the Jewish street."

3

The Collapse of Jewish Political Parties and the Rise of the Evsektsiya

[Shatov] was one of those idealistic beings common in Russia, who are suddenly struck by some overmastering idea which seems, as it were, to crush them at once, and sometimes forever. They are never equal to coping with it, but put passionate faith in it, and their whole life passes afterwards, as it were, in the last agonies under the weight of the stone that has fallen upon them and half crushed them.

DOSTOYEVSKY, *The Possessed*

These zealots must have their own way. They were like those men who walked always with their eyes on the stars and, never seeing the ground, they stumbled into pits and were grievously hurt.

BORIS BOGEN

THE immense losses, dislocations, and sheer human problems facing the new Soviet regime in the first months of the Bolshevik Revolution did not immediately result in the drastic economic measures known as war communism. Rather, the new rulers were gripped by a swelling euphoria and desire to transform long-rooted structures such as the family, illiterate peasantry, army, and bureaucracy along utopian lines.[1] However, Russia's social backwardness and resistance to change, combined with the isolation of Bolshevik leaders from the grim realities of prerevolutionary Russian society and their inclination toward grand abstractions, created inevitable anger, impatience, disillusionment, and, with the civil war, resort to authoritarian controls.[2] As early as January 1918, for example, Lenin wanted all food speculators shot on the spot. Moreover, from the very beginning, his central goal was preservation of power. The vision of a workers' state and a flourishing cooperative peasantry, imbued with a deep culture and protected by a proletariat militia, collapsed under the vehement pursuit of this goal, spreading violence and the brutalization of Russian life, ideological rebellion and the threat of "class enemies."[3]

In the great economic and social convulsions caused by the Bolshevik Revolution, many people surged to positions of authority and power; many more sank until a measure of equilibrium could be achieved. Jews, too, reacted variously. Although most opposed the regime, some were initially very useful to it and suddenly appeared in government jobs from which they had been barred under tsarism. The fall of the old regime and the Provisional Government had left a void in the ministries. Many of the old Russian intelligentsia had emigrated, and most of the Germans who had filled important posts lived in territories that were no longer within the USSR. Jews were prominent among those who replaced these vital groups. By 1921, for example, although under 2 percent of the population, Jews comprised 19.9 percent of all personnel in the Ministry of Justice in the Ukraine.[4] In the Commissariats of Trade in Moscow and Leningrad, Jews comprised over 13 percent of the staff.[5] Jews were also important in filling posts in the Foreign Ministry in the early 1920s and later, in building administrative structures in the non-Russian states such as Belorussia and the Crimean Republic. According to the census of 1920, Jews had a 70.4 percent literacy rate— the highest of any large national group in the Soviet Union—and more than double the average for the Soviet population in general at the time.

This new prominent position of Jews was also reflected in their membership in the Communist party. In 1922, there were 19,564 Jewish Communists, 5.2 percent of the party membership.[6] They also became visible—and hated—as were other minority people such as the Poles and Letts, in the ranks of the first secret political police, *Ve-Che-Ka, Cheka* for short, (the All-Russian Commission for Suppression of Counterrevolution, Sabotage, and Speculation). With the removal of legal barriers, already enacted by the Provisional Government, Jews also streamed into the universities.

Jewish students, so long as they were not children of the stigmatized bourgeois or "declassed" groups (see Chapter 7), represented a persecuted minority, and were welcomed into the universities. By the same token, these new opportunities offered by the Bolsheviks favorably predisposed such students to the regime. The zeal to study can be seen in a few statistics: In 1923 (the first year for which Soviet figures are available), 47.4 percent of all students at institutions of higher learning in the Ukraine, where 60 percent of all Soviet Jews lived, were Jews, as compared with 10.7 percent in 1913.[7] (Jews constituted 5 percent of the total population of the Ukraine.) Furthermore, they joined faculties of universities in quite large numbers, especially in newly opened institutions.

Some Jews also felt great hope—even exultation—in the glowing prospect of a new, fairer social order under communism. A more measured optimism was expressed by those who were suffering personally but who still hoped for redress of injustices. The largest numbers were still living in impoverished shtetlach and trying to recover from the atrocities of the pogroms and civil war. In the welter of other vast problems facing the regime, the problems of these Jews drew relatively scant official attention, but that scant attention and subsequent improvisations reflect, in microcosm, the gaps between theory and reality so conspicuous in the larger Soviet setting. Jewish Communists who were called upon to bring the Bolshevik message to Russia's Jews were, like their superiors in the larger setting, ignorant of the needs, fears, and traditions of the people they were to transform. Armed with Marxist slogans and theories, they assailed Jewish communities, eager to overturn and sovietize the old life.

For a time the Evsektsiya could be mocked or ignored. Not all of the Jewish towns could be covered at once. However, the transformations were inexorable, and the crisis of the civil war, war communism, and the elimination of Jewish political dissidence by 1921, which otherwise might have provided Jews with a natural, organically grounded leadership, left many of the Jewish communities bereft, traumatized, suddenly wrenched from all familiar institutional and cultural supports and largely at the mercy of a new breed of Jewish commissars. The huge gap separating them from the communities existed because of two earlier Bolshevik shortcomings rooted in Marxist misperceptions of Jewish life: they had engaged in very little agitation or propaganda among the Jewish masses prior to the October Revolution, and almost no Bolsheviks were available who were familiar with Jewish life or Jewish traditions, or who knew Yiddish. Most politically active Jewish workers and intellectuals had joined the Bund, and the more assimilated intellectuals had joined the Mensheviks. There were, of course, leading Bolsheviks who were of Jewish origin. For example, of the twenty-one members of the Central Committee as of August 1917, six were of Jewish origin: Lev Kamenev, Grigori Y. Sokolnikov, Yakov Sverdlov, Leon Trotsky, Moisei Uritsky, and Grigori Zinoviev.[8] At the party congresses held between 1917 and 1922, between 15 and 20 percent of the delegates were of Jewish origin.[9] However, these Jewish Communists did not think of themselves as Jews and were completely estranged from Jewish life. Typical of their lack of interest in Jewish life and rejection of any trace of Jewish consciousness was Trotsky, who felt no kinship with other Jews, or sense of being persecuted as a Jew until the Nazi assaults began. These non-Jewish Jews were internationalists who believed they had transcended the "Jewish condition."

Bolshevism attracted marginal Jews, poised between two worlds—the Jewish and the Gentile—who created a new homeland for themselves, a community of ideologists bent on remaking the world in their own image. These Jews quite deliberately and consciously broke with the restrictive social, religious, and cultural life of the Jews in the Pale of Settlement and attacked the secular Jewish culture of Jewish socialists and Zionists. Having abandoned their own origins and identity, yet not finding, or sharing, or being fully admitted to Russian life (except in the world of the party), the Jewish Bolsheviks found their ideological home in revolutionary universalism. They dreamt of a classless and stateless society supported by Marxist faith and doctrine that transcended the particularities and burdens of Jewish existence. Such Jews exhibited vehement hostility toward other Jews such as Bundists, Zionists, and observant Jews who proudly proclaimed or expressed their Jewishness, and became extremely zealous officials in the new regime.

But at first they were plunged into unfamiliar waters with the establishment of a Commissariat for Jewish National Affairs (abbreviated as *Evkom*) in January 1918, one of several similar national commissariats set up within the People's Commissariat for National Affairs under Stalin. The People's Commissariat was to initiate Soviet legislation on the national question and recommend measures for the economic and cultural uplift of nationalities. Evkom's task was to bridge the gulf between the Bolshevik regimes and the Jewish masses. Late in 1917, in conversations with Lenin, Semen Dimanshtain, who was to become the first Commissar of Jewish Affairs, had said that party forms for work among the Jewish proletariat would be needed to compete with existing Jewish socialist parties.[10] Lenin warned against "falling into

Bundism" and suggested that a conference of all Jewish parties be called for the purpose of explaining the nature of the Soviet government and new opportunities for developing the culture of the Jewish masses. Such a meeting was held, but the Bolsheviks failed to convince the audience to cooperate with the party.[11] Moreover, Evkom had a great deal of trouble finding qualified people to join its staff. Dimanshtain said that, at the time of the organization of Evkom, "whoever had taken up this work did not know the life of the Jewish worker. Several didn't even know Yiddish. We had to set up as secretary of Evkom a man who didn't understand a word of Yiddish." In 1919 he admitted that "the Russian Bolshevik party did not have any work among the Jewish masses," and that in fifteen years of the existence of the party, only its program was translated into Yiddish—into wretched Yiddish—and a few leaflets."[12]

In early December 1917, two Communist arrivals from America began to plan publication of Yiddish material that would be "friendly to the Soviets," but it was impossible to find any relevant materials in Yiddish or a Jewish editor who knew Yiddish who was willing to work for the new regime. Finally, two emigré anarchists from London were enlisted. One knew no Russian, the other, no Yiddish. They were given dictionaries and began preparing a newspaper when they were told that a Jewish Commissariat had just been formed and that they were to attach themselves to it.[13] Other members of the Commissariat were recruited from the ranks of the Left Poale Tsion and Left Socialist Revolutionary party—also without experience in Jewish affairs, but who supported the platform of the Soviet government.

Dimanshtain's background was in sharp contrast to that of the others in Evkom. He had had an unusual ideological journey—from intense Talmudic studies at famous *yeshivot*, to Hasidism, rabbinical ordination, illegal socialist circles in Vilna, arrest and exile in Siberia, and escape to Paris and activity there in the Bolshevik organization. He admitted that in 1918 there had been great obstacles to the Bolshevik conquest of the Jewish proletariat:

A handful of Jewish communists, we had to wage a hard struggle for the Jewish working masses against parties heretofore exercising exclusive influence over them, having at their disposal complete teams of experienced party workers and an extensive press, and enjoying the benefits of a rich past, a "hallowed" national tradition.[14]

To add to its difficulties, Evkom was not sure of its specific tasks and had no experience in organization or tactics. At its first two public meetings in Petrograd, speakers were shouted down by Bundists. It then created a number of departments to try to deal with specific problems: culture and education, press, provinces, refugees, economic work, and a campaign against anti-Semitism.[15] Much attention was devoted to resettling refugees; Evkom even directed them to local kehillas for kosher food and lodging. Evkom also channeled letters from abroad for Jews and helped in the reuniting of families. For a short time, the blurring of purpose and slow start in "implementing the October Revolution in the Jewish street" may have reflected awareness of recent tsarist persecution of Jews, as well as resistance by Jews to Bolshevism. Some believed that Lenin had ordered Dimanshtain "to go slow on the Jews."[16] The presence of non-Bolsheviks on Evkom also created diverse, even conflicting ideas, ranging from creating non-party Jewish workers' soviets to reconstructing Jewish national life on a proletarian-socialist foundation.[17]

Evkom's first enterprise was the amateurish newspaper, *Di varheit* (The Truth), written in chaotically spelled Yiddish. It appeared on March 8, 1918, and then irregularly for a few months. Of the three members of the original editorial board, only one knew Yiddish. For a short time, destitute nonparty writers such as Shmuel Niger and Daniel Charney, who could not find paid work anywhere else, worked for *Di varheit* before leaving the Soviet Union.

The experiences of Evkom in actual contact with Jewish life in 1918 quickly revealed the gap between existing Jewish realities and the Bolshevik task of bringing the message of the Revolution to the Jewish masses who, it was said, "had been lagging far behind the revolution [and] had not grasped its meaning."[18] "Special national tasks" did not exist for Jewish Communists, but Jewish communities most certainly did exist, with an extensive network of homes for the aged, hospitals, orphanages, schools, libraries, and synagogues. The dilemmas were soon apparent. Revolutionary propaganda could not eliminate the need for such institutions, but the Bolsheviks, ideologically speaking, could not keep them functioning. What did the "dictatorship of the proletariat in the Jewish street" mean in the case of these indispensable, traditional communal institutions and services? How could they be reorganized to fit into a Communist mold? Would they be abolished?

Under the chaotic circumstances of 1918, Evkom had to administer existing services, "without thereby disrupting the proper functioning of the work,"[19] despite all the inconsistencies and contradictions involved. Moreover, the Jewish Commissariat's manifesto of June 1918 which had recommended the establishment of local Jewish workers' and soldiers' soviets in every city to deal with Jewish communal functions, reflected a concern for "Jewish national life"—though not along Bundist or Zionist lines:

We, the Jewish working masses, now have an opportunity to shape our internal life according to our own desires and interests . . . Our community, our schools, all our communal institutions [now] serve every interest but that of the broad popular masses. Many among the Jewish masses still trail along behind the bourgeois Zionists, who confuse the minds of the poverty-stricken strata of the people in the interest of an "all-Israel policy." Others . . . still cling to the Bund (who) . . . together with the Russian bourgeoisie, wage a shameful struggle against all the achievements of the revolution, against full national and social emancipation . . .

The Jewish Commissariat's task is to rebuild Jewish national life on proletarian-socialist foundations. The Jewish masses now have full freedom to control all existing Jewish public institutions . . .[20]

Evkom's local agencies were told to keep a watchful eye on the Jewish schools, to give aid to the needy masses, administer hospitals and homes for the aged, and organize the fight against anti-Semitism. The attitude of Evkom to the kehillas, however, "must be negative; without disrupting their activities or impairing the work, efforts must be made to reorganize them on the basis of the dictatorship of the workers and the poor."[21] These were difficult goals to implement. The Evkom relief program and the fight against anti-Semitism created no conflict, but the complex functions of the kehillas and the strong and intimate relations with the Jewish masses baffled and frustrated Jewish Communists. Meanwhile, the continuing influence of Jewish socialists drew their vehement attacks. Completely different worlds were colliding.

Thirteen local Jewish Commissariats (Evkomy) were established, but only in Vitebsk and Dubrovna were there substantial Jewish populations. In these local Evkomy nonparty members, especially from the Left Poale Tsion, were at first welcome, but the conflicting demands of Soviet politics and the daily necessities of Jewish life enmeshed the Communist administrators of Jewish affairs in a tangle of disputes and bureaucratic rivalries. These have been vividly described by Samuil

(Shmuel) Agursky, one of Dimanshtain's aides, who was commissioned to survey the operations of the local Jewish agencies in July 1918. By the time he reached Smolensk, the local commissariat was being "turned by local Left Poale Zionists into a nationalist office which the Smolensk soviet was forced to close."[22] Agursky undertook to reconstitute the commissariat but claimed he could not find the requisite Jewish proletariat. In Orsha, crowded at the time with Jewish refugees, Agursky lectured to a few dozen people on "The October Revolution and the Jewish Workers," and somewhat sheepishly had to chair the meeting and introduce himself. Only one person asked a question, and after he answered it, Agursky was left alone in the hall.[23] Dejected by the inability of the Communists to make contact with Jewish workers, Agursky began to believe that all Jewish work was a waste of time, that his mission was doomed to fail. But he grimly hung on and went to Vitebsk, which had a Jewish population of almost 60,000. At meetings, he addressed crowds as provincial Commissar for Jewish Affairs, but they shouted him down and refused to support Evkom schools either with teachers or students until some children were won over by gifts.[24]

In his extensive accounts of the Jewish commissariats, he described the efforts of the local Evkom in Vitebsk to deal with the specific needs of a Jewish old-age home after the Commissariat of Social Security took over its operation:

. . . the Vitebsk Commissariat of Social Security introduced the same regulations as governed all such homes, and all were supplied with the same food. It so happened that the meat allotted to the Jewish institutions was almost exclusively pork. Of course, it is no great calamity for people to eat pork. But the old Jewish people not only stopped eating meat; they stopped eating altogether; they refused to eat non-ritual food and simply starved to death. The Jewish Commissariat protested the situation . . . in an article entitled "Social Security or Social Murder?" . . . but nothing was done.[25]

Finally, in June 1919, the chairman of the Central Executive Committee, the so-called President of the USSR, Mikhail Kalinin, who was keenly interested in Jewish affairs, ordered a special investigation into the situation and the guilty commissar was prosecuted and punished.

Agursky made his survey immediately after non-Communist members had been expelled from the central Evkom. The first rupture came with the Left Social Revolutionaries, who were eliminated from the Commissariat, the soviets, and the government after their uprising in

Moscow in July 1918 was crushed. The Social Revolutionaries, strongly opposed to the Brest-Litovsk Treaty and Soviet subservience to Germany, had assassinated the German ambassador, Count Mirbach. Then came the turn of the Left Poale Tsion, which had opposed the Bolshevik seizure of power, but did not want to obstruct the socialist experiment once it had started. At first its help was eagerly sought, especially in filling the Jewish commissariats of the cities, but complications soon arose. At the national kehilla convention in early summer 1918, a Poale Tsion delegate named Rabinovich, who was also on the central Evkom, was accused of trying to protect the existence of the kehillas[26]—to which the Bolsheviks were vigorously opposed. He and the remaining Left Poale Zionists were quickly expelled from the central Evkom; they lingered a bit longer in the local Evkomy. Thus ended the short-lived experiment in coalition commissariats.

In August 1918, when Evkom moved from Petrograd to Moscow, the name *Di varheit* (German) was changed to *Der emes* (Yiddish for "truth"), in an effort to seem more authentic to Jewish workers. *Der emes* was designated as an organ of the Communist party, in order to sidestep a restriction of the Brest-Litovsk Treaty which forbade distribution of government newspapers such as *Di varheit* in occupied areas.[27] Its circulation, however, was only about 5,000 and scarcely affected the pulse of Jewish life. The Jewish intelligentsia and politically conscious workers continued to be conspicuously hostile, while some of the contributing writers and typesetters burned the papers as fuel.[28] The appearance of *Der emes* launched a more aggressive Bolshevik approach to Jewish life and foreshadowed the liquidation of political opposition. This change was soon followed by a fateful debate on the nature of the so-called Jewish Sections.

The plans of Evkom had originally spoken of the creation of Jewish Soviets or of Jewish Sections within Jewish Soviets, which would be subordinate to regional Soviets; in turn, the regional soviets would be united into a federation. A projected All-Russian Congress of Jewish Soviets would determine "general policy on all questions touching on Jewish social life."[29] Such a concept, however, was strikingly similar to the national program of the Bund and Faraynigte, which were regarded as "bourgeois." Moreover, a Congress of Jewish Soviets would not result in a Bolshevik majority in such soviets. The decision was then made, apparently with the approval of Lenin,[30] to create Jewish Sections within the party.

Certain Jewish Sections, Evsektsii, or generally referred to in the singular, Evsektsiya, of the party came into being as early as August 1918, some of them formed by the local Evkomy with the help of non-Bolsheviks.[31] Dimanshtain was in charge of both the Central Bureau of the Jewish Evsektsiya and the Central Evkom and controlled both budgets. Evkom was supposed to deal with administration, and the Jewish Sections, with enlisting the Jewish masses, but their functions overlapped. On October 20, Dimanshtain called a conference of Evkomy and Evsektsiya in Moscow in order to coordinate activities, raise morale, and familiarize the central leadership with the local activists (see Photo 3.1). Interestingly, of the sixty-four delegates who attended, thirty-three were non-Bolsheviks, of whom twenty-eight were teachers in Yiddish schools.[32] In the discussions of political problems, the national question, and cultural matters, the non-Bolshevik delegates, who had limited voting power, created an uproar by demanding that the supervision of education be removed from Evkom and restored to the kehillas and that all speeches be in Yiddish. They also protested against being banned from voting on all issues except education. But a Communist fraction caucused and decided that the tasks of the Evsektsiya were to agitate among Jewish workers, "carry out the dictatorship of the proletariat on the Jewish street," and act autonomously on all matters in Jewish social and political life. Dimanshtain explained that the party could not conduct its work in many different languages, thus necessitating the Evsektsiya. He also made it clear that the Jewish Sections did not constitute a separate party, but were merely a part of the Communist party. Nor were the Sections to elect their own officers—they would be appointed by the party and answerable to it.[33] The voting delegates then agreed that

there is no longer any place in our life for the various institutions which have so far been running things in the Jewish street, or for Jewish communities elected by universal, direct suffrage and the secret ballot.

At a time of perilous struggle, there can be no compromise of any kind with the bourgeoisie; all such agencies and institutions injure the interests of the broad Jewish working masses by lulling them with sweet words about so-called democratic principles.[34]

A council of Evkom was then empowered "to take the necessary steps to systematically liquidate all bourgeois institutions" (see Chapter 4).

3.1 First Conference of the Evsektsiya, Moscow, October 1918. YIVO.

The Sections were intended to be part of the Communist Party, but generally party members did not recognize their special legitimacy or that of Evkom. They were simply a cog in the party apparatus. Some Sections were even attacked for their "nationalistic deviations"[35] at a time when the party was liquidating the autonomous nationality Sections in the areas liberated from German rule (Belorussia, Lithuania, and Latvia) and transforming them into territorial Communist parties. Since Soviet Jews lacked a territorial base and since there was no territory with a Jewish majority, no Jewish territorial party was formed. To many ardent party members, the existence of Jewish Sections seemed anomalous—a needless problem and a nuisance.

    While the Jewish Sections were struggling to define themselves, recruit new personnel, and bring the Communist message to "the Jewish street," the Bund and socialist Zionists were undergoing severe internal crises and external pressures which eventually destroyed their unity and independence.[36] Their breakdown gave the Evsektsiya control over Jewish communities and cleared the way for the destruction of traditional Jewish life, the Zionist movement, and Hebrew culture.

The last chapter in the life of Jewish socialist parties was enacted during the Red Army's struggle to achieve victory during the civil war, during the harshness of war communism, and the liquidation of all of the non-Bolshevik socialist parties.

From the summer of 1918 on, Bolshevik survival needs spawned drastic policies known as "war communism," under which all private and public wealth and manpower were conscripted, all private trade banned, manufacturing and distribution of goods nationalized, and grain forcibly requisitioned. These decisions were "not in the party's 1917 ideology or program . . . but in response to the perilous military situation that suddenly confronted the Bolsheviks with the outbreak of the civil war. . . ."[37] They were drastic measures taken under siege, but "subsequently acquired a higher rationality in the minds of many Bolsheviks . . . regarded not only as necessary, but principled . . . a valid, if painful road to socialism."[38] These ideas were assailed by other socialists, as well as some Bolsheviks, who believed that the transition to socialism would be relatively painless. In an effort[39] to answer such attacks, Nikolai Bukharin, a leading Bolshevik theoretician and editor of *Pravda*, concluded that the "costs of revolution" involved the collapse of all productive and social forces and would require coercion and force in the creation of a new order.[40]

The first application of forced labor involved middle-class men and women sent to dig trenches for the defense of Petrograd against the Germans. Wages were paid in kind since money had lost virtually all value. Food and grain were requisitioned from the peasantry. Many atrocities and brutalities were committed by the revolutionaries as well as by their adversaries.

After 1918, Bolshevik defense of the Revolution escalated to the use of terror not only against bourgeois enemies but against other socialist parties. Cheka was created for the purpose of "combating counterrevolution and sabotage." The transfer of the capital from Leningrad to Moscow conferred on the Cheka the attributes of a large and independent department of the state under Felix Dzerzhinsky, the chief security officer, who set up headquarters in the premises of a large insurance company on Lubyanka Square and began hounding all "wreckers" of the Revolution. By 1920, there were 4,500 Cheka agents in Russia.[41] They had a completely free hand in their searches, arrests, trials, and judgments in "the defense of the Revolution."

In April 1918, the Japanese landing at Vladivostok signalled the danger of foreign intervention, but also provided hope and a rallying point for all elements in Russia which were opposed to the Bolshevik regime. In the spring and summer of 1918 Moscow swarmed with Allied and German agents, fragmentary groups from right and centrist political groups, and the surviving parties of the Left plotting against the Soviet government. The right-wing Social Revolutionaries openly agitated to overthrow the Bolsheviks and accept Allied aid in the war against Germany. The Mensheviks, torn by internal dissension, temporized. By June 1918, both parties were expelled from the All-Russian Central Executive Committee (VTsIK), and in July 1918, the Left SR's planned to seize power. The Bolsheviks put down this rising as well as widespread provincial revolts by prosperous, independent farmers (kulaks). By this time, the regime was well on the way to a one-party state. The ensuing civil war led the Mensheviks to denounce counterrevolution and foreign intervention, but Cheka played a cat-and-mouse game with the opposition parties, in turn harrying and patronizing them, alternately arresting and releasing their leaders and making their organized existence almost but never quite impossible. In December 1919 at the Seventh All-Russian Congress of Soviets, the Menshevik leader Yuli Martov attacked violations of the Soviet Constitution and demanded freedom of the press and assembly, and the abolition of executions without trial and official terror. Lenin responded by saying that "terror and the Cheka are absolutely indispensable." The Mensheviks maintained party offices a bit longer, issued news sheets through friendly printers, and controlled some unions, but many of their leaders were arrested during the civil war as "counterrevolutionaries." At the Eighth All-Russian Congress of Soviets in December 1920, Lenin said that it had been shown that "the proletariat can only be united by an extreme revolutionary Marxist party, only through a ruthless struggle against all other parties."[42] Then, in March 1921, at the Tenth Party Congress, after the Kronstadt revolt, Lenin completely eliminated all of the non-Bolshevik socialist parties in Russia. In May 1921, he asserted the need for a regime of terror:

After the imperialist war of 1914–1918 . . . it is impossible not to apply terror. . . . It is either . . . White Guard bourgeois terror, or it is the Red proletarian terror. There is no in between . . .[43]

The Mensheviks and Social Revolutionaries were given the choice of prison or banishment. It is against these developments that the struggle for survival of Jewish socialist parties was carried on.

We have seen that initial Jewish opposition to Bolshevik rule weakened when and where Jews felt protected from pogroms. This realization was felt very keenly by Jewish socialist parties, which were strongest in the areas of the pogroms. Aware of this strength, the Communists were "strongly tempted . . . to seek a quasi-alliance with non-Bolshevik Jewish groups,"[44] especially in the Ukraine and White Russia. There, Bolsheviks at first used the Jewish elements in socialist parties to sovietize the Jewish communities, then to absorb and liquidate the parties themselves.[45]

A large bloc of the Bundist movement—probably over 20,000—had left Russia and was already part of a rising Poland. Those who remained in Soviet Russia began the tortuous road of splitting and capitulation. The dispersal of the traditional leadership and membership and the recruiting of new members who had not experienced the expulsion of the Bund from the RSDWP in 1903, the commitment to cultural autonomy, or the Bund's adherence to Menshevism, created a new kind of Bund in 1918. Pro-Bolshevik tendencies[46] began surfacing in a few Bund organizations, and the November 1918 revolution in Germany, which seemed to herald worldwide revolutions, at least in Europe, made a profound impression on Bundists as well as on other revolutionaries and stimulated pro-Bolshevik tendencies. Yet there were dilemmas and reservations. Bund conferences in December 1918 urged participation in freely elected soviets, but only if the Bund could maintain its political independence. Bundists also declared their opposition to the "Bolshevik dictatorship," and called for freedom of speech and the press, the supremacy of the soviets, cessation of terror and a democratic constitution.

But the pulls toward Soviet power became stronger, "strengthened by demonstrations among the Jewish people that the Red Army would save them . . . evidence that strengthened the positions of left elements in the Bund and Faraynigte."[47] "One shouldn't be left on the outside," they argued. "With whom can we go?" Others argued "like Gedali in Babel's story," that they "must not soil their hands," but continue caring about a "clean conscience."[48]

In the Ukraine, especially cruel dilemmas faced the Bund. Its basic opposition to the Bolshevik seizure of power became untenable as it had to accept what it saw: that it was only under the shield of the Red Army that Jews were safe from the horror of spreading pogroms. It will be recalled that it was the pogrom excesses that radicalized Jewish youths and workers in the Ukraine who wanted vengeance and who volunteered to serve in the Red Army, even though the Red Army itself was not entirely free of pogromizing. Jewish Red Army groups formed in the Ukraine as well as in White Russia, and a special recruitment section of the Red Army called "Evvoensek" was set up to enlist Jewish youth and conduct intense propaganda among Jewish volunteers.[49] In Yiddish, it prepared brochures, posters, and agitators, calling on the Jewish people to bind itself to the Red Army, "with specifically Jewish arguments."[50] In the Red Army, a Jew, it was said, "can die with a rifle in hand."

Special Jewish military units in Red Army ranks were officially opposed because it was feared that the separation of Jews from non-Jews would intensify anti-Semitism. The Evsektsiya specifically opposed the idea because it would "provoke pogroms" and "will prove detrimental, from both the political and practical standpoints." Separate units were also opposed on the grounds that Jews as individuals would be perceived as avoiding the Red Army altogether. The issue was hotly debated, especially in the Ukraine, and by the Jewish socialist parties. Several Jewish communities such as Odessa had their own self-defense groups before the pogrom waves and some Jews fought with Red partisans, but most communities were defenseless, prompting Trotsky, the commander of the Red Army to write to Moishe Rafes, a Bundist who joined the Ukrainian Komfarband (see below), lamenting the fact that "Jewish working masses were so ill-prepared to fight." Trotsky personally was in favor of establishing special Jewish units if only to counter the widespread feeling that Jews were shirking service at the front. He seems also to have been concerned about the anti-Semitism aroused by the presence of Jewish political commissars in the Red Army. Finally, on May 10, 1919, in response to persistent appeals for Jewish units by the Poale Tsion party to high Bolshevik officials, including Lenin himself, Trotsky authorized Jewish battalions, urging that they merge with those of other nationalities to avoid "national alienation and . . . chauvinism."[51]

Nedava concluded that no separate Jewish units were formed because the Evsektsiya "sabotaged" Trotsky's proposal, but Smoliar documented the existence of several such units: "Ber Borokhov," formed by Poale Tsion leader (later historian) Zvi Fridland, and "Bronislaw Grosser," formed through the Bund. Smoliar also noted that in the Karol Battalion in Minsk, 70 percent of the men belonged to Poale Tsion, 10 percent to the Communist party, 2 percent to the Bund, and 18 percent non-party soldiers.[52] In the struggle to take Vilna, a large proportion of the forces were Jews.

The Red Army shield forced some Bundists as well as these masses to support the Red Army while trying to make a distinction between it and the Bolshevik regime. The Kiev Bund had rejected the takeover of Kiev by the Bolsheviks in February 1918, but when they returned in 1919, their ideological differences began to fade under the stark realities of the pogroms. In January 1919, the Ukrainian Bund split into three factions, mirroring a similar split in the Ukrainian Social Democratic Workers' party. In February, after much painful soul-searching, leftist elements saw no effective alternative to the Red Army and Bolshevik power: they made "a revolution within the Bund" and created a Communist Bund (Kombund) as an independent party of the Jewish proletariat, believing that they could defend their national demands, including national autonomy, and bypass the Jewish Sections. Moishe Rafes, a leading Ukrainian Bundist, became their spokesman, but the Ukrainian Communist party refused to recognize the Kombund or even the idea of a Jewish Communist party, which Rafes proposed. Increasingly "subjected to the heavy pressure of agitation for 'unity,' [Jewish socialists] were gradually maneuvered into fusing with the Communists, in the belief that a certain degree of autonomy would be preserved in Jewish affairs."[53] Like the Bund, the Faraynigte could not sustain its unity, and also broke into factions, some leaning toward union with the Bund and the formation of Jewish Soviets, others looking to Poale Tsion. A few elements united briefly in May 1919 with the Kombund in the Jewish Communist party in the Ukraine to form the Komfarband, but the Ukrainian Communist party still refused to accept any autonomous groups within it and insisted that the Komfarband transform itself into Jewish Sections of the party, subject to direct party control and discipline. However, most individual members of the

Ukrainian Komfarband either refused to enter the party or were not admitted to it.[54]

Bitter debates followed within the Komfarband on organizational and national questions. Dimanshtain, meanwhile, succeeded in having the Central Committee of the Russian Communist party press the Ukrainian Communist party to accept the Komfarband, especially since its members were active in the struggle against Denikin's White forces in August 1919.[55] In the same month, the fusion was accomplished; however, the Komfarband could not be an autonomous organization but would transform itself into Jewish Sections of the party, subject to direct party discipline and direction. Of the 4,000 members in the Komfarband, only 1,757 joined the Ukrainian Communist party in 1919, which then had about 55,000 members. There were fewer than 7,000 Jews in the UCP, indicating that most Jewish Communists had not previously affiliated with a Jewish party.[56]

A similar development occurred later in Belorussia, where a Kombund was created in April 1920. Here the Bolshevik party was particularly weak in the cities, whereas the Bund was strong. The Bolsheviks calculated that a temporary toleration of the Bund and limited cooperation with it would be necessary to insure the maintenance of Bolshevik power in Belorussia.[57] The Belorussian Evsektsiya also planned to induce the pro-Bolshevik Bundists to give up the idea of national-cultural autonomy and a separate organization. Finally, against all Bolshevik tradition, a compromise led to the formation of a Jewish Communist party in Belorussia, which endorsed "special institutions" for the "development of Jewish national-cultural life," but this was hardly more than a paper organization and lasted only a few weeks.

At the same time, the Belorussian Bund was undergoing its own internal crisis,[58] even though it had solid support among the numerous Jewish artisans and factory workers and was well aware that the Communist party aroused little or no enthusiasm. Here, too, the German revolution and intermittent Red Army control of Belorussia in 1918–19 created conflicting positions within the Bund that threatened its unity. These issues were discussed at the Eleventh Bund Conference in Minsk in March 1919. The composition of the delegates revealed that many who came were newcomers, participating in a Bund conference for the first time. The Red terror and relentless nationalization of property that was hurting small Jewish shopkeepers and artisans were condemned, but the protection of the Red Army could not be gainsaid. The influential and dramatic Esther Frumkin also condemned the terror, but began to believe there was only one choice: "We cannot give up power to the bourgeoisie," she said. "The Red Army is our army—its faults, our faults. There is no way back."[59] A resolution of the left faction asked for more autonomy in local government and democratization of the soviets, but urged Bundists to take government posts (about half of those who attended the conference already had government jobs) without accepting responsibility for government policies. This conference managed to avoid a split. Even the Left Bundists were hostile to the Evkom and Evsektsiya, assailing the Jewish Communists as "national-Bolshevik comedians" and "assimilationists" and refusing to enter the Communist party.[60] All factions of the Belorussian Bund, however, supported the Red Army and declared a party mobilization of all members over twenty-five early in 1919 to meet the threat of invading Polish forces. Poale Tsion, as well, which led the Jewish socialist parties in organizing armed resistance, also intensified its general recruitment drive. Volunteers were sent to Orsha and Minsk in May 1919 and later, in June 1920, there were plans to send forces to the Warsaw front, but Polish victories in parts of Belorussia, fear of Polish pogroms, and the retreat of the Red Army from Warsaw blocked any further military activity.[61]

Like the Russian White forces, the Poles had identified the Jews with Bolshevism and began a systematic persecution which pushed Jews to seek the protection of the Red Army just as had happened in the Ukraine. Meanwhile, starting with small isolated towns and working toward large cities such as Vitebsk, Gomel, and finally Minsk, Bolsheviks rigged elections and dissolved Bundist and Poale Tsion organizations.[62] At the Twelfth Bund Conference in April 1920, the left faction of the Bund, which had a majority, declared itself a Belorussian Kombund, joining the Communist party as a separate autonomous organization of the Jewish proletariat "to carry out the tasks of the socialist revolution among Jews," and demanded that the Jewish Sections be absorbed into the Kombund. A minority of the delegates walked out, warning that the Kombund would soon be swallowed up by the Communist party, and began to identify itself as a Social Democratic Bund.[63] Thereafter, many Bundists in both factions withdrew from all political activity; most of the veteran Bundists vanished from the political scene and with them, the characteristic Bundist activism, independence, and discipline. Even so, resistance to fusion strained and stretched old attachments. Kombund members like Esther Frumkin could not wrench themselves away completely. She clung tenaciously to the uniqueness of Jewish workers and *their* world and *their* need for a mass Jewish organization:

This Jewish world [has] . . . a specifically Jewish religious life and a Jewish nationalism, . . . an *Agudas Yisroel*, plain Zionists and *Poale Tsionists*, . . . Hebraists, Tarbut schools . . . EKOPO, OZE, ORT,* *Kultur-Lige*, . . . pogrom victims, American relatives, *heders* and *yeshivos*—in short, our Jewish microcosm.[64]

Because of such a richly diverse Jewish life, Esther (as she was known) held that only the Bund could effectively reach the Jewish masses with a Communist ideology; the Jewish Sections were merely a technical, bureaucratic apparat and could never appeal to Jewish workers or answer their needs.

Local Bund groups, which wanted to absorb the Jewish Sections into an enlarged Bund, were particularly intense in their pressure on their national representatives not to yield to the Bolsheviks. But outside of Bund control events overwhelmed such debates. Serious divisions within the Central Committee of the Communist party erupted in 1920–21; a wave of strikes swept over Petrograd in February 1921 and the Kronstadt rebellion followed in March. Hard-line Communists grew increasingly impatient with small groups wanting to retain their identity.[65] However inevitable Communist party control of the Soviet Union seemed, Komfarband elements fought for autonomy and resisted absorption and dissolution. The struggle dragged on until March, when the unconditional merger of the Komfarband with the Communist party was voted. Even so, many local Bund groups balked at the decision: the Mogilev organization rejected it as a "crime," the Gomel group deplored the action which "snapped the golden thread of the Jewish labor movement."[66] But the tide of events was too powerful. In a painful and emotional conference on March 5, 1921, in Minsk, Komfarband delegates, representing 3,000 members, gathered formally to dissolve the Bund, a task they knew the Bolsheviks would do anyhow, because by this time all non-Bolshevik political parties had been liquidated. There

---

*EKOPO was the Committee for Jewish Relief, created in 1916 to aid war victims;
OZE was the Society for the Preservation of the Health of the Jewish Population;
ORT was the Society for Artisan and Agricultural Work Among Jews, founded in St. Petersburg in 1880. It exists today as the Organization for Rehabilitation and Training (ORT), though not in the Soviet Union.

were attacks against "betrayals," poignant defenses, individual struggles to maintain old loyalties, and the bittersweet memory of a glorious past history of Bund achievements.

Yet there was also the vision of a new world on new foundations and a stubborn faith that the Bund could preserve its influence in the party and would help bring this vision to realization. As Esther Frumkin, who at first had opposed entry into the party, said dramatically, "We must spin our thread anew."[67] Rakhmiel Veinshtain, another Bund veteran, who also made his way tortuously to fusion, admitted that "although not a single one of us has ceased to be a Bundist, we face the dilemma of independent existence or Sections, with the hope that we will be able to remold the Sections and suit them to the needs of the Jewish proletariat."[68] The final resolution, which approved the fusion, predicted that the Jewish labor movement, within the ranks of the Communist party, would "sooner or later assume the normal and appropriate forms which were given to it earlier by the Bund."

Overwhelmed by a sense of guilt and loss, delegates continued working on explanations, rationalizations, and exhortations to Bund members:

Jewish workers! The Bund is not leaving you, but remains with you. It leads you under the banner of the All-Russian Communist Party. Carry your love, your trust, your faith in the Bund into that great alliance where the movement of the Jewish proletariat will emerge in time.[69]

This guilt haunted the old Bundists for a long time as they tried to salvage what they could of their honor and influence. Veinshtain fought successfully to have three Bundists in the Central Bureau of the Jewish Sections. Those Bundists who wanted to become members of the Communist party could do so if approved by a certain commission—an arrangement criticized by some Soviet historians because ex-Bundists "could not outlive their petit bourgeois nationalistic traditions," as expressed in "the idealization of the historical part of the Bund."[70] However, by 1921, most Bund members had either withdrawn from political activity altogether, or were living outside areas of Soviet control. There was a drop in Bund membership when the Bund adopted a Communist platform, and a further drop when the Belorussian Komfarband was absorbed into the Communist party. Agursky claims that only 2,000 former Bundists entered the party in 1921, out of an estimated 11,000 members then living under Soviet rule. The great Jewish labor center in Minsk provided only 175 members, and Moscow, only 115.[71] In the Communist party purges of 1921–22, Jewish members of the party and many former Bundists, Mensheviks, and members of other parties were expelled. Former Bundists were especially hard hit and after the 1921 purge, "many of the former Bundists remained outside the party ranks."[72]

The Bundists who had joined the Communist party and survived were doomed to live a self-divided life, loyal to Bundist beliefs and the idea of a separate Jewish organization, but reluctant to admit their past affiliation because of the persistent Leninist taint on the party and numerous political tests and checks to see if they had freed themselves of "petit bourgeois" beliefs. Any hope of their representing specifically Jewish interests had already been foreclosed by the Eighth Congress of the Russian Communist Party, in March 1919, creating a unitary centralized party and subordinate central committees in various regions, and by the resolution of the Third All-Russian Conference of Jewish Sections in July 1920, which totally rejected any notions of autonomous Jewish Sections. "The Sections," as Schwarz observed, had only one function: "to see to the execution of party orders, and this remained their function so long as the party leadership thought a special Jewish 'apparatus' necessary."[73]

There is still only fragmentary evidence regarding the numbers of former members of the Bund and Faraynigte in the Evsektsiya after the purges, and intense controversy over their motives in joining and their roles in controlling Soviet Jewish life. However, Gitelman concludes that without their infusion, the Evsektsiya could not have functioned or survived as long as they did.[74]

Whatever their hopes for the Jewish proletariat under the new banner of Communism, and however misguided they were in thinking they could maintain the special character of the Bund and the Jewish labor movement, the presence of former Bundists—and to a lesser extent, the Faraynigte—in the Jewish Sections gave them highly intelligent people who had had experience in Jewish work, something which the Sections had lacked in 1918–19. Four ex-Bundist leaders—Veinshtain, Esther Frumkin, Rafes, and Alexander Chemerisky—became closely identified with work in the Evsektsiya at higher levels and with the radical transformation of Jewish life. Ex-Bundists also served in lower levels of Evsektsiya work, probably representing a fairly large proportion of the 2,000 or so in the Evsektsiya structure.[75]

The Social Democratic Bund continued to lead a shadowy existence until 1923, occasionally harassing the Evsektsiya at meetings, but inevitably declining. Meanwhile, Poale Tsion was also absorbed after its own struggle to create a Communist faction, known as EKP, and unsuccessful efforts to form a Jewish Communist party together with the Bund. When the Comintern insisted that it drop its Palestine program, a small faction of EKP dropped its Zionist commitment and joined the Russian Communist party, while the rest of EKP and one wing of the Hekhalutz pioneering movement continued their legal existence until 1928.[76]

Charged with nothing less than the total economic, social, and cultural reconstruction of Russian Jewry, after much wrangling over organizational, ideological, and personnel questions, twenty Jewish Sections were established throughout the Soviet Union by October 1920; by August 1921, there were sixty-six. However, there were several large centers of Jewish population where there were no Sections at all—especially in the Ukraine where the party was determined to eliminate them.[77] In 1921, as both the Communist state and party grew stronger and consolidated fields of control, most Jewish traditional institutions and services that had survived the dislocations of civil war were destroyed or sovietized and drawn into the jurisdiction of Yiddish soviets, Evkom, or the Evsektsiya. The others stubbornly resisted, but were eventually crushed.

4

The Campaign against Traditional Jewish Life, 1917–29

The Poles, my dear Sir, shot because they were the counter-revolution. You shoot because you are the revolution. But surely the revolution means joy. And joy does not like orphans in the house. Good men do good deeds. The revolution is the good deed of good men. But good men do not kill. So it is bad people that are making the revolution. But the Poles are bad people too. Then how is Gedali to know which is revolution and which is counter-revolution?

ISAAC BABEL, *Gedali*

And don't be amazed, my teacher . . . that I left our house. You know better than anyone that if our house flowered in your time, it withered in mine. In your time, the light from the tower was dazzling. It glittered like gold. . . . But in my time, not only was the light gone, but the house itself was in ruins. . . . We sat down to our own poor meals by ourselves, and it was melancholy at our tables.

DER NISTER, *Unter a ployt* (Under a Fence)

THE long-range Soviet goal has been to create a fully atheistic society. From this view, the church and synagogue have been seen as a kind of social vice, catering to the displaced needs of the ignorant and backward masses, and diverting them from socially useful activity, while the clergy has been viewed as a parasitic element paid to cater to an undesirable addiction.[1]

In eliminating the "social opiate" of religion, the Bolsheviks have sometimes temporized and sacrificed ideological rigor for short-term political gains. They have also argued over the pace of change and over the roles assigned to government and the law as against party agencies in combating religion. The party and Komsomol antireligious agitation and propaganda pressed for a continuous and intense struggle and opposed any collaboration between the state and churches. The pragmatists in the state bureaucracy, on the other hand, tended to favor a more moderate policy and were quite willing to "sovietize" religious organizations and reward those that cooperated in realizing Soviet aims. On the whole, although there were intermittent antireligious campaigns, the harsh, destructive attack on religion did not come until 1929, after Stalin's victory in the succession struggle following Lenin's death.

Theoretically, antireligious policy in the Soviet Union is based on the writings of Marx, Engels, and Lenin as well as current ideological spokesmen, on decisions of the Communist party, and on specific government legislation. However, there are also "various oral and local instructions, which are not reflected in the formal legislation . . . [so that] the Soviet believer simply does not know where he stands in relation to the secular authorities. His situation varies from uncertainty through threats to direct persecution."[2] From the very beginning, Soviet policy toward religion has been curiously irregular and inconsistent, reacting to a complex interplay of ideological and pragmatic considerations. Neither the party's ideology nor Soviet constitutional principles of "freedom of conscience" and "separation of church and state" can explain the meandering course of Soviet church policy and the wide differences in the treatment of individual religious groups by the regime.[3]

Moreover, the tenacity and resilience of religious beliefs among the Soviet people, the frequent intertwining of religion with nationality and culture, and the reaction of foreign opinion have tended to limit the impact of literal Bolshevik atheistic ideology. Internal security needs have also aborted Marxist dogma. These influences have not necessarily been compatible or consistent with one another and have had varying force since 1917. However, the attacks on Jewish religious (and thus cultural) institutions, literature, and values have been particularly vehement, publicly declaimed, and continuous.

The first official act dealing with religion was the "Declaration of the Rights of the Peoples of Russia" of November 2, 1917, abolishing all national-religious privileges and restrictions. This was aimed especially at the preeminent position of the Russian Orthodox Church and equalized the status of all religious cults in the Soviet Union. In December

1917, all religious organizations were ordered to transfer their schools, seminaries, and institutions to the People's Commissariat of Education.[4] A decree of January 23, 1918 ("On the Separation of Church from State and School from Church")[5] gave every citizen the right to profess any or no religion. Citizens were free to study and teach religion privately, but the teaching of religious dogmas was prohibited in all schools. Religious groups were denied property rights, thus they had to lease their property from the state. Property could be leased if a group of twenty (dvadtsat) persons would assume responsibility for the property and its upkeep. The dvadtsatka was also charged with making all repairs and paying all expenses needed to maintain the property.

This measure decreed the complete secularization of the state, the confiscation of all religious property and funds, and the withdrawal of legal status from churches and church organizations, including synagogues. It dealt a particularly harsh blow to the Russian Orthodox Church—the state church in tsarist Russia—but during the early years of Bolshevik rule, not all of its provisions could be enforced because of massive resistance and insufficient force where the Bolsheviks were in control. Moreover, until after the end of the civil war, the regime had many enemies from within and without and had neither the will nor the resources to create any more by deliberately antagonizing believers. However, as the regime stabilized its rule, some Soviet officials began to think of ways to use churches and synagogues for Soviet purposes.[6]

The decree on separation of church and state was subsequently refined to restrict religious freedom and give great sweep to "scientific antireligious education" and organized antireligious propaganda by party members. During the early period of NEP (New Economic Policy—see Chapter 7), the campaigns were slowed down, but by 1923, policy makers felt that NEP had fostered the growth of bourgeois and clerical-national ideas such as Pan-Islamism and Zionism, Catholic activity among Poles, and Baptist influence among Latvians and Estonians.[7] A stepped-up antireligious drive was then resumed, with intermittent slowdowns until 1929, when it reached a severely destructive pitch.

The assault on Jewish religious life was particularly harsh and pervasive because a Jew's religious beliefs and observances infused every aspect of his daily life and were invested with national values and feelings which the Bolsheviks mocked, denounced, and were bent on destroying. Family relations, work, prayer, study, recreation, and culture were all part of a seamless web, no element of which could be disturbed without disturbing the whole. In this web, the synagogue served as house of prayer and study and social center. Traditional Jewish life had been shaken by the force of secular, socialist, and Zionist ideas even before the Bolshevik Revolution, but in 1917, most Jews in Russia still adhered to traditional structures and values: the semi-autonomous kehilla, rabbinical courts, kosher slaughtering of animals, religious schools, synagogues, *khevras* (societies) for the support of widows, orphans, the indigent and aged, and the binding power of halakhic law. This culture could not be put into a Marxist-Leninist mold, although some awkward attempts were made and failed. Moreover, the Evsektsiya activists, who were charged with carrying Bolshevism to the Jewish masses, were bearers of a new vision and faith which had to triumph. They were impatient with and often intolerant of competing or dissenting value systems. All of the traditional Jewish institutions and loyalties which clashed with or encumbered the Bolshevik drive had to be re-formed, sovietized, or destroyed according to party doctrine and for party purposes. The pre-Bolshevik opposition of Jewish socialist parties to these institutions because of their "bourgeois-clerical" attributes seems to have added a special vehemence to the actions of the Evsektsiya. And yet, some of the Evsektsiya members were divided about means and uncertain about ends. Until 1921, when the final liquidation of the Jewish socialist parties took place, there was considerable conflict and disagreement over what measures to take, how to replace the needed services that were being abolished, and how to deal with community resistance. Nor was there as yet any clear conception as to what form Jewish life would take under Soviet communism. Many of the Evsektsiya activists had strong antireligious feelings, which translated into harsh campaigns, but there were gradations of hostility and complicated feelings growing out of the sense of new power in the hands of Jews who just yesterday and for centuries past had had no power at all.

Some of the Bundists, for example, still felt a residual regard for Jewish religious practices and ambivalence about their own role. The Bund had been not so much antireligious as areligious. It had opposed the submission of rabbis and communities to the bourgeois establishment in the kehillas, which were accused of exploiting Jewish workers and controlling the religious life of Jews. Yet during the pre-Bolshevik period, some Bundists had already faced the difficulty of applying strict Marxist formulations to the Jewish "proletariat" or "bourgeoisie": stall and shopowners were often as poor as their workers and Jewish cobblers, tailors, and draymen were improbable candidates for the Russian industrial proletariat. Bundists had lived within the culture of Jewish workers—many of whom were observant—and early Bundist self-help funds, called *kassy*, and meetings were organized within the synagogue. Vows not to become scabs were often taken before a Torah scroll. Bundists had often been involved in bitter controversy with the Jewish community, but they were not isolated from it. Interestingly, they even advocated Saturday as a day of rest. More significantly, although Bundists might be atheists and attack rabbis, they rarely attacked religious customs or religious culture to which, indeed, many of them felt emotionally attached. They did not wish to deny religious freedom to any individual but favored complete separation of church and state. Nor could they bring themselves to forcibly seize synagogues or houses of study *(batai medrashim)*. Even the restless and provocative Esther Frumkin, who *did* take a particularly strong antireligious line, wanted to return the houses of study in Vitebsk after they had been seized by the overzealous Evsektsiya in 1921.[8] Early in her life, she had written tenderly about the appealing tradition of candle-lighting on Friday night. But, as a contribution to the antireligious campaign, she had written a pamphlet called "Down With Rabbis and Priests" and publicly agitated against rabbis and synagogues. Yet, at the same time, she had to admit that no Jewish socialist party fought with as much vigor and devotion as those Jews "wrapped in their prayer shawls." Though she was a granddaughter and wife of rabbis, her fiery passion seems to have been rooted in her conviction that rabbis were responsible for the scandalous submission of masses of Jews to their lot of abject poverty and oppression.[9] She wanted above all to transform Jewish life, to free the Jewish poor, and create a new Jewish proletarian culture. She may also have felt the need—as so many Jewish Communists did—to exhibit unmistakable hostility toward Jewish religious institutions and practices in order to prove her new allegiance and show dramatically that she was not showing favoritism to her own people. Esther hammered away at this theme:

You do not understand the danger Jews face. If the Russian people begin to feel that we are partial to the Jews, it will be harmful to Jews. It is for the sake of Jews that we are completely objective in our dealing with the clergy—Jew and non-Jew alike. The danger is that the masses may think that Judaism is exempt from anti-religious propaganda. Therefore, Jewish Communists must be even more ruthless with rabbis than non-Jewish Communists are with priests.[10]

This sensitivity was associated with the experience of a number of Jewish activists who had been reviled by peasants for attacking Russian Orthodoxy but not Judaism. A dark side of this new surge of anti-Semitism was intimated by Gorky, who deplored the activities of the "Evseks" as being "devoid of all tact," adding that he knew of cases in which Jewish Communists were purposely sent to persecute the Russian church and priests "in order that the Russian peasants should see with their own eyes that Jews are desecrating their holy places."[11] It is known that Esther and other "Evseks" were greatly embarrassed by Gorky's criticism, but this aspect of their new mission was only one facet of their complex predicament.

The Russian Orthodox Church, whose leaders believed that Russia had fallen under the power of godless men, frequently blamed its troubles on the Jews. As a result, while the Jews in the Evsektsiya carried out confiscations of churches, they were acutely aware of their "duty" to be even more zealous when they dealt with synagogues. But when they showed that zealousness, they aroused suffering and self-division among Jews; and when they showed themselves as passionately committed Bolsheviks in whatever they did, they reinforced existing anti-Jewish feeling, especially among adherents of Russian Orthodoxy.

At the same time, the "Evseks" who remained and were added after 1921 were under Bolshevik pressure to carry out antireligious measures. This pressure was complicated by the prevailing party disdain of the whole Evsektsiya structure. Thus, burdened by an unpopular, alien ideology, by small numbers, by an acknowledged weakness both in Jewish community life and within the Communist party, and yet defined as an arm of the Bolshevik power, and experiencing power for the first time, the Evsektsiya members went forth with their complex tasks into a complex Jewish world (see Photos 4.1, 4.2, and 4.3). Here, a formidable array of traditional institutions and loyalties balked their advance: the intricate synagogue and kehilla structures, the force of traditional Judaism, networks of Jewish schools and teachers, social, cultural, and economic secular organizations, the numerous Zionist organizations, and the Hebrew cultural movement—all of which formed trusted and familiar sources of loyalty and authority to their members,

4.1 Kaplan looks back nostalgically to the old shtetl culture: "The circle grows higher and better." A wedding celebration, from B. Sures, *Anatoly Lvovich Kaplan: Ocherk tvorchestva* [Album of his works]. Leningrad, 1972. Kaplan's *Album* was published on the occasion of his seventieth birthday, covering works from 1928 to 1969. Widely known for his illustrations of Sholem Aleikhem's stories.

and all of which were opposed to the Bolshevik ideology. They were harassed and coerced into submission or disappearance ultimately, but they resisted more vigorously than is generally realized—until 1929, and even thereafter under the Stalin dictatorship. Moreover, some residues of traditional Jewish culture survived surreptitiously in certain families and were to influence children and grandchildren in the 1960s and 1970s.

The first act of the new government, based on the January 23rd de-

4.2 "Sunday, Monday, Tuesday, Wednesday—Potatoes
Thursday and Friday—Potatoes
Tsimmes and *kugel*—again with Potatoes
Sunday, however—Potatoes" (Kaplan's *Album*)

cree, that directly affected the religious life of Jews was intended to
close and confiscate synagogues. A circular of February 28, 1919, spelled
out circumstances under which prayer houses could be closed: in cases
where there was a shortage of housing, medical and sanitation services, or cultural-educational institutions; or at the instigation of "the
mass of people."[12] Confiscation, however, was rare until 1921–22, when
the antireligious campaign became very intense. One of the first confiscations involved a synagogue in Vitebsk in 1921.

4.3 "Bread, Wine and Fish Make the Table Festive" (Kaplan's *Album*).

The incident began with claims that there was a shortage of buildings for Soviet Yiddish schools although there were 77 synagogues in the city, half of which were said to be empty. The local Evkom invited representatives from local synagogues to turn over a number of synagogues that were concentrated in one courtyard. When they refused, local Communists began to clear the synagogues of Torah scrolls and religious books. Orthodox Jews then began occupying the synagogues, remaining inside from morning till late at night. The Communists then decided to close the synagogues, but worshippers resisted. Dressed in prayer shawls, they gathered in the court and held protest meetings and demonstrations. A detachment of fifteen men was sent to "liberate" the synagogues but they were beaten back by mud and stones. Finally, a cavalry unit forcibly evicted Jews from the buildings, which were then converted into a Communist party "university," a club, kitchen, and dormitory.[13] Antireligious actions in 1921 also erupted in Gomel and in Minsk, where two Jews were killed during a forcible seizure of the synagogue. The 1921 campaign was described as "a bitter military operation . . . a grandiose attack on the camp of the ancient enemy . . . a sort of national movement of the Jewish proletariat against *its* bourgeoisie."[14] In 1922 the campaign spread to the Ukraine.

The events in Vitebsk were presented by the Yiddish-language Communist press as an example to be followed elsewhere. Particular interest was expressed in taking over the choral synagogues in big cities, which had large and modern buildings and served a relatively well-to-do, moderately Orthodox community. The Choral Synagogue of Minsk was confiscated at the beginning of 1923 after a series of staged meetings and officially inspired letters to the editors of local Communist papers.[15] In June 1923, the Choral Synagogue in Kharkov was confiscated and converted into a Jewish Communist club after an extensive propaganda campaign, including a mass petition from "Jewish toilers." The local Evsektsiya proclaimed the day a holiday. Special meetings were held at places of work and a workers' march to the synagogue was organized, ending with a group carrying a red flag into the building. The Moscow *Emes*, aiming to expose the "counterrevolutionary nest" that had been closed, said that Torah scrolls in the building had been dedicated to the tsar.[16]

In the first half of 1923, the Moscow Evsektsiya conducted a campaign to close the Choral Synagogue there. *Der emes* published a series of articles against this "center of clericalism," urging workers to adopt resolutions that would turn the synagogue into a workers' club. In response, a petition from the congregation pointed out that such a decision would constitute persecution of the Jewish religion and was thus contrary to Soviet law which guaranteed religious freedom. The authorities were also reminded that only eight people had asked to turn the synagogue into a club, in sharp contrast to the thousands of worshipers who were being deprived of a house of prayer.[17] The Moscow Synagogue remained open, as did others during this period, following appeals of congregants. For example, a petition from 2,000 Jews in Kherson[18] asks the authorities to allow them to retain one of the six synagogues—Novo-Nicolaevskaya on the First of May Street, where "permanent and registered members" regularly attend services, but which is threatened by a takeover by "an insignificant number of youths, mostly craftsmen," in order to establish a club. An "improperly organized meeting of the craftsmen" voted on the question, but only 80 of the 300 people who came voted, according to the petitioners. The rest left in protest, showing that "the majority of the craftsmen are against disbanding the synagogue." The petition further points out that those interested in a club are not at all interested in Jewish culture; furthermore, the craftsmen already have a club of considerable capacity. Nor would the synagogue be suitable: "it is only a box with four walls, without any chimneys or flues, or stoves. Partitions are impossible because the area as a whole is much too small. Moreover, loss of the Novo-Nicolaevskaya Synagogue would mean the loss of two other synagogues next to each other in a courtyard. The existence of a prayer house under the same roof as an atheist club is inconceivable. If the confiscation takes place, "what of the wishes of the 2,000 undersigned constituting a religious community, whose rights are guaranteed by the Soviet Constitution?"

There were countless petitions of this sort in 1921–22, when local Evsektsiya decisions on confiscations were drastic. Although their resources were extremely stretched out and "woefully inadequate," they "had the full force of Soviet power to fall back on . . . when all other expedients failed."[19]

During this period, in the drive to close down Jewish religious schools under the January 23d law, a new technique known as the "social trial" was introduced by zealous Communists to expose the bourgeois nature of Jewish religious institutions and Jewish holidays. The "Trial of the Kheder" took place in Vitebsk in January 1921 and the "Trial of the Yeshiva" a little later in Rostov. In Vitebsk the officials distributed four hundred tickets to people wishing to attend the trial and planned to start at 7 P.M. on January 8. But, by 6:30, there were over 5,000 people shouting to stop the trial and threatening to close the Rekord Cinema where the trial was to be held. Thousands of other angry Jews were assembled in the Zhorier and Zarecheer prayer houses adding to the protests. The officials were threatened physically as well as verbally and retreated. The trial was called off and a "better organized" one scheduled later when the kheder was "sentenced" to be liquidated.[20]

One of the most bizarre of these show trials took place on the eve of Rosh Hashanah 1921, in the large hall of the District Court of the Evsektsiya in Kiev,[21] where, ironically, the Beilis trial had been held in 1911. Soviet newspapers called on Communists and non-party Jews to attend stage-managed trials. The first of the "defendants" was an old woman who said she sent her children to kheder where, the court said, "their ideas were darkened by the study of religious and other counterrevolutionary subjects." When the judge asked her why she didn't send them to Communist schools where they would be freed from religious superstitions, the woman answered that she was not a "low-class shoemaker or tailor," but had come from a family of rabbis and *mohels* (circumcisers) and could not "poison her own children with Communist teachers." After she was led out of the courtroom, a witness, dressed as a rabbi with traditional beard and sidecurls, was then brought in. When asked why he "poisoned Jewish youth with religious fairy tales and chauvinistic ideas," he answered: "I'm doing this deliberately to keep the masses of people in ignorance and bondage to the bourgeoisie." When someone in the audience shouted that the witness was "a lying ignoramus," he was immediately arrested. Another "witness" was called, a stout man bedecked with gold and diamonds. He declared that the Jewish bourgeoisie used religion to keep the Jewish masses in slavery and numbed their desire for freedom from the yoke of capitalism.

A local Hebrew teacher, Moshe Rosenblatt, rose to defend Judaism and remind the court that just ten years before, in the very same room, similar attacks on the Jewish religion were made by the anti-Semitic Black Hundreds: "Today you, like real anti-Semites and haters of Jews, are repeating the same insults." When the audience broke into a storm of applause, Rosenblatt, too, was arrested. The Evsektsiya prosecutor then summarized the "case against the Jewish religion" and asked for a "sentence of death on the Jewish religion." The judge brought in the desired "verdict."

Such trials were widely publicized and supposedly impartial, but they were not always successful from the Bolshevik point of view because they did not gain many adherents. Rather, the trials backfired. Party "testimony" was too flagrantly staged and drove most Jews to stronger opposition by the insulting, mocking nature of Bolshevik arguments. The number of trials diminished during the mid-twenties, when the antireligious campaigns were toned down. In 1924 the Thirteenth Party Congress resolved that they were to be conducted only with agitprop and educational methods.[22] By then, the compromises of NEP and foreign policy considerations, and the need for American Jewish funds for agricultural resettlement, caused one of numerous reorientations to come. In March 1924, Rakhmiel Veinshtain of the Evsektsiya Central Bureau explained that the Evsektsiya were not to alienate the "petit-bourgeois" elements of the Jewish population, but to "neutralize" them.[23] The last-known religious show trial—an attack on circumcision—was held in Kharkov in 1928. This is particularly ironic since many Jewish Communists themselves have clung to this ancient ritual and have resorted to all sorts of subterfuges to have their sons circumcised. Here, it seems, is a doctrinal limit that has been transgressed.

For a time, as the religious rituals and observances were assailed at show trials, meetings, lectures, public debates, and in numerous articles in the press, Jewish Communists tried to fill the religious void with crude and often grotesque forms of Red Judaism. "Red Haggadahs" were devised for Passover, in which the history of the October Revolution and deliverance from the slavery of capitalism replaced deliverance from Pharaoh.

In an effort to create a Communist substitute for the traditional Haggadah, a "Haggadah for Believers and Atheists" (*Hagodeh far Gloiber un Apikorsim*) was prepared by M. Altshuler, with illustrations by A. Tishler, in 1927. In the new interpretation, Passover, the traditional Jewish festival of freedom, is seen as a holiday used to chain the masses and indoctrinate them with hatred of Gentiles, and thus had to be abolished, in the Communist view. Instead, their Haggadah emphasized the theme of the class war. For example, the traditional portion over the burning of leaven is recast:

May all the aristocrats, bourgeois, and their helpers—Mensheviks . . . Cadets, Bundists, Zionists . . . and other counter-revolutionaries—be consumed in the fire of the revolution. May those who have been burned never rise again. The rest . . . we abandon and hand over to the jurisdiction of the GPU.

The passage on the washing of hands is rendered:

Wash away, workers and peasants, the entire bourgeois filth, wash off the mildew of the ages and say—not a blessing—but a curse: May annihilation overcome all the outdated rabbinic laws and customs, yeshivas and heders, which blacken and enslave the people.

The Hallel has become:

Sing the "International" and say—
Down with the mildew of the ages!
Down with clerical nationalistic festivals!
Long live the revolutionary workers' holidays.[24]

Communists also tried to persuade Jews to bake *khalla* (a braided loaf of white bread served on the Sabbath and holidays) in the shape of a hammer and sickle and set up "Living Synagogues" which preached Communism as the Mosaic Torah translated by Lenin. But none of these experiments ever caught hold. Indeed, Jewish workers, who despite their socialist orientation, still observed holidays and the Sabbath and wanted their sons circumcised, deplored these travesties—much to the disappointment of the Evsektsiya. Typical was the complaint that "the less conscious . . . Jewish worker at first did not understand what the Jewish Communists want of the rabbi and the kehilla, of the *minyan* (ten men needed for a prayer service) and synagogue . . . The rabbi, it seemed to him, is an innocent creature. Unlike the priest, he was never to be found in the tsarist regime."[25]

Moreover, most rabbis and religious teachers existed in great poverty and near destitution—as did the Jewish artisans and stall and shop-keepers—but to the Evsektsiya zealots, all of these and the whole keh-illa structure were dogmatically fixed into the condemned "bourgeois-clerical" class, regardless of economic realities. The kehilla, with its ra-mified substructures and services, was the most difficult for the Evsek-tsiya to understand and control. It penetrated to the very core of tra-ditional Jewish life and held communities together; its very complexities angered and frustrated the Jewish Communists. There was no Marxist formulation for these unruly, deeply rooted life forms. They would have to be destroyed. But this proved easier to declaim than to accomplish.

The decree abolishing kehillas was issued by the Central Jewish Commissariat in July 1919 and approved by Stalin, Commissar of Na-tionalities. But, as Agursky warned, "It would have been senseless simply to close the kehilla because the Jewish poor, who came to the kehilla for aid, would have suffered."[26] The adaptations varied. Often, in places where there were no Evsektsiya or Evkom, kehillas could function openly. In Vologda,[27] for example, the community managed charity, religious schools, and a kosher public relief kitchen which re-ceived supplies from Soviet officials without charge. Part of the public bath was set aside for a Jewish ritual bath (*mikva*), and the former offi-cial rabbi was recognized as the representative of local Jews. Some keh-illas existed under different names, and some of their functions were taken over by other institutions. In Vitebsk,[28] for example, a "Syn-agogues Committee" dealt with matters of welfare, education, and cul-ture. In the small town of Sevyezh near the Latvian border, there was a "Jewish Committee" that regulated synagogues, ritual baths, pay-ment of fees to rabbis, ritual slaughterers and beadles, management of the cemetery, and aid to the poor. Taxes were imposed on the whole

Jewish population. *Emes,* however, complained that the committee did not concern itself with the local Soviet Yiddish school, which was having a difficult time. In certain cities,[29] an influential rabbi such as the Lubavicher Rabbi in Leningrad, could serve as spiritual leader beyond his official area. This rabbi also made an appeal in 1924 to revive communities that had stopped their work, and some cities such as Gomel did indeed re-establish community activities. The Moscow rabbi by virtue of his access to central authorities, who were more liberally disposed than local officials, could sometimes act on behalf of other communities.

The resistance to liquidation was tenacious, and was undoubtedly strengthened by the relaxation under NEP. It is difficult to measure the extent of this resistance for generally there were no official data on the number of Jewish religious communities, but in October 1925, 418 registered Jewish communities were reported in the RSFSR.[30] An Evsektsiya statement dated September 1, 1926, reported the existence of 1,003 registered communities, with 137,437 members in the Ukraine[31]—12 to 13 percent of the adult Jewish population—as well as small, unregistered communities. These are quite astonishing figures, five years after the communities were to have been liquidated.

Synagogues were still being confiscated in 1924, but the closures stopped in 1925–27 during the relaxations of the NEP period. An antireligious pamphlet reported that between 1917 and 1927, 23 percent of synagogues (366 out of 1,400)[32] and churches had been closed, but these figures are much too low. Some cities had had over one hundred synagogues and the total number as well as the confiscations were greater.[33] The figure of 1,400 very probably referred only to the Ukraine, a figure which was reduced to 1,034 by 1927, according to *Bezbozhnik* (The Atheist) (see Photo 4.4).[34] After 1927, confiscations were carried out on a much greater scale, some by the Evsektsiya, some by city councils, and by local and regional soviets.[35]

In the Ukraine, many synagogues were closed by the Evsektsiya, which threatened to take action against members of the synagogue committees if they complained to the central authorities. Several synagogues in Kiev were confiscated on the pretext that the Jewish community was unable to look after the buildings properly. In Bobruisk the city's three great synagogues were seized and their Holy Arks smashed and burned. Elsewhere, the synagogues were turned into clubs after requests by "Jewish toilers."[36]

4.4 The cover of an issue of the journal *Bezbozhnik* ("The Godless"). On the right is a caricature of Jehovah, wearing a prayer shawl and phylacteries. Next to him is Allah, and in the center, a figure of Buddha. Courtesy Joseph B. Shechtman, *Star in Eclipse*, 1961.

Despite these closures, most Jews who still wanted to attend synagogue could do so in 1928, but a sharp change took place in 1929 which profoundly affected the lives of all religious persons in the Soviet Union. The year 1929 marked the onset of harsh economic policies and forced collectivization under Stalin and a correspondingly severe regimentation of all Soviet life (see Chapter 10). The new laws were approved by the USSR Central Executive Committee on April 8, 1929 and allegedly provided the use of churches and synagogues for "religious needs," but barred them for social, educational, and cultural functions. However, the interpretation of "religious needs" was squeezed very tight.

Two laws were passed in 1929, which still remain in force, further defining the rights and duties of Soviet citizens in religious matters and the status of religious cults. These laws permit Soviet citizens over eighteen to belong to two kinds of religious groups, called religious societies (consisting of at least twenty members) or groups of believers (consisting of fewer than twenty members), but the right to establish a group of believers and prayer meetings in the homes of such believers has seldom been granted. Such meetings are usually held secretly. Moreover, meetings which under the law are permitted to religious associations are often blocked whenever officials deem it expedient to do so. Leases can be withdrawn without notice, buildings can be condemned as "unsafe," members of the dvadtsatka can be harassed by threatening job, housing, and educational disabilities. A continuous workweek was also decreed in 1929 to "facilitate a more successful struggle against religion," and in 1932 the observance of a religious day of rest was made more difficult by depriving the accused of ration cards and housing. Religious propaganda conducted by religious associations was declared illegal.[37]

The declassment of all clergymen, including rabbis and religious teachers, further hampered efforts to keep religious life alive, but from the Bolshevik point of view, was introduced in order to hasten its dissolution by penalizing religious leaders. In 1918, a category called *lishentsy*, or declassed, was adopted, depriving them of civil rights and access to housing, food rations, medical aid, and educational opportunities for their children. They were also subject to abusive attacks and public defamation. In the intensified campaigns of 1929–30, rabbis, religious teachers, *shokhtim* (ritual slaughterers) and *mohalim* (ritual circumcisers) were arrested, exiled, and sometimes executed.[38]

Many rabbis, however, conducted services clandestinely, like Spanish Marranos of old. Some, in 1926, dared to convoke a rabbinical assembly in Korosten. Religious schools and yeshivot were also denounced and baited but some managed to sustain a camouflaged network for several years. The Lubavich Yeshivah kept alive by moving from Orel to Kremenchug to Rostov-on-the Don, to Nevel, where many students were thrown into jail, then to Kharkov, back to Rostov, and again to Kharkov, where it eventually succumbed to the Stalin terror.[39]

In 1924, an American rabbi visited the Soviet Union and when he returned to America, reported that rabbis' apartments in Minsk had been requisitioned, synagogues turned into clubs, and Jewish cemeteries and historical sites desecrated or turned into public parks.[40] Thirty rabbis were arrested as a result, charged with instigating anti-Soviet propaganda in America.

The attitude and actions of Soviet Russia toward Jewish religious life as reported by visitors and in the press were discussed and argued by numerous Jewish and non-Jewish spokesmen in the United States and England. They ranged from early confidence that the Bolshevik commitment to separation of church and state and long tradition of Jewish rather than state support of religious institutions would protect Jews, to fear for the physical survival of observant Jews. The investment of American Jewish financial aid in the Soviet Union in the mid-1920s was mooted, as well as a variety of counters in negotiations with the Soviet regime. The Chief Rabbi of England, for example, believed that removal of the ban on religious instruction should have been the "indispensable condition" of any Western Jewish cooperation with any Soviet scheme of colonization. Others feared to lodge any protest lest JDC relief work be stopped; still others, that American recognition of the regime would hinge on a more tolerant Soviet attitude toward religion generally.[41]

Within the Soviet Union, up to 1929, there was still a margin of flexibility. Local Communists themselves sometimes bent to the wishes or protests of communities, and from time to time, complaints to the central authorities resulted in the return of prayer houses to their original users. However, most Jews looked upon the antireligious attacks with increasing anxiety. The activities of the Evsektsiya were especially painful, for their actions against deeply rooted Jewish institutions and leadership posed a mortal threat to the very core of traditional Jewish life and to values for which Jews had been willing to die in centuries past. The vehemence of the Evseks in the antireligious campaign took on the fanaticism of a political theology and the implacable hostilities of war. The fabric of Jewish solidarity, already cracking in the pre-Bolshevik period under the hammer blows of ideological controversy, class antagonisms, and reformist pressures, was being torn asunder by the aggressive frenzy of Jewish Communists. This warfare was essentially a clash of generations. Jewish youths were being won over by revolutionary fervor and the stampede into the ranks of the Young Communist League—the Komsomol—which helped the Evsektsiya. Sometimes antireligious demonstrations on sacred days of severe fasting and prayer, such as Yom Kippur, caused near civil war, especially in small towns. Demonstrators disrupted services after marching in torchlight parades, breaking into synagogues with axes and saws, presenting clowns and music for entertainment and ostentatiously eating bread before the stunned congregation. In Odessa, fist fights broke out and the Cheka arrested the whole congregation. In Minsk, on the eve of Yom Kippur, during the solemn Kol Nidre service, youths from the Union of Militant Atheists arranged street demonstrations and carried placards reading "Down with rabbis and priests." Such primitive outbreaks caused painful rifts with parents and anguish among older Jews, vividly described in Haim Hazaz' classic *Gates of Bronze*.[42] Brooding over the Jewish hunger for redemption, Hazaz dramatizes the conflict between traditional Jewish and latter-day Jewish Communist messianic hopes, visions, and blindnesses. He describes the floundering incomprehension of the shtetlach. Shops are closed, rabbis arrested, beggars beaten up, the sacred Sabbath desecrated by Jewish youths driven on by a kind of apocalyptic destructiveness. They will cleanse out the old and bring a new world to birth.

For Jewish Communists, this new world would also have to be cleansed of two other tenacious remnants of "bourgeois-clericalism"—Zionism and Hebrew. In these campaigns, the Evsektsiya cracked wide open two tragic fissures in prerevolutionary Jewish life: the intense conflict between proponents of Yiddish and those of Hebrew, and the rabid anti-Zionism of the Bund and Faraynigte.

5

The Campaign against Zionism and Hebrew Culture

Sometimes when I fall ill with a fever and I look around and see that I have no one to leave the few books to, that I am the last . . . I fall into a black melancholy. . . . You write something in Hebrew, you have a new idea—there is no one to whom you can show it.

BARUCH SHPILBERG

ZIONISM in tsarist Russia began to attract large numbers of Jews in the early twentieth century, living in an illegal twilight and challenging the Jewish Bund and religious orthodoxy in Jewish communities. The movement lost many Jews to emigration after the pogroms of 1905–6 and later, but recovered again after the March 1917 Revolution, which removed its illegal status and ushered in a brief but remarkable period of growth, further enhanced by the Balfour Declaration of November 1917.

When the Bolsheviks took power, Zionism was unquestionably the dominant movement in Russian Jewish life, and although there were substantive ideological differences within the movement, it did not suffer the tortured splitting and ambivalence of the Bund in 1918–19. A core of Socialist Zionists and others had already gone to Palestine after 1903, and although the Helsingfors Conference of Russian Zionists in 1906 accepted the principle of national autonomy and equality of rights for Jews and all other nationalities in the Russian Empire, the dynamic in Zionism was Palestine. If there was to be a Jewish class struggle, as Borokhov anticipated, it would be fought there. Thus, emigration out of Russia and preparation for that emigration made Palestine the center of gravity for Zionists rather than Soviet Russia or any other Diaspora.

Jewish nationalism rather than the international proletariat was the compelling loyalty. Positions on domestic political issues assumed considerable significance among Zionist groups after the Helsingfors Conference, but were eclipsed by the Balfour Declaration and expectations that a Jewish homeland in Palestine would soon have international acceptance.

All of the main currents in Russian Zionism prior to the Bolshevik Revolution had been identified with or were close to political movements opposed to Bolshevism, and during the Kerensky regime Zionists gave their support to such parties and to a separate peace with Germany. For its part, the new regime regarded Jewish nationality and Jewish nationalism as reactionary ideas at odds with the interests of the Jewish proletariat. For Lenin and other Bolsheviks, Zionism was tainted as "bourgeois" and linked to religion. Ironically, Lenin had attacked the anti-Zionist Bund for being seized by the "Zionist" concept of a Jewish "nation," and was convinced that, although there would be transitional changes, the ultimate fate of Jews would be assimilation. Whereas Zionists viewed Jews as a distinct national people, Bolsheviks saw them as surviving and persisting only because of the persistence of anti-Semitism and external persecution. Thus, although the clash did not come immediately, Zionism and Communism were plainly on a collision course in Russia.

On the larger scene and in terms of foreign policy, Bolshevik theories about world revolution and the nature of imperialism and capitalism also set one ideology against another. Palestine had been conquered by Britain, considered by the Bolsheviks as the bastion of imperialism and capitalism, thus placing Britain close to the Russian border. In the Bolshevik view, the occupation by Britain was part of a British scheme for the dismemberment of the Ottoman Empire, to be followed by the destruction of revolutionary Russia.[1]

However, this hostility to Zionism was sometimes muted, sometimes denied, sometimes compromised, and in the very early stages of the regime, largely ignored because of other more urgent pressures. For the first few months, there was no interference with Zionist activities. In December 1917, Joseph Trumpeldor, the much loved visionary soldier and leader of *Hekhalutz*, the Zionist pioneering movement, received permission to establish a Jewish battalion to defend Jews against pogroms.[2] Hekhalutz colonies were spreading throughout the country. A "Palestine Week," proclaimed in the spring of 1918, was successfully celebrated in hundreds of Jewish communities, and Palestine emigration centers in Petrograd, Minsk and other cities functioned freely.[3] The Zionist press published its material unmolested, and there were many campaigns to mobilize capital for the upbuilding of Palestine. Zionists, however, were cautious and, not wanting to arouse Communist hostility, played down domestic issues. At a Zionist conference in Moscow in May 1918, the sixty delegates endorsed a resolution of neutrality on domestic affairs.[4]

The Jewish Communists in the Evsektsiya, however, mainly from the Bund and Faraynigte—old enemies of Zionism—picked up their former battles with zeal and at this time began to denounce the "counterrevolutionary essence" of Zionism and its "concentration of petty bourgeois elements." Dimanshtain was particularly active in elaborating critiques of Zionism in numerous articles and speeches, arguing that Jewish workers now had every opportunity open to anyone else, while bourgeois Zionists were "resisting the 'progressive' forces of the socialist revolution."[5] The Evseks stepped up their drive and in February 1919 Zionist headquarters in Petrograd reported that Zionist offices in many parts of Russia were being requisitioned and Zionist periodicals banned. In the following month, at a Zionist conference in Petrograd, many delegates complained of frequent administrative interference with their activities, but stressed the fact that local Jewish Communist officials rather than government agencies were generally responsible for the raids.[6]

In Great Russia, the persecution of Zionism came almost a year later than in the Ukraine. In 1919 the Jewish population in the RSFSR did not exceed half a million—most of them refugees who had been expelled by the tsarist regime during World War I, for whom Zionism had great appeal. Thus, the Jewish Sections had considerable difficulty recruiting Jewish cadres in this area, making it possible for Zionist activity to continue without undue harassment during the first half of 1919.[7] Moreover, there was no Komfarband in the RSFSR. The undermanned Evsektsiya concentrated on the suppression of the independent Jewish communal and social welfare services, but at its second conference in June 1919, delegates also demanded the dissolution of the "counterrevolutionary . . . clerical and nationalist" Zionist organization.[8] In the RSFSR proper, this appeal met with no immediate response and the Evsektsiya was highly critical of the government's failure to act vigorously. In the Ukraine, however, before late summer, when Denikin's army took over much of the region, the former Bundists and members of the Faraynigte, still in the Komfarband, sent a memorandum to the Ukrainian Commissariat of Internal Affairs, insisting that it was "absolutely necessary to liquidate the activities of the Zionist party and all its factions."[9] The Commissariat responded quickly and vigorously. Two days later, the homes of scores of prominent Zionists in Kiev were searched by the Cheka, accompanied by members of the Komfarband who spoke of these actions as a "Jewish civil war."[10] A July 12 decree ordered fifteen Zionist organizations, as well as the *Tarbut* (Culture), a Zionist sponsored school system in Kiev, to be closed down.[11] After the Red Army re-occupied the Ukraine early in 1920, repressive measures were resumed. In the wake of the bloody pogroms, this anti-Zionist drive intensified efforts of Jews in the Ukraine—especially in the small towns—to leave for Palestine.

Alarmed by the full-scale attack on Zionism at the Evsektsiya conference, the Zionist Organization requested official certification of legality from the All-Russian Central Executive Committee of Soviets (VTsIK) in July 1919, maintaining that Zionist activities were directed at transforming Jewish merchants and tradesmen into farmers and artisans in Palestine. Since VTsIK had not issued any decree declaring Zionism counterrevolutionary, the presidium of the VTsIK instructed all Soviet organizations "not to hamper" Zionist activities.[12] This permitted a semilegal existence but did not exclude administrative repression, as was soon made clear. On September 1, 1919, the Cheka sealed the central Zionist office in Petrograd, arrested its directors, confiscated its documents and cash, and closed down the Zionist weekly, *Khronika Yevreiskoy Zhizny*, (Chronicle of Jewish Life).[13] Arrests followed in Moscow and Vitebsk, but all those arrested were soon released and the Zionist office in Petrograd was re-opened and the confiscated money returned. Zionist publications were silenced, but Zionist leaders were somewhat heartened by the uneven course of official policy and convened an All-Russian Zionist Congress on April 20, 1920, in Moscow. Special traveling permits were even granted to out-of-town delegates. The first two days passed uneventfully, but on the third day, seventy-five of the 109 delegates and guests were arrested—technically not because Zionism was illegal, but because the congress was not licensed and because the delegates allegedly expressed pro-British views.[14] By this time, the new regime had eliminated all non-Bolshevik parties and was bent on destroying all political dissidence. At the same time, an occasional nod would be made to Jewish public opinion abroad, especially in America, in order not to jeopardize the urgently needed relief.

The imprisoned Zionists were held in the notorious Butyrka jail in Moscow for three months without formal legal proceedings. In mid-July, sixty-eight were released through the intervention of representatives of the Joint Distribution Committee, who were on a mission to Moscow at the time.[15] The remaining seven were sentenced to hard labor for varying periods, but were released after pledging never again to engage in Zionist activity. The Zionist Central Committee then decided to move underground. On July 1, 1920, a secret memorandum was circulated to all local Cheka offices ordering the harassment, but not the unlimited persecution, of the Zionist movement, apparently out of concern lest a massive anti-Zionist campaign cause an outcry against the Soviet Union among world Jewry.[16]

Impatient with the seeming half-hearted government drive, the Evsektsiya at its third conference in July 1921, declared that there was

no longer any ground for a cautious attack on Zionism. It is necessary to put an end to the vacillation of the old official attitude toward the general Zionist party and to all its cultural and economic organizations. It is essential that a total liquidation be carried out, notwithstanding the socialist phraseology of the *Tseirei Tsion* and Zionist socialists.[17]

The composition of the Evsektsiya had substantially changed by this time, with the infusion of enthusiasts from the Komfarband and new recruits of the Communist party. Even so, the threatened total liquidation did not occur. A protracted relaxation of pressure and repression was felt for most of 1921 during the early phases of Lenin's New Economic Policy (NEP—see Chapter 7).

In February 1921, in conversations between George V. Chicherin, the Soviet foreign minister, and David Eder, a British MP and Zionist leader who tried to negotiate a legal status for Russian Zionism, it seemed apparent that even though the government did not want to root out Zionism completely, the Evsektsiya were serving the government well in depicting "any harassment of Zionism as the spontaneous and justified expression of progressive Jewish opinion"—one episode in the "civil war in the Jewish street."[18] Chicherin argued that Zionism was not being discriminated against in the Soviet Union, unless it was "bourgeois" or "criminal," and that "the *Poale Tsion* social-democratic movement and the *Poale Tsion* Communist movement . . . have always had the authorization to propagate their Palestinian ideas. . . . As for persecution, if sometimes repression has been ordered against some bourgeois elements among the Zionists, it was the consequence of crimes committed by these elements, but the repression was never directed against the principles of Zionism itself."[19] The demise of Russian Zionism was thus interpreted as a natural death in a progressive socialist society, not an instigated planned campaign for its liquidation—exactly the same "explanation" for the officially directed destruction of Jewish culture in the Soviet Union in recent years.

After some of the older leaders such as Jabotinsky and Trumpeldor had emigrated to Palestine, Zionist leadership and activity shifted to the youth movements, *Tseirei Tsion* (Young Zionists), *Hashomer Hatzair* (see Photo 5.1), and *Hekhalutz*. In 1920, succumbing to pressures and fear of exposure, Tseirei Tsion split into two wings, one supporting the government, the other anti-Bolshevik, moving underground. By 1922, it constituted the mainstay of the Zionist movement, with particular strength in the Ukraine.[20] On April 30, 1922, at a conference of the right-wing movement in Kiev, fifty-one youths were arrested. Thirty-seven were brought to trial, the first public prosecution of Zionists in the Soviet Union and the occasion for a full-scale attack on Zionism. Twelve were sentenced to two years at hard labor, fifteen to one year; the rest were released.[21] In September 1922, over 1,000 Zionists were arrested in Odessa, Kiev, Berdichev, and other Ukrainian cities.[22] Harassment and arrests continued throughout 1923–24, albeit with confusing signals to those who could not see the baseline policy or who needed the prop of illusion. In the summer of 1924, with an obvious, calculated nod to Western Jewish interest and concern, the Soviet government invited the *Histadrut* (the General Labor Federation in Palestine) to participate in the International Agricultural Exhibition in Moscow in 1923. The Palestine pavilion attracted tens of thousands of enthusiastic Jewish visitors from all parts of the Soviet Union and aroused Zionist youth demonstrations. The Histadrut exhibit also coincided with a meeting between two delegates of the Histadrut, David Remez and David Ben Gurion, who came to Moscow by official invitation, and Solomon Lozovsky, chief of *Profintern*, the Communist Trade Union International. The visitors wanted to know the official party view on Jewish emigration to Palestine. When Lozovsky was told of the Palestine Communist party's opposition to emigration, his terse reply was: "That is an anti-Communist position."[23]

5.1 Hashomer Hatzair Scouts, Kremenchug, 1917. Courtesy Itai.

But this seemingly accommodating tone was suddenly quenched by a wave of arrests on September 2, 1924, between midnight and dawn, when several thousand of the most active Zionists were jailed after secret trials and then scattered to obscure parts of Russia—the Solovetski Islands in the White Sea, Kirghizia in central Asia, and Siberia. This crackdown was meant to deal a massive blow to the underground Zionist movement, but the movement was hardly dead. A month after these arrests, after Simchat Torah services, Jews were startled by the sight of Jewish youngsters marching in formation outside the synagogues, singing *Hatikvah* and chanting Zionist slogans. Tens of thousands of Jewish children, undoubtedly urged on by Zionist adults, began sending letters and petitions to Soviet officials requesting that Hebrew be taught in the schools. Meanwhile, youths of fourteen and fifteen took over leadership of the clandestine cells. Zionists continued to needle and even harass the Evsektsiya, disrupting their meetings, circulating brochures (100,000 in the Ukraine in 1924) which attacked

Evsektsiya policies, and calling for a new regime of the "toilers themselves . . . freely elected Jewish soviets, cooperatives, and the right to
maintain ties with Palestine."[24] Zionists hammered away at the dismal
economic outlook in the Soviet Union as proof that the regime was
unable to solve Jewish economic problems. In the tug of war between
the Zionist underground and the Komsomol, Zionists were more successful in penetrating the rival organization; at times they even rose to
key posts, using Komsomol's physical facilities, stationery, and equipment to promote Zionist clandestine work.[25] But the harassment and
persecution intensified. Any competitive youth movement that threatened the Komsomol was intolerable.

There is no doubt that had the anti-Zionist campaign been relaxed,
many Jews would have joined or rejoined Zionist groups, thus threatening Communist control. The movement was steadily being crippled,
but the fear of its influence agitated the Evsektsiya and undoubtedly
worried the regime. Chemerisky, in October 1924, cautioned the All-
Ukrainian Conference of Jewish Sections that "the Jewish youth in the
shtetls is not in our hands. Even in such a city as Kremenchug the
Zionists penetrate our schools."[26] Almost daily, articles in the Moscow
Emes called upon the authorities to give more rigorous support to the
fight against Zionism and to prohibit any vestiges of Hebrew or Jewish
emigration:

The great want in which the Jewish small town population lives creates a favorable basis for the development of Zionism, whose influence on the petty-
bourgeois elements of the Jewish youth is now very large.[27]

Continuing to the end their efforts to get the government to intercede
against the Evsektsiya and legalize the movement, on May 25, 1925
several Zionist leaders sent a memorandum to Peter (Pyotr) Smidovich,
the acting head of VTsIK, asking for an end to all persecutions and
permission to emigrate to Palestine for those who wanted to leave. A
special session of the VTsIK was held in June, after which Smidovich
advised the Zionists to submit ideas for a legal emigration society to
VTsIK for approval. This was done and the proposals were also sent
to the Commissariat for Internal Affairs. Simultaneously the Evsektsiya
sent a memorandum to the Politburo listing its reasons why the Zionist
program should be rejected. Finding it easy to cast blame elsewhere,
Smidovich told the Zionist leaders that "your own people are causing
all kinds of hindrances." Negotiations continued but no emigration

agency was created.[28] However, the government characteristically exploited this process to its own advantage. A World Zionist Congress was soon to meet and the economist Yuri Larin told the Zionists "that the government was not eager to incur the wrath of world Jewry because of a handful of Russian Zionists." Larin even offered to let Russian Zionists send a delegation to the forthcoming congress if they agreed to say publicly that the Soviet government championed Jewish rights and to ask all Jews to support the Crimean colonization program. In exchange, the regime would legalize an emigration agency and permit the reestablishment of the Tarbut organization and Hebrew schools. The Zionists, in turn, insisted that all persecutions cease, that the imprisoned Zionists be freed, and that the Evsektsiya be restrained. These negotiations continued for over six months, ending March 16, 1926, when more than one hundred leading Zionists in Moscow were arrested and subsequently sentenced to three years' exile in Kazakhstan. Several were later deported to Palestine.[29] No further negotiations were attempted.

These decisions involved domestic considerations. No dissident, unassimilable minority would be allowed to function in an increasingly regimented society. The regime was not at all interested in reaching a modus vivendi with the Zionist movement, but at the same time did not want to alienate Western Jewish opinion, which was still somewhat sympathetic to the Soviet "experiment" and, more importantly, was sending large sums of money to the country for various projects (see Chapter 7). So, a line was developed and later perfected: to create the impression that the regime was negotiating or acting in good faith but was blocked or swayed by Jews inside the country who, in this case, opposed Zionism or refused to make concessions, i.e., to bend to the regime's will, and who would then be described as anti-Soviet. For this purpose, although the dénouement for the Zionist movement was inevitably approaching, the regime tried to create a front organization out of Hekhalutz.

Hekhalutz was a Jewish pioneering youth movement, largely molded by a Labor Zionist philosophy and the inspiring leadership of Joseph Trumpeldor (see Photo 5.2). Its members sought to become productive workers building a just society in Palestine. Centers sprang up in the Ukraine, Bessarabia, Poland, and Lithuania. In the early twenties, the Hekhalutz program of training for settlement in Palestine on collective agricultural farms offered a certain appeal to the Soviet regime's ideol-

5.2 Vitebsk Hekhalutz Garden Group, 1920. Courtesy Tsentsiper.

ogy, and Hekhalutz was permitted to grow. By the end of 1923, there were 75 groups in the Soviet Union with about 3,000 members. In August of that year, disregarding Evsektsiya's objections, the Commissariat on Internal Affairs issued a charter to the "Labor Federation Hekhalutz".[30] Some of its members refused to accept the offered legal status, fearing infiltration by Communist agents, and formed a separate, illegal group, but others persisted in sustaining the organization's life and work in existing colonies. The latter had to walk an ideological tightrope expressed in the overstretched, hyperbolic, often turgid language of their Russian-language newsletter, called *Gekholuts* (Hekhalutz), which first appeared in Moscow in June 1924[31] and was described as the "organ of the Central Committee of the All-Russian Labor Organization." *Gekholuts* praises the growing strength of the workers' movement in Palestine but deplores the "class backwardness" of many workers. *Hakhshara* (preparation for settlement) is viewed as "the most active counterbalance to the notorious Jewish adaptation." The transition to productive labor must also be achieved in the Soviet Union. "Our attitude toward the problem," it was stressed in the lead article, "is not sufficiently serious yet" and the large Jewish masses in the country must "reeducate themselves" and become "conscious workers, organizers, creators, and fighters." Collectivism remains one of the main principles of the "essence of Hekhalutz. All our measures and undertakings must be directed toward preparing comrades for 'Chevrat Ovdim' [a brotherhood of workers]—that is, 'a labor society.' " The Hekhalutz movement is credited with being a pioneering vanguard, but its ideas are described as "foggy and romantic" until 1923–24, when it fully realized the necessity of the class struggle and the "injection of revolutionary virus." According to *Gekholuts*, Hekhalutz is now fused to the general worldwide proletarian class struggle. Its "individualistic-anarchist ideas" have been tempered by the Russian Revolution and its psychology has been "collectivized."[32]

Palestine is seen as an undeveloped country that will undergo modernization on its way to join the forces of world revolution and communism, but it becomes dimmer and more and more distant in the life plans of Hekhalutz youths, as can be seen in another article dealing with a conference in the summer of 1924. In it, there is a wistful reference to an "echo" from the call to "the broad working masses beckoning them to work for Jewish collectivist Palestine," but also a quick qualifier and withdrawal:

Although the conference did not represent all the khalutzim [pioneers] of the Soviet Union and is cut off from the Palestine working class, nevertheless, it expressed the ideas with which thousands of people living in the USSR and Palestine are filled. . . . The conference threw a sturdy bridge of hakhshara across the deep gulf that lies between the sickly shopkeepers' middle-class economy and the strong life of farmers digging the soil and stone workers in the communes. . . .[33]

By "connecting the lessons of the Great Social Revolution [in the USSR] with the categorical urges of small Jewish Palestine," solidarity between working-class Palestine and Soviet Russia is cemented. Moreover, the regime's efforts to proletarianize Jewish petty traders and "unproductive" elements are viewed as identical to those of Hekhalutz. Thus, the "legal" Hekhalutz was fused to Bolshevik aims and lost its own in the wearing down process, as had happened to the Bund earlier.

Yet the glowing dream of Palestine still filled the minds and hearts of thousands of Jewish youths, and the regime knew it. Its own land resettlement for Jews, which was launched in 1924, and Birobidzhan (see Chapter 13) in 1928, used Zionist phraseology in its efforts to win support and drain away the powerful feelings Palestine stirred. Some Zionist youths responded. For example, Dan Pines, the leader of the legal Hekhalutz, appeared at the first general meeting of the Soviet resettlement agency OZET and promised to support its activities. Some members hoped to convert these settlements into Zionist colonies, but *Emes* warned against Hekhalutz participation.[34] In fact, both wings of the movement soon began to suffer. Arrests started in 1924 and were intensified in 1926. In March 1926, Hekhalutz House in Moscow was raided and arrests there were followed by arrests in Leningrad, Nezhin, Poltava, Simferpol, the colonies in the Kherson province and in the Krivoi Rog region of Crimea.[35]

Ten colonies are reported to have existed in 1925, a number with Hebrew names such as Tel Khai, Mishmar, and Ma'ayan. Hebrew was used by both branches of Hekhalutz and even *Gekholuts* emphasized that Hebrew was the language of the Jewish working masses returning to life in Palestine. The colonies are described by David Bergelson in his trip through the Crimea in 1926 as "remarkably well-organized communes, full of vitality," but whose members were "strange creatures: seemingly from here and yet not from here . . . one foot in Crimea and the other in Palestine."[36] The liquidation of the colonies began in 1926 and ended with that of Mishmar in 1928, when *Gekholuts* was also closed down. Its sponsor, the "official" Hekhalutz and the small residual Left Poale Tsion also came to an end in the same year. Their usefulness to the regime was over now that Birobidzhan was to replace Palestine as a Jewish national territory.

Linked and yet separate to some degree from Zionism was the campaign against the Hebrew language. Yet there was nothing intrinsically antagonistic or threatening to Communist ideology or Soviet policy in the Hebrew language. Zionists, of course, wanted a Jewish national revival based on Hebrew. As the language of the Bible and synagogue, it might be considered subversive if used and perpetuated by religious Jews. However, the regime at first did not have any ideological opposition to Hebrew. The battle was joined largely by the anti-Zionist ex-socialists now in the Evsektsiya who seized upon Hebrew as an implacable enemy and who urged Soviet officials to make war on it.[37]

There is a great deal of evidence to indicate that Soviet policymakers were at first either somewhat sympathetic or indifferent to the continued use of Hebrew, or else too busy to be concerned at all with language feuds of a small minority. In time, it became officially excommunicated, but the question whether this hostility derived from the nationality policy of the regime or from the Evsektsiya continues to be debated.[38] The Evseks, in their zeal to be exclusive agents of the class struggle among Jews and press the complexities of life into an iron frame, hailed Yiddish as the language of the masses and excoriated Hebrew as the language of bourgeois-capitalists, Zionists, and rabbis. Thus they conveniently submerged or avoided the fact that the Hebrew prophets and most of the major Hebrew writers were themselves poor and wrote for the masses, and that there was a large secularist, non-Zionist and anti-Zionist literature in Hebrew. Conversely, the Evseks would not face the fact that there are many religious works in Yiddish and bourgeois, religious Yiddish writers.

Very likely the Evseks' inability to influence the Jewish masses, combined with their sudden power and need to express it, gave their drive against Hebrew, as against Zionism, special vehemence. It has also been suggested that the addition of Moishe Litvakov and Esther Frumkin to the Central Bureau of the Evsektsiya in July 1920, may have contributed to the intense campaigns. The language battle fueled and was fueled by the ideological battle, but "the most radical Yiddishists could not match the Evsektsiya in the fury of their anti-Hebrew campaign."[39]

Obviously, the struggle over Hebrew was not in the forefront of needs and problems facing most Jews in the early twenties, but those who fought in it invested it with great intensity. For the defenders of Hebrew, indeed, it was a life-and-death struggle for a culture of immense value, whose destruction would mean a rupture in Jewish history without parallel. Pre-Bolshevik Russia, moreover, had seen a neo-Hebrew movement associated with Haskalah and the later developments in fiction, poetry, and journalism. Lebensohn, Mapu, Gordon, Smolenskin, Abramovich (Mendele Mokher Seforim), Ahad Ha'am, Klausner, Bialik, Tchernikhovsky, and lesser writers had contributed to this historic stream, and the liberating force of the March 1917 Revolution opened up new springs and channels. In the anticipated Jewish national reconstruction, Hebrew literature, publishing, education, and scholarship were expected to play a significant role after March 1917, and began to do so. At the beginning of the Bolshevik Revolution, there were also large-scale plans for the the publication of Hebrew books and journals, but they soon had to be aborted. Even so, in the period 1917–19, more than 180 books, pamphlets, and reviews appeared in Russia in Hebrew,[40] the bulk of them in Odessa. In the first few months of the new regime, a number of journals including *Hashiloah*, *Hatekufah*, and *Barkai*, and a Hebrew newspaper *Ha-Am*, as well as anthologies and translations, were published but were soon closed down.

Odessa was the center of Hebrew culture, pivoting around the figure of the great poet Khaim Nakhman Bialik, who was gallantly striving to maintain his publishing house Moriah, to provide short popular works in Hebrew for the children and adults in the Tarbut schools, and to write as well. A thriving Hebrew Teachers' Association, *Hamoreh*, existed in the Ukraine, but was able to publish only one of its journals. In Moscow, to which a number of Hebrew scholars and writers were gravitating, the publisher Avraham Steibel hoped to carry out his old dream of translating the great classics of world literature into Hebrew. Works by Tolstoy, Romain Rolland, Turgenev, and Oscar Wilde were already completed. For a time, Evkom even shared the Moscow villa of the well-to-do Persitz family, famous patrons of Hebrew and publisher of *Ha-Am*. Shoshana Persitz was a Zionist leader who supervised a kosher kitchen, shared by Zionists and Evkom. But the days of this strange co-existence as well as those of *Ha-Am* were numbered. On December 7, 1917, the editor Benzion Katz wrote in an editorial: "The Russian Revolution surpasses in its savagery all the negative features of the French Revolution. . . . We have only one hope, that the reign of this new Inquisition will not last long."[41] The newspaper had to suspend publication in June 1918 and before the end of the year, Steibel's translation projects and *Hatekufah* had moved to Warsaw. Authorities confiscated type already set for Flaubert's *Madame Bovary* and Zola's *Germinal*. In June 1919, all managers of print shops were told that all works being printed, "relating . . . to Zionist and clerical organizations must be reported to the administration," and that such publications "must be withheld and confiscated."[42] When the Communists consolidated their control of Odessa in January 1920, a delegation went to Abram Merezhin, a leading Jewish Communist and member of the Odessa Soviet at the time, asking for permission to carry on *Barkai* as a purely literary review, but he declined.

The Hebrew secular school movement, which had blossomed during the days of the Provisional Government, was steadily battered after a brief interlude of activity. There was no legal ban, but the anti-Hebrew zealots in the Evsektsiya used various decrees and resolutions regarding the "mother tongue"—Yiddish—to destroy Hebrew. In August 1918, for example, the Commissariat of Jewish Affairs restricted the study of Hebrew in the second grade and in all new schools subsidized by the government. On November 12, 1918, the Commissariat announced that wages of teachers teaching Hebrew in elementary schools would be paid only until January 1, 1919. Evsektsiya members seized upon these measures to close down government as well as Tarbut schools that taught Hebrew, or absorb Tarbut schools into the government system.[43] They assailed Hebrew as the language of rabbis, exploitative capitalists, and Zionists—all class enemies—and declaimed the Soviet creation of a new proletarian culture in Yiddish. In this crusade, they were strengthened by ex-Bundists from the Komfarband, and by Moishe Litvakov, who became editor of *Emes* during this period. Litvakov, a former member of the Ukrainian Faraynigte, who once had Zionist leanings and had owned a large personal library in Hebrew, had undergone a complete turnabout in his outlook and wanted a radical transformation of Jewish culture in Soviet Russia. His articles and editorials in *Emes* savagely attacked Hebrew and Zionism.[44]

At the same time, the lovers of Hebrew fought back stubbornly, but with diminishing means, trying to find crevices within the decrees or general Communist principles with which to justify Hebrew. For example, the Communist party had stated time and time again that, while it opposed national autonomy and national schools, it supported "the right of the population to receive education in its own tongue." On December 1, 1918, the People's Commissariat of Education published a decree legalizing schools for national minorities while keeping them within the framework of Communist control. The minimum number of students required in an age group was twenty-five. This decree seemed to allow room for one of the Jewish languages—Hebrew—and gave some hope to those struggling to save the language. Why, precisely, was Hebrew being discriminated against? What was the basis for the discrimination?

Discussions, meetings, and interventions sought to clarify the matter. Then, in May 1919, the First All-Russian Convention on Education approved a resolution stating that, "pre-school education cannot be conducted in a language other than the mother tongue, that is to say, the language that the child actually speaks, without taking into consideration the nationality to which he belongs."[45] If applied literally, this would mean the end of the Hebrew school, for, although Hebrew was spoken in some Jewish homes, Yiddish was the primary language.

By June, the Evsektsiya at its second conference declared war on the Hebrew schools and petitioned the Commissariat of Education to close them. The Commissariat acquiesced, saying that "the mother tongue of the Jewish toiling masses in Russia is Yiddish and not the ancient Hebrew language." This decree in effect closed down most of the surviving schools and dissolved Tarbut. A large public meeting was held in Moscow to protest this decision.

The main speaker, Rabbi Jacob Mazeh, formerly a Crown Rabbi in Moscow, was devoted to the Zionist cause, especially to its youthful members. Mazeh had received an invitation from Anatoly Lunacharsky, the People's Commissar for Education, to visit him in Yaroslav and discuss the question of Hebrew schools. While waiting for Lunacharsky in an outer office, Mazeh was amused to read in a local newspaper that the commissar in a speech the previous day had referred to the prophet Amos and the other prophets as communists. Mazeh told Lunacharsky that he had come on behalf of the parents, teachers, and pupils of a Hebrew school in Gomel that had been shut down. Lunacharsky dispatched a telegram asking why repressive measures were taken and then heard Mazeh patiently explain the importance of Hebrew to the civilized world and most especially to Jews. He cited the new law and asked why Hebrew fared worse than other tongues. "Even prior to the revolution our teachers were enunciating and disseminating the doctrines of liberty and freedom. If you shut down these schools, sir, you will be doing to death those very principles which we fought and died for." Lunacharsky answered evasively:

I don't know anyone who is disputing the value of Hebrew except your own brothers—the Yiddishists. They maintain that since Hebrew is the language of the bourgeois and not of the masses, it can have no rightful place in public schools. And am I not forced to agree with them. . . . However, I am interested in your assertion that Hebrew is the language of the proletariat. That is new to me. You do have a poet, Bialik, I recall now—did he arise from poor stock?[46]

Mazeh said, "From the very poorest, sir. And the same thing is true for almost every important Hebrew writer."

Various other meetings were held with Lunacharsky, who made ultimate policy decisions on education, and Lev Kamenev, a half-Jew who was a member of the party Central Committee and was remembered as someone who had protested anti-Jewish violence by Bolshevik soldiers and interceded later in behalf of the Hebrew theater *Habimah*. Lunacharsky's real attitude in the matter is hard to determine.[47] At times, he assumed a neutral position in the controversy; at times he pleaded ignorance of the issues. Mostly, he seemed eager to put the onus on the Evsektsiya, as in the conversation with Rabbi Mazeh. However, Lunacharsky's deputy, the historian Mikhail Pokrovsky, probably influenced by the Evsektsiya, was strongly opposed to Hebrew schools, and following a meeting with the Collegium of the Education Commissariat on July 11, 1919, a new decree, possibly the work of Pokrovsky himself, defined Hebrew as a "foreign language, not one of the languages of the masses of the RSFSR."[48] Instruction in the Hebrew schools was to cease immediately and students were to be switched to Yiddish. Hebrew was now to be restricted to universities, special institutes, and pedagogical institutes for training Yiddish teachers.

In the Ukraine, in the areas controlled by the White armies, Hebrew schools managed to struggle on a bit longer, but in the spring of 1920 when the Red Army took Odessa, the schools there, too, were closed down. During 1921, in the early months of NEP, vocational classes in Hebrew were possible, but all study material and teachers would need prior approval of the Evsektsiya and the social status of the students would have to be reported to the Evsektsiya each month. Teachers prepared new texts, "social in content," but these efforts were fruitless. Harassment and arrests continued. A Jewish Workers' School in Moscow using Hebrew as the language of instruction functioned until 1921, when it was closed down.

The Evsektsiya and the Jewish Commissariat sometimes tried to lure Hebrew teachers to other schools, and occasionally veiled threats and economic need proved effective. But many refused to accept the bait. Some began teaching in the approved Yiddish schools, smuggling in the study of Hebrew and Palestinian songs, and in Moscow, Kiev, and Kharkov, as well as in smaller towns, there were underground study groups.[49] Still prosperous Jews could afford to teach their children Hebrew or have tutors, but the attrition was unmistakable. Teachers could no longer earn a living, and the shutdown of the Hebrew presses created the same crisis for Hebrew writers.

The Hebrew presses were nationalized in 1919 and used to publish materials in Yiddish. The confiscated print shops were handed over to the Evsektsiya, giving the Jewish Communists another powerful weapon in the war against Hebrew. Many writers and teachers, finding no other alternative to survival, tried to leave Russia, but for most, that option, too, was blocked by the Soviet ban on emigration. Among the exceptions was Bialik, who tried various interventions, including that of Gorky, who often spoke of his indebtedness to Jews and who was a great admirer of Bialik. Permission was finally granted Bialik and eleven other writers, including Ben-Zion Dinaburg (Dinur) and Saul Tchernikhovsky and their families, and they left Russia in May 1921.

Interventions on behalf of Hebrew (as well as Zionist activity) came from abroad but were deflected by the argument that "all questions of the culture and spiritual life of the Jews are determined by the Jews themselves," that the Soviet government was merely a "passive observer." There was also a memorandum from a group of Jewish and non-Jewish scientists and literary figures in 1924 to Stalin, People's Commissar for National Affairs, complaining of the persecution of the language although there was no official ban. In the summer of 1925, Professor David Shor, the well-known pianist, and engineer Yitzhak Rabinovitch, both Zionist leaders, met with Smidovich, requesting that imprisoned Zionists be released, that emigration to Palestine be permitted, and that Hebrew be granted the same rights as other languages. Smidovich told them that since "there is no law prohibiting the study of Hebrew . . . there is no need of a law permitting it." Evidence of repression of Hebrew was produced: teachers arrested, books confiscated, parents arrested for teaching "the counterrevolutionary language." They were told that there was no longer any support for Hebrew, except among a small group of fanatical Zionists who "continue to harass the authorities with their petitions and to confuse the minds of a number of innocent children in clandestine youth movements."[50]

This type of official rationalization for elimination of programs of Jewish substance was to become commonplace in subsequent years and has served as justification for the nonexistence of Jewish culture in recent years. First have come the official measures of liquidation, and then the ex post facto "explanation." There may not be an explicit ban on a certain activity, but all understand that it is impermissible. Yet some Jews have always been found who have searched for the "gray areas" that lay between what was not illegal technically but was ideologically forbidden, risking arrest, exile, expulsion from work or school, and enduring the great stresses of anxiety, fear, and exposure by informants. In the defense of Hebrew, there was much sacrifice and risk, with occasional flickers of hope (see Photo 5.3).

In 1924–25, there were "petition campaigns" in many towns and cities

5.3 Hebrew Circle, "Will of the People," Uman, 1922. Courtesy Itai.

and hundreds of petitions from Jewish children, spurred by Zionist youth movements, requesting and demanding that Hebrew be introduced into their schools. Some were threatened with expulsion from school, even arrest, and the agitation led to increased arrests of Hebrew and Zionist activists at the beginning of 1926. Yet Yehuda Livrov, a leader in the Hebrew underground, maintained that there were still "tens and hundreds" of illegal Hebrew classes for children and adults.[51] Another wave of arrests took place in January, but Hebrew teachers and activists were heartened by the news that Gorky, who had left the country in 1921, was returning. He was remembered as a champion of Hebrew and, in contrast to their past disregard, the regime was now planning lavish receptions for him. It was decided to hold a second underground Tarbut conference and use the occasion to appeal to him. The conference was convened in mid-June 1928 and thousands of Jews who loved and taught Hebrew gathered in a pine forest near Tver (now

Kalinin). A long, eloquent letter was addressed to Gorky, lamenting the impossibility of meeting him face to face and describing the plight of Hebrew:

A Jewish community of three million people in Russia has not one single Hebrew newspaper, weekly, monthly journal or Hebrew publishing house . . . Anyone desirous of taking a Hebrew book from a library must receive special permission from the Yevsektsiya. . . . But it is rare for such permission to be granted. . . . Throughout Soviet Russia there is not even one school where the Hebrew language is taught. . . . Children or adults who study Hebrew in their own homes are punished. . . . All our requests and pleadings are like a voice crying out in the wilderness. . . . We have come to you, dear and courageous fighter for freedom of culture for all peoples. Raise your voice in protest against the oppression of our ancient culture.[52]

There was no reply, however. Gorky may never have received the letter, or if he did, his answer may never have been delivered. But secret meetings of teachers and surreptitious lessons for students continued into the thirties and and beyond. In 1930, for example, in Moscow, the poet Avraham Krivoruchka (Kariv) founded an underground teachers' seminary. Ten men and two women attended, meeting in the home of a peasant who was told that they were preparing for the *Rabfak* (Workers' School). The school lasted for a year and a half until mid-1931, when the police discovered it and arrested the students.[53]

Most such efforts were completely wiped out by the Stalin terror. But love for Hebrew in Soviet Russia could not be destroyed, as we learned later when writers and others picked up their Hebrew in a fever of excitement during the struggle for the creation of the State of Israel (1947–48), and in the 1950s after Stalin's death, when many Jewish prisoners were released, some of whom had clung to Hebrew and helped to nourish the Hebrew renaissance of the 1960s and 1970s (Chapters 27 and 30). These were truly the children and grandchildren of the earlier generation of the lovers of Hebrew.

Some of the older writers and scholars continued their work for a few years under the new regime, often at immense sacrifice: Yehuda Leib Levin, Yeshayahu Nissan Hacohen Goldberg (Yaknehaz), Shlomo Berman, Eliezer-David Rosenthal, Chaim David Rosenstein, Eliezer Breiger, Yaacov Teplitzky, Yisrael Greenberg, and Ben Zion Fradkin. They passed Hebrew journals, articles, and stories from hand to hand; some continued to teach in small, clandestine circles; some were able to obtain Hebrew material from Palestine and send their work there.

In the letters that have survived there is expressed a great yearning for new works—even words—in Hebrew and, as the censorship became tighter, fear that very detailed instructions were not being followed. In 1925, Greenberg wrote to a friend in Berlin: "Not more than five pages in one envelope . . . lest I be endangered. . . . Erase the name of the article and my signature. Please do not forget all these details."[54] All of these older men lived in great poverty and died in the Soviet Union before 1935. Some of their work has been salvaged and published in Israel, but countless manuscripts have perished.

A few scholars specializing in Hebrew law were able to send their articles to Palestine with official permission. For example, from 1928 to 1930, Ze'ev Markon wrote for the journal *Hamishpat* (The Law) and could receive the journal as long as it was "scientific and apolitical." After the end of NEP and freer economic opportunities, Markon is found living "frugally by manufacturing buttons on a machine which overpowers his cramped apartment."[55]

Rabbinic literature possibly endured for a longer time than did secular literature in Hebrew, accumulating in private libraries and synagogues, and from time to time liturgical works and Jewish calendars were printed. Jacob Ginzburg of Bobruisk was particularly resourceful in obtaining the necessary permits from reluctant Communist authorities, managing to produce 100,000 copies of religious texts in one year, 1927–28.[56] A rabbinic collection entitled *Yagdil Torah* (May the Lord Enhance the Torah) which came out in 1928 was used by Lunacharsky in Soviet foreign propaganda as proof that the Hebrew language had not been outlawed—a curious example of the official unwillingness to admit the banning of what it was in effect banning, for foreign opinion purposes.

The hard reality of the policy, however, was felt not only by those who disliked the regime and suffered, but those defenders of Hebrew who accepted communism enthusiastically, yet who also suffered. These were young writers, many starting out on their careers after the Revolution, who believed that Hebrew would and must have a firm place in the new Communist order. They looked upon the official Yiddish culture as an aberration foisted on the authorities by the Evsektsiya and attacked the official disapproval and suppression of Hebrew as illogical and senseless.[57] How could one be hostile toward a language in which the principles of social justice and other revolutionary ideas had been expressed in ancient times?

They argued: "We are Soviet writers, writing in Hebrew, and we are strangled. For 200 languages there is room in the Soviet Union. Should only Hebrew be disqualified?" *Their* work, they said, came out of revolutionary springs and had nothing to do with the traditional "bourgeois-Zionist-religious-capitalist" evils the Evsektsiya was attacking.[58] An impassioned pamphlet, *The Hebrew Communist*, for example, appeared in Odessa in 1919, expressing "profound attachment to the ancient tongue and to the young revolution." Judaism is identified with redemption and revolution. There is a call for Hebrew communes and a "Red Hebrew Culture." The author of the pamphlet, Eliezer Steinman, also published a non-Zionist Hebrew periodical, but only one issue appeared. Besides Steinman, among those called "Hebrew Octobrists" were Moshe Hyog, Zvi Preygerzon, Shimon Trebukov, Avraham Krivoruchka, Mili Novak, and Yosef Tsfatman, all of whom seemed to have utopian visions of what a true communist order could achieve for Hebrew.[59]

A poignant effort to celebrate the new life in the Soviet Union in Hebrew was symbolized by a collection of poems called *Tsiltselei Shama* (Clashing Symbols), published in Kharkov in 1923. As its name suggests, the work was intended to break a silence, but the battle for publication went on for at least a year. The Evsektsiya delayed permission to publish as well as to hold a literary evening of poetry readings. Heavy, protracted, and nerve-wracking meetings with the Evseks beset the young writers and only 100 copies were eventually allowed instead of the 1,000 requested.[60] Curiously, although the Kharkov group wanted new beginnings, severed from the Jewish past, the title of the collection is taken from Psalms 150:5—"Praise Him with Clashing Cymbals."

One of the first to receive a copy of *Tsiltselei Shama* was David Ben Gurion, who was visiting the agricultural exhibition in Moscow in 1923. Attached to his copy was a letter addressed to comrades in the Workers' Publishing House in Palestine, describing the group's work in a "lonely sea of indifference and hostility," and their future of Hebrew "very, very restricted." They write of their "orphanhood," and ask for literature from Palestine.[61] The poetry itself, however, has no specific Jewish elements.

The Evsektsiya indeed was now making irrational war on a language, but the regime, too, was lending its strong arm, and the argumentation was tendentious, as can be seen in the twisting story of a booklet entitled *Gaash* (Storming), which contained poems by Mili

(Shmuel) Novak, one of the young Soviet poets. The booklet was published in Kiev in 1923 and somehow reached Palestine despite the censor's evaluation:

The booklet . . . is an attempt to give expression in Hebrew to the trends of our modern communist poetry . . . The verse is clear-toned, acute at certain points. One of the poems sounds like a hymn to October . . .
    To whom are these poems directed? Obviously, in other circumstances, in Palestine, [it] might serve as propaganda material for the communist party. But in . . . our life [it] . . . is . . . literary-philological nourishment for the clerical-bourgeois segment of the Jewish public. It is clear that this publication is undesirable.[62]

One protracted effort lasting three years, from 1923 to 1926, finally resulted in the ambitious compilation called *Bereshit* (In the Beginning), a 200-page anthology of work by twelve writers.[63] The book was ultimately printed in Berlin because of the lack of Hebrew vowel symbols and paper in the Soviet Union, as well as fear of Evsektsiya sabotage. Among the contributors were Hyog, Trebukov, Novak, Krivoruchka, Yocheved Zhlezniak (Bat Miriam), Tsfatman, Yitzhak Cohen, and Yitzhak Simovsky (Norman). Of special interest are authorized translations of several stories by the famous Russian-Jewish writer Isaac Babel who wrote in Russian. The sense of living in two worlds, expressing the pain of the new crushing the old, is caught in his story "Gedali." An old shopkeeper, Gedali asks the Red Cavalry fighter what has happened to the "International of good people" and adds pensively: "The Revolution—we will say 'yes' to, but are we to say 'no' to the sabbath?"

Some writers in *Bereshit*, in an elegaic mood, lament the dying Jewish tradition; others accept the Revolution as the sole new reality and Hebrew as a value in itself or tool of the redemptive revolution. Some move forward with the revolutionary tide. The direction is not always clear, but the poets stand "in the footsteps of the world revolution. . . . All our bridges have been burned behind us."[64]

A second volume of *Bereshit* was prepared but never printed. Yet even as late as 1927, the young writers refused to give up the struggle or run away, as they said the older writers had done. In Leningrad in that year came another declaration of faith: "We have grown up in the bosom of the Revolution. We do not wish to wander over alien countries, to fall from the workbench of the new life. Russia, which put its imprint on all Hebrew literature for the last 100 years, will again bring forth a new spirit and provide new foundations for the golden thread of our old-new literature."[65] Influenced by the revolutionary poetry of Mayakovsky and Blok, they felt the pulse of new beginnings but could not create in the leaden uncertainty of the times. In 1927, realizing that their main enemy was the government, they petitioned the authorities to pronounce a clear policy:

If our language, for reasons we are unable to understand, is really harmful and counterrevolutionary, then we demand its suppression by law. But if national policy permits the existence of all languages, then we demand a law forbidding its persecution.[66]

The Hebrew writers in Leningrad also turned to "brother writers" of the world in 1927, pleading for help: "We are turning to you, the Hebrew writers of the world . . . because we are broken and without hope. . . . We demand that you do all that is possible to wipe out the terrible persecution in the Soviet Union. Organize demonstrations, bring up the question in workers' organizations. Save us!"[67] All but one of the group that signed the letter were arrested and two of them— Y. Matov (Saarony) and S. Sosensky (Sh. Rusi)—were exiled to Siberia for three years. After 1927, publication abroad remained the only but hazardous outlet for Hebrew writers, especially in two journals in Palestine, *Ketuvim* and *Gilyonot*.[68]

Krivoruchka, who became extremely active in the Hebrew language underground, had at first welcomed the Bolshevik Revolution as "a rising new dawn," one who greeted the spring "after a long and angry winter," but his hopes for a Soviet Hebrew culture collapsed after a few years and he resorted to underground activity. He was a member of the group around *Bereshit* and sent many of his poems to Palestine where they were published in *Maariv, Moznayim,* and *Gilyonot.* In a poem written in 1933, we feel his deep longing:

In the veil of night's magic sleep
My rebellious soul rests
Under vine and fig tree
In the hills of Galilee and Judah,—
Morning will come to me here
Lonely sevenfold . . .
Oh, the wretched awakening
From the sweet and unreachable
Like the land of Ophir that is no more,
Like the lost Atlantis . . .[69]

Krivoruchka was able to go to Palestine in 1934, but many of the writers were forced to remain in Russia, pained by the collapse of their dreams for a new society, endlessly subjecting themselves to self-examination, fated to eke out a bitter existence, face imprisonment, exile, and squalid deaths. Some simply disappeared. But for as long as possible, they clung to Hebrew. Hyog, for example, labored over Hebrew translations of Pasternak's *Safe Conduct* and Babel's stories, but could not get them published. He lost his post in the army and membership in the party and was dismissed from numerous jobs. He was arrested in September 1948, served eight years at hard labor, and died in 1968.

Zvi Preygerzon, a mining engineer, who wrote with great feeling about the disintegration of shtetl life in *The Travels of Benjamin IV*, was imprisoned in 1949 for seven years in a camp in the Arctic Circle, but never gave up his devotion to Hebrew. His *Yoman Hazikhronot* (Diary of Remembrance), is an important historical document not only for its details of conditions in Soviet camps and the behavior of prisoners, but for his unfailing attachment to Hebrew. "Even when I was in prison," he later wrote, "I swore that I would not forsake the Hebrew language, and I have kept that [vow] until today. . . . Until my very last breath, I will devote heart and soul to the Hebrew language."[70] Wherever he was imprisoned, he sought the company of Jews who knew Hebrew or Hebrew songs, which he collected. One prisoner remembered that "in isolation, he would talk to himself in Hebrew in order not to forget it."

The poet Elisha Rodin also had an unquenchable passion for Hebrew. "Go to Hebrew," he wrote, "all you who thirst for the Kingdom of Heaven." He, too, yearned to go to Palestine and received a visa but when it had to be extended, permission was denied. Some of his work, however, was published in Palestine, including the poems *Laben* (To My Son), in memory of his only son who was killed during the war.

During their years of suffering, these writers were partly sustained by handwritten or mimeographed work in Hebrew—*samizdat*—which passed from hand to hand through an underground network—very much in the way Jewish cultural material has to be disseminated today. They also occasionally received letters and literary work from friends who had gone to Palestine, often by circuitous, ingenious channels. Some exceptional lyrical poetry was written by Chaim Lensky, the most gifted of the poets—"the nightingale without a nest"—from prison in

Siberia, and saved from oblivion by later emigrés and brought to Palestine. Lensky too was arrested (in 1934), released and re-arrested, finally perishing in a camp sometime in 1942–43 at the age of 38.

The outstanding prose writer, and the only one known to have produced a full-length novel during this period was Avraham Friman,[71] whose great novel *1919* was written in four or five parts, of which three were published in Palestine. The remaining parts were presumably lost. The book draws a picture of Jewish life in the Ukraine in 1919, a year of bloody pogroms, but, instead of dwelling on Jewish suffering, Friman writes about a new fighting Jew Solomon, who organizes self-defense units and saves his town while other Jews are immobilized by ideological squabbling and political impotence. Friman too suffered great physical as well as spiritual distress, living in Odessa in a miserable attic, close to starvation. He was arrested in 1934, released, re-arrested, and exiled for ten years to Kamyshlov, a remote town beyond the Urals. He died in 1953.

The lonely helplessness of the furtive Hebrew writer was movingly described by the writer Baruch Shpilberg of Berdichev:

Sometimes when I fall ill with a fever and I look around and see that I have no one to leave the few books to, that I am the last . . . I fall into a black melancholy . . . You write something in Hebrew, you have a new idea—there is no one to whom you can show it.[72]

Even a few Jewish Communists like the complex, enigmatic Shlomo Niepomniashchi, who had studied in the yeshivas of Russia and Palestine, confessed that he was "a slave to Hebrew forever," that no one could uproot Chumash and Rashi from his soul, but that he had to "cruelly choke these sentiments."[73] Yet he begged his friends to send him Yiddish and Hebrew publications from abroad and apparently swallowed them whole, remaining the "yeshiva boy who trembled over a point in biblical exegesis," after having served so many strange gods. If the writer Haim Hazaz was not exaggerating, even Jews in the Cheka, he said, while on official business, carried with them Bialik's poems.

The hopes for Jewish scholarship in Hebrew under the new regime were also short-lived. Most of the organized scholarship in the pre-Bolshevik period was in Russian, and there was some in Yiddish, but research in Hebrew also existed, especially in the area of folklore and local history.[74] One of the first of the new projects was *He-Avar* (The Past), a Hebrew historical journal, edited by Saul M. Ginsburg, historian, folklorist, and editor of *Ha-Am*, the Hebrew newspaper noted earlier. Ginsburg "hoped that the newly opened archives could be exploited and asked his readers to collect material for the folklore sections of the journal." Two issues were printed, each a book of over 200 pages, containing material from communal archives and letters of important personalities. But in the summer of 1918, Jewish Communists took over the press which was printing *He-Avar* in Moscow and stopped publication of the journal. "Other Hebrew publications stopped about the same time due to a combination of difficult conditions, administrative chicanery, and a tendency to move this sort of work to the then independent Ukraine or to . . . Poland."[75]

The study of Hebrew was permitted certain students in universities and also for a short time in the institutes for training Yiddish teachers. In the twenties, Bibles and other Hebrew religious books could still be printed, but scholarship in Hebrew ended in 1918[76] except for rare dissertations written by non-Jews. In 1929–30, harsh measures were taken against academic Jewish institutes and journals engaged in research in Yiddish (see Chapter 8), including the Jewish Department of the Belorussian Academy in Minsk. Among the Minsk scholars was Jehiel Ravrebe who had been a minor Hebrew poet in his youth and had taught Hebrew to teacher trainees in Minsk. By 1930, he "was completely discredited," and began working in Leningrad libraries, becoming a consultant on Hebrew manuscripts in the Public Library there in 1935. Sometime later, possibly in 1938, he was arrested and exiled.[77]

Part of the Hebrew catalog of the Academy of Sciences Library was published in 1936, and Volume I of the Hebrew manuscripts in the Oriental Institute in Leningrad, prepared by Jonah Ginstburg, may have been published posthumously in 1966, when it was ready for publication, but this has not been determined.[78] Hebrew is taught officially at the Institute of International Relations in Moscow and several other scholarly centers and Hebrew publications from Israel are accessioned in special library collections, but these facilities are largely unavailable to Jews in the Soviet Union,[79] and those who study Hebrew today are generally punished if discovered (see Chapters 30 and 31).

The Jews of Bukhara, who have lived mainly in Uzbekistan and Tadzhikstan, and whose language is a dialect of Tadzhik, called Parsi, were also involved in a struggle over Hebrew, specifically, to retain Hebrew as a language of instruction in their schools after the Revolution. Yiddish was completely foreign to them. Bukharan Jewish children had been educated in the traditional khadarim and yeshivot and some studied Hebrew in the pre-Bolshevik state schools. Their dialect was written in Hebrew script. But once the Soviet regime established control in the early twenties, there was a fierce struggle between the local Communists and Jewish school officials over the continued use of Hebrew. The People's Commissar of Education Lunacharsky was appealed to, and through his intervention, Hebrew was allowed to continue, but only until the academic year 1922–23,[80] when it was replaced by Tadzhik and Parsi. Yet, at the end of the twenties, there existed in Samarkand alone thirty-two synagogues and the continued use of the Hebrew script in writing Parsi. The conversion to the Latin script was started in 1929, but this process, too, occasioned stormy debates until 1934, when an official conference "confirmed" what had already been decreed in 1931–32.[81]

An even more outstanding exception to the general withering of Hebrew was the phenomenon of Habimah, the Hebrew theater. It was the dream of theater in the Hebrew language that inspired a Hebrew teacher in Bialystok named Nahum Zemakh to found a drama company in 1914 and take his players to Vilna and Vienna, where a Zionist Congress was then meeting, and to demonstrate cultural Zionism in action. For several years, the impoverished little troupe lived from hand to mouth and played in shabby, unheated quarters. One of its members, David Vardi, wrote a laconic, despairing entry in his diary on September 9, 1918, after the group had moved to Moscow:

We held a general meeting of Habimah today and discussed the food situation. It was decided to send two members to the countryside around Moscow to buy flour and potatoes. Otherwise we shall simply die of hunger. Moscow is getting emptier and emptier. . . . Jews are turning away for fear of pogroms and Bolshevist decrees.[82]

A month later, in the midst of the hunger and dislocations of the Soviet seizure of power, Habimah had its "evening of beginnings," as it was called, in the residence of a former nobleman in Arbat Square, requisitioned and given to Habimah as part of the Moscow Art Theater. Seventy people packed the audience including leading figures in Jewish intellectual circles, agents of the ubiquitous Evesktsiya, and a number of non-Jewish stage personalities including the great Konstantin Stanislavsky, world-famous director of the Moscow Art Theater. There were two short speeches by Rabbi Mazeh and the director Evgeny Vakhtangov, one of Stanislavsky's most talented pupils. Four one-act plays introduced Hannah Rovina, who was to star in *The Eternal Jew* and *The Dybbuk* and later went on to become one of Israel's greatest actresses. The Habimah repertoire created some of the best interwar theater in Europe, despite continuing adversities. The group sustained itself as a collective, with roles, choice of plays, and management in the hands of members. During the early twenties, which coincided with the period of the civil war and the pogroms in the Ukraine, the choice of a play such as David Pinsky's *The Wandering Jew* in the language of the Bible, was both fitting and dramatically stirring. After *The Wandering Jew*, literally all of theatrical Moscow began to take an interest in Habimah, and when the Evsektsiya launched a campaign to close down the theater because it was "nationalistic and anti-Soviet," Gorky and Lunacharsky came to its defense. But Dimanshtain condemned it as "a caprice of the Jewish bourgeoisie" and the government subsidy was stopped. A memorandum, signed by well-known figures in the theater, including Stanislavsky, stated:

Russian art is in the debt of Jews who throughout the epoch of Tsarism . . . were denied the opportunity of developing their national creativity. . . . Language cannot be bourgeois, proletarian, reactionary, or progressive. Language is a means of expression of human thoughts. An actor cannot be forced to play in a language that is out of harmony with his soul . . . [and] with the part he is playing. What is important is for the acting and the stage impersonation to find an echo in the souls of the spectators; this is what *Habimah* is achieving.[83]

Amazingly enough, the subsidy was restored as a result of a decision by Stalin, who rejected the protest of the Evsektsiya and said, "I do not object to the granting of a subsidy."

Vakhtangov's genius reached a new high in the production of Ansky's classic *The Dybbuk* which, in a translation by Bialik, had its premiere in January 1922 and became an international theatrical sensation. But the death of Vakhtangov soon after this triumph left a huge artistic void and placed the theater in a difficult situation. Zemakh became the director temporarily, but the larger, nagging questions were these of identity and repertoire. What precisely was Habimah? For a time Leivik's *The Golem*, based on an old legend of a man who creates an artificial creature, supplied an answer. Indeed, the golem, who eventually developed a will of his own, became for some Jews a metaphor for the Revolution, which turns from the intentions of its creators to become a creature of rampaging violence. The Jewish Communists meanwhile kept up their protests against Habimah. The company floundered and despaired until a flattering offer of a European tour raised morale and postponed necessary decisions. After a farewell performance of *The Dybbuk*, the company left Moscow on January 26, 1926, never to return. Many of the members eventually re-established Habimah in Palestine. Thus, except for the isolated writers, stubborn Hebrew underground cells, occasional reprints of liturgical works, and the teaching of Hebrew in institutes and universities[84] connected with linguistic and archeological studies, Hebrew culture was destroyed for almost half a century the day Habimah left. That is, until recent years when many Jews have begun or resumed their study of it, some of them influenced by old Zionist prisoners who were already in prison by the time Habimah left.

The first Zionist prisoners, most of them eighteen or nineteen years old, were sentenced to exile in the spring of 1924.[85] The verdict was generally handed down by the so-called Committee of Three, a special GPU committee in Moscow. There was no trial, only an investigation and the signing of a document by the accused, which, in fact, was the verdict—a process which has continued to this very day. The usual period of exile was three years, and most prisoners were sent to remote places in Asiatic Russia. They were "free" in their places of exile, but were required to sign in once a week or more at the local GPU office. Living quarters were in the homes of local residents. The six roubles and twenty-five kopeks they received each month were not enough for rent; thus it became necessary to find work or obtain help.

At the end of this first exile, prisoners were further restricted to certain places, called "minus," for a time.[86] "Minus 100," for example, forbade an exile from living within a hundred kilometers of certain major cities. "Minus" also generally lasted three years. However, such a sentence could sometimes be exchanged for a special exit permit to Palestine, much sought after, which the prisoners called the "GPU's aliyah." These were stopped in 1931, after which conditions of exile became much worse. It often happened that at the end of the period of exile or during the "minus" there was another "trial" and another period added to the exile's sentence. Life in exile was miserable, gloomy, and full of despair, but in the first few days,

The exile did not fully sense its bitterness and agony. Just the opposite. On arriving at his place of exile, he walks around with a feeling of relief. After being imprisoned in the hell of a Soviet prison . . . he began to believe there would be a change in his status, that he would be allowed a certain freedom . . . since he was permitted to leave his room, walk around as he wished, be in the company of friends, exchange letters, read books and newspapers and discuss political matters. Some said jokingly that exiles had more freedom than "free" citizens.[87]

But this excitement was short-lived. Exile was one big prison, for everywhere one was under GPU surveillance. The exile's letters were copied and all the intimate details of his life reported by the landlord to the GPU. One exile, for example, received a letter with a note accidentally left inside: "Put copy of letter in File Number . . ." Comments were often attached to letters ("Mr. so-and-so wrote to you," or "You mentioned Mr. so-and-so in your letter.") In this second exile, the prisoner would have to report to the GPU once, sometimes twice a day, and because he could not leave his village or town, the exile often could not get work. Where there were opportunities, the GPU would set a trap. The exile would report and be threatened with rejection and loss of livelihood or transfer to a more remote exile if he refused to sign a document denying his convictions, or refuse to become an informer. Anti-Semitism also contributed to the general misery. When, for example, Zionist exiles came to the GPU office in Izma to receive their stipend, the head of the GPU suddenly announced that, in his opinion, "since all Jews are rich, they don't need to be supported," and gave the Zionists less than the others. A complaint was sent to officials, which was intercepted. A short time later, seven youths in the Zionist movement were grabbed, thrown onto a sled with their hands tied behind them while local peasants looked on, and sent to a distant wasteland.[88]

Some of the Hashomer Hatzair scouts at 17 and 18 were arrested carrying Zionist literature from one city to another, from Moscow to Grodno and Bobruisk, for example, and were then imprisoned, generally with prostitutes and criminals. However, they were able to receive food packages from home. After a year, some were released through the efforts of Gorky's wife. All under 18 were allowed to go to Palestine if they could pay 500 pounds sterling. The rest were sent to Siberia, among whom were young Jews who were never released. Young Zionists in Azerbaidzan and other parts of Asiatic Russia in the early twenties went about their Zionist activity quite freely. The resident Moslem population was quite tolerant. However, those who left to go to Moscow or Leningrad for university studies were arrested and imprisoned.[89]

Hashomer Hatzair documents reveal that for their members, the most difficult punishment was the "politizolitor."[90] This was actually a prison for political prisoners. The first politizolitor, known for its disgracefully harsh conditions and its cruel administration, was in Solvetski. This was a camp around an old monastery that was built at the beginning of the fifteenth century on the Solvetski Islands in the White Sea. Most prisoners never returned from there, because they could not survive the treatment and conditions of the prison. In the years following, other politizolitors were set up with slightly improved conditions. Imprisonment in a politizolitor was also usually for three years, and after that the same pattern of exile and "minus" followed. For activists sent to the politizolitors, there was no possibility of having the sentence changed to an exit permit for Palestine.

Until the murder of Kirov in December 1934 and the onset of massive purges (see Chapter 14), there were differences between the treatment of political prisoners such as Zionists, and criminals, who were treated with great brutality, but after that time, all prisoners and exiles including Zionists, were considered "enemies of the people" (see Map 24.1).

In this dark landscape, a luminous figure stands out, known to all prisoners for her steadfast interest in and care for them. She was Yekaterina Pavlovna Peshkova, the ex-wife of Maxim Gorky and a woman of the old Russian intelligentsia. Peshkova helped to found the "Red Cross for the Aid of Political Prisoners" in 1923, when the Soviet Union was interested in developing relations with capitalist countries, and gave vital aid to thousands of political prisoners and exiles.[91] The "Peshkova" agency helped deliver food packages, clothing, money, medicine, helped families keep in touch with prisoners, and often succeeded in transferring them to less harsh places of exile. Peshkova's small office on Kozvenski 24 in Moscow was always full of prisoners' families. Peshkova wanted to know the specific conditions in each place of exile. She saw many of the exiles personally and always found words of encouragement when things were not going well. Her loyal assistant was a young Jew named M. V. Vinaver, who was in charge of running the office. In Kharkov, Peshkova had a representative in the Ukraine, Sandormirskaya. Her main function was to help prisoners up to the time of their exile. In many instances Sandormirskaya succeeded in having prisoners released on bail until the verdict was handed down from the Committee of Three of the GPU in Moscow.

Zionist movement members were often in touch with Peshkova directly from their places of exile. Often, family members turned to her when they were in Moscow, or made special trips to see her. Their main concern was to get help in receiving exit permits. In the memoiristic literature, it is said that "there was hardly a Prisoner of Zion who was under the jurisdiction of the GPU who was not helped by Peshkova's agency."[92] Among these were some who emigrated to Palestine in 1934—the last group from the USSR before the war.

In prison and exile, Zionists soon learned that they were not alone, and that some of their heroes—Ber Borokhov and Khaim Nakhman Bialik, for example—were known to imprisoned Ukrainian Social Democrats and Armenian nationalists. Moreover, banishment to the eastern provinces had certain advantages. Occasionally, it was possible to reach Palestine by taking the escape route through Afghanistan and Iran. Besides, police and postal authorities far from Moscow attached no importance to letters between prisoners and correspondents in Palestine. Hebrew newspapers and books from Palestine were received quite regularly; they were then condensed and synopses transmitted to a center, from which, in turn, they were distributed to Zionist cells throughout Russia.[93] Zionists' letters from prison were rarely forwarded to addresses in Russia proper; nor did Zionists, fearing reprisal, acknowledge that they had relatives. Instead, the prisoners would write to someone in Palestine who, by using Aesopian language, could keep in touch with relatives in Russia.[94]

Meanwhile, as the imprisoned Zionists were undergoing their ordeal, Jews in Russia proper were suffering vast economic upheavals.

6

Uprooting and Resettlement
on the Land, 1922–28

The Jewish people faces a great task, that of preserving its nationality, and this requires the transformation of a considerable part of the Jewish population into a compactly settled agricultural peasantry. . . . Only in this condition can the Jewish masses hope for the survival of their nationality.

MIKHAIL KALININ

Τ H E Revolution not only destroyed traditional Jewish religious and cultural life but shattered the old economic and social roles and relationships that had formed a precarious but familiar Jewish economy in tsarist Russia. This economy had involved most Jews as petty traders and artisans exchanging goods with peasants in the hundreds of market towns (*shtetlach*) of the old Pale of Settlement. In a determined effort to "productivize" these Jews, the regime embarked on a huge land resettlement project in 1924, which transformed many thousands of Jews into farmers. This project truly revolutionized Soviet Jewish life and proved to be a highly successful if short-lived experiment. Undoubtedly some Soviet leaders had recalled earlier tsarist attempts at Jewish colonization[1] in order to change the "unproductive" nature of Jewish occupations in the Pale of Settlement and "fuse" Jews with the rest of the population. However, the tsarist efforts were often wholly cynical and, in any case, were defeated by the May Laws of 1882, which prevented Jews from owning rural property. Most of the surviving settlements were ravaged by civil war and famine in 1919–21, particularly in the province of Ekaterinoslav.

When a representative of ORT (Organization for Rehabilitation and Training) visited the remnants of these colonies in the Ukraine after the civil war, he described them as ruins, with homesteads crumbling, trees dying, and the very bodies of the settlers shrunken to skeletons.[2] In fact, in 1919–20 an ORT survey of conditions of life for Jews generally—three million in the rump Soviet state—reported "unprecedented want and disorganization."[3] Pogroms and the ravages of civil war had devastated their shtetlach in the Ukraine and White Russia, where most Russian Jews lived, and the upheavals of war communism wrecked forever the old social and economic relationships. Under war communism, which the Bolsheviks waged from 1917 to 1921, the government conscripted all private and public wealth and manpower and banned all private trade. Even small shops were nationalized, overwhelming the small-scale traders, craftsmen, and *luftmenshen*, leaving them destitute. It has been estimated that between 1918–21, 70 to 80 percent of Russian Jews had no regular income.[4]

Ideological pressures exacted a further toll, for the prerevolutionary Jewish occupational profile was condemned and penalized by the Bolsheviks. Wedged into the pre-tsarist economy as merchants, petty traders, and artisans, an estimated two million such Jews were now stigmatized as economically undesirable and "declassed," thus in need of finding "useful" occupations (see Chapter 7).

Massive primary relief for the country as a whole came from the American Relief Administration (ARA), the American Friends Service Committee, and other relief agencies. In 1921–22, the American Jewish Joint Distribution Committee (JDC) contributed almost four million dollars toward the operations of ARA, and much of this money was spent where many Russian Jews lived.[5] JDC appropriated an additional $1,250,000 for child feeding, adult feeding, clothing, and fuel, and $1,240,000 for a "reconstruction program to be inaugurated by Dr. Joseph Rosen," discussed below. Many Jews, especially in the Ukraine, were almost totally dependent upon food remittances from relatives in America, lists of whom were being sent by *landsmanshaften*, (societies of members from the same town or country in Europe), and which JDC tried to service.

Meanwhile, the agency was trying to evaluate its ongoing programs and existing needs by having on-the-spot surveys. During 1920–21, Boris D. Bogen, JDC Director of Relief Activities in Russia, traveled throughout Jewish communities in Moscow, Kiev, Proskurov, Odessa, Petrograd and Ekaterinoslav, observing the ravaged land and people and the extent of JDC activity. From his impressions, we have a graphic picture of the immense needs, the suffering, and stoicism. Among others, Bogen visited child-care institutions in Petrograd, where 560 children—all pogrom victims from the Ukraine—Biala, Zhitomir and Kiev— were housed in five buildings, in ten "internats." "I visited eight of these internats," Bogen wrote, "and while the general appearance is far from satisfactory, the improvement over the last six months is remarkable. The children, as a whole, look very healthy, though I am told many of them are tubercular and are suffering from scrofula. . . . Their health will continue to improve with better feeding."[6] JDC had sent 300 pairs of shoes and Bogen made arrangements to have blankets, sheets, and pillow cases sent as well.

From Odessa, on February 7, 1923, he wrote:

I have just revisited Kiev and found general conditions there somewhat improved as compared with four months ago. There are more shops open, there is more traffic in the streets, and business appears to have picked up somewhat. Unfortunately, however, a considerable part of the Jewish population has not yet materially benefited . . . and still suffers from the . . . economic disruption following years of war, civil war, banditry, and pogroms. Kiev, as the center of the worst pogrom area, naturally contains the largest number of pogrom refugees . . . Five thousand children, one-quarter of them Jewish are registered . . . as homeless and live on freight cars at the station, in the ruins of buildings, or God knows how. There are many hundreds of intellectual workers, teachers, professors, musicians and artists, who are so badly paid that they practically face starvation, yet stick bravely to their work. . . . There are thousands of destitute families, pogrom sufferers or victims of the deplorable economic conditions who have not been able to find a means of livelihood.[7]

At the same time, the JDC was also contributing $2,000 monthly to Evkom, the Commissariat for Jewish National Affairs, for food, clothing, and fuel for 2,000 children in homes set up by Evkom. Evkom also had set up the Jewish Social Committee (*Idishe gezelshaftlikhe komitet*) or *Idgezkom*, which worked as a nonparty umbrella organization of pre-Bolshevik welfare groups to help the homeless, orphaned, and unemployed. Much of the money and personnel involved in this work were supplied by American Jewish organizations, especially JDC.[8] Under the terms of the partnership with Evkom, JDC was permitted to grant subsidies to institutions conducted by Orthodox and nonpartisan groups. Houses for the sick and infirm, homes for the aged, and similar agencies were rehabilitated and medical services were restored. Over ten million pounds of food, clothing, and medicine were sent to Russia as well as large cash grants through Idgezkom; money was also collected for individual food remittances,[9] tractors, horses, cows, and farm implements.

Yet even in the matter of relief, the Jewish Communists insisted on administration on a class basis, causing the non-Communist groups to pull out in 1921.[10] However, JDC aid was still vital and the Evsektsiya was apparently pressured to continue accepting it. Idgezkom, however, was dissolved in 1924. But American Jewish aid was far from over.[11] From time to time, both Rosen and Bogen complained of interference from Evkom or the Evsektsiya, and there were increasing difficulties after both agencies were dismantled, as the regime toughened its line and was too proud to admit dependence on foreign aid, or feigned self-sufficiency. Rosen, however, was especially skillful in negotiating continuation of his work until 1938.

Meanwhile, Russian ORT, a pre-Bolshevik organization, founded in 1880 to provide agricultural and vocational training for Jews, was allowed to continue its work in the early 1920s creating farm plots, courses in horticulture, and nurseries, and extending credit to some artisans and cooperatives despite the economic chaos and its own stringency. But Russian ORT alone could not handle the overwhelming crisis and called on Western help. A flood of endorsements and financial pledges came in, and ORT bureaus for the purchase of seeds, tools, and machinery were set up in various European cities. ORT had maintained vocational schools, employment agencies, and workshops, but its most basic aid in the 1920s was to agriculture—to the remnants of the old tsarist colonies and to new ones ORT created.

It was to the land that Jews now flocked in desperation, with or without help. A visionary plan to establish Jews on the land and make them "productive" had gripped the imagination of some Soviet leaders in the early twenties, but no official steps were taken until 1924. However, Jews themselves, in the chaos and misery following the civil war, turned to simple truck farming wherever they could, often finding patches of land to work on the outskirts of their towns (see Photo refs. on p. 129). Some also received parcels of land as confiscated big private estates and land holdings of the imperial treasury and churches were being divided up in a haphazard way, particularly in the Ukraine.[12] Some took land, for example, in 1918, in Lyubavichi, near Smolensk, where the economy had been based largely on flax, but was now totally destroyed. There some Jews seized a nearby estate and organized it into an agricultural collective called "Pakhar" (the Plowman). But their success was short-lived because neighboring peasants laid claim to the land and the collective decayed. However, individual Jewish farmers were able to hold on to some strips of land which gave them a partial livelihood, supplemented by carting, handicrafts, and trade in *samogan* (home-distilled liquor).[13] Other farm communes involving as many as 20,000 Jews were started in Gomel province in 1918–20 but were little more than small vegetable gardens. Economic destitution drove eight million Russians from the cities to the countryside in 1917–20, making land hunger very acute and often leading to hostility toward Jewish newcomers.[14] In some colonies, Jews starved to death.

In Belorussia, the most backward of the western regions, in the period 1918–20, thousands of Jews sought to obtain land to escape food shortages and the devastation caused by the German and Polish invasions, but most were able to have seasonal settlements only, growing potatoes and vegetables for home consumption. During this early period, settlers "received no help from public or governmental organizations . . . nor any vocational guidance. . . ."[15] Evkom urged more financial support from the central government but none was forthcoming yet.

The Jewish settlements were tiny islands in the vast countryside and remained so even after the state began distributing plots "in perpetual toiling usage" to those ready to work them. Jewish settlers were generally given uncleared land involving costly and backbreaking work. Yet the widespread destitution among Jews made the unfamiliar struggle with an often unyielding nature the only option for survival. In despair, Jews waited for some sign of hope—mainly news of available land. "No sooner does someone in the shtetl mention something about the possibility of land settlement, than the entire Jewish population begins to stir. Plans are discussed, meetings are called, and scouts are sent out. Their few miserable possessions are sold and they are ready to leave."[16] Yet the situation of Jews in many of the little towns was so wretched that they couldn't afford to travel to the farms: A report from Stepenitse in the Kiev province read:

The economic situation . . . is terrible. Altogether, the population of 800 people includes forty artisans and thirty petty traders. The rest lives from undefinable occupations, from pennies they receive from America, from service as porters, and so on. . . . Only eighteen families . . . have registered for agricultural labor, not because they are unwilling to register, but because they are so poor that they cannot afford to travel to, and still less to establish themselves on the land."[17]

During the civil war, some Jews tenaciously held on to their parcels of land with the energy of desperation. The migratory movement was particularly strong in 1922 (the year of the famine) among the Jewish communities of the Kiev, Podolia, and Volhynia regions. Driven by hunger, scouts set out for the Odessa region, the Crimea, and the Ukraine to find land. Sixteen different groups totaling 775 families founded new settlements in the region between the cities of Balta and Odessa in the period 1922–24. In the Crimea, some settlements were founded by *khalutzim* (Zionist trainees bound for Palestine) who had succeeded in leasing several abandoned estates from the government. The migrants in the Ukraine (about 800 families) at first converged upon the old Jewish colonies in the Kherson and Ekaterinoslav regions. By 1923, in eastern Ukraine, almost 3,000 Jewish families were growing cereals, beets, flax, hops, and tobacco on small plots near their former towns. Moreover, in some towns, artisans and small traders worked nearby patches of land without giving up their homes and trades.[18]

Some in the old colonies clung to their ruins; others returned to reassert their claims. With the financial help of the Jewish Colonization Society (ICA) and JDC, some recuperation of the old colonies took place. ORT furnished technical advice as well as economic aid to the old colonies in southern Ukraine and between 1918 and 1921 created new settlements in Berdichev, Kamenets-Podolsk, Vinnitsa, Cherkassy, and Novgorod-Volynsk.[19] Jews by the thousands crowded into ORT offices in various cities, wherever they could, in the midst of the civil war in the Ukraine, straining to get help.

Meanwhile, Communist leaders as well as Jews themselves were seeing land resettlement as a solution to dire economic need. The cultural functionaries, too, among the Jewish Communists were especially aware that Jewish cultural life was tenuous and vulnerable without a territorial base and organized communal life, and took seriously the idea of organized settlement of Jewish masses on the land. A land base, they believed, would "base Jewish culture on the foundations of the ruling ideology and place it beyond the tactical considerations and needs of the moment."[20] Moreover, some of the Evsektsiya activists, in their search for ways of integrating Jews into a new economy, were eager to combine modernization ideas with the preservation of Jewish ethnic identity and the development of a new Jewish culture. They believed that mass agricultural settlement would not only "productivize" Jews but retain their Jewish identity more effectively than would industrialization.[21]

Dimanshtain was particularly conspicuous in promoting land settlement. Initially, at the First Conference of the Jewish Sections in October 1918, he proposed the idea as a way of allaying anti-Soviet feeling among Jews. But at the Second Conference in June 1919, he emphasized the economic advantages of putting idle Jews to work in a productive way, thus saving them from hunger, and cutting down on antisocial speculators.[22] Mikhail Kalinin, a member of the party central committee, and head of state from 1938 to 1946, who felt deeply about Jewish suffering and wanted the Soviet regime to act wholeheartedly to give Jews a fresh start, was also enthusiastic about land resettlement. But in the midst of his remarks to the conference, when he began to speak of pogroms, he broke down and wept and could not finish his talk.[23] Some of the hypersensitive Jewish Communists opposed Dimanshtain for seeming to put a national tone on Jewish reconstruction, but following the conference, Evkom submitted a plan for the creation of Jewish agricultural communes and cooperatives (artels), which was approved by the Commissariat of Agriculture in July 1919. The Commissariat then issued an appeal to Jews:

The Soviet Power has liberated you from the burden of disabilities. You have become free citizens. You can live where you please and do what you please. But in a Socialist State there is no room for speculation and so-called "free commerce". . . . The Soviet Power stubbornly fights speculation and free commerce, and thereby, against its own will, deals a heavy blow to the Jewish masses which, owing to the Tsar's policy, have until now been forced to live by petty trade and other precarious occupations. But while it deprives you of your shameful and unprofitable business, it gives you . . . the right and opportunity to take up healthy, honest, and productive work, including agriculture. . . .[24]

This reveals an early official Soviet commitment to resettlement, but the civil war and Polish occupation of large parts of the Ukraine and White Russia stopped any planning.

Meanwhile, the work of Dr. Joseph Rosen and the JDC "reconstruction program" moved into the foreground of land resettlement. Dr. Rosen was a Russian-born agronomist with an international reputation, who emigrated to the United States in 1903. He joined the JDC Russian unit in 1921 and served with the ARA as JDC representative. When the ARA ceased its operation in the Soviet Union, Rosen remained with JDC and is associated with the whole dramatic saga of Jewish resettlement on the land until it was brought to an end in 1938. He returned to Russia in November 1922 and invited some of his scientist friends, a number of whom were Jewish intellectuals with Menshevik leanings, to work with him in helping the desperate Jewish masses. Rosen arranged to have corn seed imported from the United States and several million acres were sown with this corn in the Ukraine. He also procured eighty-six modern tractors—the first that Russia had seen since the war—complete with spare parts and American Jewish mechanics to work them. From December 1922, JDC sent relief and a growing amount of constructive help including livestock, pure seed cultivation stations, and farm implements to Russia under a special agreement with the Soviet government. Such a separate contract enabled JDC to be rid of their "uncomfortable partners, the Jewish Communists, who employed their power to make life miserable for conforming Jews."[25] Housed in the great Mirbach Palace, autonomous, and with brand new credentials, JDC work now went forward energetically under Rosen, eased from time to time whenever necessary by the interventions of Olga Kamenev, the wife of Lenin's long-time associate.

In his first letter (November 27, 1922) to his New York office, Rosen was very optimistic: "The attitude of the Government is very friendly in every way, and they are particularly interested in helping us carry out the agricultural work." The official agreement between the government and JDC was signed on December 11, 1922, acknowledging JDC's earlier contributions and its interest now in "reconstructive relief in the field of reestablishing the economic life of Russia."[26] According to the agreement, two million dollars would be available until November 1, 1923, for food distribution kitchens, maintenance of children's homes, schools, the financing of cooperative and loan organizations, and agricultural help. The ports of Riga and Simferopol would be open, and the government was to provide transportation for the movement of supplies, and facilities such as offices, garages, and storerooms.

Among the implements distributed were 1,000 plows, 2,000 barrows, 1,400 cultivators, 400 buckers, 500 mowing machines, 500 seed cleaners, and 300 wagons.[27] Much livestock had been lost during the war and had to be replenished. The government provided JDC, which earmarked $100,000 for livestock, with twenty special trains to transport

6.1 Early settlers build roof for community shelter. Universal Jewish Encyclopedia.

3,000 horses from Zhitomir to Kherson and Nikolaiev. One thousand cows were also bought and distributed, mainly to families of widows and children. JDC also undertook a large-scale seed-breeding program with the full cooperation of officials. Rosen quickly noted the deterioration of seed quality and organized 252 seed-breeding stations and plots where seed from America, Germany, Denmark, and Norway was planted. He reported that these stations "have produced sufficient quantities of seed (corn, barley, wheat, oats, and potatoes) to be distributed among farmers next year to enable them to plant not less than three million acres."[28]

In Rosen's first reports to JDC, one sees glimpses of the human and social-economic stresses of the time. The eighty-six tractors purchased in the United States revolutionized the primitive scenes in the colonies and gave the work dramatic impetus. All Russian agricultural organizations were extremely interested in the tractors. "We plowed 100,000 acres of land during the season—very good acreage for 86 small tractors," Rosen wrote. "We accomplished three seasons' work in one season, and taught about fifty people, mostly Jewish farmers, to operate

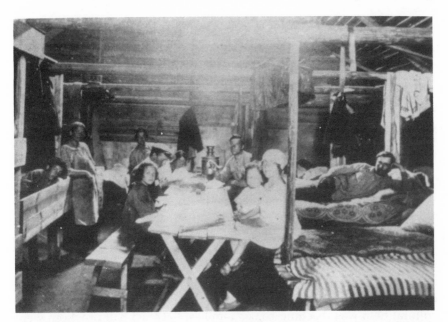

6.2 Log cabin of early settlers in Jewish farm colony. Universal Jewish Encyclopedia.

the tractors. It was absolutely impossible to do this work for Jewish farmers only. We made it a rule, however, that no plowing would be done for any villages which participated in pogroms." There were petitions from many villages asking to have plowing done and "expressing regrets for the criminal activities of some of their villagers."[29]

The land of widows and orphans was plowed first, then the land of people with no horses or plows, then communal lands. In each of the thirty-six Jewish colonies, the land was prepared for fall seeding—not less than 1000 acres.

The Jewish colonies during this embryonic period were quite small: two groups of twenty families each from Cherkassy settled in the colony Dobroye; another twenty from Cherkassy settled in Novo-Poltavka. Six hundred from Gaisin, Podolia, settled in Lvovo. One hundred and fifty families went to the Crimea. Another one hundred and fifty families settled on government land in the province of Odessa (see Photos 6.1 and 6.2).[30]

In the first flush of his enthusiastic plunge, Rosen believed that considerable numbers of Jews were leaving trading for farming and re-

TABLE 6.1
Movement of Jews to the Land from
Provinces, 1922

Name of Province	Number of Jewish Families
Vitebsk	697
Smolensk	838
Gomel	857
Minsk	720
Chernigov	87
Volynia	150
Kiev	550
Podolia	2,080
Odessa	2,491

corded the movement of Jews to the land in 1922 from various provinces as shown in Table 6.1[31] There were also 6,718 in the old farm colonies of Kherson and Ekaterinoslav. Rosen estimated that JDC agricultural help was reaching 50,000 families, "at least half of whom were non-Jewish."

The attitude of Russian and Ukrainian peasants toward Jews coming to farm the land varied. For most it was a strange, bewildering sight. A Soviet Jewish author commented: "At first . . . the attitude of the peasants was not so much hostile as skeptical: 'What kinds of farming people are they? Surely they won't work themselves, they'll go in for speculation.' But this attitude soon vanished as the peasants became convinced that Jewish toilers really work the land themselves, with their own hands and in the sweat of their brow, suffering great privations."[32] Maurice Hindus, who was born in a Russian village and revisited the Soviet Union many times saw "something painfully yet sublimely picturesque in these Jews, age-old city folk . . . in stark conflict with the forces of nature . . . No wonder that the *muzhiks* (Russian peasants) . . . asked themselves what was happening. They seemed not resentful, nor jealous, nor fearful of competition. They were merely amazed and amused."[33] From time to time they even took up new devices and methods used by Jewish farmers. There are also some reports of peasants appropriating land and, not being sure they were acting within the law, asking Jews to join in. Deep resentment and protests were also heard, particularly in 1924.

In July of that year, allocations of farm land were better organized and although, technically, only tillers of the soil were entitled to a share in the land distribution, the decrees gave Jews special consideration: "During the distribution of the reserve areas of the Republic, the requests of individual Jews and Jewish collectives are to be satisfied in the same measure as those of the local population, although the former have not been engaged heretofore in tilling the soil."[34] The average allotment was from one to one-and-a-quarter acres per person. This special consideration aroused resentment among Ukrainian and White Russian peasants whose own land hunger was scarcely being appeased, but it demonstrates the interest and goodwill of officials in trying to cope with the severe economic problems of Jews.

This interest was substantially bolstered by the creation in August 1924 of an official agency to resettle Jews on the land: the Commission for the Settlement of Jewish Toilers on the Land—KOMZET in Russian, and KOMERD in Yiddish. A non-Jewish old Bolshevik, Peter Smidovich, was named head. Other members were commissars and well-known Jews and non-Jews. On January 11, 1925, a "Society for the Agricultural Organization of Working Class Jews in the USSR" was created—OZET in Russian, GEZERD in Yiddish—to help recruit colonists and create support for the colonization work. A majority of its executive board consisted of KOMZET members,[35] but party control was inevitable when Dimanshtain became head in 1927.

The vital foreign aid came through a formal agreement[36] between the government and JDC, which was signed November 29, 1924. This called for the creation of a Russian-based subsidiary of JDC called the American Jewish Joint Agricultural Corporation—Agro-Joint—with Rosen to direct management and field work—and its expenditure of "not less than $400,000 during the fiscal year 1924/25," exclusive of help to existing colonies. It was "to establish Jewish settlers and their farms in new places and to organize them in collectives and cooperatives." Material aid would be given to individual as well as collective farms, and to their "cooperative, industrial, credit, and saving societies." Agro-Joint would also instruct farmers "in all matters pertaining to farm management and cooperatives (see Photo 6.3)." JDC would hold all of the stock.

After extensive KOMZET investigations and protracted discussions, certain areas in the Ukraine and the Crimea were selected for concentrated Jewish colonization. In the Ukraine, it was felt that the nucleus of old Jewish colonies in the districts around Kherson, where Zaporozhe and Krivorog Jews formed an absolute majority,

6.3 Staff of Agro-Joint. Universal Jewish Encyclopedia.

could be expanded and qualify for the designation "Jewish administrative regions." Eventually, three Jewish national districts were
created in the Ukraine: Kalinindorf, Novo-Zlatopol, and Stalindorf (see
Map 6.1).

The Crimea at first seemed an even more promising area because of
its fine climate and sparse population, but the land finally chosen lacked
water. Rosen himself had been very enthusiastic about resettlement
possibilities in the Crimea, a project which also excited some Jewish
Communists. Bogen too had reported in 1923: "There are unusual opportunities for our people . . . such as may never occur again. Free
land, low transportation costs—people don't have to adapt to foreign
conditions or learn new languages. Relations between various nationalities in the Crimea have always been peaceful—especially between
Tatars and Jews."[37] In the Crimea in 1923, however, according to a
JDC staff member, "the situation . . . is exceedingly bad because there
is absolutely no business and very little food. . . . As soon as the next
crop proves good, the Jewish people will be helped, as they always
handled the grain and agricultural marketing business."[38] Within a short

time, however, with Agro-Joint funds and American well-drillers, the desolate prairies were transformed into functioning Jewish farms and villages and their wheat, used for seeding purposes as well as bread, was soon able to compete with the best in Russia.

Districts were assigned and Jews now rushed to apply. Rosen selected a staff of capable young Russians, many of whom were graduates of agricultural schools. Tracts of land were selected and surveyed and some portions were prepared so that when the first group of settlers arrived in the spring of 1925, they already had a grain crop. The next step was the planning of entire villages, building of houses, schools, medical dispensaries, the drilling of wells, and the granting of loans for seed, livestock, and farm machinery.[39] Staffs of Agro-Joint specialists were assigned to various districts to give technical instruction to the new farmers and to deal with numerous problems.

From these humble beginnings and with an initial appropriation of only $400,000, there developed a quite extraordinary agricultural settlement program, with the government share gradually increasing. In 1924, Agro-Joint supplied about 89 percent of the funds, and KOMZET, 11 percent; by 1934, Agro-Joint supplied only 24 percent and KOMZET 76 percent.[40]

The average cost of establishing a family on the land amounted to about $800, which neither the state nor the settlers could bear. Recruited mainly from among impoverished petty traders and artisans who could not be drawn into the New Economic Policy (NEP), many of the settlers had no capital. They were not used to manual labor and generally had no farm experience. Exhausted by long privation, they subsisted for months on meager food and housing. Harried by shortages of all kinds, they had to accustom themselves to the vagaries of nature, phlegmatic oxen, the lack of public baths (especially in the Crimea), medical care, and schools. Some had to live in dugouts during the first months and cook under the open sky.

The government provided free land (650,000 acres in 1925–27) for tilling, tracts of timber land, and some credit for water supplies and the purchase of implements and seeds. The settlers also were allowed reduced transportation rates and were exempt from taxes and military service for three years. Funds for housing, livestock, machinery, and basic necessities were covered by Agro-Joint. Moreover, its staff helped families register for land allotments and then lived with the bewildered

MAP 6.1
Areas of Jewish Agricultural Colonies

Among the Colonies Not Shown

Aufbauen	Larina
Avoda	Lvovo
Amurzet	Mishmar
Chebotarka	Mozir
Chongar	Nai Lebn
Dobroye	Novy Zerya
Hashakhar	Oktyabr
Kachkarovka	Ratenstadt
Kadima	Razsviet
Kalininsk	Royter Poyer
Kamenko	Tel Khai
Khaklai	Zaporozhe
Khislovitz	Zavet Lenina
Kurman	Zhurtchan

LEGEND

● JEWISH FARM SETTLEMENTS IN T
  UKRAINE AND THE CRIMEA

⊙ NEARBY CITIES

Adapted from Martin Gilbert, <u>The Jews of Russia</u>, 1976,
pp. 25, 33; and AGROJOINT SOURCES, YIVO.

settlers, giving them practical help in their day-to-day problems of building houses, schools, stores, and bathhouses, digging wells, and learning to use new tools and equipment. Agro-Joint also aided cooperative loan associations, or *kassy*, which extended credit to the settlers.

In a long article[41] on the settlements, published in the *Jewish Daily Forward* in 1925, Louis Fischer, a well-known journalist and Soviet sympathizer, outlined the genesis of a colony: A group of Jews in a town forms an *artel* (cooperative), adopts a set of bylaws, and registers with local authorities. Each member buys a share, if possible, for 400–500 roubles, and a representative goes to the proper Soviet official to negotiate the granting of land. The average settlement consists of about fifty families. Fischer found that applicants were "mostly former merchants, artisans, and government employees," and that they were "happy, enthusiastic . . . less nervous, and energetic" as they prepared for their new life. Some 20,000 families, or about 100,000 individuals, had expressed interest in land settlement, and registered with special government commissions. "In many small towns . . . almost every Jewish family registered, and there were calls as well from far off centers such as Vologda, Vyatka, Archangelsk, and Baku. The largest number came from towns in the old Pale of Settlement: Gomel, Vitebsk, Odessa, Chernigov, Kiev, Ekaterinoslav. Fischer also believed that many Jews fled from the tax and psychic burdens of NEP: "The colonist never sees that horrible nemesis, the tax inspector . . . he is no more an outcast but has joined the honored class of those who vote and rule Russia. His sons and daughters are on a par with . . . the proletarian class" (see Photos 6.4, 6.5, and 6.6).

In the early years at least, Agro-Joint had excellent working relations with the KOMZET people it dealt with, representatives in Moscow, Kherson, and the Crimea, "all representatives of our own selection," according to Rosen.[42] Moreover, he reported that KOMZET was absolutely scrupulous regarding JDC funds and was altogether enthusiastic about the measure of government and party support. These impressions in the first flush of enthusiastic activity, however, were to undergo considerable change later.

The early excitement was intensified in the first inspection trip Rosen and Boris Bogen took to the colonies in the Ukraine, where they were "fascinated beyond measure by the spectacle of new life being born out of the soil."[43] Although uprooted from age-old places and habits, Jews were beginning a new life and making relationships with non-Jews. The men also visited the Crimea and were enthusiastic about the promise of Jewish colonization there and by rising feeling for a Jewish Crimean republic. They were also stirred by the great joy of some Jews who could scarcely believe the new treatment they were experiencing. They heard comments such as, "This is worth something: To be a man, the equal of all others. To be respected and to have enough for life—is there more to be asked for? It is only the Communist Jews who make life miserable; of the government we have no complaint."[44]

Bernard Kahn, the European director of JDC, also found much to hearten him despite the primitive conditions he found in the Agro-Joint colonies in the Ukraine and the Crimea he visited in midsummer 1925. In the old colony of Avodah, people were still living in a large

6.4 Jewish students, professionals, and shopkeepers form an Agro-Joint colony. Universal Jewish Encyclopedia.

6.5 Mikhail Kalinin with Jewish farmers in Lenindorf, Crimea.

6.6 A teacher and students talk informally in a Jewish farm colony school.

shed; in the newer one, established by dense Jewish towns in the Kiev district, three families were living together in a room. In the new colonies of Trudowaja, Schisn and Smirnowa, people were living in huts, their tables and beds made of clay, hardened mud, and boards. But the livestock was "well-maintained." In Aufbauen, only able-bodied working males had come, and all were still living in barracks. Yet, despite the great hardships, there were already signs of productive activity in some of the colonies—dairies, cheese factories, cattle herds, and well-tended fields and gardens. Kahn was deeply touched by what he saw: "Oft does the heart ache when one sees these pioneers . . . huddled in huts and dugouts with hardly a roof over their heads . . . [but] well-cultivated fields, nicely kept cattle, gardens in bloom, and courageous faces." He also believed the colonies would retain their Jewish quality. Although concerned with material tasks, the Jew "comes to the land to become a Jewish peasant. A strong Jewish tendency is felt throughout all the colonies." He was also heartened by "close family life" and "lack of interference by the government."[45]

In September 1925, Dr. Rosen reported to a large United Jewish Appeal conclave in Chicago that "not one man, woman, or child [in the colonies] wanted to go back [to the towns]. . . . There was bewilderment as to why I should ask so silly a question." A Moscow surgeon was even more fulsome: "It frees the souls of all Russian Jews. It gives us all a sense of relief. On the soil, the Jew lives in his village, he can worship in his synagogue, he can raise his head."[46]

Here one hears the Western Diaspora Jew overwhelmed by his own romance with the Jewish man-with-a-hoe. However, the feelings of a Russian-born woman, Markoosha Fischer, the wife of the journalist, were sharply different. She observed that it was difficult for small-town women to accustom themselves to hard physical labor and the life of peasants. They often cried while milking cows. These were not merely the tears of a difficult adjustment process. Many felt it degrading to be peasant women. In prerevolutionary Russia they had considered the peasant an unfortunate, demeaned human being. If the new settlement process was to be a success, something had to be done to ease the women's lives:

> The colony in which I settled [Mrs. Fischer wrote] was in the open steppes with not a single tree for miles around. It was freezing in the cold winter and mercilessly hot in the summer. The houses had clay walls which required frequent whitewashing. Lumber was rare in the treeless steppe, and the floors were made of a loam. . . .
> It was a difficult job to provide food for hundreds of kindergarten and school children amidst the dire scarcity which prevailed in the district. . . . No less strenuous was the constant traveling from one colony to another over bad, muddy roads in primitive horse carts.[47]

Mrs. Fischer helped to open a dozen kindergartens and provided wholesome hot meals for school children in several villages within a radius of about thirty miles.

The differing perspectives on resettlement can be seen in the views of outsiders and Westerners like Kahn and Louis Fischer and insiders like Peter Smidovich, Chairman of KOMZET, for example, who was concerned about the reaction of non-Jews to Jewish settlements. He intimated to Fischer that "the work of Jewish colonization should proceed with as little publicity and agitation as possible," since the government did not want to give the impression that it was "discriminating in favor of Jews."[48] Merezhin, too, of KOMZET, in a meeting with an Agro-Joint representative in 1925, stressed the point that Jews would

be settled on land that had not been previously settled "to avoid possible strife with peasants."[49]

Undoubtedly eager to will the settlement program to success and
minimize such problems, Fischer did not detect any opposition to the
Jewish colonies. Quite the reverse. In the southern Ukraine, he found
much land available so that "peasants cannot possibly resent its appropriation by Jews as they might, and do, in White Russia, where a land
famine exists."[50] And Kahn, in a reference to the twenty-five colonies
in the Crimea, found Jews living with "neighboring Tatars, Germans,
and Russians on friendly terms," with Tatars freely offering horses and
wagons to the Kadima colony in gratitude for help from Agro-Joint.[51]
Yet problems did exist and persisted and could not be wished away,
especially in the Crimea.

Plans for Jewish colonization in the Crimea were widely publicized
in 1925 and 1926 (see pp. 146–49). Huge sums of money were needed
and the publicity created a backlash of anti-Semitism. It was thought
apparently that the "Russian Riviera" would be a farmer's paradise;
but Jews were allotted land, not in the south, where the climate and
soil are favorable, but in the harsh north, thinly populated, an arid
steppeland of raging winds and saline soil. These facts were stressed
in Soviet publications of the mid-twenties that dealt with anti-Jewish
reactions and in the confidential reports of the JDC, Agro-Joint, and
KOMZET. The reclamation of this land was very costly and, moreover,
the administration of the Crimean ASSR did not particularly welcome
the arrival of Jewish settlers.[52] As of January 1, 1932, even with considerable aid from Agro-Joint, only a little more than 5,000 Jewish farm
families were settled in the Crimea, less than one-third of the number
planned. This project, as it developed, was devoid of any ideological
goal and reflected the winding down of "Jewish national" fervor in
agricultural schemes. Yet the myth lived on. There was a persistent
rumor in the twenties about the founding of a Soviet Jewish Republic
in the Crimea and the idea nourished a heated debate in world Jewry
on the question: Crimea or Palestine? But by the end of the decade, it
was clear that a shift had been made to Birobidzhan (see Chapter 13).

In the first few years of resettlement, Agro-Joint provided the lion's
share of financial aid and other help for the Jewish colonies, especially
in the Ukraine. Of the almost fourteen million roubles (about $7,000,000)

spent on the settlers up to August 1927—chiefly in the form of loans at low interest—more than half came from Agro-Joint; over one million roubles from ICA and ORT.[53] By 1929, twenty-two and a half million roubles had been spent on the agricultural settlement of Jews, of which almost 75 percent had been raised and donated by Jewish organizations abroad. This aid reached a peak in 1927–28 and fell off thereafter, as donors and experts anxiously watched wavering signals and the subsequent collectivization of Soviet agriculture.

Apart from the three large organizations supporting Jewish colonization (Agro-Joint, ICA, and ORT), projects were also supported by a number of smaller organizations, especially IKOR, whose members were chiefly Communists and Communist sympathizers. In order to avoid duplication, the main settlement areas were divided among the organizations as follows: the areas in the Crimea and around the Jewish settlement of Sdeh-Menuchah (changed in 1927 to Kalinindorf) in the Ukraine were given to the Agro-Joint; the areas around the towns of Zaporozhe and Mariupol in the Ukraine to ICA, and the areas around Odessa to ORT.[54]

Although the population in the areas was multinational, five Jewish administrative districts were created in the contiguous areas of settlement: three in the Ukraine (Kalinindorf, Novo-Zlatopol, and Stalindorf), and two in the Crimea (Freidorf and Larindorf). A number of settlers gave up and returned home, but a genuine class of Jewish farmers survived the rigors of a new life in the colonies and excelled in their work. Many won prizes at exhibits. Jewish farms were among the first in the USSR to use tractors. In the moorlands in the northern Crimea, they pioneered vine and cotton plantations. There were Jewish agricultural schools and professional agricultural handbooks in Yiddish and Yiddish agricultural magazines (*Der yidisher poyer* and *Dos sozialistishe dorf*). In 1925 and 1926, two collections of material dealing with the problems and achievements of Jewish farmers were published (*Evreysky krestyanin*—The Jewish Peasant), edited by Yuli Golde, who had worked in Palestine before World War I, and became active in the Jewish land resettlement program.

Religious traditions and Zionist influences were felt in the colonies until collectivization. Fisher, for example found that in all of the Jewish colonies, "Saturday is the day of rest. Even youths said they did not want to ride on Sabbath." In a number of colonies he found a Sefer

Torah and *minyanim* for services. As to Zionists, in spite of arrests and harassment, they still had considerable influence among Jewish youth in the smaller towns and used the Jewish colonization projects to propound their ideas. Since OZET was ostensibly a nonpartisan organization, Zionists tried to use it as a forum, warning that resettlement in the Soviet Union was only a "temporary political expedient designed to . . . lure American Jewish capital." Sometimes, however, they joined OZET colonies in the hope that they could use their experience later in Palestine, or disseminate their views.[55] Evidence of their influence is the fact that at least 13 of the 217 Agro-Joint colonies, especially in the Crimea, had such Hebrew names as Mishmar, Avodah, and Kadimah. Had the character and physical base of such colonies not been drastically changed by collectivization (Chapter 10), they rather than Birobidzhan might have drawn Jews into a compact territory and possibilities for a Jewish autonomous society.

Colonization in Belorussia is conspicuously missing from many accounts, although Belorussian Jewry was eager and ready for resettlement on the land. Instead, it was fated to be the stepchild in the overall scheme. Actually, agricultural possibilities in the region were scant and, economically, it was the most backward region in European Russia. Jews left Belorussia in large numbers in the late 1800s, mostly for America, and continued to leave in the Soviet period to go to other republics.[56] For many of those who remained, however, there was a strong desire to have their own agricultural settlements and territorial national autonomy within their own republic. For these projects vast foreign capital would be needed for the huge task of draining the marshlands and clearing the forests, but large empty tracts of arable land were not available in Belorussia.[57] Moreover, Moscow favored transferring Belorussian Jews to the large empty lands elsewhere, creating conflict between Moscow and the region from the very beginning. At the first conference of Jewish farmers in Minsk in December 1924, the local Belorussian agricultural commissar Prishchepov clashed with Chemerisky, secretary of the Evsektsiya Central Bureau.[58] Nevertheless, during a registration early in 1925, 34,035 Jews were prepared to farm, including shopkeepers, artisans, and laborers, but only 34.6 percent were willing to settle outside Belorussia. Some of these were resettled in the Crimea, but most eventually returned to Belorussia.[59] The vast capital needed to drain the marshlands was not forthcoming, but some Jews in Belorussia were resettled in small, dispersed farms. As of 1926, there were 38,305 such Jews, probably many of whom had been farmers before the Revolution.[60]

By 1929, over 9,000 Belorussian Jewish farm families were on the land, specializing in dairy farming, fodder crops, and orchards. The introduction of tractors made possible the replacement of draft horses by dairy cattle. In the Mogilev and Bobruisk districts, most of the settlers were individual farmers living near small towns and receiving aid from ORT; in the Minsk district, collectives predominated. Many more Jews wanted to farm, and local Belorussian Jewish leaders pleaded and argued with central Soviet bodies for funds and support, but by 1928, Birobidzhan was in the forefront of official plans, vital foreign aid was not forthcoming, and Belorussian resettlement hopes withered away.[61] Collectivization in 1929 began to break up existing colonies and discouraged new settlers from leaving their homes. Belorussian Jews did not succeed in obtaining the interest and support among Western Jews or the official backing that was vested in the Ukraine and the Crimea.[62]

Yet despite the many vicissitudes experienced and the clashing ideological positions, the advocates of a Jewish-return-to-the-land movement saw much to encourage them in the late 1920s. According to OZET, by 1928 the Jewish peasant population had reached almost 220,000,[63] up from 155,400 in the 1926 census—nearly eight percent of the total Jewish population. By 1931, approximately nine percent of the Jewish population (51,910 families, or 250,000 persons) lived on farms in European Russia,[64] not counting the Jewish farmers in the Caucasus and Central Asia. Figures vary somewhat, but by 1930, at least 10 percent of all gainfully employed Jews worked on farms, the highest proportion ever recorded[65] (see Table 6.2).

Such a transformation in Jewish life clearly portended a great revolution in the Jewish economic structure elsewhere and aroused feelings of astonishment, admiration, and gratification, especially in left-wing circles in the West. Jewish colonization also drew the ardent support of certain Soviet leaders and Jewish officials. However, the projects became entangled in furious debates among Jewish Communists over the question of the economic and social modernization of Soviet Jewry.

TABLE 6.2

Jews in Agriculture, 1921–39: Various Estimates

A.			B.	
1923	75,911		*1921–22*	50,000
1924	94,158		*1923*	75,000
1925	120,288			
1926	141,780		*1925*	100,000
1927	165,500		*1926*	120,000–112,161
1928	220,000		*1929–30*	300,000

S. M. Schwarz, *The Jews in the Soviet Union,* 1951, p. 268, based on OZET figures.

Estimates from Shapiro, *The History of ORT,* pp. 135, 378 (citing U. Golde, OZET, and KOMZET sources).

C. *1931*		D. *1939*	100,000–125,000
Ukraine	172,000		
Belorussia	47,000	(in kolkhozes) L. Zinger, *Dos*	
Crimea	21,000	*banayte folk,* 1941, p. 89.	
Birobidzhan	5,000		
Western Great Russia	6,250		
Other parts of Great			
Russia	3,750		
Total	255,000		

Y. Lestschinsky, *Dos sovetishe idntum,* 1941, p. 209, based on Y. Kantor, *National Development among the Jews in the USSR* (Russian), 1934, pp. 134, 135.

One approach saw the modernization of Soviet Jewry as a gradual process, starting with agricultural colonization. The other approach emphasized large-scale industrialization and the promotion of what was called national consolidation and cultural development, leading to a shared Soviet political allegiance or political integration.[66] The second approach urged a very rapid industrialization-urbanization and assimilation, and opposed the "nationalist" view as slowing down ultimate political integration.[67] The leadership of Evsektsiya tried to avoid both extremes, but at times actually supported both positions, believing that both served the same end—the strengthening of the dictatorship of the proletariat.[68] The movement to settle Jews on the land was seen as the chief instrument through which economic modernization and national consolidation could be achieved. Such a program, moreover, could also divert Jews from the Zionist appeal of Palestine. With a territorial base on Soviet land, there was the possibility of "creating the objective conditions" which would force a redefinition of the Jewish people.

Some Jews, however, both in and outside the party, were very enthusiastic over the national implications of the KOMZET plan, submitted late in 1925, to resettle 100,000 Jewish families on the land and were extremely critical of the Evsektsiya's cautious hedging. They began thinking about the possibilities of a Jewish nation on Soviet soil. Among the more outspoken of these advocates was Abraham Bragin, one of the non-Communist founders of OZET, a well-known journalist and agricultural expert who had not fully quenched his former Zionist feelings. Bragin was convinced that the new Russia must exhibit its resources, accomplishments, and ideals to a doubting world and prove that the new order was a living, productive reality. Overcoming enormous handicaps, he had succeeded in obtaining a government grant for the successful agricultural exhibit in 1923; it had opened on the scheduled date—a cause for considerable wonderment in Russia, where few things were done on time. Later, in his speech[69] on the opening day of the GEZERD conference in 1926, Bragin recalled his Zionist past, and in subsequent debates, argued that industrialization for the impoverished Jews was impractical because of the undeveloped state of the Soviet economy. He further argued that agriculture offered the only way out, the "foundation for national self-determination of the Jewish nation, as set forth in the policy of the Communist Party." Generally regarded as the first person to formulate the idea of a Soviet Jewish republic,[70] Bragin deplored the Evsektsiya policy of propagandizing the idea of autonomy in order to enlist foreign Jewish support while keeping a timid silence at home "at a time when history demands a clear and detailed definition of the question."[71] He shocked his audiences by charging that the Revolution "had passed the Jewish question by. Therefore, the question of a republic. . . . is a question only of the state's formulation of our affairs in the same manner in which they are formulated for all other areas and peoples."[72]

This argument soon became entangled in a discussion of a Jewish culture, "proletarian in content and national in form," a phrase coined by Stalin in his address before the Communist University of the Peoples of the East in May, 1925. In this address, Stalin did not deal specifically with the problem of Jewish national culture but generally with national culture in a socialist society, hammering out the now famous formula: "We are building a proletarian culture . . . which is socialist in content [and] assumes different forms and modes among the various peoples. . . . Proletarian in content and national in form [i.e. in language]—such is the universal human culture toward which socialism is marching." It was in that year also that Stalin formulated his position to give Jews land: "The Tsar gave the Jews no land. Kerensky gave the Jews no land. But we will give it."[73] During this period Jews both in Russia and the United States were excited by the hope that just as other large minority nationalities now had their Union Republics, Autonomous Republics, or Autonomous Provinces, Jews, too, would soon enjoy a similar status. But the Evseks wavered.

Alexander Chemerisky, the first secretary of the Central Bureau of the Evsektsiya, weaved from one position to another, reflecting the shifts and uncertainties of an ambiguous policy. In 1924, he had said that the Evsektsiya was not opposed in principle to the idea of an "autonomous area" although it might be premature until "colonization in contiguous land areas" was achieved. Later, after the KOMZET plan for the settlement of 100,000 Jewish families was approved, he was bolder: "What is at stake here is nothing less than the creation of a great class of Jewish peasants who will make over completely the appearance and economic basis of the Jewish population"—and that with sufficient funding "the basis could be laid for solving the problem of territorial autonomy."[74] Then, in the fall of 1925, he not only discussed "the question of statehood, of a republic," but went so far as to declare that "in principle," the idea of a Jewish soviet state "had never been denied."[75] Again, in 1926 in a book on the Jewish masses and the Communist party, Chemerisky wrote that Jewish territorial autonomy could materialize whenever "a considerable Jewish majority is established in some continuous territory," and that the "rural placement of Jewish masses . . . can provide this opportunity."[76] Still hewing to the orthodox formula, however, he made it clear that any extraterritorial autonomy in the field of education and culture was harmful and unnecessary. The culture of the victorious proletariat was by definition identical (socialist) for all nationalities and merely expressed in different languages. However, if the Jewish people should reconstruct its socioeconomic structure along Communist lines and be concentrated in a specific region, it might be considered a nationality deserving of territorial autonomy and entitled to express in its own "national form" the common "socialist" culture of all Soviet peoples. But Chemerisky, above all, was concerned about transforming Jews economically and drawing them to socialism through cooperatives, agriculture, *and* industry. His interest in creating a Jewish peasantry as a base for autonomy was apparently only a temporary one—too risky to pursue, since for some the *national* idea had assumed an alarming significance. The national question was thus to be modulated into the more basic economic one: Jews would have to solve their national problem by bringing new productive forces to work.[77] Nation remained a territorial concept, not to be confused with the preservation of the Jewish people as such, a concept which was, after all, considered petty-bourgeois.

In Belorussia, many leading Jewish Communists had hoped that Jewish land resettlement would create the basis for the development of an autonomous Jewish life, but the failure of substantial colonization and lack of support from central bodies frustrated these hopes. Many of these spokesmen were later purged as "nationalists" for wanting to keep Belorussian Jews in Belorussia.[78] The most intense interest in the possibilities for a Jewish republic, however, is associated with the Crimea. The Crimea resettlement was also eventually swallowed up by promotion of Birobidzhan, but the vision, not to say myth, of a Jewish republic there lived on even after the number of settlers declined in the mid- and late thirties, only to revive again after the war (see Chapter 19).

The prime mover of the Crimean project was Yuri Larin, chairman of OZET and a prominent economist. Larin optimistically projected a vast resettlement scheme that would involve over a million acres and 220,000 Jews (a figure he later raised to 400,000) by 1929. He believed that former traders and other "unproductive elements" should migrate to the Crimea, while *kustars* (artisans) should be moved to industrial centers. Although he expressed reservations about the creation of national republics as a full solution to the nationality problem, he strongly defended the rights of national minorities.[79] He also vigorously opposed the Birobidzhan project as unrealistic, and advocated instead large-scale colonization in the Crimea. His position "seems to have been based on his hard-headed appraisal of the economic situation rather than on any romantic visions of Jewish autonomy or nationhood."[80]

The Communist literary critic Moishe Litvakov, generally so harsh in his desire to demolish every residue of Jewishness, was romantic as he spoke of the Crimea as "our Palestine . . . for surely you can't compare the Jordan to the Dnieper," nor were "our" Moslems [the Crimean Tatars] like the Palestine Moslems, who opposed Jewish settlement.[81] Abraham Bragin envisioned even more: concentrated Jewish settlements along the shores of the Black Sea from Odessa to Abkhazsk. Their enthusiasm was shared by the journalist Fischer who wrote of the vast expanses of empty land, the "friendly" Tatar population, and the presence of other ethnic minorities—German, Czech, Lettish, and Estonian—all "accustomed to strangers." He also pointed to the absence of any history of anti-Semitic outbreaks in the region.[82]

Kalinin above all gave the Crimea project his ardent support, electrifying many Jews at the OZET Conference of November 15–20, 1926,[83] with his emotional appeal that the USSR give Jews their chance for national survival. By destroying petty trade, the Revolution had brought economic ruin to the Jewish masses, he declared. Now, with the government's land settlement policy and help from foreign Jews, the Jewish poor could be rehabilitated. He pointed out that while both the Crimea and Siberia had vast expanses of available land, Jews were better suited to the climate of the Crimea. Settlement there would help them make the transition to village life and attract foreign capital:

The Jewish people faces a great task, that of preserving its nationality, and this requires the transformation of a considerable part of the Jewish population into a compactly settled agricultural peasantry numbering in the hundreds of thousands at least. Only in this condition can the Jewish masses hope for the survival of their nationality[84] (see Photo 6.7).

Some of the Evsektsiya leaders pounced on Kalinin's unorthodox outburst, openly attacking his views. Chemerisky, however, was more subtle, more equivocal, explaining Kalinin's position in what was termed "a flash of dialectic inspiration": as a member of the former ruling nation, Kalinin must encourage oppressed-nation nationalism; as members of the formerly oppressed nation, the Evsektsiya leaders must encourage proletarian internationalism.[85] For Chemerisky the important precondition to any talk of "nation" remained the concentration of Jewish toilers in one place—the practical economic base:

The way Comrade Kalinin may talk and needs to talk as the representative of the government . . . is one thing, and the way we must talk is another . . . Why do we have to agree with his view about the preservation of the nation? The party has issued no such directive.[86]

6.7 Mikhail Kalinin speaking at the First All-Union Congress of GEZ-ERD, Moscow, November 1926. Courtesy YIVO.

But Jewish feeling and memories could not be crushed. According to one non-Communist observer, the conference came to an end at a banquet where Hasidic melodies and folk songs were sung. "At this time," he wrote, "there were no Communists or non-party people—only Jews, plain Jews, united in Jewish song, in Jewish joy . . ."[87]

A young Komsomol activist at the time, Hirsh Smoliar, who was present at the conference, recorded[88] the strong feelings Kalinin's speech elicited, and the stormy discussions and speeches it aroused. Many delegates were excited and enthusiastic, especially since "the words came from a man who represented the highest party and government authorities." But the morning after his speech there was a separate meeting of Evsektsiya and Komsomol delegates to formulate tactics for fighting dominant nationalistic tendencies in GEZERD.[89] The Central Bureau of the Evsektsiya had already adopted a resolution endorsing the idea of "Jewish territorial autonomy," but warned against "nationalistic overestimation" of this autonomy. Even so, there lingered Kalinin's emotional appeal to Jews and his insistence that the government was interested in preserving the national feeling of every people, and that the Soviet Union "must become the fatherland of the Jewish masses, ten times a more genuine fatherland than any bourgeois Palestine."

At the separate meeting of the Evsektsiya and Komsomol delegates—although the full story was not learned until thirty years later when Smoliar met with Yasha Rives, Chemerisky's secretary—Chemerisky reported that the Central Bureau of the Evsektsiya saw no future in the Crimea, that other areas must be found. The members were shocked by the suddenness of this decision. What was not known at the time was that Chemerisky had been called by the party secretary Stalin and told that he, Stalin, had rejected the the Crimean project.[90] Smoliar recalled the "remarkable, laconic statement of Stalin, that Jews would have land." But not the Crimea. His rejection of the region, however, was never communicated to Jews, and, after the war, Jewish leaders who believed the Crimea could become a refuge for those made homeless were denounced as "enemies of the state" (see Chapter 19). They, too, had remembered the myth of a Crimean Republic.

In the tortuous ideological word-spinning produced at the OZET Conference, one feels both the internal and external tensions and pressures battering at Jewish activists. They were not only wracked by articulated conflicts but were unable to comprehend shifting, often unseen mutations in official Soviet thinking about Jews, to which they had to bend, and which they felt they had to anticipate. No resolutions could be passed at the conference. Moreover, even at the Sixth Evsektsiya All-Union Conference the following month, Jewish Communists could not hammer out a position on the Soviet Jewish question, on what processes and forms productive Jewish life would take. One historian has described the conference as "the scene of the clash between Evsektsiya neutralists, Nationalists, and assimilationists."[91] Chemerisky continued his weaving, stressing industrialization as the main road to socialism, but wanting to assure the continuation of land resettlement as long as industry could not absorb all Jews, and further qualifying his fluid non-position by warning that "a great mass of peasants might develop dangerous political aspirations," i.e., "the idea of a national state," with the Jewish petty bourgeoisie seeking "to imbue the peasantry with an up-to-date nationalist ideology."[92] Industrialization would surely lead to assimilation, but that, he believed, was less of a danger than nationalism.

Esther Frumkin and Dimanshtain still believed that the Jewish people could consolidate themselves into a nation under communism, even without a territory; assimilation was still far off, even if a distant goal. But Esther was opposed to further resettlement on the land, convinced that the Jewish road to socialism was the direct one—industry.[93]

The turns, switches, and uncertainties seemed finally at an end in March 1928 when the Presidium of the Central Committee, the highest Soviet authority, decreed that Jews could develop national autonomy only in Birobidzhan. After this time, despite misgivings by some Evsektsiya members, the campaign for Jewish colonization centered on Birobidzhan. Meanwhile, beyond these ideological twists and leaps, there remained the practical work of resettling and maintaining Jews in the Ukraine and the Crimea, a process that continued into the thirties while rarefied ideological debates continued. Agro-Joint did not cease its work until 1938, but by that time many of the Evsektsiya activists who had labored to find economic solutions for Soviet Jews had been purged, imprisoned, exiled, or killed by Stalin (see Chapter 14).

The back-to-the-land movement had clearly revolutionized Jewish life in the Soviet Union, reversing the modern historic trend from village to city. Such a reversal, long advocated by Zionists to achieve Jewish economic "normalization," had not been achieved anywhere else to such a degree—not even in Palestine at the time. But the achievement was punctured at the very moment it was most successful, by forced collectivization, industrialization, and the confused simultaneous call to settle Birobidzhan—clashing goals which diffused energies and clouded the focus and intentions of the government's economic and political policies. Obviously, the future of Soviet Jews was not a high priority for Soviet policymakers and plans were improvised, as with other aspects of Soviet policy, until the regime came under Stalin's absolute control. His struggle for power after Lenin's death undoubtedly overlapped and reflected some of the uncertainties and ambiguities of the "Jewish policy of the late twenties." However, even discounting the many crises facing the new regime, we see in this early period a checkered, contradictory, unpredictable pattern of decisions affecting

Jews that would be repeated later. The dialectical process was not creating a synthesis but rather a choppy and confused scene of half-starts, aborted programs, and sudden shifts which dazed Jews and produced torrents of words by people maneuvering to master events or shape them.

The land resettlement program temporarily solved the problems of many Jews, but many more still languished in the shtetlach, struggling to survive.

7

Jews under the New Economic Policy (NEP), 1921–27

We are in a condition of such poverty, ruin, and exhaustion of the productive powers of the workers and peasants, that everything must be set aside to increase production.

LENIN

When we came to a town and observed the economy of the kustars, we were shocked by the desolation and need. . . . When we look at the shoemakers, tanners, and hosiery weavers . . . what do we find? The majority of them are idle . . . just wandering around.

Der emes, July 3, 1928

WHILE Jewish farmers were learning to cope with the land, the natural elements, and a completely new environment, masses of Jews in the shetlach were sinking into destitution and despair. These were the so-called "unproductive" Jews—petty traders, the unemployed, and the "declassed," a term used for those who lost civil and voting rights, housing, educational, and medical rights, and were stamped in derogatory terms. The Revolution had worsened their suffering, and the land resettlement programs scarcely touched them, but instead, stimulated a response from "productive" workers. Of the 15,000 families in the Ukraine who had registered for settlement in 1925, 71 percent were classified as "productive" (workers, *kustars* [artisans], and agricultural workers). Of 7,000 families registered in Belorussia, 60 percent were so classified.[1] With the end of the civil war and the closing of war industries, the ranks of petty traders and unemployed had swelled. JDC estimated that 830,000 Jews were classified as *lishentsy*, or "declassed."[2]

Declassed persons formed the lowest class of citizens, for they suffered not only moral and social degradation, but very tangible economic disabilities as well. They were required to pay higher taxes and higher rates for water and light as well as higher rents. Their children could be accommodated in schools only after others had been provided for. Moreover, they would be admitted to hospitals only if space was not required for soldiers, workers, and peasants.[3]

Petty traders and shopkeepers in the Pale of Settlement scarcely merited the term "declassed," since most of them were in a continual state of semistarvation, but the new regime made no careful distinctions. They were "exploiters," as were Jewish artisans, who generally had to sell their products as well as make them, and who often had family members and apprentices to help them. In some towns, the number of declassed Jews was as high as 60 percent.[4] In the 1926 elections to the shtetl soviets in the Ukraine, Jews constituted 81.5 percent of all lishentsy, and in elections to city soviets in the same year, they made up 68.8 percent.[5] For the distribution of the Jewish population from the early years of the Bolshevik Revolution until 1926, see Map 7.1 and Tables 7.1 and 7.2.

The profoundly disruptive impact of the Revolution on small Jewish communities has been documented in the famous Smolensk Archive. According to the census of 1926, there were 94,445 Jews in the Western Oblast (region), of whom 12,887 were in the city of Smolensk. The rest were largely scattered among the small towns in the region. The plight of the village Jews is described in a report of the village of Lyubavichi in 1925. The population of Lyubavichi had declined from 1,302 to 967 between 1921 and 1925, although the non-Jewish population had been increasing steadily. "Before the Revolution," the report notes,

the economy of the village . . . rested on two bases: flax and . . . the rabbi. This was an important center for the preparation of flax, which was processed here and shipped by rail. It was also the residence of the famous Rabbi Shneyerson, and a center of Chasidism. Chasidim poured into the village of Lyubavichi every day from all sides, including a number of merchants, who supplied the local population. Artisanry and handicrafts flourished, despite the scornful attitude toward productive work on the part of the "court" (the rabbi and his clique).

TABLE 7.1

Centers of Jewish Population, 1919–26

Name of City	Republic	1919–1923	1926
Moscow	RSFSR	86,171 ('23)	131,244
Leningrad	RSFSR	52,374 ('23)	84,480
Rostov	RSFSR	45,000 ('20)	26,323
Kuibyshev (Samara)	RSFSR	40,000 ('20)	
Saratov	RSFSR	20,000 ('20)	
Smolensk	RSFSR	15,000 ('20)	
Kiev	Ukraine SSR	111,000 ('20)	140,256
		129,000 ('23)	
Odessa	Ukraine SSR	190,000 ('20)	153,194
		130,000 ('23)	
Kharkov	Ukraine SSR	54,000 ('20)	81,138
Kremenchug	Ukraine SSR		28,969
Poltava	Ukraine SSR		18,476
Vinnitsa	Ukraine SSR		21,816
Berdichev	Ukraine SSR		30,812
Dnepropetrovsk (Ekaterinoslav)	Ukraine SSR	73,350 ('20)	
Zhitomir	Ukraine SSR		30,000
Minsk	Belorussia SSR		53,686
Gomel	Belorussia SSR		37,700
Vitebsk	Belorussia SSR	39,714 ('23)	37,000
Bobruisk	Belorussia SSR		21,600
Mogilev	Belorussia SSR		17,100

Sources: S. M. Schwarz, *The Jews in the Soviet Union,* 1951, p. 230; *Soviet Census of 1926;* Z. Y. Gitelman, *Jewish Nationality and Soviet Politics,* 1972, p. 265; Y. Lestschinsky, *Dos sovetishe idntum,* 1941, pp. 79, 80, 85.

The imperialist and civil wars undermined the economic foundation of the village. Flax did not appear at the markets. The court of the rabbi and the nest of Chasidim were destroyed. Most of the population were deprived of their former sources of subsistence. The impoverishment of the population began. . . .[6]

These Jews, indeed, constituted a "prostrate body" which the state was slow to help. A temporary expedient for all of the country—a very uncommunistic strategy called NEP—forced upon Lenin, gave them only temporary and scattered relief.

Peasants who had been in a state of near revolt because of the policy of grain requisitioning and the appalling famine of 1920–21 forced Lenin to scrap war communism and give peasants incentives to produce more

TABLE 7.2
Jewish Population, 1923–26

Republics and Areas	1923	1926*
Ukraine	1,483,000	1,574,000
Belorussia	423,000	407,000
RSFSR and rest of USSR	525,000	603,000 (incl. Kazakh SSR and Kirghiz SSR)
Azerbaidzhan, Georgia, and Armenia		51,000
Turkmen SSR		2,000
Uzbek SSR and Tadzhik SSR		43,000
TOTAL	2,431,000	2,680,000

*Source: S. M. Schwarz, *The Jews in the Soviet Union*, 1951, p. 15.

food for the hungry towns. In March 1921, in a speech to the Tenth Party Congress, he said, "We are in a condition of such poverty, ruin, and exhaustion of the productive powers of the workers and peasants, that everything must be set aside to increase production."[7] The result was Lenin's New Economic Policy (1921–27). NEP replaced the state seizure of farm goods by a graduated agricultural tax, which took only a fixed proportion of the peasants' surplus. This meant that peasants could market whatever they kept, thus re-creating free trade in agricultural produce. At first such trade was limited to local fairs, but later a class of NEPmen came in existence, who dominated retail distribution. NEPmen were essentially brokers who knew how to find buyers and sellers at the right moment and advise them on prices.

Though not intended to do so, the NEP also exerted a powerful influence on industry which likewise had declined. If the peasant was to be encouraged to increase production, any surplus could be sold on the open market and industry had to manufacture goods for him to buy. The first step in that direction was government encouragement of industrial cooperatives. Under NEP, the centralized state management of industry gave way to a system of "trusts" in which the state retained control over large-scale industry, transport, and foreign trade, but allowed a large measure of private initiative. Private enterprises and cooperatives, involving up to fifteen workers (almost 90 percent of all enterprises) were outside state control under NEP. Every factory, whether government-operated or privately owned, had to pay for everything it used, leading to the re-introduction of currency and bank-

MAP 7.1

Jewish Population Centers in the Early Years of the Bolshevik Revolution

JEWISH POPULATION IN RUSSIAN
EMPIRE IN 1897:

PALE OF SETTLEMENT	4,899,300
OUTSIDE OF PALE	316,500
TOTAL	5,215,800

JEWISH POPULATION IN SOVIET
TERRITORY, 1926:   2,680,000

(1,981,000 IN AREA OF PALE)

LEGEND

       PALE OF SETTLEMENT, 1835 – 1917

●   CITIES OF SUBSTANTIAL JEWISH
    SETTLEMENT IN THE 1920 s

Adapted from Martin Gilbert, The Jews of Russia,
1979, p. 19.

ing operations—a reversion to capitalism, in effect. Lenin was realistic about the crisis that had to be faced and acted quickly to save the Revolution. A decree of December 10, 1922, restored to former owners all those enterprises which had been nationalized but which had not yet been taken over by the state. Small nationalized enterprises were leased to cooperatives and private persons. By September 1, 1922, out of a total of 7,100 enterprises, over half, involving 68,000 workers, were in private hands or cooperatives.[8] NEP also forced the return to a free labor market. Forced labor under war communism was abolished and the wage system was re-introduced. Although many doctrinaire Bolsheviks cringed at the time, the state no longer undertook to supply the needs of great sections of the population. Beneficial results were immediately evident as both agriculture and industry began to recover. Outside the Soviet Union it appeared that NEP was the first step in a complete turn-about to a capitalist economy.

By 1923, a "Jewish NEP" was introduced. The Central Bureau of the Evsektsiya turned its face to the shtetl and announced a policy of reconciliation with the "petit-bourgeois" elements.[9] Special Evsektsiya detachments were sent to work in selected towns and, although most of the activists knew no Yiddish, they believed they could solve the political and economic problems of shtetl life in short order, lingering religious and Zionist feelings notwithstanding. But they found a very melancholy scene. Many of the energetic Jews had fled certain towns, leaving a disproportionate number of widows and others dependent upon charity. A study of the shtetl Monastyrshchina in the Ukraine, which was quite typical, showed that fully one-third of the population was classified as "half-beggars"—some shopkeepers, religious teachers, widows, and those without any way to make a living.[10] There was virtually no cultural life nor Soviet schools of any kind. Shtetl youth was in a particularly despondent state and many families relied on money sent from America. A Jewish Communist leader M. Kiper, in an article in *Der emes*, February 2, 1924, described their condition as "hopeless."

Dr. Boris Bogen, head of the JDC Russian Department, made an extensive survey of the needs of Jewish communities in 1922–23. His steady stream of reports accents the grinding poverty still clinging to many Jewish communities. In April 1923, for example, Kremenchug, which had a population of 100,000, over half of whom were Jews, "is now in awful condition—ruined, dirty, [with] miserable houses with broken windows, miserable people, hopeless and sick. . . . Most of the population depends, of course, upon the relief from America. . . . Last summer there were three ARA (American Relief Administration) kitchens feeding a host of Jewish children, among them many with all the symptoms of extreme starvation. . . . At present the situation has improved." The population had shrunk to 66,403, of whom 37,633 were Jews.[11]

For the destitute artisans, JDC cooperated with the Jewish Colonization Association in contributing to eighty-two *kassy* (mutual aid and loan associations) in various towns, while JDC contributed independently to them, thereby benefiting 20,000 families, according to Dr. Rosen. These sums helped a shoemakers' cooperative in Vinnitsa, a woodworkers' cooperative in Zhitomir, a metalworkers' cooperative in Odessa, and a milk producers' cooperative in Ekaterinoslav in August 1922.[12] Up to January 1, 1923, JDC also aided 42 trade schools and three agricultural schools involving almost 4,000 Jewish boys and girls in Minsk, Gomel, Mogilev, Vitebsk, Kiev, Kharkov, Kremenchug, Ekaterinoslav, Chernigov, and Zhitomir.[13]

However, in towns such as Habno in the Ukraine, which had a strong Jewish militia and had escaped the worst ravages of the pogroms, NEP temporarily restored trade to the prewar level.[14] Shutters were taken down from shops and goods again appeared behind counters. Smaller plants that had been nationalized were returned to their former owners. But in 1923 the currency was still unstable and swiftly depreciating, commodities were scarce, and prices were high. As it turned out, the commercial boom was sporadic and short-lived. By the end of 1923, the state taxes imposed on private establishments became ruinously high and state-produced goods began to compete with NEP produced goods. In Habno, for example, a tannery with an annual turnover of 6,000 roubles had to pay eight different taxes amounting to 160 roubles a month.[15] A case under official investigation in the summer of 1925 in the district of Proskurov, which had suffered severely during the pogroms, showed that while the entire stock of merchandise owned by the poor shopkeeper was valued at 17 roubles, his taxes amounted to 40 roubles. Unable to pay, he was condemned to a six-month prison term. Some persons were summoned to court for tax arrears of a few kopeks. Because of the persecutions of tax collectors, some Jews pursued their trade clandestinely. But Jewish NEPmen often "would be glad enough to scrap their little miserable trading enterprise and turn proletarian if only they had the opportunity."[16] Nor could they have real peace of mind so long as their activity reinforced old social and religious prejudices against Jews.

The burden of taxation was apparently felt from the very beginning of NEP. When Louis Fischer, the American journalist, traveled to Zhitomir, Berdichev, and Vinnitsa in December 1922, and to Minsk, Vitebsk, and Gomel in March 1923, he wrote that "NEP was just beginning to have its full effect. The air was filled with the spirit of activity and prosperity. . . . Nevertheless, I heard here and there faint, whispering complaints that 'taxes are exorbitant.' " It is true that "early in 1924, government stores and government-favored cooperatives were being pushed to the wall by their private competitors," but that after the Thirteenth Party Congress in April 1924, there was the "signal for a grand offensive against private trade." Government trusts, syndicates, and factories, which were practically the only source of manufactured goods, began to discriminate against private merchants. NEPmen were asked to pay cash and COD for goods, while cooperatives received credits and discounts. NEPmen were given the "last and worst choice," and often found it impossible to buy anything. This situation "worked particular havoc with Jews," forcing many to close down. The prevailing feeling was "sooner or later the tax collector will get me." Besides, some were tired of the "nervous, nerve-wracking hustle and bustle of petty trading and peddling . . . and tired of being considered pariahs and parasites."[17] These frustrations, Fischer believed, created the greatest driving force behind the Jewish movement of agricultural colonization."[18]

In the small towns, there was a similar economic struggle, with somewhat different variations. Self-taxation was being imposed in shtetlach in White Russia to cover 50 percent of the expense of digging wells, plastering sidewalks, building bathhouses, and remodeling schools. The Yiddish press, according to a JTA (Jewish Telegraphic Agency) cable of November 22, 1929, was reporting that "impoverished Jews were unable to pay." The overtaxing by tax inspectors during this time was a chronic and continuing complaint, based on unrealistic estimates of earnings of kustars, new strictures on loans, and drastic, slashing measures against the surviving kustar.

Tax officials decided, for example, that since barbers work ten hours each day, six days a week, and since they shave 100 customers, each shave taking six minutes, barbers must earn 500 roubles a month, an absurd figure. There was also a decision adopted at an all-Ukrainian convention of Jewish loan associations at Kharkov, "not to grant loans to Jewish kustars who are classified as not sufficiently poor."[19] This was a "blow to thousands of kustars who get loans in cash and raw materials." Deprived of raw materials, they will become "helpless declassed." But the Communists maintained that "we must apply the class difference principle in our credit system."[20] Zealous Jewish Communist students at Minsk University also invoked the "class principle" in opposing OZET in White Russia for sending ex-traders into Jewish collectives.[21] But in the Berdichev region, Jewish Communists complained that "local Soviet organs are neglecting the interests of the declassed," and urged greater help for them. A JTA cable in late 1929 reported that only 1,750 declassed Jews in the area (with a Jewish population of 70,000) had found work.[22] A report to the executive committee of the Western Oblast in August 1929 further documents the large number of "declassed" Jews: in Nevlya, they constituted 80 percent of all those deprived of voting rights; in Klintsy, 76 percent; in Starodub, 72 percent, and in Pochinok, 77 percent.[23]

Agro-Joint contributed somewhat to the industrial training and absorption of Jews into "productive labor," but Jewish lishentsy were not being reduced appreciably. From 1924 to 1930, Agro-Joint assisted 84 institutions (57 technical schools and 27 short-term training courses), which altogether graduated 4,500 young Jews who were placed in metalworking, wood-working, printing, and other trades.[24] Almost a million roubles were thus invested.

A special problem for Communists and Evsektsiya representatives particularly was that of the Jewish artisan—the kustar. The party could never make its peace with the kustars because they did not fit neatly into the Marxist paradigm of class structure and class conflict. The kustar was an artisan who worked in his own home, using his own or his customer's raw materials, and sold his product on the market or directly to a customer. There were kustars who employed hired labor and apprentices as well as those who worked alone. Thus they were at least partly traders and condemned as "exploiters." Kustars formed nearly 10 percent of the Jewish population of the Ukraine and White Russia and as much in Moscow and Leningrad. Many of them were left in the same dismal situation as shopkeepers until the advent of

NEP and struggled to survive through clandestine trading. Yet in many areas of the country, they were the only suppliers of processed foods and consumer goods. Moreover, their economic activity could not be nationalized because they were so widely dispersed and slipped in and out of hard economic classifications. Here, too, the Communists compromised. They encouraged kustar cooperatives as a way of fighting the NEPmen until such time as the kustars could become full fledged proletarians. Reflecting Nikolai Bukharin's idea of drawing peasants and small producers into cooperatives and then gradually into socialist and communist forms, some Communists identified the kustars with the middle strata of the peasantry.[25] The Twelfth Party Congress in April 1923, moreover, had urged that there be greater reliance on local resources and initiative—which some Jewish Communists interpreted to refer to the kustars. The Central Bureau of the Evsektsiya was eager to conquer the shtetlach, where so many kustars remained in their misery, untouched by the Revolution, and temporarily argued down their opponents in the Ukraine and White Russia: "We cannot allow a hostile void to continue. . . . We have the chance to win in the shtetl, and attract the poor . . . should we not seize it?"[26] Rakhmiel Veinshtain, the ex-Bundist, spoke for those anxious not to alienate but to neutralize the "petit bourgeois" elements of the Jewish population and create a friendly attitude toward the Soviet regime and the proletariat. Others argued that such work was in itself petit-bourgeois and urged that kustars be allowed to emigrate.

Arguments rocked back and forth, but for a short time the Evsektsiya tried to deal with the special problem of the kustars. A powerful argument was the harsh economic fact that state industries in the early and middle twenties were incapable of supplying the country with the goods it needed and that the artisan was still economically useful. For a time, he even lost his degrading declassed label. Many kustar cooperatives of all kinds emerged—consumer, producer, and marketing—which artisans themselves formed or which they were forced to join. The small manufacturer, theoretically protected under NEP, often felt squeezed by official pressures and gave way to the kustar cooperatives, which were given favorable treatment by the government—especially in the allocation of raw materials. In White Russia, for example, in 1926, only 5 percent of all craftsmen had joined cooperatives and were allotted fully 80 percent of available raw materials.[27] Yet the regulations binding on kustar cooperatives and government interference frequently proved ruinous. A typical difficulty in the small town of Molev is described in the Moscow *Emes* of February 1, 1923:

[M]embers of these cooperatives have worked beyond their strength, labored twelve hours or more daily, only in order to produce without help from outside workers. . . . To stop these evasive methods . . . the district offices of the craft associations imposed the law of the eight-hour day . . . and determined that no craftsmen should be allowed to work after 6 P.M. It was believed that in this way artisans would be forced to maintain hired labor . . . and keep up production. . . . But the artisans preferred to curtail production or even liquidate it completely, rather than hire workers. . . . In general, the organization of production in our time involves so many difficulties that everyone finds it more profitable to trade . . . rather than to produce. The result is that the majority of workers and artisans in Molev spend more of their time in the market than in the factory. . . . In short, speculation increases at the expense of production.[28]

The party attitude toward artisans became more positive after the Fourteenth Party Congress in 1925, when their status was edged up to that of the peasants, who, it was believed, would reach socialism by way of cooperatives. (Agricultural cooperatives were reinstated in May 1921 as a means of educating the peasants toward socialism and leveling out inequalities that threatened the development of a rich peasant class.) Kustars having only one helper or two apprentices were almost on the same footing as wage earners. Like them, they were entitled to vote and have their own mutual aid societies which gave members medical and legal help, clubs, educational services and, in cases where there were three assistants, credit was made available. Thus, for a time, some Jewish tailors, tanners, knitters, brushmakers, booters, and hatters, among others, improved their lot.

Moreover, the situation of the artisan was considered relatively better than that of the trader. A study of three small towns in the provinces of Kiev and Chernigov, which was made by Agro-Joint toward the end of 1926, reported that "the artisans, constituting about thirty percent of the population, were economically the strongest element. Tailors and shoemakers were earning about fifty to sixty roubles a month, and occasionally even as much as one hundred and fifty roubles."

When the NEP was at its height in 1926–27, it is estimated that Jews (who constituted about 2 percent of the population) were supplying 40 percent of its craftsmen and 20 percent of its trademen.[29] But there was still a great deal of unemployment and artisans lived in dread of government interference. Moreover, the new laws against employment of outside labor militated against the training of qualified apprentices and thus of skilled artisans.[30] The 1926 decision of the Union Planning Commission (Gosplan) to class the needle trades with those private industries whose further growth was considered undesirable and leather craft as superfluous because of the state leather industry[31] hurt Jewish artisans in those fields. There was also some competition from peasants who manufactured for the market during the winter. Many artisans were driven into trade and even, as reported in Odessa, a kind of subcontracting, with work parceled out to home workers who were found working in unsanitary conditions up to eighteen hours a day— very reminiscent of the plight of Jewish immigrants to America in the 1880s and later. Six hundred such workers made shoes in their homes in Odessa this way.[32]

In 1926, the official census showed that over a million registered Jews were earning a living, but that 96,000 were still out of work.[33] Moreover, there were 70,000 unregistered de-classed Jews and 60,000 impoverished petty traders and unregistered artisans without work. One Evsek estimated that about 370,000 Jews were in fact without work during that period, and that more than a million Jews were in extreme need.[34] In towns such as Kremenchug, among the registered unemployed, more than 56 percent were Jewish workers. Yitzhak Sudarsky, an Evsektsiya leader in the Ukraine, visited towns in Volyn and in Podolia and found 80 percent of the handworkers jobless. "It wasn't easy," one of the Komsomol leaders recalled, "for the Evsektsiya to convince party and government authorities of the dire situation facing the Jewish masses in the towns. The facts bearing on their situation came late and were placed before meetings of the central committees of the Jewish Sections in Moscow, Kharkov, and Minsk in the spring of 1926.[35] Handworker cooperatives and kassy were organized, largely through the efforts of the Central Bureau of the Jewish Youth Section of the general Union of Communist Youth, and a decree was passed so that many Jewish youth were trained to qualify as factory workers, especially in the Donbas region. They were admitted to technical schools and there learned necessary skills.[36] In the Ukraine, according to Dr. Singalovsky, head of Berlin ORT, in 1927, 31.5 percent of all students in technical schools in the Ukraine were Jewish.

Meanwhile, the situation of the shtetl Jew continued to be desperate throughout the course of NEP and even later. The agronomist Frucht, in a talk to Jewish farmers in 1927 told them: "The towns are full of Jewish poor who die three times a day from hunger." And a correspondent in the Ukraine wrote in *Emes* of July 3, 1928, that "When we came to a town and observed the economy of the kustars, we were shocked by the desolation and need. . . . When we look at the shoemakers, tanners, and hosiery weavers . . . What do we find? The majority of them are idle . . . just wandering around."[37] Their condition continued to remain precarious, even after the adoption of the Five Year Plan. In various articles[38] written in 1929–30 by the veteran Jewish journalist Boris Smolar, the plight of the Jewish artisan is prominently featured. Smolar believed that the government's measures were "crushing" the artisan, that he must join a cooperative or forfeit his rights, and that the "house-cleaning" of cooperatives was forcing out all small ex-traders. He noticed the word "kulak" being used against the individual Jewish artisan, and observed official coercion to join the cooperatives and the conspicuous zeal of Jewish Communists. Russian ORT was giving up its relief work among Jewish artisans, but foreign ORT was still trying to support them with sewing machines and raw materials (see Photo 7.1).

The role of the Evsektsiya in the Soviet pullback to private enterprise seems to have been beset by problems of interpreting party dogma and of pacing, of carrying the dragweight of ideology into a period when it had to be loosened up, then of loosening up and not snapping back quickly enough for the new official anti-NEP policy. The Evseks considered the petty Jewish traders and artisans examples of antiproletarian elements in the Communist class war against parasites and capitalists. In Soviet parlance, they and their family helpers constituted a "nest of speculators." Many qualified artisans became luftmenshen when their sewing and hosiery machines were taken away from them.[39] At the same time, some activists in the Evsektsiya were deeply involved in questions of national-cultural autonomy and were criticized because economic matters were neglected and the application of NEP was much delayed in Jewish towns. "In an atmosphere of super-carefulness and self-control," they delayed activity that might have saved the artisans and petty traders, especially referral of these vital matters to executive committees of the party in cities of the Ukraine.[40] Then, once loosened in their approach to the kustars and the poor in the shtetlach, they

7.1 The Red Banner Knitwear Cooperative, Minsk.

concentrated on these groups, "involved in the rehabilitation of the most 'backward' elements of Soviet society."[41]

It was in the area of economic reconstruction of Soviet Jewry—so vital for its future—that the Evsektsiya "were closely watched and regulated by the Party," and "had the least autonomy and minimal flexibility."[42] The party itself throughout the 1920s was involved in intense debates about how to modernize the country, shifting from one solution to another, often choosing several simultaneously. The Evsektsiya were like shadows, uneasily trying to shift and jump with the party. This uncertainty and need to please Communist policymakers very possibly reflected their confusion over future official "Jewish policy" and their inhibition about bringing specifically Jewish problems before non-Jewish bodies. They also had to deal with the strong animus against Jewish NEPmen, for, despite the official campaign against anti-Semitism, NEPmen soon became synonymous with Jews and were portrayed negatively in some of the Soviet literature of the time, including three novels: *The Tale about Max the Dwarf* (1926) by Mikhail Kozakov, Yuli Berzin's *Ford* (1927), and *Minus Six* (1930) by Matvei Roizman.[43]

There were also lampoons of "cosmopolitan" Jews in *The Moon in on the Right Side* by Sergei Malashkin.

Resentful customers and party members began to accuse Jewish shopkeepers of profiteering and of diverting the scarce merchandise for their own benefit. Of course, there were some big speculators, but they were few. More numerous were those small-fry middlemen, retailers, and peddlers, uprooted by the Revolution, who enjoyed a hectic and ephemeral success in the brief period of prosperity.[44] For some Jews, the short NEP experiment created a heady draught of freedom; for others, swift retribution. Well-to-do Jews, for example, could now take the curative baths at Evpatoria and enjoy lodgings in the tsar's former palace of Yalta, where in the past an occasional Jewish musician was terrified of being exposed as a Jew. Some NEPmen could also briefly flaunt their wealth in expensive restaurants and shops, but even they led a precarious existence and seemed to sense that their exhilarating tenure would be fleeting. Some of the wealthier Jews, together with others, were accused of speculation and were arrested and exiled to Siberia.

Resentment of Jewish NEPmen was especially sharp in Moscow which came to be known as "a Jewish city."[45] The Jewish newcomers milled through the business center and filled the amusement places. Seeing so many of them closely packed in unaccustomed places, residents were sure they were now a majority. Typical of this antipathy is the following observation made in December 1926 by Professor Juri Klyuchnikov who worked for the People's Commissariat for Foreign Affairs:

. . . You can see how all over Moscow small bread and sausage booths run by Jews have been set up. Here you have the main source of dissatisfaction: here we are in our city, and along come people from somewhere else crowding in on us. When Russians see how Russian women, old people, and children freeze in the streets . . . bent over the stands of the Mossel'prom [government operated chain stores], and when they see these rather warm booths with their bread and sausage, they feel some discontent. . . .[46]

Between 1923 and 1926, Moscow's population had increased from a million and a half to two million, while the city's Jewish population had grown from 5.7 percent (86,171) of the total population to 6.5 percent (131,200)—seen by many as a "Jewish invasion."

But Moscow, under NEP, had also become a gay and lively city:

The streets were crowded; the stores were open and their windows glowed with fine wares; the traffic moved again in a steady stream of horse-drawn vehicles and even automobiles. . . . The people were much better dressed, and shoes and stockings were on the feet of the women who . . . had gone barefoot. New hotels were open and cheerful-looking restaurants extended savory invitations to the passer-by. . . . The operetta theater . . . had been sold out, though it had seats for two thousand. . . . The gypsies sang and played . . . and night life in Moscow seemed again the vivid thing I remembered from my youth.[47]

However, such scenes were soon to disappear. The days of the traders and artisans, moreover, both for good and ill, were numbered. A huge industrialization plan, known as the First Five Year Plan (1928–33) was now set in motion. Factory proletariat were to be bearers and pillars of the new order and traders, artisans, and middlemen were to be transformed into industrial wage earners. This new economic upheaval caused sudden, drastic changes throughout Russia and pitched Jews into new kinds of work and relationships. NEP and NEPmen disappeared.[48]

8

Yiddish Culture in the Soviet Mold: Soviets, Courts, Schools, and Scholarship

For some the now is good enough—
And that is fine for them!
But what shall I do
when I always
see before me
phosphorescent questions flashing:
Where?
Where to?

I am already tired
of hovering,
of flickering,
of swimming,
of soaking in strange seas.

DAVID HOFSHTEYN,
translated by Allen Mandlebaum

I T was during the early twenties that the first territorial enlargement of Soviet Russia occurred, prompting Communist leaders to make concessions to national minorities, including Jews.[1] It will be recalled that between March and November 1917, Lenin switched from his position of rejecting the demands of national minorities for political independence to a promise that the subject peoples of the tsarist empire would enjoy national equality and self-determination "even to the point of separation and the formation of an independent state." However, when the national minorities moved to take advantage of these promises, the Bolsheviks reverted to their original stand.

In the course of the civil war, with the help of local Bolshevik organizations and the backing of the Red Army, Lenin offered each nationality a government consisting of his own trusted emissaries and reserved for himself the right to determine which nation could separate itself from Russia. Between 1918 and 1920, the Bolsheviks created on the periphery of Russia several "Soviet Socialist Republics" (Belorussian, Ukrainian, Georgian, Armenian, and Azerbaidzhan), while within the RSFSR itself they carved out several "autonomous republics" (Bashkir, Volga German, and Kazakh), and a number of "autonomous regions" (Chuvash, Tatar, and Karelian). Each of the republics assumed the posture of an independent state and set up a government and constitution and, following the model of the RSFSR, eliminated the private ownership of land and all other means of production and assured political power to the "working class." But while they posed as independent political entities, each of these republics expressed "complete solidarity with the existing Soviet republics" and readiness to enter with them "into closest political union for the common fight, for the triumph of the world communist revolution."[2] Early in 1919, all republics unified their military commands and economic, labor, financial, and railroad administrations. By the end of the civil war, the unification process affected all major media of communication and transportation.[3]

The promised autonomy never materialized, however. The Eighth Party Congress held in March 1919 pronounced "one unitary centralized Communist Party with a unitary Central Committee directing all the work of the party in all parts of the RSFSR." Decisions of the Russian Communist party were binding upon all other sectors of the party regardless of their nationality composition. In 1920, Stalin, who was in charge of the nationality policy, expressed the redefined Bolshevik policy of self-determination in the following way:

We are in favor of the secession of India, Arabia, Egypt, Morocco, and other colonies from the Entente, because secession in this case would mean the liberation of those oppressed countries from imperialism and strengthening the position of revolutions. We are against the separation of the border regions from Russia since [it] . . . would involve imperialist servitude for the border regions, thus undermining the revolutionary power of Russia and strengthening the position of imperialism.[4]

Party members were ordered to help the non-Russian minorities "catch up" with Great Russia by developing administrative and cultural institutions, schools, and a press through which a new Soviet culture could be created, as Stalin had formulated it: "national in form, socialist in content." In some cases, it was even necessary to devise alphabets for certain languages that had never been reduced to written form. These efforts were pursued vigorously by the party, which was determined to appear as benefactor and liberator. By February 1922, all Soviet republics, which were independent in theory, delegated their rights in the area of foreign relations to the RSFSR; in May, they gave up their rights in foreign trade. Then on December 30, 1922, the Union of Soviet Socialist Republics (USSR) was created comprising the Ukrainian, Caucasian, and Russian federated republics—a decision which further aroused nationalist feeling among Russia's non-Russians.

The formation of the USSR brought into sharp relief the practical need for a thorough re-examination of the party position on the national question. This was done at the Twelfth Party Congress in April 1923, by which time Stalin, the party general secretary, was gaining virtual control of the party apparatus. The Twelfth Party Congress created a Council of Nationalities to reflect and express the special needs of diverse nationalities. The Congress also recommended special legislation providing for the use of minority languages in all government agencies and institutions serving the local population and national minorities. Kalinin was particularly vehement in his denunciation of the "inconsiderate treatment of minority nationalities" who were made to feel like "stepdaughters."[5] It was also expected that development of national cultures would buttress the military security of the Soviet borders, populated by non-Russian nationalities, and secure the loyalty of the border peoples.

Like NEP, the policy of fostering minority cultures was intended to make concessions to popular feeling. But the process was enormously complicated by the fact that minorities differed greatly in economic and cultural development, and by the emergence of new minorities as well as newly organized national majorities. Moreover, prior to the establishment of the USSR, the Great Russians had dominated the life of the country and would resist becoming a minority nationality in the republics where they were only a numerical minority. Stalin himself admitted the preponderance of Russian influence at the Twelfth Congress. Moreover, nationality differences were crosscut by the urban-peasant cleavage, which was especially deep in the Ukraine and White Russia. There the urban population was chiefly Russian and Jewish, while the peasants, chiefly Ukrainian and White Russian, were hostile to Jews and Russians and to the new regime with which they were identified. A new minority nationality program would, it was hoped, win them over to communisn.

The new nationality policy was designed to play an especially important role in White Russia and the Ukraine—where most Jews were concentrated. According to the census of 1926, 76.1 percent of the entire Soviet Jewish population lived in the Ukraine (1,574,000) and Belorussia (407,000). The RSFSR added 21.8 percent. In the early twenties Bolshevik leaders still believed that revolutions would break out in the West. It would thus be vital to capture the loyalties of the White Russians and Ukrainians still living under Polish rule through policies of "Belorussianization" and "Ukrainization" in the areas controlled by the Soviet Union. For example, in the Ukraine from 1919 to 1922, the Ukrainian language technically had the same status as Russian, but the new ruling on August 1, 1923, showed a clear preference for Ukrainian as the language of official usage, with Russian having special political and cultural importance. Party cells, courts, and soviets were now to conduct their business in Ukrainian or Belorussian. However, native Ukrainians and Belorussians, though they felt the danger of russification, understood that *their* national minorities—Russians, Poles, and Jews—would not want to assimilate into Ukrainian or Belorussian culture. They wanted Ukrainians and Belorussians in party and state posts, but did not demand the integration of national minorities.[6] In 1923–24, the party policy of "nativization" of cultural and political institutions in the national republics meant the creation of nationality soviets to give limited recognition to nationality needs, mainly linguistic.[7] Large minorities were also entitled to carefully defined political and cultural expression in local administrative agencies, courts, and schools. In the Ukrainian and, to a lesser degree, in the Belorussian republics, a policy of "Yiddishization" of soviets in areas of "compact Jewish settlement" was undertaken by the Evsektsiya in 1925.

The Jewish soviets were involved in cultural and administrative matters, public health and sanitation, public improvements, and social organizations.[8] They were set up in those districts and communities where Jews constituted a majority or a large minority. However, they were not meant to serve purely Jewish interests or to devise Jewish policies, as such. Rather, the Jewish soviet differed from other soviets only in the language—Yiddish—in which it served the Jewish population. Its role "as an organ of the dictatorship of the proletariat was not diminished by a hair,"[9] and following Stalin's formula, it was to be socialist in content, Yiddish in form. Between 1925 and 1932, Yiddish soviets assumed some importance in the Ukrainian SSR, less so in the Belorussian SSR, and very slightly in the western (Smolensk) province of the RSFSR. Later, they declined and were generally not mentioned except in connection with "Jewish districts" in the Crimea and Birobidzhan.

Most of the Jewish soviets were organized in the Ukrainian SSR. Here, because of the large Russian minority, the rights of non-Ukrainian local minorities were acknowledged very early; in 1925, there were already 250 non-Ukrainian soviets of various kinds.[10] (A minimum of 500 non-Ukrainians, or 1,000 Ukrainians, were entitled to form a soviet at the smallest administrative level—the village, or market town.) In the same year, there were thirty-eight so-called Jewish soviets, but they represented less than 10 percent of the Jewish population in the Ukrainian SSR. Jewish soviets could be formed only in areas where Jews had a numerical majority—chiefly in small towns and villages. Since almost 75 percent of Jews in the Ukrainian SSR were dispersed in large cities, Jewish soviets for the urban Jews were virtually precluded.[11] Besides, there were somewhat veiled instructions against urban soviets for Jews at an Evsektsiya conference late in 1926.[12]

There were 130 Jewish soviets by 1927,[13] and 168 by 1932, mostly in market towns—still representing only a little over 11 percent of the Jewish population in the Ukraine. Not only were many Jews urbanized, but many also were barred from voting in soviet elections because they were classed as bourgeois, religious, Zionist, or NEPmen. Efforts were made to enfranchise artisans and petty traders but in the 1926 elections to the shtetl soviets, 81.5 percent of all declassed persons were Jews, and in elections to city soviets in that year, they made up 68.5 percent of those ineligible to vote.[14] In the whole of the Ukraine, where the average percentage of the voteless was only 4.6% in 1926, Jews constituted almost half of the ineligibles.

At first, the Evsektsiya pushed ahead energetically with the Yiddishization drive. Both oral and written transactions in the Jewish soviets were in Yiddish and in some cases Yiddish was used in communications to other government agencies, requiring some non-Jewish soviets to have a special department to handle Jewish business,[15] but the official use of three languages—Ukrainian, Russian and Yiddish—in the Ukrainian SSR was bound to create confusion over which language to use. Indeed, as early as 1926, a party resolution placed limitations on the official use of Yiddish, declaring that it be used only where there was "an overwhelming and absolute majority" of Jews. This policy, as well as the increasing flight from the small towns of young Jews who were coming under Communist influence, halted the growth of Jewish market town soviets. After 1928, their decrease was visible and rapid.

In the villages, however, because of the encouragement of Jewish agricultural colonization in the late twenties and early thirties, the number of Jewish soviets increased up to 1932 when 113 were reported.[16] One of the major areas of settlement was in the province of Kherson where the first Jewish regional soviet and the only fairly large unit in the USSR administered by a Jewish soviet was established in 1927. Out of a population of 18,000 farmers in the region, some 16,000 were Jews. The regional seat was Kalinindorf, where the regional soviet was convened for the first time in March 1927. It was an occasion for much rejoicing—some 3,000 guests as well as delegates attended, many of whom hoped for more such soviets in the future, possibly even a Jewish autonomous republic. Two other regional soviets were created a few years later, but Jewish colonization efforts in the Ukraine were weakened by desperate economic conditions—many farmers fled back to their small towns—and by the conflicting demands of an official switch to industrialization and the campaign for Birobidzhan in 1928.

By the late thirties, Yiddish had yielded to Russian in the Jewish regional soviets in official transactions, announcements, and ordinances.[17] Experimentation with Jewish soviets in the market towns of the Ukraine ran an ambivalent course, with some Jewish Communists exhibiting great enthusiasm over Jewish self-government, while party resolutions warned against the danger of peasants perceiving the soviets as instruments of "Jewish domination."

In the White Russian SSR, which had the second largest number of Jews, the thrust was somewhat different. The republic had been set up as a multinational state with four official languages (White Russian, Russian, Polish, and Yiddish), but instead of envisioning soviets, officials planned to adapt the entire political, cultural, and social machinery to the needs of the four nationalities on an equal basis—a virtually impossible task and one that was in conflict with Belorussianization. Only twenty-seven Jewish soviets as such were created in White Russia, most of them in small towns where most White Russian Jews were concentrated, and in many of which they were a majority. In the census of 1926, over 90 percent of Belorussian Jews named Yiddish as their mother tongue. The recognition of Yiddish was thus of great importance, and in the 1920s Yiddish was widely used in official announcements, posters, street and shop signs, and inscriptions on buildings. Despite the "Belorussianization" policy, both Jews and many non-Jews were accustomed to using Yiddish in their daily life, and continued to use it until the middle thirties when it gave way under economic and ideological pressures. The June 30, 1934 issue of *Der emes*, the Evsektsiya newspaper, commented on the disquieting decline in national minority activities and official neglect:

This paper has been receiving letters, reports and articles every day from Jewish workers, bitterly complaining about the deplorable state of political and cultural services and reporting that enthusiasm for their liquidation is spreading like wildfire. . . . They have abolished special staff for national minority affairs on executive committees and education departments. They abolish national clubs and libraries. All this is called "raising the level of work." In Mogilev, Jewish schools are already being merged with White Russian schools; some Jewish schools are being closed.[18]

The establishment of law courts for national minorities during the 1920s was another expression of the new interest in the intricate and urgent nature of the nationalities problem. The first Jewish court was set up in Berdichev in May, 1924, and the second in Kiev a few months later. By the end of 1925, there were 15 in the Ukraine, rising to 46 by 1930.[19] Whereas the ratio of Jewish soviets to the total number of national soviets was low, the percentage of Jewish courts among all the courts for national minorities was high (63 percent in the Ukraine in 1927 and 60 percent in Belorussia for 1926–27.)[20] It has been argued that Soviet authorities encouraged them in order to undermine the authority of the rabbinical courts,[21] which had been widespread before the Bolshevik Revolution and lingered on in some places where Orthodox religious Jews were making a last-ditch effort to hold on to old ways. Some Jewish Communists, moreover, favored the "Sovietizing" role of the courts in the liberation of the shtetl poor from the influence of the "class enemy" and religious "superstitions."

The Yiddish courts were opened mainly in those towns that offered Communists the best potential for political activity among Jews, not necessarily where there were large concentrations of Jews. The process of organizing the courts was usually a long and tiring one.[22] The initiative generally came from the local activists of the Evsektsiya, who would explain the value of the courts to the local population in the form of announcements, articles, and letters to a local newspaper. Then the local authorities (usually the town soviet and court) were approached and, finally, the agencies in charge of nationalities policy. In the Ukraine, the territorial principle was adopted and a minimum of 10,000 nationals within an administrative unit were needed to merit a court. In Belorussia, the principle was non-territorial—the courts were to serve national minorities regardless of residence.

Organizationally, Yiddish courts were not independent but functioned as sections of a People's Court and were closely supervised. Inasmuch as Jewish lawyers generally refused to take any part in the work of the Yiddish courts, most of the judges were artisans or industrial workers. Both criminal and civil cases were heard by the Yiddish courts if the parties so wished, or if cases were directed to them. Many Jews, especially in the early years, did not comprehend the scale of the political changes that were occurring and did not understand the function of the Yiddish courts. Others—both secular and observant—avoided using them because they did not have much faith in Soviet justice or opposed the elimination of rabbinical courts. The Soviet press did its best to interest Jews in using the new courts, but Jews came to understand that they were not Jewish courts, but Soviet courts using Yiddish. Criminal cases dealt with libelous gossip, fighting, theft, forgery of documents, desertion, charges against teachers for punishing children, and illegal trade. Civil cases dealt with property claims, social, i.e., class status, housing disputes, nonpayment of bills, and divorce. During the period of industrialization and collectivization (1928–33), some of these categories disappeared and new ones emerged—many especially involving needy parents not entitled to state pensions or requisite class status. Of the thousands of cases brought to the Yiddish courts (over 6,000 in Belorussia in 1926, and over 20,000 in the Ukrainian SSR in 1927), many dealt with establishing social, i.e., class status— a matter of enormous importance—the outcome of which often determined the fate of a whole family. A large number of such cases involved the support of parents.

The cases reveal dire poverty, economic dispossession, unemployment, and the desperate search for a livelihood among Jews, especially in the twenties and early thirties. Many cases involved actions against declassed Jews who were expelled from towns and evicted from their apartments, those whose ration cards were confiscated and whose children were expelled from schools. Rabbis and religious teachers were accused of being tools of rich men and of causing children to suffer. Some Jews, however, continued to bring their problems to rabbis for a *Din Torah* (religious judgment) through the late 1920s. They asked, "Why should Jews appear in courts when one can reach a peaceful agreement at the rabbi's?" But those who did were attacked in the press.

Like the Jewish soviets, the Yiddish courts were perceived and intended by some to be a conspicuous symbol of Jewish national expression in the first socialist state in the world. But the meaning of autonomy diminished to a matter of language; neither the courts nor the soviets could decisively or deeply influence the development of Jewish communities since the concessions to national minorities were soon swallowed up by Stalin's drive against the opposition led by Bukharin, by the increased russification of Communist leadership, and attacks on the nationality policy as chauvinistic and harmful to proletarian internationalism. By the early 1930s, Yiddish courts were in decline. Moreover, many legal codes had not been translated into Yiddish, and it became increasingly difficult to find court personnel who knew Yiddish and had the right political or class status. The industrialization campaign also caused a great dispersal of Jews and accelerated assimilation. A new generation of Jews did not learn Yiddish and had no use for Yiddish courts. Newspapers gradually stopped discussing them and they silently disappeared. Yiddish schools, however, lasted much longer.

According to some sources, there were about 12,000 Jewish children still receiving clandestine religious instruction in the Soviet Union as late as 1929, and about 800 in yeshivot.[23] Some illegal religious schools persisted even to 1938, but by the early 1920s vast numbers of Jewish children were thrown out of *khadarim* without having any new schools to go to. Trials and denunciations of religious teachers and rabbis accompanied the closings, but not until 1930–31 was the regime able to provide a sufficient number of Soviet schools for all children—including Jewish children—and to make primary education compulsory. Up to this time, many Jewish children remained without any schooling at all. The Evsektsiya, meanwhile, fashioned a Soviet Yiddish educational philosophy and school network.

A leading ex-Bundist in the Evsektsiya, Esther Frumkin, had formulated the necessity of a Yiddish folk school as early as 1909 while she was still an active Bundist.[24] Later, after she joined the Evsektsiya, she urged the building of Yiddish schools to popularize the principles of proletarian education and Communist doctrines, but warned against "the emergence of nationalistic Yiddish deviations . . . and ideologies which are foreign to the proletariat."[25] Presumably, these referred to using Yiddish for its own sake and Zionism. Another leading Jewish Communist, Mikhail Levitan, who was head of the Bureau of Education of the Evsektsiya, in a progress report to a conference of the Evsektsiya in 1923, reported that the Soviet Yiddish schools had already done much to "become a revolutionary factor" in Jewish life: schools now remained open on the Sabbath and Jewish religious holidays; aetheistic and internationalist ideas were replacing religious, nationalistic and petit-bourgeois elements; Jewish teachers and textbooks were being purged of undesirable orientations; teacher training institutes were being established with a great many Communists enrolled.[26] However, Levitan also admitted serious problems that held back progress, including the exhaustion of funds and the struggle against Russification tendencies evident among some Jewish workers and party members.

In the four-, seven-, and nine-year Yiddish schools set up by 1923, only 20 to 25 percent of Jewish school-age children were enrolled. It was obvious that new schools could not be created as quickly as old ones were destroyed or taken over. The teacher, for example, was an important figure in the Evsektsiya scheme of things and was often the only Communist sympathizer in the shtetl who had the political knowledge and sophistication to do political work among the shtetl youth and poor. But such a teacher himself was often russified and opposed the conversion of Russian schools into Yiddish schools, on the grounds of principle as well as fear of losing his job.[27] Moreover, the old secular teachers of pre-Bolshevik days who knew and loved Yiddish were suspected of "Yiddishism" and were not hired. Jewish Communists, on the other hands, generally lacked pedagogical training and genuine feeling for Yiddish. As for the Jewish masses, they were largely unmoved by the sovietized Yiddish school, or ambivalent. Some felt that such a school, in which traditional Judaism was vehemently attacked, was more dangerous than a general Soviet school, where the propaganda war against religion would not be aimed so pointedly at Judaism.[28] Others believed that in spite of a curriculum largely drained of Jewish substance, the Yiddish school at least maintained the Yiddish language and deserved Jewish support. For a time in 1922, a transitional year, some Jewish parents sent their children to khadarim as well as to Soviet Yiddish schools.[29]

The Soviet government claimed that it was promoting national cultures, but in the case of Jews, an extraterritorial minority without a compact land base, Jewish culture with its complex history and religious and Hebraic roots, was essentially stripped down to a sovietized use of Yiddish. The Yiddish schools reflected this formulation—at first fairly broadly—but noticeably narrowed in the early bristling thirties.

The twenties were a period of progressive educational experimentation, greatly influenced by the educational philosophy of John Dewey. The approach was known as the "Complex Method," the Soviet version of the project method, in which the project or "complex" was simply a center of interest such as nature, work, and society, rather than a specific subject.[30] Communist doctrines were inculcated rather subtly and indirectly, in contrast with the more blatant propaganda a few years later. For example, in the fourth grade, a widely used text called *Arbets kinder* introduced the section on worker protection with several short pieces by the well-known Yiddish writers, Sholem Aleikhem and Abraham Reisin. However, the questions[31] that followed were not based exclusively on the readings, but involved visits to nearby factories and investigation and personal observation by the student. Typical questions were: Who owned the factory before the Revolution and who owns it now? How is the health of the workers protected now? How many hours does he work now compared with prerevolutionary times? The students divided into groups and wrote a collective composition, using ideas from the stories, their visit to the factory, and the experiences of their parents. This text also dealt with the oppressed life of Jews under tsarism—which the texts of the 1930s rarely did—compared with the improvements under the Soviet regime. New problems and deprivations were not mentioned, but many transmitted anti-Jewish canards were refuted and positive achievements of Jews noted.

The very concept "Jewish history" had no place in the curriculum, but any course in the history of the class struggle included elements describing the struggle of Jewish artisans against their employers and of Jewish workers against Jewish or other bourgeoisie. Pogroms against Jews were described not as a national tragedy but as counterrevolutionary, bourgeois weapons. In the second grade, children were warned against "non-hygienic customs such as kissing the Torah," while in the fourth grade, children learned about agriculture in the USSR and Palestine to dramatize the "utopianism and harmfulness" of Zionism.

A course in Yiddish literature was required, but here, too, Communist criteria guided the selections. For example, excerpts from the great Yiddish writers were selected—Sholem Aleikhem or Mendele—that satirized or criticized traditional Jewish life, in contrast to the advances of Soviet society.

The philosophy of the Yiddish schools, as of all Soviet schools, stressed preparation for a useful life of labor. A generally permissive atmosphere was encouraged: all punishment was abolished, and, in the early years, there were no examinations or homework.[32] Children were encouraged to study those subjects which interested them, and to do independent work without becoming egotistical or damaging the goal of collective activity. Children were also introduced to many forms of work and machines and made frequent visits to factories and farms. In secondary schools, more specialized subjects were introduced.

Dr. Boris Bogen, the JDC representative, has left a vivid vignette of a class studying coal, but spending most of their time studying the life of the miners, their hardships and dangers, the good coal does and the evil it can do:

In this school, Jews moved with their heads scraping the clouds, and had little or no consciousness of physical needs. And though the children had for sleeping quarters one small cottage in which they were huddled miserably . . . and though there were no washing facilities whatever, the dreaming teachers were quite content. When, later, we undertook to improve the housing, the teachers looked upon our work as something to be tolerated, but which really had nothing to do with the fundamentals of education.[33]

Lenin's wife Krupskaya was very influential in articulating the early Soviet educational philosophy and meshed the ideas of Dewey with Lenin into a new mix which aroused great enthusiasm in certain American circles. The Yiddish schools adopted the same philosophy and were specifically guided by directives issued to the Jewish Bureau of the Commissariat of Education at the first convention of Jewish educators in Moscow in July 1920, 75 percent of whom were Communists. The convention, in turn, was directed by the Evsektsiya to free Jewish education "from those cultural traditions that are the result of a different epoch" and to "develop among the Jewish people a communist ideology . . . and to prepare it for the rebuilding of society."[34]

Local Jewish Communists aided by the Central Bureau of the Evsektsiya and local chapters of the Jewish Commissariat struggled to rebuild and then expand the Yiddish school system. From 1921 to 1924 the supervision of the schools was in the hands of the Central Bureau of Jewish Education, and after 1924, in bureaus of Commissariats in the RSFSR, the Ukraine, and White Russia. The problem of "Jewish content" was a sticky one for all those involved and required a purging of "the spirit of Yiddishism, petit-bourgeois Folkism" and "the spirit of nationalism without the proper Marxist orientation."[35] By 1921, the Education Bureau of the Evsektsiya was claiming considerable success in replacing a "spirit of Yiddishism" with a spirit of communism. Yet the Jewish Communists were aware that no matter how much the undesirable elements were purged, the teaching of Yiddish and the use of materials from Yiddish literature were likely to have some *Jewish* value. Indeed, it was inevitable that "the majority of Jewish children who did not attend the Jewish schools became more estranged from Jewish life than those who did attend."[36] Absence of religious instruction and elimination of all national aspects of Jewish life left the Yiddish language the only experience that clearly gave Jewish students a sense of themselves as Jews.

Prior to the Bolshevik Revolution, it was chiefly the non-Zionist sector of the Jewish labor movement in Russia—particularly the Bund—that had given full recognition to Yiddish and used its literature as a way to educate and indoctrinate Jewish workers. This movement was largely non-religious and secular, and negatively linked Hebrew with rabbinic teaching, traditional religious ideas, and Zionism. Those former Bundists who joined the Bolsheviks now partly controlled the cultural institutions which the new regime sponsored for the Jewish population and brought their views of Yiddish literature as an educational and political instrument into the Bolshevik era, thus helping to lay the foundation of Soviet policy on ways to develop Jewish culture.[37] The introduction to an anthology of literary criticism and historical studies called *Yidishe Literatur*, published in 1928, acknowledges this debt, but goes on to attack the negative class influence on pre-Bolshevik Yiddish writers. The editor Levitan admits that although Yiddish literature was oriented to the Jewish poor "whose interests fit within the proletarian ideology," the literature was created by the intelligentsia, ideologically near the petit bourgeoisie and even the middle class.[38] One of the aims of the textbook was to point out this contradiction—something which apparently was never done in dealing with Lenin's own middle-class origins.

From the Communist point of view, "Jewish content" had to be drained out of readings, but the Yiddish language itself contains many Hebrew words. It is also saturated with folk expressions and idioms that cannot be ideologically straitjacketed, and with Jewish "national" elements that could not be completely purged from the materials used, especially in the early years of the Yiddish schools. A sampling of the readings in Yiddish, grouped according to themes such as the village, the town, the city, war and revolution, include works selected and taught from a Communist ideological angle, but ranging from the classical writers Sholem Aleikhem, Mendele Mokher Seforim and Peretz, to later ones such as Sholem Asch, Abraham Reisin, and H. Leivick and Soviet Jewish writers, David Bergelson, David Hofshteyn and Peretz Markish, all of whom matured before the Revolution. A textbook called *Yiddish*, compiled by Elihu Spivak and published in 1923, contained poems and stories for children on nonpolitical themes by both Soviet and non-Soviet writers, including a well-told story of the Biblical Joseph, Peretz' translation of "Chad Gad'ya" and Mani Leib's "Ingl Tsingl Khvat."[39] In the pedagogical institutes, a book by N. M. Nikolski called *Ancient Israel*, published in 1919–1920, speaks very positively about the history of the Jewish people and "the best literature of the ancient Israelites [which is] preserved and is known to the whole world."[40] But in Nikolski's *Jewish Holidays*, published in 1925, the author passed from higher Biblical criticism to a Marxist attack on "religious superstition" and argued that the aim of the Jewish holidays was to dull the class consciousness of the Jewish workers.[41] All of the writers associated with Hebrew—for example, Khaim Bialik, Yitzhak Katznelson, and Y. D. Berkowitz—were omitted.

Many important writers in the history of Yiddish literature were also excluded—figures such as Yehoash and Moshe Leib Halpern. Almost no Yiddish writer outside the Soviet Union except Sholem Aleikhem, Mendele, and Peretz were studied, and they were selectively useful mainly for their critical and sometimes satirical descriptions of the shtetl, which could be contrasted with Soviet reconstruction. One story by Peretz, called "Di Shtreimel," which was included in many of the workbooks, paints a rather unsavory picture of a Hasidic rabbi, quite rare in Peretz' work. Old religious traditions were attacked from the earliest grades on.

The study of the Yiddish language occupied an important part of the early curricula but linguistic analysis was also ideologically slanted and wrenched from Hebrew roots and borrowings.

Yiddish orthography also had its ideological dimension. Words had to be "de-Hebraized." Beginning in 1921, instead of the traditional Hebrew spellings, Yiddish words were spelled phonetically, and the five final Hebrew characters reserved for certain word endings were discarded. Even more complex than the revised spelling, however, was the lexical problem—the problem of vocabulary—which the Communists pushed and pulled in order to create a "class" language, "socialist in content and national in form." Efforts were made to show that the emergence of a Jewish working class had reduced the inventory of Yiddish words of Hebrew origin, referred to as the creation of the "rabbinic-merchant aristocracy."[42] However, many Hebrew words in Yiddish have no archaic or religious origin, and because it became impossible to eliminate all of them, they were replaced by Slavic words. But which Slavism? Jews were getting directives from Moscow, but lived largely in the Ukrainian and Belorussian republics. They were under pressure, as were other minorities, to enrich Yiddish with Russian loanwords. Were there now two or three Soviet Yiddish literatures? To paraphrase Orwell, "All languages were equal, but the Russian language was more equal than the others." By the early thirties, advocates of the integrity of a language were drawn into cultural politics and condemned as *natsdemy* (national democrats)—a serious charge at the time. No serious effort, however, was made to abandon the Hebrew script and replace it with the Latin or Cyrillic alphabets—which was the case with other minorities.

Since the Communists were interested in Yiddish solely as a sovietizing instrument, Yiddish schools were made available only to Jewish children whose parents spoke Yiddish in the home, not to every Jewish child. In many areas of the Ukraine and Belorussia, Jewish children were forced to attend Yiddish schools often against their will. The well-known Soviet Jewish writer and statistician Yakov Kantor wrote that "in 1924–1928 no consideration was given in many places to the wishes of the children and their parents."[43] The Jewish Communists themselves were divided on the issue. For some of the Evsektsiya activists it was *not* clear that Yiddish was not an end in itself; others, like Chemerisky, favored giving the parents a choice if the child knew both Yiddish and Russian; while a few, like Larin, favored giving parents complete freedom of choice. The more coercive policy eventually won out and as a result, a substantial number of Jewish children were denied admission to general schools.

Educators and politicians had different stakes to protect: the educators urged forcible enrollment in Yiddish schools because it would strengthen the Yiddish school system and the school budget, while the politicians were afraid such a policy would be unpopular with the Jewish masses.[44] The pull of Russian further complicated their task. Russian was the language of a culture much stronger than the secular Yiddish culture of the USSR, and those families who expected to move about or settle in the large cities knew they would need Russian, not Yiddish. For them, learning Russian as a second language in the Yiddish school was not the answer; they needed it as their first. Besides, a graduate of a Yiddish school who wished to continue his education had to know Russian thoroughly before taking entrance examinations to secondary schools, which were conducted in Russian. Indeed, the language problem for Jewish children was extremely difficult for other reasons. Besides Yiddish and Russian, which was taught from the fourth grade on, German was taught in the higher grades, and in the Ukraine and Belorussia, Ukrainian or Belorussian was introduced in the second grade.

Yet, despite these problems and the destructive upheavals in the old Pale of Settlement which obstructed the development of a Yiddish school system, there was measureable growth in the number of schools and the number of Jewish students attending.[45] The need for Yiddish schools was greatest in Belorussia, where, according to the census of 1926, 90.7 percent of Jews there gave Yiddish as their mother tongue. In the Ukraine, the figure was 76.1 percent, and in the RSFSR, 50.3 percent.[46] Table 8.1 shows the number of Yiddish schools, pupils, and percentage of Yiddish-speaking children enrolled in White Russia, the Ukraine, and the RSFSR, where available, for selective years.[47] No official statistics were published after 1933. In 1937, according to *Emes* of June 24, 1937, there were 30,000 pupils in Yiddish schools in White Russia, a drop of 6,501 from 1933.[48]

The RSFSR had relatively few Yiddish schools because in tsarist times most of the territory (except the western provinces) that later became the RSFSR was outside the Pale of Settlement, and Jews who lived outside the Pale were generally more Russified than those in the Ukraine and White Russia. Thus, the Jews who lived in Leningrad and Moscow

TABLE 8.1

Schools, Pupils, and Yiddish-Speaking Children

Year	Number of Schools (Primary and Secondary)	Number of Pupils	Percentage of Yiddish-Speaking Children in Yiddish Schools
	White Russia		
1922	106	10,745	22.0
1926	175	22,535	44.5
1928	190	26,020	54.6
1930	209	28,310	—*
1932	334	33,398	64.0
1933	339	36,501	—*
	Ukraine		
1924	268	42,000	
1926	—*	58,384	
1928	668	79,000	
1930	996	83,414	
1934	—*	85,489	
1935	—*	73,412	
	RSFSR		
1924	83	10,000	
1926	118	12,193	
1927	—*	6,315	
1928	129	—*	
1931	110	11,000	

*No official data available. No official statistics were published after 1933.

went to general rather than Yiddish schools. In the large cities of the Ukraine and White Russia, the Yiddish-language school was also virtually nonexistent.[49] Since the schools existed solely to attract Yiddish-speaking children and youth to communism, there was no need to establish them where Russian or another language had already penetrated. In the smaller localities and Jewish agricultural colonies, where Jews formed the majority of the population, the Yiddish schools were strong—indeed, there was no alternative except for the few scattered stubborn and surreptitious religious schools that still persisted.

Soviet writers on the subject of Yiddish schools and some Yiddish writers abroad wrote fulsomely of the achievements of the Soviet Yiddish school compared to what had existed earlier and to Jewish schools in other countries. Typical was the praise of S. Klitenik, who wrote:

. . . the rapid growth of the Yiddish schools continues . . . It is quite superfluous to point out that not one highly developed capitalist land could point out such a thing to us. . . . We are creating a Soviet revolutionary proletarian Jewish culture which is rapidly expanding.[50]

Others pointed to the baleful fascist and capitalist influences in Polish schools, as contrasted with the impressive facts about Soviet Yiddish schools. It is rather startling to note that more Soviet Jewish parents sent their children to Jewish i.e., Yiddish, schools than did American, British, and perhaps even Polish Jewish parents during the 1920s.

The conscious decision of the government to expand the Yiddish school system was made in 1925—the year of intense Ukrainization and Belorussianization—and a time of vehement anti-Zionist and anti-clerical agitation. The Smolensk Archives of the Smolensk District Communist party reveal that the party complained bitterly that their educational work among Jewish youth suffered greatly because most of them spoke only Yiddish. One report states that "completely different results may be expected if the educational work, both among the Komsomols and the Jewish pioneers, were to be conducted in Yiddish."[51] Another report describes instructions to numerous Komsomol and Pioneer units to use Yiddish in order to attract Jewish youth who didn't know Russian.[52] Shimon Dimanshtain, the former Commissar of Jewish Affairs, also confirmed the new party emphasis on Yiddish in an interview he gave to one of the leaders of the Palestine Communist party during this period. Dimanshtain himself had wanted Jews to forget Yiddish and begin to speak Russian, but by 1925 or so he too began to realize how deeply attached Jews were to Yiddish and concluded that the party must use it as a way of reaching Jews and bringing them to communism.[53]

The growth of Yiddish schools was also linked to the current fostering of the Ukrainian and White Russian language, literature, and history: Ukrainian and White Russian nationalists favored Yiddish schools as a way of preventing Jewish children from becoming carriers of russification. The curricula at the Jewish teachers' seminaries and the Jewish departments of several universities prepared teachers for Yiddish schools as well as functionaries for Yiddish courts, soviets, and collective farms.[54] Besides teachers' seminaries, there were also *technikums* (technical institutes) and professional institutes in Yiddish covering the fields of industry, agriculture, transportation, art, printing, and machine building. There was a Yiddish section in the Pedagogical Faculty of the White Russian State University at Minsk and Yiddish sections in a number of city museums as well as two Jewish state museums in Odessa and Minsk.[55]

Jewish history as such was not taught in any of the schools except in the pedagogical institutions, but was taught as part of Russian, Ukrainian, or Belorussian history. In 1928 two Jewish teachers submitted a proposed curriculum for teaching Jewish history four hours a week and recommended an appropriate textbook, but their plan was not accepted;[56] nor was any course in Jewish history offered even after the school reform of 1931, which elevated Russian history to a position of great importance and allowed the history of the local dominant minority nationality to be studied.[57] Judah Dardak, a Communist educator, proudly recalled, "The very concept 'Jewish history' has no place in the school. The general course in the history of the class struggle had sections dealing with the struggle of Jewish craftsmen against the boss. . . ."[58] The Jewish teacher was advised to highlight the pogroms as a natural bourgeois and counterrevolutionary manifestation rather than a national tragedy.

Jewish Communists may have been inordinately proud of the Yiddish schools, but within the party and state machinery, forces were churning toward radically new ideological positions. The growth of the schools was in itself problematic. The number and proportion of Jewish children enrolled did not compare favorably with other national minorities attending schools which used their languages. At the end of 1927, only 55.5 percent of Jewish pupils in White Russia, 49.6 percent in the Ukraine, and 8 percent in the RSFSR were in Yiddish schools, whereas among Germans, Georgians, Ukrainians, White Russians, Armenians, and Kazakhs, the enrollment in their language schools was close to or over 90 percent.[59] By July 1932, 53 percent of all Jewish students attended Yiddish-language schools—probably the highest point reached.[60]

This relatively low figure can be variously interpreted, depending upon the weight given to educational and economic changes, the motives and instincts of Jewish parents, the development of generational conflicts, and official shifts in policy. It will be recalled that the early experimental period in Soviet education rejected technical mastery and factual information in favor of developing and instilling a sense of solidarity with exploited masses. This philosophy was subjected to vehement criticism in 1930–31 for its ideological slackness and failure to create the trained, Communist manpower needed for a modern state. The Complex Method was abandoned in 1931, and a much more aggressively propagandistic educational philosophy was adopted, aligned with the consolidation of Stalin's power and the push for massive industrialization. The earlier philosophy was condemned as "left opportunism" in favor of the "easy-going project method" and replaced by one which stressed specialized technical mastery. Schools were now to "prepare fully developed members for communist society" by having students learn to operate machines and fully understand productive processes in factories and farms.[61] Yiddish schools followed suit. Yiddish literature was still studied, but much more narrowly than before, having been purged of certain writers who were labeled "bourgeois," "Menshevik," or "nationalist."

Coercive measures to force Jewish children to attend Yiddish schools were no longer used, yet their numerical growth continued (despite the low proportions mentioned earlier) reaching a peak in the years 1932–33, when about 160,000 Jewish children were attending elementary and secondary schools, factory schools, and institutions of higher education.[62] After that, there was no official abandonment of Yiddish schools, but a cooling down of interest and effort. The campaign against them "grew very slowly and unevenly."[63]

Supervision of Yiddish education had been entrusted to Central Bureaus of Jewish Education in the various Commissariats of Education and involved Evsektsiya members. However, after the dissolution of the Evsektsiya in 1930, there was no specifically Jewish body to be concerned with the state of the Yiddish schools or Jewish affairs generally, and, thus, however ambivalently, nobody to look after Jewish interests. The fate of the schools now fell to indifferent, local Ukrainian, Belorussian, or Russian officials, and their decline soon began. By the middle of the thirties, Jewish children in the schools were being cut off from their past, from Jews and Jewish literature in other countries, and from all substantive Jewish culture except language. The school had become a Soviet indoctrination tool, denigrating the Jewish past and provoking shame and revulsion toward all of pre-Bolshevik Jewish life. The institution that had been invested with so much hope for reconstructing Jewish life without destroying the threads of the past had become a caricature of itself.

The reasons for the decline and ultimate end of Soviet Yiddish schools are still a matter of some controversy. Schwarz found that the movement away from the old shtetlach to the large cities was one of the major factors. The larger the city, the less important was the Yiddish school. He also believed that "Ukrainization" and "White Russification," with preference to their respective schools, was "done at the expense of the Jewish school."[64] Russifying influences, too, were drawing many Jews to send their children to Russian schools. Halevy, on the other hand, argues that most Jews did not leave their traditional areas of residence for cities such as Moscow and Leningrad, but that there was an "official policy of suppression" responsible for the decline. Beginning in 1929, Stalin assumed greater power, crushed the opposition, and placed more emphasis on "socialist content" than "national form." The drive against "bourgeois nationalism" diminished the use of non-Russian languages and literatures in order to advance "the hegemony of the proletariat in linguistics." Orthographical changes had, in effect, already denationalized Yiddish.[65] Lipset believes that Yiddish schools began to decline when Stalin gave up policies of Ukrainization and Belorussianization, which had indirectly helped to expand the Yiddish system. This happened toward the end of the 1920s when Stalin began to brutally suppress "National Communists." The Yiddish journalist Ben Zion Goldberg noted the "cooling of the air" despite an absence of a new party decision and reported that it was ascribed to "the inefficiency or personal resistance of minor officials, who were failing in their duty."[66]

Benjamin Pinkus has concluded that the decline was largely due to "political decisions taken at various levels of the Soviet governmental system," including the difficulties facing pedagogical institutes in Vitebsk, Minsk, and Odessa in preparing teachers, budgetary and other financial problems, the campaign against nationalist deviation, and the processes of urbanization and migration, especially from the towns in Belorussia and the Ukraine. The "severest blow to Jewish education . . . was struck in the second half of the thirties," when purges swept away the Jewish cultural leadership.[67]

In the shifting sands of Soviet policies affecting Jews, it is hardly likely that Yiddish schools could survive when all other cultural activity was being destroyed. The purges following the assassination of Kirov in 1934 (see Chapter 14) ended the work and life of almost every important figure in Jewish educational and cultural activity, including Litvakov, Esther Frumkin, Agursky, and Veinshtain, and Jewish teachers and scholars, dealing a massive, near-mortal blow to Jewish culture, Soviet style, and pulling the Yiddish schools down at the same time. In 1937–38, the columns of Der emes "were full of items which testified to the crumbling of the system,"[68] often ascribing the problem to a negligent local official or administrator. As Jewish institutions were closed down, Jewish children began leaving the schools in large numbers. In some places, the principals had been arrested and there was no leadership to assume authority. Many schools were closed before the German invasion, and in the Soviet-annexed areas in 1939–40, Jews were pressured to attend Russian schools after a more sympathetic beginning. Any remaining schools were destroyed by the Nazis.

Soviet-sponsored scholarship in Yiddish[69] after the Revolution developed gradually, at first leaving the field to "bourgeois" scholars, then building its own superstructure. As an officially recognized minority in the Ukrainian and Belorussian republics, Jews were encouraged to take part in what was called "Soviet cultural construction."[70] However, as with all other aspects of Jewish culture, the absence of a Jewish territorial base and compact population area, combined with the disdain for Yiddish among many intellectuals, seriously limited the building of Yiddish-language scholarship. When the work first began, in the early twenties, it was largely to standardize Yiddish spelling, grammar, and terminology, including the phonetic spelling of Hebrew words, under the leadership of Isaac Zaretsky. During the Belorussianization drive, a Jewish Department was created within the Institute for Belorussian Culture in 1924 in Minsk, later upgraded into an Institute within the Belorussian Academy of Sciences. Commissions were established in history, literature, language, and economics-demography. Government support for Belorussian and Jewish culture were both welcomed and needed.

By the middle of 1926, there was enough material in Yiddish for the first issue of the academic journal of the Jewish Department called Tsaytshrift, hailed as a major event by Soviet Yiddish scholars, and reflecting great hope for Jewish culture and scholarship in Belorussia.[71] A second issue came out in 1928, with contributions from scholars in

Leningrad (Zinberg and Ginsburg), Kiev, and Moscow, and from Max Weinreich, a founder of YIVO (Yidisher visenshaftlekher institut—Institute for Jewish Research) and Israel Sosis. A Marxist historian and ex-Bundist, Sosis was now a member of the Evsektsiya and headed the historical commission. His most important work on Jewish history is *The History of Jewish Social Trends in Russia During the Nineteenth Century*, published in 1929 in Yiddish. While he stresses economic forces in the intellectual, social, and ideological ferment involved in the Haskalah period and during the rise of socialist and Zionist parties at the end of the century, the work is well-rounded and shows a grasp of the complexities of Jewish life in Eastern Europe.[72] He refuses to divide Jews into exploiting and exploited classes and avoids the doctrinaire polemical tone generally found in Communist literature. Sosis' book came out just one year after the Evsektsiya conference in 1928 demanded an end to the previous "ideological slackness" and the subordination of Jewish scholarship to the needs of "militant Marxism", and contains an unsigned preface warning the reader not to be misled by "basic defects" and "errors" of the author.[73]

One of Sosis' most ambitious projects was to collect *Responsa* literature bearing on Jewish social conflict, a small part of which appeared in *Tsaytshrift's* second issue—a high water mark in efforts toward Jewish cultural autonomy, according to one scholar.[74] The literature commission stressed folklore and research on the Yiddish classics of the nineteenth century.

The Ukrainian counterpart of Minsk developed somewhat later mainly because of considerable anti-Jewish feeling and because the Ukrainians "had to be prodded to help their minorities," but Jewish scholarship there "proved to be the most strongly based and the longest lasting."[75] A "Chair for Jewish Culture" was upgraded into an "Institute for Jewish Culture" in the Ukrainian Academy of Sciences in Kiev in 1929. At first headed by Nahum Shtif, who also edited its first semiacademic journal, *Di yidishe shprach*, the Institute is largely associated with the name of Joseph Liberberg, a party member and capable administrator. Liberberg succeeded in expanding the work in Kiev to Odessa, and in founding a bibliographic center with all-Union coverage and a press archive for Jewish newspapers and periodicals from all over the world.

In the Russian Republic, organized Jewish research based itself on the universities, but the research at the University of Leningrad was done in Russian—not acceptable to the Jewish activists—while in Moscow, the research in Yiddish was carried out on a smaller scale than in Minsk and Kiev. The framework was provided by Jewish sections of the pedagogical faculties of the Second Moscow State University and the Communist University for the National Minorities of the West, whose members formed a scholarly society, the "All-Russian Society for Studying the Jewish Language, Literature, and History." The leading figure in the society was Moishe Litvakov, the editor of *Der emes* and zealous advocate of carrying class war into all branches of Jewish culture. His position and the time—1928—"a time of increasing political harshness" lead one to "assume that there was a political raison d'etre for the new organization."[76] This was also the year of the Second All-Union Conference of Jewish Cultural Workers in Kharkov. Over forty delegates attended and there must have been lively debates, but these were not reported. What emerged was Litvakov's views of Soviet Jewish scholarship strained through the hardening screen of Soviet ideology. Jewish scholarship is viewed, not as a branch of worldwide Jewish scholarship, but like Soviet scholarship generally—a weapon in the class struggle. Older Jewish scholars and writers such as Simon Dubnow and Ahad Ha'am, as well as YIVO scholars and existing independent societies in the Soviet Union, are attacked for serving "reactionary" and bourgeois interests. The reviews of foreign Yiddish publications were to become negative "to the point of viciousness."[77]

In 1929, Max Erik, an outstanding scholar of Yiddish literature from Poland, who settled in the Soviet Union, and Yakov Kantor, a demographic specialist and statistical analyst, did an important analysis of the 1926 census data of Jews in the Ukraine, but, as Alfred Greenbaum has said, "From 1929 on, Soviet Jewish scholarship was increasingly affected by the contemporary political and ideological problems of Soviet intellectual life . . . [and] for Soviet-sponsored writers, publicists, critics and scholars there was . . . growing pressure to conform or at least to pretend to be in tune with the new society. For scholarship in general the criteria of objectivity and autonomy were now discredited." Objectivity was to be exposed as a facade for hostile class interests. The social sciences and humanistic disciplines were now to "fight the remnants of the old society at home and its bourgeois allies abroad."[78] Anticipating these changes were the purges in the academies of science in the Ukraine and Belorussia to counteract allegedly subversive "nationalism." The two prerevolutionary Jewish societies, the Jewish Historical-Ethnographic Society and the Society for the Spread of Enlightenment (or Promotion of Culture) among the Jews of Russia (OPE), which published material in Russian and continued their work after 1917, were closed down late in 1929, after which time Jewish scholarship came more and more under party control. Yiddish literature similarly began in a bloom of hope which began to wither in the late twenties.

9

Yiddish Literature and Theater, 1917–30

I have come from the baths; one has to keep washing and purifying oneself here if one wants to avoid the extreme limits of life.

MOISHE KULBACK

A profoundly important aspect of Soviet Jewish culture was Yiddish literature, and the dangling of hopes for expanding Jewish cultural expression in the Soviet Union is no more poignantly shown than in the experience of Soviet Jewish writers. Early dreams of a great flowering of Yiddish literature after the Bolshevik Revolution were shared both by young Soviet writers and older writers who had left the country and returned several years later. The most creative figures, who became known as the Kiev Group—David Bergelson, Der Nister, Peretz Markish, David Hofshteyn, Aaron Kushnirov, and Leib Kvitko—had started their literary careers before World War I.[1] They were deeply rooted in Jewish life and classical Yiddish literature, and were in close touch with Yiddish writers and literary developments in the great Yiddish centers, Warsaw and New York. The upsurge of hope after the March 1917 Revolution also inspired a belief that writers would be able to experiment with new styles and forms befitting the new age.

The outbreak of the Revolution seemed to many poets and artists to be the last great earthly struggle that would deliver men and reshape human life everywhere. A Promethean faith gripped many writers, composers, and artists, as well as Marxists like Trotsky with his "limitless creative faith in the future" and confidence in man's ability to raise himself to a new plane, to create, if you please, a superman."[2]

The early years, from 1917 to 1928, have been described as years of "searching" in Soviet literature, years in which there was a relatively wide tolerance of writers and their work, an atmosphere in which literary problems could be debated and in which writers could work without the restrictions of an official writers' organization.[3] Writers were searching for new forms and styles, for a renewal of literature in the wake of the immense changes and sense of hope the Revolution had aroused. This phase of natural growth and spontaneous experimentation seems to have reflected Lenin's conviction that art is not a weapon wielded by a party or class but "belongs to the people," and "ought to be intelligible to these masses and loved by them." He rebuked those "who have been soaring and soaring in the empyrean of 'proletarian culture'" and instead, reminded party workers that "much real dirty work remains for us to do in order to attain the level of an ordinary civilized state of western Europe."[4] Universal literacy and the accessibility of all great art to the Russian masses were the primary goals sought by Lenin. He did not develop a systematic philosophy of aesthetics, as Trotsky did, but there seems no question that he did not want to put art into an ideological straitjacket.[5] This flexibility and openness determined the first phase of revolutionary Russia's groping steps in art and literature and freed writers from the coercive power of the state and party doctrine. The somewhat permissive atmosphere was also the result of Bolshevik concern with political consolidation and economic reconstruction and an expression of the relatively optimistic and humanistic reading of Marx's theories of culture by men who "insisted that a new culture must follow rather than precede a new proletarian society." Until the advent of such a society, the arts were obliged to "absorb the best from past culture and provide an independent reflection of reality in a complex era of transition."[6] Although controls began to set in quite soon, even at the time of Lenin's death in 1924, two-fifths of all publishing was outside government hands.[7]

A precursor of the subsequent "proletarian culture" was the brilliant theorist and critic Alexander Malinovsky, better known as Bogdanov, who had joined the Bolsheviks in 1903 and helped edit their journal *Novaya zhizn (New Life)*. Bogdanov believed that the ultimate key to the future lay in the technological and ideological culture of the future, already being created by the proletariat. His organization for the creation of a proletarian culture *(Proletkult)* enjoyed great popularity during the period of the civil war and war communism and published twenty journals during those difficult years. *Proletkult* would soon have a new life, but late in 1920, Lenin subordinated it to the Commissariat of Education and Bogdanov himself was censured for trying to bring about "immediate socialism" in the cultural sphere, totally severed from the bourgeois past.[8] *Proletkult* was soon abolished altogether—for the moment.

Prior to the Bolshevik Revolution, Yiddish literature in Russia had displayed no sympathy for the Bolshevik brand of communism. Among the forty-nine periodicals in Yiddish, not a single one had identified with the Bolshevik cause. Even after the Revolution, in 1918, most of them were still anti-Bolshevik. It was only in 1919 that thirty out of fifty-eight publications passed into the hands of Bolshevik functionaries; by 1922, the whole of the Yiddish press had succumbed, but ideological demands had not yet become stringent. Indeed, throughout the twenties, there was a remarkable flowering of Yiddish poetry and prose as well as literary criticism and philosophy. Many of the younger writers were sympathetic, even partisan, to the Communist cause, while the older ones could look back as well as forward. The poets wrote with heartbreak about the pogroms, and their work was also filled with Jewish images and allusions that every Jewish reader would understand.

The new state took pride in its lavish support of culture, and publishing firms did not have to worry about sales or profits. Writers, too, were assured of government stipends and did not have to worry at first about heavy censorship. The artistic and intellectual creativity of the early years of the Revolution, despite the rigors of war communism and the civil war, once again prospered during the relatively permissive period of the New Economic Policy (NEP) 1922–27. Besides the strikingly original poetry and music that was created, there were revolutionary contributions to film art by Eisenstein and revitalization of the Russian theatre and ballet. Moreover, the government encouraged the return of those who had opposed the Revolution, or were noncommital, and for a time they were accepted as "fellow travelers" or somewhat less.

The Yiddish publication figures are impressive, leading one historian to observe that

Neither in scope nor in effort could parallels be found in the centres of Yiddish literature outside the Soviet Union. . . . [T]he most effective appeal during this time was the range of opportunities which [the writers] thought lay open to Yiddish culture in the Soviet Union. . . . They believed that only a government which insured the growth of Yiddish culture and literature by financial support could guarantee its future.[9]

Even during the turmoil of the civil war, between 1917 and 1921, about 850 Yiddish books were published in the Soviet Union. In 1926 Bergelson declared that Soviet Yiddish literature had achieved supremacy in the world of Yiddish letters, citing a total of 451 Yiddish publications throughout the world, of which 208 appeared in the Soviet Union.[10] In 1928 alone, a total of 238 Yiddish books was published, with an aggregate circulation of 875,000.[11] Daily newspapers and periodicals in Yiddish appeared in Kiev, Kharkov, Odessa, Minsk, and Moscow. All of this activity characterized the unprecedented creative and economic opportunities unfolding in a new society and induced a number of emigré writers and artists to return to the Soviet Union, among them Maxim Gorky, Ilya Ehrenburg, Serge Prokofiev, and the Jewish writers Bergelson, Peretz Markish, Kvitko, and Der Nister.

Yiddish literature reflected the searching and creative experimentation that characterized early Soviet literature, but was expressed through the sharpened consciousness of searing Jewish experiences: the passing of the shtetl, the agony of Jews during the Revolution, and pogroms. The rupture with a vanished Jewish life was physically and sometimes ideologically absolute, but emotionally that life could not be crushed out. Half-mocking, sometimes tender images of the past float through the early Yiddish poetry:

> In my soul a little mouse scratches
> My father's or grandfather's melody.
> But my own holy Sabbath's door
> Profane week has latched with a star.[12]

and surface again in howling pain during the war.

The beginning of Yiddish literature in Soviet Russia[13] was closely bound up with writers who matured before World War I and came under the influence of modernist literary movements—expressionism, symbolism, and futurism—and the Russian avant-garde poets, Pasternak, Mayakovsky, and Esenin. In 1912–13 a group had formed in Kiev, among them David Bergelson and Der Nister (The Hidden One, the pen name used by Pinkhas Kahanovich), prose writers, and Peretz Markish and David Hofshteyn, poets. Most in the group were well-grounded in traditional Jewish learning. Bergelson and Hofshteyn had started their careers in Hebrew, but as they turned toward Yiddish, they separated from the larger Jewish community, hoping "to move beyond the folk character of earlier Yiddish writing, its preoccupation . . . with folk motifs, references, and language." Their first important collective work was a miscellany called *Eygns* (Our Own) in two volumes (1918–20), considered "the outstanding literary phenomenon in the first years after the Revolution, and perhaps even until the middle of the 1920's."[14] *Eygns* was an anthology of poetry, fiction, drama, and criticism, edited by Bergelson and Der Nister, with special importance given to poetry. Besides Hofshteyn and Markish, the poets represented were Osher Shvartsman, Kadia Molodovsky, Lipe Reznik, Leib Kvitko, and Yehezkel Dobrushin. In their work, there is a striving to break with the classic poetic forms and with the idyllic or melancholy lyricism of Yiddish poetry after World War I, but, although *Eygns* must rank as "the first serious post-revolutionary literary achievement," and although there were certain innovations in the poetry, literary historians question whether the works can be "attributed, even in the formal sense, to Soviet literature":[15]

With eyes wide open these poets put into words the horror, the suffering, the brutality to which the people of their generation had been exposed as human beings and as Jews. Despair, the desire to belong somewhere, and the search for solutions to national and social problems made some poets both inside and outside Soviet Russia accept the Revolution; among these were Markish, Kvitko and Hofshteyn. But this acceptance was basically ambivalent.[16]

Eygns writers pondered over the aesthetic aspects of literature, recognizing the "strain between those who wanted to protect their own artistic way and others who required literature to be the servant of propaganda at the service of the regime." They were opposed to the idea that a creative person "must be the mirror of the colorful and cheerfully charged life of Jewish workers," or that the writer "must become a guide in our peaceful upbuilding and struggle for freedom."[17] They did not believe that the Revolution per se would bring forth its own literature or that the proletariat would create its own poetry through the class struggle. Six of the contributors to *Eygns* left the Soviet Union for Berlin and Warsaw in the early twenties: Bergelson, Markish, Molodovsky, Der Nister, Kvitko, and A. Katsizne; three— Yehezkel Dobrushin, David Hofshteyn, and Lipe Reznik went to Moscow. The disruptions of revolution and civil war, the material shortages and hunger as well as the future uncertainties of life in the Soviet Union, rather than ideological or political considerations, generally determined the decision to leave. In the early twenties, at least, those who left and those who remained considered themselves colleagues.[18]

Besides *Eygns,* there were other Yiddish literary journals of a high quality in the early twenties, including *Der shtern* (The Star), published in Minsk; *Di royte velt* (The Red World), published in Kharkov; and *Shtrom* (Stream), published in Moscow. Hofshteyn, Aaron Kushnirov, and Yehezkel Dobrushin founded *Shtrom* in 1922, an outgrowth of literary evenings and readings by young writers in Moscow, in which some of the Kiev Group participated; for a time, Yiddish authors from abroad were also invited to contribute. These young writers accepted the new regime but stood firmly on two issues which soon set them apart from the fiery advocates of "proletarian literature": they favored artistic autonomy and felt a deep concern for Jews under the new regime. In its opening statement, the magazine described itself as "a literary and art monthly . . . containing contributions from the best Yiddish writers, poets, and artists from Moscow, Kiev, Warsaw, Berlin, and New York. *Shtrom* aims to unite all responsible Jewish creative elements that are today forging the aesthetic values of our epoch." *Shtrom* seemed the ideal instrument to bridge both past and present in Jewish life. It has been said that "the contributions to *Shtrom* are often ripe with Yiddish sensibility and wit, Yiddish tonality and tradition. But everything is also responsive, eager toward the new Russia; nothing openly or tacitly hostile to the Bolshevik regime."[19] *Shtrom,* however, lasted only two years. Its writers were attacked by Moishe Litvakov, member of the Central Bureau of the Evsektsiya and literary commissar of the new Yiddish literature, who had already written a critical article in the first issue of *Eygns* (1919). Litvakov was to become the chief "Octoberizer" of Yiddish writers. His youth ranged from yeshiva training to philosophy studies at the Sorbonne, revolutionary agitation in Russia, and journalism. A keen and discerning literary critic, he edited an anthology of Yiddish writing in 1919 and three years later became editor of *Der emes,* the Yiddish organ of the Evsektsiya. Litvakov expected active help from the writers in strengthening *Der emes* with its declared propaganda message and when he was ignored, he attacked them for "shutting themselves up in their own world and in their artistic problems" and threatened to remember old accounts.[20]

Other harsh, strident voices appear in the work of the very young Yiddish poets, Itzik Feffer and Izi Kharik, who fought in the Red Army and became members of the Communist party. Feffer was perhaps the most "political" of the Soviet Yiddish poets. A printer's apprentice at twelve and self-educated, he became a true child of the Revolution, joining the Red Army and the Communist party at nineteen. For all his youth, Feffer quickly became "an aggressively influential member"[21] of the Kiev Group and an active propagandist, condemning symbolist and modernist writing, and demanding "plain, but firm and secure steps" from his fellow writers: "Do I have the right to sit here and sing songs, do I have the right to sing on paper? My brothers sing with axe and hammer, and axe and hammer wait for me."[22] In his later writing, especially during World War II, he affirmed Jewish life, but in the twenties he was convinced that communism would comprehensively solve the Jewish problem. When critics in the late twenties found "Trotskyist tendencies" in some of his poetry, he showed that he could skillfully adapt to official requirements and hastened to make amends. In 1930, he said "We must with sharp political poems drive away the lyrical mumble. . . . We build the poem, as one builds a house, as the Party builds its theses."[23] Some of his poems are paeans to Stalin. Yet he could not crush his own lyric gifts, though much of his poetry is full of political clichés and sardonic thrusts at the old Jewish life. Nor was he spared the fate of a whole generation of Yiddish writers who perished during the "Black Years."

Literary politics began to embitter the Soviet cultural scene in the mid-twenties and involved not only heated debates over literary principles, but struggles for control of literature and for full and open support of the Communist party. At first, party resolutions were deliberately ambiguous. However, the more ardent supporters of the regime ("On Guardists") wanted to bring literature under a stricter discipline, and in June 1923, in the first issue of their magazine *On Guard*, called for writing which would explicitly reinforce communism and help push the Soviet people into a full proletarian class consciousness.

In 1925, still equivocal, the Central Committee of the Communist party passed a resolution which, while denying the possibility of neutral art, recognized the difficulty of composing rules to govern literature. By this time, however, there were acrimonious disputes between those who were loyal to "proletarian" principles in literature and those who insisted on artistic autonomy. The dividing line was sharpened after 1925 when an All-Union Association of Proletarian Writers was formed. Simultaneously, in Kharkov, Kiev, Minsk, and Moscow—the four centers of Yiddish cultural life—there arose Yiddish sections of the "proletarian" writers' associations that wanted control of Yiddish literary life and created an atmosphere of fear and intimidation. The "proletarian" critics were themselves embroiled in bitter personality and literary feuds and in competitive struggles to appear most legitimately "proletarian."

Some of the writers at first defied Litvakov and in an open letter to *Der emes* affirmed the authority of literature over propagandistic writing, a position which was also asserted in the second issue of *Shtrom*, but its early eclectic character broke under sharpened quarrels between those who wanted artistic autonomy and those who wanted literature to serve proletarian needs and interests. The latter group won and formed a Jewish Section of the Association of Proletarian Writers in 1925 in Moscow. Their two Yiddish literary collections, *Nayerd* (New Earth) and *Oktyabr* (October) were important indications of trends to come but they did not end differences between Soviet Yiddish writers. Some of those quarrels can be seen in two Yiddish monthlies that also appeared at the time: *Di royte velt*, which was published from 1924 to 1933 and *Der shtern* from 1925 to 1940. *Di royte velt* attracted some writers who had formerly been linked with *Eygns* and had re-immigrated and so-called "fellow travelers,"[24] who were sympathetic to the regime but not fully committed. For a time, it also published works by Yiddish writers from America. *Der shtern*, meanwhile, became the stronghold of the "proletarian" writers in Belorussia. In 1928, a third literary monthly *Prolit*, the official organ of the Yiddish members of the Ukrainian Association of Proletarian Writers appeared, lasting until 1932.

Literary debates and arguments often became heated and acrimonious, blocking the development of Yiddish literature. Moreover, personal prejudices and feuds were inflamed by rigid ideological stands. The increase in all publications issued by government publishing houses contributed to the energy, often fierceness, of the literary struggle. Moreover, the absence, in the twenties, of a clear literary dogma by the Communist party helped to sustain the arguments.

The position of the party at the time was that art and literature must serve class interests, but that there is no single literary rule, school, or group that can speak for it. Fellow travelers, for example, were not to be eliminated, for the party wanted to broaden its relationship with writers who had a positive approach to the new regime. In other words, it would not insist on "political purity." The party even attacked proletarian writers and critics for their "arrogance."[25]

David Hofshteyn's turbulent life reflected the literary and political oscillations and clashes of many another Soviet Yiddish writer. Hofshteyn was born in 1889, in the small town of Korostyshev in the Ukraine, went to kheder until he was nine, then studied Hebrew and Russian with a private tutor. From 1909 he studied as an extern student in the Kiev Gymnasium for several years and then at the Kiev Commercial Institute. He married in 1914, but his wife died in 1920, leaving him with two small children. Besides his work in *Eygns*, Hofshteyn was the head of the influential Jewish cultural league *(Kultur-Lige)* in Kiev. In 1920, after the establishment of Soviet rule in the Ukraine, he left Kiev and joined the Moscow circle of Yiddish writers, becoming editor of *Shtrom*. He had greeted the Revolution with enthusiasm, but had been one of those who refused to work for Litvakov's *Der emes*. In 1920–22, five volumes of his poetry were published in the Soviet Union, including many elegies for Jewish communities that had been devastated by pogroms. He left the country in 1922, staying briefly in Berlin, but returned the following year to begin the difficult weaving that was to characterize the experiences of Yiddish writers, at first telling writers in America about great hopes for Jewish renewal after so much suffering, for "new cultural forms," and about the exciting artistic and literary activity in Kiev despite the great material hardships and need.[26]

Hofshteyn's difficulties began when he refused to recognize his "error" in arguing in favor of Hebrew. In January 1924, a group of non-Jewish writers sent a memorandum to the Soviet government protesting against the persecution of Hebrew. The memorandum was co-signed by Hofshteyn as a member of the central committee of the Kultur-Lige and editor of *Shtrom*. The president of the central committee of the Kultur-Lige called a special meeting to deal with the matter. Hofshteyn refused to recant and a resolution was passed attacking him for "having excluded himself from the family of Yiddish writers who work in behalf of the working masses." The *Shtrom* editors removed him from their staff and a vehement campaign against him was started (see Photo 9.1).[27]

In this darkened atmosphere, Hofshteyn again left the Soviet Union, once more to Berlin ("emptier than before") and Palestine. From Tel Aviv in 1925 he wrote an enthusiastic letter to the American Yiddish poet Liessen: "I am in Eretz Yisrael. This alone means so much to me that I am ready to repeat the words a thousand times. I have no others and look, meanwhile, for none, much to my great surprise."[28] In Palestine, he wrote poetry, essays, and dramas in Yiddish and Hebrew, including "Saul" and "Messianic Times." He was published in several

9.1 David Hofshteyn, 1889–1952.

journals and worked in various field jobs, but he could not make a living for his second wife and new daughter (the other two children remained in Russia) and once more returned home. In 1926 he wrote a remorseful letter to *Der emes* asking to "find my place among you who are building a new life for the toiling Jewish masses,"[29] and was received back by the Moscow writers. But the first half year after his return, he couldn't get any work and wrote a desperate letter to Daniel Charney describing his extreme want and desire to go to America. He admitted that he had taken upon himself a "great burden" because of the memorandum.[30] Soon thereafter he began working with Itzik Feffer in Kharkov and Kiev where they helped to start the "Yunge gvardye"

(Young Guard), a Communist Yiddish literary group of young writers organized around a journal with the same name. Hofshteyn now found himself compelled to praise all Soviet achievements, even to the point of describing Birobidzhan's primitive forests as the Promised Land.

In 1927 he joined the Yiddish Section of the Ukrainian Proletarian Writers' Association (UPWA) and in the following year became an editor of its organ *Prolit*. He wrote critically of the symbolism of Der Nister but disagreed with the crude attacks of the "proletarian" critics and writers, admitting in a letter to Charney that although "I take part in such things, I do so mechanically and do not feel good about it." (At the time there was a harsh campaign against the Russian writer Pilnyak, whose works warned of the dangers to individual freedom under Bolshevism.) The regime, meanwhile, refused to allow Hofshteyn's wife and child to return home. He became very apprehensive and asked his friends in America not to publish his translations of certain Russian poets in *Tsukunft*.[31] Even so, his differences with the proletarian writers sharpened and he was expelled from the UPWA in 1929 because "his errors in recent times have shown that he has not liquidated his former petty-bourgeois nationalistic interpretations."[32] A "Cycle of Occasional Poems" was published in Kharkov in the same year—an indication, he said, of adjustment to "reality," not a reflection of my "inner being." Deep within him, he began to feel the lack of genuine roots in contemporary Soviet Yiddish literature.

As early as 1926, Hofshteyn had a frightening premonition of what was to come: "The ruler of the great land, he is almighty and all-powerful . . . the choice of sacrificial victims lies in his hand. . . . Let us then . . . silently and gravely bow our heads . . . and hearken and obey."[33] His writing in the thirties did indeed become hackneyed and "obedient," as was to happen to others; nevertheless, he, too, became a victim of the Black Years, 1948–1953.

David Bergelson, one of the *Eygns* group and generally considered the greatest of the Soviet Yiddish prose writers, had also challenged Litvakov in the early period and then had to bend. He wrote a sharp reply to Litvakov's criticism of the first *Eygns* in 1919, and like Hofshteyn, refused to work for *Der emes*, left the Soviet Union, but subsequently returned. His growth as a literary artist and experiences as a Jew in a turbulent time also reflect his fluctuating attitudes toward the Revolution and the ultimately coercive power of the state against which the writer could not prevail.

Bergelson was born in 1884, in Okhrimovo, a small town near Uman in the Ukraine. His father was a successful lumber and grain merchant and something of a scholar in Hebrew religious literature; his mother, too, had literary interests and was fond of making up stories. Their comfortable home saw a lively stream of visitors—Polish landowners, Jewish estate managers, commission brokers, and others whom Bergelson undoubtedly drew on later in his stories. His parents both died while he was still a young child and he lived for several years with brothers in Kiev, Odessa, and Warsaw. He continued his intense immersion in Yiddish, Hebrew, and Russian literature, which he had started in Okhrimovo, and became part of the youthful Russian-Jewish intelligentsia. Yiddish, however, was his first language, and although he wrote in Russian and Hebrew, all of his later and greatest works are in Yiddish. His earliest stories, written before he was twenty, reveal a profound sympathy for the poor and exploited, a distaste for the vulgar, especially shrewd grain dealers, and evoke an atmosphere of futility and melancholy that reminds one of Chekhov. Bergelson's Yiddish was and remains distinctively his—spare and impressionistic. His novel, *Nokh alemen* (When All Is Said and Done)[34], published in 1913, was hailed by Yiddish critics as a masterpiece. The novel deals with the disintegration of Gedaliah Hurvitz, a wealthy, cultivated Jew and the rise of coarse, aggressive businessmen, but centers mainly on Gedaliah's daughter Mirele, a moody, restless, unhappy young woman who is repelled by the emptiness and banality of the life around her but cannot bestir herself to change it. Nothing like her had appeared in Yiddish fiction.

During the war, Bergelson did not write anything. The tsar had banned all Yiddish and Hebrew printing and Bergelson was deeply depressed by the widespread carnage. But during the first Soviet occupation of Kiev, where Bergelson lived, the central element of Jewish life, the Jewish Kultur-Lige blossomed and the future of Jewish culture seemed promising. Writers argued whether they should create a *modern Yiddish* literature or a *modern literature* in Yiddish. Bergelson argued for the former. His antagonist Moishe Litvakov was interested in a "universalistic" literature beyond a particular tradition, in the service of a Marxist ideology. Both wanted a conscious break with the past—from the atrophied shtetl and traditional Jewish life. Both welcomed new verse forms and new themes—the city, the introspective self, nature—but whereas Litvakov wanted the new art to create the new social reality, Bergelson defended artistic freedom. For him, art could follow the Revolution, but could not make or lead it. The new literature would have to wait out the Revolution.

In *Opgang* (Departure), published in 1920, Bergelson again depicts the sleepy monotony of a shtetl "with virtually no emphasis on social conditions, economic effects or political remedies," and again sees his characters bereft of meaning in life, or hope.[35] In the same year, the Kultur-Lige press was nationalized and the Evsektsiya took control. The continuing civil war and savage pogroms upset him deeply and after a brief visit to Moscow, he left for Berlin in 1921. There he and Der Nister edited a journal called *Milgroym* (Pomegranate) and Bergelson contributed stories to the New York *Forverts* and the Warsaw *Folkstsaytung*. Der Nister returned to the Soviet Union in 1926, Bergelson not until 1933. In 1926, he seems to have overcome his ambivalence about the Bolshevik Revolution by leaving *Forverts* and writing for the Communist *Morgen freiheit* and the pro-Russian monthly *In shpan* (In Harness). He summoned all of the Yiddish writers throughout the world to orient themselves to Moscow, declaring that the only hope for Jewish literature lay in the emerging Jewish center in Moscow.[36] Yet in his novella of that time, *Birger-milkhome* (Civil War), the tone is enigmatic and ironic, far from a decisive commitment to the Bolshevik cause. One critic has suggested that Bergelson "is clearly trying to whip up a certain enthusiasm for the revolutionary idea . . . yet what finally strikes the reader . . . is the depth of his skepticism, distancing, and questioning."[37]

Many of his short stories published in the late twenties vibrate with subtly nuanced, varied, and fully realized characters and scenes he had observed: the decline of the little Jewish towns and traditional life, the chaos of the civil war, the heavy weight of anti-Semitism, shifting political loyalties, idealistic motives clashing with survival needs. Nevertheless, individual life stories remain idiosyncratic and never fall into stereotypical images. In *Penek* (1932), the social injustices in the shtetl are attacked along class lines through the sharpened perception of a child—Bergelson's first clearly Marxist critique of the social structure of a shtetl. In 1933, he went to Birobidzhan for two months and wrote an enthusiastic account. He then returned to Moscow, apparently convinced that the future of Jewish life would develop best under Soviet communism. Shmuel Niger, the Yiddish literary critic, describes this optimism: "The new Bergelson is new in the sense that he wants to persuade us and himself that his dissatisfaction with the world is a class feeling, that there are no ugly and fine individuals, only ugly and fine social classes; he is new in the sense that he strives to become an optimist, a believer."[38] In the course of the subsequent ever-tightening Stalinist censorship, apparent in the second volume of *Penek* and later, Bergelson shifted as did other writers, trying to find official acceptance, at times demeaning himself, swallowing self-regard and his own strict literary standards, finding some release during the more relaxed war years when he became active in the Jewish Antifascist Committee (see Chapter 17). All of his efforts, however, proved unavailing. He was arrested in 1949 and executed in 1952, together with all of the leading Jewish writers and intellectuals of the time (see Chapter 22).

Markish and Kvitko also left the country in the early twenties and returned several years later, by which time they could no longer write with the former artistic freedom—and ambivalence—or for a small literary elite. The artistic autonomy of *Eygns* could not mesh with the growing conformity heralded by Litvakov and other literary commissars. Peretz Markish, the most colorful, impetuous, and talented of the Kiev Group poets, struggled against these pressures, as did the others. Markish was born in Polonnoe, Volhynia, received a traditional Hebrew education, and sang in a synagogue choir for several years. He was drafted into the Russian army during World War I and served until he was wounded. In Kiev, shortly after the outbreak of the Revolution, he met several Soviet Yiddish writers; later in Warsaw, he was associated with *Di Khaliastra* (The Gang), a group of modernist writers. He was strongly drawn to the stirring idealism of the Revolution, that was sweeping away the old moldering life and promised a reborn world. But weaving or cutting into his exuberance are tones of sadness, even despair. During 1921–26, while he was in France and Poland, he wrote again and again of the pogroms in the Ukraine. He returned to Russia in 1926, full of ardor for the new order and eager to take his place in a communist society, but he was soon caught up in the disputes and feuds that raged on in the mid-twenties (see Photo 9.2).

Litvakov insisted that "the folkloristic beauty" of Jewish culture be separated from and safeguarded against "the reactionary laminations" that had accumulated over the years.[39] The model that was held up at the time was Elie Shekhtman, who "has rearmed himself and is drawing nearer to proletarian literature: in his novel *Ploughed Furrows*, he has rid himself of his former 'objectivism,' of his petit-bourgeois 'humanism'; instead of bewailing the decline of the rich, he now justifies

9.2 Peretz Markish, 1895–1952.

their annihilation and extinction."[40] Some of the militantly politicized critics and writers were undoubtedly compensating for being "latecomers"—Jews of petit-bourgeois origin and traditional Jewish upbringing, or emigrés, and expressing early sympathy for the Bund or Trotsky, which they now had to expunge. In 1927, the UPWA declared that "all vestiges of nationalistic afterpains that are still in evidence among Jewish writers, and which can only lead to isolationism and helplessness, must be eradicated."[41] Markish was one of the first of the important Soviet writers to feel the criticism of the proletarian attackers, first for his story "Kustars," which appeared in *Di royte velt* in 1928 (Number 10). He referred to this later in a letter to Opatoshu when he referred to himself as "having been put under a kherem" (ban). The story was described as "anti-Soviet," but Markish did not capitulate and a commission of writers in the Ukraine selected by the party judged that it was a good story, worthy of being published in a large edition of 20,000.[42] In the same year, Markish was attacked by Litvakov—who was himself possibly trying to curry favor with "proletarian" critics—for the "political error" of having earlier contributed to the less politically constrained journals. In 1929 Markish was again subject to attacks. Meanwhile, in April 1928, the official organ of the Yiddish members of UPWA, *Prolit*, began to appear. Jewish proletarian writers' associations were also active in Moscow, Kiev, and Minsk, and were generally supported by the Evsektsiya. Very possibly more insecure than their Russian superiors, these Yiddish subcommissars "sometimes forced themselves to act against their own inner convictions and therefore with special venom."[43]

These literary struggles and intensified arguments among Jews in other fields reflected the larger Soviet cultural scene, which by the midtwenties witnessed vitriolic debates over the nature of art, cinema, theater, and music as well as literature in a socialist society. In the early twenties Bogdanov's Proletkult movement generated doctrinaire, aggressive organizations of "proletarian" writers, musicians, and painters who attacked those trying to preserve artistic freedom. In literature, the proletarian groups organized their first conference in 1925 as a forum to attack "fellow travelers," advocates of "bourgeois" values and individualism and to drastically redirect and control culture. The party meanwhile remained officially aloof, but the Russian Association of Proletarian Writers (RAPP) demanded strict party control of literature and began a relentless persecution of some of Russia's greatest writers: Boris Pilnyak, Eugene Zamyatin, and Vladimir Mayakovsky. It also attacked Gorky and drove Isaac Babel into silence. Hundreds of manuscripts lay unprinted in the state publishing house because RAPP disapproved of their contents and authors.

This polarization between "left" and "right" factions in the arts during the mid-twenties was partly a generational struggle between young militant Communists and older, culturally sophisticated Bolsheviks, partly the result of Stalin's growing power and the emergence of a bureaucracy submissive to him.

Some writers like Markish admitted some of their errors, but also rejected ridiculous charges. Others courageously held to the integrity of literature, but then had to bend if they wanted to work at all, indeed to live. One critic has concluded that "It is hard . . . to estimate the extent to which the 'campaigns of correction' suffered by Yiddish writers were a sort of charade to which critics drove themselves and the extent to which the critics genuinely believed their simplistic slogans. Probably both."[44]

The effects of these campaigns on the writers were permanently harmful. In the degradation of standards and nerve-shattering anxieties that poisoned a writer's personal and creative life, literary freedom became impossible. Writers lived increasingly in an atmosphere of distrust, fear, tension, and sometimes betrayal. The self-censorship that is at the core of every writer of integrity became tainted with fear and the pressure to please a hierarchy of critics and editors. "Alien class tendencies" and "dangerous ideological elements" had to be intuited by writers, and removed; or they were combed out by editors, who then held the author's ideas as hostage against the future. It is impossible to know how much was written for the desk drawer, in crushing secrecy and silence. One can only guess at the emotional and physical toll exacted by the strains and cruelties of living such splintered lives.

Specifically, what faults did the "proletarian" critics find in Yiddish literature of the time? One of the active writers and critics in the "proletarian" camp summarized some of the more glaring literary sins:[45]

1. The trend toward individualism and symbolism, as writers cut themselves off from "real life";
2. Idealization of gradually disappearing classes and emotional involvement in their fate;
3. A passive attitude toward "our reality";
4. Epicureanism and glorification of the passing moment;
5. Lack of self-definition, neutralism, going along at a distance—a general evil.

To these "sins" we may add the continuing attacks on "nationalist" and "petty-bourgeois" deviations and the ever larger list of "sinners." Markish, Shmuel Halkin, Der Nister, Lipe Reznik, Leib Kvitko and Moishe Kulbak became vulnerable. A few weeks after Kulbak returned to the Soviet Union in 1928, he wrote an Aesopian postcard to a friend in Vilna: "I have come from the baths; one has to keep washing and purifying oneself here if one wants to avoid the extreme limits of life."[46]

A climax in the ideological struggle between "proletarian" critics and

writers and their adversaries occurred in 1929, a time of forced industrialization and collectivization and merciless purges of "nationalist"
party members, especially in the Ukraine and Belorussia where most
Yiddish writers worked. By this time, any pessimistic views about the
condition of Jews in the Soviet Union and doubts about the new order
were declared harmful. References to pogroms were "nationalistic";
symbolism and other nonrealistic literary styles were considered re-
gressive and dangerous.[47] Praise for party leaders was strongly encouraged, creating a lot of bombast and empty rhetoric. Contacts with Yiddish writers outside the Soviet Union were disturbed or broken off.[48]
There was also, in 1929, the ominous "Kvitko Affair." Kvitko had published a series of poems in *Di royte velt*, the journal he edited, satirizing
Litvakov for his oppressive censorship and attacking Jewish Communist zealots. For weeks Kvitko was assailed for his "counterrevolutionary act,"[49] a campaign that coincided with a stepped up attack on Pilnyak and veiled warnings to those Yiddish writers who had publishing
contacts outside Russia.[50] Resolutions against Kvitko were passed by
the party Central Committee in the Ukraine and by the Central Bureau
of the Evsektsiya. Finally, Kvitko and his "accomplices" were removed
from their editorial posts.[51] In 1930, his poetry was found to be defi-
cient in "socialist realism"; he was accused of being a "rightist" and
for a time went to work in a tractor factory. After he was reinstated,
his poetry appeared in "improved" editions—markedly hackneyed and
mediocre, adhering to formula. Later his reputation was based chiefly
on his stories for children.

When Kulbak published the first part of *Zelmenyaner* (Zelmenian),[52]
his great novel of Jewish life, in *Der shtern*, in 1929–30, he was attacked
for employing irony and sarcasm toward his youthful Communists.
Litvakov himself was not immune and came under attack from the rabid
critics in Minsk for supporting "nationalist" elements in literature and
being a hidden "lover of Hebrew." Der Nister's remarkable story in
the symbolist genre, "Unter a ployt" (Under a Fence),[53] first published
in *Di royte velt* in 1929, was assailed as "reactionary." In the same year,
at a public meeting honoring Markish's great epic of Jewish life in the
Pale of Settlement during World War I and the Bolshevik Revolution,
Dor oys, dor ayn (A Generation Goes, A Generation Comes), Litvakov
attacked Markish for having a "national apologetic point of view," for
singling out only Jews as heroes and neglecting the class struggle in
the shtetlach. Markish admitted "a few errors," but rejected the idea

that he was obliged to have non-Jewish revolutionaries in his work. "In a Russian story," he said, "where Russian revolutionaries are described, there are no such arguments."[54] Indeed, as Chone Shmeruk has pointed out, "Markish, and surely other Jewish writers as well, lacked the proper artistic tools and background to create non-Jewish heroes . . . [which would have been] mere shadows compared with Jewish figures of undiluted vitality," a problem Litvakov surely understood.[55] Yet Litvakov now had to defend himself against the "young 'proletarian' critics [who had] no faith in him."[56]

The writers suffered under the buffetings and trials of 1929. In a letter to Opatoshu, Markish deplored the fact that "many ugly things reported in the press in my name are lies, but not one word has appeared in sympathy with Leivick,"[57] who had left *Morgen freiheit* over the issue of the Arab riots in Palestine. But within the country, Markish was becoming "cautious in the selection he made" and "introduced textual changes" in collecting earlier poems so as to meet anticipated critical tests.[58] Other writers, too, were apprehensive. Hofshteyn, for example, sometime in 1929, wrote to Liessen, urging that he not publish his Yiddish translations of Russian poets in *Tsukunft*. "Now," he wrote, "is no time to bargain. I'm sending you a clipping which will make clear how it goes for those who write for the outside press."[59] This was apparently the third time Hofshteyn had made this request. His wife and child were still in Palestine, unable to return, and Hofshteyn was struggling to earn a living, bowing to new pressures while keeping some shreds of his integrity. His dilemmas were surely felt by many other writers at the time. He had not only abstained from attacks on his friend Kvitko because of their abusive character, but had courageously defended him in a letter to many writers and functionaries, including Litvakov. Yet in March 1928 he had joined *Prolit* and become its literary editor and general factotum for a short time. "I have a secretary, a phone, and an office," he wrote to Charney somewhat sheepishly, and, ashamedly, am "making concessions."[60]

Der Nister in the same year already saw himself suffering terrible punishment in his remarkable story "Unter a ployt." Der Nister (see Photo 9.3) was born in Berdichev and grew to adulthood steeped in Hebrew studies and cabalistic lore. Well before the First World War he had gained a reputation as a rare literary artist in the symbolist tradition, increasingly the target of proletarian critics. He wrote in the secretive, concealed way of the mystic Nachman of Bratzlaver, a style

9.3 Der Nister (Pinkhas Kahanovich), 1884–1950.

which gave rise to the pseudonym by which he is generally known—
Der Nister, or the hidden one.

Many of the Soviet Yiddish writers identified the shtetl with stagna-
tion and religious superstition, but not Der Nister. Living in relative
seclusion and often penury, he continued to write tales of the fantastic
and mystical, going even beyond Peretz in seeking the deep mysteries
of cabalism, and refusing to harness his work to Communist doctrine.
His marvelously complex and suggestive "Unter a ployt," published in
1929, was called by a proletarian critic "the most reactionary in all his
questionable work."[61] In the 1930s he had to turn to his brother in
Paris for financial help, and for a time, justified his existence as a writer

by writing reportage—"technical work," he called it, "which required his soul to be turned upside down."[62]

Der Nister never rushed to join the chorus of praise for Stalin and everything in the Soviet system. Even as critics found his early work full of "veiled hints and secret allusions," which concealed his "wavering irresolution in regard to the revolution," Der Nister remained silent.[63] For years he did not publish anything. His novel *Di hoypt shtet* (Capital Cities), published in 1934, describes vast reconstruction projects in the fashion of the thirties, but there is no reviling of the Jewish past which other Jewish writers felt compelled to demonstrate. His great masterwork, *Di mishpokhe Mashber* (The Mashber Family), a rich, vividly rendered story of Jewish life at the end of the nineteenth century, deals centrally with the profound spiritual struggle of God-seeking Hasidim. After many unsuccessful efforts to "turn his soul upside down," in moving from symbolism to realism, he finally "found a way," as he wrote to his brother. "I want to give my all to this book. It includes my whole generation—what I saw, lived,and imagined. . . . [I]f I do not write [this book], the man within me is destroyed . . . I am erased from literature."[64] Only one volume of the three-volume work was published in the Soviet Union in 1939.[65] Toward the end of the war, Der Nister was caught up in the momentary hope for a Jewish home state in Birobidzhan, and went there for a short time (see Chapter 22), but soon "decoded the signs" of the shattering of the hope and returned to Moscow.[66] In 1950 he perished in a prison camp.

In the correspondence of the twenties between these writers and their friends in the United States, the literary and ideological conflicts are alluded to, sometimes openly deplored, sometimes muted. One can also feel the pulls, pushes, and self-divisions of the writers. Hofshteyn, for example, "absorbed in penance days," once more considers the possibility of leaving the Soviet Union, but knows he cannot leave again. Litvakov had warned that there would be not just a "wall" between him and other Yiddish cultural activists, but an "abyss". Yehezkel Dobrushin writes to Leivick about the intense interest in literature, the many books and the growth of libraries, the "huge appetite" in schools for readers, and his great hopes for the future of Yiddish literature and folklore research; Kvitko writes of his hardships in Hamburg, working as a longshoreman from six to five, living in a dangerous neighborhood, in need of some money (he returned to Russia in 1925). Nahum Oyslander writes to Leivick of the earnest "searching" of Yiddish writers to find a new way, of his belief that the many discussions and literary gatherings are a demonstration of such searching; and his regret over the "unnatural and awkward" rupture between some American Yiddish writers and Soviet writers. Hofshteyn writes to Niger that his criticism and separation have caused "a great heartache to many intellectuals here," then goes on to make several requests, including sending to Palestine his *Purim shpiel*, which cannot be published in the Soviet Union. Markish writes that "people here love a writer, that he [the writer] has it better here than in the whole world if he will only work and leave politics to others," and admits that he didn't find the cultural atmosphere in Warsaw congenial, yet the first years of his return to the Soviet Union were "very difficult because [he] had to adjust to strenuous literary debates and discussions." The production of Peretz' "A Night in the Old Market" arouses intense debate, which is described in several letters. There are harsh words about "that worm-like Litvakov" and the "renegades" associated with him, frequent expressions of gratitude for gifts of money and books from the American writers and gossip about the Moscow State Theater. In a letter from Dobrushin to Leivick, there is a reference to Hofshteyn's critical review of Leivick's "Falling Snow" in *Der emes* (May 9, 1926), Dobrushin's fears that Hofshteyn is "disoriented," and that writers are tempted to "prod him about all his transgressions." Dobrushin asks Leivick why he "is so far from *Di royte velt*, which," he claims, is getting "better and better"; he also wants writers to take a stand against the "bluff-accomplishments of Zionists" and "exhaust the sweet nationalism that has begun to water down our literature and divert it from its hard galut [Diaspora] reality."[67] All of the letters from the Soviet writers invariably end with the urgent plea, "Shreib, shreib!" (Write, write!).

Some of these writers had known each other before the war; some had answered the call of their friends and visited the Soviet Union. For a time Menachem Boraisha, Leivick, Mani Leib, and Abraham Reisin wrote for the *Morgen freiheit*, creating great enthusiasm for Soviet Yiddish writers, while the creative work of American Yiddish writers was published and studied in the best Soviet journals. Even after Leivick and Opatoshu, for example, became critical of Soviet work, Oyslander and Dobrushin encouraged them to offer their works for publication in Soviet journals. There was even discussion of a joint work in modern

Yiddish literature and a joint organization, but toward the end of the twenties, Soviet power over the arts, especially literature, was too restrictive for such a venture.[68]

By this time, repressive controls and censorship began to contract the whole field of Soviet literature, Yiddish and otherwise, and the greatest writers of the time—Pasternak, Mandelshtam, Akhmatova, Paustovsky, Tsvatayeva, among others, suffered in various ways. However, in a society where the arts—especially literature—have such immense importance and are so passionately cherished by the people, and where the tradition of pre-Bolshevik Russian literature has been so revered, a large body of privately written, unpublished, underground literature has developed parallel with repression—circulated clandestinely or smuggled out abroad.[69] Among the Yiddish writers, too, such works "for oneself alone" have been produced, away from the prying eyes of censors, expressing their deepest and truest interests, themes, and creative impulses. Some of these were shown to close friends who later emigrated to Israel. The writer Eliezer Podriachik, for example, has written of the "hidden archives" he himself has seen and read, of a work on Sabbatai Zevi by Kushnirov; of several parts of a work by Der Nister called *Fun finftn yor* (From the Fifth Year), dealing with the Revolution of 1905 and a disappointed revolutionary who seeks solace from tormenting questions in a mystical religious quest leading to cabalism. He has also disclosed Marrano-like phrases and references from Biblical and Jewish historical themes and heroes deftly tucked away in socialist-realistic stories required in the thirties.[70] Fine lyric poetry can be found in otherwise toneless praise of Stalin, and a "spiritual richness" reminiscent of the best in Yiddish literature in underground works.[71]

On the general Soviet literary scene, writers like Zamyatin and Pilnyak who were repelled by the soulless bureaucrats and machine madness that characterized the Five Year Plan, and who could no longer write freely, fell under stepped-up attacks by RAPP, which increased its grip on literature as it waged "vicious warfare" against "neobourgeois and kulak" literature, all the while enjoying the full support of the party.[72] In connection with these campaigns, the Soviet journal *Literaturnaya gazeta* stressed that in the expression "Soviet writer," the adjective was "not a geographical but a social concept," that Soviet writers were those who involved themselves and their work with socialist reconstruction.[73] In anticipation of blows to come, many writers began to slide into demeaning, protective self-criticism and self-censorship which were to reach grotesque proportions in the thirties.

Perhaps the most shining moments in the generally bleak history of Soviet Yiddish culture are to be found in the Yiddish theater. Especially bright was the beginning in 1919 after the very long tsarist ban on the Yiddish theater. In the thirties, when there were twenty state Yiddish theaters, Shlomo Mikhoels, the great actor of the Moscow Yiddish State Art Theater (GOSET), looked back wistfully to the beginning: "In the era when worlds perished and new worlds took their place, a miracle occurred, a tiny miracle perhaps, but for us Jews it was big: the Jewish theater was born."[74] In 1918, the Commissariat of Education's Arts Department had created a theater section under Trotsky's sister. Existing theaters were nationalized and thousands of new theaters were established for new audiences of the proletariat and peasants. Separate ethnic groups, Jews among them, were also granted theaters, and the experimental, gifted young German-trained Alexander Granovsky was assigned to start a studio in Leningrad for training Yiddish actors. The early repertoire deliberately and selfconsciously broke with the traditional Yiddish theater of Eastern Europe, but quite soon the works of the three classic Yiddish writers—Sholem Aleikhem, Peretz, and Mendele Mokher Seforim—were to provide material for GOSET's most exciting productions. Marc Chagall[75] designed many of the sets which electrified audiences and created the distinctive style of the Yiddish theater (see Photo 9.4).

For Chagall, as for many other intellectuals and artists, the Bolshevik Revolution promised a new age for art—and for a short time in 1917, there was talk of a ministry of culture in which Chagall would head the section on fine arts, but Chagall's wife Bella urged her husband to avoid any political involvement and the young couple instead went to Vitebsk, their hometown. In August 1918 Lunacharsky, the Commissar for Education and Culture, gave his approval to Chagall's project for establishing an academy of art in Vitebsk, and for two years Chagall was busy organizing exhibits, festivals, a museum, and a "people's art school" which would "bring art down into the street," and rouse painters on the road to revolutionary art. He was completely absorbed by his work and was a popular, singularly creative teacher and painter, but

9.4 Marc Chagall working on a study for a mural in the State Jewish Theater in Moscow, 1920–21. Courtesy Harry N. Abrams, Inc.

there was opposition to his avant-garde ideas among party circles and other painters and he resigned and left for Moscow in 1920.

He had already designed a few sets for plays using some of the radical techniques and effects that were to thrill audiences of GOSET: geometric forms, dislocation in space, objects and figures floating in air, slanting walls, metal spirals rising from platforms—all conveying great vitality, the dizzy whirlwind of the first days of the Revolution, and the complete overthrow of commonplace reality.

A meeting with Granovsky brought Chagall to the Yiddish theater and revolutionary innovations. Granovsky soon realized that Chagall's antirealism would create the radical changes he wanted and gave Chagall a free hand. Their collaboration was difficult at times, for Chagall wanted to decide on every detail of production, even the gestures of the actors. Granovsky's small company in Leningrad settled in Moscow in November 1920 as a State Theater.

GOSET opened in a tiny hall seating ninety people with a performance of three miniatures by Sholem Aleikhem—*The Agents*, *The Lie*, and *Mazeltov*. The audience was dazzled. While still a young man in Vitebsk, Chagall had been pained to see Sholom Aleikhem's plays acted as vulgar farces and felt that "the author's curious airy humor, which saps the firm foundations of reality demanded an entirely different interpretation."[76] His sets for *Mazeltov* had all sorts of side scenes and magic symbols on the fire screen; his cabaret railway carriage for *The Agents* was an abstract structure and his side scene for *The Lie* had a reclining street lamp, behind which an actor dove headfirst.

During rehearsals, Chagall convinced the actors, Mikhoels in particular, that his style expressed the spirit of the author. "More than once," Chagall wrote later, "Mikhoels came up to me, eyes and forehead bulging, hair disheveled. A short nose, thick lips. He follows your thought attentively . . . and, by the acute angle of his arms and body, rushes toward the essential point. Unforgettable!"[77] How far Chagall put his imprint on the entire theatrical performance is shown by his joking remark while he was busy with Mikhoel's make-up. Whoever saw the actor agreed that his dominant feature was his remarkably compelling eyes. "Oh!" Chagall exclaimed, "Solomon, Solomon, if only you didn't have a right eye. There's so much I could do."[78]

Chagall's monumental murals which filled the auditorium of the new theater also inspired wonder. These were Chagall's largest paintings in oil on canvas and were fastened to the walls. They surge with hasidic-like fervor, magic, and dance. The largest of them—*Introduction to the Jewish Theatre*[79]—measured twelve by thirty-six feet. Four panels on one wall were devoted to the four arts that, in Chagall's view, have their place in Jewish culture: music, drama, dance, and literature, represented by a musician, a wedding jester, a woman dancing, and a Torah scribe. Painted from floor to ceiling, the murals were an entirely modern work, swirling in a blaze of color and rhythm, full of turbulent fantasy and soaring lightness.

The old material provided form and content for the productions, but the old values and institutions were mocked and parodied. One of Granovsky's targets was Avrom Goldfaden's familiar *Koldunye* (The Witch), produced as a kind of Purim carnival, making the characters grotesque or mechanical, allowing the players to climb, jump, and tumble in a frenzy of movement and tension that galvanized audiences. As one theater historian has written, "The group was hurling itself against an adversary that was still vital to them; the adversary . . . was internal, for they were trying passionately to destroy the culture that had formed them. And if the enemy had not seemed so . . . lively and tough, the fight would not have been so exciting and creative."[80]

The climax of GOSET's savage attack on the old shtetl culture came in 1925, in a dramatic version of Peretz' surrealistic and controversial play *Bay nakht oyfn altn mark* (At Night in the Old Marketplace). Dress and sets suggested the grimness and decay of the old oppressed and oppressive life: skeletons in rags, the dead rising from graves, ghosts marrying under a black canopy, and the *badkhen* (jesters) screaming "Your God is bankrupt!"[81] Other less aggressively biting productions followed as the Yiddish theater shared in the glow that made Moscow the world center of theater. But, like so many other artists of his time, Granovsky overestimated official tolerance of experimental work. In 1928, the year that began Stalinist repression, he was charged with "right-wing deviation" and "bourgeois formalism." He was still allowed to take the company on a tour of Western Europe that was a great triumph, but while in Berlin, news came that he had been removed as GOSET's artistic director. His name was removed from all billboards and posters and his company now had to undergo a complete readjustment to his loss, to heavy censorship, and the constraints of socialist realism. Its exuberant energy and unique style vanished forever. Their greatest actor, Mikhoels, replaced Granovsky as director and the company began maneuvering the tightrope between ideological requirement and artistic integrity. The Central Committee decreed that:

Playwrights and directors must make Soviet youth spirited, optimistic, devoted to their country, believing in the victory of our cause, unafraid of obstacles, and capable of overcoming any difficulties. . . . The Soviet theatre owes all its successes, all its achievements, to the Communist Party and its wise, truly Marxian solution of problems.[82]

In the struggle for appropriate material, Russian theaters increasingly put on classics which could be interpreted to show class conflict or the decadence of the bourgeoisie. *King Lear*, with Mikhoels in the leading role, was GOSET's most memorable production in this genre and received great acclaim on its European tour (see Photo 9.5).

Since the theater was a "secular domain untainted by the influence of 'Jewish clericalism' and free from any possible counterrevolutionary blemish, it could serve as a perfect instrument of Soviet culture."[83] Generous material and technical resources were lavished on it. Government financial support made it possible for the first time for Jewish dramatic art to train future performers and directors in special schools in Kiev and Minsk as well as Moscow. By the mid-thirties, there were twenty professional theaters with eleven in the Ukraine alone. There were also traveling troupes, a special children's theater in Kiev, and several theaters in the farm collectives in Kalinindorf and Stalindorf.[84] Birobidzhan had its own theater and Moscow, Kiev, and Minsk had drama schools attached to their theaters. After 1935, however, the great burst of creative activity in the Jewish theater subsided during the years of the purges, and one theater after another began to disappear. There was a brief revival after the war but many Jewish theater critics and actors were attacked as "rootless cosmopolitans" and "antipatriotic" in 1948–49, and were arrested and imprisoned or killed. All Jewish professional theaters were liquidated in 1949 (see Chapter 22). The Jew-

9.5 A scene from *King Lear*, performed by the Moscow State Yiddish Theater.

ish State Theater in Moscow was last billed in a newspaper notice of November 1949. Since that time only a few traveling troupes and amateur groups have been permitted to play in cities and towns with Jewish populations.

The decline of Soviet forms of Yiddish culture was very possibly heralded by the dissolution of the Evsektsiya in March 1930, following several months of uncertainty. However that may be, one can be more certain that the economic and social upheavals caused by massive industrialization and collectivization of agriculture in the 1930s greatly diminished, indeed, all but destroyed, the possibilities for such a culture.

10

Proletarianization: Collectivization of Agriculture and the End of the Jewish Colonies

COLLECTIVIZATION of agriculture (1928–32) and the First Five Year Plan (1928–33) created vast, irreversible transformations in Soviet society and in the lives of Soviet Jews. They also mark the period of the ascent of Stalin to absolute power, the beginnings of a terror state, repressive bureaucracy, and recurring purges to wipe out real and imagined "enemies." The question whether Stalin inherited a system that resorted to violence and brutality and extended and deepened it, or whether he created a wholly new order based on terror and a personal dictatorship far different from Lenin's conceptions is still a matter of some controversy. Nevertheless, many historians interpret Stalinism as a fundamental break from Leninist communism and, thus, a discontinuity.[1] However that may be, the origins, background, and personal characteristics of each man differed sharply and each gave Soviet communism his individual stamp.

For Jews, as has already been suggested, whatever foundations or plans had been laid for a continuing identifiable Jewish life in the Soviet mold were now to be undermined, cynically exploited, as in the case of Birobidzhan (see Chapter 13) and the Jewish Antifascist Committee (see Chapter 17), or destroyed. Ultimately, under Stalin, Jews were left with no institutional base, coherent organization, or viable program around which such a life could be sustained, notwithstanding catch phrases and slogans which were intermittently flung out to quash foreign criticism, appease anxiety about anti-Semitism, or mask transient concessions. Ironically, the man who conceived and directed these assaults—Stalin—was the first Soviet Commissar of Nationalities who gave practical definition to the resolution of the Tenth Party Congress in 1921, by affirming "the right of national minorities to free national development," and by defining proletarian culture as "socialist in content and national in form." He also predicted the end of any differentiated Jewish culture and life through inevitable assimilation in his essay "Marxism and the National and Colonial Question" (1913).

Born into an obscure shoemaker's family in the Caucasus and educated in the tribal traditions and seminaries of his native Georgia, Stalin[2] had none of the broad access to European culture and the circle of cosmopolitan Marxists that Lenin enjoyed and appreciated. Despite his fixation on the attainment of power and the organization of an elite disciplined party, Lenin had had many friends among nonparty intellectuals and many years of experience in Western society. He could be and was, of course, ruthless, wiping out intraparty opposition groups in 1920–21, and resorting to terror during the civil war, but he was not despotic by nature and could bear criticism as well as be self-critical. Stalin, by contrast, was a provincial, dogmatic, xenophobic man, spiteful, and capricious, a man who pursued his grudges implacably.[3] In Lenin's time, if offended, he would sulk and stay away from meetings for days. Lenin warned his comrades that Stalin often acted out of anger or spite, that he was impulsive and rude, and, indeed, that he should be removed as general secretary of the party. Unlike most of the Bolshevik leaders who were well-educated, Stalin had been only half-educated at an Orthodox Russian Seminary. He was ignorant of foreign languages and cultures and was considered intellectually mediocre by his colleagues. Lenin viewed him mainly as a valuable and reliable subordinate, an adroit party intriguer, and a man who knew the party apparatus well. Slowly, Stalin worked to become second only to Lenin in the party machine and the Central Committee, and, during Lenin's illness (1922–23), schemed to become his successor. Frustrated by illness, and isolated from party decisions by Stalin, Lenin could not arrest his rise to power. His famous last testament, urging Stalin's removal and warning against party schism, was suppressed until 1956. After Lenin died on January 21, 1924, Trotsky, Krupskaya, and others were not only forced to suffer this concealment but even to support Stalin by declaring publicly that no such will existed.[4]

In the last year of Lenin's life, the actual leadership of the party had passed into the hands of the so-called Troika: Stalin, Zinoviev, and Kamenev, united to a large extent by fear of Trotsky, who was still War Commissar and a popular and charismatic leader. In the bitter intraparty struggle for power that followed, Kamenev and Zinoviev joined Trotsky and formed a "united opposition." "Trotskyism" thereafter became a major heresy[5] and in 1927, Trotsky, Kamenev, Zinoviev, and many of their followers were expelled from the party. Kamenev and Zinoviev were later re-admitted, but Trotsky was exiled to Alma-Ata in Central Asia and in 1929 was deported to Turkey, the first stop on his long journey to exile and death in Mexico in 1940 at the hands of an assassin.

Ironically, during Stalin's struggle with this "Left" opposition, he publicly supported an essentially moderate and cautious course in domestic and foreign policy and criticized the "superindustrializers," as he called them, in that opposition. He even opposed their proposed hydroelectric project on the Dnieper River, liking it to a peasant's buying a gramophone instead of a cow. Yet in an astonishing turnabout, such a project would become the symbol and proud achievement of his drastic industrialization program. In agriculture, too, he agreed at first with most of the party leaders in wanting to encourage and strengthen the small, prosperous farms and keep NEP while slowly adding collectivist elements. He strongly opposed the more radical elements that wanted to return to war communism. In 1925, at the Fourteenth Party Conference, he had said: "The important thing is not to incite class struggle in the village . . . to unite with the great peasant masses. . . . What we need now is not a maximum squeeze but maximum flexibility, both in political and in organizational leadership."[6] It was understood that by permitting the peasants and petty bourgeois elements to prosper, the state would be unable to increase its capital investment in industry; thus, the development of heavy industry and an industrial proletariat would have to be deferred somewhat. The Fifteenth Congress in 1927 called for greater industrialization and partial collectivization, but in no sense the imposed, wholesale collectivization that Stalin adopted a year and a half later.[7] Indeed, at this congress, following several stormy demonstrations organized by the radical Left, Stalin deceived his rightist allies and laid the groundwork for the new line of forcible collectivization and stepped-up industrialization. The resolutions for "the gradual transfer of scattered peasant households to the system of large-scale production in the form of peasant cooperatives" . . . and for "displacing the capitalist element in the village" were to become much more than verbal concessions to the more radical Communists. As interpreted by Stalin, who was left with the final decisions regarding amending the land tenure laws and the elaboration of the Five Year Plan for industrialization, the omissions and ambiguities of the resolution cleared the way for a swift and shocking reversal of Soviet economic policy.[8]

It is not certain precisely when Stalin changed his mind so completely. The immediate cause may have been the food crisis which began to reach dangerous proportions at the end of 1927 and early in 1928. There was a serious shortfall in grain deliveries. The smaller farms produced only enough for their own needs, while the more productive kulaks refused to deliver grain at the low prices set by the state. Party members were instructed to take energetic measures to extract grain. The tempo and intensity of these measures were determined by Stalin, now in control of the party machinery. As for industrialization, the low productivity and absence of capital investment would be overcome by a vast industrialization at the expense of the farmers. Since foreign capital was not forthcoming, the level of consumption of the main sector of the population—the peasantry—would have to be reduced, and the peasants, actually expropriated.

As the process accelerated, Stalin may well have determined to achieve uncontested power over the Soviet state. By means of the rapid collectivization of agriculture, the state would have economic and political control of the peasantry, and by means of forced industrialization, it would control the production, labor, and movement of masses of people. In these convulsions, the party and state bureaucracy, also controlled by Stalin, feared him, served him, obeyed him, and made him into a cult figure, but they, too, were destroyed in periodic sweeping purges, devoured not so much by "the Revolution" or Thermidor, as by a single man—Stalin.

In what was to become a titanic struggle against the Russian peasants, beginning in December 1927, raids were unleashed against their land and grain was confiscated. In May 1928, Stalin called upon party members to choose between "suicide" and rapid collectivization and development of heavy industry. At a July meeting of the Central Committee, he said that while it was an "unpleasant business," since the Soviet Union had neither colonies nor ready capital to industrialize rapidly, it had to resort to exacting a "tribute" from the bulk of its population—the peasants.[9] This frank and blunt announcement was followed by a ruthless and bitter war against the million or so kulaks, the most resourceful and prosperous peasants. Party members who showed any leniency toward them were purged. The poorer peasants were flung into the struggle against the kulaks, and in the incredible chaos and violence that followed, peasants of all classes suffered. Thousands of party agents, police, and army units were ordered to the countryside to eliminate the kulaks as a class, and in the process thousands were arrested and killed, and millions deported. Before they "joined" collectives, peasants killed their cattle, pigs, and horses and burned their crops, causing a drastic reduction in production. Official response to peasant resistance was brutal: confiscation of kulak property, deportation, and the death penalty for any "theft" of state property. These draconian measures created a famine in which five to ten million peasants perished. What the party Congress had envisioned as a stretched-out plan for collectivization was dropped for a swift, ruthless, and devastating process.

Throughout the country, toward the end of 1929, the collectivization process became more and more destructive, for which "a mass mobilization of all forces at the disposal of the party and soviet organizations" was demanded.[10] Those who concealed grain surpluses were put on trial, and "very severe measures" were taken against "those better-off elements who might attempt to follow the example of the kulaks."[11] In the chaos of vaguely defined instructions, confused peasants, exhortations to push for collectivization against the imminent threat of attack by "imperialist enemies," with poorly equipped cadres to implement the changes, and total lack of any coherent policy on organizing the new *kolkhoz* (collective farm) structures, Soviet peasants suffered untold physical and economic abuse. Nor could the existing Jewish colonies endure for long. The more prosperous farmers were evicted, imprisoned, or deported, and their property confiscated.

For a time, the Evsektsiya had maintained that the Jewish colonies would be exempted from forced collectivization and that state control of the settlements would be confined to the so-called "contraction" system—obligatory delivery of grain to the government at fixed prices—but this lasted only for a time. Moreover, at first, foreign organizations such as Agro-Joint seemed not to worry overmuch about collectivization. In fact, in 1928, the JDC created a new instrument for raising funds: the American Society for Jewish Farm Settlements in Russia, with James N. Rosenberg as chairman. This group was to advance an annual sum of $900,000 in the form of a loan for settlement purposes, in return for Soviet government bonds bearing 5 percent interest. An additional $100,000 would be an annual nonreturnable contribution which the government was to match with 500,000 roubles per year. By 1933, the society had loaned $4,725,000 to Russia, which was later repaid. However, disturbing news broke into this agreement within a short time, and collectivization inevitably struck the Jewish colonies and spread over several years.

One of the first changes to come was a report to the society's executive committee, dated August 1, 1929, noting that 45 Jewish kolkhozes, involving 3,000 persons, had been established in the region, and that an additional 2,180 Jews had been similarly resettled in other parts of the Soviet Union.[12] On August 13, 1929, there was a meeting of KOMZET dealing with materials on the collectivization of Jewish settlements.[13] Throughout the fall and winter of 1929, dispatches from the Jewish Telegraphic Agency (JTA) reported the alarming and sudden changes which collectivization and government confiscations created. On October 16, 1929, a cable from Moscow read:

21 Jewish wirtschaften in Larin region Crimea ruined because government—aid of militia arrested their livestock, fodder, even pillows for 9000 ruble unrepaid credits. Larin region owes government 140,000 rubles—crop in last two years unsatisfactory. . . . Declassed Jews receiving machinery from relatives in America. Can't use them unless they enter cooperative collectives now during Soviet "cleaning." KOMZET contemplating appeal to nullify expulsion of those receiving machinery. Emes today demands expulsion from artisan collectives of all ex-traders who are now kustars.[14]

On November 12, JTA cabled[15] reports that "Jewish colonists in Jankoy and Evpatoria regions now facing extreme repressions because of not delivering their bread to government." Dzhankoy was 79 percent behind schedule and Evpatoria, 65 percent. December 1 was the deadline, "but if they follow schedule Jewish colonists will be without bread for winter." In Odessa, "out of ordinary repressions" were reported. There, colonists gave the government 700 tons of bread, leaving only two tons for the entire year for themselves.

In the same cable, harsh measures against kustars earning more than 1,500 roubles a year were revealed. They "will be thrown out of dwellings, according to new Commissariat of Interior Project." It was also proposed to "dispossess kustars who use hired help regardless of income."

Later that month[16] JTA predicted two movements against colonization, one against "foreign religious organizations," the other "against

GEZERD settling ex-traders on the land." Foreign organizations were accused of "discouraging collective farming offenders (critics)." Clearly intending to modify the activities of Agro-Joint, ICA, and ORT, these Communists began hurling phrases such as "We don't know whether a viand of lentiles [sic] is worth a birthright," telling KOMZET to have "severer control of bourgeois ideology of foreign organizations." Members of the White Russian Evsektsiya warned that "Jewish colonies be cleared of speculants, exploiters and undesirables who have penetrated on the land due to GEZERD misinterpreting the word declassed in pure nationalistic light."

The first open effort to express prevailing views among many Evsektsiya leaders to oust "foreign religious organizations" came at an OZET conference of 188 delegates in the Moscow region on December 4, 1929, where there was a "demand that KOMZET refuse further relief for Jewish colonization from foreign organizations."[17] Avrom Merezhin argued that funds from Agro-Joint were not charity but a loan. The "internationalizing" of Jewish colonies was also urged by A. Bailin, a Jewish Communist leader in White Russia, who was identified with the effort to colonize White Russia instead of Birobidzhan. He told the White Russian Government Executive Committee that "we must now seriously revise existing Jewish collective farms."[18]

The need for tractors was apparently a key element in pushing collectivization, and colonists who required any government aid, including tractors, sooner or later had to join collectives; otherwise they could not survive. The journalist Boris Smolar faulted Agro-Joint for removing many of its tractors from Kherson, leaving only two, and thus giving the local soviet the opportunity to "force collectivization upon the Jewish colonists."[19] Fearing repression, colonists in the Kherson region began to submit to grain requisitions; many remained without bread. In Evpatoria colonies numbered 22, 60, 62, and 63, Jewish settlers were already applying for bread at Agro-Joint offices, according to a JTA cable dated November 24, 1929.[20] The same cable reported that four settlers in the Khaklai colony in the Crimea, who were regarded as "able, loyal settlers," were arrested and sent to prison for three years because they hadn't met government requests. The purpose of the arrest was "to show neighboring non-Jewish peasants that Jews also are arrested." Merezhin was trying to "moderate excesses."

In trying to grasp the full implications of these drastic measures, Agro-Joint leaders expressed great anxiety over the future. In a JTA cable[21] (from Warsaw) late in November, it was reported that the entire Kherson region was now "100 percent collectivized." The Agro-Joint central office in Kherson was closed down, and agricultural supervision was being taken over by a state agronomist. The "entire character of Agro-Joint activities must change," the JTA correspondent believed. "Helping the individual Jewish colonist now [is a] matter of [the] past because all individuals must now join collectives. . . . Helping the collectives is neither A.J. mission . . . nor is government anxious to let A.J. have free hand in collectives."

Many Jews were leaving their colonies. A colony of seventy-one in Evpatoria was being dissolved and returning to Mozir, where they had come from. A similar exodus was reported from two neighboring colonies. Others were joining collectives unwillingly. For those who remained "plain bread was now ideal." The colonist "cannot dream of meat or fats; he has nothing to sell for cash . . . the government gives him credits in seeds. . . . He has no money for shoes or clothing. . . . He has milk, but doesn't want to be considered a kulak, limits himself to one cow, and sells milk for kerosene and matches."[22] In collectives, milk could not be sold individually. Smolar found many Jewish children in the Crimean colonies eating only dry bread. A JTA cable of November 25, 1929, reported the "entire property of several Jewish colonists in Dobroye and Nikolaev region confiscated and auctioned because [they] did not give government enough grain." Jewish youths in colonies "were returning to the city in masses," according to Crimean KOMZET representative Lozovsky.[23] Depression was spreading all over the Crimean colonies, except the Zhurtchan section, which was not yet collectivized. The situation was "especially bad in Kalinindorf," where collectivization was being pushed strenuously.

In the Ukraine, the activity of Agro-Joint was not as great as in the Crimea, and Jewish colonies there were much more vulnerable than in the Crimea, where, according to Smolar, the government "has no bait with which to entice colonists," such as tractors or credits. In Jewish colonies where Agro-Joint, ICA, and ORT were still active, there were, as yet, no collectives. But, significantly, Smolar reported that in the Zaporozhe region, the government tried to take away thirty-five ICA tractors. However, they were rented to KOMZET as a delaying tactic.

Local decisions also affected Jewish settlers, as, for example, the one to expel "all Gypsies, Jews, and thieves from the village of Kosobrovsk in the Ukraine," made at a "peasant meeting when the question of 'cleaning Soviet apparatus' " was discussed.[24] At the same time, two-thirds of party members in Mozir were expelled by a "Communist Party cleaning commission," because they had assisted Jewish ex-traders in local artels and had been "helping Mozir Jews to organized themselves around the synagogue as the agency of American Jewish capitalism."[25]

Collectivization in White Russia was also forced, and as elsewhere, meant not only severe economic and social losses, and the loss of personal initiative and pride, but the loss of a distinctively Jewish character to the Jewish colonies, for collectivization meant merger with non-Jews. Jewish Communists themselves were at first divided on the issue. Late in 1929, JTA cables[26] reported that the "merging of Jewish collective farms with non-Jewish [was] meeting with tremendous opposition in White Russia resulting in split GEZERD [OZET] ranks there." Communists "with more nationalistic inclinations are bitterly against compulsory process." The opposition was branded as "right-wingers and opportunists." Internationalization of the colonies was also opposed. On December 19, 1929, a JTA cable from Moscow reported that the Jewish colonies of the White Russian collective "Razsviet" sent a memo to Minsk OZET saying that they "do not want to toil on the soil any longer," and will liquidate the colony because of the compulsory merging with non-Jews.

As the juggernaut of collectivization pushed ahead, foreign contributions to Soviet agricultural projects dwindled and there was increased official pressure to cut down or close down the activities of Agro-Joint. Those Communists who had from the beginning resented Agro-Joint's superior agricultural technology and efficiency, coming as they did from the capitalist world, were now defining the new policy. Moreover, by 1929, the Russian-language monthly organ of OZET, called *Tribuna*, which had originally permitted a variety of views, and whose character was determined by OZET, now became an outright Communist organ, "expressing faithfully the line of the party and the Soviet authorities and serving as a tool for the internationlist education of the masses."[27] The formula "Organ of the Jewish People" was also dropped from Tribuna's cover that year and replaced by "Workers of all countries unite!" OZET now began to enlarge its non-Jewish membership and was describing itself as an internationalist organization.[28] The organization also declared that there were no more poor Jews who wanted to settle the land and that industry's demand for labor made Jewish organizations such as OZET and KOMZET unnecessary.[29]

The Jewish press in the United States at the time was full of articles debating these issues and reporting growing anti-Semitism in the Soviet Union. Some were critical of Agro-Joint for being neutral about everything but resettlement and inhibiting protests against the persecution of Judaism and Zionism. Leo Glassman, a former Jewish correspondent in the Soviet Union, was particularly strong: If, he said, "the fate of the colonization enterprise hangs by a thread so thin that it can be snapped by a protest against injustices practiced against Jews . . . then American Jewry has a right to stop and speculate as to the wisdom of the undertaking."[30] Agro-Joint was also criticized for giving up relief work for "productivization."[31] Positions were further entangled by differences about diverting American Jewish support away from Palestine and the whole question of official American recognition of the Soviet Union.

However, these hotly debated arguments had no effect on Soviet policy. Collectivization went on inexorably and Agro-Joint had to adapt while trying to maintain its presence. Early in 1930 Rosen admitted that "we must adapt our plans to the general policy, which means collective ownership of fields, vineyards, implements, livestock, and barns, but not collective houses."[32] Yet he still believed that the situation in the Crimea, Krivoy Rog, and Kherson was much better than in Birobidzhan, where "great havoc" was caused during the "collectivization epidemic." However, government measures became more drastic and in February 1930, JTA reported that 70 percent of the Jewish settlers in the Crimea had gone, many forced to become members of kolkhozes. The collectivization process also spread to the old settlements in the Ukraine.

In the autumn of 1930 every peasant was ordered to hand over his entire grain crop except for immediate family needs and bring the rest to a government warehouse. The farms already collectivized were easily controlled by the government, but the situation facing the individual farmer was harsh. He was generally forced to sell his livestock in order to meet the government requisition, and thus "thinks it better to join a collective," giving it all his property, "having no other way out." "This allows the government to bend and break him."[33]

Rosenberg, the president of Agro-Joint, saw this same process engulfing the Jewish colonies, leaving Jews in their colonies with only fifteen poods of bread per person. By late 1930 the Jewish colonies in the Kalinindorf region in Kherson were already controlled by Jewish soviets, and a bread tax was being carried out very strictly. Rosenberg believed that the colonies would have to be fed by Agro-Joint in spite of the fact that the crop for the past year was very good. Agro-Joint apparently had "great difficulty" with the local soviets, and decided to close its main office in Kherson.[34]

This process was also going on in the Crimea. Agro-Joint was told not to build any more individual barns or houses, and its help generally began to lose its importance. The government budget provided the collectives with tractors and credits, yet Agro-Joint was in a dilemma. Not only was there acute need of bread, but there was fear of expulsion of ex-traders from the Jewish colonies. Moreover, the government and KOMZET were exerting continuing pressure on Agro-Joint to extend aid to Birobidzhan, but Rosen declined.

In scattered colonies there was some resistance to the severity of collectivization as observed by an American visitor in the early thirties.[35] At the Larina kolkhoz, in the office of the agronomist, several Jewish farmers who still clung to their individual farm holdings were struggling to regain good land which had been taken away by the local land commission, instead of the poor land they were forced to take. To testify before the commission would be to invite suspicion, to be pleading the cause of kulaks. The kolkhoz was also depriving them of the right to use the tractor, which Agro-Joint had given the colony to be shared by all settlers.

The paradoxes of life for Jews at this revolutionary time were also evident: bearded men ploughing fields, pictures of Lenin alongside white-wigged Jewish grandmothers, a placard of the Komsomol brigade juxtaposed against the traditional menorah.[36] The colonists told visitors of the great uprooting from their familiar lives, ("like tearing out a tree from the earth"), the early hardships, adjustments, and acceptance of the inevitable. "Mi lebt," (One lives) was a common phrase. Jewish youths, however, were fiercely loyal to the new regime and enthusiastic. At the colony of Novy Zerya (New Dawn), near Krivoy Rog, a young girl of twenty, the president of the soviet, was described as "sharp as an eagle's eye" and "smarter than any man in the village." Jewish parents were upset because their children had pledged their "viexotnoy den" (day of rest) to the shock brigades, but proud of their school achievements.[37] The youths barraged a visitor with rhetorical questions: Had she observed the construction going on all over Russia? Was there not greater development going on in Russia than elsewhere? Did she find another people who had so much to look forward to?[38]

Older and still-observant Jews feared that internationalization of their colonies would not only affect their religious life but would lead to the expulsion of many Jews.[39] They also knew that they would have to give up observance of the Sabbath and Jewish holidays. Even so, religious observance, even in the kolkhozes, held on tenaciously. Moreover, the first action of the government was disarming. Since "Collectivization Day" fell on Yom Kippur and since it was understood that the Jewish members would not celebrate the official festivities, but mark their own, the Executive Committee of the Supreme Soviet changed the date for the Jewish kolkhozes, so that the "Jewish members could participate in celebrating their holiday of their own free will."[40] But this gesture was only a deceptive moment before the coming antireligious hurricane.

The antireligious campaign began in the fall of 1929 with a wave of terror against the Russian Orthodox church and spread to all religious organizations and groups, first striking the cities, then the countryside. Religious observance was regarded as a brake upon collectivization and was to be uprooted by force. Observant Jews likewise were punished or intimidated. Already, in December 1929 in the Borisov region, there were demands that Jewish colonists who did not milk cows on Saturday be expelled as "undesirables."[41] In the early thirties, as was happening in the cities, synagogues in the colonies were converted into meeting halls. For example, in the Krivoy Rog Jewish Center, a handsome stone building that had formerly been a synagogue, an American visitor described the changes:

The raised platform on which one reposed the Ark of the Covenant, the Torah, and the pulpit were now bare. A white sheet extended across the wall . . . used as a screen when a picture was on the program. A piano stood against it. The people who filled the auditorium were attired in field or factory clothes, soiled, smelly. The huge room which had once resounded to the chanting of people absorbed in holy prayer . . . was now alive with the buzz of conversation . . . [and] crowded with the noisy animated youth of Russia.[42]

On the program were new songs and old Yiddish ballads, with new words that mocked traditional pieties. A typical new colony song dismissed the traditional Sabbath:

Oy hob ich a fatter (Oh have I a father)
Hat ehr a pahr pferd (Has he a pair of horses)
Und yedem Shabbos (And on every Sabbath)
Hahkt ehr auf dem erd (He ploughs the field with them).[43]

However, the destruction of traditions was uneven. In some of the colonies, older men and women were still seen coming out of the small synagogues on Saturdays, dressed in their best, with men carrying small velvet bags for their prayer shawls. In a number of homes, women wore white aprons, still lit candles, and served *khallah* covered by a white napkin. One former Hebrew teacher in the Krassin colony acknowledged that "Shabbos [was] his Viexotnoy Den, as it has been to all Israel, for over a thousand years."[44]

In 1932, the Yiddish organ of the "godless," *Der Apikoires,* in its summary[45] of the "anti-High Holidays campaign," complained that the Jewish members of the kolkhoz "Forward to Socialism" in Khislovitz did not work on both days of Rosh Hashanah, and that after a search of several weeks they were pleased to have found a cantor for the services. The periodical also reported that in a tailors' artel, only six out of twenty-nine workers went to work. A similar situation existed in a shoemakers' artel.

In the course of time, however, the harsh administrative measures against religion, the constant antireligious propaganda, and the fear of resisting the main tide of opinion weakened the hold of High Holiday observance. The decline took its greatest toll among Jewish youth who worried about educational opportunities and future jobs. Jewish prayer houses and synagogues diminished in number and sanctions for worker absenteeism became more severe.

In the United States, there were agitated discussions in Jewish circles over the mounting reports of religious persecution and reprisals. Typical was a report by Glassman:

But the outstanding example that impressed itself on my mind more than any other was in Kherson. . . . Here Bolshevik cruelty was brought down to its finest point: the Jewish children were told that if they stayed out on Passover, their ration cards for bread would be taken away from them. I leave it to your own imagination to visualize this. Had I not been in Soviet Russia and investigated this personally, I would have refused to believe that such inhumanity was possible.[46]

Both Christian and Jewish leaders joined in worldwide protests against the antireligious campaign, and Stalin pretended to disavow it in his much-publicized "Dizzy with Success" article, published in *Pravda*, March 2, 1930. There he blamed and condemned local "excesses" but they did not stop.

Beyond the "de-kulakization" and the deportations was the terrible, artificially created famine of the winter of 1932–33, affecting especially the southern Ukraine, where many Jewish colonists perished, but also the northern Caucasus, the Volga region, and Central Asia. Among other writers, the novelist Sholokhov describes some of the horrors in *Virgin Soil Upturned*, as does Pasternak in his unpublished memoirs:

In the early 1930's, there was a movement among writers to travel to the collective farms and gather material. . . . I wanted to be with everyone else and made such a trip with the aim of writing a book. What I saw could not be expressed in words. There was such inhuman, unimaginable misery, such a terrible disaster, that it began to seem almost abstract, it would not fit within the bounds of consciousness. I fell ill. For an entire year I could not write.[47]

As the juggernaut of collectivization charged on, the work of Agro-Joint was being wound down and certain of its assets were being transferred to OZET and the Soviet Red Cross throughout the early thirties. However, as late as the mid-thirties, kolkhozes were still applying to it for loans, technical advice on agricultural matters, schools, hospitals, day nurseries, and social and institutional planning. Some scattered courses were still being offered.[48] When an American JDC staff member visited the surviving Agro-Joint colonies in 1935, she found evidence of these services and needs, streams of visitors requesting guidance from Agro-Joint and tangible achievements, but also uncertainty.[49] It was difficult to assimilate so many disparate elements, to know how to read the fast-changing scene.

At Dzhankoy, which had been the hub of Agro-Joint activity in the Crimea, there were factories and workshops supplying colonists with lumber, tractors, farm implements, and machinery. Electrification plans were causing great excitement.[50] The Agro-Joint colony of Ratenstadt in the Kolay district had already been collectivized. Some farmers seemed content, but may have been afraid to complain. Each family had been allotted an acre for its own vineyard, and the vast nursery of fruit trees was shared in common by Jews, Tatars, and Germans. The supplies at the cooperative store were "meager." At the same time, a number of the older children were preparing for the university.[51]

At Kalininsk, one of the oldest colonies in the Crimea, an aged couple showed their home of three rooms with pride. The cheap iron beds were covered with clean white coverlets; the windows were curtained, and the plain wooden tables were brightened with colored cloths. When asked if he was able to make a living, the man said:

Oh yes, my son as head of the kolkhoz does very well, and although I am too old to work very much in the fields, I have already twenty-two working days to my credit so far this year. We own a cow; and my daughter, who is a widow, also has a cow. I have one sheep, one steer, and about a dozen chickens. . . . We have sixty apricot trees in our own private orchard. . . . We have no pigs; we are good Jews. We market our apricots and our surplus milk and eggs.[52]

The members of this kolkhoz pooled their farm implements and horses, and the Soviet farm tractor center supplied the colony with tractors, machines, plants, and seeds. The individual farmer kept his garden and some animals and could market certain products, but this kolkhoz was quite small—there were only twenty-six families at the time—and quite prosperous. Each family was credited each month with the number of working days contributed, against which it could buy some of its daily necessities in the kolkhoz store. In addition, there was apportioned out of the crop yield of the farm a quantity of wheat, barley, oats, and a yearly cash payment based on kolkhoz profits, of about 400 roubles per family.

Agro-Joint advice was still being sought on a variety of problems: technical information on agricultural problems, schools, hospitals, day nurseries, and institutional planning, but its days were numbered. Pressure to shift to the Birobidzhan project failed. Rosen made a trip there in 1934, but he was not favorably impressed with the area or the program and JDC did not offer any help.

In the same year, in a survey of ten years' activity,[53] Agro-Joint could boast of having helped over 250,000 Jews resettle on the land and retrain as artisans. In that period, Agro-Joint had spent twenty million roubles in the form of loans to settlers, already fully refunded by the government. Of the six million "non-returnable" allocations for land surveys, instruction, and water supply systems, a substantial amount had been returned. A reorganization of the credit system in the USSR had led to increasing government responsibility for financing loan kassy and subsidizing trade schools, some of which were being transformed into "Technikums."

By January 1935, the indebtedness of Jewish agricultural collectives amounting to eleven million roubles (about 6 million dollars), was written off by a Soviet decree, which released all farm collectives from debts amounting to 435 million roubles.[54] The eleven million roubles represented advances made to the Jewish colonies by Agro-Joint, which the government had been paying back.

The government, meanwhile, was steadily taking over Agro-Joint work. In 1936, out of 7,168,000 roubles spent by Agro-Joint for agricultural work, only 2,175,000 roubles came directly from the agency's funds. The rest was allocated by the government and covered by the settlers themselves.

Yet Rosen clearly wanted Agro-Joint to retain some role, and in the autumn of 1937 he thought KOMZET and OZET could take over the work of Agro-Joint, but leave it with some management role or level of participation.[55] However, the purges of 1936–38 (see Chapter 14) claimed many active members of OZET and KOMZET, and in 1938, the agencies themselves were finally closed down together with the activities of all foreign colonizing agencies, including Agro-Joint.

In summarizing twelve years of Agro-Joint work,[56] Dr. Rosen's appraisal was cool and level-headed: Life in Russia, he said, was still "very difficult, the standard of living is still very low; there is still a great deal of misery and suffering. . . . Nor has our own path . . . been strewn with roses. We have had our full share of troubles, disappointments, heartbreaks, and heartaches, from without and from within." Yet he acknowledged a "tremendous change for the better." The Bolshevik Revolution, he said, "was neither made by the Jews, nor for the Jews, nor against the Jews. Our people in Russia were simply caught between the millstones of history and were confronted by a dilemma—either to be crushed and turned into historical dust, or to extricate themselves by a determined effort of readjustment . . . to the changed conditions, no matter how painful and tortuous this process should prove to be. . . . Russian Jewry was unable to save itself without outside help." He was still eager for Agro-Joint to retain some role, but at a joint meeting of Agro-Joint Trustees and directors of the ASJFS (American Society for Jewish Farm Settlements in Russia) on January 21, 1937, he declared[57] that "as far as the Russian Jews are concerned, the job in Russia is completed—it could be completed this year or in

1938. . . . [The] government is prepared to take over the entire organization, including our assets and staff . . . and carry on the work. . . . But, because of the present international situation, it would not be wise to end now." In July 1938, Rosen himself left and the last of the Agro-Joint staff (fewer than 100, all of whom were Soviet citizens) disappeared, their whereabouts unknown.

Subsequently, the generous aid from American and European Jewry was disparaged as a capitalistic venture to gain money by charging interest on loans and by exploiting the economic difficulties of the thirties.

The great experiment in land resettlement for Soviet Jews as a way of solving their economic distress and old "unproductive" ways of making a livelihood was now at an end. From a crest of 10 percent of the gainfully employed Jewish population on the land in 1930, the figure dropped to 6.7 percent in 1935, and to just over 6 percent in 1939. According to the estimates of the demographer Lev Zinger, there were only 25,000 Jewish farm families still on the land at the beginning of 1939—about 125,000 Jews—all of them on kolkhozes,[58] and all under great pressure to produce ever larger quantities of food and fiber with the lengthening work day. With the forced collectivization and industrialization push, hopes for a secure and lasting Jewish peasantry which might have provided a territorial base for Jewish autonomy crumbled.

11

Proletarianization: The First Five Year Plan and Industrialization, 1928–39

I consider them [our fathers] the most unfortunate generation of Soviet people. They were too young to appreciate the change of epochs, at the same time nothing linked them with the old one; it was the new one that raised them, they became its flesh and blood, to it they gave their physical and spiritual powers, including inner freedom and independence of thought. And when the string on which they were threaded like beads, in strict order, broke, they were scattered helplessly in different directions, without ever having understood what had happened to them and preserving till the end of their days only the memory and the yearning for the string: they may have been cramped on it, but at least they had known exactly where they were.

ILYA ZILBERBERG

Everywhere there were new elections for the running of housing, trade, industry, and municipal services. Commissars were being appointed to each, men in black leather jerkins, with unlimited powers and an iron will, armed with means of intimidation and revolvers, who shaved little and slept less.

The people in the cities were as helpless children in the face of the unknown—that unknown which swept every established habit aside and left nothing but desolation in its wake. . . . All around, people continued to deceive themselves, to talk endlessly. Everyday life struggled on, by force of habit, limping and shuffling. . . . Ordeals were ahead, perhaps death.

BORIS PASTERNAK, *Doctor Zhivago*

SIMULTANEOUSLY with collectivization of agriculture came the drastic upheavals of stepped-up industrialization, defined as a Five Year Plan (1928–33). The NEP reached its peak in 1925, but "its decline cannot be dated precisely . . . as official statements on the subject were ambiguous or deliberately misleading."[1] As late as 1929, Stalin "indignantly denied rumors . . . that NEP was to be ended," and statements that it was still in operation were heard in 1931.[2] But in 1930, private trade became the crime of speculation and the employment of labor for private gain became illegal. Moreover, by 1926, heavy taxes, surcharges, and confiscations of private property indicated that the private sector in the Soviet economy was under attack. Grave distortions in pricing, procurement, and state control over certain industries and commodities in conflict with the private market created a "goods famine." More centralized planning and centralized state control over the market were believed necessary to transform the economy of the Soviet Union, to make it a strong industrial and military power—the first truly successful working-class state in history.

Stalin called for a staggering 176 percent increase in industrial output and a 70.5 percent increase in real wages—grandiose and fantastically unattainable goals, which the government pressed upon the Soviet people in the name of socialist aspiration and glory. In December 1929, a congress of "shock brigades" adopted a call to fulfill the plan in four instead of five years—an accelerated program which was adopted as official policy.[3] In 1931 Stalin said, "We are fifty or a hundred years behind the advanced countries. We must make good this distance in ten years. Either we do so, or we shall go under."[4] The price was very heavy in human misery and created intolerable pressures, shortages, and great disorganization, but the country was transformed. Large-scale industry was mainly financed by investing the confiscated wealth of the peasants in the forced collectivization, systematically reducing consumption to subsistence and often less. The standard of living of workers actually declined by 50 percent or more during the first plan, but the country built machines, factories, railroads, dams, and armaments in a nationwide frenzy of work.[5]

Behind the "pell-mell heavy industrialization through wildly escalated targets, menacing exhortations, recurrent crises, makeshift measures, and wasteful imbalances" erupted "the last, and most fateful of the factional struggles inside the the Soviet Communist party after Lenin's death in 1924."[6] Stalin's extremist policies were bitterly opposed by his erstwhile allies—Nikolai Bukharin, Aleksei Rykov, and Mikhail Tomsky—all senior Politburo members, who realized that Stalin's policies were "politically dangerous, economically disastrous, and, in the fundamental coercive aspects, incompatible with socialism."[7] But their fear of public factionalism and splitting and their refusal to carry the struggle to areas of their support gave a fateful victory to Stalin. Moreover, Stalin had been perceived by many high officials as "a man of the cautious center" whose ultimate excesses could not be imagined at this time. Bukharin and Kamenev understood that Stalin's line was "disastrous for the revolution as a whole," that he was "an unprincipled intriguer who subordinates everything to the preservation of his own power," a "Genghis Khan" whose policy would lead to civil war, in which revolts would have to be drowned "in blood."[8] But they failed to outmaneuver him and bring him down.

For Jews, as for others, the dislocations and adjustments were very severe. They, of all people, had heard the call to "productivize" very early in the Revolution, but did not move into acceptable "proletarian" occupations in large numbers until the advent of the Five Year Plans. The pre-1928 period lacked both a clear policy and program leading to their proletarianization, and agricultural resettlement as a solution was aborted.

Prior to the Revolution, most Jewish factory workers lived in Lodz and Bialystok, which were now part of Poland. Yet there was a small Jewish pre-Bolshevik industrial proletariat in Belorussia and the Ukraine, which grew to 40,129 in the Ukraine, and 10,639 in Belorussia.[9] There were also over 3,000 Jewish factory workers each in Moscow and Leningrad. Many former Jewish artisans and traders had also become salary or wage earners, and they were classed as proletariat. By 1926, there were 150,000 Jews in industry, of whom 20 percent were physical laborers, including Jews working on the railroads and in coal mines.[10] There were also 241,000 salary earners (nonmanual)—mostly government employees.[11] Thus, a Jewish proletariat was forming, largely made up of white-collar workers. If Jewish farmers (over 6 percent of gainfully employed Jews) are added, fully half of the employable Jewish population in 1926 were in "productive" work. But the other half had not found a place in the Soviet economy and lived from hand to mouth or worse. Almost 10 percent was unemployed and 7.8 percent had no definite occupation.[12] Proletarianization among Jews as a whole lagged far behind the rest of the population before the start of the First Five Year Plan, and, with the exception of Moscow, the percentage of gainfully employed was lower among Jews than among the total population.

Soviet Jews desperately required economic, social, and sheer physical rehabilitation, but each effort thus far had been piecemeal and/or aborted. It was industrialization that would finally absorb Soviet Jews into the economic mainstream of Soviet life and conquer unemployment, but it was this process which also destroyed any possibility of Jewish national-cultural reconstruction. Nevertheless, the call to industrialize was somehow supposed to lead to the "national consolidation" of the Jews.

The First Five Year Plan produced a huge demand for labor in the industrial centers of Great Russia and in the new industries springing up in the larger cities of Belorussia and the Ukraine. It now became necessary to liquidate the "declassed" and "nonproductive" categories and hasten the migration of Jews out of the old Pale into Great Russia where they could become wage and salary earners. In 1928, the first year of the Plan the condition of Jews was described as "catastrophic."[13] Certain Soviet officials began to recognize the economic crisis facing the Jewish poor and began to give special attention to Jewish youth. Fragmentary efforts to draw Jews into industry—especially Jewish youth among the poor—had been made in 1926 in the Ukraine by the Council of People's Commissars, but the influx into factories was slow and unorganized.[14] In 1927, placements in industry were found for a mere 1,427 Jewish poor and youth.[15] By February 1928, the Commissariat on Nationalities approved vocational training for the Jewish poor and Jewish youth to qualify them as proletariat. The Labor Commissariat and related Commissariats in the republics were instructed to channel them into mechanized tailoring and shoemaking operations, construction projects, sugar factories, and forestry.[16] Placements rose to 5,969—but this was still very inadequate.

The beginnings of more systematic planning were made in 1928–29, but, reminiscent of the beginnings of Jewish farming, were made not by the government, but by KOMZET, which was authorized to establish special vocational training classes for young Jews.[17] KOMZET was also instructed to organize the "planned transfer" of Jewish youths to the Voikov Metallurgical works in Kerch, the Crimea.[18] KOMZET offices in Moscow, Belorussia, and the Ukraine issued thousands of orders expediting the admission of Jewish youths to vocational courses and apprentice schools. Some were also placed in construction projects.

Vocational training, however, did not ensure the actual placement of a trainee. In 1930, industrial plants in the Urals were highly favored for placement, but the lack of preparation and "marked reluctance of local management and labor to accept the newcomers," were especially criticized at a special conference called by the Ural Provincial Committee of Communist Youth to discuss the poor results of the placement of Jewish trainees.[19] There were no dormitories for the newcomers nor any organized plan for employing them and their meager earnings were often insufficient even to pay for the cost of food. Moreover, the involvement of KOMZET, which had been set up to resettle Jews on the land, in industrial placement, exposed the absence of a long-range plan for Jews.[20]

At the same time, many Jewish artisans clung to their crafts tenaciously through the late 1920s and tried to avoid the status of declassed persons by refusing to train apprentices or to engage journeymen. When they shifted to industry, most of them pursued the old trades in the traditional Jewish fields: needle and allied branches, leather, printing, and food industries. In 1929, for example, Jewish membership in the needleworkers trade union in White Russia was 86.2 percent; in the leather and printing trades, it was over 70 percent.[21] These industries were by then mechanized, but tended to be smaller (employing up to 2,000 workers) than metal plants or mining industries, which drew comparatively few Jews.[22] (Only several dozen Jews were to be found in the railroad and postal and telegraph industries by 1929.) In 1931, Jews still constituted 60.9 percent of all tailors and 48.2 percent of all leatherworkers, but only 11.1 percent of all metal workers and 1.4 percent of coal miners.[23]

The plight of the Jewish artisan and the "declassed" in general remained perilous during the first years of the Five Year Plan and is fully documented. The journalist Smolar who traveled widely and wrote numerous articles[24] believed that the government's insistence that an artisan join a cooperative or forfeit his rights was "crushing" the artisan, and that the "house-cleaning" of cooperatives was forcing out all small ex-traders. The word "kulak" was being used against the individual Jewish artisan, forcing him into cooperatives, or often unemployment. Meanwhile, Jewish lishentsy still constituted a critical problem in 1929–30.[25] In February 1930, the government reinstated voting rights to two categories: those families that had suffered during the pogroms and those whose heads had served in the Red Army. However, Rosen estimated that approximately 300,000 Jews still remained in the lishentsy category, for whom a "productive occupation" would have to be found "either through land settlement, or cooperative shops of the mutual aid societies." He even conjectured that for some emigration would be the only alternative.[26]

Because of the changed official attitude toward lishentsy, the Central OZET, which was preparing new harsh restrictions, postponed its July 1930 convention to November. In June of that year, Agro-Joint assigned 100,000 roubles[27] to the Kiev regional soviet to assist declassed Jews in the region to organize garden, poultry, and dairy collectives near small towns. At first, it was planned to have all-Jewish projects, and later, to mix them.

The government also began to modify its policy toward artisans. Ezekiel Grower, assistant director of Agro-Joint, cabled in June 1930 that a new decree was helping Jews in small towns become artisans, as part of the government industrialization process.[28] Artisans in artels were to be given the same rights as factory workers. Moreover, the decree urged the discontinuance of forced mergers of artels and "cleansing" actions. Declassed Jews were also to be helped, within limitations. The All-Soviet Artisans Association ordered the reinstatement of all expelled lishentsy in artels, but no voting rights. Lishentsy were to pay a special price for shares in the artel and would not be able to get so-called deficit goods from the cooperative, such as bread, sugar, butter, and other foodstuffs, but could get nondeficit goods.

These considerable numbers of Jews were now largely left behind, neglected or bypassed by the Evsektsiya and government in the simultaneous campaigns for collectivization, Birobidzhan, and industrialization. Intermediate remedies had to be provided by Agro-Joint, or, to a lesser extent, by ORT.

In order to expedite the shift of Jewish workers to state factories, Agro-Joint expanded its industrial division to teach and upgrade skills in Jewish trade schools and cooperative workshops set up by Jewish mutual aid societies.[29] Courses lasting from six to twelve months were established in woodworking, shoemaking, needle trades, and metal and lathe working, and many special projects were established especially to attract declassed Jews, such as the manufacture of meter-sticks, files and metal tools. In Kiev there was a sawmill project; in Tiraspol, a shop for the manufacture of belting; in Znamenka, a brush and suitcase factory; in Odessa, a button and woodworking factory. Projects of various kinds were created in numerous towns, including Vosnesenka, Valegotsulovo, Dubossary, Anan'yef, and Krivoy-Czero.

At the time, of the 25,000 Jews working in the cooperative shops of mutual aid societies, about 30 percent were beginners just learning a trade. Agro-Joint gave credits amounting to 640,000 roubles to 23 loan societies for the purchase of lumber, motors, and the extension of knitting, furniture, textile weaving, brick making, pottery, and tool shops.[30] Altogether, 1,036,000 roubles were appropriated by Agro-Joint for its industrial division in 1933. By the end of the year, in addition to the general training and upgrading, over 5,000 Jews had been placed with various government industrial plants.[31]

The evolution of a transformed Jewish economy can be seen in the changes that took place in several cities in Georgia, as observed by Mr. F. E. Landes,[32] Agro-Joint inspector for technical assistance. The frail beginnings were made by the All-Georgian Jewish Committee for Technical Assistance of the Jewish Poor, which was organized in 1929 with a capital of 16 roubles. The committee consisted of eleven men and three alternates elected by a general assembly of artel members for three years and "approved by various Soviet organizations." By May 1930, when Landes made his first visit to the area, the committee had helped to put into operation several artels employing 600 Jewish workers in Tiflis, 120 in Kutaisi, and 55 in Sukhumi—all of whom had been considered declassed. In 1931, Agro-Joint sent in a "planned supply of raw materials" and the committee greatly expanded its work. By November 1931, it was actively involved in 82 artels specializing in needleworking, shoemaking, the manufacture of paper boxes, chemicals, sporting goods (for which there was a great demand in the Caucasus), toys, and glass manufacturing. Of the 2,568 people employed, 2,053 were Jews, almost half of whom were women. Landes also visited several confectionery artels which made fruit-filled and hard candies and imitation tea made from cranberries, which was shipped to Siberia and the Far East. There were 157 persons in these artels, many of them Jews.

Inadequate raw materials were the chief problem. Tailors, for example, didn't have enough needles or yarn and had to keep repairing old clothing. The Tiflis knitting factory was a very popular workplace (593 Jews out of a work force of 792 worked there) and Agro-Joint not only contributed knitting machines, but helped to equip a medical department and dining room. In 1931, Agro-Joint contributed 100 tons of mercerized yarn to the committee, some of which went to the Tiflis factory. In 1932, this was increased to 200 tons.

The Georgia committee also struggled to deal with a number of social problems and tried to raise the general cultural level.[33] It had its own physician who gave medical aid to declassed Jews not yet employed and its own medical assistance insurance fund for members. In 1931 it was planning to provide five ambulances to small towns in Georgia and cash aid of 25 roubles per month to the needy. The committee was also trying to combat illiteracy, especially among Jewish women and the declassed. In 1932, it had plans to set up a chain of libraries and radio sets in artel clubs.

The committee exerted special pressure upon the declassed Jews who were described by Landes as "absolutely unfamiliar with industry." Up to the time of the Bolshevik Revolution, 95 percent of the Jews of Georgia were petty traders. After Georgia was sovietized (February, 1921), virtually the whole population was declassed. Hunger was widespread; the change to acceptable "productive" work was painful. The Georgia soviet approved the plans of the Georgia committee and in two and a half years, "rooted from the depths of necessity," tremendous progress had been achieved. The committee applied to Agro-Joint for help for the first time in May 1930, requesting equipment it could not obtain in Russia, not money. The next year, it began to use credits made available from the state bank.

Jews in the cities and those who could move there or go to the huge industrial complexes that multiplied in the early thirties fared much better than did the Jews in the shtetlach. An important factor in their success was the Jewish educational level—a 70.4 percent literacy according to the 1920 census, more than double the average for the Soviet population at the time, rising to 72.3 percent by 1926. In the early years of the regime, Jews filled many administrative posts and civil service jobs. Moreover, because of unparalleled opportunities and their hunger for higher education, they poured into universities and technical institutes of all kinds. In 1923, Jews made up almost half of the total number of students in institutions of higher learning in the Ukraine—18,488—though they constituted only a little over 5 percent of the population. In the RSFSR, in faculties of medicine and economics, by 1929, they comprised over 60 percent (see Table 11.1).[34] For the year 1928, there were 14,061 Jewish students in the RSFSR, making up 12.5 percent of the student population although Jews comprised less than 1 percent of the total population (see Table 11.2).[35]

Several shifts in these trends occurred in the late 1920s but they can

TABLE 11.1

Jews in Institutions of Higher Education in the RSFSR as of September 15, 1929, by Faculty

Faculties	Number of Institutions	Number of Jews	Total Number of Students	Jews as % of All Students
Industrial, Technical	58	3,798	31,134	12.2
Agriculture	39	638	18,792	3.4
Pedagogy	22	2,194	21,947	10.1
Medicine	16	1,410	15,000	9.4
Economics (incl. Law)	16	2,301	13,620	16.9
Art	8	511	1,945	26.3

be interpreted variously. There was a marked movement, especially of young Jews from the Ukraine and White Russia to the big cities of the RSFSR—Moscow and Leningrad—and to their universities and technical institutes. By 1929, the number of Jewish university students in the Ukraine had fallen from 18,488 in 1923 to 9,525 in 1929.[36] A similar drop occurred in White Russia. It has been argued that "the principal reason for the steady drop in the number of Jews in the student body . . . was the Soviet policy of discriminating against citizens of 'bourgeois' origin in the sphere of university admission, [and] unlikely that the decline was primarily the result of Jews from the Ukraine studying in the RSFSR."[37] However, the shift to the RSFSR certainly accounted for some of the drop. Moreover, Jews barred from the universities because of their class designation were enrolling in workers' faculties, or Rabfaks (see below) in increasing numbers in order to qualify for universities.

TABLE 11.2

Jewish Students in Soviet Schools, 1928

Republic	Number of Jewish Students	Jews as % of All Students
RSFSR	14,061	12.5
Belorussia	1,216	27.5
Ukraine	6,878	26.3
Other Areas	1,250	—
USSR (totals)	23,405	14.4

The new breakneck industrialization plan made it essential for one to have the identity of a worker, a full-fledged member of the proletariat. Young Jews who were barred from universities and from the worker category because of their ambiguous or tainted family background now had to make strenuous efforts to create a worker classification. They did this through a regulation of the so-called Workers' Faculties, or Rabfaks, which permitted someone of "bourgeois" origins to become a worker by working in a factory for three years.[38] Young Jews flocked to plants for this experience, increasing those in Rabfaks from 7,429 in 1925 to 14,533 in 1929 in the Ukraine; and in White Russia, from 471 in 1926–27 to 747 in 1928–29.[39] Frequently such Jews were resented as "non-proletarian intruders" and "careerists" and were also subject to anti-Semitic slurs, but the students hung on. They needed to be "workers."

Such a selective class admission practice had begun in 1923, but had to be changed several times because of the poor academic performance of the early students and the increasing demand for specialists. In order to facilitate the growth of a Soviet intelligentsia based on the working class, many measures were taken to encourage the entry of working-class students into the universities, including dropping the requirement of a secondary school diploma, use of Rabfaks to help coach students in secondary school subjects, and quotas based on class selection.[40] During the NEP period, Communists had been particularly concerned about the lack of proletarian elements in the universities and bureaucracy and began the practice of checking out backgrounds and expelling "bourgeois" students. Questionnaires were designed to elicit a detailed picture of the student's work experience, trade union affiliation, role in the Revolution and civil war, social origins, party standing, political orientation, and parents' occupational history. Jewish students, too, now had to certify to their "proper" social origins, and "proletarian" background. Since the Rabfaks admitted people who had worked for three years, a large number of Jews of "bourgeois" origin used this means to enter universities and then move into technical, managerial, and administrative positions, which were formally proletarian categories—all of which were urgently needed in the vast economic and social changes of the First Five Year Plan. The approved occupations also included salaried positions in the liberal professions, and writers, artists, and musicians, whose livelihood now depended on state stipends. The employment opportunities for graduates of the technical institutes, which had been virtually closed to Jewish students in tsarist Russia, can be seen in the high percentage of Jewish students enrolled in technical faculties in 1927 in the RSFSR alone, in relation to the total Jewish student population: 43.6 percent, or 9,663 students.[41] This percentage increased as positions in engineering, metallurgy, mining, chemistry, and factory management, etc. opened up under the Five Year Plan. Although considerable numbers were attracted to medicine and law, the traditionally "Jewish" subjects, Jewish students gravitated toward the industrial-technical subjects closely tied to the planning and management of the Soviet economy.[42]

Feverish activity swept the country after the First Five Year Plan was launched. Every factory, scientific institution, school, government office, theater, department store, restaurant, sports club, shoe repair shop, and writers' association submitted its own Five Year Plan. When people got together, they first talked of the food shortages and then what they were going to do under the plan. Boris Mironov, the foreign press censor, with a flair for anecdotes, told foreign correspondents that the government was considering Five Year Plans submitted by midwives and rat exterminators.[43]

As all private shops were closed down, food and many everyday staples became scarce. Large quantities of lumber, butter, eggs, and meat were shipped abroad in exchange for foreign machinery. Ration cards were introduced, but little could be bought with them. Government stores were bare and long hours of queuing up in many different lines for many hours of the day yielded little. It took infinite patience and ingenuity to produce a meal, but the shortages were never mentioned officially and the Communist press in foreign countries published ecstatic reports of "Socialist Plenty." Yet most Russians gave themselves unsparingly to the great task of rebuilding Russia. "Those years were hard years," a sympathetic observer wrote:

yet they were good years, full of exhilaration and renewed hope in the possibilities of socialism. A superhuman effort was being made to create happiness at the cost of maximum human sacrifices. As in the first years after the Revolution, people now starved and froze for the sake of a better future. The present offered little. But the future promised much. To the scientist it meant ideal research laboratories, to the architect new beautiful cities, to the physician a modern hospital in every Soviet village, and to all a wonderful free life. What if there were no shoestrings and razor blades today? Tomorrow there would be razor blades and shoestrings for everyone.[44]

A young American Jewish woman, the niece of Litvakov, was in Moscow during this time with her husband, as were numerous Americans. She worked in a foreign translation publishing house; he, in a factory. They, too, experienced great hardships, including food and housing shortages, but they found Moscow "full of life."[45] When they first arrived in 1932, they were met at the railroad station by relatives in a horse and buggy. Cattle moved in the streets. Their main foods consisted of bread, cornstarch, farina, soybeans, beets, and cabbage. There was virtually no meat or milk. But life was exciting, nevertheless, and there was tremendous enthusiasm, especially among the young, about building a better world for the future. By the time they left in 1937, the great Moscow subway was near completion and the cattle had gone. But the purges were also under way and many foreign students and workers were leaving.

Other observers have noted that people bore hardships with little grumbling, or, if they grumbled, they did not consider their hardships senseless or hopeless. Most Jews also suffered, but some shared in this exultant expectation. Those with children going to college or working in offices and those who submerged the government's attacks on Zionism and Judaism were grateful that Jewish children "were as good as anyone else in the Soviet Union." Pale and tired from overwork and often hungry, like other Russians, such Jews would take fire in passionate figuring about the future. The figures meant schools, theaters, books, hospitals, housing—a promise to make the Soviet Union the first country where everyone without exception would enjoy everything that life can give to a human being.

Except for the disenfranchised NEPmen and those accused of being "class enemies" and "oppositionists," there were plenty of jobs available. In the late twenties, thousands of Jewish traders, middlemen, and artisans went to work for a wage. Between 1926 and 1931, the number of Jewish proletariat almost doubled—from 394,000 to 787,000.[46] Many Jews poured into factories spontaneously, causing a steep rise in the number of Jewish wage earners (manual workers) from 153,000 in December 1926, to 342,000 in 1931.[47] Another 445,000 were classified in 1931 as "salary workers," (white-collar workers, employees of government bureaus, and administrative personnel), as compared with 241,000 in December 1926. The growth in the number of white-collar workers was not a specifically Jewish phenomenon, but a reflection of the burgeoning Soviet bureaucracy and the tendency to recruit white-collar workers from the cities, where over 80 percent of the Jewish population lived by 1931.[48]

The increased proletarianization of Jewish life thus accompanied a shift to cities, particularly to those outside the old Pale of Settlement (the Ukraine and White Russia): Moscow, Leningrad, Kharkov, and new industrial centers, reflecting not only the advance of proletarianization, but also the scattering of the ghetto population of the Ukraine and White Russia. By 1923 Moscow, with 86,000 Jews and Leningrad, with 52,000, had become the largest centers of Jewish population after Kiev and Odessa, with 129,000 and 130,000, respectively.

The influx of Jews into Russian cities outside the Pale was already evident after the Revolution and continued afterward. By 1926 there were 131,000 Jews in Moscow and 84,500 in Leningrad; moreover, the census of that year showed that many were recent arrivals in the very cities in which very few Jews had been allowed to live in tsarist times. Between 1926 and 1931 the number of Jewish manual laborers increased from 14.2 percent to 21.8 percent in Moscow, and from 24.9 percent to 31.9 percent in Leningrad.[49] By the early and mid-thirties, a large number of these Jews had moved into managerial and semimanagerial positions, including manual laborers who had worked their way up. As the Soviet bureaucracy increased, the number of government employees of every nationality increased, but the predominantly urban Jewish elements, generally better educated and having a higher proportion of clerical, professional, and other salaried workers, were quite conspicuous.

In the areas of the old Pale—the Ukraine and White Russia—between 1926 and 1931, the number of Jewish manual workers doubled, an increase exceeding that in salaried workers. Outside the Pale area, the reverse was true: the number of Jewish salaried workers was more than twice the number of manual workers (wage earners), reflecting outmigration and the trend toward white-collar status (see Table 11.3). Already by 1929, Jewish white-collar workers constituted 78.2 percent of the total number of Jewish employees in Moscow, and 68.1 percent in Leningrad; in the Ukraine, the figure was 55.7, and in White Russia, 46.3 percent.[50] By 1931, more than half of the 787,000 Jewish wage and salary earners in the Soviet Union were in the white-collar category as clerks, managers, planning, technical, and administrative personnel.[51] Moreover, Jews in the so-called "commercial class," which was almost totally liquidated by 1931,[52] filled positions as business agents in state and cooperative commercial enterprises and in state wholesale establishments and retail stores.

TABLE 11.3
Jewish Wage and Salary Earners, 1926–31[53]

Area	December 1926	April 1931
Ukraine		
Wage Earners	93,200	195,000
Salary Earners	126,500	189,000
Totals	219,700	384,000
White Russia		
Wage Earners	25,200	52,000
Salary Earners	25,500	34,800
Totals	50,700	86,800
Other Republics		
Wage Earners	34,600	95,000
Salary Earners	89,000	221,200
Totals	123,600	316,200
USSR Total		
Wage Earners	153,000	342,000
Salary Earners	241,000	445,000
Grand Totals	394,000	787,000

With its emphasis on sexual equality and the emancipation of women, the Bolshevik Revolution opened up vast educational and economic opportunities for Jewish women, many of whom had lived restricted lives because of traditionally religious or tsarist limitations. They became particularly conspicuous in government and state positions, industrial enterprises, and the liberal professions and tended to advance more rapidly than their non-Jewish opposite numbers.[54]

In 1935, the number of Jewish wage earners was said to exceed over one million, thus achieving in large part the proletarianization of Jews so long sought by the Bolsheviks. By this time, nearly half the Jewish workers had been drawn into larger industries and about a quarter into artisan-type industries, such as printing, needle trades, tobacco manufacturing, woodworking, and tanning—fields in which Jews had worked prior to the Revolution.[55]

The outmigration of Jews from the Ukraine and White Russia continued in the late thirties (the percentage of Jews dropped to 50.8 and 12.4, respectively, by 1939), while 32.1 percent of all Jews lived in the RSFSR by 1939). Unofficial estimates indicate that there were 300,000 to 400,000 Jews in Moscow and 350,000 Jews in Leningrad at that time.[56]

TABLE 11.4
Classification among Economically Active Jews

| | 1934 Number of | | 1939 Number of | |
Field	Jews	Percent	Jews	Percent
Civil servants and state employees	420,000	33	520,000	37.2
Liberal professions	100,000	7.8	180,000	12.8
Manual laborers	300,000	23.6	300,000	21.5
Farm employment	110,000	8.7	100,000	7.1
Artisans	210,000	16.6	200,000	14.3
Middlemen	30,000	2.5	—	—
Miscellaneous	100,000	7.8	100,000	7.1
Totals	1,270,000	100	1,400,000	100

Source: Lestschinsky, Dos sovetishe idntum (1941), pp. 170–71.

Wage earners of previous years acquired higher skills or were up-graded through on-the-job training and moved into nonmanual jobs (see Table 11.4). In addition, there was a larger pool of educated young Jews from newly opened secondary schools. The rising proportion of Jews in manual (i.e. wage-earning) jobs (about 600,000) to salaried jobs (almost a million and a half) had transformed the Jewish economic profile by 1939. By that time, proletarianization of Jews had reached its natural limit, and most of the floating, "nonproductive" population had found work in industry, transportation, commerce, and public service.[57]

The traditional Jewish drive for intellectual advancement was spurred by the new opportunities. Lestschinsky observed that "Aspirations to higher positions played a greater role among Jews than among non-Jews. The notion that Jews could be professors raised fantasies of Jewish mothers and young people. Jews had never dreamt of such status."[58] By the late thirties, many such aspirations were being realized, as can be seen in Tables 11.5 and 11.6.[59] There were 3,020,000 Jews at this time (1939), constituting 1.78 percent of the total population.

These vast material changes, however, should not be seen as a flowing, uninterrupted process. The statistics alone do not reveal the traumas of millions of individual lives among Jews and others, the breakup of families and communities, and, most of all, the spreading chill of

TABLE 11.5

Numbers and Percentages of Jews in Occupations, 1939

Occupational Field	Number of Jews	Percentage of Jews
Physicians	21,000	16
Artists and actors	17,000	11
Engineers, architects, and technologists	25,000	10
Cultural workers (journalists, librarians, etc.)	30,000	10
University professors and scientific workers	7,000	9
Nurses and other medical personnel	31,000	8
Accountants and bookkeepers	125,000	8
Primary and secondary school teachers	46,000	5
Intermediate technical personnel	60,000	7
Agronomists and other agricultural specialists	2,000	1

TABLE 11.6

Urbanization Trend among Soviet Jews, 1926–39

Republics	Percentage of Jewish Urban Population	
	1926	1939
Ukrainian SSR	77.4	85.5
Belorussian SSR	83.6	87.8
RSFSR, Kazakh, and Kirghiz SSR's	94.2	88.9
Azerbaidzhan, Georgian, and Armenian SSR's	96.7	87.3
Turkmen SSR	100.0	87.1
Uzbek and Tadzhik SSR's	98.5	88.9
Average for USSR	82.4	87.0
Total Jewish Urban Population	2,190,000	2,628,000
	Percentage of Jewish Rural Population	
Average for USSR	17.6	13.0
Total Jewish Rural Population	490,000	392,500

Source: S. M. Schwarz, *The Jews in the Soviet Union*, 1951, pp. 16–17.

fear that enveloped the country as Stalin's grip tightened. The economic advances of Jews, as of others, were undercut or conditioned by the power rivalries of new cadres of bureaucrats, the ascent of new cadres to power, the siren call to Birobidzhan, the accelerating regimentation in all phases of life, and, finally, the destructive purges. In literature, we have already described the zeal of the proletarian critics in the late twenties and their attacks on "petty bourgeois" and "nationalist" deviations. In the early thirties, Yiddish literature had to be preoccupied with industrialization and the regeneration of Soviet man and society and had to imbue their work with positive messages and idealized figures abstracted from the Five Year Plan.

Yiddish literature indeed had a double task. Whereas Russian literature had the task of guiding workers and peasants into socialism, Yiddish literature had to first make Jews into workers and peasants and then guide them to socialism.[60] The entry of Jews into occupations that had previously held no prestige value for them involved deep inner anguish and struggle, especially for older Jews who, while accepting the realities of the Soviet regime, still tried to keep their bridge to the old life. No literary propaganda, however, was needed to make Jews enter the administrative offices and professions, for the old reverence for education and for the security and prestige of the professions were self-propelling. However, it was the factories, mines, and hydroelectric projects that had to provide grist for the writer's mill.[61]

In H. Orland's novel *Aglomerat*,[62] for example, the main theme is the struggle to build a blast furnace for the Kerch metallurgical combine, juxtaposed against the theme of shtetl youths in the Ukraine in a shock brigade. Their parents pray that the factory will fail so that their children can return home. A rabbi from the town even brings some money for a return ticket for one boy. A few weaken but most of the Jewish boys and girls are finished with the old life and resist his appeal. More important than remaining Jewish and going to synagogue is the new hope that Jews will be equal—that the new generation will have enough food and a chance to go to school and have work. Socialism must prove victorious. Personal interests and ambitions are subordinated to the interests and goals of the group—the factory collective. When a young Jewish member of Komsomol is forced to give up evening classes for the sake of overtime in the factory, he does so willingly: "What is more important at this moment? There is only one possible answer: the interests of the factory, the interests of the workers' collective, the interests of the country. All these come first!"

The same fiery enthusiasm for the regeneration of humanity mixed with the joy and excitement of construction is found in Peretz Markish's drama *Der finfter horizont (The Fifth Level)*,[63] which describes the experiences of two Jewish coal miners on the fifth underground level in a coal mine in the Donbass during the First Five Year Plan. When the time comes to plan for a May Day demonstration, the Jewish miner Shapiro wants to take the whole demonstration down into the mine and celebrate there: "Let us demonstrate through the tunnels and on the fifth level, and then to the Anatoliev vein. And we shall see that the very bowels of earth will tremble with the First of May!"

All of the organs of propaganda—including literature—were now harnessed to the belief that the future lay resplendent, that all citizens would find the sacrifices worthwhile. For example, in a novel called *Fabrika Rable* by Mikhail Chumandrin, the former owner of a chocolate factory is shown supporting the Soviet order. After a party conference that seals the fate of his business, Rable, a Jew, says:

. . . despite this, I love the U. S. S. R. . . . Any restoration would be stupid. What for? To have the Pale, the percentage norms in the universities, pogroms? This is why I don't want to see a repetition of the Denikins, the Kolchaks, and interventions. Enough, I want to work and, of course, make money. . . .[64]

But even his desire to make money is socially directed: "The principle of profit is not important to me. The setting up of the goal and its fulfillment, that is what fascinates me. The process in itself. . . ."

As Jews were caught up in the national obsession with quotas and worker output, and as large numbers of them moved into new cities, the possibilities for Jewish cultural reconstruction dwindled. The Evseks had been concentrating on the shtetlach, then simultaneously on Birobidzhan and the Five Year Plan, but their energies were scattered and their numbers too thin to have any effect on the Jewish factory proletariat. As the economist Lestschinsky wrote, "Programs were not thoroughly or efficiently prepared, or worked out through political or economic institutions. . . . Things were in chaos, thrown together. The Evsektsiya had no coherent program or direction. It simply followed events."[65]

The question of Jewish identity and consciousness again remained ambiguous. Jewish settlers were going to Birobidzhan (see Chapter 13) to build socialism, but they were also going to a Jewish territory, which became a rallying point for Jewish culture. On the other hand, the industrialization drive was aimed at creating the new Soviet man, an international proletarian and, thus, denationalized. The new Jew "who has become an actual fact," was personified in the character of David Margulies in Valentine Katayev's novel *Vremya vperyed* (Time Forward), written in 1932. Throughout this story of the socialist construction of Magnitogorsk, Margulies, the conscientious engineer, emerges as a Soviet ideal type—neat, well-organized, selfless, and fully integrated. The word "Jew" is never mentioned.[66]

Magnitogorsk was one of the highly publicized vast industrial centers in the Ural Mountains created during the First Five Year Plan. There were 40,000 Jews working there—"all of them new arrivals in a strange environment and with relatively few contacts with one another. This feeling of isolation was doubtless responsible for the partial failure of the directed emigration of trained young Jewish workers to the Ural region." In 1928–29, only 538 of 1,220 young apprentices assigned to schools in the area actually reached their destination, and only 350 remained (see Photo 11.1).[67]

11.1 Jewish youths going to Magnitogorsk in early thirties.

From time to time, writers in *Der emes* deplored the weakening of "Jewish work," noting that it "was treated like a stepchild by the Communist apparatus"; that hundreds of new Yiddish books lie unread in a closed cupboard; that "national work is being buried, thrown into a trap, with the key thrown away"; that in Minsk, where there are 311 Jewish workers, "only six read Yiddish papers." The appeals of russification were also described: "The Jew," one writer declared. "cannot live in two cultures. . . . The Jewish worker smells the odor of emancipation and tears himself away not only from the physical but also the spiritual ghetto." Many workers began to realize that the Russian language, not Yiddish, was the way to economic betterment and absorption into the new society.[68] The way to intermarriage and cultural melding was now open.

The Soviet drive to industrialize forced Jewish Communists to rationalize a new formulation for the future of Soviet Jewry and shift their earlier assumptions and views. They now had to see industrialization as an inevitable process of economic leveling which would give proletarian status to Jews and fuse them into the Soviet mainstream. It was now accepted that proletarianization would finally "normalize" the Soviet Jewish condition. Indeed, by 1930 the Evsektsiya was abolished.

The geographical upheaval of the Jewish masses that accompanied the proletarianization process uprooted Jews from a Jewish milieu and flung them into a strange, often hostile world, hastening assimilation and intermarriage. They experienced "great tension in coping with the languages of the majority—the first requirement for feeling comfortable about one's work. But perhaps more deeply was the strain in dealing with strange things"—tools, machinery, and techniques that were completely new to many Jews.[69] Moreover, industrialization dissolved any lingering sense of a Jewish community and the strong traditional bonds of Jewish family life. Family unity was ruptured and individual members were often separated by vast distances. Moreover, anti-Semitism again began to erupt and the government did nothing to curb it.

12

Stalin's Iron Age: New Controls,
Repression, and Anti-Semitism, 1929–34

The great majority of us are required to live a life of constant, systematic du-
plicity. Your health is bound to be affected, if, day after day, you say the
opposite of what you feel, if you grovel before what you dislike and rejoice at
what brings you nothing but misfortune.

BORIS PASTERNAK, *Doctor Zhivago*

Do not bear down hard on us,
No one knows what we went through.
It is altogether a miracle that
 we somehow preserved our human image.

DAVID HOFSHTEYN

THIS influx of Jews into new fields and positions as well as new
geographic areas touched off recurring waves of anti-Jewish feeling.
The main sources of the new anti-Semitism in the late twenties, when
unemployment was still quite high, lay among the dispossessed and
declassed urban middle classes and penetrated into certain strata of
industrial workers, university students, Communist youth, and the party
itself. Almost the only means of social mobility had become the factory
and Communist party. In such a situation of intense competition, anti-
Semitic charges were hurled against the Jewish newcomers. Those Jews
who came into factories rarely had mechanical skills, but they were
generally more literate and more used to handling simple tools than
the largely illiterate peasantry who surged into factories after 1928. But
they were in an essentially alien world in which flesh-and-blood Jewish

factory workers summoned up the earlier vivid images of the Jew as money-lender, trader, Christ-killer, profiteering NEPman.

The problem had been attacked legally in July 1918, when the Soviet Criminal Code specifically made anti-Semitism a criminal offense. At that time, the Council of People's Commissars issued an order calling for the destruction of the anti-Semitic movement "at its roots," by outlawing "pogromists and persons inciting to pogroms." However, enforcement could not keep pace with the offenses. One of the first to raise the issue of rising anti-Semitism had been Kalinin, titular head of the state, who wrote in July 1926: "There are many letters and written questions addressed to speakers at public meetings . . . which refer to the Jewish question in general and to the transfer of Jews in the Crimea in particular. Some are clearly reactionary, bigoted, and anti-Semitic. . . ."[1] Later in November, he asked why "the Russian intelligentsia is perhaps more anti-Semitic today than it was under Tsarism?" Anti-Semitic incidents in the mid-twenties became so frequent and violent that the Soviet press was compelled to take notice. A Soviet journalist Mikhail Gorev discussed the question in a number of articles in *Komsomolskaya pravda*, the Moscow Young Communist paper,[2] and Maxim Gorky and other noted writers wrote articles deploring the anti-Semitic tendencies of some of their colleagues. Gorev, for example, wrote about a Comrade Grifeld from Smela: "In 1925–26 I worked in the Smela sugar refinery. Anti-Semitism there was very widespread. It happened that a 'Jewboy' greenhorn would be put on the running gear, the carriage made to roll full speed, and then the 'Jewboy' would be ordered to jump off the racing wheels. Then another entertainment was invented—greenhorns would be doused with hot water. Or the fellows would form two lines and, yelling and shouting, would hurl the Jew back and forth between the two lines."[3]

In his *Against the Anti-Semites* (1928), Gorev confirmed the eruption of anti-Jewish abuses, including acts of violence. During this period, numerous anti-Semitic incidents involving workers and even party workers were reported in the daily press and in special pamphlets. Newcomers to the factories, and easily identified by their appearance and language, numbers of Jews were abused verbally and physically. The Jewish sociologist Jacob Lestschinsky observed that "Anti-Semitic atrocities were so savage in 1927–28, the Communist party had to take extra measures against this plague."[4] Conductors were required to stop trolley cars and have militiamen arrest passengers—sober or drunk—

who uttered anti-Semitic invectives. Not even a prominent poet like Sergei Yesenin could escape censure and a trial by literary colleagues for having indulged in an anti-Semitic slur while drunk. Officially, the regime tried to shield Jews against outbreaks of official anti-Semitism as well as organized social outbreaks. Schools, factories, farms, and government offices were instructed to expel guilty persons, but anti-Jewish feeling persisted.

A short Russian novel called *The Man Who Kisses the Ground*, by Mikhail Kozakov, which appeared in 1928, presents some of the aspects of anti-Semitism of the period, from the passive variety exhibited by a commissar who feels that an eligible Jew should not be given a leading factory post for fear that this would arouse anti-Semitism, to the violent type shown by a group of workers who mutilate a Jewish beggar.[5] An agitprop play *The Trial Against Anti-Semitism*, by M. U. Mal'tzev and published in the same year, further illustrates the new forms of anti-Semitism as well as the means by which they were countered. Three Russians are on trial on charges of anti-Semitism brought by a Jew, Abraham Shapiro. A former petty tradesman, Shapiro has decided to settle on the land in the Crimea. While applying at the local registry for a copy of his birth certificate, a clerk has incited a peasant and a worker to anti-Semitic remarks. The clerk says that "The Jews are everywhere—in the factories, government houses, publishing houses. . . . I am for the Soviets, I am also a member of a trade union. But I can't stand Jews."[6]

A peasant testifies that he has heard that Jews are getting the best land and that they are taking over the government and factories. Witnesses are brought in and the prosecution proves with figures that the Jews are not running the country. The accused are found guilty. The clerk is expelled from her trade union and sentenced to two years' imprisonment; the other two get stern reprimands. The play not only condemns anti-Semitism but shows that Shapiro is in the process of becoming a productive worker and eagerly uses his new opportunities: "I shall go to work and then I will know that I live like a man on solid ground and not somewhere in the air."[7]

As compared with strident popular anti-Semitism of the NEP period, recriminations against Jewish "usurpers" diminished in the early thirties. The First Five Year Plan created millions of new jobs and in the frictions and hostilities of minority nationals flung together for the first time in the workplace, most of the victims of violence were non-Europeans.[8] Even so, the party was concerned, for anti-Semitism had penetrated into the ranks of industrial workers, who before the Revolution had been thought relatively free of prejudice. In the daily press as well as in special pamphlets, numerous anti-Semitic incidents involving workers and even members of the party were reported.[9] Even during the early months of 1930, when there was fuller employment, the Soviet press carried many reports of anti-Semitic incidents.[10] Stalin himself issued a tirade against "anti-Semitic bestiality" in reply to an inquiry from the Jewish Telegraphic Agency in January 1931 (but not published in the Soviet Union until 1936). The daily paper of the All-Ukrainian Trade Union Council reported numerous anti-Semitic episodes in sugar refineries and distilleries and other factories in the countryside. Some Jews were beaten up, poisoned, pelted with bolts and wrenches, blinded with wood shavings, and even axed to death.[11] Young Communists, ambitious to climb into improved roles, especially resented those Jews who used the factories as stepping stones to advanced institutes and universities—the more so if Jewish students did better than they academically.

Some anti-Semitic episodes involving Komsomol members in 1929 were described by Chemerisky, the secretary of the Central Bureau of the Evsektsiya:

In the Mechanical Works No. 13 in Bryansk, a gang of young workers constantly baited a young Jewish worker, Furmanov. In the gang there were six Komsomols. . . . A general anti-Semitic feeling runs very high in this plant. Recently an informal discussion was held with workers on the subject, and this is what Comrade Ilenkov . . . writes about it:
"The workers who attended the discussion may be divided into three groups of different strength: (1) Those strongly contaminated with anti-Semitic prejudice . . . (2) The bulk of the audience, who tacitly agreed with the arguments and speeches of the former. (3) A tiny minority, who timidly tried to reason with the first group. Party and Komsomol people in the audience kept silent. . . . The impression was obtained that they were all in agreement with the anti-Jewish statements.[12]

Admissions to the Pedagogical and Medical Faculties in Smolensk University in 1929 indicate that the Jewish group was the largest of the minority nationalities. Occasional actions to suppress anti-Semitism and other residues of "national chauvinism" crop up in party protocols. On December 28, 1929, for example, during a quarrel over a radio tube, the manager of the club in one of the dormitories called one of the students a "zhid." He was expelled from the university, but not before his action was defended by a group of Komsomol students.[13]

Sometimes Jews themselves challenged their attackers, as in the case of a Jewish youth,[14] a top student in a technological institute in Kharkov sent to Odessa in 1929 to work in a factory as an engineer under supervision. There he suffered abuse from some of the other engineers, but waged a fight and won. The anti-Semitic engineers were fired and he seems to have won the respect of his co-workers.

There were numerous instances of Komsomol violence. One account in a Communist youth paper conveys the atmosphere of fear and intimidation that must have been the lot of many Jewish students:

At the Surveying Institute (in Kharkov), the Jewish Workers' Faculty student Sh. was obstinately hounded for months, day in and day out, behind the closed doors of the student dormitory. Among his fellow students Sh. lived the life of a hunted animal. Every one of his steps, gestures, casual remarks brought down upon him an avalanche of coarse taunts and vile abuse.

Lyashenko, a young surveying student and member of the Komsomol, abused Sh. simply because he happened to be the only Jew in the dormitory. Sh. . . . was kept awake at night, forced to lie awake in bed with his eyes wide open. To awaken him, they hit him on the head . . . doused his head with icy water, prodded his bare heels with a pair of compasses. The result of this persecution was that Sh. suffered repeated and protracted fainting fits.[15]

Time and time again Komsomol members were involved in such episodes and frequently demanded the introduction of the hated tsarist weapon, the *numerus clausus*, for Jewish students.

The Communist leadership tended to blame this agitation on "backward elements" from the country, newly employed in factories, but as a rule, it was either the status conscious, class-indoctrinated youth who resented the influx of "socially different Jews" or vociferous and self-assertive elements among Communist youth. This generation had reached adolescence during the civil war or even later—youngsters who were ignorant of the tradition of a free labor movement and looked with suspicion on anyone who seemed "different." The hostility grew partly out of the feeling that Jews were using the factories as a stepping stone to admission to institutions of higher learning, but did not stop when these youths themselves entered universities, technical institutes, and other specialized schools. These conflicts were sharpened because, by the mid- and late twenties, higher education fell within the reach of children of workers and peasants and, in roundabout ways, of children of lower middle-class ("nonproletarian") families. Among those of lower middle-class origin were numerous Jews considered "bourgeois" and thus in need of a worker identity. Work in a factory became the magic key to proletarian status.

Another source of anti-Jewish feeling reported by an American journalist[16] was the help sent Soviet Jews by relatives from the United States in the form of remittances which were then used in the so-called Torgsin shops. In these shops one could buy better and more abundant supplies than were available generally, with gold or foreign currency. Until 1936, they produced a large *valuta* (currency, thus foreign currencies here) revenue from abroad. Anyone who had the tiniest bit of gold—a ring or bracelet—could exchange it for Torgsin tokens and secure food and other items. "The percentage of Jewish people standing in the Torgsin queues . . . was very high. Anti-Semitism . . . took on a new lease on life when Russians saw their Jewish neighbors cooking good food which they never had a chance to buy. A few years later, in the great purge, countless Jewish families suffered for their past enjoyment of a little food bought with money sent from abroad."[17] By 1936, it was a crime to communicate with relatives abroad. Torgsin shops were closed down, and those who had used them were arrested and sent to prison camps.

Reports in America about mounting anti-Semitism in the Soviet Union began to appear in the late twenties. The American Jewish leader Louis Marshall wrote to Joseph Rosen of Agro-Joint on May 28, 1928, saying that he had recently read "from responsible sources" reports of "a recrudescence of anti-Semitism. . . . It is said that this feeling of hostility against Jews is permeating the proletariat and is to some extent encouraged by those in authority."[18]

In 1929, JDC, in answer to a questionnaire dealing with the situation regarding Soviet Jewry, replied, "In many cases they are pushed out of factories, workshops and mines by their antisemitic co-workers. . . ."[19] In June 1930, Rabbi Leon Fram wrote:

I remember seeing during a visit in Soviet Russia a Russian play which was a satire upon the inefficiency of Russia's factory managers. There was a scene in which a government inspector came to the factory manager to find out if he was doing anything to eliminate the usual evils of Russia's bureaucratic industry. "Have you eliminated anti-Semitism from this factory?" asks the reporter.

"Yes, sir," answers the manager briskly, "there is no more anti-Semitism in this factory. We have discharged all the Jews."[20]

There were heated debates in the United States over the issue of anti-Semitism, with some arguing from a strong anti-Soviet or Zionist bias; others deploring the "silence" of American Jewry; still others refuting the charges of Soviet anti-Semitism. Some non-Jewish circles in the United States used the conflict between Stalin and Trotsky to heat up anti-Semitism and charge that Jews were "running the Communist International." Obtaining hard, verifiable information was difficult, a situation that gave rise to imagined abuses as well as fantasies. In some Jewish circles, for example, there were hopes that when the United States recognized the Soviet Union, it might be possible to arrange for the emigration of certain Soviet Jews over fifty. Some Jews even believed in the possibility of strengthening "progressive" forces in the Soviet Union aimed at the overthrow of Stalin. For their part, "American officials were extremely careful in dealing with the situation of Soviet Jews."[21]

The Evsektsiya, during what was to be their last chapter, combated the "right deviation" of chauvinism more vigorously than anti-Semitism, and "attacked Jews who blamed all of their ills on the alleged anti-Semitism of government and party officials, as well as those who wanted to hush up manifestations of anti-Semitism."[22] The late twenties and early thirties witnessed many denunciations of various "oppositionist" groups, especially those guilty of "Trotskyism," and since many Jews in the party showed strong support or sympathy for Trotsky, an anti-Jewish bias overlapped ideological hostility. Trotsky himself in 1937, in his essay "Thermidor and Anti-Semitism," accused the Stalin regime of anti-Semitism (see Chapter 14). As for the regime in the early thirties, in contrast to the NEP period and earlier, it discontinued the campaign against anti-Semitism and stopped publications on the issue.[23]

Collectivization and industrialization introduced movement controls over the population and new rigid controls over the work force. In 1930, workers, in effect, were riveted to their jobs, forbidden to leave without permission of the managers but subject to transfer at the will of authorities. In February 1931 came the work certificate, containing details of the worker's social origins, training, type of employment, fines, and reasons for dismissals. The most encumbering document was the internal passport, introduced ostensibly to control the overcrowding in large cities, but locking the urban population into a vast check-and-control system.

Collectivization ushered in a large-scale movement from country to town, especially among the richer farmers who, "in anticipation of being classified as kulaks, moved away from the villages and others who fled from the rural districts in . . . fear of disorders and a general collapse of the rural economy."[24] The subsequent famine in 1932–33 and 1933–34 forced other millions on the move. These near-chaotic conditions, and the desire to check the influx of the "class enemy" into the cities, and the severe housing shortage in the cities as a result of the industrialization plans were the alleged reasons for passage of the Passport Law on December 27, 1932. Internal passports were to be subsequently issued in 1933 to all urban residents sixteen and over by the local authority or militia at the place of permanent residence of the applicant. Once thought to typify tsarism and despised by all the Russian revolutionaries, the internal passport system was revived by Stalin, and still functions in the Soviet Union today. The document requires name, date of birth, nationality, permanent residence, and place of work. Upon registration, a person is required to produce papers showing the nationality of both parents. If both parents are of the same nationality, the children automatically assume that nationality. If the parents are of different nationalities, the sixteen-year-old selects one of the two.

The Russians have a ditty which runs, "Without a document, you're an insect; but with a document, you're a human being."[25] There are all sorts of documents—the passport, the work book, the institutional work pass, a character reference, and special purpose permits (to stay at a hotel, take a vacation, receive medical treatment, enter a library, etc.), but the internal passport is the quintessential document because it contains vital information about one's birth, parentage, ethnic or national group, marriage and divorce status, and residential registration with the local police. This internal passport and the residential permit, called the *propiska*, are the basic elements that control population movements in the Soviet Union.

The designation of nationality on the passport has sometimes been interpreted as acquiescence in and recognition of the national pride of the many national groups in the Soviet Union, but in view of the official Soviet doctrine of increased assimilation of these groups, or "Sovietization," the retention of this item, especially as it is applied to Jews, has a dubious if not suspect rationale. Internal passports must be produced when one applies for a job, admission to a school, and on occasions of birth, marriage, and death.[26] Existing national and ethnic prejudices often operate in the decisions of all-powerful bureaucrats examining the documents, and in the case of Jews, the designation "Evrei" has often been used to block access to employment, promotion, and schooling. For this reason as well as for personal reasons, an uncounted number of Jews have not identified themselves as Jews in the recent censuses. Thus, it is impossible to know exactly how many Jews there are in the Soviet Union. The figure of three million is generally used as the most accurate approximation, but 2,151,000 is the figure given in the census of 1970.[27]

Legally, there is no possibility for Jewish descendants of homogeneous marriages to change the designation *Evrei* (Jewish) on their passports. They may, however, choose not to identify themselves as Jews to census takers.[28] In the latter situation, because the concept of Jewish nationality is difficult to define, the data is gathered through respondent self-identification.

There is no doubt that Jews have suffered from the contradiction of having a designated nationality without the status and advantages accruing to other national groups: territory, cultural channels of expression, their own language, press, and schools. Moreover, the scattering of the Jewish population need not necessarily have excluded it from these benefits other scattered groups enjoy. In unpublished discussions on nationality theory held in 1966, some participants held that the desire to remain a nation survives dispersal, or can exist despite the lack of a common language or a common economy, despite Stalin's earlier formula, but Jews alone have remained outside the category "nation."[29] In these discussions, Jews were dismissed by someone as never being able to develop into a nation because of their "historically formed dispersal and social composition," a reference apparently to "some imbalance due to dependence on industry alone."[30] There would seem to be some serious imbalance in this kind of formulation.

In addition to population controls, Stalin imposed an extreme cultural and social regimentation in the early thirties—changes that had no precedent in the often repressive history of the Russian people. Past service to the party and Marxist convictions lost all meaning in Stalin's demands for a "new Soviet intelligentsia," obedient and technologically competent. One historian has observed that "The destruction of a living Russian culture was made complete in 1930 with the suicide of Mayakovsky, the formal abolition of all private printing and Stalin's sweeping demand . . . that the first five-year plan be expanded into a massive 'socialist offensive' along the entire front."[31] Deliberately kept uncertain about what was required of them, creative writers and thinkers twisted, twirled, and circled helplessly, creating the new ersatz culture of "socialist realism." Such a cultural regimentation exploited and manipulated the thinking and talents of individuals in order to create a uniform and obedient society with a supreme, infallible leader. The "cultural revolution" not only undermined early literary traditions and brought proletarian writers to power, but shattered the old intelligentsia and existing cultural institutions. "Socialist realism" became the required style and substance in all of the arts and the catchall slogan of Stalin's Iron Age.

In the industrialization fervor, the factory and the machine became the primary metaphors for society, and writers were not only required to remold their work, but to remake themselves. A number did field work in factories and construction sites in an effort to dissolve their former special status and "class prejudices" and merge with the proletariat. Working-class opinion became the touchstone of good and evil. Writers began to read their latest works before factory workers and worked as consultants on collective histories of industrial enterprises. Universities invited workers to participate in the choice of professors.[32] There was, of course, strong pressure from above to destroy all vestiges of bourgeois individualism and enter into the spirit of the new age, but there seems also to have been some inner-directed movement as well.[33] Some of the pressure also came from a newly emerging class of young proletarians who hungered for power of their own. There was a push from the bottom—pressure from working-class Communists to move up the economic and political ladder and to create their own intelligentsia through a class war aimed at the old "bourgeois" intelligentsia.[34]

The switch to a class war concept of cultural revolution had been argued earlier but was accepted as official dogma in 1928 with the attack on the prosperous peasants and mining engineers and technicians in the Shakhty Trial. "This trial marked a turning point in Soviet policy toward the bourgeois specialist. . . . From this time, the technical intelligentsia ceased being seen as the Party's natural ally in industrialization, and became a potentially treacherous group whose real allegiance was to the dispossessed capitalists and their foreign supporters."[35] The purpose of the trial, according to an NKVD official, was to mobilize the masses and intensify their vigilance against the intelligentsia as a *class enemy*. Successful industrialization now required proletarian engineers and a population alert for signs of wrecking and sabotage among the bourgeois intelligentsia.[36]

Specialists—many of them nonparty members—employed by the government, earned very high salaries and enjoyed special privileges, such as housing priority and access to higher education. Moreover, NEP had marked not only a retreat from the leveling of the civil war period and a retreat from revolutionary ideas, but had sharpened the economic gaps and exposed widespread unemployment in the cities, especially of unskilled workers and the young.[37] The bourgeois elements, it was held, were fighting for their own schools, their own art, theater, and cinema and using the state apparatus to maintain their positions. Thus, working-class Communists demanded more of the economic and political spoils. Their class war concept reflected real tensions between the materially disadvantaged and the privileged. The ensuing struggle strongly resembled that of the Red Guards in the Cultural Revolution in China in the 1960s.

The composition of the Communist party itself foreshadowed this upsurge: by 1930, 56.3 percent of party members were of working-class origin and 46.3 percent worked in proletarian occupations. "Bourgeois" socialists were steadily replaced by "red" specialists, and ideology and politics invaded the purest of sciences. Literature made heavy use of conventional formulas and slogans, attacking "wreckers" and "saboteurs" threatening the new society, or the theme of the bourgeois-gone-astray-under-capitalism ending up in antisocial crime, occasionally finding salvation in socialism. The literary upheavals of the "cultural revolution" which occurred in the years from 1928 to 1931 not only damaged Soviet literature but embroiled writers in bitter polemics and personality conflicts. A number of the antagonists and victims were Jews, as has been described earlier (see Chapter 9).

Increasingly, writers feared the spreading power of the police, with its own secret service, counterespionage, and network of agents who promoted denunciations, false accusations, and endless investigations.

Communist critics now made a stand for the inclusion of art in the Five Year Plan, and they and members of RAPP (Russian Association of Proletarian Writers) organized "all creative activity along lines similar to industrial activity": they wanted a captive literature produced on an assembly line.[38] Books had to show the heroism of socialist construction and the new Soviet man as bursting with energy, a builder and technician, with full confidence in himself and the future, and pride in his country. Leopold Averbakh, a Jew and a leading figure in RAPP, and others at first exerted heavy pressure on writers to write in this vein, resulting in works of very low quality and creating "an atmosphere of insufferable monotony."[39] Averbakh himself fell into disfavor in 1932 because he did not show enough enthusiasm for such a regimented literature and defended some of his literary protégés who had exposed disillusionment and denigration within the party itself. Averbakh had said the "Bolsheviks are not afraid of the truth," but all literary sins of the time were heaped on his head and RAPP, which he had headed since 1927, was liquidated in April 1932.[40]

Having himself grown disillusioned with the regime, the petty and vulgar bureaucracy and rampant materialism, as well as suffering profound personal problems, Mayakovsky, who had been hailed as *the* poet of the Revolution, committed suicide in 1930. The irony in his poem "Home" tells us how he felt about the new order:

Along with reports of pig iron
    and steel
I want to report on verse production
    on behalf of the Politburo

From Stalin.[41]

Besides RAPP, all other literary groupings were dissolved in 1932, including the apolitical Union of Writers, which had been especially concerned about the economic welfare of its members. The principal figures of this union were the great writers Pilnyak and Zamyatin, who were pilloried as enemies of the state in a vicious campaign of vilification. Pilnyak's nerves broke. The "attack and his reduction to recanting impotence might have served as a model for later literary campaigns and purges"—he was simply associated with enemies of the Soviet Union.[42] This technique would be used later, like a steady tattoo, against the Yiddish writers.

The end of RAPP and other groups was variously interpreted—some believed it would usher in a period of greater artistic freedom—but it actually signaled the complete control of all literature and the arts by the party. It was two years before the full impact of this decision was felt. Meanwhile, some of the disgraced "bourgeois" scholars and writers had been tentatively "rehabilitated"—with the same suddenness as a momentary truce Stalin had made with technical experts after issuing a statement of reconciliation to the "bourgeois engineers" in June 1931.[43]

After RAPP was abolished, the staffs of publishing houses, magazines, newspapers, and boards of censorship were changed and all writers were urged to join a general Union of Writers. Within the union, all literary affairs fell to a Committee on Art, which began to function like a state ministry, with its system of awards, penalties, and surveillance.[44]

The theory of socialist realism was now to become official doctrine sanctioned by this union and by the First All-Union Congress of Soviet Writers, convened in Moscow in August 1934. Of the more than 500 delegates, the majority were party members, including ten Yiddish writers. There were also some prestigious foreign guests, including the American Yiddish writer, Joseph Opatoshu. There were 113 Soviet Jewish delegates at the Congress—almost 20 percent of the total. Twenty-four of them wrote in Yiddish, the rest in Russian, including Pasternak, Babel, and Ehrenburg. Of the Yiddish writers, only eight had the right to vote: Bergelson, Markish, Hofshteyn, Kvitko, Feffer, Kharik, Yashe Bronshteyn, and Y. Khatskels.[45]

Andrei Zhdanov, who would declare cultural war on "rootless cosmopolitans" after the war, first emerged at this congress as the party's new authority on cultural affairs. He gave the main address, which outlined the future form and content of all Soviet literature: "In the age of the class struggle, a non-class . . . apolitical literature does not and cannot exist." Soviet literature had to be a class-permeated literature, whose heroes would be "active builders of a new life."[46] Socialist realism was now mandatory for all writers.

The formulation was accepted by an overwhelming majority, but a number of the Jewish delegates expressed independent opinions during the debates. Lev Kassil, for example, "dared to speak against the general tendency . . . to run down Western literature and called on delegates 'to learn seriously from foreign writers.' " Ehrenburg expressed his pride at being a "rank and file Soviet writer," but admitted that the Soviet negation of European literature was "simply provincial."[47] Pasternak, who was of Jewish origin, was reported to have been hesitant and dispirited, expressing loyalty to the regime, but avoiding the jargon of others and warning writers not to be enticed by status and wealth.[48] As the spokesman of the Yiddish writers, Feffer's remark chimed in with the prevailing line, consigning the classical Yiddish writers to a dead past and portraying the trajectory of Jewish literature as "the poor literature of a poor tribe, without a country, history or great literary tradition of its own."[49] Brief compliments were paid to Bergelson, Hofshteyn, and Markish.

It was left to Isaac Babel,[50] perhaps the greatest Jewish prose artist of the time, who wrote in Russian, to laconically allude to the shrinking space left to the Soviet writer. He had already been hailed for his sharp, impressionistic series of short stories based on incidents in the bloody campaign of Semyon Budenny's Cossacks in Poland in 1920, called *Red Cavalry*. Babel's Cossacks are ignorant and ferocious, but also graced by a kind of violent beauty, which he, a thin, bespectacled Jewish youth from a past haunted by pogromizing Cossacks, admires. They will somehow bring about the new order that will make them all brothers. But the prose is far from reportage or the flatness of Communist dogma. Rather, it is a highly individualistic style of bright images, startling metaphors, slanting incongruities, irony, and piercing flashes of Jewish pain and suffering.

A protégé of Gorky, whom he met in 1916, and to whom he said he "owed everything," Babel gained approval and popularity in the mid-twenties and enjoyed a brief period of comfort and privilege. However, increasingly he had to meet the demands of exacting and dogmatic editors and censors who cared nothing about literary artistry, while he could spend hours over a sentence. Then, in 1928, he was attacked by Marshal Budenny himself, who said that Babel was a "worthless and vicious hack." For a time Gorky defended Babel's integrity as a writer, but his difficulties grew worse. Several years went by and he had nothing new to show in published form—a dangerous situation in the early thirties. A playwright named V. V. Vishnevsky, who had helped to bring Averbakh down, wrote a black-and-white corrective to Babel's *Red Cavalry*, showing Budenny's Cossacks as "men of high morale who knew what they were fighting for." At the Writers' Congress in 1934 people asked why Babel remained silent. Was it possible he no longer approved of the regime?

At the 1934 Congress Babel spoke about the necessary right of a writer to "write badly." He admitted to his silence, of which he said he was "a past master," and in his typically ironic manner, told the delegates that he had been spending all of his time "searching for a new style suitable to our epoch."[51] He subsequently wrote a few plays and movie scripts, but they were not vintage Babel. His alienation from the growing repression was climaxed in 1939 when he was arrested and never heard from again—a victim of Stalin's purges. A certificate delivered to the family shortly after Stalin's death gives March 17, 1941, as the date of his death, but does not mention the cause or place. In 1954, Babel was "rehabilitated" and cleared of all criminal charges. A selection of his works, a carefully censored and expurgated edition, was published in Moscow in 1957.[52]

Another Jew who wrote in Russian, Osip Mandelshtam,[53] considered by some to be the greatest Russian poet of the twentieth century, was also resisting authority in the early thirties by insisting on retaining his artistic integrity and by refusing to extol the glories of the Stalin state, despite the sordid material conditions he and his wife were forced to endure. He scarcely mentions the Five Year Plan in his *Journey to Armenia*, but writes sympathetically of a schoolteacher who has been expelled from a collective farm. He was also eagerly heard at crowded poetry recitals, but was provoked by hecklers asking his opinion of contemporary Soviet poetry. After 1933, none of Mandelshtam's work was published. His *Journey to Armenia* was attacked for ignoring Armenia's achievements, but he refused to recant. His age had become menacing—"the wolfhound age springs on my back"—and he sensed his own doom. Then in November he composed his notorious "Poem on Stalin," with its references to the "Kremlin's mountaineer" with fingers "fat as worms" and "cockroach mustache." In May 1934 Mandelshtam was arrested, imprisoned in Lubyanka, and exiled for three years to the small town of Cherdyn in the Urals. He failed in a suicide attempt in his second place of exile, Voronezh, where he died in 1938.

The early thirties also witnessed the discarding of earlier experimental methods and programs in Soviet schools, which were declared to be a "source of ignorance . . . counter-revolutionary attitudes and 'wrecking.' " Curricula were drained of any hint of Jewish tradition, holiday celebrations, or any element of *folkstimlikhkeit* (shared intimate popular culture), and all the textbooks "overflowed with eulogies of 'construction,' descriptions of nature and blatant Stalinist patriotism."[54] By 1933–34, Jewish children began to fill Russian schools and a rapid decline set in throughout the Yiddish schools. Even in Birob-idzhan, not more than 20 percent of the Jewish children attended Yiddish schools. Any agitation to send children to Yiddish schools was regarded as a "dangerous deviation."[55] Soviet Jews now in the United States recall warnings to parents: "Don't send your kids to the Yiddish school." At work, "they say to a man, 'Look, you want to advance on your job, don't send your kids anymore to the Jewish school. It's reactionary.' "[56]

Jewish scholarship also suffered in the 1930s. For example, *Evreiskaya starina* (Jewish Antiquities), the journal of the Jewish Historical-Ethnographic Society, which had originally been started and edited by the historian Simon Dubnow, and was revived by Lev Sternberg after Dubnow left, lapsed for four years and appeared again in 1928, "with an emphasis on East European Jewry. . . . The last issue appeared in 1930 . . . largely devoted to literary and cultural history . . . [and showing] signs of haste, such as numerous errors in transliteration."[57] The popular historical journal *Evreiskaya letopis'* (Jewish Chronicle), had already ended publication in 1926, possibly because of its interest in Hasidism.[58] Dubnow, who had left Russia in 1922, was invited to write a memoir from Berlin, but the invitation was denounced in an article by Niepomniaschi in 1929 and provided a pretext for the closing down of both the Jewish Historical-Ethnographic Society and the Society for the Spread of Enlightenment among the Jews of Russia,[59] known as OPE, both of which had carried on significant research in Russian in prerevolutionary Jewish scholarship, and had continued publishing, sponsoring lectures, and maintaining libraries and archives in the early Communist period in Leningrad. Joseph Liberberg, who became director of the Department of Jewish Culture in the Ukrainian Academy of Sciences in Kiev, took over their archives.

Any hint of nationalist feeling, "pessimism," or "dwelling on the past" was condemned, but even other subjects such as economic reconstruction at a time when views on "productivizing" Jews were still unsettled could be potentially perilous. Scholars such as Hillel Alexandrov, who tried to steer a middle course while still condemning the ideas that were clearly out of favor, were brought down in 1933.[60] Lev Zinger, who had worked as a statistician for ORT and later became an outstanding Soviet demographer, fell into the ideological never-never land in 1932 because he was "particularly cautious on Birobijan, which he depicted as a place of migration only for the Jewish poor," without much prospect for a large migration.[61] One of the scholars who attacked it, I. I. Weizblit, head of the Jewish Institute in Kiev until 1931, himself had been attacked (in 1930) for calling land settlement wasteful and nationalistic in the Five Year Plan era. He later published a retraction, but was removed from his position at the Kiev Institute.

As Stalin rapidly obliterated the distinction between state and society, and as all institutions, services, intellectual, and artistic pursuits were becoming politicized, semi-autonomous functions such as existed in the remaining churches and synagogues were eliminated. In 1929, the campaign against religion intensified. On April 8, the USSR Central Executive Committee approved a law restricting the use of churches and synagogues to prayer and "religious needs," but not for social, cultural, educational, welfare, or other functions.[62] In the following month, the use of residential city buildings as prayer houses was banned and throughout the year more than a hundred synagogues were closed. In some cases, the prohibitive costs of upkeep caused closings: electricity rates for prayer houses were four times higher than the regular rate, and the cost of heating, land taxes, and insurance were also much higher.[63] By late 1931, not a single synagogue remained in Kiev, but appeals to Moscow were successful in having one reopened.

The Evsektsiya outpaced the party in some of these repressions. In the late 1920s, for example, the Evsektsiya launched a campaign to force Jewish synagogues to donate ritual objects to provide funds for the First Five Year Plan. Churches were similarly requisitioned. Many devotional books and religious objects were thus eliminated. At times local officials and the Evsektsiya were overruled by higher authorities for their overzealous excesses, but it is likely that "these 'excesses' . . . were instigated, or at least welcomed by the same authorities who later rescinded some of the 'excessive acts' in a fraudulent demonstration of magnanimity."[64]

The onslaught against Judaism stirred prolonged and stubborn resistance among some Jews, especially the *Bratslav* and *Chabad* groups of the Hasidic movement and the leader of the latter group, Rabbi Joseph Isaac Schneerson, who had formed an underground network of Hasidic circles, schools, and social welfare programs, which moved from Rostov-on-the-Don to Nevel, then to Kharkov to avoid the police. Schneerson was arrested in July 1927 and sentenced to death for counterrevolutionary activity and spreading anti-Soviet propaganda abroad. However, following worldwide protests, he was allowed to leave the country at the end of 1928 and continued his efforts to send relief funds and books into Russia from Latvia.[65] Before his arrest, Schneerson had helped to organize artels of Jewish artisans who wanted to observe the Sabbath and maintain kosher kitchens, but non-Jewish workers were then brought into the artels and voted for Saturday work. Some older observant Jews and rabbis could not accept this decision and left, finding work as night watchmen in some of the large cities. During their long vigils in deserted factories and office buildings, they prayed and studied.

In April 1929, a decree was issued empowering the NKVD to register a religious association if petitioned by twenty or more persons of eighteen years or over. However, over one hundred paragraphs of restrictions and bans and ways to liquidate the associations made the decree a grotesque travesty. Yet the tenacity of observant Jews was strong. At the end of 1929, according to reports reaching American Jewish agencies, about 12,000 Jewish children in 189 localities were receiving religious education in clandestine schools, and about 800 students were attending yeshivot.[66]

American Jewish organizations wrestled with unseen and inscrutable forces inside the Soviet Union: Would protest intensify anti-Semitism and destroy whatever fragile contacts they had within the Soviet Union? Would help to beleaguered observant Jews be illegal and threaten the lives of the very ones being helped? Was it safe to send help to Schneerson's agency in Riga? The organizations divided on what approach would provide the safest and most beneficial approach.[67] Moreover, Soviet Jews themselves were locked into positions where they had to defend their government.

In February 1930, American Jewish organizations received reports of the arrests of several rabbis in Minsk, including Menachem Gluskin, Mendel Yarcho, and Gerz Maisel. On February 26, the American Jewish Congress called together a conference of representatives of 250 leading national and central Jewish organizations to protest the persecution of Jews and other religions in the Soviet Union; the arrested rabbis were released, probably as a result of this pressure, but they publicly denied any persecution. "Some rabbis abroad," they said, "have joined the worst enemies of the Jewish people and Jewish religion in unjustified anti-Soviet attacks, saying that the Soviet government persecutes the Jewish religion. . . . We don't need such protection in the Soviet Union. We can't separate our fate from the fate of the Jewish nation, regarding which the Soviet government is the only one conducting an open fight against anti-Semitism. We are against the anti-religious . . . propaganda of the Communist Party, but justice requires, however, that we should say that the Communists are openly . . . fighting anti-Semites."[68]

On the larger Soviet scene, the late twenties and early thirties were marked by internal party and general ideological struggles, all of which affected Soviet nationality policy and attitudes toward the Jewish national minority. In the course of the struggle against the so-called right deviation, every national demand could be interpreted as nationalistic and thus dangerous to the security of the Soviet Union. As early as 1927, Russians or russified Ukrainians began to replace Ukrainians in party posts in the Ukraine.[69] In 1929 many Ukrainian intellectuals were arrested on charges of national deviation. The appeal of Soviet nationality policies to nationalities abroad also began to fade and much was made of the military capabilities of the Soviet Union. An atmosphere of possible war against the USSR was used to justify growing government and party centralization and downplay national expression. Many Jewish Communists were attacked for idealizing the Jewish labor movement—the Bund particularly.[70] Both nationalist and assimilationist trends had appeared in Evsektsiya, but ultimately their diverse views were swallowed up by the dictates of party policy in 1930, when the Jewish Sections were abolished (see below). Yet they were required to find a safe channel for the promotion of Birobidzhan between 1928 and 1930 which somehow avoided the Scylla and Charybdis of "nationalism" and "right deviation." The period was a treacherous one. Intellectuals were being purged in Armenia, the Crimea, and Turkestan, and in Belorussia there was a massive purge of party leaders accused of "national democratism." The end for the Evsektsiya was fast approaching.

In the fall of 1929, party leaders in Belorussia threatened to strike at the Evsektsiya leadership which had worked closely with the Belorussians.[71] Many of the Jewish Communists in Evsektsiya now began to assume an exaggerated anti-nationalist posture and to attack each other for nationalist deviations. They became embroiled in vehement literary disputes of the time and strained to purge themselves of the forbidden deviations: defending Jewish interests against party and state, failure to understand anti-Semitism as a *class* phenomenon, tolerance of "petit bourgeois moods and motifs in literature."[72] A flood of self-criticism amounting to self-flagellation paralyzed Evsektsiya work in many localities. Phrases such as "Jewish environment" and "social reconstruction of the Jewish population" were forbidden, while the dangers of "Jewish chauvinism" were considered more serious than anti-Semitism,[73] as Evsektsiya activists contorted language and forced themselves to demonstrate their super-orthodoxy.

The spiralling debate within the Evsektsiya over Jewish settlements, Yiddish institutions, and modernization alternatives for Soviet Jews twisted to a stop toward the end of 1929 as the goal of rapid industrialization swept finely calibrated arguments to the dustheap. Apprehensive and often intimidated by stronger men, anxious about personal and career stakes, and divided within their own ranks, the Evsektsiya could not stand four-square behind a clearly defined direction for Soviet Jews. Maneuvering the shoals of Soviet political life, trying to avoid heresies—a daily problematic—struggling to keep their jobs, and tossed by sudden changes in ideological nuance, Evsektsiya activists, after 1929, lost their footing altogether and became politically impotent. With a few exceptions, most paid a heavy psychological toll trying to walk a constantly shifting ideological tightrope. Nerves frayed, they resorted to recriminations, accusations, and breast-beating confessions of error. The writer Peretz Markish summed up the situation as "very strained and aggravated. . . . In general we don't know what world we're in."[74] But the Evsektsiya itself was caught unaware of its own doom. Plans were made for an Evsektsiya conference in December 1929 or January 1930, but it was never held. Early in January, the Central Committees of the Communist parties of the various republics met and decided on a "reorganization," including the dissolution of the Evsektsiya and other national sections.

There was no formal announcement of the dissolution as such, but on March 9, 1930, Semen Dimanshtain, prominent Evsektsiya leader, officially announced the end of the national sections of the party as part of the general reorganization of the Central Committee. In *Der shtern* of March 12, he spoke of the need to draw nationality work and the organization of state and party more closely together. Elsewhere he called for "new forms" in "so-called Jewish work" under the stepped-up industrialization drive and volunteers to replace the professional Jewish activists. After March 9, the Evsektsiya disappeared from the masthead of *Der emes*, and the paper became an organ of the Central Executive Committee of the Soviet of Nationalities. Dimanshtain complimented the Evsektsiya on its accomplishments in the past, but explained that new conditions dictated new structures and that "national peculiarities" had been reduced essentially to language differences with the advance of Sovietization.[75]

The gigantic industrialization drive had focused the party's attention not on the Jewish colonists or kustars, who had preoccupied the Evsektsiya, but on industrial workers, who were scarcely touched by the Evsektsiya.[76] Its programs to promote Yiddish in the trade unions, for example, were completely futile. In the frequent party shifts on policies of economic modernization, the Evsektsiya responded obediently. But by 1930 the party no longer had any use for it. Moreover, as the regime moved toward centralized decision-making and planning, it did not need to make concessions to national minorities, as it once did. Pluralistic allegiances and seemingly competing loyalties had no place in the new Stalinist order.

It has been argued that, from the beginning, the Evsektsiya was a temporary modification of the fundamental Bolshevik position on the nationality problem, and that it had been regarded, at best, as a mere technical apparatus with a limited life, for bringing Bolshevism to the Yiddish-speaking Jewish masses. The party had obviously never intended it to be more than that. Officially Jews had been defined as one of the small "fluid national groups" with which the party was not centrally concerned. Often they were treated as a subproblem of the large national minorities among whom they lived in compact masses—the Ukrainians and White Russians. Nor did they figure significantly in varied discussions of the "national problem" in the Soviet Union. Yet the various improvised programs for Jews such as the campaign for compact settlements on the land in Belorussia, the Crimea, the Ukraine, and Birobidzhan, and the creation of Yiddish schools, soviets, newspapers, journals, courts, and theaters had aroused vast hopes for a Jewish national life in the Soviet Union. For many of the Evsektsiya workers, moreover, their struggle for a rational, sovietized Jewish economy and culture was earnest and determined, if often perverse and wrongheaded and unnaturally subservient to the wishes of the party, anticipated as well as real. It can even be argued that the Evsektsiya prolonged Jewish activity and certain levels of Jewish consciousness by their very efforts to wrench a new concept out of a badly battered and traumatized Jewry—a *homo Sovieticus Judaeus*, as it were—though at an incalculable cost.

That a number of the Evsektsiya activists, particularly those from the Bund, were initially convinced that such a culture could be created under Bolshevik communism and then had to watch that belief atrophy and die, makes the tragedy all the more poignant. The others who believed that the Jew could strike new roots by assimilating himself completely in the new society watched the advancing menace of popular and official anti-Semitism with bitterness and chagrin. Ultimately, the Evsektsiya served only the regime's purposes. The party exploited the genuine resentments and antagonisms of Evsektsiya activists, especially former Bundists, toward bourgeois Jews and let them do the party's own destructive work, thus avoiding the suspicion of anti-Semitism and proving the existence of a pro-Bolshevik element among Jews.[77] The party then succeeded in intimidating the Evsektsiya by raising the specter of "right-wing deviation," the ghost of the Bundist past with its call for Jewish autonomy. In the first edition of the Great Russian Encyclopaedia (1932), the dissolution of the Evsektsiya is explained as necessary "in order to overcome once and for all the nationalist tendencies still observable in the activity of the Jewish Sections."[78] All margins, rationalizations, stretched out formulations, and nervous lurching were now suddenly ended.

The Communist party played down the importance of the reorganization of the national minorities apparatus, and the dissolution of the Evsektsiya was glossed over as a routine administrative matter. Some scholars maintain that this decision did not mean a basic shift in the Soviet policy toward Jews,[79] but others believe that it was, indeed, a turning point, clearly signaling the party's refusal to tolerate even the mildest forms of Jewish separatism[80]—"an effective means of further weakening a separate Jewish political and cultural consciousness and of amalgamating Jewish . . . life with Soviet life as a whole."[81]

As all matters affecting Jews now became more and more the concern of party and government organs, the possibilities for any distinctively Jewish life faded. And yet, those organs kept fanning Jewish hopes while extinguishing the forms that had aroused them and condemning "national" feeling and thinking that expressed them. No time was lost in 1929–30 for one of the recurring Soviet switchbacks that bewildered Jews and deprived them of any sense of equilibrium. The call for Jewish autonomy in Birobidzhan was now to fill the dead space left by the end of the Evsektsiya, and the "crime" of Jewish national feeling was simultaneously waved as a crusading officially motivated slogan.

Mass prosecutions of prominent Jews, predominantly Communists and fellow travelers, followed close on the heels of the shutting down of the Evsektsiya and in 1930, "a first warning was given the Jewish Commissar Dimmanstein [Dimanshtain] who had come out in the press against a 'total collectivization in the national areas' in an attempt to save from collectivization the Jewish farming settlements in the South of Russia."[82] Dimanshtain also expressed the belief that national differences would persist for a long time and warned against Russian chauvinism[83]—courageous acts in a dangerous time. Ultimately, he, too, perished with most of the other Evsektsiya activists several years later. Yet, before their demise and despite the danger of the nationalist "heresy," the Jewish Sections were obliged to support Jewish colonization in Birobidzhan, while balancing collectivization and industrialization at the same time.

13

Birobidzhan, 1928–40

. . . Chains your granddad used to wear,
Cold Siberian chains;
Now this land is yours, I swear,
Yours are all its gains . . .

Hills and boughs here know no woe,
Peace now fills our view.
In the taiga children grow,
Lucky ones, like you.

To the Kremlin tidings go,
Bright ones, child, I vow!
We'll let Comrade Stalin know
You are sleeping now!

Sleep, my child, shut both your eyes,
Now the hills grow dim;
Over us an eagle flies,
Be, my child, like him.

ITZIK FEFFER, "Birobijaner Viglied,"
   translated by Morris U. Schappes

O FFICIAL Soviet promotion of Birobidzhan overlapped simultaneous efforts to settle Jews on the land elsewhere and "productivize"
them. When the search for a territory for large-scale Jewish agricultural
colonization began in 1924, the national significance of such efforts was
scarcely alluded to by Jewish Communists. The notion of national Jewish revival through agricultural resettlement came primarily from the
chairman of the Presidium of the Central Executive Committee of the
U.S.S.R., Mikhail Kalinin, who, as titular head of the Russian state,
lent great prestige to the idea. It will be recalled that at the first convention of OZET (The Society for Agricultural Settlement of Jewish
Workers) on November 17, 1926, Kalinin spoke of the great task facing

the Jewish people, namely "that of preserving its nationality, [requiring] the transformation of a considerable part of the Jewish population into a compactly settled agricultural peasantry."[1] Successful resettlement efforts were undertaken in the Ukraine and the Crimea, but the launching of the First Five Year Plan (1928–33) broke into those plans and Jews were urged to move into industry. Yet enthusiasm for a Jewish return to the land did not end. Indeed it acquired a new impetus from the sudden interest in Birobidzhan, a distant territory of some 14,000 square miles bordering Manchuria. Though a discredited failure long since, Birobidzhan is still intermittently promoted and identified even today as the Jewish Autonomous Region. Indeed, it has a very special place in the history of the Jewish experience in the Soviet Union.

Many different motives converged on the choice of this remote, sparsely populated territory on the Amur River, named from the two tributaries of the Amur—the Great Bira in the east and the Bidzhan in the west. The area, somewhat larger than Belgium, had been annexed by Russia in 1858, but repeated efforts to colonize it had failed. By the mid-twenties, there were only about 30,000 inhabitants, mostly descendants of Trans-Baikal Cossacks planted there by tsarist authorities, Koreans, Kazakhs, and a primitive tribe called the Tungus. Much of the area, especially in the northeast, is mountainous, covered with thick virgin forests of oak, pine, and cedar, but there are also large swamplands. The climate is very severe with long harsh winters and short intolerable humid summers with their swarms of flies and mosquitoes. The Amur is frozen from the end of November to the end of April. In the spotty arable areas, grains, soybeans, and potatoes can be grown. The principal city is Birobidzhan, formerly the station called Tikhonkaya on the railway line to Khabarovsk (see Map 13.1).

As a border province, Birobidzhan was often infiltrated by Chinese from the far side of the Amur—a practice which alarmed Soviet leaders and led some of them to consider the area for Jewish settlement.[2] "In ten or fifteen years," it was said, "the Chinese will come in a dense mass." Cooperation between Chiang-kai-shek and the Chinese Communist party had just ended and increased this threat. Moreover, Japan seemed ready and willing to detach the Far Eastern provinces from the Soviet Union.

The First Five Year Plan included exploitation of the natural resources of the Far East—iron ore, graphite, magnesite, coal, and gold—but the massive state and party propaganda campaign, especially in

MAP 13.1
Birobidzhan—Jewish Autonomous Region

the crowded cities, which was aimed at attracting settlers, played on the Jewish desire for agricultural work. The government seems to have calculated that Agro-Joint would shift the burden of its work to Birobidzhan, thus keeping up the flow of foreign capital.

The acute competition for land in the Ukraine and the Crimea and the still unsolved problem of Jewish poverty in the late twenties also gave impetus to a search for a new territory with a sparse population. An expedition of 180 people, including scientists, first explored in the Azov Sea area, north of the Caucasus, and the steppes of northern Kazakhstan in 1927.

The expedition also spent a month and a half in Birobidzhan, chiefly in the steppelands, which offered some possibility of settlement. Elsewhere, the area was forbidding and the report[3] warned of swamps, a lack of roads, overflowing rivers, heavy rains, and "a proliferation of vermin." The expedition especially warned against "partial, spotty colonization" and recommended colonization based on "a strict plan. . . . aimed at achieving a dense population . . . over a period of years," to start in the southern and southwestern part of the region along the

Amur. Great emphasis was placed on the need to prepare the region by developing a highway network that could carry heavy motor trucks and tractors as well as access roads and bridges over the rivers. Colonists would also require prepared lots, with fixed boundaries, water supply, and drainage. For a full year before the arrival of settlers, land would have to be turned over and made ready for sowing, and walls and roofs of houses would have to be completed. A phased schedule for the arrival of advance scouts, workers, and families was proposed, with the first 100 families coming in 1929, 2,000 in 1930, and 2,000–3,000 per year in the following years. The report stressed not only the importance of systematic preparation and colonization of new settlers, but the need to plan for the agricultural settlement of the local population, described as "a fundamental prerequisite" and "rather complicated." Finally, the report warned that "the population knows about the forthcoming agricultural utilization of the region and is alarmed and apprehensive with respect to it."

The expedition returned to Moscow on August 23, 1927 and a preliminary report was sent to the government early in 1928. It completed its investigation in the spring of 1928 and produced a multivolume report, which apparently was never discussed and mentioned *only after* the Birobidzhan plan was approved.[4] In March 1928, the Birobidzhan region was allocated to KOMZET "for the purpose of the dense settlement of free lands by working Jews," with the possibility of forming a "Jewish, national, administrative-territorial entity" in the region.[5] Settlement by non-Jews was at first barred.

Curiously, not only was Birobidzhan not born of Jewish initiative, but the project was strongly opposed by leading KOMZET members such as Yuri Larin and Abraham Bragin, who felt that the climate was too harsh, the soil unsuitable for cultivation, and the area too far from the centers of Jewish population. They argued in favor of the Crimea. Larin also said that to achieve the five year goal of settling 9,000 families in Birobidzhan, the government would have to allocate at least 20 million roubles, whereas in 1928–29 only 3.3 million had been allocated. Larin contrasted this "unrealistic program" with the situation in the Crimea and the Ukraine which were financially underwritten by foreign organizations. He also argued that the "unhealthy ballyhoo . . . raised around Birobidzhan is in inverse proportion to the real significance of the area for the Jewish poor," and that instead, workers and kustars were emigrating "for nationalistic reasons."[6] Melech Epstein, a sympathetic American Communist visitor at the time, attended the OZET convention late in 1930 and made this interesting observation:

I was present at the meeting of the Communist caucus on the eve of the Gezerd [OZET] convention, and I witnessed the antagonism of the delegates to the Birobidzhan project. But they were overruled by the party representative and, of course, none of them dared to speak his mind at the open convention. Abram Merezhin, secretary of OZET, was later removed from his post and accused of sabotaging the party decision.[7]

According to Dimanshtain, the Birobidzhan project was proposed by the Commissariats of Agriculture and Defense and was supported by Chicherin and Stalin and, according to others, by the "highest Party organs, not by the Evsektsiya."[8] The prime considerations were strategic: to strengthen the far eastern frontier politically and militarily against an expanding Chinese population and an ambitious, expanding Japan.

In March 1928, representatives of OZET came to Khabarovsk to help prepare the way for settlement of Birobidzhan.[9] Several hundred horses, plows, tents, food, and fodder had been brought to Tikhonkaya, which had been converted into a center for the distribution of provisions, but living quarters, cultivable land, and wood for building had not been arranged for the first settlers. The original area designated for settlement was in south Birobidzhan, in the Amur District, but the Cossacks there objected and a site in the north called Birofeld, closer to the Transsiberian railway was picked. This was a fairly level area, but there were no trees for construction and no drinking water. The only road to Tikhonkaya was muddy and full of pits.

Disregarding the warnings of the Commission against haste, the authorities rushed the first Jewish colonists to Birobidzhan immediately, with dire consequences. The first settlers—numbering 654—came from Kazan, Minsk, and Smolensk, and arrived between April and June 1928.[10] Four hundred and fifty of the original contingent were sent to Birofeld despite the situation there, but the rest were sent to a rice plantation in the Amur District, near a Cossack village. The plantation was put on the agenda unexpectedly—"a straw in a drowning purpose"—because there was widespread despair, and there seemed the possibility of joining the nearby villages. Allotments were made and plans for the digging of an irrigation canal were discussed but slowly faded. Conditions were untenable. Soon telegrams called desperately for tents because no quarters had been prepared, and described starvation of horses and settlers because there was no fodder or food; illness and mounting tensions demoralized the newcomers.

Among those sent to Birofeld were twenty-two men, six from Kazan, ten from Smolensk, and six from Leningrad, who arrived on May 28. After spending two days in tents in Tikhonkaya, they went to Birofeld in a caravan of wagons filled with tools, food, and fodder, a journey of several days. Mud clung to the wagon wheels and the reins broke under the strain of horses pulling the wagons. Eventually, the men themselves had to push the wagons, laboring one whole day to cover twelve kilometers, and drenched by a torrential rain. Seven returned to Tikhonkaya in disgust and frustration.

Victor Fink who accompanied the IKOR (American Association for Jewish Colonization) mission to Birobidzhan in 1929 reported that:

The settlers—who on top of everything were unaccustomed to farm work—found themselves in the taiga forest in extremely painful conditions. . . . Of the settlers of 1928 only a little more than a third were left . . . by the end of the year. The same thing was repeated in 1929. But even of those few settlers who were left . . . the majority were concentrated around Tikhonkaya Station [the future city of Birobidzhan] and in some other small settlements along the railway, and not "on the land."[11]

At the railway station, which had become a bottleneck of settlers, people crowded into filthy barracks, lying about squashed together in two-storied cots—bachelors, young women, old men, large families with babies. Single women, who had fallen into a helpless position, began to turn to prostitution. "They had come," Fink wrote, "with the intention of working on the land, but they could not get to the land."

Hersh Smoliar in his memoirs[12] notes that a fourth of the first contingent returned quickly and described the "unheard of severe conditions" they had to endure. The Central Bureau of the Evsektsiya realized how important it was to stimulate resettlement of the Jews in Birobidzhan, and, above all, to prepare them by giving them a Jewish political stimulus. However, how this should be achieved concretely was not worked out. Among members of the Evsektsiya, there was considerable informal discussion of the importance of bringing to the resettlement program a vision of a full-bodied Jewish culture along socialistic lines, but there was a pervasive fear of falling into the danger of Jewish nationalism.

After the experiences of first contingent had been digested, however, in 1928, the Central Bureau decided to send party and Komsomol organizers to Birobidzhan.[13] Yankel Levin was first recommended to be the party organizer and Smoliar, to represent the Komsomol. I. Lezman filled Smoliar in with respect to the hardships to be expected and the great pioneering opportunities to be found. Smoliar felt called upon to respond as a "mobilized soldier," and agreed to go, but made a speech which was not received sympathetically by the Central Bureau members. In it, he said that the Birobidzhan project needed two essentials: fervor for the upbuilding of the Jewish state like that of other people, and the development of cadres of idealistic youth who wanted to build Jewish national life, in other words, "communist khalutzim." Esther Frumkin disapproved, saying he "was hiccoughing Zionism." Litvakov, who was pleased with Smoliar's work as night editor on *Emes*, was also dissatisfied. Chemerisky, who would later try to arouse interest in Birobidzhan by speaking in near-Zionist terms ("To a Jewish Land"), put off the appointment and did not send Smoliar.

What was the attitude of native peoples toward the coming Jewish settlement? In the Soviet publications dealing with Birobidzhan, "it was frequently stressed that the indigenous population of the region welcomed the Jewish settlers, provided them with assistance, and in general exhibited a positive attitude toward the Jewish settlement, believing that it would bring progress to the region, help in its development, and thus be a blessing to it. . . ." But the truth of this proposition is doubtful. Indeed, in the light of the testimony of a Professor Brook, there was a 1927 report of KOMZET, according to which, "the local population knows what the shape of future land arrangements is destined to be, [and] looks forward to it with worry and suspicion . . ." The Jewish settlement brought about a land arrangement which was repugnant to the local peasants, who, from the moment of Jewish settlement were accustomed to till whatever parcel of land which appealed to them without interference or limitation."[14]

An engineer Noah London, who accompanied the IKOR delegation in 1929, noted that the attitude of local inhabitants was "neutral and expectant." Some received the newcomers warmly and helped them. But, on the other hand, there were some open manifestations of anti-Semitism. One of the first groups arriving at the railway station in May 1928 were called "Zhids" and were refused hot water, a vital necessity after a long journey in the Soviet Union.[15] "In the face of such a reception," the Soviet newspaper *Amurskaya pravda* reported, "the Jews were afraid to leave the coaches."[16] A telegram protesting this treatment was sent to President Kalinin. The official KOMZET report, however, noted later that "the Russian population offered the greatest possible help to the migrants, giving them free housing and seeds; helped them to plough and sow their fields, and offered them advice." According to this report, "the Jewish settlers were allocated land at the rate of four hectares per person and loans of up to 600 rubles per family."[17]

The first settlers had received free transportation for the journey of several thousand miles, but because conditions were so wretched, only 555 settlers arrived in 1929 and 860 in 1930.[18] The planners had projected settling 3,000 families in 1929, or a total of 15,000 persons and 60,000 by 1933. These projections were unrealistic in the extreme. Large-scale colonization in the south of the region, along the Amur, was no longer an option because there had been no preparation. New settlers were routed to the central and northern areas, closer to the railway, but conditions here for developing the land were much more difficult. In 1931, an appeal was made to Jewish ex-servicemen, reflecting the special hardships for families and the increasingly tense situation in the Far East as a result of Japan's invasion of Manchuria in 1931. Yet by the end of 1931, there were only a little over 5,000 Jews in the region out of a total population of almost 45,000. In spite of the 1928 ban on non-Jews, they were settling in Birobidzhan faster than were Jews.

Among the newcomers in 1931 and 1932 were Jews from the Ukraine, where poverty was still acute, but large numbers returned home while some cast about in the larger cities of the Far East, such as Khabarovsk and Vladivostok. In the autumn of 1931, a new decree demanded a "substantial increase in the economic growth of the region on the basis of heavy industrial enterprises using local raw materials (iron, graphite, timber, building materials) home crafts . . . road building and land amelioration,"[19] but these plans were also totally unrealistic. Meanwhile, the influx of non-Jews continued and the plan of turning Birobidzhan into a region of "integral" Jewish agricultural colonization— with no non-Jewish settlement—was tacitly abandoned. In 1932, there was a rise in the number of Jewish immigrants—up to 14,000—because of the launching of the Second Five Year Plan and a stepped up recruitment effort, but an equally sharp rise in the number who returned, some putting the figure at 80 percent.[20] Those who remained were assigned to state and collective farms, industry, transportation, professional, and white-collar categories.

The Khabarovsk survey[21] explained the "unfulfilled" migration plan on "the radical change in the economic situation in the country. Industrialization was accompanied by the liquidation of unemployment and the growth of demand for labor in all parts of the country. The economic causes which had forced Jews in the past to migrate . . . now vanished. The demand for labor . . . both in the west and in the cities of the Far East brought about the departure from Birobidzhan of a substantial number of Jews."

Because of the small number of Jews in Birobidzhan, it was apparently necessary to show a substantial number in official positions. For example, in a listing of members of the organization committee of the Birobidzhan Branch, confirmed by the Far East executive committee of the party in September 1930, ten names appear, with an asterisk after the four Jewish names: Gendlin, Rubenson, Rasky, and Shkolnik.[22] At the first conference of Birobidzhan soviets, held from September 30 to October 6, 1930, there were 124 voting delegates, 27 of whom were Jews. Among ten persons chosen to the Bureau of the Birobidzhan Party Committee on September 30, 1930, five were Jews: Yankel Levin, head of the Agitprop Committee and Birobidzhan Party Secretary, Rubashkin, Braginsky, Stuluv, and Mariasin. Between October 1, 1930, and May 25, 1931, there was a slight increase in the number of Jews in the party and Komsomol in Birobidzhan from forty-seven (9.4 percent) to ninety-five (14.6 percent).[23]

In addition to subsidies for train fare, baggage, utensils, and loans, there was considerable material help from institutions and special projects in several republics. Equipment and missions of specialists came from Belorussia, for example, in 1931. In the same year, there were special contingents from Moscow, and in 1932, from Leningrad.[24]

Generally, however, few Jews were going to Birobidzhan, but officials continued to push for clearly unrealistic targets: 50,000 Jewish settlers by the end of 1933 and 150,000 by the end of 1937—the end of the second Five Year Plan. Again, in 1933, the departures outnumbered the arrivals and, at the end of the year, the total number of Jewish settlers was only a little over 8,000—less that 20 percent of the total population.

The Jewish Sections had been split on the question of Birobidzhan. Until 1930 there were partisans for the Crimea and partisans for Birobidzhan, while the Jewish Sections of the Belorussian Communist party favored Jewish settlements in Belorussia. Eventually they were overruled by the Moscow center of the sections, and began to promote Birobidzhan publicly, if only because non-Jewish settlers were beginning to go to Birobidzhan.[25] Besides, it was hoped that Birobidzhan as a future autonomous Jewish territory would deal a heavy blow to the Zionists and turn the attention both of Soviet and foreign Jews away from Zionism. Chemerisky, for example, boasted that "the autonomous Jewish territory will be the heaviest blow to the Zionist and religious ideology." The Evsektsiya leaders denounced Zionism, but did not hesitate to use Zionist phrases, such as "Tsu a Yidish Land" (To a Jewish Land) and Herzl's famous phrase, "Oib ir vet dos veln—vet dos sein" (If you want it, then it will come to pass). At the same time, the organ of OZET acknowledged the political motivation: "The masses of the Jewish toilers, who are permeated with loyalty and devotion to the Soviet regime, are going to Birobidzhan . . . they are not only fighting for their country . . . but for strengthening the Soviet Union in the Far East."[26] Nationalist arguments, nevertheless, were used in appeals to the Jews of Russia, and still more to those abroad in the expectation of receiving moral and financial support. Zionism was condemned as a tool of British imperialism, but this new Soviet effort would presumably root Jews territorially, as other nationalities had been, and normalize their economic life.

Birobidzhan was also promoted abroad, with a special eye on American Jewry. America had not yet recognized the Soviet Union. The Five Year Plans required large purchases abroad, but the supplies of foreign currency were low. Credit and trade were vital, but could not be achieved in the existing hostile international climate. Jews in Europe and the United States were thought to have significant political influence; they could be won over to the Birobidzhan idea. Bourgeois liberals, secular Yiddishists, and Communist party members and sympathizers did indeed respond and a number of groups were formed that raised money, held meetings, and issued publications. Support came especially from non-Zionists and those who believed in Jewish territorialism, but virtually all sectors of the Zionist movement opposed it. The intensification of anti-Jewish persecution in Germany in the mid-1930s also contributed to outside support for Birobidzhan. The most active organizations were IKOR and Ambidjan (American Committee for the Settlement of Foreign Jews in Birobidzhan), which organized the colonization of about 1,400 Jews from the United States, South America, and Europe. One American committee for Birobidzhan had, at the height of its popularity, a budget of $750,000, and its annual dinners were gala events. Its guest speakers often included American senators and military officials. ORT-Farband gave limited assistance for the development of industry and workshops while Agro-Joint and ICA (Jewish Colonization Association) generally took a neutral stand. Representatives of the Argentinian Jewish organization PROKOR (Society for the Productivization of the Jewish Masses in the Soviet Union) visited Birobidzhan in 1929.

IKOR was an American society set up in 1924 to help in the agricultural resettlement of Jews in the Soviet Union. (The name derives from the Yiddish, *Geselshaft tsu Helfen der Idisher Kolonizatzie in Sovetn Farband*.) From 1924 to 1928, IKOR concentrated on aid to the settlements in the Crimea and southern Ukraine. All the funds transmitted by IKOR during this time were spent through OZET offices in Moscow. Between 1928 and 1932, IKOR shifted its focus to Birobidzhan, directing all its activities there, and becoming the chief exponent of Birobidzhan in the United States. Toward the end of 1928, the Soviet government agreed to allow IKOR the right to explore the new territory, to build and aid Jewish collective farms and industrial plants, and to organize various forms of cultural aid. In 1929, IKOR sent an investigating team to Birobidzhan, headed by William Harris, president of the University of Utah,[27] and from 1930 to 1933, Charles Kuntz, president of IKOR, was in Birobidzhan supervising the work of the organization. During this time about $300,000 was contributed by American Jews to IKOR for the purchase of American-made machinery for clearing the forests, tractors, trucks, automobiles, excavators, road-building machines, gasoline motors, incubators, canning machinery, and a complete wood-working factory. From 1933 to 1938, the emphasis was on cultural activities. A modern printing establishment was installed, a picture gallery and library were opened, and many Yiddish typewriters were distributed. At the height of its activity, between 1928 and 1933, IKOR had a membership of about 12,000, with more than a hundred local committees throughout the United States. In 1935, it began to publish a monthly in English and Yiddish called *Naylebn* (New Life) and from time to time, issued pamphlets on the developments in Birobidzhan.

IKOR sponsored the one successful project of the early years, the youth collective of the same name, the only farm in Birobidzhan that weathered the hard times of 1928–29. Its members were the first graduates of the Jewish Agricultural School in Kurasovhchina, near Minsk—highly motivated sons and daughters of pre-Soviet Jewish peasants who went to Birobidzhan inspired by the slogan "Onward to the land of the Jews!"[28] There were also some idealistic American socialists who contributed to its survival. But most foreign groups lacked direct contact with Birobidzhan. For all their devotion to the cause, they had no exact information on conditions there, and no true picture of the problems. Letters often went unanswered; shipments of material and equipment specifically marked for Birobidzhan were not transferred once they had arrived in the Soviet Union—frustrating difficulties that block general shipments today. Yet the campaign for Birobidzhan and the support it generated for the Soviet Union as a whole were extremely important to Soviet officials. They wanted good-will, recognition, and trade, and seemed more interested in effective propaganda campaigns for Birobidzhan than in the material help.

As for the settlers, they were not permitted to have any information about the very Jews abroad who were interested in them, except Soviet-censored news of the anti-Semitism, discrimination, and oppression in their respective capitalist societies. In keeping with the Soviet view that Soviet Jews were not part of a larger Jewry, virtually all ties with world Jewry were severed.

Clearly missing was a wholehearted official Soviet commitment to a national Jewish republic, undercut as it was by conflicting versions of Birobidzhan's future: Kalinin's voice for such a republic as against the stress on colonization for the sake of a more secure fatherland; OZET's campaign for Birobidzhan rubbing against KOMZET's efforts to resettle Jews in the Crimea. Moreover, the Soviet industrial timetable played havoc with the initial Birobidzhan idea. More and more Jews were flocking to large state enterprises in administrative and managerial positions, and Jewish labor, with promising new opportunities in the large cities, was clearly not tempted to go to a semiwilderness thousands of miles away.

Very few foreigners had actually visited Birobidzhan except persons with an official interest, such as Dr. Charles Rosen of American Agro-Joint, or A. Epstein of IKOR. Foreign correspondents generally did not travel that far, unless they were bound for China or Japan. One well-known correspondent of the Yiddish daily *Der tog*, and sympathetic to the Soviet Union, Ben Zion Goldberg,[29] however, was determined to do a story on Birobidzhan for eager readers back in America. In October 1934 he first tried to make arrangements through Intourist, but was told they had no service in Birobidzhan. Then he tried the chief press officer of the foreign ministry, a keen and knowledgeable Jew, Constantine Oumansky, who later became ambassador to the United States. Oumansky said such a trip did not come within his purview, and, like so many other upper-echelon Bolsheviks, regarded the Birobidzhan project as one of Kalinin's antics but intimated that it was possible to get there—on one's own. Goldberg then asked his Intourist guide if she could go to Birobidzhan and be his personal guide. Arrangements were finally made and the young woman proved extremely resourceful in several tight situations, including their accidental boarding of a military train from Birobidzhan to Smidovich.

The train trip took eleven days, and after having a meal at the station, Goldberg was put up in the one lodging place in town, a shelter of ten rooms for new arrivals, each housing a family with all they had brought with them—bedding, linen, kitchenware. Mostly the women were grumbling about the primitive conditions, but some said they had come for the sake of the children—so that they could grow up "in a Jewish country." Goldberg found some proud and hardy pioneers clearing the virgin forests, who said that Jews were happy to have roots in the soil. The show place was Waldheim, a settlement that looked like a well-established Russian village, with solidly built log cabins, ample gardens, and abundant food. Pioneers had also come from America, idealistic Socialists and Communists, to found an IKOR settlement which Goldberg was most eager to see, but officials kept presenting obstacles. He begged, cajoled, and threatened, and finally appealed to the highest authority in the region, who granted permission. But the settlement was in a run-down, depressed state, and "the drab ramshackle buildings, the barren waste, their scrawny animals and fowls were unmistakable signs of poverty and privation, of an unequal struggle with an unfriendly environment, of a defeat that they refused to accept." Goldberg's driver said that the settlers were wonderful people with a fine spirit, but they had had bad luck—two crop failures in a row. A Jewish organization had sent them equipment for woodwork and carpentry—perhaps they should concentrate on woodworking. The manager admitted that "they were up against it. They found it tough when they started out; then one piece of bad luck had come after another. But they were still on their feet, and fighting. And they would fight it out." He asked Goldberg "to please say that they were all happy, very happy, in IKOR." Socialism, he said, had already arrived in the Soviet Union and Birobidzhan offered the great opportunity to help build a Jewish socialist state in the Yiddish language and culture as part of the great international socialist fatherland. "Of what consequence were hard work and temporary deprivation against this great mission? Happy the man who could serve this ideal and live by it!"

But Goldberg could not find much happiness among the hard-bitten, haggard faces. Yet he had to admit there *was* something quite thrilling: the sounds of Yiddish. Yiddish was dominant and pervasive even if the quality of Yiddish culture was still quite primitive. There was as yet no theater, although an amateur group was forming, or book publishing, and no Yiddish high school. There was only a beginning, but Goldberg felt that "the beginning had a distinction not found anywhere else in the vast land. Here *all* Jewish children went to Yiddish schools; practically all Jews spoke Yiddish; the government was conducted in Yiddish. . . . Here was one spot—indeed the only spot in the world—where the language and culture of the Jewish masses was primary, not secondary; dominating, not dominated; and practically exclusive."

One of the most ardent advocates of Birobidzhan was Henokh Kazakevich, a big, strapping Jew, a party member, and something of an idealist and dreamer. In the early thirties, he was a newspaper editor and prominent figure in OZET and lived in Birobidzhan for a time with his wife. Esther, the wife of the Soviet Jewish poet Peretz Markish tells of the heated arguments Kazakevich and her husband had over Birobidzhan, with Markish intuitively feeling that "settling Jews in Birobidzhan was artificial . . . that it could never become a real homeland for Jews . . . and that it would end up in a fiasco." "Nothing could succeed," he believed, "unless the hand worked in harmony with the spirit, and could there be any doubt that the wilderness of Birobidzhan was alien to the Jewish spirit?"[30] In 1934, Markish and a group of other writers visited Birobidzhan, but came back disheartened and disillusioned. According to his wife, many of the Jews who had come to Birobidzhan from abroad were sent to camps during the purges of 1936–37.

The optimistic hopes and illusions of Kalinin were apparently shared by the Jews in OZET, who had projected a highly ambitious Second Five Year Plan in 1932, not only to develop Birobidzhan's agricultural resources, but to lay the basis for big industry, especially the exploitation of the vast forests for lumbering and a building industry that would require at least eighteen state factories. This Second Five Year cycle coincided with the worldwide depression, the rise of Nazism, the desperation of millions of Jews in Poland, Germany, and other parts of Europe to find work and refuge, but the Soviet Union was reluctant to admit such refugees.[31] Yet the Central Council of OZET adopted a resolution in 1934 noting the advantage "to bring from abroad certain contingents of qualified Jewish workers in deficit occupations, taking into consideration the drive of Jewish workers in capitalist countries to take an active part in the socialist upbuilding of the Jewish autonomous region."[32] Such a tone was clearly a nod to foreign public opinion, only a trickle of Communist stalwarts was allowed in. This was a period of rising xenophobia in the Soviet Union—of fear and suspicion of foreigners, of Soviet vulnerability to foreign criticism, fears of invasion, and swelling Russian nationalism.

For a time, the campaign for Yiddish in Birobidzhan was taken up enthusiastically. Street signs, rail station signs, and postmarks appeared in both Russian and Yiddish. Resolutions were passed making Yiddish as well as Russian the official language of the province. In 1934 a Jewish state theater was established, and a regional library, named after Sholem Aleikhem and containing a sizable collection of Judaica and Yiddish works, was founded in the city of Birobidzhan. Kalinin was consistently supportive of the project, and at a reception given to representatives of Moscow workers and the Yiddish press in May 1934, he expressed the hope that "within a decade Birobidzhan will be the most important . . . bulwark of national Jewish socialist culture."

The efforts to make Yiddish the dominant language, or at least the equal of Russian, were self-conscious and determined in the first few years, giving the settlements the aura of a Jewish culture, but Yiddish never really enjoyed the prestige of Russian. An attempt was made in September 1935 to make Yiddish the compulsory language for clerical work and official correspondence, but according to news items in *Der emes* in 1936 and 1937,[33] only two of the fifteen Jewish collective farms carried on their work in Yiddish, courses for civil servants in Yiddish dissolved, and important personnel in the Secretariat of the Regional

Executive Committee had no knowledge whatsoever of Yiddish. Officials in the Regional Health Department and Land Department were accused of avoiding Yiddish with workers and visitors and treating it with disrespect. Much specialized technical work was still in Russian and many official accounts were being kept in Russian. According to *Der emes* of April 2, 1937, even Yiddish theater announcements were in Russian. Street signs were often badly misspelled. Readers of the *Birobidzhaner shtern* complained that even when Jews were a majority at workers' meetings, they spoke Russian—a "deviation of the Leninist line on the national question."[34] In August 1934, the *Shtern* ran a leading editorial deploring the fact that there was not a single courthouse operating in Yiddish.[35]

Throughout the thirties, at all sorts of meetings—party, governmental, local, and regional—demands were made that the use of Yiddish be "encouraged," and "intensified," but the momentum ebbed quickly. Unexpected support sometimes came from strange quarters. For example, a military commander, a Latvian non-Jew, demanded that the neglect of Yiddish be redressed by himself as well as others. He taught himself Yiddish and used it publicly at a party conference in June 1934.[36] The conference resolved that Yiddish penetrate into public and governmental spheres, but the counterforces were too strong.

The Yiddish press in Birobidzhan also fell away from early high hopes. The circulation of the small *Birobidzhaner shtern* (Birobidzhan Star), which had started in 1930, dropped to about 1,000 by 1939, and a quarterly called *Forpost* (Vanguard), which was started in 1936 just before the purges, came out irregularly until 1940, when it was dropped altogether. At a conference of Jewish cultural workers in August 1938, it was reported that courses at the Medical College and Railway Training School were conducted in Russian, while Yiddish and Jewish literature were often ignored owing to a "lack of specialists."[37] By then, of course, the purges had shattered the leadership and core idea behind Birobidzhan.

The Jewish schools, however, which used Yiddish as the language of instruction, held out more promise. Esther Rozenthal-Shneiderman, who had come to Birobidzhan as a pedagogical expert, wrote proudly of the growth of the Yiddish schools. Whereas in 1931–32, there were only 250 students altogether, in 1934–35, there were 1,114 in all schools. In January 1936, there were 450 teachers, and 300 more preparing to teach.[38] There were numerous conferences of teachers and school inspectors came to Birobidzhan from Khabarovsk to borrow copies of pedagogical materials.

Religious observances vanished quickly in Birobidzhan, although a few fragile efforts survived for a time. Otto Heller, a Communist writer who visited Birobidzhan in 1930, was amused to see "a strange-looking, glass-covered hillock of earth" near the experimental station at Birofeld, which turned out to be a kind of igloo erected in 1928 by the first settlers for prayer. "Evidently," commented Heller, "they were not yet freed from their shtetl [ways]. This 'synagogue' was the first structure they erected—possibly the most unique Jewish prayerhouse in the world. Now it stands empty. No one prays in it even on holidays."[39]

A. Epstein, an officer of IKOR, who also visited Birobidzhan in 1930, reported[40] that on Rosh Hashanah all of the Jewish settlers of Amurzet were at work, except one old man and four old women who prayed at home. At Waldheim, where he spent Yom Kippur, he saw Jewish men and women "nonchalantly eating lunch." Yet in 1932, a local settler named L. Shub, in an article called "Let us Strengthen our Anti-Religious Work," disagreed: "When Rosh Hashanah and Yom Kippur approach, a number of Jews run around like poisoned ones looking for a place in which to pray. Last year they prayed secretly in a shed in the Immigrant Reception building; today. . . . [they] have more *chutzpah*—they actually gathered at the office of the chairman of the city soviet and asked him for a place to pray. Most likely they did not report to work on those days."[41]

Another observer reported the existence of two *minyanim* in 1933 and the baking of matzos in the town of Birobidzhan at Passover, despite the "energetic propaganda" of the Atheist Society, which included a lecture on the subject, "Jewish Clericalism and Its War Within the Workers' Movement," special antireligious courses in the schools, and the dispatch of antireligious propagandists to various places.[42] A visitor from Poland in August 1934 noticed a group of non-Jewish Sabbatarians, who observed the Saturday Sabbath, did not eat pork, and tried to live by Biblical law. They had come to Birobidzhan, assuming that since it was a "Jewish state," they would be able to live according to the Law of Moses. At the same time, there apparently was substantial intermarriage of Jews with non-Jews, including Chinese and Koreans, and burial of Jews with non-Jews.[43]

Yet much was done to give Birobidzhan a "Jewish" cast. Jewish collective farms and Jewish village councils were established; Jews served in key positions in the region, including L. Zavilovitch, secretary of the regional executive committee, and his assistant deputy Pevzner. At the first regional conference of soviets held in the town of Birobidzhan, December 18–21, 1934, there were 160 Jewish delegates out of a total of 323.[44] Professor Joseph Liberberg, former head of the Jewish Section of the Ukrainian Academy of Sciences in Kiev, was chairman of the Birobidzhan regional executive committee. By the end of May 1935, nine out of eleven members of the Communist party bureau of the town of Birobidzhan were Jews, including its secretary Matvey Khavkin and his deputy Dickshtain.[45] Among the thirteen members of the presidium of the executive committee of the town administration seven were Jews. Again, Soviet sources accented the presence of Jews in "key positions," although at the time Jews constituted only 15 percent of the region's population.

Vigorous efforts were made to induce writers and intellectuals to go to Birobidzhan, and during the thirties some Yiddish writers answered the call and lived there for a time: Yosef Rabin, Emmanuel Kazakevich, Yehiel Falikman, B. Olievsky, Aron Vergelis, Tuvia Vergelis, and Lyuba Wasserman, among others, but only Wasserman remained for any length of time. Chiming with the Stalinist grip on literature in the thirties, David Bergelson moved from the richness and complexity of his earlier work to an uncritical glorification of the Birobidzhan experiment and cold contempt for any vestige of Jewish tradition in his *Birobidzhaner* published in 1934. He stayed in Birobidzhan for several months and wrote[46] glowingly of Jewish settlers developing the area and themselves, especially of former *luftmenshen* who strike out in the primeval forest, chop down trees, build huts, dig wells, and erect homes. Physical hardships and the plague of insects run through the narrative, but the human satisfactions dominate. His favored characters reject Jewish "nationalistic nonsense" and "moldering religious beliefs."

Among the 530 delegates to the First Congress of Soviet Writers in Moscow in August 1934 was Nahum Fridman, a Jewish cultural figure in Birobidzhan, who mentioned the arrival of some writers but admitted that "so far, the Soviet Jewish writers have not responded properly to the Government proclamation [of the establishment of the JAR]. . . . The Jewish Autonomous Region is a tremendous building enterprise of the Soviet Union and one ought to go there not as an observer but in order to take part in its construction."[47] He, too, touched on the Japanese threat: Jewish writers should arouse the enthusiasm of Jewish workers, and in particular urge the youth "to build the Jewish Autonomous Region as an outpost of Socialism on the border with Japanese imperialism." In February 1936, the visit of Lazar Kaganovich, a Jewish member of the Politburo, to Birobidzhan, greatly heartened the Jewish leadership of the region. He talked enthusiastically about creating a Jewish cultural center there which would have meaning for Jews everywhere (see pp. 307–8). Acting on his suggestion to broaden the use of Yiddish, Khavkin, the secretary of the party in the Birobidzhan region, issued a call to all Yiddish writers and Jewish scholars, urging them to settle in Birobidzhan, but the appeal fell flat. Later, after the war, the response would be better, but what had been built up was gone.

One is bound to speculate that the Jewish response to Birobidzhan might have been heartier had a genuinely national feeling been aroused. "If," as Solomon Schwarz has said, "a spirit of pride and devotion had been inculcated in the Jewish youth, hundreds and even thousands of hardy pioneers could have been trained to go out to clear the land, build the roads, and improve the soil,"[48] but the Communist leadership was unwilling to invest the colonization effort with a Jewish national purpose. It was afraid of organizing Birobidzhan as a Jewish national movement. No attempt was made to establish any special autonomous Jewish agencies for directing the transfer of the Jewish population or the planning of the settlement program. The project also lacked a coherent, consistent operational plan. But the myth of national autonomy had a life of its own—a myth which was strengthened in May 1934 when Birobidzhan was created as a Jewish Autonomous Region (JAR) while the real Birobidzhan was fast becoming a failure, with its tiny Jewish minority, its unattractiveness, and its inability to arouse Jewish emotion within the Soviet Union.

There was, however, intense enthusiasm in some circles of Western Jews over this announcement, coming as it did when Nazism took a firm grip on Germany and when European anti-Semitism swelled with the deepening economic depression. For a time, well-known Jewish intellectuals such as Reuven Breinen and Chaim Zhitlovsky and the poets Reisen and Levick gave their support to Birobidzhan, "but soon repented under the influence of the sharp pro-Arab position of IKOR and *Morgen freiheit*."[49] The *Jewish Daily Forward* and *Tsukunft* were sharply critical because of the remoteness of Birobidzhan, the harsh climate and the dangers of attack from Japan. A number of writers questioned the sincerity of the Soviet government regarding its interest in Soviet Jewry altogether.

The JAR label, moreover, although it may have excited foreign Jewish opinion, concealed an actual radical change in the character of Birobidzhan. Instead of urging the impoverished and uprooted Jews of the decaying shtetlach to come to Birobidzhan, there was to be recruitment of experienced workers, farmers, and artisans. In June 1934 Dimanshtain, in calling for a semi-mobilization of productive workers for security considerations, explained the "higher" state interests:

This is a stage that is higher, as compared with the past work of Komzet, when it was basically a question of liquidating the declassed condition of the Jewish poor. . . . For every conscious participant in socialist construction the whole significance of the defence of the Far East against intervention is quite clear. One of the fundamental factors in the strengthening of [this] defence is the necessity of settling the region with reliable, seasoned people.[50]

Kalinin, in responding to the May proclamation,[51] still held tenaciously to his earlier thesis of 1926 on preserving Jewish nationality, but shifted his attachment from the Crimea to Birobidzhan as "the only means of a normal development for this nationality, . . . the most important guardian of the Jewish national culture." He admitted the disappointing figures but hoped that if only 4,000 Jews would immigrate each year, within ten years, quite a lot could be achieved. But security needs were overtaking Kalinin's ardor and any residue of official interest in a Jewish Birobidzhan.

The basic challenge facing Soviet foreign policy was how to provide security for the militarily weak but rapidly industrializing territorial base of the Revolution in the face of German and Japanese aggressiveness. Dimanshtain put the security argument baldly in his 1934 statement: "The stronger we are in the Far East, the more remote becomes the danger of war." The Soviet Union had to secure its eastern provinces with an industrial buildup as well as increased armed forces. Non-Jewish labor must have its role as the recruiting advanced. Dimanshtain said:

The republics must give up the best people, who are best suited for the new and difficult work of construction in the Far East. . . . The slogan 'The whole of the U.S.S.R. is building the JAR' means . . . that together with the Jewish settlers what is indispensable is to create non-Jewish cadres also that will help carry out more quickly the plans of construction of this extremely rich border region. We are not setting ourselves the goal of building up in the JAR a Jewish majority in the near future. We are convinced that this will come about. . . . But that is not our fundamental goal. . . . Our foremost aim is the expansion and consolidation of socialist construction.

The influx of non-Jewish settlers had already been foreseen in 1932 and 1933. However, after the "catastrophic" year 1933, there was a great burst of enthusiasm and activity during 1934–36, propelled by the autonomy status and official encouragement, and especially by Jews in key cultural positions in Kiev. This change was reflected in every aspect of life in Birobidzhan, from the raw population increases to the rich diversity of cultural life. Whereas in 1933, 3,000 Jews came to Birobidzhan and 4,000 left, in 1934, 5,250 Jews came, of whom 2,000 remained. (The official plan aimed at 10,000 new settlers in 1934.) In 1935, there was an unprecedented increase: 8,344 came, both quantitatively and qualitatively noteworthy. This figure represented over 80 percent of the goal, and although some of the new settlers were non-Jews (including skilled workers such as cabinet workers), there were 6,000 Jews. The growth of the Jewish population by the end of 1935 was the largest of any single year—to 14,000—and there were no returnees during that year. Moreover, among the new settlers were many highly qualified Jews: more than 600 agronomists, doctors, teachers, and cultural activists. In 1936, there was again a so-called "mass-emigration" of 8,000, and according to Professor Liberberg, at a GEZERD (OZET) meeting in Moscow, the JAR tripled the percentage of Jews in two years. Among a contingent from Zhitomer were a group of musicians determined to develop an orchestra in Birobidzhan.[52]

For strengthening Birobidzhan, labor was recruited—some have even said it was forced by 1936—to provide trained manpower. KOMZET and OZET began to recruit kolkhoz foremen, tractor drivers, and Jewish workers in the big industrial cities for factories and collective farms in Birobidzhan. But in spite of strenuous campaigns, there were only about 20,000 Jews in Birobidzhan in early 1937, a net increase of less than 12,000 in three years. The planners had envisioned a Jewish population of 43,000 by that time.

The changing nature of Birobidzhan can be seen in the increasing non-Jewish elements in the population. By late 1936, the population had grown to a little over 60,000, of whom Jews comprised about 30 percent. The fact that many of the newcomers (over 8,000 in 1935 and

8,000 in 1936) were non-Jews, and that a number of older Jewish settlers left in 1936 did not seem to trouble Soviet officials.[53] Rather, it
was used as a spur for arousing Jews to go. Indeed, 600 Jewish families
and 1,000 single persons, making a total of about 3,000 persons, went
to Birobidzhan in 1937, among them more officials and tailors than
farmers, suggesting that many had been recruited. There were also many
specialized workers (145 structural workers, 120 metal mechanics, 23
drivers, and numerous "cultural" workers), suggesting that they had
been mobilized and persuaded to go.[54] The *Vilner tog* of December 27,
1936, also reported that some Jews from Poland, America, Latvia, Lithuania, and even Palestine went to Birobidzhan during the year, but the
purge trials following the assassination of Kirov (see Chapter 14) dashed
all possibility of encouraging Polish Jews and foreign refugees to come
to Russia, assuming genuine Soviet interest, which was not evident.

However, Communist propaganda, emphasizing the *national* significance of the Jewish colonization of Birobidzhan did not flag. On August 29, 1936, the Presidium of the Central Committee of the USSR
extolled "Jewish statehood" as if it had already materialized: "For the
first time in the history of the Jewish people, its burning desire for the
creation of a homeland of its own, for the achievement of its own national statehood, has been fulfilled."[55] The Central Committee also declared that Birobidzhan was becoming the cultural center of the entire
Jewish working class, and that the 15,000 Jews there would far surpass
the rest of Soviet Jewry in its cultural progress, if not in the world.
Following this quite extraordinary announcement, *Der emes* cautioned
against ignoring the rest of Soviet Jewry and urged the upbuilding of
cultural institutions for all Soviet Jews.[56]

At the time, the changing nature of official policy in Birobidzhan was
not grasped, but later this realization could not be evaded: "As was
characteristic of Soviet realities in those years, in connection with Jewish social policy in the Soviet Union, there never openly arose the
question of the causes of deep changes in the scope and character of
the new and conspicuous rhythm of construction in 1935–36 in the
Jewish region. . . . We were left with a faded explanation: all failures
. . . were caused by all sorts of right-wing opportunists, left nihilists
and enemies of the people, and all successes came out of the 'deus ex
machina' of a correct party line and a firm Bolshevik leadership".[57]

This "firm Bolshevik leadership" was to be removed shortly. Meanwhile, the resolution of the Central Committee had a rousing effect on

certain segments of Jewish opinion abroad, for it also spoke of the eagerness of "Jews in foreign lands" to emigrate to Birobidzhan. In 1936, Ambidjan secured permission for an initial quota of a thousand families from Poland to settle in the Jewish Region. This contract was not rescinded but none of the Polish Jews was allowed to enter.[58] The Jewish Autonomous Province, or Region, also figured in the Constitution (the "Stalin Constitution") adopted by the Congress of Soviets in December 1936. Under this Constitution, the JAR, like other regions, had the right to send five delegates to the Council of Nationalities, one of the two chambers of the Supreme Soviet, the highest organ of state power. However, what was not realized by foreign sympathizers was that only Union and Autonomous Republics—not National Autonomous Provinces or Regions—could enjoy statehood. Moreover, Stalin, who had kept silent on the question of the Jews since 1913, when his essay "Marxism and the National Question" appeared, had written off the transformation of Birobidzhan to a republic. In his famous speech late in 1936 defining the three conditions under which autonomous regions become republics, two clearly made Birobidzhan ineligible: the requirement that a given nationality have a majority within the population, and that it have a population of not less than a million. For the promoters of Birobidzhan, however, it was hoped that, among other appeals, the image of a Jewish state would help in the recruiting of Jewish settlers, especially for Birobidzhan's collective farms.

From the beginning, it was emphasized that agriculture must be the economic foundation of the Jewish province, but the proportion of the Jewish farm population had been declining, and the province could not feed its growing population unless agricultural colonization increased. In 1936 Khavkin stated that only 2,500 Jews, or about 17 percent of the total Jewish population, lived on collective farms. A year later, the Jewish rural population apparently had not increased; there are no official statistics after 1936, but one report in 1937 refers to 15 kolkhozes with only "about 500 Jewish families."[59] In the recruitment effort planned by OZET in March 1936, the plenary session "advocated the dispatching to the province of experienced kolkhoz foremen, kolkhoz rank-and-filers, tractor drivers, etc. to be taken from suburban and other collective farms." Central Committee directives of August 29 underscored the agricultural priority. Kalinin particularly reproached officials in Birobidzhan for underestimating agriculture and charged them with "the fundamental task of creating through collective agricultural labor a physically and morally healthy generation of new people who have cast aside the specific survivals . . . of a wretched past." He is quoted as asking, "What are we doing? Creating a Jewish people in the cities and a non-Jewish society in the field?"[60] A new impossible projection was set: no fewer than 150,000 settlers for the period from 1936 to 1942, of whom 40 to 50 percent were to be collective farmers.

Yet agricultural productivity as a whole lagged and continued to be a weak element in the region, partly compensated for by the high quality of certain products of the experimental fields, which far exceeded the average in the region and indeed for the whole of the Far East area. For each year 1935 and 1936, each hectare of land on the Jewish farms grew as follows: wheat by one-third; oats more than doubled; rice almost doubled; potatoes by two-thirds. This was "a significant output, but not decisive and not enough to end the problem. For our own self-sufficient land base, it was still wide of the mark."[61] The real problem was the dearth of proper soil. The necessary improvements that were perceived during the exploratory expeditions were never made, especially the matter of drying out the swamps and clearing the tree stumps. Much raw earth still had to be turned over. "The total effort was modest and the danger to the structure became more and more serious."[62]

As late as 1938 Der emes described the bleak conditions of land settlement: "Some collective farms are established in districts where there is a scarcity of land suitable for cultivation. Some are in out-of-the-way places where there are no roads. . . . The cattle was imported in the winter but no sheds or fodder had been provided for. . . . Most of the settlers are people who have never done any farming and there are no instructors to direct them."[63] Late in 1939, detailed information on Jewish collective farms was given in a pamphlet issued by the Emes Publishing House and intended for new settlers. It reported eighteen (out of a total of sixty in the region) with the most recent two numbering ninety-one families—379 people.[64] Out of the five districts in Birobidzhan, the Jewish collectives were largely consolidated in two, the most notable being the two oldest farms—Waldheim and Birofeld, known for its dairies and apiaries. The others such as Amurzet and Stalinsk had mixed populations. Schwarz estimated the total number of Jews on collective farms in 1939 at no more than 3,000, about one-sixth of the Jewish population in the region as a whole.[65]

Over the years, Jewish labor built up the town of Birobidzhan, which boasted paved streets, electricity, buses, shops, a hospital, theater, and several schools. The bulk of the Jewish population lived in the city, estimated at 9,000 or 10,000 in 1935 and an overly generous 20,000 by *Der Emes* in March 1938. Jews worked here in white-collar occupations, industry, and transportation. Outside the city, they were employed in machine shops, sawmills, lumber yards, brick works, lime kilns, and quarries. The green and rose marble of Birobidzhan was used in the construction of the famous Moscow subway. "The spirit and pulse of the town were like those of a large city," one writer has observed. "To build and grow became the leitmotif of the town and indeed the whole region." In 1935–36 there were thirteen full-fledged Yiddish schools and twelve mixed schools in the city. Both Russian and Yiddish were obligatory in both types of school. The middle school was a particular source of pride. In 1935 a three-story brick building was erected—the first of its kind—to house the 600 Jewish middle school students. By 1937, the enrollment had increased to 800. The Yiddish Pedagogic Institute, which had opened in October 1932 with 78 students in its three year course, enrolled 215 in 1936.[66]

A number of specialized technical institutes in metallurgy, agriculture, and health also showed marked increases in enrollment, with a number of students coming from Moscow, Kiev, and Kharkov. The Kiev Institute for Jewish Proletariat Culture provided a number of experts who spurred the work of a Scientific Commission in Birobidzhan, which did far-ranging research in such fields as geology, statistics, geography, history, Yiddish bibliography, and the formation of a Birobidzhan archive.

The State Jewish Theater in the region was perhaps the best loved cultural attraction of all. In April 1934, 25 members of the Moscow Theater and six musicians and an orchestra conductor arrived in Birobidzhan, together with technical and mechanical personnel and several wagonloads of costumes. The opening featured a program devoted to Sholem Aleichem and took place on June 2, 1934, to a packed hall. As the theater became more popular, it was enlarged and often went to rural districts to play for farmers and their families and military units near the Amur River frontier. In 1935, the Leningrad Vocal Ensemble and the famous composer Yosef Milner came to Birobidzhan; in 1936 another musical ensemble came from Zhitomir.

The buoyant hopes for the region were sustained at the time and aroused to a new pitch of enthusiasm by a visit on February 9, 1936, by Lazar Kaganovich, the secretary of the Central Committee and commissar of communications, "whose iron hand was felt all over the land."[67] Kaganovich was one of Stalin's closest co-workers, a member of the Politburo and skillful troubleshooter. He brought official greetings to the Jews of Birobidzhan who felt greatly honored by a visit[68] from an important Soviet figure "who never hid his Jewishness."

At a meeting of city party activists, Kaganovich gave a two-hour inspirational talk followed by an analysis of the achievements of the "Lenin-Stalin national policy" and its struggle against Bundist national parties and Zionism. He then paused to "reflect on the work of the JAR and the responsibility of Bolsheviks in the region to develop socialism, to create new men, national culture and language, to realize without deviation Stalin's national ideology." As was customary in those days, the meeting ended with resolutions passed unanimously "to the beloved teacher and leader of the workers of the world—to Comrade Stalin and his trusted co-worker, Comrade Kaganovich."

Kaganovich spoke at every opportunity with great seriousness about developing the Jewish national language and culture—even about food! At a festive evening at the Birobidzhan State Theater, devoted to Sholem Aleikhem's "Goldgreber", he declared, "The time has come to bring to the stage the heroic moments in the history of the Jewish people." His remarks were so "unbelievably new and astonishing, they awakened unimaginable, joyous hopes." A resolution was quickly adopted to name the theater after him, and the decision was officially confirmed on August 11, 1936, by governmental action. Kaganovich thus became in effect the guardian and protector of the JAR, a role not altogether consistent with his image as an iron commissar.

His visit was also bound up with a project to convene a Yiddish-language conference; in fact, the idea came from him. For many months, there were elaborate preparations, in which Professor Joseph Liberberg took a leading role. There was extensive press and radio publicity and consultation with experts on the main subjects for the agenda: consistency of dialects, orthography, grammar, punctuation, newspaper and literary Yiddish. Discussants were to be important philologists and scholars from the whole of the USSR. The conference was scheduled to open February 9, 1937, marking the anniversary of Kaganovich's visit. But the sweeping purges of 1937–38 destroyed this project, together with many others.

Another project connected with Kaganovich's historic visit was the creation of an earth fund by the end of 1936 to advance the work of improving the land. Kaganovich even helped with budgetary details; these plans were officially confirmed on August 29, 1936. For the year 1937, 25 new kolkhozes were projected and the area to be sowed increased from 42,000 to 100,000 hectares. Kaganovich also demanded that the official language of the region be Yiddish and that "proper and obligatory forms for the administration" be worked out as soon as possible.

All of these developments gave the Jewish activists "not only satisfaction, but a sense of triumph and new, visionary horizons." Dimanshtain, too, was carried away and wrote in *Forpost*, "Already the transition has taken place from craftsmen's work (kustarish)—from small deeds—from the mobilization of forces—to a highly developed government upbuilding of the Jewish region with an unprecedented driving force."[69] Dimanshtain also contrasted the two existing Jewish efforts to rebuild a national life, one in Palestine, "linked with imperialist England . . . [where] Jews will pay for the sin of Zionism . . . and face catastrophe," and Birobidzhan, where "for the first time in the history of the Jewish people, under socialism, they are developing sovereign, soviet, national upbuilding, a process which grows from year to year."[70]

Under the surface of this rhetoric and activity, however, other forces were set in motion that would soon throw the Birobidzhan project into a shambles. The first blow struck Professor Liberberg, at a time when he was still involved in plans for the conference on Yiddish. Liberberg also served as chairman of Birobidzhan's Regional Executive Committee, the highest position in the regional hierarchy.

Suddenly in August 1936, he was called to Moscow. Only two months later, in the second issue of *Forpost* in October, was there any information about Liberberg's disappearance. The article said that he had been "unmasked as untrustworthy, counterrevolutionary, and a bourgeois-nationalist." This was the beginning of the frightening terror of the Yezhov (chief of the NKVD) years, which started at the end of 1936 and persisted until the beginning of 1939 and took an appalling toll in Birobidzhan. Liberberg's arrest agitated many Jews of the region and made them apprehensive. He was a much-loved and trusted leader who had contributed greatly to the ideal of creating a Jewish national existence in Birobidzhan. All who worked with him were now to pay a heavy price.

Yet on September 15, 1936, the third plenum of the Regional Party Committee opened, and the delegates celebrated the historic Central Committee resolution of August 29. Liberberg was no longer in Birobidzhan and no one as yet knew of his fate. Ironically members called for energetic upbuilding of socialist Jewish national culture, for the need to "speak a good Yiddish."[71]

The purges of 1936–38 were to deplete the Jewish leadership of Birobidzhan. At the end of 1936 and the beginning of 1937, there was a drastic shake-up in the personnel of the local government and party administration. An anonymous review in *Forpost* (1937, no. 2) branded both Khavkin and Liberberg as "wreckers" and the main obstacles to the growth of the region. It said further that Trotskyists had done their utmost to hinder the work in Birobidzhan, but that now the cause was safe in "the hands of the flaming patriots" of the JAR. Especially significant was the need to scapegoat the agricultural failure: "The wreckers' activities were particularly felt in the agricultural colonization of the province and in the setting up of collective farms, where they aimed at sabotaging all plan objectives."[72] Yesterday's loyal leaders were attacked as spies, Japanese agents, and contemptible schismatics who "neglected the needs of the settlers, and thus contributed to their mass exodus." The April 10, 1937 *Birobidzhaner shtern* accused Khavkin of "rupturing the regional party organization and described him as a "shameful intriguer, flatterer and embezzler of state money."

Liberberg was never heard from again. He was replaced by M. Katel—the head of OZET in the Ukraine—but he, too, was soon arrested. Soon the governing cadres began to be decimated. In May 1937, Khavkin was seized and shipped to a labor camp. Yaacov Levin was denounced as a Trotskyist. Secretaries of the regional committee and many workers in the field of Jewish culture were purged. By the beginning, of 1937 the governmental machinery was quite completely Russified. The cleansing drive went on apace. According to a *New York Times* dispatch from Moscow dated June 14, 1938, seventeen inhabitants of Birobidzhan, including seven with apparently Jewish names, were shot; the *London Daily Telegraph* of September 22, 1938 quoted a Moscow publication to the effect that "a Jewish counter-revolutionary and Zionist organization" had been "unmasked" by the secret service. A second group of leaders including Katel was also purged.

However, purged Jews were succeeded by other Jews to prove that "these 'cleansings' were not intended to tamper with the basic concept of a Jewish Autonomous Region—though they severely damaged it—but were the outcome of national rather than local causes."[73] At the climax of the Yezhov purges, a new and ominous feature was introduced: the immigration department of the NKVD became responsible for the transportation of Jews,[74] subjecting all potential settlers to strict scrutiny.

OZET, whose magazine *Tribuna* had often reported on Birobidzhan, was abolished in the summer of 1938 and official information on Jews there ceased almost totally. For example, the census of 1939 disclosed the total population of Birobidzhan as 108,419, but gave no precise figures on the Jewish population. Similarly, *Der shtern* for January 10, 1939, reported 113 schools at the beginning of 1938 (25 of them Jewish), with 15,834 students, but gave no figures for the number of Jewish students. Publications hailing the growth of Birobidzhan continued, but the actual number of Jews could be ascertained only by inference.

In spite of the decimations caused by the purges, during the spring and summer of 1938, there were "celebrations" in Birobidzhan and elsewhere in the Soviet Union, marking the ten years of settlement in the region and four years of its status as an autonomous region. On May 7, for example, in Moscow there was a celebration by OZET, featuring a speech by Shkolnik, the president of the Birobidzhan city soviet; and in August, there was a celebration in the editorial offices of *Der emes*, at which Nikolai Bigler, the chairman of the Regional Executive Committee, spoke about a "Jewish Republic" and cultural center in Birobidzhan.[75]

The extravagant rhetoric continued. In a special broadcast on Birobidzhan in connection with the All-Union Agricultural Exposition in Moscow in August 1940, there were glowing reports:[76] "The history of this region is a wonderful tale about transformed men, emigrants from little towns and villages. They clear the forest and cultivate the land. The agricultural achievements are outstanding. . . . Their work is excellently paid and the earnings of the medium family reach 12,000 roubles a year and hundreds of centals [each cental is 100 pounds] of various produce. The region also has many industrial undertakings . . . mills, tanneries, cloth-cutting workshops, etc. Coal mines and gold fields are also exhibited." The broadcast concluded by asking for immigrants: "Here, as in the whole of the Far East, work awaits the Soviet patriot. The country is in the reliable hands of the Jewish Autonomous Republic." On February 2, 1941, it was reported that 1,000 Jewish families were to be settled in the coming year. With the annexation of territory from Poland, Romania, and all of the Baltic countries in the years 1939–40, there was "new hope" awakened for the development of the area through the transfer of a part of the Jewish population from the annexed territories to Birobidzhan.[77] The Communist press reported that instructions had been given to the Immigration Committee of the Soviet of Peoples' Commissars of the USSR in 1940 to work out extensive plans for the settlement of the region.[78] Official representatives of this committee were sent to Birobidzhan to plan for the absorption of 30–40,000 immigrants from the annexed areas (see Chapter 15) and registration procedures for candidates were devised. In 1939–40, the annexations took place, but the German invasion of the Soviet Union in June 1941 stopped any alleged new settlement plans.

After the war, Birobidzhan was once more revived as an area of Jewish "autonomous" development and there was a brief, very intense new start (see Chapter 22), but old Stalinist patterns repeated themselves and the brutal purges of 1948–49 shattered any plans for the future. Yet the cynical designation of Birobidzhan as the Jewish Autonomous Region has remained and the Birobidzhan myth endures in Soviet propaganda to this day.

14

The Great Purges, 1936–38, and the Hitler-Stalin Pact, 1939–41

In a village on the upper Volga
Where seagulls make noise,
There lives a quiet old man . . .
Comes frost, he cracks the ice
Over fish runs for luck . . .

How can they possibly know that
In a still Arbat lane long ago
An engineer with gray hair was seized
According to order prescribed . . .
And that he was tortured, abused
In sleepless cellar captivity . . .
And then they proclaimed as error
The stolen seventeen years.

ANONYMOUS

And in the room of the disgraced poet
Fear and the Muse take turns on watch.
And the night goes on
Which does not know of dawn.

AKHMATOVA

THE Great Terror created by the purges of 1936–38 established Stalin as unchallenged dictator of the Soviet state. Robert Conquest, the authoritative historian of the period, has summarized three distinct features of the Great Purge: "above all, its immense scale, in which millions perished and every member of the population was held under immediate threat; secondly, its methods, and in particular the extraordinary device of the confession trial, with the ruler's leading critics publicly denouncing themselves for treason; and, thirdly, its secrecy— apart from the public trials and a few announcements of other executions, nothing was officially said of the whole vast operation."[1] The barest facts of the terror were long concealed, denied, rationalized, or misunderstood inside Russia and among fellow travelers and Communists abroad. However, journalists such as Oswald Garrison Villard and Eugene Lyons as well as Yiddish newspapers were reporting news of the purge trials in the West. For twenty years the Russian people were told that a vast conspiracy, led by party leaders, had penetrated every part of Soviet life with the help of foreign powers to crush the Soviet state and restore capitalism. The conspiracy had been discovered, its leaders had confessed and had been fairly tried and punished. It was only during the Khrushchev period, especially in the years 1961–64, that the first admissions of mass repression and falsified confessions were made in articles and memoirs. The existence of a vast labor-camp system was also then publicly revealed for the first time.

The de-Stalinization process was phased over eleven years, from 1953 to 1964. At first the principle of collective leadership was upheld against Stalin's cult of personality. Then, Lenin's role as victorious founder and leader of the party was glorified at Stalin's expense. The legend of Stalin's achievements, his pictures, statues, and writings began to disappear, culminating in Khrushchev's extraordinary speech at the Twentieth Party Congress in 1956, in which the most sweeping charges were made against Stalin. He was accused of inaugurating a reign of "the most cruel repression," practicing "brutal violence" against everyone who opposed or criticized him, gaining confessions "with the help of cruel and inhuman torture," and causing the arrest and shooting of 70 percent of the party's members between 1934 and 1938.[2] However, these charges were heard only by a carefully selected audience of 1,436 high party functionaries. Khrushchev's address was not published inside the Soviet Union, but the speech was made known to thousands, perhaps millions of party members before the Central Committee issued a special circular ordering all copies of the speech returned under special guard to Moscow.[3] It was also leaked out abroad.[4]

In October 1961, at the Twenty-Second Party Congress, Khrushchev launched the next phase of de-Stalinization—the liquidation of Stalin's memory. Stalin's remains were removed from the hallowed mausoleum on Red Square and his name was obliterated throughout the Soviet Union. These decisions cleared the way for open discussion of Stalin's terror inside the country.

Stalin's purges of the thirties made of Russia a terrorized and totalitarian state. Scholars have speculated about the reasons for these dreadful events, without reaching definitive answers, but the need to cover up economic failures and eliminate all possible opposition to his power by creating the spectre of conspiracy, were surely important motives. Stalin's own paranoid, delusional make-up, a man who everywhere saw "enemies," "two-facers," and "spies," undoubtedly provided the central motivation. Anyone slightly or potentially critical of him was suspected and then accused of hostile and treasonable intent, therefore, guilty of conspiracy. Moreover, besides providing Stalin with uncontested power and complete subservience from the party and population, the trials prepared the way for the Soviet-Nazi Pact of 1939.[5]

There had been four major purges in the 1920s to remove the politically weak, unfit, or dangerous, but the purges of 1936–38 were of an unprecedented scale, not only in the huge number of party victims, but of nonparty casualties, in the spectacular "show" trials and in the dramatic, undoubtedly rigged confessions. Throughout the revelations in his 1956 speech, Khrushchev established the year 1934 as the crucial date—the year of Sergei Kirov's assassination. However, a foreshadowing[6] of the massive purges came in 1928 in the Shakhty district of the Donets basin, where the secret police (OGPU) arrested and brought to trial several German non-Communist engineers, who were accused of counterrevolutionary plots, sabotage, and collusion with Germany to obstruct the Five Year Plan. A second rehearsal came in Kharkov, with a "show" trial of forty-five prominent Ukrainians, accused of organizing peasants to resist collectivization and plotting with emigrés in Poland and Germany to create a separatist Ukrainian state. The third trial in 1930 involved an "Industrialist Party" charged with sabotaging industrial expansion and conspiring with France. In 1931 former Mensheviks were charged with conspiring with foreign powers, and in 1933, a group of British engineers were blamed for certain failures of the Five Year Plan. Most of the defendants received long prison terms or exile. Another "purification" purge occurred between June and November 1933, to cleanse the party of "alien and hostile elements"—an ominous harbinger of persecution of national minorities.[7] Sporadic acts of sabotage in the thirties in factories were attributed to foreign spies and "wreckers" organized by anti-Stalin "oppositionists."

The irreversible turning-point in Stalin's drive for absolute power occurred in 1934, specifically in the developments during and following the Seventeenth Party Congress held January 26–February 10 in Moscow. Up to that time, the party had been exempt as a target of terror. It had its own Control Commission for testing political loyalty and discipline, which acted as a brake on Stalin's efforts to use terror against it. Moreover, at the Congress itself Stalin did not control the Central Committee that had been elected. Some, in fact, wanted to oust him as a member; others wanted to replace him as General Secretary with Kirov. However, he manipulated the results of the voting as well as neutralized the opposition of a number of the delegates who were disturbed by the horrors of collectivization and the frenzied pace of industrialization. Since the last congress in 1930, Stalin said, the Soviet Union had achieved a "world-historical victory," and had become a great industrial power with a thriving agriculture. Moreover, the Second Five Year Plan, adopted in 1933, promised more moderation. Some of the delegates were also soothed with Stalin's famous words, "Life has become better, Comrades. Life has become gayer." The "revolution from above," proclaimed by him in 1929, was now officially achieved and in party history, the 1934 Congress became known as the "Congress of Victors." Among the old Bolshevik leaders, particularly Bukharin, who had read *Mein Kampf*, there was undoubtably a felt need to close ranks in the face of the growing Nazi threat. In any case, there was, according to Bialer, "the sense of relief that the worst is over, that a more moderate policy will henceforth be pursued."[8]

However, this perception was a mirage. Stalin was already perfecting his craftiness in stage-managing events and facades. He reinforced the Control Commission with his own men and drew up an "enemies" list of those who opposed him or threatened him as rivals. Khrushchev, in his speech at the Twentieth Party Congress, revealed Stalin's demand for "absolute submission" after the 1934 Congress: "Whoever opposed this concept or tried to prove his viewpoint and the correctness of his position was doomed to removal . . . and to subsequent moral and physical annihilation. This was especially true during the period following the Seventeenth Party Congress, when many prominent party leaders and rank-and-file workers, honest and dedicated to the cause of communism, fell victim to Stalin's despotism."[9]

One such man was the young and popular party boss in Leningrad, Sergei Kirov, who was murdered on December 1, 1934. Kirov had opposed Stalin's harsh repression of Trotskyites and other former oppositionists. Officially, Stalin blamed Kirov's murder alternately on foreign powers, the Right Opposition, and on Trotsky and Zinoviev. (In 1956 at the Twentieth Party Congress, Krushchev hinted that Stalin himself ordered Kirov's death.)[10] Mass arrests, forced confessions, deportations, and the execution of thousands followed. After Kirov's assassination Stalin "skillfully built an atmosphere of hysteria, of siege, of imminent danger which clearly had no foundation in reality, but which permitted him to start a general purge."[11]

Gorky, among others, is known to have tried to induce Stalin to institute new reforms without a purge,[12] but Stalin drove ahead relentlessly. He replaced the old head of the GPU with Genrikh Yagoda and surrounded him with agents and spies. (At the show trial of 1938 he was "unmasked" as one of the organizers of Kirov's murder.) Then, after Kirov's murder, there was a secret trial of Kamenev and Zinoviev in 1935, followed by many sudden arrests. In the same year, a decree was passed authorizing reprisals against children over twelve of "enemies," including execution. A new wave of "purifications" started in January 1936, with a relentless cycle of denunciations, arrests, and expulsions, leading to the spectacular trial in August of sixteen "Old Bolsheviks," including Zinoviev and Kamenev, as well as a number of other leading Jewish Communists. These new victims were accused of organizing a "terroristic center" under Trotsky, directed against Stalin. All sixteen were sentenced to death and promptly executed. These cataclysmic events were briefly camouflaged in 1936 by the announcement of a new Constitution—the Stalin Constitution of 1936—which was in force until 1977. It guaranteed basic freedoms of speech, press, assembly and religious worship as well as the right and duty to work and the right to numerous social benefits. It also promised universal and equal suffrage and the secret ballot—which had been previously denounced as counterrevolutionary. However, all of the provisions were cynically ignored or violated in the engulfing terror. People were not only expelled from the party for having suggested that the pace of development had been too fast, or for mentioning difficulties, but Stalin's suspicion, hatred, envy, or caprice could and did fall upon anyone without the slightest basis and with frightening suddenness. Yet, ironically, there was widespread feeling that, not Stalin, but Yagoda or Yezhov, who succeeded him, were to blame for the waves of arrests and disappearances. Even in Soviet prisons the legend grew that Stalin was being deceived, that he knew nothing, and that fascists had wormed their way into power.

In the meantime, Stalin had to deal publicly with the rising threat of Nazi Germany in 1934, particularly after Hitler's purge of the S.A. on June 30, and sanctioned certain projects in collaboration with the West: the Soviet Union joined the League of Nations, concluded a pact with France and, in the person of Foreign Commissar Maxim Litvinov, a Jew and sincere anti-Nazi, became the strongest advocate of collective security. Another zigzag in Soviet foreign policy took place in 1935–36. Stalin reversed the former implacable Communist hostility toward moderate socialist and liberal parties and launched the briefly reassuring and welcome Popular Front. But the West was inert in facing the aggressions of Hitler and Mussolini. In March 1936 Hitler marched into the Rhineland, but neither England nor France nor the League challenged him. It has often been argued that Stalin thereafter had to seek an agreement with Hitler to buy time and that the timidity of the West caused the Soviet Union to give up the policy of collective security. The subsequent purges, thus, were necessary to destroy all possible opposition for the eventual struggle against Hitler. However, these purges did nothing to strengthen the Soviet Union, but, instead, destroyed "the basic cadres of the Communist party, the Soviet government, the Red Army, the economic agencies, and all the other public and social organizations,"[13] among them Jewish cultural institutions and virtually all Jewish cultural leaders.

Internal and external pressures converged in 1936–38. The connection between the purges and preparations for a Nazi-Soviet Pact can be traced. Virtually all of the old Bolsheviks had strong anti-Nazi views and would severely criticize Stalin if he were to make a deal. At the same time, if Hitler attacked Russia, Stalin could be accused of having been largely indifferent to the rise of Hitler and, in fact, of helping the Nazi cause by stubbornly insisting in 1930–32 that German Social Democrats were "social fascists" and ordering German Communists to war against them instead of making common cause in an anti-Nazi coalition. Kennan argues persuasively that in this dilemma, "the only way out [for Stalin] was the physical annihilation of anyone else who had ever had any aspiration to leadership within Russia—anyone who had ever opposed him in any way . . . anyone who could possibly profit from the inevitable political embarrassment." Out of a complex of reasons, "these considerations" must have contributed substantially.[14]

Within a few days after the German occupation of the Rhineland in March 1936, Stalin gave secret orders for the preparation of the first of the three great purge trials. Yet, while thousands of Jews were being purged from the party and government, and while plans for a deal with Hitler were ripening, there were a few official pro forma denunciations of anti-Semitism in November 1936 by Stalin and Vyacheslav Molotov, chairman of the Council of People's Commissars at the time. Stalin's statement was unearthed from a reply to a query sent to him by the Jewish Telegraphic Agency in 1931, in which he said that "anti-Semitism, as an extreme form of race chauvinism, is the most dangerous survival of cannibalism." He also assured Jews throughout the world that "according to the laws of the USSR, active anti-Semites are punished with death." Molotov contrasted Stalin's attack and "our fraternal feelings toward the Jewish people" with the "cannibalism" of the Nazis.

These statements were obviously intended for foreign consumption, aimed especially at Jewish readers in the West growing increasingly alarmed by the spread of Nazism and reports of anti-Jewish actions in the Soviet Union. There were, at the same time, frequent vehement diatribes against Nazism in the Soviet press, but no attention to its core of anti-Jewish hatred or to anti-Semitism generally. Not only did Stalin personally have a strong anti-Jewish animus, he was himself purging the party and government of Jews, and preparing for an agreement with the arch anti-Semite Hitler. Moreover, the Nazis were effectively weakening the internal unity of many countries by appealing to anti-Semitism and the alleged links of Jews to communism. For their part, the Communists in the Soviet Union were no longer taking their once prominent campaign against anti-Semitism seriously.

Meanwhile, other disturbing and deflecting events occurred. Gorky, the popular writer who had once been "one of Stalin's few intimates," and who had urged "a softening and humanization of the regime," died under mysterious circumstances (probably from being poisoned) in June 1936, and the draft of the new Constitution was published. In August, the public trial of Kamenev and Zinoviev opened. Bukharin among others was named as co-conspirator. Stalin slyly left for the Caucasus, "leaving the onus of the imposition of the death sentences to be formally incurred by the . . . court."[15] Sixteen "Old Bolsheviks," including Kamenev and Zinoviev were swiftly executed.

N. I. Yezhov, who replaced Yagoda in the fall of 1936, presented Stalin's case against Bukharin and the others, accusing them of a "monstrous conspiracy" being plotted against the state. Bukharin countered by accusing Stalin and Yezhov of a monstrous conspiracy to destroy the regime created by Lenin. The Central Committee voted against Bukharin's (and Rykov's) expulsion and the case against them was temporarily dropped, but Yezhov and Stalin now began to prepare for new waves of arrests and trials. In 1937–38, according to Khrushchev, "383 . . . lists containing the names of many thousands of Party, Soviet, Komsomol, Army and economic workers were sent to Stalin. He approved these lists."[16] In the typical cycle of killing the killers and killers of killers, in order to annihilate evidence of mass murder, Stalin removed Yezhov in 1938, accusing him of arresting too many innocent people!

In the wake of the 1936 trial, many other founding fathers of Russian Communism were implicated in the "confessions" and "testimony," leading to a new trial of seventeen in January 1937. All of these defendants "confessed" their guilt in conniving with Nazi Germany and Japan to dismember the USSR. Thirteen were sentenced to death and executed; four received long-term sentences, but their ultimate fate has never been made known. The next trial, held in secret in June 1937, claimed several army commanders, including Marshal Mikhail Tukhachevsky of civil war fame, accused of heading a "military conspiratorial organization." A hemorrhaging of the Red Army followed—estimated losses run as high as 35,000 men and half of the officer corps—perhaps as many as 15,000.[17]

The last "show" trial in March 1938 was the climax to the earlier trials, involving twenty-one former members of the Right Opposition, led by Bukharin and Rykov. Among the defendants was the former head of the secret police—the NKVD—Genrikh Yagoda. All were charged with sabotage, espionage, attempted dismemberment of the USSR, and conspiracy to kill Soviet leaders, and all were executed, except three who were given long prison terms.

The human costs of the trials, arrests, and executions, aside from the economic, intellectual, and military costs, were and still are incalculable. Estimates of the number of victims range from three to nine million. Khrushchev himself admitted that the nation was hard put to survive the events of 1937–1938: ". . . our march forward toward socialism and toward the preparation of the country's defence would have been much more successful were it not for the tremendous loss of cadres suffered as a result of the baseless and false mass repressions in 1937–1938." One undoubted result, however, was Stalin's conquest of absolute power.

A new era of the all-knowing and faultless leader Stalin was achieved by a fiendishly skillful manipulation of propaganda and what has been characterized as the "retroactive lie." All wisdom and genius in everything from politics, economics, and history to military strategy and leadership, science, art, music, and literature were shown to be possessed by Stalin. Giant pictures and statues of him were everywhere in the country, providing an image of omnipotence; even the Constitution of 1936 was named for him. The net of the secret police stretched far and wide, but it was not permitted to grow too powerful and thus become a threat to Stalin. His private secretariat, his appointment of competing police officials, and a military intelligence apparatus that competed with the police, plus intricate systems of surveillance kept everyone watching everyone else.[18] Not only was the old party crushed; all trust among comrades was poisoned.

In covering the trials, at first the sheer volume of details, involving incidents of trivial as well as significant scale, descriptions of localities, and reports of conversations led American correspondents and the American diplomatic corps, including Ambassador Joseph E. Davies, to write home that the testimony rang true. The fantastic piling up of detail in the stenographic reports of the trials submerged the grotesque accusations and self-flagellation until the facts could be sorted out and checked. In the 1936 trial involving a "Trotskyite-Zinovievite United Center," for example, one defendant claimed to have flown to Oslo to meet Trotsky at a certain time, but the Norwegian authorities insisted that no foreign plane landed in Oslo at that time. The Communists then said that the landing was made in a private airfield. A meeting of conspirators was said to have taken place at a Hotel Bristol which was torn down fifteen years before the alleged meeting, but the prosecution asserted that there was a Cafe Bristol.

The trial of the "United Center" was open, but violated the most elementary rules of judicial procedure. No material evidence or documentary proof of the guilt of the accused was presented to the court.

The entire case rested on the "depositions" and "confessions" of the accused. Moreover, the defendants were deprived of the right to defense counsel. A number of foreign lawyers offered to defend them, but were denied. The charges were plainly fantastic. Old Bolsheviks now turned conspirators were accused of blowing up Red Army trains, poisoning workers, preparing dangerous bacilli, planning to partition Russia and give parts to Germany and Japan. How was it possible for Russians to believe these charges? Torture and fear of reprisal against their families, especially threats against children, pressed defendants to accuse and abase themselves. Moreover, "the vast majority of the Soviet people believed the testimony of the accused and approved the sentences they received."[19] The press of the time in fact carried many letters applauding Stalin's action and decrying the treason of the defendants. Few at the time, except the prisoners among themselves in the Gulag, dared to ask how it was possible for so many tried revolutionaries to fail in their alleged plots so consistently. Nor did any of the defendants balk at confessing their crimes. "With the exception of a few minor clashes, they vie[d] with each other in making a 'clean breast' of it, in incriminating themselves and their associates."[20] There were veritable orgies of self-accusation and massive appeals (except in the case of Radek and Shestov) for clemency. Yet not all of the confessions came overnight. Radek took three months; Nikolai Muralov, who put down the Moscow uprising of the Left SR's in 1918, took eight months. Bukharin resisted pressure for three months and, apparently, agreed to go to trial only under the threat of retaliation against his young wife and son.

In 1937, the storm broke over the main body of foreign Communists—from Germany, Hungary, Romania, and Poland—many of whom lived a somewhat bohemian existence in the dingy corridors of the Hotel Lux in Moscow.[21] Some of those arrested were Jews, but this fact did not save them from charges of fascist espionage any more than it did the great Jewish general Yona Yakir. An interrogator is quoted as saying, "The Jewish refugees are Hitler's agents abroad."[22] Arthur Koestler, who had been an ardent Communist and had spent a year in the Soviet Union, but was at this time becoming uneasy about Stalin's course, learned, while he was in England, that several of his closest friends and his brother-in-law Dr. Ernst Ascher had been arrested.[23] Ascher, a German Communist, had worked at a state hospital in the Volga German Republic. He was accused of injecting syphilis into his patients and of being an agent of a foreign power. One of Koestler's friends, Alexander Weissberg, a physicist, was employed at the Ukrainian Institute for Physics and Technology. He was arrested in 1937 and charged with hiring twenty bandits to ambush Stalin and Kaganovich on their next hunting trip to the Caucasus, but he refused to sign a confession, was imprisoned, and then, after the Nazi-Soviet Pact was signed, was turned over to the Gestapo. His wife, a ceramist from Austria, was arrested in 1936 and accused of inserting swastikas into the pattern of teacups she was producing and hiding the guns intended to be used against Stalin. She was confined to Lubyanka prison for eighteen months while interrogators pressured her to testify against Bukharin, but she refused, made a suicide attempt, and was saved by steadfast exertions of the Austrian consul in Moscow.

These were typical experiences endured by foreign Communists in the Soviet Union. They were to become hapless, shocked victims whose idealism and illusions about the Soviet Union had become a nightmare. But the greatest reservoir of Western liberal and Communist political idealism was undoubtedly invested in the struggle against fascism in Spain, and this, too, Stalin destroyed. As Kennan has said, "Soviet attention turned less and less to the defeat of Franco and more and more to obscure, bitter, underground feuds with those elements of the Spanish Left Wing which were resistant to Soviet influence and domination."[24] By early 1937, Soviet military aid tapered off and Stalin began to ruthlessly purge those Communists who had fought in Spain on the charge of "Trotskyism."

In her memoirs of the time, Peretz Markish's wife Esther writes that "the year 1937 crept in on us like a beast of prey on soft padded feet." It can be compared "to the year of the deluge, the plague, the eclipse of the sun."[25] It was a year of death, arrests, and soul-shattering events. N. A. Mikhailov, the new editor of a Komsomol paper who later became first secretary of the Komsomol, called a meeting of Jewish staff members and suggested that they take Russian names, but the indignant Jews refused. The paper was about to publish a poem of Markish and he was urged to sign it "Pytor Markov," but he, too, refused. Esther's brother Shura, a journalist, was arrested and sentenced to eight years in a camp. Under torture he confessed to belonging to an underground organization. With a touch of irony, he wrote: "Our organization was so clandestine, not one of the members knew any of the others"—a confession which apparently satisfied his interrogators, but only briefly. During the war, when some political prisoners were being released, he received a second sentence of ten years for attempting to build an airplane—within the confines of his camp—in order to fly off and join Hitler!

In the massive waves of arrests and murders, the anti-Jewish thrust was conspicuous, a further signal from Stalin to Hitler that the Soviet state was now ready to come to terms with him. Shmuel Ettinger notes that in the early 1930s, because of the acute shortage of educated people and specialists, anti-Semitism was not a very acute social problem, but a new, quite intense anti-Jewish campaign began in 1936–37, "when the first signs of Stalin's rapprochement with Hitler appeared. . . . A side effect of this effort was the expulsion of Jews from the state apparatus, the diplomatic service, the party Central Committee, and Stalin's personal secretariat."[26] The purges of 1936–38 made the Jews a particularly easy target in the denunciation of a generation of active Communists who had personified the internationalist tradition of the party. This tradition was now branded as the disguise of traitors and spies working for foreign military intelligence. Russian nationalism, which had previously been condemned as "great power chauvinism," now seemed vindicated and spread quickly in the Communist party. Since the leading and most sensationally publicized personalities denounced at the trials had been Jews—Trotsky, Zinoviev, Kamenev, Radek—treason to the fatherland easily became identified with Jewish figures. Moreover, the drumbeat of accusation throughout the trials against Trotsky, the Jew, as the guiding genius of the counterrevolutionary plot was especially ominous. The defendants—strong, dominating Bolshevik leaders—were described as meekly awaiting instructions from the exiled "starik"—the old man—who allegedly sent letters to them in invisible ink via motion picture magazines. "Through Trotskyism I arrived at Fascism," confessed Zinoviev. In the final speech of Prosecuting Attorney Vyshinsky in 1936, "Judas Trotsky" was accused as the very center of the vile conspiracy: "It is not an accident," he said, "that the Trotskyites are playing this role of vanguard of the anti-Soviet Fascist forces. The descent of Trotskyite groups into the anti-Soviet underworld, its conversion into a Fascist agency, is merely the culmination of its historical development."[27] The sudden elimination of so many Jews as "traitors" cast doubt on the trustworthiness of Jews in general—an old prejudice now dressed in a new cloak.

However, it was the destruction of all of the cadres of Jewish cultural workers and agencies that dealt the most severe, irreparable blow to the hope for some sort of identifiable Jewish life. A whole generation of Jewish Communists involved in Jewish affairs was liquidated in the massive purges. Afterward, "not a single person with any authority whatsoever was left at liberty in Soviet Jewish journalism, culture, or even science. . . ."[28] By 1938, virtually every important figure in "Jewish work" was killed or had died in prison: Dimanshtain, Litvakov, Levitan, Veinshtain, Rafes, Chemerisky, Agursky, Sosis, and Liberberg,[29] and the cultural and political leadership in Birobidzhan (see Chapter 11). Almost all Jewish newspapers and periodicals, including *Der emes*, *Der shtern*, *Di royte velt*, and various children's newspapers such as *Zy greyt* and *Yunge gvardia* were, or soon would be, shut down. All works in Yiddish devoted to the Jewish labor movement were confiscated and taken out of circulating libraries, and the Jewish scholarly institutes attached to the Academies of Science in Minsk and Kiev were shut down, with sudden arrests of leading figures. KOMZET and OZET were also closed down and the activities of Agro-Joint and ORT were declared illegal.

Nor were "nonparty immigrants" spared. For example, Max Erik, an outstanding literary scholar who had emigrated to the Soviet Union from Poland in 1929 and directed the Institute for Jewish Proletarian Culture in Kiev, which in 1934–35 was called "the largest Jewish scholarly institute in the world,"[30] was arrested on April 15, 1936. In letters he wrote to colleagues who had gone to Birobidzhan, he hinted at the worsening situation and the dispirited youth in the institute. After Erik's arrest, his wife was thrown out of her apartment and roamed the streets of Kiev, eventually being picked up and deported. Erik had written that "he didn't want to live through the tragedy of having one's idealism turned into barbarism," and tried to commit suicide. The attempt failed but he died in a prison hospital in 1937.[31]

The children's newspaper *Zy greyt*, which in 1934 had a circulation of 50,000 and was extremely popular among Jewish children, was closed down in 1936. Shimon Kipnis, a young correspondent on the paper at the time, has noted the rapid decline of Yiddish schools during this period as well. Kipnis also worked on the Moscow *Emes* late in 1937, by which time Litvakov was already a prisoner. By then the paper was edited by Mikhail Sheinman, who could barely speak Yiddish and was unable to write it. At editorial meetings he spoke only Russian. Early in April, Kipnis was overjoyed to get an assignment from Sheinman to go to Birobidzhan for several months to do some stories. On April 4, 1938, he stopped into the *Emes* office before his departure, but was told that the trip was off. Sheinman called the staff together and said, "Comrades! I'm going to read you a decision of the Secretariat of the Central Committee of the party. But first I must warn you that you are not to ask me any questions, because I won't answer them." Then he quietly read the decision: "The Secretariat of the Central Committee of the Communist party does not deem expedient the publication of the Yiddish paper *Emes* after April 5, 1938." A few months earlier, the Yiddish State Theater Director and actor Shlomo Mikhoels had told Kipnis in an interview in Kharkov, "Your newspaper will not have a very long life."[32]

The Jewish minority, of course, was not the only one to suffer the loss of its political and cultural leadership, but the Jewish loss was particularly catastrophic because it ended the organized life of Soviet Jewry as a recognized cultural and ethnic minority. The cultural and political elites of all national minority groups were swept away, but as the Yiddish journalist Ben Zion Goldberg put it, "in all Soviet purges prominent figures in the national culture were purged, but the culture itself was able to go on evolving under the new leadership; it was only with the Jews that things were different; in the case of the Jewish institutions . . . once closed, they were not reopened."[33] The historian Schwarz observed that, "in no other nationality did the national culture as such arouse such suspicions and such acute hostility on the part of the authorities as did Jewish culture; private persons who owned Yiddish books were subjected to harassment for this reason alone."[34] On December 11, 1937, Anthony J. Drexel Biddle, American ambassador in Poland, reported that "Stalin is expected to advance a more intensive purge against the Jewish element, stressing his distrust both of 'Ghetto mentality' and of individuals and groups with outside connections as means of offsetting impression of racial prejudice."[35]

Among those purged were most of the leaders of the Evsektsiya—a major step toward the liquidation of organized Jewish life in the Soviet Union. The incomprehension and helplessness of former activists who had risked so much in their fiery loyalty to the party and Communist ideal and were now being destroyed arbitrarily, have been conveyed in memoirs and letters which have come to light. Characteristic is a letter[36] from Shmuel Agursky, one of the founders of the Evsektsiya and one of its most zealous activists, to Shakhne Epshteyn, Jewish Communist journalist who became secretary of the Jewish Antifascist Committee during World War II. Agursky was arrested on March 4, 1938 and deported to Kazakhstan. According to *Sovetish heymland*, (no. 5, 1975), he died in Alma Ata sometime in 1938 but his son claims he died August 19, 1947. Agursky's letter was written sometime between the end of 1938 and June 1941. He writes:

You know how much my articles and books have benefited the Party both here and abroad. You know how many bitter enemies I have made because of my constant fight against the Jewish and non-Jewish petit-bourgeois parties and their apologists. You know well the vicious hunt which the Litvakovs and others conducted against me and how many times they tried to discredit me. . . . *'I assure you that I am the victim of horrible and base slander and not a criminal, nor an enemy of the Party and the Soviet Union. . . .'* For more than three years already I have suffered physically and morally, since my ouster from public life. For more than a year I have been regarded as an 'enemy of the people' and my whole revolutionary past has been besmirched and disgraced by vile and criminal elements.

Agursky then tries to unravel the campaign of vilification and begs his friend to try to clear his name. The details do much to unveil the thick net of suspicion, double-dealing, mistrust, fear, and terror of the time.

Agursky traces his fall to March 1936, when a campaign of incitement was begun against him by Litvakov, the editor of *Emes*, who had found an "unfortunate phrase" of three lines in an article of Agursky's in *Emes* sometime in 1924. These lines were "incorrectly translated" and made the basis of a charge of Trotskyism, which was referred to the highest party authorities in Belorussia. Agursky was "completely rehabilitated," but in June 1937, a "new and vicious campaign" was started against him in Minsk where he was accused of being a "disguised Bundist," although he had struggled against Bundism for fifteen years. Agursky took this charge to be a signal to destroy him. People began demanding his expulsion from the party as "an enemy of the people." No one would speak to him. He became ill and had to be hospitalized for a "nervous condition." Later he found that the agitation against him had begun "on direct orders from Vasily Sharangovich, secretary of the Central Committee of the party in Belorussia, who himself was sentenced to death in 1938 in the Bukharin trial. Why did Sharangovich press for his "unmasking"?

In the spring of 1937, according to Agursky, many emigrants from Poland and western Belorussia were arrested, including an Abraham Damesek, a Yiddish journalist and secretary of the editorial board of *Shtern*. When interrogated, Damesek confessed that he was a member of a "Bundish Nazi-fascist organization" which existed in Minsk under the cover of the journal *Shtern* and that the editors . . . [Khayim] Dunets, [Yasha] Bronshteyn, [Izi] Kharik and [Moshe] Kulbak (all outstanding Yiddish writers and critics), were the leaders. . . . On the basis of Damesek's fantastic 'evidence' they immediately arrested Bronshteyn and brought Dunets back to a Minsk gaol from the distant camp where he had been deported." Dunets then confessed that "on his initiative a Bundist Nazi-fascist organization had been created in Minsk, which . . . had undertaken the murder of the leaders of the Party and the Soviet regime." Minsk was allegedly the center of this organization with branches in other cities. The alleged leaders of the Moscow group were Litvakov, Alexander Khashin, and Oskar Strelits, all Yiddish writers. Kharik, Bronshteyn, and Kulbak were named as "active terrorists" and were arrested in August 1937; Litvakov was also arrested as a terrorist and "confessed to everything," even to the extreme of declaring himself a Gestapo agent. Litvakov also informed on A. (Elijah) Osherovich, a leading member of the Evsektsiya in Belorussia, and labeled Agursky an "active" terrorist. Osherovich was then arrested and confessed to being "an agent of the Polish security service" and the leader of the "Bundist Nazi-fascist organization."

In the seventy-two pages of typescript containing Osherovich's "confession," there are four pages filled with names of people he had identified as belonging to this organization and carrying out his orders. Among those names are the Jewish activists, Esther Frumkin, Veinshtain, V. Nodel, and others, who were arrested in January 1938. Osherovich also identified Agursky as someone "he had sent to America during the years 1919–1921 to conduct Bundist activities." Agursky says that when he read the charges, he was aghast, but could not confront Osherovich personally for he had committed suicide in the Minsk prison.

After his temporary "rehabilitation" in 1936–37, Agursky was told to resume writing an official history of Belorussia that he had already started. He was even given a new apartment, when suddenly on March 4, 1938, he was arrested on the charge that he was a "Polish spy." At first he thought this was nothing but a poor joke; then he demanded evidence and Osherovich's "evidence" was produced. Fruitlessly, he tried to defend himself from the slanderous accusations, but to no avail. His case was turned over to a military prosecutor and Agursky apparently had some hope that he might receive a fair trial by a military tribunal, but after nineteen months' imprisonment in a Minsk prison, he was told that a "Special Board" had decided to deport him to Kazakhastan for five years "for participating in a counter-revolutionary organization."

Agursky's son, Mikhail, who left the Soviet Union for Israel in June 1975, recalls[37] that the Belorussian NKVD in 1937 was instructed to organize a great separate trial and made suggestions of names of defendants, "but all were rejected by Moscow without any explanation until a Jew was included and the whole affair given a Jewish colouring. It was in this connection that Agursky was arrested." According to Mikhail, his father was subjected to cruel torture in the Minsk prison. Since his cell was separated by a thin partition from the torture cell, he could not escape the groans of the victims. His family knew nothing of his fate until October 1938, by which time most of those charged with participation in a "Jewish fascist center" had been shot or imprisoned. Late in 1939, Agursky was exiled to Pavlodar in Kazakhstan where his family joined him after the war broke out. In 1947 Agursky requested rehabilitation, but this was refused and on August 19 of that year he died of a cerebral hemorrhage. After Beria's arrest in 1953, Mikhail wrote to Voroshilov, the chairman of the Presidium of the Supreme Soviet, requesting his father's posthumous rehabilitation. Many of the investigators themselves had been shot and in 1955 a mass rehabilitation began. Agursky's turn came in April 1956, and in August he was posthumously restored to party membership. Like most of the Jewish Communists purged, Agursky had cultivated illusions about the nature of the Soviet state and had worked ardently and conscientiously to serve it, but the state had found him expendable. The shocked helplessness, anguish, and suffering of these men and women who disappeared in the anonymous, appalling wretchedness of the Soviet Gulag were for a long time experiences sealed from the world, but can now be read in Shalamov's *Kolyma Tales*, Solzhenitsyn's *Gulag Archipelago* and Ginzburg's memoirs.[38]

An estimated five to nine million persons were arrested in the purges of 1936–38, a grisly projection of Stalin's paranoid fears of conspiracy and suspicious nature, combined with his ruthless drive to complete power over state, party, and society.[39] His own psychopathological needs expressed both in internal and external affairs were then and until his death to be the dynamic in Soviet policy, creating a "historical mutation far beyond the intent or grasp of any of the traditional Bolshevik thinkers."[40] Soviet society was now to be in the grip of permanent and pervasive terror. Moreover, the staggering human losses severely weakened the country's capacity to withstand the coming test of total war. Survivors of these purges not only experienced the bitterest kind of anguish over the deaths of their comrades and the insane waste, but lived through the travesty of a pact with Nazi Germany after having heard the vilest denunciations of those who had allegedly conspired to meet with Nazis.

Deprived of spokesmen, semi-autonomous agencies, newspapers, and publications, and with almost two-fifths of Russia's Jews dispersed outside the old Pale of Settlement (see Tables 14.1 and 14.2), Jewish group cohesion was no longer possible and individual Jewish identity was

TABLE 14.1

Jewish Population Centers in 1939 prior to Hitler-Stalin Pact—Estimates*

Republic	City	Jewish Population
RSFSR	Moscow	400,000
RSFSR	Leningrad	275,000
RSFSR	Rostov	40,000
Ukrainian SSR	Odessa	180,000
Ukrainian SSR	Kiev	175,000
Ukrainian SSR	Kharkov	150,000
Ukrainian SSR	Dnepropetrovsk	100,000
Ukrainian SSR	Vinnitsa	25,000–28,000
Ukrainian SSR	Zhitomir	30,000
Belorussian SSR	Minsk	90,000
Belorussian SSR	Gomel	48,000–53,000
Belorussian SSR	Vitebsk	45,000–52,000
Belorussian SSR	Bobruisk	22,000–28,000
Belorussian SSR	Mogilev	20,000–27,000

Source: S. M. Schwarz, The Jews in the Soviet Union, 1951, pp. 225, 229, 230, 231, 236.

*Census figures on Jewish population by individual cities were never released.

TABLE 14.2

Size and Distribution of the Jewish Population in the USSR, as of
January 1, 1939 and Changes, 1926–1939 (to nearest thousand)

Republics	Population	Change from 1926 to 1939	Percentage Change
Ukrainian SSR	1,533,000	−41,000	−2.6
RSFSR	948,000		
Kazakh SSR	19,000	+366,000	+60.3
Kirghiz SSR	2,000		
Belorussian SSR	375,000	−32,000	−7.8
Azerbaidzhan SSR	41,000		
Georgian SSR	42,000	+33,000	+64.7
Armenian SSR	1,000		
Turkmen SSR	3,000	+1,000	+49.0
Uzbek SSR	51,000	+13,000	+34.2
Tadzhik SSR	5,000		
Total Jewish Population	3,020,000	+348,000	+12.7
Total Population in USSR	170,467,000	+23,439,000	+15.9

Sources: S. M. Schwarz, *The Jews in the Soviet Union*, 1951, p. 15; L. Zinger, *Dos Banayte Folk*, 1941, pp. 36, 40, 126.

sustained at great sacrifice and even risk. Such fragile Jewishness as could survive was stricken by the Nazi-Soviet Pact of August 1939.

An inconspicuous portent of the coming change in Soviet foreign policy appeared in mid-April 1939, when *Izvestia* stopped publishing Ilya Ehrenburg's dispatches from Paris, which had been carrying strong denunciations of fascism, and whose books had been ceremoniously burned in Berlin. Then on May 3, 1938, Litvinov, the Soviet foreign minister—a Jew who favored cooperation with the West against Hitler, and who was referred to by the German radio as "Litvinov-Finkelstein"—was dropped in favor of Vyacheslav Molotov. "The eminent Jew," as Churchill put it, "the target of German antagonism was flung aside . . . like a broken tool. . . . The Jew Litvinov was gone, and Hitler's dominant prejudice placated."[41] On August 23, 1939, the Nazi-Soviet Non-aggression Pact was signed and announced to a stunned world. The Kremlin Hall where the pact was signed was decorated with a swastika banner alongside the red flag; Stalin personally toasted Hitler's health. In November, when Molotov addressed the Supreme

Soviet, he said that Germany was now interested in making peace, whereas the Western powers were eager to continue the war. When, a few weeks later, Hitler and Ribbentrop congratulated Stalin on his six- tieth birthday, Stalin replied that Soviet-German friendship had been "cemented by blood."

The pact enabled Hitler to invade Poland without fear of a Soviet challenge. Moreover, according to a secret protocol appended to the treaty, "the spheres of interest of both Germany and the USSR" were to be "bounded by the line of the rivers Narev, Vistula, and the San," thus giving the Soviet Union eastern Poland "in the event of a territo- rial and political transformation" of Poland.[42] Latvia, Estonia, Finland, and Bessarabia were also assigned to the Soviet sphere. Lithuania was added later. The motives of each partner have been debated heatedly and variously interpreted, but there is no question that the treaty marked a turning point in world history and was the prelude to World War II. A week after it was announced, Germany invaded Poland.

For Europe's Jews, the treaty was the beginning of the road to anni- hilation. Soviet Jews at first found it incomprehensible, but then under- stood that it provided the very grounding for increased harassment and isolation as the most suspect minority in the regime. The promi- nent Soviet dissident Andrei Sakharov said that anti-Semitism entered into the policy of the "highest bureaucratic elite" at that time.[43] The leaders of the Soviet Union were now embracing Hitler, the ideologist of extreme anti-Semitism who had already threatened the elimination of Jewry in case of war. On January 30, 1939, he had warned publicly that "if the international Jewish financiers inside and outside Europe should again succeed in plunging the nations into a world war, the result will be . . . the annihilation of the Jewish race throughout Eu- rope."[44]

Within the Soviet Union itself, all anti-Nazi and anti-fascist publica- tions disappeared from bookstands and editors began to cut any dis- paraging remarks against fascism or Nazi Germany in novels and pe- riodicals. In his *Memoirs*, published some twenty years later, Ehrenburg refers to a number of such details which were deleted from his book *The Fall of Paris*, published in early 1941. Most of the articles he wrote at the time for *Izvestia* were turned down and he was finally told to send no more dispatches from Paris, since "in every line the editors discovered slanting references to the Fascists, whom our wits called our 'deadly friends.' "[45] Even those Jews who argued that the pact was a bitter necessity could not swallow the new image of the German fascists, whom they had "regarded since our Komsomol days . . . as something hostile, evil and dangerous. . . . This change was not necessarily expressed directly but it penetrated our souls from the many pictures of Hitler at Molotov's side, the news of Soviet oil and grains streaming to Fascist Germany."[46]

Articles on Jewish problems outside the USSR—generally dealing with anti-Semitism, which was interpreted as a capitalist aberration—stopped appearing in the press after the signing of the pact, and anti-Nazi films depicting persecution of Germany's Jews such as *Professor Mamlock* and *The Oppenheim Family* disappeared from Soviet screens.[47] Soviet silence on Nazi anti-Semitism reduced or eliminated apprehension of dangers ahead for Soviet Jews and encouraged the spread of anti-Semitism within the Soviet Union itself, sparked by indigenous forces and deep-rooted anti-Semitism in the newly annexed territories (see Chapter 15). The Third Reich in fact was congratulated for its systematic battle against the Jewish religion and newspaper readers were urged to support their new ally in its struggle against religion.[48] In the documents on Nazi-Soviet relations during the period of the pact, published after the war, there is no reference at all to the "Jewish problem" and its bearing on these relations.[49] Soviet leaders were obviously aware of the significance of the Jewish issue in coming to an understanding with Hitler, and Litvinov's dismissal was intended to remove an obstacle, which Hitler later told his generals was "decisive."[50] Yet despite the absence of the issue in official records, on July 24, 1942, a year after the German invasion of Russia, Hitler told his entourage that "Stalin had broached the delicate subject of 'Jewish Bolshevism' with Ribbentrop in Moscow . . . [and] had made it clear . . . that he would oust the Jews from leading positions the moment he had sufficient qualified Gentiles with whom to replace them."[51] We know that Stalin had a strong personal dislike of Jews. By sharing these feelings with an arch anti-Semite with whom he wanted to avoid war and divide territory, he could also dispel any misgivings about communism's alleged identification with Jewry. Stalin's decimation of the Jewish intelligentsia in 1936–38, and his drive for empire and pan-Slav nationalism also apparently led Hitler to think of Stalin as a modern tsar rather than an exponent of "Jewish" Marxism.[52]

Soviet Jews knew that the Soviet Union was fattening the German economy with oil, phosphates, and grain, but did not know that these products were being fed into the German war machine which would soon be turned against them and their country. Nor were they permitted to have any news of the persecution of Jews in western Poland, or elsewhere in Europe. Many of the Jews in eastern Poland, moreover, soon after the pact was signed, fled to western Poland, thinking that their lot would be better under Germans than under Russians. But it was not only Jews who were shocked and confused about the significance of the pact. The Soviet turnabout had to be rationalized to the Soviet people. Yesterday's enemy was suddenly harmless.

The brunt of the new Soviet strategy was an attack against "the ruling classes of France and England." The official Soviet gloss during this period was that Jews, Ukrainians, and White Russians had been rescued from an oppressive and backward Polish regime which had been unable to defend its citizens.[53] A new Soviet line had to be suddenly devised to undo the Nazi propaganda up to August 1939, which had hammered away at the connection between Jews and communism. "Communism in the twentieth century," Hitler had written in *Mein Kampf*," is in fact nothing but an attempt by Judaism to take over the whole world." The Soviet Union, it was alleged, was ruled by "an international Jewish clique" and inspired by "the opium of Judeo-Marxism." Nazis even tried to prove that Lenin came from Jewish stock. The Russians had to improvise a new line swiftly. On August 24, the day after the pact was signed, *Pravda* explained to its readers in an editorial that "the proper conditions for the developing and flourishing of friendly relations between the Soviet Union and Germany must be created. . . . Political and ideological differences must not constitute an obstacle to the establishment of good neighborly relations between the two countries." On October 9, 1939, *Izvestia* stated that "The war against Hitlerism should not be supported, because war cannot be supported purely because of hatred of an ideology. This would plunge us back into the dark period of the Middle Ages." An especially tasteless item, with anti-Semitic overtones, appeared in an article in *Pravda* on October 17 dealing with the creation of a Polish Government-in-Exile in Paris: "At the Great Synagogue of Paris, Sikorski addressed the Jewish Parisian bankers. The synagogue was decorated with the flag of the white eagle, duly approved by the Chief Rabbi, as this bird is generally not eaten by observant Jews. In the past, Polish Jews used to be deathly afraid of the Polish aristocracy and the pogroms. Now, however, it appears that Jewish bankers have nothing to fear from General Sikorski."[54] Later in the month, on October 31, Soviet Foreign Minister Molotov in an address to the Supreme Soviet cheered the elimination of Poland ("the monster brought into the world by the Versailles Treaty") and railed against France and England for continuing the war: "One can sympathize with Hitlerism or be disgusted by it, but all intelligent men must realize that an ideology cannot be eliminated by war. A war 'for the destruction of Hitlerism' under the false slogan of struggle for democracy is, therefore, nonsense or even criminal."

The Soviet difficulties involved in reversing public opinion were frankly expressed by the German ambassador to the Soviet Union, Count Friedrich Schulenburg, in a cable to the German Foreign Office less than a month after the pact was signed:

Since anxiety over war, especially the fear of a German attack strongly influenced the attitude of the population here in the last few years, the conclusion of a nonaggression pact with Germany has been generally received with great relief and gratification. However, the sudden alteration in the policy of the Soviet Government, after years of propaganda directed expressly against German aggressors, is still not very well understood by the population. Especially the statements . . . that Germany is no longer an aggressor run up against considerable doubt. The Soviet Government is doing everything possible to change the attitude of the population. . . . The press is as though it had been transformed. Attacks on the conduct of Germany have not only ceased completely, but the portrayal of events in the field of foreign politics is based to an outstanding degree on German reports and anti-German literature has been removed from the book trade, etc.[55]

The populations of eastern Poland and the Baltic states were also confused by the significance of the pact, none more so than the Jews in those areas who could not possibly fathom their future under Soviet rule.

15

Jews in the Soviet-Annexed Territories, September 1939–June 1941

We had a few hundred thousand refugees at that time in Bialystok, and we had many discussions, sometimes deep in the night, trying to find out what to do . . . should we accept the passport or not. . . . There was general confusion. As a matter of fact, many went back to Warsaw because we remembered the Germans from the First War. We didn't know what we may expect this time.

DR. LEON FRIEDMAN

THE German invasion and quick conquest of Poland in September 1939 activated the Soviet-Nazi Pact and brought eastern Poland under Soviet rule. Professing a "sacred duty" to liberate the people there, the USSR incorporated the territory into the Belorussian and Ukrainian SSR's before the end of the year. In June 1940, during Hitler's conquest of Western Europe, the Baltic countries likewise became Soviet Socialist Republics, the northeastern districts of Romania were added to the Moldavian SSR, and northern Bukovina was annexed to the Ukrainian SSR (see Map 15.1). The Jewish population now under Soviet control had swelled from 3,020,000 in 1939 to over 5,000,000 (see Table 15.1).

When the Red Army entered these annexed territories, Soviet authorities rapidly began to integrate the populations within the administrative, economic, social, and cultural frameworks that had crystallized in the USSR during the 1930s. Life in the new areas took on a definite sovietized pattern and all vestiges of the former regimes were wiped out. For Jews this meant the extinction of a traditional religious and cultural life and an official policy of Ukrainization and White-Russification, which generally brought into prominence anti-Semitic nationalists. Moreover, the presence of many Jewish refugees from western,

MAP 15.1

Jewish Population in the USSR, by Republic, 1939, and Soviet Annexations, 1939–40

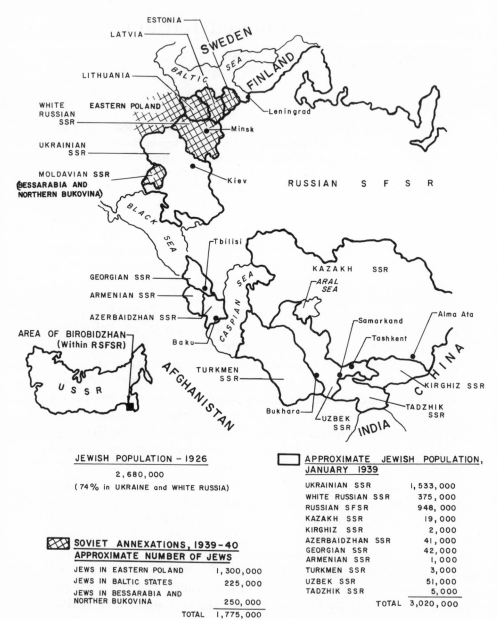

JEWISH POPULATION – 1926

2,680,000

(74% in UKRAINE and WHITE RUSSIA)

SOVIET ANNEXATIONS, 1939–40
APPROXIMATE NUMBER OF JEWS

JEWS IN EASTERN POLAND	1,300,000
JEWS IN BALTIC STATES	225,000
JEWS IN BESSARABIA AND NORTHER BUKOVINA	250,000
TOTAL	1,775,000

APPROXIMATE JEWISH POPULATION, JANUARY 1939

UKRAINIAN SSR	1,533,000
WHITE RUSSIAN SSR	375,000
RUSSIAN SFSR	948,000
KAZAKH SSR	19,000
KIRGHIZ SSR	2,000
AZERBAIDZHAN SSR	41,000
GEORGIAN SSR	42,000
ARMENIAN SSR	1,000
TURKMEN SSR	3,000
UZBEK SSR	51,000
TADZHIK SSR	5,000
TOTAL	3,020,000

TABLE 15.1

Approximate Number of Jews in Territories Added to
USSR, 1939–40

Eastern Poland	1,300,000
Baltic States	225,000
Bessarabia and No. Bukovina	250,000
Total	1,775,000
Total Soviet Jewish Population Prior to German Invasion, 1941	5,000,000–5,300,000*

*Some estimates are as high as 5,500,000.

Nazi-occupied Poland who tried to make contact with their families in western Poland increased the suspicion of the already suspicious NKVD and eventually resulted in mass arrests and deportations. Among those active in establishing Soviet rule in eastern Poland were Nikita Khrushchev, first secretary of the Ukrainian Communist party and I. Serov, head of the secret police in the Ukraine.[1]

The Jewish minorities in the annexed areas had been subject to discriminatory treatment and popular anti-Semitism, and at first, expected their situation to improve with the change in regime. Most of the 1,300,000 Jews in eastern Poland had greeted the Red Army with great relief, but initial feelings soon gave way to disappointment and bitterness as harsh ideological and economic measures were introduced.[2] These Polish Jews became sovietized at a time when the national status of the Soviet Jew had begun to disintegrate. At the same time, the intensive political, social, and recreational activities of the new regime had a certain appeal to some Jewish youth and workers and gave them educational and job opportunities which they did not have before. "In some places, the arrival of Soviet units actually prevented anti-Jewish rioting,"[3] and in the early stages of the Soviet occupation, there was widespread sympathy and help from local Jews. Jews entered the local militia and in a few towns, served on the temporary administrative committees. Soviet authorities even accepted the help of Bundists and Zionists at first. Jewish officers and soldiers of the Red Army spoke Yiddish to the local Jewish population and promised them a glorious future under Soviet rule.[4] Visits by Red Army men to Jewish homes on Saturdays and holidays were not uncommon.

Economic, cultural, and political changes, however, soon reversed the early optimism. The Jewish middle class was rapidly pauperized under Soviet nationalization and many had to be supported by relatives and friends and the sale of personal belongings. The greater part of the Jewish intelligentsia, with the exception of teachers, also lost their means of livelihood. Some moved to the Ukraine and White Russia and found work in industrial plants and collectives; others registered for work in the coal mines in the Urals and Donbas region, but harsh conditions and barely subsistence living conditions drove many of them back. Sovietization also involved the closing of many synagogues, Jewish organizations, and institutions, and the arrest of Zionists, Bundists, and "bourgeois" elements. Jewish youths were pressed to join the Komsomol and fall into line with the new order.

Soviet policy also stressed Ukrainian and Belorussian nationalism, causing Jews to lose their initial status and hoped-for improved political and economic conditions. They were not given their proportional share in representative bodies—for example, in the national assembly of Belorussia, there were only twenty Jews out of 1,495 members.[5] Nationalization, moreover, and heavy taxes were very burdensome, especially in large cities such as Bialystok, Lvov, Pinsk, and Rovno, where the native populations were inundated by streams of refugees from western Poland.

Adaptation to the Soviet way of life was especially difficult for Jewish refugees. German atrocities against Jews in western Poland commenced as soon as their forces gained control and thousands of Jews had fled eastward hoping to find safety in the Soviet zone. Their presence aggravated existing food, housing, and job problems despite the efforts of the local population. The Soviet authorities were at first rather well-disposed to the refugees, but they soon became a political, administrative, and economic problem and Soviet policies became increasingly harsh.[6] These decisions were determined by security considerations and the related complications regarding border crossings. The final borders in Poland between the USSR and Germany were drawn on September 28, 1939, but Jews continued crossing the border throughout October and were generally not stopped, even when forced to cross by the Germans.[7] Nor did the waves cease after November 11, when the Soviet authorities required special permits for refugees crossing into their zone, without which reprisals could be severe.

The turmoil of these sudden changes can be glimpsed in the experiences of a Jewish writer Julius Margolin, who had fled from Lodz hoping to reach Romania and Palestine.[8] At Sniatin, only three miles from the Romanian border, he encountered the Red Army. Jewish stores there were doing a thriving business and Jews, glad to have Russians instead of Germans, joined in a welcoming program. Many in the parade hailing the Red Army were Jews. Poles saw this as a "Jewish demonstration." The soldiers set up their headquarters in the white building of the Zionist movement, still bearing the Star of David. Margolin and others finally got permission to go on to Lvov, the capital of western Ukraine. There, panic-stricken refugees and soldiers jammed the streets. Refugees were registered along with Polish army officers, but "when it became clear that the Soviet army was occupying Poland, not liberating her, the Poles began to flow back en masse towards the German zone." People talked in whispers about the chances of escaping to Hungary or Romania, but "we were already encircled; all the frontiers were closed except for the partition line between eastern and western Poland."

Unable to get a travel permit to Romania, Margolin went to Pinsk, but fearing the local NKVD, moved on to Sniatin and Lvov again, then to Lida, on the Lithuanian frontier, where there were refugees everywhere. Many like Margolin hoped to reach Vilna, the legendary Jewish center and mecca for refugees at the time, and thence receive a transit visa for Palestine. (On October 10, 1939, a Soviet-Lithuanian Agreement had transferred Vilna to Lithuania, a step that seemed to offer Jews a gateway to the free world and Palestine.) Late in December, a guide helped Margolin and a small group to Vilna by sled, but they were stopped at a police barrier and told to go back to Lida to work. Instead, Margolin decided to go back to Pinsk, where he observed the process of sovietization at first hand.

First, the Polish government was not merely dismissed, but disappeared without a trace. The Polish farmers were deported in the bitter cold. Rumors circulated that mothers were throwing frozen corpses of their children out of padlocked cars. Wealthier peasants, intellectuals, and socially active people and officials were also deported. Then came the turn of the Jews. Local Communists helped to draw up a list of "leisure elements," mostly shopkeepers and lawyers who were expelled. The liquidation of Jewish educational, publishing, and political bodies followed. By the beginning of 1940, those who survived became employees of the Soviet administration, part of a forced-labor system. In retrospect, life under the Polish government seemed quite good. A Belorussian peasant said, "For twenty years the Polish government tried to make Poles out of us, and they didn't succeed. In two months the Bolsheviks have made Poles out of us."

Quite soon Soviet authorities made a sharp distinction between local residents and refugees, since most of the refugees balked at the sovietization process. Most of them considered their stay under Soviet rule temporary, while Soviet authorities intended to convert them into Soviet citizens. Often officials at employment offices refused to register refugees for work and insisted they go into the Soviet interior.[9] Clinging to the large cities, they aggravated existing housing and food problems. Local resources were stretched and the efforts of the Joint Distribution Committee and local agencies to assist were rebuffed. In a few towns, Soviet authorities established free kitchens, but they were totally inadequate for the needy thousands. There was only one such kitchen in Bialystok in November 1939 for the 33,000 registered refugees.[10] Moreover, there was little available shelter and many had to sleep in fields, woods, railroad stations, empty freight cars, and synagogues. "Most fortunate were those who found quarters in the Halutz [Zionist pioneering movement] shelters, where it was clean and possible to get warm food."[11] Government regulations often forced refugees who had been sheltered in an apartment or public building to leave. "Several hundred refugees who lived in the headquarters of the Merchants Association in Bialystok were driven out in the middle of the night so that the offices could be used for a new tailor's cooperative."[12]

Early in 1940 there were reports[13] of starvation and spreading epidemics in Soviet-annexed Poland, especially in Lvov, as a result of shortages of food, water, and proper medicine. On March 25, the Bucharest correspondent of the *New York Times* reported starvation in eastern Poland as a result of the almost complete despoliation of its reserves. The situation was aggravated by the refusal of the Soviet government to admit outside relief. According to a Paris dispatch of March 21, approximately 200,000 penniless Jews, including women and children, were wandering from village to village in Galicia, begging Ukrainian peasants for bread. The situation facing Polish Jews became very acute as a result of the decree invalidating Polish currency in March. Reports from Lvov, Stanislawow, Bialystok, Stryj, and Grodno indicated that Jewish youths deserted these cities for the Soviet Union proper.

Trapped between the lash of Nazi savagery in the west and Soviet harassment in the east, and often unable to penetrate the full realities of the time, refugees floundered, shuttled back and forth in confusion and fear, desperately searching for safety.[14]

Accounts by eye-witnesses testify to the panic and uncertainty of the time. In some cases, border guards stopped refugee crossings in October: "About the fifteenth of October, the borders were suddenly shut tight. The sentries were no longer friendly, and frequently towns and villages near the border were searched for refugees who had somehow got across. . . . Those caught were shipped back to Nazi Poland. Soviet border guards shot at anyone trying to get back. . . ."[15] Moreover, in the German-Soviet negotiations over the final boundary lines, there were several switches back and forth, catching Jews in the disputed towns. For example, some refugees who had fled in September and October across the San River toward Lvov and Sokal into the Soviet zone were told the area would be given to Germany. They trekked over 200 miles to Holoszyce, then Grodek, which fell officially under Soviet rule, and were safe there until subsequent deportations.[16]

By November, Jews in the no-man's land of the border towns became victims of Nazi brutality and Soviet indifference. In the bitter winter of 1939, local Jews "did their utmost to help them, frequently sharing with them their crowded quarters and last piece of bread. . . . When finally the refugees had reached a point of desperation, they stampeded past the Soviet guards. Several were shot, but most of them got across after overpowering the sentries by sheer weight of numbers." At Drohyczyn, the refugees had to cross the Bug River in rowboats, "frequently under a hail of bullets from both Nazis and Soviets."[17]

The incomprehensibility of events for Jews caught in German-Soviet diplomacy can also be viewed from the perspective of a man already confined to the Warsaw Ghetto. An astute observer of the disintegrating life around him, he cannot fathom the efforts of Soviet officials to obtain manpower. In a diary entry for December 23, 1939,[18] Chaim Kaplan, a well-known Jewish educator, notes that a Soviet Commission is in Warsaw to arrange for "Slavic emigration." He wonders if there is a formal ban against Jews. Is the border being closed because "undesirable elements" such as financiers, middlemen, and black marketeers are unwanted? At the same time, only 800 of 2,000 who applied for work inside Russia and received 50 roubles and two changes of linen returned to the registration agency to accept the work and make the journey. Later, on January 5, 1940,[19] Kaplan notes that the emigration of non-Jewish Poles is permitted, but that they don't want to leave either. When a Russian official is asked, "Why do you exclude Jews?" he answers, "The conqueror does not consent to any privileges for his hated Jews." Again, according to Kaplan, there seems to be a shift by January 16, when he notes that Russia will take Jewish craftsmen.

Meanwhile Jews were expelled from Nazi-controlled Poland with particular ferocity and driven to frontier areas bordering Lithuania and Soviet Poland or left to find refuge in the Soviet zone. A Vilna dispatch of November 6, 1939 reported[20] that 1,400 Jews, mostly women and children among thousands who had been driven into frontier areas bordering Lithuania and Soviet Poland, were stranded in a forest near Brok following the closing of the Soviet border. They were finally permitted to cross after pleading with border guards not to shoot them. A Copenhagen dispatch reported that all Jews in the Suwalki district were expelled, with many marooned near Soviet territory. Some were later admitted to the Soviet zone. There were German-Soviet discussions of population transfers at the time and on November 15, the Soviet Union officially protested forced expulsions into their territory.

Survivors have described both the humane as well as cruel treatment they received at the hands of Soviet border guards, after the border was officially sealed. Already in December 1939, moreover, there were reports of severe punishment meted out to Soviet soldiers and officers who smuggled refugees into the Soviet zone, some of whom had accepted bribes.[21] In November–December, reports that the Soviet Union was pressing officials in the zone to expel all refugees considered harmful to Soviet interests were categorically denied. Previously, however, in November, a Soviet delegation had arrived in Kaunas (Kovno) to arrange for the transfer of about 100,000 White Russians and Jews from Vilna districts. Between 8,000 and 10,000 Jews had previously emigrated to the Soviet Union from Vilna seeking to emigrate to Palestine by way of the USSR, but they were not given transit visas.[22]

Because of the fluctuating situation at various border crossing points, it is impossible to know the exact number of Jews from Nazi-occupied Poland who found refuge in the Soviet zone when the border was technically closed, but it is believed to have been about 300,000 to 350,000.[23] Some of these were extradited as well as forced back by Soviet officials, while others continued their struggle to go east after the border was closed, virtually until the German invasion of the Soviet Union in June 1941.[24]

One of the most painful experiences of Jews in eastern Poland was their exposure to Soviet silence about Nazi anti-Jewish atrocities and Soviet cordiality to the Nazi regime. Writers among the refugees were shocked to find that all anti-Nazi publications had disappeared and that they themselves were forbidden to write about their own experiences.[25] One leftist writer Moshe Grossman showed an editor a yellow badge (such as those the Nazis were forcing Jews in western Poland to wear) which a refugee had showed him and urged Grossman to write an article on the subject, but the article was suppressed. "The supreme authorities have banned it," the editor explained.

Polish and Polish Jewish Communists were generally denounced as Trotskyists. They soon learned that their ideas were of no account and that their anti-Nazi opinions were completely out of order, and, in fact, dangerous. A large number were imprisoned. No discussions were permitted at meetings of factory or party cells. A witness to a meeting[26] held in the market place of Zaremb Koscielny, where most who attended were Jews, reported that a Polish Jewish Communist delivered a speech bitterly attacking the Nazis and their persecution of Jews. The chairman, a captain in the Red Army, tried several times to stop him and finally drove him off the platform.

Late in 1939, a collection of literary contributions by twenty Yiddish writers from the newly annexed territories appeared in Minsk under the title *The Liberated Brothers*, but there was no reference permitted to the Nazi menace under whose shadow they had recently lived, and in a book of poetry by a "liberated" Jew that appeared in Minsk in 1940, one poem called "The Hangman" referred not to Hitler but to Marshal von Mannerheim of Finland.[27]

When the refugee writers met Soviet Yiddish writers, they had to exchange experiences furtively; no criticism of the Soviet-Nazi Pact and no talk of the unfolding Jewish tragedy could leak out. Those who could not yield to the Soviet line stopped writing.[28] Yet for a brief time, whatever contact was possible between Soviet Jews and those in the annexed territories before the German invasion of Russia in June 1941 gave the former a glimpse of an intense and varied Jewish cultural life which had been destroyed in the Soviet Union. "Even Jewish Red Army soldiers," one historian has observed, "were deeply moved by the . . . pithiness and vivacity of Jewish life, the devotion and adherence to tradition, which they encountered for the first time in their lives when they visited synagogues, or were invited to Jewish homes."[29]

Soviet Yiddish writers, including Kvitko, Feffer, Markish, and Hofshteyn were sent in Writers' Brigades to help instruct and indoctrinate the new citizens, especially the refugee writers and intellectuals.[30] The

Soviet writers wrote fulsomely about the liberation of the "western areas," but there were slippages from the official scenario on both sides. For example, at a reception in Bialystok,[31] when some of the refugee writers made a great show of demonstrating their new loyalties, Motl Grubian drank a toast to "the life of the great Jewish nation." Zelik Akselrod, a Soviet poet from Minsk, was deeply stirred when he heard Moshe Kusevitsky, a renowned Warsaw cantor, give an operatic recital. When he heard complaints that Soviet authorities were closing down all existing Yiddish schools in Minsk, he suggested—somewhat rashly—that parents sign petitions to save the school system.[32] But there were penalties. Akselrod was reprimanded by the local political commissar for "manifesting Jewish nationalism." Later, he moved to Vilna and joined with another Soviet Jewish poet Elia Kahan in a protest against the closing down of the last Vilna Yiddish paper, the *Vilner emes.*[33] Both men were promptly arrested and imprisoned.

Some of the Soviet writers subtly alluded to their misgivings. Markish, for example, who helped a number of Polish refugee writers resettle and re-establish their careers, did not paint an especially rosy picture for the future.[34] The authorities had no intention whatever of encouraging the further development of Jewish culture by the Polish Jewish intelligentsia. In the eyes of the Soviet regime, the refugees from Poland were not only Jews, they were also aliens, because they had not undergone Soviet ideological preparation. Markish told the writers that shoemakers were needed more than writers—a harsh remark that wounded some of the writers. But others understood his point. Some, including Rachel Korn, Chaim Grade, and Efraim Kaganovsky, were able to get to Moscow with his help. Markish also extended help to Moshe Broderzon's Jewish Miniatures State Theater of Poland[35] and the Yiddish Theater of Ida Kaminska.

Feffer also is known to have momentarily overcome his caution, boasting at one meeting with refugee writers of his rabbinic ancestry and explaining "Back to the past! We are now celebrating the 800th anniversary of Judah Halevy. Judah the Maccabean and the Hasmoneans are national heroes and revolutionaries."[36] Feffer was also very helpful to refugee writers from Poland and the provinces later annexed from Romania. Some were at first encouraged by this solicitude, but there was little anyone could do to stop the sovietization drive. The refugee writers had to fall into line. Yiddish newspapers and periodicals with large prewar circulations were replaced early in the occupation by a few Soviet-style publications. In Lvov, for example, the Communist daily *Royter togblatt* replaced all other Yiddish papers in September 1939.[37] In all of the western Ukraine, only one Yiddish daily was to be found in June 1941.[38] The only Yiddish paper in western Belorussia had a meager circulation of 5,000.

Soviet-style literature, however, was abundant. Special branches of the Soviet Union of Writers were established in Bialystok and Lvov and the works of poets and novelists who were ready to serve the regime filled numerous journals.[39] The printing of children's literature also increased, and Yiddish state theaters and theater troupes were formed in Lvov, Riga, Chernovtsy, and Bialystok. The actors received a fixed salary and did not have to worry about technical matters such as costumes and the sale of tickets. Artists were given rooms in which to exhibit their work, and a club where tea and meals were served— a very important matter in those days.

The new Yiddish schools set up under Soviet authorities (for example, thirty in Lvov, and forty-three in Bialystok, including four full-time high schools) and special institutes for the training of Yiddish teachers at first aroused high hopes for the future of Yiddish culture.[40] However, the real intentions of the regime became apparent quite soon. The number of Yiddish schools decreased, and in those which still functioned, Yiddish was replaced by Ukrainian, Belorussian, and Lithuanian. Jewish libraries ceased to exist as separate institutions and undesirable books were purged, even burned.[41]

In their antireligious campaign, Soviet authorities insinuated their dogmas in antireligious periodicals, at conferences, meetings, and in oral persuasion. They also acted directly to close synagogues, arrest rabbis, prohibit the sale of religious objects and prayer books. Moreover, the "Godless League" received large budgets for its antireligious propaganda. Jews were forced to work on the Sabbath and religious holidays and religious personnel were pressured into leaving their posts. As in the Soviet Union itself, efforts were made to create the impression that Jews themselves wanted religious activities to cease. Especially vehement were the campaigns directed against Hasidim; by contrast, there were awkward efforts to train so-called "red" rabbis who would be loyal to the new regime.[42] Many of the synagogues were decorated with pictures of Lenin, Stalin, and Molotov. While Lithuania was still ostensibly independent, about 2,000 Polish yeshiva teachers and students crossed the border into Vilna where JDC provided them with shelter, food, and clothing.[43] The synagogue assumed an important role, being the only legal remnant of the former Jewish communal network, the only available meeting place for Jews—as in certain cities of the Soviet Union today. There the Jewish refugees could find food and shelter, and from there some Zionist youths could go to Vilna and then attempt to get to Palestine or the Far East.[44] By the end of October 1939, there may have been as many as 100,000 Jewish refugees in Vilna and its vicinity,[45] but no more than 2,250 were able to leave, by way of Moscow and Odessa to Turkey, through Intourist, which insisted on being paid in foreign currency.[46] The British White Paper of 1939 also blocked emigration possibilities.

Arrests of Zionists, Jewish socialists, and Bundists continued apace. Occasionally, there were reports of the release of Zionists after they had taken an oath of loyalty to the government. They were not, however, permitted to work.[47]

The inability of thousands of refugees to find work led to an often desperate decision to return to Nazi-occupied Poland. These returnees included not only declassed merchants and artisans but Polish Communists and those who lost all hope for survival in Soviet Poland.[48] The sudden devaluation of the Polish zloty in December 1939 and then the total elimination of Polish currency gave added impetus to this tragic return. Many simply became destitute. Others were afraid they would be permanently separated from their families in western Poland. This fear intensified late in 1939 when the refugees were faced with the choice of Soviet citizenship or return to their former homes.

On November 29, 1939, Soviet citizenship was extended to eastern Poland and all residents who lived there as of November 1 and 2, when the territory was incorporated into the USSR, became Soviet citizens. Refugees could also become Soviet citizens, but their passports imposed certain restrictions on residence and freedom of movement. Special commissions of the NKVD were set up in April–May 1940 to register the refugees, and most decided to return home.[49] Some apparently also tried to register with German commissions that were present as well, but they refused to register Jews.[50] At the time, there was a Nazi-Soviet population exchange agreement,[51] excluding Jews, and Soviet authorities decided on a grim solution to the refugee question. They wanted a "fast and complete change in the status of refugees" from refugee to Soviet citizen. Such a transfer of loyalty would be a political and diplomatic triumph for Stalin and would serve as a weapon in Soviet propaganda against the Polish government.[52] A "Repatriation Census" was carried out to determine the status of the refugees. Those who refused to accept Soviet citizenship—a semi-official source puts the figure at 250,000, but some estimates are higher[53]—were expelled to remote camps and villages in the Autonomous Republic of Komi, Kazakhstan, and Siberia. Suspicion of the refugees was so great that even those who accepted Soviet citizenship received passports stating that their holders were not allowed to live in big cities or near the border.[54] Stalin undoubtedly viewed the refugees as a "dangerous element," with contacts in the West, generally a bourgeois background, and of dubious or unreliable loyalties.

Deportations of Polish ex-officers, former government functionaries, persons of so-called "bourgeois" origin, intellectuals, and families of individuals who had gone abroad took place between February and April 1940. Many Jews associated with the Bund, Zionist organizations, religious life, and "bourgeois" occupations were deported in April. The third deportation in June–July 1941 consisted mainly of refugees from western and central Poland who had fled to eastern Poland.[55]

Arrests and deportations were conducted according to previously prepared lists, based on the political past and economic background of those listed. Witnesses have reported raids "night after night" rounding up refugees who refused Soviet citizenship. "Frequently families were separated in the rush, since refugees were given only two hours to pack forty kilograms of their belongings. In one case, during the temporary absence of a prominent Labor Zionist, who had all his papers ready to leave for Palestine, his wife and thirteen-year-old son were seized in Bialystok at one o'clock in the morning and shipped to a labor camp in Siberia."[56] In the drive to round up Jews who had not accepted Soviet passports, some Jews tried to hide, but police threatened families and friends and hiding places were revealed.[57]

The deportees consisted of those who had been arrested and imprisoned prior to their deportation and those who were directly deported to the Russian interior. "The majority of those in the first group were sentenced to forced labor and transferred to labor camps, mainly in Siberia and the far North, and were under direct and continuous NKVD control."[58] Those in the second group were sent "either to remote and isolated rural settlements (*posiolki*) or into collective farms (free exile)," and were periodically supervised by the NKVD.[59] Those sent to camps were generally sentenced for five- or eight-year terms. Such transports generally consisted of men. Those sent to rural settlements were generally family groups, and included many old people and children. The disease rate from dysentery, typhoid, malnutrition, and unsanitary conditions was quite high and the death rates in both types of transports reached as high as 66 percent.[60]

Packed into unheated freight cars, the deportees traveled for days without food and often without water. Their life in labor camps was harsh and often inhumane, and Jewish inmates were often subject to physical attack and abusive anti-Semitism, while the life of families in the wild Siberian wastes was difficult in the extreme.[61] Camp inmates generally worked ten to twelve hours a day at woodcutting, mining, road and railroad construction.

The history of the deported Jews remains to be written, but a number of survivors have recounted their experiences. The following is an unpublished account[62] by a Polish Jew who found himself in eastern Poland and experienced the sufferings, rumors, and lack of information verified by countless others:

When the war started in 1939, the Polish government gave an order that all men up to the age of 45 should go to the East where the government would try to create a new army. I went with my two brothers to Bialystok. . . . We didn't know that Hitler and Stalin had signed a treaty to divide Poland, and . . . suddenly we were in the Soviet Union. Because of my knowledge of several languages, I was able to obtain work in the foreign department of a bank. Each day the director of the bank insisted that I should take a Soviet passport.

We had a few hundred thousand refugees at that time in Bialystok and we had many discussions, sometimes deep in the night, trying to find out what to do, to answer the simple question—should we accept the passport or not. . . . The majority, I would say, refused. Well, there was general confusion. As a matter of fact, many went back to Warsaw because we remembered the Germans from the First War. We didn't know what we may expect this time.

One night, I believe it was the 20th of June 1940, 250,000 former Polish citizens who refused to accept the Soviet passport were sent to the northern part of Siberia, the part called Komi ASSR.

The trip by train took about four weeks, with 50–60 people in each car. Food was very limited, but the passengers suffered chiefly from lack of water. The train was stopped in open fields so that people could relieve themselves. When they reached the village Mandacz in Komi, they were told that they would have to "start a new life and build a new town." Mandacz was set in 400 square miles of forest. The prevailing temperature is forty degrees below zero, with winter starting at the end of August and lasting for ten months. Some in the group tried to run away but came back after they found skeletons in the forest.

The work involved was chiefly felling trees, but most Jews had never done this sort of work and when they admitted their ignorance they were asked, "Where is your culture?" The "highest culture," apparently, was the skill needed to cut down trees and the knowledge of which parts could be used for railroad ties, which for telephone poles, which for furniture. For this group, as for thousands more, food needs were severe, and did not necessarily abate after the Soviet-Polish amnesty in August 1941, when all the deported Polish Jews were allowed to go to Central Asia.[63]

Birobidzhan would have been an obvious solution for the deported Polish as well as other Jews who were to come under Soviet control, but reports were contradictory. At first it seemed that Soviet officials tried to encourage Jews from the annexed territories to settle there. In October 1939, for example, Radio Kiev encouraged Jews in Galicia to emigrate there,[64] but on November 11, the *Morning Journal* reported that a plan to send them to Birobidzhan had been dropped. However, rumors of a possible migration continued. On December 3, it was reported from London that 9,000 Jews in the Bialystok region had been selected for resettlement in Birobidzhan, but there is no confirmation that they were ever sent.[65] In the fall of 1940, special offices for the registration of potential settlers were opened in Bessarabia and north Bukovina, but apparently no more than a few hundred actually settled in the JAR.[66] It was also reported on February 9, 1941, that Jewish Communists in Lvov, Drohobycz, Brod, Kolomyja, and other cities had requested the Soviet authorities to deport Jewish refugees from Nazi-controlled Poland to Birobidzhan, rather than to Siberia,[67] but there is no evidence that there was any response to this request. The Soviet mistrust of refugees and anxiety about security in Birobidzhan apparently precluded an open door there.

Soon after the Polish refugees began to be deported, in the summer of 1940, Jews in the Baltic states also came under Soviet control—about 250,000 in Lithuania,[68] 95,000 in Latvia, and 5,000 in Estonia (see Map

15.1). From October 1939 to June 1940, Lithuania, Latvia, and Estonia were ostensibly independent states, although Soviet army units were stationed there, and Soviet absorption would soon come. Vilna, which had been a part of Poland, was incorporated into Lithuania under Soviet pressure and the Soviet takeover of all three Baltic states was completed in the summer of 1940. It was supervised largely by Vladimir Dekanozov, a top figure of the Soviet secret police, Andrei Vyshinsky, the prosecutor of the Moscow purge trials, and Zhdanov, who had succeeded Kirov as party leader in Leningrad and would be Stalin's adviser in postwar Russia. "The lessons learned in the sovietization of the Polish territories were efficiently applied in the Baltic states, and the secret police apparatus was extensively used."[69] By the beginning of August 1940, all three Baltic states officially became Soviet republics, including large Jewish centers such as Vilna (Vilnius), Kovno (Kaunas), and Riga.

The fate of the Jews of Lithuania was enmeshed in the conflict between Jews and Lithuanians during the Lithuanian struggle for independence after World War I and the continuing tensions afterward, especially in the period between Germany's attack on Poland and the invasion of Russia. Jews were described as opposing Lithuanian independence and pogroms erupted in 1918–19, leaving a trail of anti-Semitic attitudes, economic measures, and even attempts to revive the ancient notorious blood libel[70] (the false accusation that Jews murder Christian children so as to obtain blood for making Passover matzo). The overt and latent symptoms exploded with great ferocity during the Nazi occupation, decimating virtually all of Lithuanian Jewry.

In early 1939, Lithuanian policy was drawn closer to that of Germany, but in an annexe to the Molotov-Ribbentrop Agreement of August 23, 1939, Lithuania was transferred to the Soviet Union's sphere of influence. On October 10, the great Jewish center of Vilna, which had belonged to Poland, and was under Soviet control for three weeks, was given to Lithuania, in return for which the Soviet Union obtained military bases in the country. The Lithuanians as a whole hated the Russians from whom they had freed themselves only twenty years earlier, while the Jews, though they were unsympathetic to communism, had feared a Nazi takeover and greeted the Russian army with relief. For a time, until June 15, 1940, when the Soviet Union occupied Lithuania, there was considerable prosperity in the country,[71] bolstered by the presence of Russian soldiers, funds for Jewish refugees, especially from the American Joint Distribution Committee, and the economic agreement between Lithuania and Germany. Anti-Semitism subsided momentarily and Lithuanian Jews were lulled into thinking that what had happened in Germany and Poland would not and could not happen to them. The refugees from Poland, however, reminded them of the rioting in Vilna when the Lithuanians entered the city, but the point was not regarded seriously. Then, Poles, who formed the great majority of the population, blamed Jews for the rising price of bread and rioters broke into Jewish shops in Vilna. The disturbances spread and Lithuanian police joined in the attacks. Finally, the threat of Soviet intervention persuaded them to bring matters under control. Work permits were not given to refugees and in January they were ordered to move to the countryside.

Besides using Vilna[72] as a way out to Palestine, Jewish refugees, picturing an independent Lithuania, believed they could live freely as Jews, while some had moved to Vilna fearing arrest in Soviet-controlled Poland. The flight of Jews up to mid-November was unobstructed, but from mid-November to mid-January 1940, the frontier was blocked. Guards were stationed along hundreds of kilometers of the new border between the Soviet Union and Lithuania. Yet there was some illegal crossing especially by Zionist youth groups eager to get to Palestine by way of Romania. The refugee wave brought to Vilna many leaders of the Polish Jewish parties—Zionist and Bundist—including Menakhem Begin, a *Betar* (Revisionist Zionist Youth) leader, and some of the youths who were later to become leaders of ghetto revolts: Mordecai Anielewicz, Mordecai Tenenbaum, Haika Grossman, and Abba Kovner.

Various local and foreign refugee aid groups tried to ameliorate the straitened conditions of the refugees and find new homes for them, but most routes were cut off following the German invasion of Western Europe in May 1940. Unexpected help came from the Japanese consul in Kovno who issued Japanese transit permits to Jews until August 31, 1940, enabling 2,180 to travel to Vladivostok on the Trans-Siberian Railway and from there to Kobe, Japan.[73] During the summer and autumn of 1940, about 1,200 Jews passed through Odessa on their way to Palestine. However, despite intense individual and group efforts, few Jews in Lithuania ultimately survived. Of the 250,000 Jews in Lithuania, only about 4,000 were saved by emigration and escaped from the coming Nazi assault, while several thousand more survived in the Soviet Union itself after the Soviet deportations in June 1941.[74]

Meanwhile, a flood of events had overtaken Lithuania and its Jews. On June 14, 1940, the Soviet Union presented an ultimatum to Lithuania, accusing her of kidnapping Soviet soldiers and signing a military pact with Estonia and Latvia, and demanding a new government friendly to the Soviet Union. On June 15, without waiting for a reply, Soviet units crossed into Lithuania, and on June 17, a new Soviet-controlled government took power. All organizations and parties except the Communist party and its affiliated organizations were banned. During July many influential public figures and newspapermen were arrested. Lists of "unreliable elements," including Zionists, Bundists, and all the refugees in Vilna, were prepared and put into a category called "The Jewish National Counterrevolution"—names that were used in subsequent deportations.[75] A Communist list of candidates was elected to the *Seimas* (Diet, later Supreme Soviet) and on August 3, Lithuania was formally annexed to the Soviet Union.[76] Economic and cultural sovietization followed, with all the attendant dislocations and declassment. The economic measures deprived many Jews of their property and livelihood. Of the 1,593 enterprises nationalized in Lithuania, 1,320 had been owned by Jews.[77] Some who tried to hide their merchandise and trade on the black market were brought to trial as bourgeois parasites. Jewish unemployment increased and in the winter of 1940 the Soviet authorities launched a big campaign aimed at mobilizing the unemployed to move to the interior of the Soviet Union. The Soviet Yiddish press alleged that 30,000 volunteered to go but this figure cannot be verified. At the same time, anti-Semitism was outlawed and the number of Jews in government posts increased markedly. There was also an increase in the number of Jews as teachers in high schools, actors, and journalists.[78] Moreover, Jews made up about 16 percent of the Communist party in Lithuania, and the identification of Jews with communism was strongly felt in the popular Lithuanian consciousness—a feeling which the Nazis later exploited. This feeling, combined with prewar Lithuanian anti-Semitism and hope that the Nazis would give them their independence, created the special ferocity with which some Lithuanians killed Jews during the Holocaust.

Soviet deportations to the interior of the Soviet Union started just before the German invasion. Beginning June 14, 1940, about 30,000 people were deported from Lithuania, including 6,000 to 7,000 local Jews and refugees. It is not known how many survived,[79] but, as was the case with other Jews so deported, they stood a much better chance of survival than those who remained, for *their* annihilation was virtually total.

Latvian Jewish life between the wars has been described as lively, diverse, and colorful, spreading over a wide spectrum of political and cultural bands. Latvian Jews played a pioneering role in the history of the Zionist movement, the Bund, and in Jewish religious life. Some Latvian Jews were close to Russian culture, others to German, but most knew Yiddish and many, Hebrew. Half of Latvia's 95,000 Jews lived in Riga, a renowned Jewish center which was to provide the first Jewish activists in the Soviet Union in the 1950s (see Chapter 27). A fascist coup in 1934 weakened the community through a policy of economic and social discrimination and political repression. Thus, when Soviet forces moved in, the Jewish population was relieved, though not enthusiastic.

Soviet policy at first moved slowly so as not to offend Latvian national feeling. Communists—Jews among them—were, of course, jubilant. Characteristically, however, attacks soon hailed down on "anti-Soviet elements," including Zionists, Bundists, and religious leaders. In the summer of 1941, Soviet authorities arrested 6,000 Jews, including some refugees, and sent them east, leaving Latvian Jewry without its traditional leadership[80] for the coming life-and-death struggle with the German invaders. Only those who were able to emigrate, or flee, and those who survived in the Soviet Union, lived to see the end of the war. As in Lithuania, the destruction of Latvian Jewry during the Holocaust was almost total.

The fate of Estonian Jews[81]—about 4,500—was brighter, because most of them were inside the Soviet Union by the time Germans occupied the country. Like other minorities in Estonia, Jews had enjoyed full cultural autonomy from 1926 on. The process of systematic sovietization began in 1940 and working-class Jews could join the new government, military, and police. As in Lithuania, the fear of Nazi occupation and Nazi atrocities, reported by refugees from Poland, was temporarily put to rest. However, the mass deportations carried out by Soviet authorities in mid-June 1941, just before the Nazi invasion, came as a severe shock. Tens of thousands of Estonians were deported to the northern Urals, among whom were about 500 Jews—former factory owners, Zionist activists, and others who were classified as "dangerous elements." The fate of other Jews subsequently became linked with that of other Estonians in the bitter two-month fighting against the Nazis. Over one hundred Jews fought in the Estonian regular army, but usually suffered from the anti-Russian feeling, which spilled over into attacks on Jewish soldiers. On June 28, Soviet authorities in Estonia decided on a large-scale evacuation of resources and population; in this process, about 1,000 Jews remained under German occupation. Those who were evacuated, experienced, like other refugees, the rigors of Siberia and then the strangeness of life in Central Asia. The earlier deportees were generally put into huge labor camps and worked at felling trees and piling lumber. A number of prisoners were interrogated, "tried" in absentia, and sentenced to five or ten years' imprisonment. Wives and children, separated from them by enormous distances, were exiled to the Kirov district of Siberia or to Novosibirsk. Death rates among elderly parents and children were high.

Some of the Jewish survivors of the Estonian troops joined the Estonian unit of the Red Army created in the Ural region in December 1941. They were joined later by Jews serving in other Soviet military formations and in September 1942 a combined Estonian 8th Rifle Corps was created. At the beginning of the campaign for the liberation of Estonia in June 1944, about 250 Jews were in the corps.

The Soviet annexations of northern Bukovina and Bessarabia were made in the summer of 1940 at the expense of Romania. On the night of June 26, the Soviet Union delivered an ultimatum, demanding both areas, and on Germany's advice, Romania yielded. Hungary and Bulgaria as well demanded and received portions of Romanian territory, losses which drove Romania into Germany's orbit and inflamed an already highly charged popular anti-Semitism and fascist elements. Romania eventually recovered northern Bukovina and Bessarabia (losing them again in 1944), but the huge territorial losses in 1940 unleashed waves of massacres in Romania and smouldering anti-Jewish feelings in all of the annexed areas, including those annexed by the Soviet Union.

There were approximately 300,000 Jews in the annexed provinces, characterized by a strong Jewish consciousness and Yiddish and Zionist cultures. (In the early 1970s, many of the first emigrants to Israel came from these regions.) These areas were incorporated into the Ukrainian SSR and the newly created Moldavian SSR and included major Jewish centers such as Kishinev and Czernowitz (Chernovtsy). The Soviet claim to Bessarabia was based on historical and "legal" rights, while in the case of Bukovina, it was claimed that most of the people were Ukrainian, "bound by cultural and historical ties to their brethren in the Soviet Ukraine."[82] Russian culture had been strong among Bessarabian Jews through the inter-war period, while in Bukovina, which had been part of the Austrian Empire, many Jews were attached to German culture. As was true of non-Romanians in other parts of Greater Romania, which was created in 1918, those in Bessarabia and Bukovina—and especially their Jews—were seen as opposing national integration.[83] Soviet Communism combined with Russian irredentist claims to Bessarabia created another dimension of fear and hostility, and Jews were readily linked with Bolshevism.

There is still some controversy over the actual extent of Jewish involvement in the Romanian Communist Party, and, specifically, in Bessarabia.[84] Very likely, before 1940, regardless of the figures, one popular perception was that there was a Judeo-Communist threat while, at the same time, petty Jewish tradesmen, estate managers, and religiously Orthodox Jews had left negative images of Bessarabian Jews going back to tsarist times. Yet, following the annexations, there were reports of some Jewish businessmen fleeing to Bucharest on June 30, only to confront widespread anti-Jewish rioting and pogroms, as well as the flight of Jews to Bessarabia.[85] In both areas evacuated by Romanian forces, there were assaults upon Jews and Jewish property. In some towns even those Jews who were in the Romanian army were tortured and murdered. In August, laws were passed nationalizing and redistributing land; in the administrative changes that followed, many Ukrainians were appointed to important positions in northern Bukovina,[86] while in Bessarabia local anti-Jewish elements likewise arose.

About 120,000—possibly as many as 160,000—Jews in Bukovina came under Soviet authority; most of them "accepted the new situation with relief after their recent trials and tribulations. . . . High hopes and great enthusiasm characterized, in the early days, not only left-wing Jews, but also wider Jewish groups, such as the Yiddishists, and especially the lower classes."[87] Some veteran Communists were disappointed by the policy of Ukrainization, but certain Jewish doctors, accountants, engineers, and jurists were given jobs in the new regime. Yet there were apprehensions about the preferential treatment of Ukrainians, some of whom had only recently led pogroms against the Jews. Jewish anxiety was heightened by the very friendly relations between the Soviet Union and Germany, dramatized on November 7, 1940, the anniversary of the Revolution, when German army officers shared a platform in Chernovtsy with Soviet leaders. Jews were also shocked by the swift destruction of Jewish communal institutions and harassment and arrest of many community leaders. Zionist youth groups disbanded or went underground. The activities of the Bund, which operated mainly in the field of education, came to a halt and many of the most active Bundists were deported during the summer of 1941 to the Komi ASSR and other remote areas of the USSR. Some activists were tortured and coerced into signing confessions of their "counterrevolutionary" crimes.[88]

During the expropriation of business and industry, some Jews were locked up and their goods sold or transported elsewhere. In certain cases, there were house searches and arrests and exile. Fear of being labeled "bourgeois" and "enemy of the people" led many middle-class elements to try to appear proletarian by removing ties, expensive clothing, and jewelry, and especially by seeming eager to take any work. A number of young Jews found jobs in manufacturing cooperatives and state services; Jewish lawyers and doctors generally were able to find positions under the new regime. As in the Soviet Union under NEP, Jewish craftsmen and small-scale traders continued operating family businesses but were heavily taxed.

Culturally, some Jews had high hopes for Yiddish culture and education under the new regime, but except for the Yiddish theater they were disappointed. Yiddish writers were constrained by canons of "socialist realism," on which visiting veteran Soviet Jewish writers Feffer and Hofshteyn lectured them. Hebrew literature, of course, was totally eliminated and many Yiddish works in libraries were classed as "unsuitable." For a time, Yiddish schools aroused great enthusiasm, but there was a serious shortage of textbooks and a drum beat of political indoctrination which alienated many students and parents. As one early enthusiast commented after eleven months of communism; "Today I do one job only: I burn my dreams one after the other." On a visit of Feffer[89] to Chernovtsy where he met Yiddish activists, he asked, "Why do we need another Yiddish paper? Take the *Shtern* [published in Kiev] for the present—and as for the future, we'll worry about it later!" Both he and Hofshteyn told local writers they were only now entering a new phase, and that the "broad horizons on Soviet Jewish literature" were still lacking locally.

Those writers who used Russian or Ukrainian found it quite easy to be published, but few such writers were Jewish. There were a number of very successful Yiddish literary evenings particularly in Chernovtsy, but these generally featured Soviet writers.

As in the other annexed areas, there was a speedy dismantling of all Jewish communal organizations. Some Zionist youth groups tried for a time to hold meetings in the local cemeteries and public parks, but a large number were arrested and deported east in the summer of 1941. Bundists, as well, and industrialists, landowners, merchants, businessmen, and professionals whose documents showed that they were suspect for "social" or "security" reasons, were also deported—estimates range from 3,000 to 10,000. The Soviet recasting of Jewish life came to a sudden stop with the outbreak of the war (June 22, 1941), and the reconquest of the region by German and Romanian troops, but the Soviet deportations continued for a few days afterward. Many Jews of Bukovina saw them as "the epitome of everything that occurred under the Soviets in 1940–41, the symbol of that eventful year."[90]

The retreat of the Soviet army from Bukovina was hasty and disorganized. As elsewhere, Communist party and government officials were helped to evacuate, but there was no organized general evacuation plan.[91] Ironically, many Jews in Bukovina, together with ethnic German settlers, had been fervent supporters of "Germanism"; Jews indeed had helped Bukovina become a stronghold of German culture. After the headlong retreat of the Russian soldiers, some Jews fled, but most stayed behind to become victims of the murderous frenzy of Romanian killers and Nazi *Einsatzgruppen*, or were sent to the dread camp Transnistria, operated by Romanians, where many thousands perished.

The formerly Russian province of Bessarabia had been incorporated into Romania in 1918. As in Bukovina, Bessarabian Jews kept their traditions, autonomous structure, and cultural life within the framework of the All-Romanian Federation of Jewish Communities. Culturally, the deep-rooted Jewish life of Bessarabia, with its Hebrew schools and writers and Yiddish press had a strong influence on Jewish life in Old Romania and helped to buffer discrimination and subsequent suffering. Many of the Jews in Bessarabia in 1930 were deprived of Romanian nationality, while the community as a whole suffered popular hostility and official harassment. In the late 1930s, as Nazi influence and policies spread to Romania, the whole Jewish occupational and social structure began to collapse. With the entry of the Red Army into Bessarabia on June 13, 1940, life for Jews was gradually sovietized. Soviet policies "took advantage . . . of the grievances of the local minorities against the former Romanian regime," even to the point of appointing local anti-Semitic figures in the new Bessarabian administration "in order not to antagonize the non-Jewish population."[92] The Zionist movement, which had intensified its work before the Soviet takeover, was quite fully aware of the fate of Zionists in the Soviet Union, but all escape possibilities evaporated. Arrests began three days after the Soviet Army entered Bessarabia, and included people who were known to be sympathetic to the Soviet Union. Local Communists were at a loss to explain these arrests. Khrushchev said that no Bessarabian citizen would be punished for his past and that everyone should concentrate on work. Feffer, who appeared in Kishinev in uniform in July, was likewise reassuring, although he hinted at the harm done by Bundists and Zionists. Nevertheless, arrests of Zionists began on July 13, generally at night. Those arrested were kept in the Kishinev prison for seven months and then sent to labor camps for five- and ten-year prison terms in the Archangelsk District. Those Zionists not arrested were cross-examined by the NKVD and given identity cards marked with politically objectionable pasts, which deprived them of residence and work rights.[93]

Although Soviet Yiddish schools were theoretically permitted, Jewish parents discovered that, instead, the favored languages of instruction were Moldavian, Ukrainian, and Russian. Promised openings of Yiddish schools in Sgorita, Lipkany, and Britshiva never materialized. In Kishinev, there were four Yiddish schools, but in the history courses, no mention was made of Jews, except as Bundist and Zionist "counterrevolutionaries," and teachers were required to explain the greatness of Bogdan Khmielnitzki,[94] the Ukrainian leader responsible for massive pogroms in 1648–1649.

Altogether, about 275,000 Jews were deported from the Soviet-annexed territories of Bessarabia, Bukovina, the Baltic states,[95] and eastern Poland. These Jews were considered unreliable, anti-Soviet, or dangerous, and thus disposable. And yet, ironically, of all Jews in eastern Europe, they were to become the ones with the best chances to survive after the Nazi invasion of the Soviet Union,[96] which found the largest numbers exposed to Nazi mass murder. Meanwhile, the fate of those who had been deported East was very much influenced by the complications of Polish-Soviet relations after June 1941.

16

Jews as Pawns in Polish-Soviet Relations, 1941–46

They [the Jews] were not aware that they were only an instrument in the implementation of a definite policy, that once their services were no longer needed they would be regarded as an alien element and treated accordingly.

KLEMENS NUSSBAUM

A F T E R the German invasion of the Soviet Union, Polish Jewish deportees[1] found themselves entangled in the complications of Polish-Soviet relations. A needed ally against the Nazi enemy joined the beleaguered Soviet state when Stalin resumed relations with the formerly hated Polish Government-in-Exile on July 30, 1941. There was also a desperate bid for Western material and moral support in the formation of various antifascist committees. But an emerging hard Soviet political line vis-à-vis Poland can be discerned early in their relations. Both parties were concerned with the struggle against a common adversary, with the creation of a Polish army on Soviet soil, and with the future Polish frontier, questions which involved the fate of Polish Jewish refugees in the Soviet Union. Poland had never abandoned its claims to its prewar 1939 boundaries; Stalin, however, insisted on Russia's right to eastern Poland. Both sides sought to validate their territorial claims through control of local populations. This conflict was to enmesh the lives of thousands of Polish Jews in the Soviet Union.

Several distinct phases in Soviet policies can be seen:[2]

1. From September 1939 to December 1941: Jews from western and central Poland were considered Polish citizens, while Jews from the annexed territories were not. Thus, only Jews in the first category were granted amnesty in August 1941.
2. From December 1941 to January 1943: Polish Jews were not officially

denied their former citizenship but did not enjoy its full privileges. Polish authorities in the USSR were strongly discouraged from treating Jews as Polish citizens.

3. From January 1943 to April 1943: A second campaign to force Soviet passports upon Jews took place and both western and eastern Polish Jews were forced to accept Soviet passports.

4. After April 1943: The situation changed radically because of the rupture in Soviet-Polish diplomatic relations and the Soviet plan for a projected Communist order in Poland. Jews were allowed to join the Polish Communist army being formed in the USSR and claim their Polish citizenship once more.

The resumption of diplomatic relations between the Russians and Poles was followed on August 12, 1941, by a pact providing for a general amnesty for all former Polish subjects including those in camps and prisons. Among those covered were Ukrainians, Belorussians, and Jewish refugees who had lived in eastern Poland. It soon became clear that the attitude of the Soviet authorities toward these non-Polish groups differed from their attitude toward other refugees of Polish origin. In areas where there was a concentration of non-Polish ethnic groups, local Soviet military authorities began to draft men, including many Jews, into the Red Army. The Polish Government-in-Exile immediately demanded an explanation. The Soviet answer of December 1, 1941, typically veiled and devious, argued that no injustice had been committed against Polish citizens; in fact, it was said, they had been given preferential treatment: all residents of the western districts of the Ukrainian and Belorussian republics who had lived there as of November 1–2, 1939, were now Soviet citizens, but those residents who were ethnically Polish were not forced to accept a Soviet passport.[3]

This question, "Who was a Polish citizen?" was to cause increasing friction between Soviet and Polish authorities, but a signal of Soviet intentions can be read in an episode a month earlier. On November 10, 1941, the head of the Polish mission, Stanislaw Kot, lodged a complaint alleging that attempts had been made in Kazakhstan to conscript Ukrainians, Belorussians, and Jews into the Red Army despite the fact that technically they were Polish citizens. But Stalin did not budge. Those groups would not be granted the same leniency as ethnic Poles. All sorts of pressures were applied "in order to discourage their claims to Polish citizenship" and Polish authorities in the Soviet Union were strongly discouraged from treating Jews as Polish citizens.[4]

In the early period Polish Jews were useful as pawns in pressing

Polish boundary claims and countering those of the Soviet Union. In October 1941, for example, Kot wrote to the Polish Deputy Prime Minister, Stanislaw Mikolajczyk: ". . . . In the future, when the eastern frontier comes up for consideration, this influx of Jews (into the newly created Polish Army in the USSR) will be a great political argument, especially in view of the Ukrainians' systematic hatred for everything Polish. . . ."[5] The question of the loyalty of minorities in the establishment of the future Polish state seemed very important to Kot, and he considered Jews as the most pro-Polish minority of all. Poles were thus placed in the position of defending Polish Jewish refugees from the arbitrary actions of the Soviet government because of their anxiety about the future of the Soviet-Polish border. Kot discussed the question of the Jewish refugees with Soviet officials many times but they never relented. In one such talk, Andrei Vyshinsky, the Soviet foreign minister, who often repeated the point that all Polish Jews in the USSR were Soviet citizens no matter where they were born, said, "It is not even worth discussing them [the Jews]."[6] In March 1942, when Kot discussed with him the possibility of releasing Polish citizens from their jobs because of the approaching religious holidays of Easter and Passover, Vyshinsky objected in the case of the Jews: ". . . . The question is complicated by the problem of citizenship; it would be better to have these holidays without the Jews. . . ."[7] The Soviet government was bent on claiming them as citizens and preventing them from leaving the country. It made sure of these objectives when, on December 1, 1941, it announced that eastern Poland was part of the Soviet Union.

Manpower needs may have been a factor in this matter, especially in the first months of the war, but more weighty was Stalin's preparation of a forceful territorial policy after the war. His immovable stand on the citizenship of some of the former residents of Poland signaled his real intentions. In numerous ways Kot tried to obtain a reversal of the December 1941 decision. He believed the question of Jewish refugees could have considerable influence on Jewish opinion in the United States and England and tried to use this leverage against Soviet policy. When it became apparent that the Soviet Union would not reverse its decision, Kot then urged an appeal to "world public opinion" against Soviet policy.

Jewish public opinion in the United States and England was considered a significant factor in the border issue. In a letter to the Polish foreign minister, Kot wrote: ". . . . The Jewish organizations should be guided in such a way that public opinion in England and the U.S. should concern itself with the situation that has developed because of the Soviet Government's ambition to achieve a one-sided solution. . . . "[8] He also stressed the need to alert public opinion to the suffering of Jewish refugees because of Soviet conduct and the unsolved issue of future Soviet-Polish borders.

Kot also tried to involve two prominent Polish Jews, Henryk Erlich and Viktor Alter, in his efforts. Erlich and Alter[9] had been leading Bundists in Poland who were imprisoned after the Soviet Union annexed eastern Poland. Western labor organizations tried unsuccessfully to have them released. Both men were harshly grilled by the NKVD, accused of anti-Soviet subversion, and sentenced to die (ultimately the sentence was changed to ten years in labor camps). Then suddenly in September 1941, they were released. The Nazi invasion required a radical shift in Soviet foreign policy vis-à-vis Poland and the West and both men soon found themselves involved in planning a world-wide Jewish propaganda agency (the Jewish Anti-Hitlerite Committee—JAHC). As patriotic Poles and devoted Bundists, they desired such a committee to help create a free and socialist Poland and defend Jewish life. The Soviet objective, however, was to use the committee to promote American military support for the Soviet war effort. The Polish interest concerned the future Polish state and its borders. For a brief time, all of these interests seemed to converge. But the committee could not possibly bear the weight of so many disparate goals and never materialized.

Erlich and Alter submitted their proposals to the NKVD head Lavrenti Beria, who soon after their release, suggested that they apply directly to Stalin. In October, they did so and then left Moscow for Kuibyshev together with Soviet and foreign officials who were evacuated from the capital. Their plan called for the JAHC to operate in Poland, in the West, and in the Soviet Union. In Poland the committee would gather information about the Nazi persecution of Jews, secure material aid for them, and appeal to the Jewish masses to resist. Contacts with the Polish government in London would be used to reach Polish Jewry. In the West, special emphasis was put on mobilizing support for the Red Army with the help of Jewish communities. In the USSR, the committee would be active among Polish Jewish refugees, urging all who could to enlist in the Polish army, then being organized on Russian soil. Several of the members of the projected committee would be Bund members while the presidium itself would include Erlich and Alter and a representative from the Soviet Union. These activities would be arranged in close cooperation with the Polish Government-in-Exile. Both men were in constant touch with Kot, who "became convinced of their integrity and their loyalty to the Polish Government" and warned them against Soviet machinations and tricks. They were under strict surveillance and thus virtual custody of the NKVD in Moscow and Kuibyshev, but were apparently not aware of the significance of this control and freely made contacts with foreign diplomats and journalists. Their closest contacts were with the Polish Embassy, Kot especially, and it was to him that they made crystal clear their beliefs and intentions. They were, they said, representatives of the Bund, the largest Jewish political party in Poland, which had an immense stake in Poland's future as a democratic and independent state.

Erlich and Alter were considered "the most prominent Polish-Jewish refugees in the USSR," and were consulted by Polish officials on Jewish affairs. On the question of recruitment of Jewish soldiers, they opposed separation of Poles from Jews and fought against the revisionist Zionist idea of a separate Jewish Legion in the Polish army. On the issue of future borders, the Polish government hoped to use the men to gain American and Western support for their stand. The Soviet Union, however, had very different objectives and the complex relationships split open in December 1941, when both men were re-arrested and secretly executed.[10] The dire Nazi military threat to the Soviet Union, which made the Soviet-Polish rapprochement possible, seemed to have receded late in November, when Rostov was recaptured by Soviet forces and when their counteroffensive began. The desperate Soviet reach for two Polish Bundist leaders, who had not even been granted the status of Polish citizens after their release from prison, crumbled after a brief two months and familiar accusations were resumed: The Polish Jews were anti-Soviet; they were spying against the USSR.

For their part, the Poles, who had also wanted to use the Jewish leaders, had lost *their* counters and tried to warn the Soviet Union of serious consequences following the arrests. In his talks with Vyshinsky, Kot said, "Your arresting them is very unpleasant . . . it is very important for them to be released now. . . . Just think what a hullabaloo the American Jewish organizations will raise over these arrests. . . ."[11]

Later, an American Jewish leader cast a cold eye on this concern: "In

the name of so-called democracy, she [Poland] began to support . . .
the Polish Jewish Socialists—so-called Bundists. How did the Polish
government exploit the tragic Erlich-Alter affair! Naturally, the only
reason was because the Bundists were anti-Russian. . . ."[12] But Kot
could not prevail against Stalin. None of his arguments and none of
his supporters mattered. Meanwhile, the Polish passports of some Jews
who wanted to emigrate to Palestine were disallowed.[13] Strong Polish
protests against these decisions were unavailing, while the British Embassy in Kuibyshev concluded that "Russia is already decided to assure
for herself the settlement of boundaries."[14] General Wladyslaw Sikorski, Polish prime minister, wrote that the Soviet decision evoked "dismay and depression" among Polish Jews in Russia. The "sense of injustice and degradation which they have . . . suffered is at present so
intense . . . that it has produced dislike, contempt and even hatred of
Russia. . . . They have been expressing and continue to demonstrate
their attachment to Poland and the earnest desire of returning at all
costs to their homes. . . ."[15] By this time, moreover, the Russians were
not allowing Jews to join the Polish Anders army (see below), according to Sikorski.

In seeking a new understanding with the Soviet Union, a prime consideration for Poles had been the creation in the Soviet Union of a
Polish military force which would be subordinate to the Polish Government-in-Exile.[16] By the fall of 1941 a Polish army was already being
formed—with Soviet aid. The commander Wladyslaw Anders was appointed by the Polish Government-in-Exile, but was to be subordinate
in operational matters to the Supreme Command of the USSR according to a July 1941 agreement. Differences emerged almost immediately,
arising out of deep-seated distrust and differing goals and led ultimately to the transfer of Anders' army out of the Soviet Union.

From the very start of recruiting, thousands of released Polish Jewish
prisoners and exiles flocked to the numerous collection points scattered
throughout the USSR. The first units set up had a very large number
of Jews—according to Anders as much as 60 percent—arousing suspicion and dismay among Poles. Some accused the Russians of purposely flooding the army with the "Jewish element." Others, like Anders, accused the Jews of having "warmly welcomed" the Soviet armies
that invaded Poland in 1939. Professional Polish soldiers, for their part,
said Jews were "unfit for military service." Before the end of 1941, as
a result of deliberate inspections or re-examinations, many Jews were

transferred to kolkhozes or simply cashiered. If they tried again to re-enlist, they were rejected. Ukrainians and Belorussians apparently had the same experience. But in the Polish-Soviet political tug-of-war, each element, for different reasons, wanted to restrict the number of Jews in the Polish army.

In a conversation between Sikorski and Stalin in Moscow on December 3, 1941, at which Anders and Kot were present, Anders made much of the difficult conditions under which the Polish army was laboring and suggested that the whole operation be transferred to Persia. Stalin was furious at this and said, "If the Poles don't want to fight, they should leave." When the discussion subsided somewhat, Anders, in offering details about the size of the force, complained about Jews in the army, and Sikorski agreed. "They never will make good soldiers," Anders said, to which Stalin replied, "Yes, Jews are bad warriors." His concurring with Anders' and Sikorski's evaluation of the Jews as poor soldiers removed any doubt about Stalin's attitude on the matter.

Before the end of the month, Soviet authorities notified Polish army officials that recruiting in Anders' army would be open to all Polish nationals of Polish descent except Jews, Ukrainians, and Belorussians, who, on November 29, 1939, were in territories annexed by the Soviet Union, and thus were Soviet citizens. Poles, of course, would be re-cruited, but had not many of them come from an annexed territory, and were they not also Soviet citizens? The Russians said they were, nevertheless, showing "exceptional lenience," but acceptance of this ploy was tantamount to recognition of the Soviet annexation of Polish territory. In further discussions between Sikorski and Stalin, Sikorski tried to press Stalin for a clarification, but Stalin was evasive. He admitted that Jews, Ukrainians, and Belorussians would not be released from "labor divisions." "Were they not Polish citizens?" Anders once asked angrily. "They have never ceased in fact to be Polish citizens, because your agreements with Germany have been annulled," Stalin replied portentously. Then, playing on Anders' pride and prejudice, he added craftily, "What do you need Belorussians, Ukrainians and Jews for? It is Poles you need, they are the best soldiers."[17] Anders' memoirs add yet another opportunistic nuance to this bandying about the fate of non-Polish minorities from Poland: "I am not thinking of the people," he said; "they can be exchanged for Poles who are Soviet citizens. But I cannot, in principle, agree to the instability of the frontiers of the Polish Republic. . . ."[18]

The Soviet plan at the time was "the complete Sovietization of the non-Poles among the refugees." A "mass mobilization of Polish Jews into Anders' army would have severely defeated this policy."[19] In pressing their position, Soviet officials purposely tried to overestimate the proportion of Jewish refugees from eastern Poland.[20] They also spread reports about anti-Semitism in Anders' army.

In actual practice, there seems to have been little interference by Soviet agents in recruiting for the Polish army, but Stalin may have been craftily playing on Anders' own anti-Semitism, thus giving Anders the pretext for excluding Jews (except Jewish physicians and those who enjoyed the backing of influential Poles). This convenient facade was clearly understood by several fiercely patriotic Polish Jewish Bundists who left the Soviet Union with Anders' army late in 1942:

The fact is that the position adopted by the Soviet authorities was instrumental in the exclusion of thousands of Jewish youth who were fit to serve, from the ranks of the Armed Forces. However a large share of the responsibility for this state of affairs devolves upon Polish military elements.[21]

Despite his contradictory statements on the matter, Kot attached political significance to expressions of concern for Jews, warning the Polish Government-in-Exile and Anders of the damage of anti-Semitism to the Polish cause. In a cable to Sikorski on April 10, 1942, he wrote:

It should be brought to General Anders' attention that the systematic anti-Semitic policy pursued by the General Staff . . . unwittingly serves the interests of the Soviets, who are seeking to distinguish between Jews and Poles so as to create a precedent which would enable them to take over the territories in the east. . . .[22]

In a letter to a Polish general of April 30, 1942, Kot wrote:

. . . . complaints are again being voiced by Jews that a purge is being carried out in the ranks of the army so as to reduce their numbers, and that those who are healthiest are being released as sick. Is this necessary, and does it serve our interests in this time . . . ?[23]

A few days after he arrived in Moscow, Kot wrote to Mikolajczyk on October 11, 1941:

. . . . in the future, when we will be dealing with the eastern borders, this stream of Jewish recruits will be of considerable political weight, particularly when the Ukrainians' systematic hatred of anything Polish is taken into account.[24]

The variability in the Polish position, from one approach to another can also be seen in a memorandum from Sikorski to Churchill, dated March 5, 1942,[25] in which he says that the first Jews released from prison were sent directly to Polish military camps, among whom were "a considerable number of unreliable individuals, such as smugglers, speculators, etc." Then he added significantly, "The Jews in the Polish army," were an object of "vigilance on the part of the N.K.V.D." which circulated the view that because of anti-Jewish feeling they would not be able to perform well. The NKVD also spread the opinion that the Jews "are the worst element in the army, that they are always dissatisfied and that therefore, it would be most desirable for the Poles to get rid of them." But Sikorski told Churchill that, on the whole, the conduct of the Jews was "commendable . . . loyal and disciplined," and wanting to put a good face on Polish-Jewish relations, discounted Polish anti-Jewish feeling as "immaterial."

The Soviet Union and Poland, of course, pursued diametrically opposite political aims, but found it convenient to agree on restricting Jews in Anders' army for their respective ends. "The Soviet directives actually gave the Poles a free hand and served as a ready pretext which was later used to justify to the outside world the low percentage of Jews in the Polish Armed Forces."[26] The Russians, for their part, "sought to emphasize the basic political principle of distinguishing between segments of the population in the east and the other parts of Poland, thus creating a precedent for the future."[27] In this wedge, Jews lost. Many were denied Polish citizenship, Polish papers, material aid, exit visas from the Soviet Union, and the right to enlist in the Polish army.

American Jewish leaders were also drawn into the diplomatic web. In a meeting[28] on January 10, 1943 with Morris D. Waldman and Dr. Max Gottschalk, leaders of the American Jewish Committee, in New York, Sikorski tried to draw them into Polish-Soviet intrigues, obviously wanting to use "Jewish influence" to recover the Polish eastern territories. He directed criticism especially against certain Zionists and other American Jewish leaders who were showing their sympathy toward Soviet Russia. He maintained that there was considerable anti-Semitism in Russia and that the Soviet government "is behaving very badly towards the 300,000 Polish Jewish civilians who are in Russia."[29] He also held that his government had seen to it that they were favored over other Poles in having larger relief supplies and greater representation on relief committees. In "strictest confidence," he reported a conversation with Stalin (which apparently was reported to others as well) when Sikorski asked why Russia considered these Jews as Soviet citizens when Poland considered them as equal to Christian Poles. Stalin allegedly replied that he didn't understand his complaint. "Didn't the Poles have ten percent Jews before the war and should they not be glad to have only five percent left?"[30]

When Waldman asked why Poland, which had so vigorously pursued a mass emigration of Jews, should now be upset about losing hundreds of thousands without any expense, Sikorski said he had seen these Jews and "was amazed at their declaration of loyalty to Poland." He also wanted help in getting 800 Polish Orthodox rabbis out of Shanghai back to Poland! Most of all, it seems, he wanted the Committee to use their "influence with the Zionists" in damping their "sympathy" toward the Soviet Union.[31]

Polish Jews in the Soviet Union were also the subject of negotiation and manipulation by the British.[32] Before the invasion of Russia, the possible emigration of Jews from eastern Poland to Palestine caused British apprehension. Although the British White Paper of 1939 limited Jewish immigration to Palestine for the next five years to 75,000, the British were concerned about the "gravity of risk" from "the infiltration of undesirables into the Middle East" resulting from the emigration of Jews from Soviet-controlled territories. The high commissioner of Palestine urged the prohibition of Jewish emigration from Soviet territory for the duration of the war. Lord Halifax, the British ambassador to the United States, favored returning Polish nationals, formerly resident in Palestine, stranded in Russian-occupied Poland. It was finally decided to ban all such immigration and not to make the decision public but to explain to the Jewish Agency its inability to make effective arrangements to investigate possible emigrants, leaving open the possibility of exceptions.

After the German invasion, certain Jewish leaders found themselves caught between the millstones of too much support for the Soviet Union, and too little. Rabbi Maurice L. Perlzweig, for example, of the World Jewish Congress, shuttled between New York and Washington from 1941 to 1947, visiting embassies and American government officials. Lord Halifax complained about the "strenuous pro-Soviet propaganda . . . conducted in the U.S. . . . by men with Jewish names," while at the same time, the Soviet ambassador Konstantin Umansky complained about his "very thick file" on Jewish anti-Soviet propaganda.[33]

Perlzweig raised the question of the release of Jews in Russian prisons, and Umansky asked him to send him a list, but warned that it must not be too long. Perlzweig said that if he secured their release, "world Jewry will be grateful to you." Umansky looked straight into Perlzweig's eyes and said, "What do you mean by world Jewry? Don't I belong to world Jewry?" Then he added as if "to convey a warning" to be "good boys," that the question of Palestine would undoubtedly come up at the Peace Conference and that "we shall have a word to say about that."[34]

For their part, the British found that it "would suit us far better that they [Jews] should remain in the Soviet Union, where Zionism is fortunately not encouraged," and not return to Poland "since one of their main objects in so doing would be to get to Palestine."[35] The British were also alarmed by the large number of Jews in the 5th and 6th Polish divisions in Russia since they were committed to bringing Polish troops out of Russia to the Middle East.

Behind these diplomatic charades and niceties, many individual Jews suffered at the hands of Soviet authorities who controlled them. After the amnesty in August 1941, for example, many of the Jewish labor camp inmates were still kept interned, while their Polish counterparts were being released. Some who had been released were re-arrested, the accusation being that they were in contact with the Polish Embassy, even though they had been released as Polish citizens![36] Moreover, as early as November 1941, Polish Jews who arrived in Kazakhstan were mobilized into the Red Army, although they clearly expressed their wish to join Polish units. Polish Jews were consistently refused exit visas, whereas Poles could get them quite easily.[37] Soviet officials in the Ministry for Internal Affairs also often excluded Jews from the charitable activities carried out by the Polish Embassy.[38]

The American Ambassador to the USSR, Rear Admiral William H. Standley, appointed early in 1942, wrote about this marked Soviet separation of Polish Jews from other Poles in his cables to Secretary of State Hull. On September 30, 1942, he wrote:

Although a considerable number of Polish citizens have been released from detention in the Soviet Union, the Embassy has learned that generally when the Polish Embassy intervenes on behalf of Polish Jews the Soviet authorities consistently refuse to entertain such representations on the grounds that the interested persons are Soviet citizens.[39]

The cases of Alter and Erlich are mentioned in this connection. Moreover, the

Foreign Office has officially refused to recognize Polish Jewish relief workers appointed by the Polish Government on the grounds that they are Jews and cannot be considered Polish citizens.

Menakhem Begin, in his account of imprisonment in the Soviet Union,[40] describes those in Pechora camp who were not pardoned when the amnesty was announced. He and 800 other prisoners were taken on a freighter equipped with only two lavatories and run by *Urki*, criminals in charge of the political prisoners. All were infested with lice. Finally, a small number, Begin included, were dropped off at a transit camp. On his way south to Koshva, he saw hundreds of labor camps and settled for a time in a little Uzbekistani town called Dzhizak, between Tashkent and Samarkand. There he heard about the arrest of Erlich and Alter and then later their execution for having "helped the German armies," according to an official communiqué. In Begin's interpretation, the USSR needed Erlich and Alter as long as the United States stayed out of the war. He believed Stalin may have wanted to send them to the United States to mobilize American public opinion before the Japanese attack on Pearl Harbor, December 7, 1941.[41] Begin himself was at first rejected by the Polish army and felt like other Polish Jews "pounded between the millstones of the Soviet Generalissimo's dislike for the Jews and that of the two Polish Generals."[42] However, he was told by a friend who traveled thousands of kilometers from Mari in Turkmen to meet him that he would never be able to leave the Soviet Union unless he joined the Polish army. He applied personally to the Polish chief of staff and was accepted on his second try. Most Jews, however, were not so lucky.

As tension between the Polish Government-in-Exile and the Soviet Union mounted during 1942, Polish Jews were pressured to renounce their loyalty to Poland, a campaign which culminated in the passportization drive of January 1943 to force Soviet passports on Jews. This campaign imposed Soviet citizenship on all Polish Jews in the Soviet Union.[43] Those who did not accept Soviet passports willingly were imprisoned and sentenced to forced labor, among whom were Jews who had also been imprisoned before the amnesty.[44] (Most such prisoners were released only after the end of the war.)

Toward the end of 1941, the Soviets demanded that part of Anders' army be sent to the front. Anders hedged and said the men needed more training, but Stalin refused to tolerate a nonfighting force on Russian soil any longer and limited rations and equipment. An untenable situation developed and Anders' army began to leave Russia in stages, beginning in March–April 1942. Churchill had suggested that it leave by way of Persia; the Russians considered it good riddance. Only about 4,000 Jews left with this army of about 115,000 men, partly because Anders did not want them, but also because some Soviet army recruiting boards had refused to allow them to enlist. Polish military officials also obstructed the evacuation of Jews. The families of Jewish soldiers were purposely misled by false instructions, and some Jews were actually delivered directly to local NKVD authorities.[45] However, in several cases involving rabbis and a few Zionist leaders, Polish officers extended help so that they were evacuated.

The evacuation of Jewish children—almost 1,000 among the 26,000—was in itself a dramatic saga, for they were eventually taken to Palestine. A young Polish Jewess helped in their supervision on the journey to Teheran. In Cairo, funds were raised through a bazaar involving Jewish women soldiers in a British unit commanded by Mina Rogozik (Ben-Zvi), which helped make possible the final lap of their journey to Palestine under the direction of Tsipporah Shertok, wife of the future foreign minister of Israel.[46]

The Soviet-Polish amnesty of August 1941 had released many Jews in camps in Siberia and northern Russia, freeing them to go south to Uzbekistan, Kazakhstan, Tadzhikistan, and other parts of Soviet Central Asia, where the climate was mild and where there was some hope of escaping over the border into Iran. But few escaped. The great trek south took place in the winter of 1941–42, and the death rate from exposure and disease, especially in the warm weather, was high. Possibly as many as 200,000 streamed into central Asia, exposed to strange, often primitive cultures and harsh conditions. An uncounted number died of hunger, but most sources indicate a fairly high survival rate, helped no doubt by trickles at first of JDC food packages and aid from the Jewish Labor Committee and then later, when Soviet taxes proved exhorbitantly high, shipments of tea, tobacco, needles, and razor blades, which Jews could barter for food. Some of the refugees were mobilized by the local collective farms, mainly for cotton picking, "but the majority had to rely on illegal petty trade, assistance from abroad, and the relief facilities of the Polish Embassy," which supported about 70,000 Jews.[47] The largest concentrations of Polish Jews were in Bukhara, Tashkent, Samarkand, Fergana, Dzhambul, Oshsk, Frunze, Alma-Ata, Dzhalal, Abat, and southern Kazakhstan.[48]

Kot insisted on a fair and just distribution of relief and strongly opposed any separate Jewish relief action,[49] but some discrimination has been recorded. As for the Soviet Union, relief activities went undisturbed until the summer of 1942, when Polish relief representatives (including Jews) were accused of anti-Soviet activities and many imprisoned. After April 1943, the residue of the program was closed down and the remaining agents imprisoned.

The accounts of Jewish survivors of wartime experiences in Central Asia vary. Some recall episodes of great hardship and anti-Semitism;[50] others remember it as a benign time, despite the difficulties and strangeness, because they were spared the horrors of those Polish Jews who remained in Poland. In some places, the climate was milder than in Siberia, but hunger and the struggle for food were still dominant drives. In kolkhozes in Uzbekistan,[51] for example, refugees were given meager rations of from 100 to 300 grams of bread a day. "At night, at day," one survivor has recalled, "when you are awake, only food." People gave away their clothes for food. A number committed suicide. Some died from eating grass. Where they picked cotton, they ate the seeds. After the Battle of Stalingrad (February 1943), Uzbek soldiers returning from the front talked about the killing of Jews: "There has to be a reason for that," they said. Contact with Ukrainian and German soldiers had left them with strong anti-Jewish attitudes. At the other extreme, east of Krasnoyarsk, in the small villages where conditions were very primitive, the native people were very kind and hospitable, showing Jews how to use saws and axes and how to fell trees. Never having seen Europeans before, they were awed by their clothing, razors, and watches.[52] Many accounts underscore the absolute need to barter, to use the black market, or try to be paid in the form of sugar. Sugar could buy bread, but money often could not. In Alma-Ata, Jewish women worked in factories or in government bureaus as clerks while the men served in the *Trudfront* (labor batallions) for the Russian army. Children went to school. Relations with the native population were generally good.[53]

After the amnesty, Jews in Mandacz camp in the Arctic Komi ASSR, were released and allowed to work in the main city of Siktivkar, but there the food supply was so meager, people were collapsing on the street, and many died. Survivors have told of the necessity to steal food, but also of the great fear of consequences. In one account, a baker brought a bag of flour to a hungry Polish Jew, who said,

Go back. I don't need you. I want to survive. I don't want to go back to the forest. I don't want to go back to jail. I want only to survive. . . . We didn't talk about politics. . . . I would often think what did I say during the day. Maybe I said something, one word, which would take me back to the forest. Who knows? By stealing, you can get five to six months, but saying a word— ten years.[54]

Those who wanted to leave the Komi ASSR to go west to Kotlas, which is on a train line to Leningrad via Vologda, needed legal papers. Those who didn't have them tried to evade police, in some cases hiding in men's rooms on boats. From Kotlas some were able to make their way to Murashi, in the Kirov region. There, unaware of the amnesty, they sent a memorandum to a Soviet official, asking for permission to move south, where food was more plentiful and where the climate was milder. They were "amazed" that the official agreed to prepare special papers enabling some of them to transfer far south to a little town near Sochi, called Gelendzhik, settled mostly by Greeks.[55] There local officials accepted them immediately, without approval from the central government. The other Jews fanned out to other towns in the Black Sea area.

A new Communist-oriented Polish order was projected by Stalin at least as early as the time of the Anders' evacuation. While Polish men of Jewish, Ukrainian, and White Russian origin were ordered to enlist in the Soviet army, Polish Communists, a number of whom were Jews, were dispersed for training. Some were also parachuted toward the end of 1941 into Poland for the purpose of organizing the Polish Workers' Party and a partisan movement.[56] Some captured Polish officers of questionable loyalty were also given a comfortable villa near Moscow and told to prepare the organization of a Polish military unit in the USSR, which later became the First Polish Army.

After the Russian victory at Stalingrad early in 1943, it seemed likely that the Red Army would enter Poland before the other allies and plans for a new Communist Poland accelerated. The Sikorski government was denounced by the USSR for preventing active resistance to the Nazis in Poland. In April 1943, Goebbels announced that Germans had found several mass graves in the Katyn Forest near Smolensk containing the bodies of thousands of Polish officers. The Sikorski government accepted charges that Russians had executed them. Stalin refused an independent inquiry by the Red Cross and, after a prolonged and abusive diplomatic exchange, relations between the two governments were ruptured on April 25. The USSR could now throw off all pretense and announced that it "has decided to meet the request of the Union of Polish Patriots [not yet in existence] and has granted permission for a Polish military unit to be set up in the USSR."[57] Soviet control of this army was established in various ways but it took no substantial part in the fighting until it entered Poland in August 1944, after the Germans had crushed a Polish uprising.

After the rupture in Polish-Soviet relations, a major aim of Soviet propaganda was to expose the anti-Semitism of the Polish government and "to contrast it with the friendly attitudes of the Moscow-based Union of Polish Patriots and of the pro-Communist Polish Army." This new army was headed by General Z. Berling; many of its officers had previously served in the Red Army. "A strange mixture of communist ideology and Polish nationalism prevailed in this new Polish army."[58] Thousands of Polish Jews found themselves in transports converging from all parts of the Soviet Union in the formation of these new units. A large proportion of soldiers—from 12 to 15 percent—were Jews; and it is estimated that Jews accounted for 20 percent of the officer corps.[59] As almost all officers of the prewar Polish army had been executed at Katyn, or had left with the Anders army, there was an immense problem in creating a cadre of Polish officers, thus explaining the large number of Jewish officers.

Among the Jewish refugees who were recruited into the Polish army or had volunteered were young men who believed they had been saved from the Nazis by Soviet Russia. They were also impressed by Soviet propaganda dealing with the future "democratic" Poland, the elimination of the numerus clausus and anti-Semitism, and the promise of full equality for all citizens. However, there was the reality of anti-Semitism among the Polish soldiers, and in order to meet this problem,

Jewish officers were asked to change their names, to keep their Jewish origins a secret, and give their nationality as Polish in all official dealings.[60]

Nevertheless, the leadership in the Union of Polish Patriots was positively disposed[61] toward the Jewish refugees from Poland and included several Jews in its Presidium. Publications of the Union attacked Polish anti-Semitism, placing the blame on the London government and the Anders army. Friendly feelings of the Polish Communist leadership toward Polish Jews were stressed repeatedly. A recurring theme was the mutual suffering of Poles and Jews under Nazi occupation and their mutual desire to build a better Poland after the war.

Since Polish Jews could reclaim their Polish citizenship after April 1943, many refugees joined the new Polish army in the hope of returning to Poland. In the first important encounter with the enemy at Lenino in October 1943, many Jewish soldiers excelled in the fighting and received high military decorations.[62] Later, the high proportion of Jews declined, and their patriotism and heroism, at first highly praised, were soon belittled or ignored. However, at a crucial time, they were exploited for the advance of Soviet policy, an instance, according to one scholar, "of how, in certain historical periods, the skills and abilities of Jews are made use of and how, once they have fulfilled their role, they are regarded as superfluous, their merits are cancelled and erased from history. . . . They were not aware that they were only an instrument in the implementation of a definite policy, that once their services were no longer needed they would be regarded as an alien element and treated accordingly."[63]

Little information was available in the West about the lot of Polish Jews in the Soviet Union in the first two years of the war. Sporadic reports filtered out later, varying from enthusiastic pro-Soviet feeling to reports of Soviet oppression. The December 1943 issue of *Contemporary Jewish Record* reported that on September 24, 1943, at a meeting in Kuibyshev, "Polish Jewish refugees in the Urals celebrated the freeing of the Donbas region . . . and expressed their eagerness to aid in restoring the Donbas coal fields. Polish Jewish workers at a mass meeting in Chelyabinsk announced a similar desire."[64] NKVD suspicion of Polish Jews was common, however, and frequently reported, especially toward Zionists. Many were subjected to solitary confinement, incessant interrogation under bright lights in a hard chair, not permitted to sleep, forced to answer questions while suffering terrible thirst and hunger, sealed away from any contact with the outside world.

In the fall of 1944, a committee of Polish Jews in the USSR[65] was set up—ostensibly separate, but, in fact, "no more than a branch" of the Union, "from which it received guidance and directives." Among its members were well-known Polish Jews including Dr. Emil Sommerstein, Ber Mark, Moshe Broderzon, and Ida Kaminska. The committee was to help prepare an organizational framework for postwar Polish Jewry and carry on propaganda activities stressing the new era in Soviet-Polish-Jewish relations. Many of the committee's functions were of a cultural nature, and in 1945 several members of the Jewish Antifascist Committee in Moscow joined in events commemorating the Warsaw Ghetto Uprising. The revival of Jewish cultural activity in Poland, including Zionism and Hebrew, was discussed at a conference[66] in November 1945 at which Bergelson, Markish, and Feffer spoke hopefully of a new future. All were deeply moved at the time by the chanting of *El Maleh Rakhamin* (God, full of compassion), the traditional memorial prayer for the Jewish dead, including victims of the Holocaust.

Contacts continued, but the efforts of the Polish Jews to have Soviet Jews visit Poland failed. Many Soviet Yiddish writers, however, who could not be published in the Soviet Union, found an outlet in the Polish Yiddish press, especially in *Folkshtimme* and *Dos naye lebn*, which began publishing in 1945.[67] Some of the Polish Jewish writers and actors found temporary creative expression in the Soviet Union, but almost all returned to Poland, as did most other Polish Jewish refugees in 1945–46. In September 1944 and July 1945, agreements dealing with citizenship and repatriation were concluded between the Polish Committee of National Liberation and the Soviet government. Out of the million and a half Poles who were repatriated, about 140,000–150,000 were Jews.[68] Among those repatriated was Ida Kaminska, the noted Yiddish actress and former director of the Yiddish State Theater of Poland. She had returned from Frunze, capital of the Kirghiz republic, to Moscow in April 1944, and visited often with members of the JAC. She hoped for some work in the theater, but it never came. At the end of 1945 came an order that former Polish citizens who wanted repatriation had to register with the militia for foreigners by December 31.[69] Many, however, in remote parts of the Soviet Union could not leave until 1946. If they returned through the Ukraine, they often experienced not only the traditional anti-Semitism, but murder. Survivors on their way back to Poland reported the killing of Jews who left trains to go into villages to buy food.[70]

The 200,000 or so Polish Jewish refugees[71] who survived in Soviet Russia endured many hardships and vicissitudes, but they were spared annihilation. Many went to Palestine after the shocked exposure to Polish anti-Semitism in 1946. The rest were caught up in the transformation of Poland into a Communist state, but left the country during the anti-Zionist and anti-Jewish purges of 1956 and 1968.

After a brief heady exultation over the annexations in 1939–40, the Soviet Union had to brace itself for the shock of the sudden German invasion in June 1941. Soviet Jews were extremely vulnerable, having been specifically marked by the Nazis for annihilation. They were also exploited by the Soviet regime, this time to mobilize American Jewish support for the Soviet war effort by arousing Jewish national hopes. The instrument was the Jewish Antifascist Committee.

17

The Jewish Antifascist Committee and Other Illusions, 1942–43

The Soviet regime is not of a kind that will change its course because of the homage paid by prominent Jewish leaders in America to a poet and theater director.

MENACHEM BORAISHA

The dispersed Jewish population is seeking an address and we should not deny it to them.

SHLOMO MIKHOELS

DESPERATE for support of its war effort and straining for all sorts of ties and alliances, the Soviet Union made a bid for support from world Jewry, especially American Jewry, by establishing a Jewish Antifascist Committee (JAC) in April 1942. However, propaganda efforts to involve various ethnic and nationality groups, including Jews, for pro-Soviet activity, had started soon after the German attack.[1] In this earlier period there were public meetings and radio broadcasts, described as meetings of "representatives" of various Soviet nationalities, and, generally, speakers in the broadcasts later became members of the antifascist committees.[2] Jewish support was sought in the late summer of 1941, and although other similar committees were formed to mobilize support for the war, such as the Committee of Soviet Youth, the Committee of Slavic Peoples, and the Committee of Soviet Women, Jews were the only nationality to form a separate committee.[3]

The idea for such a committee may first have been conceived and developed by the Polish Jewish socialists, Erlich and Alter.[4] However, the free-ranging activities of their proposed committee, their hated

Bundist identification and association with the Second International made them dangerous in Stalin's eyes. By November-December, moreover, the Nazi threat against Moscow had been turned back and the extreme Soviet need for allies among old enemies appears to have lessened. However, the idea for a supportive, broadly based Jewish committee was undoubtedly strengthened during the Erlich-Alter affair.

The JAC was not intended to be a national Soviet Jewish organization with a domestic program, but, rather, to serve Soviet foreign policy and military needs, as part of the Soviet Bureau of Information under Solomon A. Lozovsky, director of the bureau and vice commissar for foreign affairs. Lozovsky himself, although a Jew, was only interested in the committee as an instrument of Soviet propaganda abroad.[5] However, the impact of the committee's work reverberated unexpectedly, giving rise to new illusions and hopes of a Jewish cultural revival and new waves of Jewish consciousness which to this day have had their influence.

The outreach of the committee was to world Jewish opinion. Most particularly was the great significance Soviet authorities attached to world Jewry in shaping public opinion in the West. "As the prime object of Nazi hatred, the Jews could be motivated to clamor for the opening of a second front in Europe and for America's entry into the war against Germany."[6]

Within the Soviet Union itself, the creation of the committee marked a "sensational reversal of internal policy,"[7] in that Soviet Jews were now accorded some sort of central organizational framework for the first time since the Evsektsiya was dissolved in 1930.

Lozovsky's Sovinformburo was in the Commissariat for Foreign Affairs, but the security apparatus (NKVD), headed by Lavrenti Beria, also closely supervised the various antifascist committees, including the JAC. Beria had already been involved in the earlier effort to create a Jewish anti-Hitlerite Committee using Erlich and Alter.

The first signs of the Soviet propaganda offensive appeared at a Jewish antifascist rally organized by Soviet officials in Moscow on August 24, 1941. The meeting was described in the Soviet press as a "public gathering of representatives of the Jewish people (see Photo 17.1)."[8] At this exceptional Soviet acknowledgment of a Jewish people transcending territory, outstanding figures among non-Jewish as well as Jewish intelligentsia spoke,[9] including the dean of Soviet letters Aleksei Tolstoy. The opening speech was made by Shlomo Mikhoels, famed actor and director of the Moscow Yiddish State Theater, who made a special appeal to the Jewish communities in England and the United States. Mikhoels would later become chairman of the JAC.[10] Peretz Markish, the leading Soviet Jewish poet, evoked images of earlier Jewish suffering and heroism. Samuil Marshak, who wrote for children, spoke with great emotion of the Nazi slaughter of Jewish children in the Polish town of Otwock. Ilya Ehrenburg, a highly assimilated writer who wrote in Russian, acknowledged his Jewish origins: "I am a Russian writer. . . . However, the Nazis reminded me of something else: that my mother's name was Hanna. I am a Jew, and I proudly state this fact." Shakhne Epshteyn, a Yiddish journalist, who would be the future secretary of the JAC, spoke in praise of the Soviet regime and its policy toward Jews. At the rally, there was also a resounding appeal "to our Jewish brothers all over the world":

In the countries seized and enslaved by murderous fascism, our unfortunate brothers have become the first victims. . . . Their blood does not call for fasts and prayers, but for retribution! . . . It calls not for words but for deeds. . . . On our long road of martyrdom stretching from the time of Roman domination to the Middle Ages, our long-suffering people never experienced a calamity comparable to the present one, which fascism has inflicted upon the whole of mankind, and whose main ferocity is directed against the Jewish people.[11]

This dramatic, unprecedented call was answered by many representative Jewish organizations and individuals, including a trilingual broadcast from Palestine sponsored by the Jewish Agency, and eloquent messages from leading American and British rabbis. On May 24, 1942, Mikhoels broadcast an address on Moscow Radio to the Jewish people in many lands, in which he identified himself as representing "that part of the Jewish people that is living in the USSR."[12] Under the impact of the traumatic Soviet defeats and losses and the need to mobilize maximum support for Russia's war effort, Stalin had allowed Soviet Jews to speak and be spoken to as part of a Jewish people, a sweeping, if opportunistic, departure from all previous Soviet policy.

In another radical switch of policy, the government stopped the liquidation of all houses of prayer, including synagogues. Officials were at great pains to assure the world that charges of Soviet antireligious activity were entirely without foundation. In October 1941, Lozovsky issued the following statement:

The Soviet government provides buildings for religious purposes and exempts them from taxation. The Soviet government insures that no one disturbs

17.1 Soviet Jewish leaders appeal to Jews of the world to unite against fascist aggression in a radio address on August 24, 1941. First row, left to right, Samuil Marshak, Peretz Markish, David Bergelson, Shlomo Mikhoels, Boris Iofan, and Ilya Ehrenburg. Second row, left to right, Y. Flier, David Oistrakh, Isaac Nusinov, Y. Zak, Benjamin Zuskin, Alexander Tyshler, and Shakhne Epshteyn. This appeal preceded the formation of the Jewish Antifascist Committee. Universal Jewish Encyclopedia.

the rites of believers, offends their feelings, or jeers at their beliefs. The Soviet laws severely punish those who try in any way to infringe the rights of believers. The Soviet government has secured for each nationality the possibility to perform religious ceremonies in its mother tongue. Religion is a private affair . . . in which the state does not interfere and considers it unnecessary to interfere.[13]

Throughout the Soviet Union where there were synagogues, Jews celebrated Rosh Hashanah in 1941. There were no antireligious campaigns during the Jewish High Holy Days, and the strident antireligious paper *Bezbozhnik* (The Godless), which had been issued for many years by the League of Militant Godless, was suspended.[14]

In the meantime, besides the brief use of Erlich and Alter, the Soviet

Union utilized other foreign contacts. At the end of September, Mikhoels wrote to Leon Feuchtwanger, the well-known German Jewish novelist, who was then living in the United States, urging him to carry the message of Soviet need to "all our brethren living in America . . . to all those who came from Vilna, Kovno, Bialystok [and] Warsaw."[15] Personal messages were also sent to elicit support from other well-known Jews abroad and within the next few months an active nucleus for the future JAC was built up. Members of the JAC differ as to the dates of its actual beginning, but it probably took place in Kuibyshev sometime in the first half of 1942.[16]

On April 6, 1942, JTA reported that a committee of Jewish Soviet intellectuals was formed in the USSR. On April 25, Lozovsky announced in a press conference that "the Jews had created an antifascist committee to help the Soviet Union, Great Britain and the U.S. put an end to the bloody madness of Hitler."[17] The JAC traced its origin back to the August 1941 rally. Erlich's and Alter's plan very probably played a role in suggesting a Jewish organization to maintain contact with world Jewry, but the new committee would be under direct Soviet control. The first JAC plenum was held on May 24, 1942, parallel with another public meeting referred to as the "second meeting of the representatives of the Jewish people," and a radio broadcast.

For the first time since the Revolution, Jews abroad were linked with Soviet Jewry in an officially sanctioned cause that had a high priority. Moreover, the composition of the committee itself was unique, uniting Jews who wrote in Yiddish as well as Russian, together with actors, scientists, scholars, and soldiers, most of whom had been far removed from Jewish interests for a generation. They were now aroused by the scale of Jewish suffering and the struggle against Nazism, and joined together in one body. The members included Mikhoels, Der Nister, Kvitko, Feffer, Bergelson, Markish, Hofshteyn, Halkin, and Nusinov who were devoted to Soviet Yiddish culture, and celebrated Soviet personalities of Jewish origins who considered themselves Russians but had varying Jewish backgrounds and feelings about their origins, such as Ehrenburg, Vasily Grossman, Marshak, David Zaslavsky, General Aaron Katz of the Stalin Military Academy, Dr. Boris Shimelovich, chief surgeon of the Red Army, and Lina Shtern, a well-known biologist. There were also a number of non-Jews on the committee from fields of literature, art, theater and film, journalism, the military, and science.[18] Beyond their propaganda functions, the committee carried out specifically *Jewish* activities and became, for a time, "the national Jewish representative body for internal affairs."[19]

Mikhoels, the chairman, highly regarded in general Soviet cultural circles, was in close touch with certain Soviet political figures. Nevertheless, he still felt strong bonds with Jewish traditions, Hebrew, and the Bible. It is believed that he was appointed chairman at the recommendation of Beria. Epshteyn, the secretary, was a former Bundist in prerevolutionary Russia and the United States, but joined the Communist party in 1919 and served the Communist cause in Europe and in the United States, including work as editor and correspondent for the *Morgen freiheit*, as well as in the Soviet Union.[20]

The meeting of May 1942 appealed to all Jews to take up weapons and fight the common enemy. Jewish soldiers and officers were urged to volunteer for special and demanding duties in the armed forces and become snipers, pilots, and tank commanders. Jews in the USSR and abroad were called upon to avenge the murders of fellow Jews.[21]

The JAC functioned under the auspices of the Soviet Information Bureau and more specifically, Lozovsky, deputy chief of the Bureau. Lozovsky had been active in the field of foreign affairs and propaganda in the early years of the Revolution "and was considered by Stalin as the appropriate man for handling Soviet propaganda during the war."[22] Besides serving as secretary, Epshteyn was named editor of *Einikayt* (Unity), the organ of the JAC, which began publication in Kuibyshev in June 1942. *Einikayt* was first published every ten days, but after a year when the JAC was transferred to Moscow, it appeared weekly until February 24, 1945.[23] This became a channel of communication, through which the JAC reached and was reached by Soviet Jews during the war and for three years thereafter. Because the general Soviet press published little about the experiences of Jews during the war, *Einikayt* helped to supply this material. Many letters from readers, including soldiers at the front and refugees who had been deported or evacuated, underscored its significance and popularity. Often, because of the paper shortage, copies were passed from hand to hand. Information on what Jews were contributing to the war effort and the unfolding details of Nazi mass murder were reported by several hundred reporters in far-flung parts of the country. *Einikayt* also covered general Soviet issues such as the deterioration and then breakdown in Soviet-Polish relations.[24]

The JAC became an address for Soviet Jews, and after it moved to

Moscow, it was housed in an impressive building and employed about eighty people. It collected and sent a large quantity of material abroad to Jewish newspapers and agencies, especially in the United States, and sponsored radio programs in Yiddish, Russian, and English, that were also beamed abroad.[25] The JAC also became a center of newly invigorated Soviet Jewish culture, especially of Yiddish literature, whose quality and output from 1941 to 1948 is considered by one scholar "unparalleled in the history of the Jews of the USSR."[26] A signal contribution of the committee was its revitalization of Yiddish and Yiddish publishing. The drop in publication of original Yiddish works and periodicals in the mid- and late 1930s was somewhat reversed by the addition of new territories between 1939 and 1941,[27] but during the first months after the German invasion, Yiddish publishing was virtually wiped out. The evacuation of Moscow ended the work of Der Emes Publishing House. From June 22, 1941, until June 1942, when *Einikayt* appeared, there were no newspapers or periodicals in Yiddish. Many Soviet Jewish writers volunteered to serve in the Red Army; others fled to distant towns. After coming to Moscow, the JAC brought back some of the writers and journalists who had been in eastern areas—a step "taken at the request of Sovinformburo which required Soviet propaganda in Yiddish for circulation abroad." Der Emes Publishing House began to function once more.

In an examination of the Yiddish material published during the war, Chone Shmeruk found most of the Yiddish belles lettres "pervaded with Jewish national content."[28] Publications included essays, stories, poems, and memoirs dealing with the war and its effect on Jews, documentary accounts of the mass murder of Jews, biographies of Jewish war heroes, and accounts of camps such as Maidanek and Treblinka and various Jewish underground movements.[29] In 1943, Der emes published fifty-six books and pamphlets, many in editions of 10,000 copies or more. Altogether, during the war period, the editions of Yiddish books were larger than in the prewar period. Shmeruk estimates that 100,000 books and pamphlets in Yiddish were circulated.[30] The JAC played a central role in the production of this material. Interestingly, during this entire period, there is not one antireligious book[31] in Soviet Yiddish literature—reflecting Stalin's need to mobilize the entire country, including surviving clergy, rabbis, and religiously oriented citizens, and secure their support for the stupendous war effort.

However, the heterogeneous composition of the JAC, the varied interpretations of its functions, and the deep yearning of some members for a new Soviet Jewish cultural life, inevitably led to sharp differences over the meaning of its mandate,[32] differences which broke out shortly after the committee was organized. Epshteyn, for example, was opposed to giving the committee any tasks beyond that of fighting fascism. Mikhoels, Markish, Feffer, and Hofshteyn, among others, urged a more specific Jewish focus, encompassing aid to Jewish refugees and rehabilitation of Jewish farms in the Crimea and the Ukraine. Indeed, they wanted the committee to revitalize Jewish life and direct Jewish cultural and communal life during and after the war.[33] Others regarded the committee as a temporary institution with limited functions, mainly designed for foreign consumption. The committee was also divided on the question of the value of preserving Jewish culture in the Soviet Union, with the more assimilated members, such as Ilya Ehrenburg, generally adapting to or expressing the the official Soviet position. There were also personal and power conflicts. Lozovsky, for example, served as a link between the highest Soviet authorities and the JAC. "It was mainly through Feffer's personal ties with Lozovsky and through his services to the NKVD that he was able to overpower his competitors[34]—most particularly Markish, as leader of the Moscow group of Jewish writers in the eyes of Jewish intellectual circles and Soviet authorities. Indicative of this inner struggle and the long arm of Soviet control was the decision to send Feffer and Mikhoels (instead of Markish and Bergelson) abroad. Their trip was keyed to "moral and material aid for the Red Army," the theme of a second "public gathering of representatives of the Jewish people" on May 24, 1942. The Soviet Union was called the first force in the war against Hitlerism, and Soviet Jews were praised for the example they set the Jewish people as a whole: "We Jews of the Soviet Union have set you an example. . . . The Red Army is the hope of all mankind. Jews throughout the world! Let us collect money, buy a thousand tanks and five hundred airplanes, and ship them to the Red Army!"[35] The first issue of *Einikayt* led off with an article by Mikhoels entitled "1000 Tanks and 500 Bombers."

The unprecedented visit abroad, which took Mikhoels and Feffer to the United States, Mexico, Canada, and Britain in the summer of 1943, aroused great enthusiasm and, in retrospect, somewhat naive though ardent hopes that ties with Soviet Jews might be once more re-established after the long years of silence. However, for Stalin, who authorized the mission, there was a single political purpose: to win American support for the Soviet war effort by arousing the support of American Jews, and through them, American public opinion. The visitors were given an official reception at the Soviet consultate in New York and then swept up by waves of overjoyed American Jews who saw them as miraculous emissaries of Soviet Jewry. Many prominent non-Jews also welcomed them with great warmth and at a large mass meeting in New York on July 8, 1943, Mikhoels noted the presence of Russians, Negroes, French, Italians, Ukrainians, Poles, and Czechs, as well as Jews.[36] Feffer estimated that half a million Jews in forty-six cities heard their appeal and raised between two and three million dollars for the Jewish Council for Russian War Relief. (Epshteyn mentions both figures in two different accounts). Feffer reported the larger sum. These were large amounts for American Jews to raise, especially since they were not earmarked for specific Jewish needs. But the fund-raising campaigns were a perfect means for mobilizing pro-Soviet support. Reporting to the JAC plenary session on his trip to America, Feffer said apropos this aid: "We did not deem it possible to single out Soviet Jews . . . from the fraternity of peoples making tremendous sacrifices along with us in the war."[37]

Several hundred articles in the Yiddish press covered their visit—many were overwhelmingly enthusiastic—but some Jews were wary, disturbed, and even bitterly opposed to any participation. Menachem Boraisha, for example, a well-known Yiddish writer in America, tried to warn Rabbi Stephen Wise, the foremost leader of American Jewry at the time, against meeting with the visitors. Admitting that Wise was being "guided by purely political considerations"—to change Soviet attitude and policy toward Zionism—Boraisha deplored the "hullabaloo" raised over the "mediocre" Feffer and recalled with great bitterness that "for twenty years Feffer and his colleagues were not only among those who campaigned in the most violent fashion against everything dear to you but also destroyed everything which they themselves had proclaimed as 'nationally Jewish,' the Yiddish schools, libraries, press, literature." Moreover, Boraisha refused to believe that Wise's gesture would help Zionism in the slightest: "the Soviet regime is not of a kind that will change its course because of the homage paid by prominent Jewish leaders in America to a poet and theatre director."[38] Wise nevertheless went to the meeting, as he wrote back to Boraisha, "in the hope of getting Soviet help after the war both for Palestine and the Diaspora." These hopes were fanned by actual contacts between Soviet representatives and Zionist leaders in England and Palestine, discussed later in this chapter. Many Western Jews, however, still felt outraged by the Nazi-Soviet Pact and the execution of Erlich and Alter and were worried about the effects of the rupture of Polish-Soviet relations on the fate of Polish Jews in the Soviet Union. The American socialist *Jewish Daily Forward* was particularly critical.[39]

Political considerations aside, both Mikhoels and Feffer were themselves deeply stirred by the great warmth of the Jewish masses they met, while their Jewish audiences fervently believed that a new era was dawning for Soviet Jewry. Feffer remarked that though there had been a certain "estrangement" between Soviet and American Jews, he was sure that "this is a matter of the past, and from now on the two important Jewish communities will be joined by bonds of unity." He also expressed the hope that "our coming here has created a possibility for living contact, and [that] our books will frequently reach you, and your books will reach us."[40]

Appeals to Jews of democratic countries for aid and support had come from various other Soviet Jews. Samuil Chobrutsky, president of the "Moscow Jewish community" sent a message of greeting to Jews throughout the world at Rosh Hashanah,[41] while a plea to help the Red Army was issued on October 2, 1942, by the administration of Birobidzhan.[42] Sympathy for Jews in Nazi-occupied countries was expressed by David Bergelson, who stated on September 22 that "Jews in Russia should wear the Magen David as an expression of solidarity with the other Jews, and thereby display their contempt for the Nazi anti-Jewish laws."[43] A Rosh Hashanah message sent by Moscow Jews in Tashkent to the Jews of the United States through the Jewish Telegraphic Agency on September 22, 1943, said, in part: "from the heart of the U.S.S.R. we shall, with God's help, again represent religious Soviet Jewry and establish contact in its name with the Jews of all the world."[44] At the time the Kuibyshev radio was broadcasting in Yiddish twice a week.

The sense that the formerly lost Soviet Jews were now to be reunited to the fold of world Jewry was voiced explicitly on numerous occasions by the Soviet visitors as well as their hosts. In a booklet "Calling All Jews to Action", published as a souvenir of the visit of Mikhoels and Feffer to England by the Jewish Fund for Soviet Russia, but prepared from material supplied by the JAC, Soviet writers resorted to traditional national and religious imagery, using quotations from the prayer book and references to religious sentiments. For example, they referred to an obscure "religious young poet," Israel Emiot, who wrote of the "sacred scrolls that were desecrated by the Nazis," and a Warsaw cantor chanting Kol Nidre in Moscow.[45] Mikhoels himself in his message quoted from the prayer recited on the night of Yom Kippur, ending with a plea: "We are calling upon you to fulfill your national duty toward your people."[46]

Caught up in the wartime fervor of the time, Jews especially, but others as well, were willing to overlook or ignore the unsavory evidence of Soviet past history in their eagerness to identify with a great power struggling to defeat Hitler. The war obliterated unpleasant and irksome facts of the past. For many Jews, this simplification created a momentary illusion that Soviet and Jewish interests coincided. Soviet national self-interest briefly cultivated this illusion. Even so, Soviet Jewish policy was Janus-faced, encouraging Jewish illusions, but maintaining a silence on Jewish matters with its non-Jewish citizens. "Soviet authorities confined reporting of JAC activities to the Yiddish-language *Einikayt* . . . and to foreign-language broadcasts. In an article . . which Mikhoels and Feffer wrote in a Russian periodical after their return, Jews were not mentioned, and there was no indication whatever that the visit possessed any Jewish connotation."[47] In the material for foreign consumption, which involved four weekly radio broadcasts, daily cables, and special features, two themes were especially stressed: the total absence of anti-Semitism in the Soviet Union, and the special help rendered Jews in moving them away from Nazi-occupied areas. The success of this propaganda was to be found in the American Jewish groundswell of sympathy and support for the Soviet cause. Even so, differences among Jewish organizations as to the nature of Jewish help surfaced. Some Jewish leaders, Wise among them, were willing to help in relief work, but with guarantees that certain funds would be for "specific Jewish needs." James N. Rosenberg, long-time leader of the JDC and Agro-Joint, was willing to yield on this point and criticized the American Jewish Committee, which favored a completely nonsectarian approach and feared a deadly association of Jews with communism.[48]

In general, however, many Jews in America believed that the new tactic in Soviet policy regarding Jews signified a basic change in policy. The Soviet alliance with the democracies also nurtured illusions about the Soviet role in building a new democratic world order after the war. Many Jews both inside and outside the Soviet Union believed that Soviet Jews would enjoy new freedoms and opportunities to resume their ruptured culture. Nowhere was the illusion of a new era so pervasive as in Palestine and among Zionists.

Many Jews in Palestine had their roots in Russia and still spoke and loved the Russian language and literature and had friends and relatives there. The ties were still strong. The Zionist movement itself and the first waves of emigration to Palestine at the turn of the century stemmed from Russia. Palestine had been omitted from the itinerary of Mikhoels and Feffer, no doubt to keep official hostile Soviet policy toward Zionism unclouded. But the emissaries personally seemed eager to visit there; toward the end of the war, Mikhoels told the poet Abraham Sutzkever when they met in Moscow, "When I flew to America in July 1943, I kissed the air when we passed over Palestine."[49] In Palestine itself, there was a prevailing belief that a historic reconciliation between Soviet Russia and Zionism was at hand. The warm currents that seemed to blow from Moscow satisfied deep yearnings. Every friendly gesture made by the Soviet Union had a tremendous impact in Palestine.

This hope of a new era was given fervent expression in Palestine Jewry's reply to the August 24, 1941, appeal of "representatives of the Jewish people in Moscow." In a dramatic radio broadcast to Soviet Jewry on October 3, 1941, leading figures including the Chief Rabbi Isaac Herzog, the poet Saul Tschernikhovsky, Yitzhak Ben-Zvi, chairman of the Vaad Leumi (representative council), labor leader Berl Katznelson, and the famous Habima actress Hannah Rovina expressed a tremulous excitement over the renewal of bonds with Soviet Jewry. Katznelson, for example, said, "For many years we have yearned to hear your voice. Now it has reached us . . . from those precious centers that have been razed to the ground. . . . And it sounds to our ears like a voice from the depths of Jewish history. . . . We shall continue to be one people despite all barriers."[50] So hopeful were these new signs that Palestinian Jews wanted to send physicians and Jewish fighting units to the Soviet Union. At the end of October 1941 a "Public Committee to Help the Soviet Union in its War Against Fascism" was created largely on the initiative of Palestinian Communists, and the V (victory) League followed in May 1942.

The outreach of the Jewish Antifascist Committee was also heartening, as were earlier, very dramatic contacts between leaders of the *Yishuv* (Jewish community) and Soviet officials in London and Palestine. The key Soviet figure in these talks[51] was Ivan Maisky, himself a Jew, and Soviet minister to Great Britain. A highly respected and experienced career diplomat, Maisky had already interceded in 1940 on behalf of students and rabbis in the religious academies of Vilna, including the famous Mir Yeshiva, and helped them emigrate to Palestine. Palestine Jewry through its major agencies, the Jewish Agency and the Histadrut (Labor Federation), was keenly interested in the rescue of other Jewish war refugees who had fled Nazi-occupied territories in Eastern Europe and hoped that Soviet authorities would help. They were also eager to re-establish contact with Soviet Jewry, especially with the thousands of Zionists who had been imprisoned or exiled and those who had gone underground, with whom thin ties were maintained secretly.

Chaim Weizmann met with Maisky in midsummer 1941 at the same time that two other Zionist leaders, Berl Locker and Selig Brodetsky, met with the first secretary of the Soviet Embassy in London and touched on these matters. On the legal status of Russian Zionists, the Jewish representatives were told that the Soviet government "does not recognize any movements or organizations on its territory." In September Maisky wrote to the Chief Rabbi in England and the Chief Rabbi in Palestine promising to do everything possible to enable certain Polish rabbis to leave the Soviet Union. Maisky and Weizmann met again in September and Weizmann presented the official positive response of the Jewish Agency to the August 24 appeal of Soviet Jews for worldwide Jewish unity and solidarity. Anticipating a softening of relations, David Ben-Gurion, chairman of the Jewish Agency and secretary general of the Histadrut, met Maisky in September and October to discuss the Yishuv's war effort. He explained the principal goal of Zionism as the territorial concentration of the Jewish people in Palestine, emphasizing that the labor movement in Palestine was playing a major role in the social and economic construction of the country and was already successful in establishing a socialist community. He expressed the hope that previous misunderstandings between Zionists and the Soviet Union would soon be removed and proposed sending a Histadrut delegation to Moscow to explore ways of supporting the Soviet war effort and describe more fully the role of the Jewish labor movement. He followed these two meetings with a memorandum detailing the achievements of this movement and its own war effort. He also stressed the vital role the Soviet Union would play in determing postwar Palestine, making it all the more important for Soviet leaders to understand the actual achievements of socialist Zionists in Palestine. Ben-Gurion also asked what assistance the Soviet Union would be willing to render Jewish political aspirations in Palestine. Maisky promised to relay all of the information to the Soviet government, but the possibility of a Histadrut visit was rejected—very likely for fear of reviving Jewish national feelings among Soviet Jews.

On March 2, 1942, Weizmann provided Maisky with more material, stressing the significance of Palestine as the only possible place of absorption for large numbers of Jewish refugees after the war and emphasizing its progressive character. "There are," he wrote, "no fundamental psychological barriers to mutual understanding . . . the Zionist movement has never felt antagonistic to Soviet social philosophy." Above all, out of the newly forged common bond Weizmann hoped for Soviet support and understanding of the wartime plight of the Jewish people.

A tangible expression of Jewish hope came in August 1942 in an official ceremony at the Soviet Embassy in London, when Locker presented Maisky with a check for 10,000 pounds from the Histadrut for the Soviet Red Cross. Locker spoke ardently of the way in which the working people of Palestine were following the heroic struggle of the Red Army and hoped "the coming victory would strengthen the bonds of brotherhood which were being created." Maisky seemed very pleased by all of these gestures and interested in the information submitted by Zionist leaders. Meantime important events were also unfolding in Palestine.

The V League had been founded to provide aid to the Soviet war effort and promote better understanding between the Soviet Union and the Jewish and Arab communities of Palestine. At first the Palestine Communist party dominated, but quite soon the Histadrut and Zionist workers' parties asserted leadership. The Communists, deeply hostile to Zionism, withdrew after the League adopted a resolution (August 1942) which committed it to gaining Soviet support for socialist-Zionist aspirations in Palestine. In the course of the war, funds and medical supplies were collected and sent to the Soviet Union, and V delegations went to Teheran in 1943 and 1944 and handed over ambulances, field operating rooms, and medical equipment to Soviet officials who were then occupying Iran.[52]

Of special significance was the attendance of two representatives of the Soviet embassy in Ankara, Sergey Mikhaylov and Nikolay Petrenko, at the first convention of the V League in August 1942 in Jerusalem and their subsequent visits through the country. They met with both Jews and Arabs but had different agendas with each group. Moreover, they saw more Jewish than Arab settlements and expressed great admiration for "what the Jewish nation has managed to achieve here within a short time." Jewish leaders and journalists perceived their "reservations about any commitment to Zionism, . . . though in most cases they were careful not to talk about it." Mikhaylov intentionally avoided visiting the Jewish Agency, yet during a press conference, Petrenko said that "it had long ago occurred to them to suggest broadcasting in Hebrew from Baku or Tiflis."[53] When asked about the fate of Zionist prisoners in the Soviet Union, the men "were not flustered," and promised to "consider the request." According to a prominent Jewish journalist, Yeshayahu Klinov, the second session of the V League convention was "truly Zionist in content," and the representatives were told "about our aims, our attitude toward fascism, . . . our achievements, the discrimination against the Hebrew language and Zionism in Russia, the hope for improvement in relations, the hope of seeing a mass immigration of refugees from Russia to Palestine. . . ."[54]

The Arab-Jewish conflict at the time was somewhat submerged and left-wing Arabs were reversing their negative attitude toward the allied war effort. The Soviet emissaries were interested in securing more Arab support for the war and seeing an end to Arab-Jewish discord; indeed, they urged a common front to defend Palestine. Mikhaylov proudly pointed to the Soviet Union as a model, a country of 154 nationalities which had "solved the problem of nationalities by not having any one nation rule over another and by having no antagonism between them."[55] In reply to a request for Arabic broadcasts over Soviet radio, Mikhaylov, who was a linguist, said, "We will try to do it. We will broadcast over the Soviet Radio in Arabic and also in the Ancient Hebrew language." He turned to the Jews present and added, "I know that you do not like people saying 'Ancient Hebrew' and so I shall say 'in revived Ancient Hebrew.' "[56] Klinov arranged for daily copies of the *Palestine Post* to be sent in "a closed envelope" to the two men in Ankara as well as a bulletin in Russian about events in Palestine, but noted that "most likely they will not be able to keep their word, nor have the opportunity of passing on even some of our information to the press in Russia." Yet he believed it would be worthwhile if even a few Soviet officials read such a bulletin.

Ben-Zvi's diary for August 31[57] records his impressions of his visit with Mikhaylov and Petrenko on August 26 (then conveyed to Moshe Shertok—later Sharett—head of the Political Department of the Jewish Agency and later foreign minister of Israel, 1948–56, and prime minister, 1953–55). They were able to talk with Ben-Zvi for two full hours completely alone since he knew Russian perfectly and since they had explicitly expressed their desire to see him. Ben-Zvi emphasized the desire of Jews to reach an understanding with the Arabs of Palestine, but said that the conditions of the British White Paper of 1939 had made that impossible. Mikhaylov, who had seen High Commissioner Sir Harold MacMichael, believed he was interested "in strengthening the ties between Jews and Arabs," but Ben-Zvi said that Jewish immigration could not be politically dependent on the Arabs. Mikhaylov kept coming back to the Arab complaint that Jews did not give them work on Jewish farms. Ben-Zvi tried to explain the special problems facing Jewish agriculture—its lack of a traditional peasantry, its fear of a Jewish managerial class and exploitation, its battle for an independent cooperative workers' economy, the need to absorb new Jewish immigrants into such an economy since they could not be absorbed by Arabs. However, he stressed that in areas such as urban development and transport where there was a common economy, Jews and Arabs could work together.

Ben-Zvi doubted if he had convinced them in his analysis of the complexities of Jewish self-labor, but felt that much had been gained: "I was left with the impression that the discussion had been frank and open. They were surprised by what they had seen. It seems that they actually had no idea of what was happening here. . . . One must consider this visit as a sort of beginning of new contacts with Soviet Russia. For the first time in modern history, Russian representatives saw tens of thousands of Jewish workers and fighters. . . . For the first time, they witnessed the force of the revived Hebrew language. . . . They were astonished to see the University, Hadassah [Hospital], and the vast activity in the fields of medicine and social welfare." Ben-Zvi also had the impression that the visitors realized that "Jews here were preparing the background for a Jewish State; and from this they developed an attitude of great appreciation and respect for us."[58] For the first time, moreover, Soviet representatives stood at attention for the singing of "Hatikvah" in front of the Jewish flag.

Ben-Zvi also raised the questions of Hebrew and of Zionist prisoners in the USSR, but for him the "main question" was the presence in the USSR of Jewish refugees from occupied countries, especially from Poland—perhaps as many as 400,000. "We need these refugees," Ben-Zvi urged. "You speak of the additional war effort which is so much needed. There is no need for propaganda, we are all of the same opinion. But our manpower is limited. We have contributed almost 26,000 so far. . . ." Ben-Zvi mentioned "the other front"—the Arab attacks instigated by the Mufti of Jerusalem—and the need for new manpower. "It does not make sense to waste hundreds of thousands of Jewish refugees. . . . You must make it possible for those emigrants to come to our country." Mikhaylov pursued this question somewhat, asking if Ben-Zvi was also referring to Russian citizens and if he could be certain all the refugees wanted to go to Palestine. Ben-Zvi replied that no one would be coerced, of course, but he thought most of them would want to go to Palestine.[59]

Ben-Zvi did not comment on Mikhaylov's tone in dealing with this issue, but possibly the most objective reading of the meaning of the visit is to be found in the account of the high commissioner's talk with Mikhaylov. In their talk on August 27, 1942,[60] MacMichael laid special stress on the "non-employment by Jews of Arab labor" which he said was "politically and economically idiotic," and seemed to find Mikhaylov of the same mind. According to MacMichael, he found the Jews lacking in any desire "to cooperate or come to terms with the 'Arab' " and regretted that the Arabs were not part of the antifascist movement, that "the Jews had ulterior political motives mixed up with their antifascism." MacMichael also queried him about emigration of Polish refugees in Russia to Palestine and was told unequivocally: "Never, never, would the USSR let the Jews or anyone else without very adequate and exceptional reasons leave Russia, at least as long as the war continued. The USSR regarded anyone living in the Soviet Union as a Soviet subject; he could have complete liberty as regards his religion and way of life, but as a Soviet subject his role was to stay there and work there. What good was it going to be to the Soviet Union if he left it and merely stirred up additional trouble for it by exciting the animosity of the 'Arabs'." To this MacMichael noted, "I had no answer."

After his appointment to the post of vice commissar for foreign affairs, Maisky also visited Palestine in October 1943, as an official guest of the British. For the Zionist leaders, "Maisky's visit was significant in several respects. It was the first time such a high-ranking Soviet official had visited the country with the aim of studying conditions there and holding formal talks with Zionist representatives."[61] The expected Allied victory made the issue of postwar political arrangements, including the resettlement of Jewish refugees imminent, and Jewish Agency leaders were intensely interested in having Maisky grasp the potential role of Palestine as the sole hope for those refugees.

The British high commissioner was eager to have Maisky leave after a day, out of "security considerations," but more likely to discourage talks with Zionist leaders. However, Ben-Gurion was invited to meet with him at his request and was subsequently joined by Eliezer Kaplan and Golda Meyerson (later Meir), Jewish Agency leaders. Maisky was taken to two kibbutzim near Jerusalem, where he was able to speak with many members in Russian for several hours. "He confessed great interest and asked many questions. In the evening [he] requested to be shown the old religious Jewish quarters in Jerusalem and to tour the modern sector of the city. . . . In a subsequent report to the Jewish Agency Executive Committee, Ben-Gurion stated that it was Maisky who had initiated the discussions on the postwar plans of the Yishuv during his trip, and had enquired about future settlements and the Yishuv's capacity to absorb a substantial additional immigration."[62] He was assured that some two million immigrants could be resettled. Interestingly, Maisky hinted at a new channel of communication between the Jewish Agency and the Soviet government, probably through a Soviet mission in the Middle East.

Ben-Gurion and Mrs. Meyerson were deeply impressed by the seriousness of Maisky's interest, an impression borne out by his apparently enthusiastic report to the Kremlin. Neither his visit to Palestine nor his report was ever acknowledged in the Soviet press nor in any official Soviet statement, nor were his experiences allowed to remain in his published autobiography, but Bartley Crum, in his book *Behind the Silken Curtain* (1947), revealed that Dimitry Manuilsky, foreign minister of the Ukrainian Republic, told him that Maisky "wrote a glowing report to the Kremlin about the magnificent progress the Jews had achieved in Palestine."[63] Harold Laski, the well-known British socialist, also confirmed the enthusiastic tone of the report in a conversation with Ben-Gurion in April 1944, saying Maisky "not only praised the Zionist effort in Palestine but warmly endorsed Zionist aspirations in the post-war political struggle for independence." Significantly, however, Manuilsky told Crum, who served on the Anglo-American Committee of Inquiry on Palestine, that "Your country has made the situation rather difficult by not insisting that Russia be represented on your committee of inquiry."[64]

All reference to the state of Soviet Jews was quite deliberately avoided in the discussions with Maisky, since this would have been resented as interference in internal affairs and would have endangered the cordial atmosphere that had developed, but Jewish leaders pinned great hopes on Maisky's role in paving the way for possible Soviet support for the establishment of a Jewish state in Palestine. He served as a key advisor to Stalin at Yalta and may indeed have had a role in the Soviet support of Jewish statehood in 1947–48. However, following the vehement anti-Zionist and anti-Jewish campaigns of the "Black Years," 1948–53, he was arrested in 1953 and kept in solitary confinement for a time but was ultimately pardoned. He died in 1975.

The war during these years was raging through the Soviet Union and decimating Soviet Jewry, the first Jewry to feel the Nazi machinery of mass murder and the most unprepared of all.

18

Jews and the War

We were to find out later just what the "final solution" meant, when six million Jews had been burnt in the ovens. However, at that time it sounded like a promise to end the excesses and restore order. It even occurred to me that maybe this had been brought about by pressure from us, that in signing the Pact we had made it a condition that the anti-semitic antics must cease.

ANATOLY RYBAKOV, *Heavy Sand*

Along the trench, along the grave's black rim
They've placed them, one by one.
The rifles aimed directly at their hearts . . .
And, swallowing their final breath of air,
With flickering eyes they sink into the darkness.
The dawn scoops up the snow and dips it in their blood . . .

ALEXANDER BELOUSOV, "The Martyrs"

Whither beckon you, whither drive you,
The icy wind and sorrow of the night?
The blizzard swirls, in the fields the blizzard swirls,
The portals and the gates locked tight.

PERETZ MARKISH, "To the Jewish Dancer"

The two years' grace that the Soviet Union had ostensibly gained by the 1939 pact with Germany were not exploited wisely by Stalin. The Soviet Union was completely unprepared for war and utter chaos and disorganization followed the sudden German attack on June 22, 1941. Soviet leaders had not realistically evaluated the clear evidence of Hitler's aggressions and buildup of forces in Poland and the Balkans. Stalin incomprehensibly ignored British and American warnings of the imminent invasion and continued to ship vitally needed grains, petroleum, and manganese to Germany up to the moment of the invasion.

The war provided the landscape for the first mass killings of Jews. Hundreds of small and large Jewish communities were turned into infernos of death by German *Einsatzgruppen*—mobile killing squads—which swept through the plains and forests of Poland and Russia and slaughtered over a million Jews in two sweeps, the first during June–October 1941 and the second beginning January 1942[1] (see Map 18.1). The *Einsatzgruppen* were instructed to carry out "certain special Security Police tasks which were not within the province of the Army." This meant the murder of Jews, Gypsies, asocials, "Asiatic inferiors," and political commissars. Hitler's instructions to the senior army officers on March 30, just before the invasion, eliminated any scruples the officers might have had about military honor or the so-called laws of war: "The war against Russia," Hitler said, "will be such that it cannot be conducted in a knightly fashion. This struggle is one of ideologies and racial differences and will have to be conducted with unprecedented, merciless, and unrelenting harshness. All officers will have to rid themselves of obsolete ideologies. . . . German soldiers guilty of breaking international law . . . will be excused."[2]

Altogether, four *Einsatzgruppen* of battalion strength were set up: Group A in the Baltic states, Group B in White Russia, Group C in the Ukraine, and Group D in the Crimea-Caucasus. Armed with unlimited power (they were independent of the army, which was, however, required to supply the units and, indeed, often handed over Jews to the killers) each of the four group commanders had between 500 and 900 men serving under him. Indigenous units of Ukrainians, Latvians, Lithuanians, and Estonians were added as auxiliary police when numbers had to be augmented. At their training center at Pretsch in Saxony and in the neighboring village of Duben, the units were told where they were going and what they were expected to do. The training consisted largely of rifle practice and listening to lectures and exhortations on the necessity to exterminate subhumans threatening the life of the Reich. A few days after the invasion, the squads sped away in fast cars and trucks, armed with rifles, pistols, and submachine guns. They needed no cavalry, cannon, or airplanes; there would be no reconnoitering, no surprise attacks, no armed enemy. They had merely to cover vast distances and quickly round up their prey.

MAP 18.1
Towns, Cities, and Killing Sites where Soviet Jews Were Murdered, 1941–42

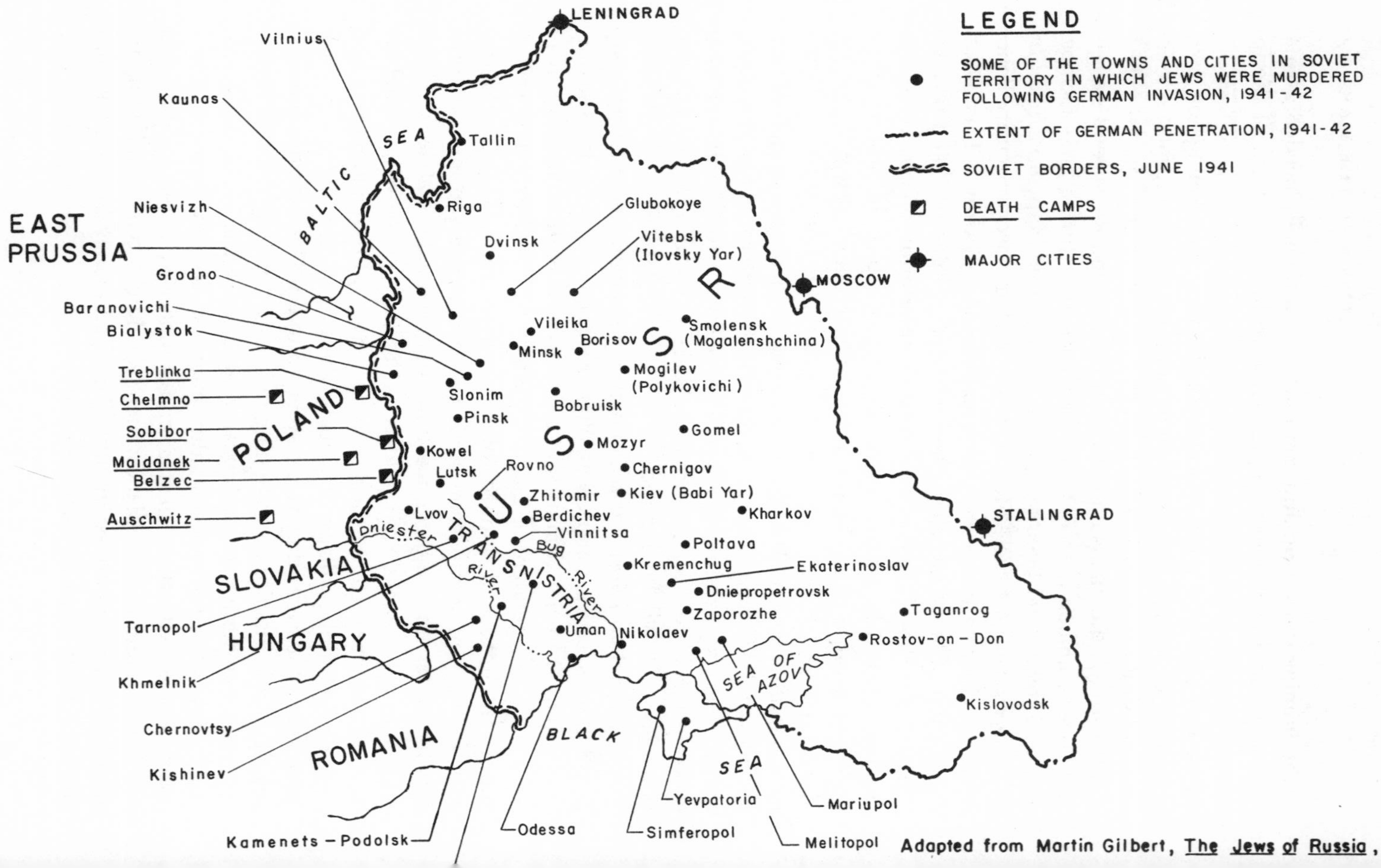

LEGEND

● SOME OF THE TOWNS AND CITIES IN SOVIET
  TERRITORY IN WHICH JEWS WERE MURDERED
  FOLLOWING GERMAN INVASION, 1941–42

--- EXTENT OF GERMAN PENETRATION, 1941–42

~~~ SOVIET BORDERS, JUNE 1941

◪ DEATH CAMPS

⬤ MAJOR CITIES

EAST PRUSSIA

POLAND

SLOVAKIA

HUNGARY

ROMANIA

TRANSNISTRIA

BALTIC SEA

BLACK SEA

SEA OF AZOV

Vilnius
Kaunas
Niesvizh
Grodno
Baranovichi
Bialystok
Treblinka
Chelmno
Sobibor
Maidanek
Belzec
Auschwitz
Tarnopol
Khmelnik
Chernovtsy
Kishinev
Kamenets–Podolsk

Tallin
Riga
Dvinsk
Glubokoye
Vitebsk (Ilovsky Yar)
Vileika
Minsk
Slonim
Pinsk
Kowel
Lutsk
Lvov
Rovno
Zhitomir
Berdichev
Vinnitsa
Uman
Nikolaev
Odessa
Simferopol
Yevpatoria
Mariupol
Melitopol

Borisov (Mogalenshchina)
Smolensk
Mogilev (Polykovichi)
Bobruisk
Mozyr
Gomel
Chernigov
Kiev (Babi Yar)
Kremenchug
Poltava
Kharkov
Zaporozhe
Dniepropetrovsk
Ekaterinoslav
Taganrog
Rostov-on-Don
Kislovodsk

LENINGRAD
MOSCOW
STALINGRAD

Dniester River
Bug River

Adapted from Martin Gilbert, *The Jews of Russia,*

When the *Einsatzgruppen* rolled over the border into the Soviet Union, of the five million Jews (including two million from the 1939–40 annexations) who were living there, 2,160,000 lived in areas overrun by the Nazis: 1,533,000 lived in the Ukraine, 375,000 in White Russia, 50,000 in the Crimea, and 200,000 in the RSFSR. The mobile units moved closely behind the army and trapped large Jewish centers in the first stages. Within five months, half a million Jews were slaughtered.[3] In the Baltic states, the change to Soviet rule after twenty-two years of national independence had been a traumatic one and served to give the German invaders a receptive territory. Tragically, many Jews in the Soviet zone and in the interior, unaware of Nazi actions, and recalling that in World War I Germans had come as quasi-liberators, expected more from the Germans than the Russians.[4] A German intelligence report of July 12, 1941, reveals a German officer's astonishment at this unawareness:

The Jews are remarkably ill-informed about our attitude toward them. They do not know how Jews are treated in Germany, or for that matter, in Warsaw, which is, after all, not so far away. Otherwise, their questions as to whether we in Germany make any distinctions between Jews and other citizens would be superfluous. Even if they do not think that under German administration they will have equal rights with the Russians, they believe, nevertheless, that we shall leave them in peace if they mind their own business and work diligently.[5]

Thus unprepared, they were physically and psychologically immobilized and vulnerable to German reassurances, ruses, and traps. Unable to comprehend their situation realistically and, completely unaware of Nazi plans for Jews, they had no time to warn each other or plan any group action separate from or together with other Russians to defend themselves.

Jews were trapped during the most potent phase of the German attack, at a time when the Russians were reeling under the relentless German advance. Inasmuch as they were being marked for "special treatment"—that is, physical destruction—was there any official Soviet policy to save Jews? During the war, defenders of the Soviet Union tried to press the point that special help was indeed given. In a pamphlet intended for world Jewry, for example, David Bergelson praised the Red Army which "evacuated the weakest elements of the local population first, among them the weakest elements of the Jewish population so that they would not fall into the hands of the Nazi thieves and butchers."[6] The Soviet writer Moshe Kaganovich at first wrote that such an order was issued by Kalinin, chairman of the Supreme Soviet, but later he admitted that he merely "had heard" and "read" about such an order. "The truth," he wrote in 1954, "is that without giving the Jewish population any preference, the Soviet government ordered the evacuation of the entire civilian population together with the factories so that only 'scorched earth' would be left in the hands of the Germans."[7] Such evacuations involved purely economic and administrative considerations. Soviet Jews, like other Soviet citizens, were evacuated because of their occupational importance, party or government position, or urban distribution. The most vital industrial centers—besides Riga and Minsk, which were lost during the first few days—were in the central and eastern Ukraine and in Moscow and Leningrad. The gigantic industrial transplantation to the Urals, western Siberia, and central Asia started in midsummer 1941—five days after the invasion—and continued into 1942, accompanied by a parallel evacuation of civilians.

Only a rough estimate of the number of Jews evacuated together with others is possible. Perhaps as many as one million Ukrainian and Belorussian Jews in the eastern regions of the republics were evacuated, despite the fact that a considerable part of both areas was under German control by mid-July 1941. Possibly another half a million Jews were evacuated from the western parts of the RSFSR. Thus, a reasonably balanced figure for the number of Jews saved by evacuation lies somewhere between one and one and a half million, out of the twelve to fifteen million Russians evacuated.[8] The principal areas to absorb the Jewish evacuees were Orenburg, Chelyabinsk, Sverdlovsk, Perm, and Ufa in the Urals; Saratov in the Volga region; Novosibirsk in western Siberia; and the Kuznetsk basin, especially the city of Stalinsk, which became a center where many Jews worked in the metallurgical and coal industries.[9] Several thousand Jewish collective farmers from the Crimea were evacuated to the Krasnoyarsk district in Siberia. The largest center, accommodating about half a million Jewish evacuees, was in the Uzbek republic. Tashkent, the capital, became a new center for Moscow Jews, and the offices of the "Moscow Jewish Community" were officially transferred there early in 1942. In the republic of Uzbekistan, Jews moved or were moved to Samarkand, Kokand, Khiva, Bokhara, and Andidzhan.[10] In the republic of Kazakhstan, about 140,000 Jews were settled, half in the capital Alma Ata.[11] It is estimated that about half the evacuated Soviet Jewish population spent the war years in the Central Asian republics, a process which exposed them to wholly new life experiences, forcing many to learn new skills and bringing them in contact with native central Asian Jews and Jewish refugees from Poland.[12]

Soviet silence over Nazi atrocities against Jews under the "solidarity and friendship" pact and the ban on criticism of Nazism were shattered by the vehemence of the invasion and the simultaneous mass murder of Jews. It was only *after* the invasion that the Soviet government began to publish information about Nazi massacres and deportations in Poland.[13] However, despite the German radio broadcasts threatening the elimination of Jews and Communists, Soviet mass media did not alert Jews to the very real danger to themselves.[14] Ignorance, incredulousness, and confusion combined to prevent awareness of the advancing peril.

The rampant chaos and confusion in western Russia in the wake of the invasion also existed at border crossings. Jewish refugees from the Baltic countries seem to have had most difficulty crossing into Russia, while in the western Ukraine, "the Dniester crossings were wide open and tens of thousands of Jews fled eastward with the encouragement of the authorities."[15] Many of these Jews, however, were later captured by Germans and Romanians on the other side of the Dniester. Jewish members of the Communist party and their families received preferential treatment, but even those who fled on foot, bicycles, and wagons were helped by military vehicles and at aid stations set up along the railroad lines of the Ural mountains and in kolkhozes. On the other hand, there was practically no chance to escape for the Jews living in White Russia and the Ukraine west of the Dnieper River. "Many Jewish families who had attempted to flee eastward on their own, found themselves, even after having covered several score kilometers, overtaken by the Germans and returned home after a few days."[16] Similarly, Jews from larger towns who had sought shelter in nearby villages and forests in the first days of the war soon drifted back home, often with the encouragement of the Germans.[17]

Many Jewish fugitives who had reached the Crimea and the Caucasus were overtaken by the German offensive in the autumn of 1941 and the summer of 1942 and were slaughtered. Such was the case in Simferopol, where many of the 10,000 victims were refugees from Kherson and Dniepropetrovsk.[18] There were also large-scale massacres in Nikolaev, Kherson, and Melitopol, and between October 23 and 25,

1941, 26,000 Odessa Jews were killed. The Crimea was the area of *Einsatzgruppe D*, under the command of Otto Ohlendorf, a 34-year-old research economist who had a doctor's degree in jurisprudence. By April 16, 1942, the whole of the Crimea was declared free of Jews, and Ohlendorf returned to Germany in June, having directed the killing of 90,000 Jews, with the help of Romanian and German soldiers.[19]

The Jewish collective farms in the Ukraine suffered almost total annihilation by the Nazis and their Ukrainian collaborators. The ambivalent, frequently pro-German, attitude of the native population, combined with native as well as Nazi-inflamed anti-Semitism, produced shattering Jewish losses in the Ukraine, Lithuania, and White Russia. In some Jewish centers such as Vilna, Kovno, Shavli, Bialystok, Riga, Minsk, Mogilev, Zhitomir, and Berdichev, ghettos were temporarily established by the Nazis and decimated in 1941–42. In most places where there were Jews, however, mass slaughter was so swift it precluded ghettos.

The most savage slaughter took place outside Kiev, where, for two days, September 29–30, 1941, over 33,000 Jews were killed in the ravine Babi Yar—a greater killing rate than that of the gas chambers of Auschwitz at their murderous peak. *Einsatzgruppe C, Sonderkommando 4A* had been assigned a special function in the Kiev area. This unit, numbering 150 men, aided by several hundred from two Ukrainian police regiments, assembled in the Kiev area on September 25, under the command of Colonel Paul Blobel. Final preparations were made for a decisive action "carried out exclusively against Jews with their entire families," as a top secret report revealed. On September 28, about 2,000 notices were posted throughout the city:

All Jews of the city of Kiev and its environs must appear on the corner of Melnikov and Dokhturov Streets (beside the cemetery) at 8 A.M. on September 29, 1941. They must bring with them their documents, money, valuables, warm clothing, etc.

Jews who fail to obey this order and are found elsewhere will be shot. All who enter the apartments left by Jews and take their property will be shot.[20]

These notices were printed in Russian, Ukrainian, and German. The street names were misspelled, but the designation near the cemetery was clear. These notices were accompanied by a rumor deliberately planted by the *Sonderkommando* that the Jews were to be evacuated and resettled elsewhere, thus giving some plausibility to the instructions.

18.1 *On the Last Road,* the famous painting by Josef Kuzkovsky, that has great meaning for Soviet Jews. It now hangs in the Knesset building in Jerusalem. Courtesy Jewish Community Relations of Philadelphia.

Since most of the able-bodied men were in the Red Army, the thousands of Jews who assembled were mostly women, children, the old, and the sick. Ilya Ehrenburg in his memoirs describes how "a procession of the doomed marched along Lvovskaya; the mothers carrying their babies; the paralyzed pulled along on hand carts."[21] The victims were ordered to remove their clothing and deposit in neat piles all that they had brought with them (see Photo 18.1). Before the shooting began, they had to run a gauntlet of rubber truncheons and big sticks. As described by the Soviet writer Anatoly Kuznetsov in his book *Babi Yar,* they were "kicked, beaten with brass knuckles and clubs . . . with drunken viciousness and in a strange sadistic frenzy."[22] The first persons selected for shooting were forced to lie naked face down at the

18.2 The ravine at Babi Yar where 90,000–100,000 Jews were slaughtered beginning September 29, 1941. Courtesy Jewish Community Relations of Philadelphia.

bottom of the ravine and were shot with automatic rifles. Some earth was thrown over the bodies and another group had to lie on top of the others. Later the victims were placed at the edge of the ravine, sixty yards long and eight feet wide, and shot in the back of the neck. Some, still writhing, were buried alive. In November many Russian Jewish prisoners of war were executed at Babi Yar. Altogether it is estimated that 90,000–100,000 Jews were slaughtered there. Later, many thousands of Russian and Ukrainian non-Jews were also killed there (see Photo 18.2).

Mass executions similar to those at Babi Yar were carried out at Ponary outside of Vilna, Polykovichi near Mogilev, Ilovsky Yar near Vitebsk, the dread Ninth Fort in Kovno, Mogalenshchina outside Smolensk, and numerous other mass killing grounds (see Photos 18.3–18.5). The cycle of death churned on in the winter of 1941–42: 11,000 old people and children in Dniepropetrovsk, 15,000 in Rovno, 14,000 in Kharkov.[23] At the time, a German economics expert Professor Peter Seraphim in a report to the Armament Inspector, deplored the irrational waste of Jewish manpower and unfortunate use of army personnel in these mass shootings, but his remarks were labeled "personal" rather than "official" and they did not change the Nazi course.

In the Bessarabia-Bukovina areas, Jews were victims of both Nazis and Romanians. There were approximately 210,000 Jews in Bessarabia lying between the Dniester and Prut Rivers. During the first week of August 1941 the Romanians began pushing Jews across the Dniester into what was still a German military area, intending to use the killing services of *Einsatzgruppe D*. After some 15,000 Jews had been driven across the river, the German 11th Army gave orders to block traffic over the Dniester bridgehead at Mogilev-Podolsk, but the Romanians blocked the way back. Again and again, the *Einsatzgruppe* turned Jews back,

18.3 Unknowingly, Jews are digging their own graves at Ponary, 1941. S. Kaczerginski, *Khurbn Vilne*, 1947.

18.4 Part of the field of slaughter at Ponary, 1941. S. Kaczerginski, *Khurbn Vilne*, 1947.

but repeatedly Jews were pushed across. In the process of being shoved back and forth, thousands of Jews died on the roadsides and ditches from exhaustion, hunger, and gunfire.[24] The Germans, meanwhile, were straining to distinguish between "ideological" killing and mere killing, and complained that the Romanians were "disorderly" and that their "technical preparation" lacked "discipline."

In Bessarabia there were locally instigated massacres in most of the towns—in Odessa alone, without the help of the German killing units, the Romanians slaughtered 60,000 Jews. Typical was an action reported in a November 16 broadcast from Ankara, Turkey, in which 25,000 Jews were herded into military barracks on October 23 and shot by Roma-

18.5 Special ladder used to carry corpses onto pyres for burning, Ponary. S. Kaczerginski, *Khurbn Vilne*, 1947.

nian machine-gunners, in reprisal for the death of 220 Romanian soldiers by a delayed action bomb.[25] Simultaneously it was reported that all remaining Jews were ordered to register, presumably for forced labor, but, in fact, they were taken outside the city and shot in anti-tank ditches. In 1944, when a visitor to Odessa asked "What happened to the Jews?" a man answered: "Oh, they bumped off an awful lot. . . . They [the Romanian police] said if so many Jews were bumped off, it was because the Germans had demanded it. 'No dead Jews, no Odessa,' they said."[26]

In October 1941 the Romanians sent 110,000 Jews from Bukovina and Bessarabia into forests in the Bug River area to be killed, under orders from General Ion Antonescu, the Romanian chief of state. From the fall of 1941 for a year, about 175,000 Jews from northern Bukovina and Bessarabia and 10,000 from the Old Romanian region of Dorohoi were deported to a region called Transnistria.[27] This was an area between the Dniester and Bug rivers under Romanian control, created as a temporary dumping ground where Jews would be assigned to forced labor and then sent "to the East." The camps in Transnistria, however, were among the most appalling in Europe and it is estimated that two-thirds of the inmates perished through hunger, disease, or by shooting.[28]

Of the 300,000 Jews in the annexed areas of Bessarabia and Bukovina, perhaps as many as 40,000 Bessarabian Jews escaped death by conversion, while about 30,000 Jews in Bukovina, considered essential to the economy, were granted exemptions.[29] Between March 15 and April 15, 1944, the Russian army overran all of Transnistria and a curtain of silence was lowered. Possibly 50–60,000 of the 185,000 Jews deported survived but the accurate count may never be known.

In the regions annexed by the Soviet Union in 1939–40, the rapid advance of the German armies made evacuation virtually impossible. Ironically, most who survived were those who had been deported earlier to Siberia. The Jewish losses in the annexed areas were searing, doubly shattering from a Jewish point of view because it was in these areas that Jewish religious and national consciousness had been strong for a full generation longer than in the pre-1940 Soviet territory. The war with its decimations gravely lessened the culturally supportive stimulus which such Jewries might have provided Soviet Jews. Even so, during the national awakening of the early 1970s, it was the remnant in the Baltic states and in Bessarabia and Bukovina that provided the most nationally conscious elements and the bulk of the emigration to Israel.

Within the pre-1939–40 Russian borders, the annihilation process was very swift. As a rule, in the first days of the occupation, the Germans placed all captured Russians in civilian internment camps, but Jews were kept isolated and frequently shot a few days later. Such a camp[30] existed in Kiev, where the barracks were so cramped that prisoners had to stand. There were no food rations. Beginning September 1941, ten to fifteen trucks left the camp each day, carrying Jews under sixteen and over thirty-five to their deaths. New captives came into the camp continuously. Camps of this type lasted only a very short time. In some towns, small groups of Jewish artisans who had survived the ghetto liquidations were concentrated in labor camps in Berdichev, Khmelnik, Kiev, Mogilev, Smolensk, Uman, and Zhitomir, some of which existed until the autumn of 1942, the rest until 1943 or the German withdrawal. In 1942–43 some Jews were found in prisoner-of-war camps, including Syrotsk, near Kiev. Some of these inmates were sent in August 1943 to cremate the bodies of the victims of the Babi Yar massacre and took part in the revolt of the *Sonderkommando* prisoners in September 1943. Only one camp near Minsk has been identified as a concentration camp, not exclusively for Jews, but containing a sub-camp for Jews.

The *Einsatzgruppen* rolled forward 600 miles into Russian territory in their first sweep, unleashing waves of massacres. Following this assault, ghettos were created mostly in the Smolensk region of the RSFSR, eastern Belorussia and western Ukraine, to accelerate the second sweep. (In very small communities, in the Crimea, Caucasus, and southeastern Ukraine, there were generally no ghettos; Jews were killed by *Einsatzgruppen* or local units.) For many Jews ghettoization and deportation to killing sites in the Soviet Union was a much swifter process than elsewhere in Europe, contracted to a span from several weeks to three months. They were segregated, registered, marked with a yellow star, permitted only hand luggage, often deprived of food, left to perish from hunger or the bitter cold of the autumn and winter of 1941, or shot in nearby woods and ravines. Ghettos[31] were set up in the most decrepit outlying areas of towns or improvised on empty lots, decayed halls, factories, huts, and warehouses. Closed ghettos were generally set up in the second month of the German occupation in places with large Jewish communities and regional towns. In camp-ghettos such as Smolevichi, Gorodok, Polotsk, Smolyany, and Kletnya, open lots were fenced in with barbed wire. No food allocations were given to Jews flung into these desolate places and they died quickly.

The ghettos were swiftly wiped out. Of the twenty-three ghettos in eastern Belorussia and the RSFSR, twelve were destroyed before the end of 1941, and six within the first two months of 1942.[32] In the Ukraine, of the seventy known concentration points, forty-three were liquidated before the end of 1941, and the rest by mid-1942.[33] The ghettos were first encircled by German and local auxiliary police, often with the help of Wehrmacht soldiers; Jews were then told to assemble, under the pretext of "evacuation", in the ghetto's main square and were taken by lorry or on foot to the killing sites, generally in nearby forests or ravines.

The largest of the ghettos was created on July 20, 1941, in Minsk, with a population of between 80,000–100,000 Jews, swollen by the addition of Jews from Igumen, Slutsk, and Uzda. "The Jews of Minsk," wrote the poet Abba Kovner of the ghettoization of the city

> were surrounded by barbed wire and imprisoned in a ghetto. The thousands of young Jews . . . gazed at this artificial wall in amazement. They viewed it only as a wild device of the Gestapo dogs which would not last long because on its other side lived tens of thousands of brothers together with whom they had built the old, solid walls. Together they had fought for socialism.[34]

Jews were registered, and according to Grossman and Ehrenburg,[35] the Gestapo seized ten men from the streets, marched them to the governor's house, and told them they were a "Jewish Committee" (*Judenrat* or Council) ordered to implement German orders. The Judenrat offices served as a meeting place for Jews to exchange news and information, and Communist party members met there and created the ghetto underground in August 1941.[36] Ilya Moshkin was the first Council chairman and, during his tenure until March 1942, when he was hanged, and later as well, the Jewish underground received help from the Council, the Jewish police, the local city underground, and the White Russian partisan movement in the Minsk area.

Hirsh Smoliar, the former Evsektsiya activist who later worked in the Belorussian Writers' Union, lived in the ghetto under the name of Stolyarevich, but, as the underground leader, was known by the code name Skromny. He met with Moshkin every Friday and established liason with the White Russian partisans, some of whom were smuggled into the ghetto as Jews left it for the forests. The Judenrat supplied the partisans with clothes, soap, drugs, food, salt, typewriters, and money. Women in the ghetto knitted clothes and the ghetto workshops produced goods for the partisans. The Minsk streets were the constant scene of manhunts and thousands of White Russian non-Jews as well as Jews were shot and hanged. "Yet, despite the wild terror and extermination of the White Russian population, the vital thread of friendship between the Jews and the rest of the population remained unbroken," according to Smoliar. He has recorded the many occasions when White Russians who lived across the ghetto fence would talk to a Jewish friend and toss in some food.[37]

The exodus of fighting Jews from Minsk assumed significant numbers between November 1941 and the autumn of 1942. Several thousand escaped, most of them armed with weapons and ammunition sufficient to supply two companies of Jewish partisans in the forests of

Slutsk and Koydanov.[38] The fighters destroyed certain Nazi communications, blew up factories, and stirred the local population to carry out anti-Nazi actions. Some linked up with Russian partisan units such as the Frunze, Dzerzhinsky, and Lazo detachments, and the 11th Minsk partisan brigade.[39] Women, children, and the aged escaped to the Burelom forest, formed a family camp, and organized a flour mill, tailoring, and shoemaking shops and a bakery to help supply the partisans.

In August 1943 when the exodus from the ghetto reached its peak—over 10,000 Jews escaped—an army of more than 8,000 Nazi soldiers surrounded the partisan region. The blockade lasted six weeks and was prepared and carried out like a full-scale frontline operation. Guerrilla resistance finally weakened and the surviving fighters scattered. Nevertheless, about 5,000 Jews survived in the forests at the end of the war.

The first mass murders in the Minsk ghetto occurred in August 1941; other large *Aktionen* took place in November when the Germans rounded up 20,000 Jews and killed them. In the same month, 7,300 Jews from the Reich arrived in Minsk and were sent to isolated camps near the ghetto. Most of them froze or starved to death during the next few weeks. Epidemics raged, but there were no serums. During the *Aktion* which began on July 28, 1942 and lasted for three days, 25,000 Jews, including members of the Judenrat, were killed, leaving 9–12,000. The ghetto was then turned into a work camp and progressively decimated. By July 1943, it was completely destroyed.

Approximately 175,000 of the 220,000 Jews living in Lithuania were murdered between July and November 1941. The remaining Jews were enclosed in four ghettos: Vilna (Vilnius), Kovno (Kaunas), Shavli, and Swieciany.[40] These ghettos were progressively reduced and liquidated in 1943–44. As in the other Nazi ghettos in the Soviet Union there was no communal structure available, but Jewish Councils "were formed at the time of the mass exterminations in the midst of sudden and drastic upheavals."[41] Thus the Judenrat leaders could not perceive German intentions before large numbers of Jews were murdered.

The ghettos of Vilna and Kovno were controlled by the Generalkommissariat of Lithuania, headed by Dr. Theodor von Renteln, and the chief of Security Police in Lithuania, *SS Standartenführer* Karl Jäger, former commander of *Einsatzkommando 3*, which operated in Lithuania from

July 2, 1941. In these ghettos and in Shavli, after the first mass exterminations at the end of 1941, thousands of Jews were temporarily exploited for labor. Germans in charge of military supplies were interested in preserving Jewish manpower for the war effort, but this proved only a temporary measure. Jäger, for example, wrote on December 1: "I intended to kill off these working Jews and their families, too, but met with strong protests from the civil administration *Reichskommissar*, and I received an order from the Wehrmacht prohibiting me from murdering these Jews. . . ."[42]

Inevitably their tenuous lease on life was also ended, but not before they were fooled into taking work certificates, thought to be life permits *(lebn shaynen)*.[43] Later, in the fall of 1943, the remnant was deported to camps in Estonia and Latvia where few survived. The Vilna Ghetto was liquidated in September 1943 and Kovno and Shavli in July 1944. A Jewish underground fighting organization, the *Faraynikte Partizaner Organizatsye* (FPO), had been formed in Vilna in January 1942, and in Kovno a year and a half later, but except for groups of fighters who fled to the forests, they were wiped out in ghetto fighting.[44]

It has been suggested that "one of the reasons for the establishment of the ghettos in the territory of the Soviet Union was the desire to separate the Jewish from the non-Jewish population," lest the ties which had developed between them during the period of Soviet rule bring about close friendship.[45] There were some strong personal and social relationships and aid, but subsequent evidence of Ukrainian collaboration with the Nazis and widespread passivity among the non-Jewish population (see below) make this theory only partially tenable. The ghetto was a mechanism widely and effectively used in Eastern Europe by the Nazis as a means of population control to accelerate the destructive process, when mass shootings or gassings could no longer keep pace with the sheer human volume. Moreover, in the areas annexed in the period 1939–June 1941, anti-Jewish feeling intensified and Ukrainian, Lithuanian, and Latvian movements enthusiastically supported and participated in the Nazi annihilation process.

The Ukraine was especially vulnerable to Nazi pressures and promises. Hetman Paul Skoropadzky, whom the Germans had made head of the Ukrainian state during World War I, appealed to the Ukrainians to revolt against the "Jewish Bolsheviks."[46] A new Russian daily *Ruskaya znamya* appeared in Berlin, filled with anti-Jewish caricatures and propaganda. Nazi planes threw thousands of copies over Russian villages and cities.[47] Nazi broadcasts urged the Russian people to over-throw the Soviet regime and usually ended with such slogans as "Death to the Jewish Bolshevist Oppressors of Russia!" Litvinov and Kaganov-ich, together with other Jewish Communists, were blamed for starting the war. A so-called "Free Ukrainians" movement in Berlin broadcast over the radio, inciting the people to organize anti-Jewish pogroms.[48]

Moreover, during the war, Nazi propaganda was often advanced by people inside the country. For example, Timofei Strokach, deputy min-ister of internal affairs in the Ukraine in 1939, and chief of staff of the Ukrainian partisan movement during the war, is described as attacking Jews when he was drunk and accusing them of not going to the front.[49] He also dismissed many Jews from their positions. On June 24, 1943, his aide Captain Ruzanov declared that "he always rails against the Jews" when "in the circle of his trusted associates" and drunk; "he is angry that they are not at the front or on the collective farms. . . . [He] has said that all Jews should be sent away but that it would be too obvious and cause too many disagreeable consequences."[50]

Ehrenburg spoke bitterly about this subject at the second meeting of the Jewish Antifascist Committee on February 20, 1943, in Moscow. It was a speech of biting sarcasm. "Yesterday," he began

I returned from a trip to the front areas around Kursk. . . . Kursk had been occupied for fifteen months. It is an awful thing, fifteen months of occupation, a life of confinement, a poisonous and infectious atmosphere—yet it did not affect the Jews. Only one Jew remains in Kursk. A nurse at the hospital de-clared that he was dead, and thus saved him from the Germans. The German flight from Kursk was a hasty one—so hasty that they left behind 900 fully loaded cars—and yet they found time to visit the hospital where there were some Jews sick with spotted typhus. They came in with lists of Jews, the last of the Jews of Kursk and shot them. . . .

One night in a howling snowstorm, I met a man with a long white beard. . . . He told me that he had killed 8 Germans with his own hands, and that a bomb fragment cut off two of his fingers. . . . I do not know whether he will be on the list of those receiving citations.

And then again I met a Jew of advanced age, the father of a famous pilot . . . and he told me: "I spoke with a certain civilian official who said to me: 'How do you explain the fact that there are no Jews at the front? Why doesn't one see Jews in the war?' I did not answer him because I found it hard to speak. That was only four days after I had received notice of my son's death."[51]

Such experiences made Ehrenburg all the more determined to tell the story of how Jews were fighting at the front, "not in a spirit of boastfulness, but in the name of our sole purpose today: the destruction of the Germans more rapidly and more completely." This was the impetus for his *Black Book* with "lifelike stories and pictures, a collection of Jewish heroes taking part in the fight for our native land."

In addition to appealing to Ukrainians with propaganda, the Nazis had prepared a Ukrainian anti-Soviet, anti-Jewish movement, including military divisions which were called "labor service" before the invasion. When the Germans invaded eastern Galicia in June 1941, they brought these units with them. At a congress of the Organization of Ukrainian Nationalists (OUN) which met in Cracow in April 1941, a resolution was adopted calling the Jews in the USSR "the most faithful support of the ruling Bolshevik regime," the "principal foe" of the Ukrainians.[52] Some factions had dreams of establishing an independent Ukrainian state and were disposed of by the Nazis. But the Ukrainian auxiliary police units and Bandera units (paramilitary anti-Soviet units led by Stepan Bandera), as well as thousands of Ukrainian pro-Nazi collaborators, contributed heavily to the torture and killing of Jews. "Pogroms," wrote Philip Friedman, foremost Holocaust scholar, "took place in the very first weeks of the occupation. They were mainly wild, spontaneous outbursts of the urban or rural population."[53] In several places, on their own, Ukrainians set up concentration camps for Jews. The principal collaboration with the Germans was through the Ukrainian semimilitary and police formations which convoyed transports to the death camps, seized Jews, and massacred them. The first SS Ukrainian division was organized in the spring of 1943 and by July numbered 28,000 volunteers. In 1944 it is estimated that 220,000 Ukrainians were fighting on the German side.[54] At the same time, it is important to balance this side of the ledger with accounts, albeit scantier, of some Ukrainians who helped hide and rescue Jews during the war.

In contrast to the spontaneous or incited anti-Semitism in the western Ukraine and Lithuania, neither in White Russia, nor the Ukraine east of the 1939 border, nor in the RSFSR proper did the Germans succeed in organizing pogroms. "Likewise the hounding and blackmailing of Jews (i.e. threats to hand them over to the Nazis) was not widespread."[55] In general, the population at large remained indifferent to the destruction of Jews out of fear, helplessness, or a reluctance to draw the attention of Nazis. The fear of Nazi reprisals was especially strong in paralyzing action. The shooting of innocent hostages was widespread. Yet there were times and places when help might have been offered. The resistance leader-poet Abba Kovner, in describing the destruction of the Minsk Ghetto, found a bitter lapse from the social solidarity Bolshevism had preached:

During the famine . . . children would slip out of the ghetto under the barbed wire in search of bread and potatoes. Few of the children returned. They went to their friends from school and from the club to ask for help, and they did not come back. . . . The Jews who lie buried in the mass grave of Minsk were not felled by German bullets alone. They were cut down by their faith, a faith so dearly cherished for twenty years, in the brotherhood of peoples, in the solidarity of the molders of freedom, in the new man.[56]

In his preface to the second collection of *Merder fun Felker*, published in 1945, Ehrenburg believed that he was citing "the facts which prove Soviet solidarity, the strength of the fraternity of peoples, which expressed themselves in the efforts of many Russians, White Russians, Poles, Ukrainians to rescue Jews from slaughter."[57] Yet he recorded only ten incidents, in which a total of twenty-four Jews were rescued. The Soviet journalist David Zaslavsky wrote, in the summer of 1943, that while others calmly witnessed the extermination of Jews, Soviet citizens were risking their lives to save them.[58] A quite different picture was given by Vasily Grossman, who late in 1943 toured newly liberated parts of the Ukraine as a correspondent of the daily *Krasnaya zvezda* (Red Star). He was shocked to find a "Ukraine without Jews . . . all have been slaughtered . . . in the hundreds of thousands . . . for the sole reason that they were Jews."[59] In chance encounters he was told that isolated Jews had been seen in Kharkov and Kursk. Grossman apparently planned a series of articles called "The Ukraine Without Jews," but none of this reportage was permitted to appear in *Red Star* and only two articles ("Ukrayna un idn") appeared in *Einikayt*, apparently because of Grossman's harsh criticism of the local population in this work.[60] At the same time, a Lieutenant Shlemin visited liberated Gomel in White Russia and failed to find a single Jew there or in neighboring towns. The absence of any official call to save Jews because of fear of inflaming German propaganda against "Jewish Bolshevism" and existing anti-Jewish feeling among the native population also diminished possible rescue activity.

The historian Solomon Schwarz believed that "one reason for the passivity of Soviet citizens . . . [lay] in conditions of Soviet life. For decades they had been drilled to obey government orders, to keep silent in the face of violence and brute force, to suppress all spontaneous leanings that might result in bringing political suspicion upon them. . . . Even when the atrocities committed against Jews filled them with horror and revulsion, they looked on benumbed, paralyzed."[61] Moreover, the government was itself silent in the face of the murderous intent and actions of the Nazis against Jews. No doubt, long years under Soviet rule conditioned many Soviet citizens against attracting the attention of authorities in any way. Above all, the fast tempo of the mass murder gave neither the victims nor their onlookers time for rescue activity. As has often been pointed out in Holocaust literature, the rescue of one Jew often involved several or even several dozen non-Jews, and one weak link could wreck a chain of helpers. Moreover, in many towns and villages where Jews were being massacred, Soviet civilians were suffering the same fate. Under the cover of destroying partisans, "antisocials," informers, and Bolshevik commissars, and avenging the killing of German soldiers, the Nazis murdered millions of non-Jewish Soviet civilians.

However, as elsewhere in Europe, there were instances of individual help at great risk: for example, Belorussian women cooperating with the Minsk Ghetto resistance movement; the case of the mayor of Kremenchug who provided Jews with false "Aryan" identity cards; the rescue of 400 families and some Jewish fugitives from Bukovina and Bessarabia in Yaruga on the Dniester as a result of efforts by the underground and their Ukrainian neighbors. Many others undoubtedly were helped, but much less information about such help is available from the USSR than from Poland or other parts of Eastern Europe. In the Crimea, however, the Tatars were specifically implicated in turning Jews over to the Nazis. The auxiliary police forces of indigenous Belorussians and Russians as well as Ukrainians, Lithuanians, and Latvians also often participated in the slaughter of Jews.

Witnesses have documented[62] considerable Jewish noncompliance with Nazi orders and acts of passive resistance, such as boycotting registration, the wearing of the yellow star, reporting for forced labor, and resettlement to and from ghettos. For example, three Jewish women were executed in Smolensk for refusing to wear the yellow star; 113 Jews were caught and shot in Radomyshl in August 1941 for sabotaging work in the Todt organization; 272 Jews were killed in Starodub (Bryansk region) for resisting the setting up of a ghetto. There are accounts of Jews striking policemen, preferring suicide to death at Nazi hands, and sharing the fate of other Jews instead of informing or accepting a proffered release. According to one *Einsatzgruppe* report, Jews in the USSR had acquired a sense of self-esteem and arrogance and were passively resisting German authorities.[63]

The *Einsatzgruppen* second sweep aimed at the complete obliteration of Jewish life in woods, swamps, and underground bunkers as well as towns and villages. Jewish resistance flared in Vilna, Riga, and Kovno, as well as in Tuczyn, Nieswiez and Bialystok in eastern Poland, but was easily crushed. Small groups or individuals fled to the swamps and forests, but there was never any possibility of bringing the scattered resistance efforts under a single command or strategy. Jewish guerrillas in the woods, no longer inhibited by fear of reprisals against the ghettos, were free, but they were also bitterly alone and vulnerable.

Everything in the Jewish experience during the war gave great emotional force to the creation of a separate partisan movement, but many factors—some external, some internal—made this impossible. In the Soviet Union, the destruction process gave Jews little time to organize channels of escape and resistance except in Minsk. But Minsk was quite exceptional. Most Jewish partisan efforts were foredoomed because of the extreme isolation of Jewish fighters and their exposure to peasant and partisan hatreds. The Soviet partisan movement was the one which offered the best chance of survival and the one to which most Jews in the forests were drawn by accident, luck, or absence of any other alternative. Yet "to get admitted into the ranks of a Soviet detachment was no easy job," a historian of the partisan movement has written. "There were some Russian units that did not admit Jews as a matter of policy. They justified this by saying that Jews neither knew how nor wanted to fight. The first requirement . . . was to have a weapon. Many young Jews had no way of obtaining arms and thus had no choice but to join family camps . . . accepting any Jew."[64] But sooner or later, Jews in the forests realized that without the Soviet guerrilla shield they could not survive. They were being killed not only by Nazis, but by Ukrainian, Polish, and Lithuanian bands.

Except for Minsk, there was no large exodus from the ghettos, but in 1942–43, as the eastern ghettos were being annihilated, small groups of Jews escaped to the woods in a desperate bid for survival and vengeance. The full story of these Jews who took to the forbidding wilderness against fantastic odds may never be written. Soviet sources are fragmentary, often contradictory or inaccessible, but many elements have been reconstructed and some excellent accounts are available.[65] Although the mortality was great, the Jewish partisans accomplished most in the White Russian forests, where, by the end of 1942, the Russian partisan movement had become an important strategic factor. By that time the Soviet General Staff had extended its field of operations to the partisans and molded disciplined cadres out of individual commands and stray details. The vast forests, marshes, and wastelands extended for hundreds of miles and created good retreats for fugitive war prisoners, escaped soldiers, and civilians. The 1941 scorched earth policy did not apply to the Polish-Russian border territories and a broad belt of villages was left from which partisans lived and supplied themselves. Hundreds of Jewish bands struggled to survive in these regions under great hazards and carried out important guerrilla missions. But they lost the struggle to maintain their Jewish identity and eventually, if they survived at all, had to merge with Russian units. This was a bitter reality Jews had to face—but only one of many they had to confront after the war.

The Jews of the Soviet Union were the first in Europe to be marked for complete physical destruction and their losses, after those of Polish Jewry, constitute the greatest of the Holocaust—approximately 1,400,000. Yet the Soviet regime, once the war was over, refused to permit the survivors to collectively mourn the dead. The singular catastrophe Jews felt they had suffered as Jews could not be openly acknowledged, expressed, or memorialized, but rather had to be merged with general Soviet suffering or mourned privately, even clandestinely. Added to the immense dislocations and traumas caused by the mass murder of whole communities and families was the bitterness felt by many Jews because of yet other Soviet postwar decisions that rebuffed Jewish needs and expectations.

19

Jewish War Losses, Traumas, and Ominous Signs, 1944–46

It is the duty of the Jews everywhere to support the Soviet people in their struggle for genuine peace. It is not only a question of gratitude to the power which saved the Jews of Europe from complete annihilation. It is in the vital interests of the Jews themselves, for only in the complete victory of the Soviet Union in the field of international cooperation is guaranteed the regeneration and further progress of all the Jewish people.

DAVID ZASLAVSKY

Toward the end of September in 1945, there was a haunting event in the still desolated city of Kiev, described by a Jewish writer:[1] "White, hungering people walked about the streets heaped with rubble and ashes from bomb attacks, still frightened, as if fascist killers were still loose. The streets were dark and gloomy. Gas lights were still not working. It was the first autumn after liberation. The building of the Kiev State Yiddish Theater was still standing, about to mark its 25th anniversary. For the first time in a very long while one could hear a free, elevated Yiddish word. From Moscow, from *Gosset*, the Yiddish State Theater, came a delegation headed by Mikhoels and Moyshe Goldblatt to greet the Kiev Theater Collective. Mikhoels quickly moved to the rostrum. . . . In both hands he was holding a crystal vase which cast its beams through the room, filled with people. But there were no flowers in the vase—it was filled with a yellow and black substance." "Before I came," Mikhoels began,

to greet our dear friends from Kiev . . . some friends from the Moscow Theater and I went to a store to buy this crystal vase. We then went directly to Babi Yar and filled the vase with earth, which held the screams of mothers and fathers, from the young boys and girls, who did not live to grow up, screams from all who were sent there by the fascist beasts.

Then, holding up the vase, he continued,

Look at this, you will see laces from a child's shoes, tied by little Sara who fell with her mother. Look carefully and you will see the tears of an old Jewish woman. . . . Look closely and you will see your fathers who are crying "Sh'ma Israel", and looking with beseeching eyes to heaven, hoping for an angel to rescue them. . . . Listen, and you will hear the Jews deported to the death camps singing the song, "We do not go the last way." . . . I have brought you a little earth from Babi Yar. Throw into it some of your flowers so they will grow symbolically for our people. . . . In spite of our enemies, we shall live.

The appalling truth of the scope of Jewish losses dawned slowly. Individuals returning to their homes found them empty and desolated. Even Jewish military officers such as Abram Granovsky were shocked:

Save this letter. All that is left of our beloved Yekaterinopol is this letter, some ruins, the graves of our countrymen, and the girl Sonya. Only grass grows on the spot where we grew up, studied, loved; our families are in the ground. . . . When the SS soldiers arrived, searching, looting, and pogroms began. All the Jews were herded into special camps. In Zvenigorodka there was a special camp for those incapable of work . . . the ill, women with babies, and children under . . . fourteen. . . . Everyone in the . . . camp was killed in April 1942. . . .[2]

From Izyaslavl:

. . . it would have been better if I had never been born. . . . I myself do not know who I am. Everything seems like a dream, a nightmare. Of the 8,000 residents of Izyaslavl only I and Kiva Feldman, our neighbor, are left. They are all gone. . . .[3]

In July 1944, Ruth Turkow Kaminska's troupe stumbled into evidence of the catastrophe overtaking Jews:

In the remains of the government house of Belorussia *Dom Pravitselstva*, we found German newspapers published in the area, in which executions of Jews were described and depicted in photographs. We spoke with people who had been partisans behind the German lines and had witnessed unspeakable happenings. In some villages parents had been forced to watch while the brains of their children were dashed out against the walls.[4]

For many returning survivors mere subsistence was out of reach. An appeal for relief for thousands of Jews who recently returned to their homes in the Ukraine and White Russia from the interior was issued October 1, 1944, by the president of the "Moscow Jewish Community" and by the Moscow representative of the "Russian War Relief."[5]

Decimated communities and grieving families might grasp the immensity of their personal and local losses, but the totality of the Jewish catastrophe took many months to absorb. The official government policy, with few exceptions, had been to suppress or omit reports of specific Nazi atrocities perpetrated against the Jews. When Jews were mentioned, it was generally in conjunction with other nationalities. For example, an official Soviet announcement issued in January 1942 described the Babi Yar massacre as follows: "Within a few days the German bandits killed and tortured to death 52,000 . . . dealing mercilessly with all Ukrainians, Russians and Jews, who in any way displayed their fidelity to the Soviet Government."[6] Ponary, the site of mass executions of Vilna Jews, is referred to as a "special camp . . . in the small town of Ponary, about five miles from the city," where "the mass extermination of its population"[7] was undertaken. No reference at all is made to Jews. In Molotov's note on German atrocities (one of three) issued in May 1942 to all governments which had diplomatic relations with the USSR, there was no specific reference to Jews: "They [the Nazis] utterly expose the sanguinary criminal Fascist plans aimed at the extermination of the Russian, Ukrainian, Belorussian and other peoples of the Soviet Union . . ."[8]

An unusual recognition of the very heavy losses borne by Jews was made on December 19, 1942, when it was stated that ". . . the Jewish minority of the Soviet population united with all the nationalities in the Soviet Union . . . have in proportion to their small numbers suffered especially. . . ."[9] Later, on October 2, 1943, London heard Moscow broadcast in English Alexei Tolstoy's article "I Demand Vengeance," in which he told of the bodies of 40,000 Russians crammed into a mine shaft near Stalino, and the filling of two large pits with the whole Jewish population of Kharkov—about 24,000.[10]

Further evidence of Nazi massacres of Jews came to light as the Red Army moved westward. On November 8, 1943, the Moscow radio reported that only one Jew was found alive in Kiev (which had a prewar Jewish population of 140,0000) when Russian forces re-occupied the city. Detailed reports of the massacre of an estimated 50,000 to 80,000 Jews in that city in September 1941 were submitted to the Kiev Atrocity Commission on November 29, 1943, by three Soviet soldiers who said they had been forced, as prisoners, to participate in burning the bodies to destroy all evidence. A Moscow dispatch of June 30, 1944, reported that 17,000 Jews in Brest-Litovsk had been massacred.[11]

Throughout the war, the JAC and the Yiddish press and radio in the Soviet Union and the United States reported the annihilation of Jewish communities, but such identification no longer appeared in official Soviet public communications toward the end of the war and after.

Officially, the Soviet government did not bring to public attention the Nazi horrors directed against the Jews. This position—which has prevailed to this very day—is reflected in the first collection of documents published in 1943 by the Soviet Government Commission for the Investigation of Nazi War Crimes, which was established in November 1942. In the Commission's first volume of *The Documents Accuse* (1941–43), there is only one reference to the mass murder of Jews—in the town of Kislovodsk in the northern Caucasus. In the second volume (1945), there are a few more: the annihilation of the Jewish population in the town of Zheleznovodsk, also in the northern Caucasus and another to Mariupol in the Ukraine.[12] Nor is there any reference to Jews in reports of the Extraordinary Commission for the Investigation of German Atrocities in Transnistria, of which Odessa was the chief regional center. Likewise, the commission that investigated Nazi atrocities in Kiev after the liberation of the city published its findings in *Pravda* on March 1, 1944 in a detailed report but there was no mention at all of the word "Jews." Between 1942 and 1945, the supreme political directorship of the Red Army issued fifteen pamphlets dealing with the horrors of the Nazi conquest, and here, too, Jews are not mentioned specifically; victims are referred to as "peaceful Soviet citizens."[13] There were, however, in the field of belles-lettres, during the war, a number of non-Jewish writers who touched on the Jewish theme, including K. Simonov, M. Sholokhov, A. Korneichuk, L. Uspensky, A. Kalinin, and V. Gerasimova; and in the field of poetry, A. Surkov, M. Tank, M. Rylsky, and P. Tychyna. After the war, there were more non-Jewish writers who dealt with the fate of Jews during the Holocaust and the attitude of the local populations, conveying a mixture of images about Jews and their behavior.[14]

After 1945, there was no further published official documentation of German atrocities in Russian until 1963, mostly consisting of German documents. Only four of the forty-six documents deal specifically with Jewish losses. One mentions the destruction of Jews at Babi Yar, and another includes the well-known map attached to the report of *Einsatzgruppe A* reporting the slaughter of Jews in Belorussia and the Baltic states.[15] In March 1965, *Yad Vashem*, the Holocaust archival center in

19.1 Vilna partisan fighters on the first day of the liberation of the ghetto.
S. Kaczerginski, *Khurbn Vilne*, 1947.

Jerusalem, requested documents in the Soviet Government Archives
dealing with the fate of Soviet Jews, but the reply on May 8 was that
the archives "relating to the crimes of German Fascism in World War
II are not organized according to the nationality of the victims."[16]

The submergence of Jewish identity in partisan units was also a bitter experience for Jews. The Soviet partisan movement was the largest
in Europe, numbering about a million and a half fighters at its strongest. It held strategic positions behind enemy lines and operated close
to the Eastern front where some of the most decisive battles of World
War II were fought. Moreover, it was active in those areas where large
Jewish communities had existed for many generations—the Ukraine,
White Russia, Lithuania, and eastern Poland. Although Soviet policy
officially fostered the formation of antifascist Lithuanian, Ukrainian,
White Russian, and other national units, it opposed the existence of
separate Jewish partisan units after 1943, such as those of Dr. Ezekiel
Atlas, the Bielski family camp, the "Kadima" group from the Bialystok
Ghetto, and the "Nekomah" (Vengeance) unit from the Vilna Ghetto
(see Photo 19.1).

The losing struggle to maintain Jewish identity in military units can
be illustrated by several examples. In Lithuania, more than 1,000 Jews
left the ghettos in the latter half of 1943 and concentrated in two areas:

The Rudniki forest, about 30 miles from Vilna, and east of the city in the forests of Belorussia. One group[17] from the Vilna Ghetto was headed by Josef Glazman, one of the founders of the Vilna FPO and for a time chief of the ghetto police. They joined a group of young people from Swieciany in the Naroch woods and joined the Jewish partisan unit numbering about fifty called "Vengeance." Glazman's hope was to form a large Jewish unit, heartened by the commander of a Belorussian partisan brigade who had urged the Jews to fight to "avenge the blood of brothers which had been spilt." "Vengeance" grew to 250 Jews by September 1943. The unit participated in operations of the Voroshilov brigade as a unit and functioned for seven weeks. It was then disbanded by order of Klimov, the highest Communist party authority in the Naroch area. He objected in principle to the existence of a separate Jewish unit, since, it was said, "the Soviet partisan movement was organized on the territorial basis of Soviet Republics and not on the basis of nationalities." Anti-Jewish feeling is also thought to have been a factor in the decision. Another element was revealed when the brigade commander Martov explained that there were people in the unit who bore arms but had no training or experience in using them, that he had to see to it that weapons were in the hands of people who knew how to use them. Weapons were then taken from most of the Jews and the few left with some arms were transferred to the Komsomolski company, but its commander refused to take them along. They were ordered to evacuate a partisan hospital nearby to a safe place in the swamps and then leave. A number, including Glazman, fell during the great German blockade of the Naroch woods.

The dissolution of "Vengeance" was not done on local initiative, but on orders from Moscow. Other Jewish units were dissolved in the fall of 1943: the unit named after Kaganovich in the Disna region, the Zhukov unit in the Kopyl region, and the Parkhomenko unit in the Minsk region, among others.

Another fighting group of about 400 Jews from the Vilna Ghetto underground under Abba Kovner, the poet who later emigrated to Israel, also tried to maintain its identity in the woods, but were told they could not form a separate unit, that "all citizens of the Lithuanian republic had to fight together," regardless of ethnic origin or religion. This time the unit was not dissolved but Russians and Lithuanians were added and Jewish commanders were replaced by Lithuanians. A document brought to Israel after the war discloses that one of the units called "Borba" (Struggle) was actually commanded by a Jew, Israel Veselnitsky, who was identified nevertheless as a Ukrainian named Vasilenko. The document also reveals that of the non-Jewish fighters, most were escaped Russian prisoners of war and recent arrivals who were given top positions.

Anti-Semitism was commonly encountered by Jews in partisan ranks, especially in the western parts of the Ukraine and Belorussia. They were often treated with suspicion and distrust; many accounts attest to discrimination in the distribution of weapons and the removal of Jewish commanders by non-Jews.[18] Jews are also known to have been executed by some commanders upon the slightest pretext, and to have been returned to the Germans after having escaped from them.[19] The Ukrainian and Belorussian partisan movements were "highly publicized" in the Soviet press,[20] but there was virtually no mention of Jewish participation except in *Einikayt* and occasionally in works of fiction.

In 1948, just before the assault on Jewish culture, a book appeared in Russian under the title *Partizanskaya druzhba* (Partisan Brotherhood), containing materials compiled by the JAC together with the editors of Der Emes Publishing House. The book "was addressed to a non-Jewish audience in order to remind the Russian people that Jews were active in the resistance and often the prime organizers of underground anti-Nazi activity." The work contains numerous firsthand accounts of Jewish partisan initiatives in the forests of Bryansk, in Latvia, White Russia, and in the ghettos of Minsk and Kovno, and the city of Odessa; the characteristics of partisan society and partisan warfare and the role of women and film makers. It was compiled with the help of Feffer and Mikhoels and may have been the last substantive volume published by the JAC. The Russian edition appeared only briefly and then was taken off the market. It was subsequently translated into Hebrew and English.[21]

A particularly cynical use of Jewish national feeling in an armed unit is to be found in the story[22] of the so-called "Lithuanian Division," and illuminates the briefly camouflaged Soviet line. In late 1941, a Soviet Lithuanian force was established within the Red Army. When the divisional standard was planted at Balakhana on the Volga, Jews volunteered by the thousands, including some who had been deported.

This unit is of unusual interest because about 45–50 percent of the fighters were Jews and because Soviet officials at first quite deliberately indulged the Jewish cast of the unit.[23] Stalin had to try very hard to convince the world and Lithuanians particularly that the nation was "genuinely involved in the war against the Germans and that it was fighting for a Soviet Lithuania." The "Jewish division adorned with some Lithuanians," as it came to be called, was a strained effort in that direction. Soviet bending of ideological rigor was, in this case, extreme. The divisional command not only tolerated Yiddish among the soldiers, but since many middle and lower rank officers were Jewish, orders were also given in Yiddish. Yiddish was used in recruitment. Public prayers were likewise permitted and evening entertainment was offered in both Hebrew and Yiddish, often ending with the hora dance. Before an action, the command organized meetings for political officers and soldiers in Yiddish, stressing the strong Jewish need to avenge Nazi murderous crimes against the Jewish people. Jews were even exempt from duties during religious holidays. The command also encouraged correspondence abroad, especially in May 1942 during the Soviet drive to open a second front. The soldiers were asked to write to relatives in America, Britain, and Palestine and to stress the necessity of a second front. The Soviet embassy in the United States assisted in locating addresses. For Jewish soldiers, this outreach had a particular significance as it widened in the direction of Palestine. Calendars, stamps, and postcards in Hebrew were cherished. "There was a certain symbolism in the letters and food parcels from abroad which were of acute interest to the Jewish soldiers, to the annoyance of the Party functionaries."

But the Jewish milieu was not disturbed. A Jewish private has recalled a rally at Tolstoy's village of Yasnaya Polyana when Jews from the 249th regiment gathered in a large clubroom: "The head of the political section spoke in Russian, but Yiddish was also used. . . . I recited Itzik Feffer's poem, 'The Vow.' The rally was designed to encourage us, to remind us of the war and our part in it. Then it dawned on us: they had arranged the whole thing just for our benefit." There were also visits with the JAC in Moscow and Jewish soldiers in other units at the front and brief painful moments with Jewish survivors of decimated towns and villages.

The proportion of Orthodox Jews in the division was quite high and except at the front, Shabbat and the high holidays were strictly observed. The relaxation of Soviet antireligious policy was reflected in the attitude of some non-Jewish officers. A Russian company commander, for example, gave one of his men, a yeshiva student, time to pray twice daily, believing his prayers would "help kill Germans." Another soldier from a yeshiva in Kovno was given special rations for his Kol Nidre eve pre-fast meal.

At first the men were slow to adapt to the rigors of training, but "in battle," a tough combat officer recalled, "I couldn't get them to take cover." Their first action came in February, 1943. A bitter blizzard covered the steppes as the 12,000-man unit was ordered to move out of its base near Bryansk. Artillery, field kitchens, mobile hospitals, and ammunition wagons sank into the snow. For five days the men slogged on until they reached the village of Alekseyevka near Orel as the Arctic winds howled. The Germans exacted great losses; more than 2,000 Jewish soldiers perished in the strategically important Battle of Orel.

In later engagements the unit fought with almost foolhardy bravery, distinguishing itself especially in the capture of Klaipeda (formerly Memel) in 1944. In twenty-eight months of combat, many decorations were won by Jews, including four prestigious awards as Hero of the Soviet Union, one to a woman medical officer Rosa Debletov, who was killed in action.

The Israeli artist Alexander Bogen, who succeeded in fleeing Vilna with the Red Army and was sent to organize partisans in White Russia, has recalled[24] with bitterness the matter of decorations. He lived in the forests for two years and made many drawings on the run, which he buried near Lake Naroch. He came to know at first hand about the exploits of the Lithuanian brigade which "opened the front to strategic German lines" in 1943 at Orel. Although many in the brigade were Jewish, Bogen recalled, "whenever a famous hero was eulogized at funerals he was always identified as Russian or Lithuanian." The names of the Jewish fighters were concealed and Lithuanian nicknames were given to Jewish parachutists and partisans. Later, when awards were made in the division, although Jews predominated, a strict quota of medals was maintained: one-third each to Jews, Lithuanians, and Russians.

There were some experiences of comradeship between Jews and non-Jews in the division, but for the most part the men lived in separate worlds. Relations between them became particularly tense when the unit re-entered Lithuania in the summer of 1944. The open hostility toward Jews of the liberated Lithuanians and the anguish of homecoming to a country empty of Jews drove some to acts of personal revenge. "The streets of the town didn't greet me," one survivor wrote. "Silently, I walked step after step, one hand on my heart, the other on my revolver—a queer feeling. Empty sidewalks, empty roads, hostile houses, not a single Jew, not even a half-Jew."[25] Others told of finding last wills of their families in the Kovno and Vilna ghettos, of visits to mass graves.

The returning Jewish soldiers are described as shocked and traumatized, exhibiting a desire to fight at extreme personal risk; behaving aggressively toward German prisoners; expressing hatred toward the local population and everything connected with Lithuania. There were also "mass outbreaks of depression, withdrawal, and hysteria"[26] among the Jewish soldiers, which threatened to damage the political image of the division and harm its own morale. The Soviet command thereupon tried to stress the German, as distinct from the Lithuanian, role in the atrocities, to re-direct informational meetings and attempt to eliminate factors which deepened depression, even to the extent of banning a lullaby about the murder of Jews in Ponary, called "Shtiller, shtiller" (Softly, softly), which had been sung in the Vilna Ghetto.

There are similarities between Soviet attitudes to partisan warfare waged by Lithuanian Jews and Soviet policies in the Lithuanian Division. During early stages of partisan activity, Soviet authorities "tended to accept . . . some national traits in those units composed of Jews."[27] However, when the Soviet-oriented partisan movement grew stronger, concessions to Jewish nationalism decreased. Four Jewish partisan battalions established in the fall of 1943 lost their explicit Jewish character in early 1944, when Jewish commanding personnel were replaced and non-Jewish partisans were increasingly assigned to them.

Except for articles in *Einikayt* and *Krasnaya zvezda* (Red Star), there was also a general silence about Jews serving in the Red Army. The central press almost never mentioned the Jewish nationality of the combatants and since many Soviet Jews carry typically Slavic first and surnames, it was impossible for the general reader to establish the full contribution of Jews to the war effort.[28] In a statement issued on the twenty-seventh anniversary of the October Revolution in 1944, the JAC expressed Soviet Jewry's pride in the fact that Jews held fourth place among the heroes of the various nationalities decorated for bravery on the battlefront by the Red Army. Outstanding deeds of heroism by

Jews figured prominently in reports of the battles of Orel, Bryansk, Smolensk, and Kremenchug. Among the many awards for gallantry were several given to Jewish guerrilla fighters. But Jews had to deter-mine this information themselves. The marked absence of official iden-tification of Jewish heroes and soldiers during the war was a cruel real-ity made more painful by the fact that non-Jews were identified by their nationality. In the official Soviet history of the war, Jews are not identified as such, but the Soviet Jewish statistician Yakov Kantor esti-mated that nearly half a million Jews served in the Soviet armed forces and that there was a high proportion of officers among them who dis-tinguished themselves in many important engagements.[29] He also es-timated that about 20,000 Jews fought in the second half of 1943 in Soviet, Polish, and independent Jewish partisan units in Belorussia, Lithuania, Volyn, and parts of Poland.[30] In *Einikayt* of January 24, 1945, there was an acknowledgment that 63,374 Jews had been decorated with orders and medals for "courage and heroism in battles against German usurpers," and that fifty-nine Jews had received the title, "Hero of the Soviet Union," but Kantor's figures are more than double these (123).[31]

The JAC sent a great deal of material to Jewish newspapers and periodicals in many countries and *Sovetish heymland*, a Yiddish journal that was started in 1961, occasionally published material dealing with the war record of Soviet Jewry. The most authoritative compilation and analysis was made by Kantor and published in the Warsaw *Folkshtimme* on April 18, 1963. More excerpts were promised by the newspaper, but Kantor died in Moscow in September 1964. Further material of his was published posthumously in the issues of May 5, 6, and 8, 1965. In the April 18 issue, Kantor had asked, "How extensive was the part played by Jews in the Soviet Army?" Their part, he concluded, was important both qualitatively and quantitatively:

Jews know that their participation was great not only because it is almost im-possible to find a Soviet-Jewish family that had not had somebody in the armed forces, but because it is equally difficult to meet a Jewish family that has not had a member killed or wounded on active service. There are some among non-Jews who think that we did not participate sufficiently in the armed forces. This view stems from the fact that however massive our participation, we Jews represented such a small percentage of the great Soviet Army that in many units there were no Jews at all, while in many others our presence, within six months of the invasion, was hardly noticeable.[32]

In fact, there were only two million Jews (as against 100 million Russians and 27 million Ukrainians) left from whom to supply the armed forces, about 650,000 of them men, of whom about 65 percent were of working age. Of the half a million Jews who fought in the Soviet armed forces, about 200,000 were killed in action.[33] Another million and a half Soviet Jews were murdered or died of starvation, disease, and torture at the hands of the Nazis, yet scarcely any official acknowledgment of this immense suffering was made at the end of the war or later.

As was true before the war, so during the war the Soviet government at no time acknowledged the declared purpose of the Nazis to destroy the Jews in Europe. No political offensive was ever launched within the Soviet Union in support of its Jews and no military action was ever taken to protect the densely populated Jewish centers.[34]

However, from time to time, specific Nazi actions against Jews were dramatized for public consumption in Britain and the United States where it was thought Jews carried political weight. Much, too, was made for the Allied public of help rendered Jews by non-Jewish neighbors. In these efforts, Ilya Ehrenburg and David Zaslavsky, Soviet Jewish writers and journalists, were particularly useful.[35]

An immense Soviet documentation of Nazi crimes against Jews was actually collected officially, but, with few exceptions, was either not made public, or confined to Yiddish readers. For example, there are extensive eyewitness accounts in *The Black Book*,[36] published in the United States in 1946, based on the work of the Soviet Extraordinary State Committee for the Ascertaining and Investigation of Crimes Committed by the German Fascist Invaders and Their Associates, and Damage Caused by Them to Citizens, Collective Farms . . . and Institutions of the USSR. (Many of the excerpts are also based on materials collected from the Russian text of *The Black Book*, although the source is not credited, except for some notes that mention the names of Ehrenburg, Sutzkever, and a few others.[37]) The State Committee collected extensive reports on the "monstrous inventiveness" of the Nazis at Auschwitz, after the camp was liberated, as a result of testimony given by survivors in December 1944 and early 1945. In December 1944, there was testimony on the atrocities in Lvov and the Janowska camp, with references to the slaughter of Jews. There was also detailed testimony from Kaunas (Kovno), described as "one of the most monstrous Jewish mass graves in Eastern Europe." Minutes of the Shaval Judenrat were found and turned over to the Soviet Extraordinary State Committee. In the Village of Tatarsk, an old farming community in the Mogilev district, Major M. Rabinovich, in the Red Army took testimony from non-Jews and presented it to the State Committee. Six hundred Jews who lived in Tatarsk in the Jewish kolkhoz Trudovik perished, together with their schools, hospital, synagogue, and livestock. Children were flogged to death with iron rods. Scenes of unspeakable torture were recorded.[38]

The Soviet State Committee also took testimony on the rounding up of Jews in Krasny, Shamovo, and Monastyrshchina, the ghettoization and destruction of Jews in Grodno, mass executions in Rogachev and Jasichi, Pinsk, Samara, Rovno, Khmelnik, Baranovka, the mass burning of the Jews of Priluki in a wooden pavilion, the mass burning of the Jews of Berdichev in a synagogue, and the slaughter of 56,000 Jews of Kiev at a ravine near Dornitza.[39] In the Golasayev woods, an eyewitness saw the woods "brightly lit with huge bonfires. We saw sumptuous set tables . . . where officers sat in parade uniforms. Near the bonfires were many small children trembling with fear. . . . I heard one German officer explain to the soldiers how the game was to be played. From a distance of twelve meters, they were to toss the children in such a manner that their heads would strike the trunk of the tree. For every cracked skull they would receive a glass of schnapps."[40]

Eyewitness accounts of mass shootings of the Jews of Kharkov were also submitted to the Soviet State Committee. In December 1941, Jews were moved from the city into barracks, an eighteen-kilometer march:

Old people, women, children went in streams; they went into the frost and blizzard, dragging along bundles, sleds; falling from exhaustion and fear. In desolate alleys, in empty lots German soldiers fell upon them, beat them, undressed them. . . . The snow turned brown with blood. . . . [In the barracks] . . . the Gestapo searched out the children and smeared their lips with some kind of liquid. Shortly after, the barracks resounded with dreadful cries. The children were in agony, threw themselves on the earthen floor. In the morning, mountains of children's bodies were loaded onto wagons. . . . In January the German command ordered all prisoners to be sent to work . . . [but] no cars arrived. Instead, a new detachment of armed soldiers brought grenades and machine guns. . . . All adults were mowed down with machine guns; the youngsters were killed with hand grenades."[41]

Similar depositions were taken by military authorities, the JAC, and Ilya Ehrenburg. Various acts of resistance in the ghettos and in partisan bands were also described.[42] But it was mainly in *Einikayt* and in belles-lettres that the Holocaust and the Jewish victimization in the Soviet

Union were revealed. As the Red Army moved westward and liberated cities, towns, and camps, there were numerous reports from the JAC revealing the stark numbers of Jews massacred during the war and the scant number of survivors in Maidanek, Treblinka, Lublin, Auschwitz, Lodz, and Transnistria. However, these reports generally did not appear in the Soviet press but were chiefly for foreign consumption.

In the first months following the German invasion of the Soviet Union, virtually all publishing houses in the country came under German control; Der Emes Publishing House was moved to Kuibyshev (until early 1943) and could not publish anything because of the lack of Hebrew type. Moreover, many of the Yiddish writers in Moscow had fled or were in the Red Army. In 1943, Yiddish publishing was resumed in Moscow and Yiddish readers could read such works as Der Nister's *Korbones* (Victims), Feffer's *Milkhome balades* (War Ballads), Polyanker's *Nekome* (Vengeance) and Markish's *Far folk un heymland* (For the People and Homeland) and an anthology he edited called *Heymland*. R. Rubin also wrote about the heroism of Jewish women during the war in *Yidishe froyen* (Jewish Women).[43] In 1944, some of Ehrenburg's material for the *Black Book* was published in a sixty-four-page pamphlet called *Merder fun felker* (Murderers of Peoples), as were stories by Shmuel Persov and sketches of Jewish partisans in Yiddish by Noah Lurie.

For Russian-language readers, two works by Vasily Grossman, published in 1942, dealt with the fate of Jews during the war: *Narod bessmerten* (The People are Immortal) and *Stary uchitel* (The Old Teacher) translated into Yiddish in 1943 and published in *Heymland*. Grossman, according to Pinkus, "was among the first to describe the relations between the Jews and the local population under the Nazi occupation. He attempted to make a clear distinction between the majority of the local population, who took no part in the destruction of the Jews, and a minority of nationalists, careerists, and deserters, who collaborated with the enemy."[44] Grossman also was the first writer to document the mass gassings of Jews at Treblinka in his *Treblinker gehenem* (The Hell of Treblinka), first published in Russian in 1942, which Der Emes Publishing House published in 1945. In the same year, it also published a second collection of Ehrenburg's *Merder fun felker* and an account of Jewish resistance in the Lvov ghetto by E. Sommer. After the war, however, there were ominous signs of a fundamental policy reversal affecting Jews.

The signs could not be clearly read at first. All Yiddish publishing houses except those in Moscow were closed down, but Der Emes House was permitted to continue, and there was a literary anthology published in Minsk and three issues of the literary almanac *Birobidzhan* in Birobidzhan. Yiddish writers petitioned to have Yiddish pre-war cultural activities resumed, but after Zhdanov's speech of August 1946 (see Chapter 20) condemning "rootless cosmopolitans," the signs became much clearer. Shmeruk counted seventeen items published by Der Emes Publishing House in 1946, several of which deal with Holocaust themes: A. Petchorsky's *Der ufshtand in Sobibor*, Smoliar's *Fun minsker geto*, Sutzkever's *Fun Vilner geto*, and S. Verite's *Ven di erd brent*,[45] several of which fell under attack following Zhdanov's speech.

Earlier there had been much eagerness over a joint publishing project involving Soviet Jewry, American Jewry, and Palestine to document the Holocaust in the Soviet Union and the exploits of Jews in the armed services and partisan groups. An arrangement was made with the JAC involving Ilya Ehrenburg[46] to set up a joint committee that would ultimately publish a *Black Book* simultaneously in each country, but the project on the Soviet side was aborted suddenly (see Chapter 20).

This documentation preoccupied Ehrenburg, a man whose Jewishness had been virtually extinguished and whose career as a popular journalist and novelist living outside the Soviet Union until the war scarcely seemed to anticipate such a deeply felt involvement. Controversial and enigmatic though he may have been, with a talent for improvising and surviving, his core experience of anti-Semitism which agitated his childhood never fully left him and flared openly during the war. The world "Jew" had meant and continued to mean that "I belong to those whom it is proper to persecute," as he once expressed it. He was sickened by the Nazi-Soviet Pact and spreading anti-Semitism in the Soviet Union during the war. The Nazi invasion of Russia finally fused his and his country's rage against Nazism.

During the war, he was one of the most popular journalists in the Soviet Union, writing principally in the military organ *Red Star*. In these articles, he explicitly referred to the annihilation of Jews in such cities as Pinsk, Mozyr, Rostov, and Stavropol. Jewish soldiers confirmed the popularity of Ehrenburg's accounts during the war. Officers would sometimes read the accounts aloud. Often soldiers would write to him for advice on personal problems. They also brought him diaries, songs, photographs, and documents they found in the shattered towns and cities where Jews had been murdered. Many individuals have testified to Ehrenburg's obsessive immersion in the catastrophe overtaking Soviet Jewry during the war, which affected him deeply and which led to his and Vasily Grossman's labored collection of eyewitness reports of Nazi atrocities and Jewish resistance. These documents were to have been published in the Soviet Union in the form of a *Red Book* and a *Black Book*.

The poet Abraham Sutzkever, who was in Vilna (Vilnius) during the Nazi occupation and escaped to fight with partisans, met Ehrenburg after the Russians liberated the city and they became close friends. Later, after the war, they were often together in Moscow where Sutzkever saw at first hand the generous help Ehrenburg extended to many young Jews, especially in finding housing for them. He also adopted a twelve-year-old child from Pinsk whose parents had been killed. He sent thousands of roubles to needy people he never saw, and answered an enormous quantity of mail. He also wrote to Khrushchev, appealing to him to provide a mass grave for Jews from Kiev who were killed at Babi Yar, but was told not to mix into such things. According to Sutzkever, Ehrenburg was also interested in the poetry of the great Hebrew poet Elisha Rodin, who had been imprisoned by the Soviet regime, and helped in the publication of his poetry in Israel. An astonishing number of letters,[47] messages, and scraps of testimony from the war zones and destroyed ghettos continued to be sent to him, some of them on cigarette paper and scraps of canvas.

During the war, he collected an immense quantity of material documenting the annihilation of Soviet Jews mainly, but of others, too. In the collection was a work in Greek on the tragedy of Greek Jewry, a long poem written in French on cigarette paper, a drama written in Hebrew, diaries of Jewish children who found refuge in churches, and Yiddish verse. The material was collected in three massive albums which Ehrenburg "dreamed about" giving to the Hebrew University.[48] But in Vilna, when he visited the Jewish Museum in 1947, he left the albums there on condition that should the museum be closed, they should be returned to him.[49] Indeed, when the museum was liquidated, the material was returned to him (see Photo 19.2).

By the beginning of 1943, he visualized a plan for the publication of three books: the first would deal with the destruction of Jews in Soviet territory (which later provided the basis for *The Black Book*); the second, proposed at the JAC plenum in March 1943, was to be a collection of accounts of Jewish heroism during the war *(The Red Book)*; and the third was to be dedicated to Jewish partisans *(The Yellow Book)*.

19.2 Artifacts and statuary saved in Jewish hideouts in Vilna—one form of resistance of the Jewish Museum during the Nazi occupation. In the background is Shmeruk Kaczerginski, the director of the Museum. *Khurbn Vilne, 1947.*

In order to implement his plan, a literary commission was established which had as its first priority the first book. In this work Vasily Grossman took an active role. A number of Jewish and non-Jewish writers and journalists, who had material from survivors, were co-opted, including Vsevolod Ivanov, Pavel Antokolsky, Lev Ozerov, and the poets Margarita Aliger, Vera Inber, Veniamin Kaverin, Lidia Seyfulin, Markish, Kvitko, and Vasily Ilyenkov. Ehrenburg later recalled: "Not a little time, strength, and heart did I give to the work on *The Black Book*. Often, reading a diary . . . or listening to an account of an eyewitness, I imagined I was in the ghetto, that there would be an 'action' today, or I am being driven to a valley or a pit."[50] For the preparation of *The Black Book*, some forty writers and journalists were involved, including some who eventually emigrated to Israel: Sutzkever, Hirsh Smoliar, Meir Yellin, and Hersh Osherovich. Ehrenburg edited at least one-third of the whole work, putting "his whole soul into it." He characterized the material in the following way: "This is not literature. These are actual unembellished accounts. Some facts which might seem insignificant have tremendous meaning because they confirm the reality of an intense Jewish pride—how unarmed Jews were able to show so much resistance to the Nazis, and how bravely they met their death."[51]

In most of both parts of *Merder fun felker*, Ehrenburg documented Nazi crimes through the interrogation of a number of German officers taken prisoner. His first words to them were: "I am a Jew." Among the letters removed from murdered Jews were often found the words: "Don't forget."

Ehrenburg compiled one more collection in Russian and French called *One Hundred Letters*. A French edition *(Cent Lettres)* appeared in Moscow in 1944, but publication of the Russian original was stopped.[52] In the course of the year, Ehrenburg also intended to issue the projected *Red Book*, dealing with the participation of Jews in the Great Patriotic War. During the summer, Sovinform asked him to write a proclamation to American Jews about Nazi savagery, showing the need for a quick victory over the Nazis, but General A.S. Shcherbakov rejected the manuscript saying, "It wasn't necessary to mention Jewish soldiers in the Red Army as heroes. That's bragging."[53] The *Red Book* was never published.

The work on the *Black Book* continued until 1946 during which many translations were planned, several of which were completed.[54] Meanwhile, a blunt decision had been made. At the height of the work of writers, editors, and translators, Lozovsky of Sovinform instructed Ehrenburg to turn over the entire project to the JAC, apparently on Stalin's orders. Work continued for several years as the contributors puzzled over delays, but the book never appeared in the Soviet Union. Such a work would have done much to create a balanced record of Jewish experiences during the war[55]—resistance, victimization, evidence to offset the ugly attacks on Jews as cowards and shirkers—but the Soviet edition never materialized.

The war transformed Soviet Jewry. The Nazi murder of one-and-a-half million Soviet Jews brought losses to virtually every Soviet Jewish family and aroused intense Jewish feelings even among the most assimilated. The evidence of rampant European anti-Semitism and the singular victimization of Jews during the Holocaust drew all survivors into a Jewish brotherhood of fate, yet within the Soviet Union itself, many Jews found themselves unwanted. Not only did they have to absorb the shocking immensity of their losses, but also the added bitterness of anti-Semitism which had spread and clung as a result of the Nazi occupation and indoctrination and earlier residues of Soviet anti-Semitism. There was great relief and gratitude for the Red Army's titanic victory over Nazism, which, they were led to believe, had alone defeated the German war machine, with minor help from the Allies, but their immediate adjustments were enormous.

The torment of Soviet anti-Semitism was experienced during and after the war not only by civilians, but by Jewish soldiers in the Red Army and in partisan units. Some Soviet Jewish war prisoners had been handed over to the Germans. Moreover, a number of Soviet high-ranking officers publicly expressed their anti-Jewish prejudices, and Jews who fled to the forests often found hostile attitudes among Russian partisans and their leaders.[56] Yekhiel Granatsztein and Shmerel Kaczerginski, Jewish partisans in Nazi-occupied Poland, testified to anti-Semitism in the Red Army,[57] especially among the Politruks, the political orientation officers. After fleeing the Vilna Ghetto, Kaczerginski reported for service to the Voroshilov Brigade commanded by a Moscow-trained Lithuanian Communist, but was turned away because he had no arms, although many Ukrainians who had collaborated with the Nazis and also had no arms were accepted unconditionally.[58] Granatsztein was accepted by the All-Soviet 66th Group, but saw other Jews with arms not only denied, but turned away after their arms were seized.

The Nazis had taunted the Ukrainians over the presumed priority given Jews in the evacuations, comparing their "comfortable" life in distant Uzbekistan with the hardships of life in the Ukraine. After the war, Ukrainians resented Jews returning to their homes and wanting possession of their property. Quite typical was the experience of a survivor from Kharkov who managed to make his way to Palestine in January 1945. He had briefly returned to the city at the end of 1944 and wrote:

The Ukrainians received the returning Jews with open animosity. During the first weeks after the liberation of Kharkov, no Jew ventured about alone in the streets at night. The position improved only after the intervention of the authorities, who reinforced the police patrols in the town. In many cases Jews were beaten in the market place. . . . In Kiev 16 Jews were killed in the course of a pogrom which took place after the murder of a Russian officer by a Christian woman who was believed to be a Jewess.[59]

A letter[60] from the British Plenipotentiary to Moscow, John Balfour, to the British Foreign Office, dated March 17, 1944, notes that "anti-Semitism in the Soviet Union is on the upward grade," though "is unlikely to become a serious problem," because of damage to Soviet international prestige and the need for all "able-bodied Jews no less than other citizens" to play their part in the arduous work of reconstruction. Samuil Chobrutsky, president of the Moscow Synagogue Board, observed privately to a British visitor to the Moscow Central Synagogue that "no Jews of any consequence had been readmitted to the reconquered territories" on the pretext that the Germans had sown the seeds of anti-Semitism and that Jews were apt to be "squeezed out of their appointments in State institutions and replaced by non-Jews." He also observed that the term "Yid," which had been banned after the Revolution, was again coming into use. Another official, a British military attaché in Moscow, believed that "anti-Semitic feeling is indeed widespread among the masses, [but] . . . that the official attitude toward Jewry is entirely favorable and corresponds with that shown towards the Orthodox Church and the Moslem religion. . . ."[61]

Officially, however, the noticeable avoidance of Jewish themes in Soviet literature indicated that the regime "did not want to deal decisively with the question of wartime anti-Semitism in the USSR."[62] Stalin never took a definite position against Nazi anti-Jewish propaganda or mass murder. Although it cannot be verified, there is a widely held belief that Mikhoels, aware of the massive scale of Jewish losses and deeply alarmed by the mounting anti-Semitism, broached the subject to him at a reception in mid-1944, to which representatives of the JAC were invited. Mikhoels is said to have appealed to Stalin to stamp out anti-Semitic manifestations, but, according to the report,[63] Stalin's reply was disappointing. He said that anti-Semitism was a kind of "time-flow" that could not be arrested at once. The implication, it seems, was that it was a phenomenon that would persist. The government contributed to anti-Jewish feeling by refusing to identify Jewish heroism as well as losses. This deliberate omission helped "support rumors that Jews were ensconced in secure and cushioned jobs far behind the front."[64]

In many cases, the loss of former apartments and jobs and the disappointment in not having any acknowledgment of the Jewish contribution to the war effort were added bitter realities. Returning Jewish soldiers and their families are known to have been given squalid basements after their return.

In the vast uprooting and dislocations after the war, the sense of homelessness was keenly felt, and some Jews hoped for a solution in the Crimea, but these hopes, too, were not only thwarted but warped by Stalin into a heinous crime (see Chapter 20). On May 9, the anniversary of the German surrender, year after year, various ethnic groups were hailed for their sacrifice—Ukrainian, Georgian, Uzbeck, Lithuanian. But Jewish soldiers and airmen were never mentioned. Waiting, listening to radios and later television sets, they sat stupefied, enraged and sometimes broke down in their embitterment. For some, this frustration became the goad that prompted the decision to leave the Soviet Union.[65]

For many Jews, even returning soldiers searching for work, there was noticeable hostility. The defector Igor Gouzenko revealed that in the summer of 1945, he was told by the chief of the "secret division of Soviet Intelligence" that the Central Committee had sent "confidential" instructions to directors of all factories to remove Jews from responsible positions.[66] The noticeable decrease in the number of Jews in high positions in the party, government, and army, which had been evident before the war, was still more conspicuous after the war. Discrimination also sharpened in universities, and the number of Jewish external (correspondence) students—which before 1940 was a virtually non-existent category—increased sharply after the war.[67] Moreover, all other major national groups could and did "give preference to their own nationality in universities located in their own national republican territories," but Jews had none (see Chapters 25 and 26 for further examples of economic discrimination in the early 1950s).

There were other keenly felt disappointments. Having experienced so many favorable signs during the war, Soviet Jews looked forward to continued official support of Jewish cultural activity after the war. But there were discouraging, even shocked rejections of appeals, one after another. A number of these appeals were made by Kaczerginski, who was in close contact with the leaders of the JAC in 1944 and 1945. He was not naive, but full of hope that Moscow would favor Jewish cultural reconstruction after the Red Army re-occupied Vilnius. He spoke to Lozovsky and other JAC officials and writers, but soon concluded that the main function of the JAC was foreign propaganda and that it could not do any work inside the Soviet Union or have local offices. He also quoted Ilya Ehrenburg who told him gloomily, "This is not a Jewish but an anti-Jewish committee."[68] In an effort to revive the Yiddish press, Kaczerginski approached Soviet-appointed Lithuanian officials, but was rebuffed. Again, in 1945, he went to Moscow to obtain permission "to issue at least one daily newspaper and one Yiddish monthly for the Jews of Russia," but without success. Feffer and Mikhoels interceded with Politburo member Lazar Kaganovich to get a favorable decision and Kaganovich promised "to take the matter up with Zhdanov," but nothing came of it. Kaczerginski did succeed in establishing a Yiddish-language school up to the third grade in Vilnius. However, all efforts to create higher grades failed, including an appeal to Kaganovich and the Central Committee of the party in Moscow. Kaczerginski was told that there was no need for a full-fledged Yiddish school since Jewish children could enter Russian or Lithuanian schools. The grade school was soon closed altogether.

For a few years after the war, there were also Yiddish classes for elementary school children (grades one to four) in Kaunas and Chernovtsy, where there had been strong and vibrant Yiddish-speaking communities, but the authorities refused to set up a Yiddish school system, and these classes soon came to an end,[69] despite interventions and petitions.

The experiences of the survivors of the Minsk Ghetto were also unexpectedly harsh. About half of the 10,000 Jews of the Minsk Ghetto who had escaped to the forests and had fought with or been shielded by Jewish partisans survived. They returned to Minsk but very few had any chance of getting their old homes back. The devastation of the city was stark. The survivors hoped for some help from the government. Smoliar and the other leaders of the Minsk underground, Nochem Feldman and Haim Alexandrovich, visited the partisan detachments camped in the fields near Minsk and decided to try to arrange a meeting with a representative of the Central Committee of the Belorussian Communist party and describe the despair of the survivors.[70] Smoliar himself finally succeeded in getting an appointment with the party secretary V.I. Zakurdayev. The secretary, however, was evidently more interested in the activity and shortcomings of the Minsk underground, but when Smoliar tried to give him detailed information, his attention waned. He absentmindedly wrote some notes and "acted surprised when [Smoliar] brought up the question [he] had come to discuss." He listened impatiently for a while, then interrupted with a blunt question: "Tell me please, how do you explain this? In our country there are tens, probably hundreds of different peoples and nationalities, even some primitive tribes. But nobody is hated as much as the Jews. . . ." Seeing Smoliar's shock, he stopped himself and told Smoliar to "write it all up." Feldman and Alexandrovich felt stung with incredulity. Alexandrovich finally said, "You went to claim the inheritance and ended up paying for the funeral!"

Smoliar saw Zakurdayev again at a subsequent meeting of the Central Committee and again, the secretary seemed especially interested in mistakes of the resistance. When Smoliar asked about housing for the homeless partisans, he was again told to "Write it up!" Smoliar did so. He also told Epshteyn and Feffer about the meetings and they advised referring the questions to "the highest authorities," as they themselves intended doing about the plight of Jews generally. Smoliar documented the situation of the Jews in the Minsk Ghetto who had returned and emphasized the urgent need for rehabilitative help. Unaware of the peril, he also sent a list of 150 names of Jewish leaders. Later he was told that the Central Committee and the Belorussian staff officials of the partisan movement had already labeled the entire Minsk underground a "nest of provocateurs" created by hostile elements. (The Minsk underground was organized independent of party authorities and, in Smoliar's words, "showed up the complete panic that had overwhelmed the entire government leadership of Belorussia, which, in the first days of the war had fled eastward, abandoning to the mercy of the enemy a city full of people.") Years later, there was a "rehabilitation" of the Minsk underground and ghetto organization.

Smoliar and the Yiddish poets Isaac Plotner and Hersh Kamenietsky of the Writers' Union finally arranged to see the premier of Belorussia, Panteleimon Ponomarenko, to specifically request the rebuilding of Jewish cultural life in Minsk. The meeting took place at midnight at Government House and after Smoliar's presentation, Ponomarenko erupted: "You are guilty of unleashing Jewish nationalism! We know how to handle that. How else can your program be characterized! And your meetings! And your gangs that go around beating up people all over town!"

This was a reference to the first Yiddish literary evening after the war in Minsk. A large audience had come, mainly soldiers and former partisans; Plotner and Kamenietsky read several of their poems on the theme of the Holocaust and Jewish resistance. Toward the end of the evening, an Air Force major asked to say a word and spoke haltingly in a mixture of Yiddish and Russian. He congratulated the poets and showed that he had lost an arm. "I'm a cripple," he said. . . . "Nevertheless, if they should need me there in the Jewish land—in Palestine—then I'll be a pilot again!" He returned to his seat amid "consternation in the hall." Ponomarenko heard about this incident and about hastily formed Jewish defense groups that were fighting off anti-Semitic terrorists and looters and thus made his accusation about Jewish nationalism. He also vented his own personal animus against Jews: "Why is it, when someone insults Ivan, no one but Ivan feels insulted; but when someone insults a Jew, the entire Jewish people feels hurt!" Smoliar answered by reminding him that Hitler had made war against the entire people, but Ponomarenko advised him to join in the "general building of socialism." After the meeting, which did not end until 2 A.M., Plotner murmured: "We have just been handed a death sentence."[71]

Smoliar, just before this meeting, had also met with Ehrenburg in Moscow and found him full of dark foreboding:

For one whole morning I sat in his study. With deep concern and attention he listened to my story about our situation in Belorussia. From him—the most popular writer in the Soviet Union—I expected to hear some word of comfort. Instead, I heard words which oppressed me like a great burden, so laden were they with pain and powerlessness.[72]

Ehrenburg described the explosive anti-Semitism everywhere and pointed to piles of letters stacked two feet high along the length of one wall: "Look at that . . . letters from all corners of the Soviet Union. From the army. From the front lines. . . . Here, read for yourself." Smoliar read at random—all complained of the same thing, a mindless, pervasive anti-Semitism. "Would there ever be an end to it?" Smoliar asked himself. "I felt as though an abyss had opened at my feet and each letter was pushing me deeper into the bottomless pit." Ehrenburg read several aloud, first one which tied his "stomach in knots" from a Jewish colonel on the Western front:

Imagine it, dear Comrade Ilya Grigorevich. We are all huddled in the trenches. Soon I will have to give the command to attack. And here come those damn planes with the black crosses. . . . We dig in. . . . But it wasn't bombs they dropped. It was leaflets—whole clouds of them. . . . Only a few words on the sheet: "LOOK AROUND YOU SOLDIER! DO YOU SEE MANY ABRAHAMS"

That's all. And you know it was enough to make some of the men look around. And not knowing which soldier was a Jew and which wasn't, to come to the poisonous conclusion that 'no Jews are at the front.'[73]

Ehrenburg was also bitterly pessimistic about the Jewish Antifascist Committee when Smoliar indicated that he was going there. "It won't do you any good . . . there's nobody there that will fight back. I never even stop in there any more." Among other disappointments, he said that the JAC had agreed to publish the *Black Book*,[74] and that he had given them much of his own material, but they had "wasted it by sending it abroad in dribs and drabs as propaganda." They had done nothing to stop the spreading epidemic. And "something has got to be done about the anti-Semitic plague in our country!" he said with great agitation.

A few days after this conversation, Smoliar spoke to a Mr. Shkiryativ, Chairman of the Central Control Commission of the All-Union Communist party, and told him about the pile of documents Ehrenburg had been collecting. "What can we do?" he said. "Once Comrade Stalin says that the Jewish cadres have not justified themselves, then the secretary of the regional committee is free to say '*Bey zhidov, spasai Rossiyu!*'" ('Beat the Jews and Save Mother Russia'—the slogan of the pogromizing Black Hundreds of tsarist times).

Smoliar concluded from this that "the anti-Jewish 'inspiration' came from the very top. The practical implementation of this 'saying' . . . was not accidental." The insulting words of Zakurdayev and Ponomarenko now fell into place. They formed part of a larger official design. Markish and G. Zhits, the editor in chief of *Einikayt*, were also plunged into a deeply pessimistic mood, and when Smoliar told Zhits what Shkiryatov had said, he replied angrily, "Well, and what did *you* think he would say?" Ehrenburg had demanded that Jews *do* something, but Smoliar asked himself "What could we do in *our* times, in *our* circumstances? To whom could we turn, when all the elementary requests of Jews were labeled 'nationalistic'?"[75]

Where indeed? Many Jews had been relying on the Jewish Antifascist Committee and were turning to it for help and leadership, but were finding it uncertain, vacillating, and coming to the end of its usefulness to the regime.

20

Collapse of JAC Projects and Signs of the Cold War, 1944–47

Communism has nothing in common with cosmopolitanism, that ideology which is characteristic of representatives of banking firms and international consortiums, great stock exchange speculators and international suppliers of weapons.

N. BALTIYSKY

THE official repression of Jewish suffering and sacrifice during the war intensified the pain and frustration of many Jews and was to give poignant meaning to the later struggle for recognition of the reality of Jewish national feeling. The expectations that had been aroused by the JAC were also steadily nibbled away, ultimately leaving Soviet Jews stripped of all institutional shields and channels of expression. Signs of an official shift could be discerned—if one knew how to read them—toward the end of 1944, when the Soviet victory was clearly in view. The fate of Soviet Jewry was to be locked into a global strategy that dictated the course of events, making the hopes that had been aroused during the war pitifully inconsequential. This strategy evolved as differences between the Allies grew sharper, and when the alliance ruptured, the Soviet Jewish role of outreach to the West for the sake of the war became expendable. The process of contraction started in 1944 but at first the signs were uncertain, inconsistent, and difficult to gauge.

The JAC was still very busy meeting with individual Jews and Soviet officials and hoped not only for a continuation of its activities, but also planned for additional functions and responsibilities, unaware that its third plenary meeting in Moscow on April 2, 1944, would be its last.

At that meeting[1] Mikhoels, in his opening remarks, emphasized the

tragedy of Jews during the Holocaust and the heroism of Jewish soldiers and partisans. He also spoke confidently about continuing contacts with Jewish communities outside the USSR. Epshteyn gave a detailed account of the number of Jews among the decorated soldiers of
the Red Army, stressing the high percentage of Soviet Yiddish writers
who had died in battle. He also condemned those who had accused
the Soviet population of anti-Semitism and, significantly, opposed what
he termed "emotional" and "nationalistic" attitudes among Soviet Yiddish writers. A special point was made of the demand for JAC material
by the Jewish world press and JAC contact with more than 300 writers
and journalists within the USSR.

At this plenary session, seventeen new members were added to the
Committee, including the novelist Vasily Grossman, the poet and partisan fighter Abraham Sutzkever, and the Lithuanian refugee poet Chaim
Grade.[2] Several high-ranking officers of the Red Army were added and
a Praesidium created. The Praesidium was enlarged between April and
August by the addition of high-ranking officials in the Soviet state administration, suggesting an official brake on any possible "nationalistic" deviations.

Streams of letters and individuals came to Mikhoels asking for help
and advice. When Sutzkever visited him in Moscow in June 1944, he
found the hall full of "Jewish soldiers, partisans, people who ran away
from death camps, actors from Birobidzhan and plain miserable Jews
who arrived in Moscow from Central Asia and did not have a roof over
their heads."[3] Soviet Jews continued to believe the JAC would serve
them in the future.

This hope was echoed in numerous messages between Soviet Jewry
and Jews in the United States and Palestine, sent toward the end of
the war. The traumas of survivors and evidence of mass murder were
reported. A Rosh Hashanah greeting to the Jews of the United States
was sent on September 17, 1944, by the "Moscow Jewish community"
in the name of the "religious Jewry of the Soviet Union," hailing the
victories of the combined Allied armies at the same time.[4] Throughout
1944 and early 1945, there were exchanges of cables between the JAC
and members of the World Jewish Congress dealing with reports of the
Jewish dead, rejoicing in the Allied victory, mourning Roosevelt's death,
and, at least on the Western side, information about a forthcoming
conference to deal with the problem of Jewish refugees.[5] The Soviet
government's decision to join the Intergovernmental Committee on

Refugees, announced on February 4, 1944, was hailed in many American circles, and the inauguration of a news service by the Jewish Telegraphic Agency to the Jewish press in Moscow was seen as a very hopeful sign of further common understanding and cooperation between American and Soviet Jewry.[6] In its New Year greeting to the Jews of America in January 1945, the JAC appealed for close unity between the two Jewries. Assurance that the Soviet Union would support Jewish independence in Palestine was given by the Soviet press attaché in Teheran to a delegation of the Palestine Victory League on December 17, 1944. The League delegates, returning from Teheran, where they had delivered a shipment of gifts for the Red Army, reported in Tel Aviv that the Soviet authorities had invited the Jews of Palestine to send a delegation to Minsk to establish Jewish orphanages there for children of war dead. The V League also reported that "a special bureau for Jewish religious affairs has been established in Moscow."[7] Another encouraging sign came from the Lenin State Library announcement on February 14. For the first time since the Revolution there was "the establishment of direct contact with publishers in Palestine for the purpose of securing Hebrew literature for its Hebrew section."[8]

A tantalizingly inconclusive process also involved the possibility of strengthened links between world Jewry and Soviet Jews, apparently starting late in 1943. On February 4, 1944, there was a cable[9] from Rabbi Irving Miller of the American Section of the World Jewish Congress to the JAC, in response to a query from the Committee, regarding the summoning of an Emergency Conference in May 1944 with an agenda "including all problems dealing [with] Jewish rescue, relief, and rehabilitation [in the] countries controlled or overrun by [the] enemy." Miller then expresses the sincere hope that the JAC will find it possible to accept the invitation. We have no record of a reply. On March 27,[10] another cable greets the "representatives of the Jewish people in Russia" on the occasion of its third plenary meeting and "rejoice[s] in the growing cooperation between us, of which the joint publication of the Black Book marks [the] beginning."

The date of the conference was changed to November, and on September 22, 1944, another cable was sent, this time to Mikhoels of the JAC, "urgently" requesting a Soviet Jewish delegation to the conference, and noting that WJC "would be glad to send a delegation to Russia."[11] Apparently there was no answer to this cable either. Again on December 26, 1944, another cable was sent to Mikhoels, saying that sending a delegation to Moscow "was urgently necessary in view of [the] liberation [of the] Balkan countries." In an explanation to the censor, the WJC points out that it is "anxious to send a delegation to Moscow in order to place before the Russian Government the proposals for rehabilitation now being submitted to all the U.N." and to discuss these "in view of the special Russian responsibility in the liberated areas of eastern Europe."[12]

Meanwhile, Dr. Nahum Goldmann, president of the WJC, had been informing Ambassador Gromyko[13] in Washington about the forthcoming conference and the WJC invitation to the JAC. On January 12, 1944, Gromyko said he thought "the chance of the delegates coming from Moscow were good, the chief difficulty [being] transportation." Goldmann had the impression that Gromyko would "urge his government to permit a delegation," although he did not commit himself. When Gromyko asked about the number of delegates, Goldmann said that "they would not be on the basis of population, or the Russian delegation would swallow the whole conference." The conference, he explained, "will be rather informal and the chief thing is to have representatives from every country." Gromyko also wanted to know whether there would be delegates from England and Palestine. Goldmann said there would be and promised to send him a memorandum. At this meeting, there was a curious half-bantering, half-serious exchange which throws a sharp light on the severely literal Soviet attitudes toward loyalty—a subject that was to poison the life of Soviet Jews in the years ahead. Gromyko asked Goldmann whether he represented the whole Jewish people, to which Goldmann countered: "Do you represent the whole of the Russian people?" Gromyko looked surprised and Goldmann said, not very tactfully, that he knew thousands of Russians who did not recognize him as their spokesman or ambassador. "Those," the ambassador said, "are traitors to Russia." Stretching the analogy, Goldmann said, "It's the same with me. There are many Jews who do not recognize anyone of us because they do not recognize the existence of the Jewish people." The ambassador laughed and said he understood, but precisely what he understood from this gauche exchange is not clear.

On January 15, Goldmann wrote to Gromyko and gave him more details.[14] He first listed the communities and organizations which had been, and would be, invited, including the JAC. Then he sketched the matter of numerical representation. As this item seems to have become a sticking point in later negotiations, it should be noted. Goldmann said that "the number of delegates from each country is not strictly fixed; we expect to have one or two delegates from the smaller communities and three to five or more from the larger ones." He left the number of delegates from the USSR to be determined by Soviet Jews themselves. He stressed the fact that this would be a conference representing all the Jewish communities of the world to discuss problems of postwar Jewish rehabilitation, reconstruction of Jewish life, and restoration of Jewish rights and property. He also noted that Palestine Jewry would be represented, but that the "Palestine problem will not be discussed in detail . . . as this is the prerogative of the Jewish Agency for Palestine, but [that] the Conference will certainly express its general views on the subject." In expressing the desire to have representatives from Soviet Jewry, Goldmann stressed the importance of "bringing Russian Jewry into closer contact with the Jewish communities all over the world."

On April 14, 1944, Goldmann had another conversation with Gromyko,[15] in which he asked him "to make inquiries in Moscow as to the number and position of the Jews, whom the Russian armies may have found alive in Bukovina, Transnistria and Bessarabia," and "the number and status of Jews in Czechoslovakia, Romania and Hungary." Goldmann also asked if Gromyko had received any information about the Russian delegation to the forthcoming conference, noting that he had cabled twice without any reply. Gromyko indicated that he would inform Goldmann if he heard anything. The ambassador asked a number of questions about Palestine and was favorably impressed with Goldmann's account of Benes' reports to Stalin, which involved discussions with Soviet leaders on Palestine.

On February 27, 1944, a bilingual interpreter attached to the British Naval mission at Archangel and a Jew, Lieutenant Penn, had a long talk[16] with Samuil Chobrutsky, president of the Moscow Synagogue Board. In the course of the talk, Chobrutsky turned to the forthcoming WJC emergency conference and said that "he was in negotiation with the authorities to enable a delegation of seven to nine Jewish representatives to attend on behalf of the Jewish community in the USSR. The delegation, as at present advised, would include a partisan and Mikhoels." The president did not know whether he would himself be allowed to take part in the delegation and thought it "improbable" that permission would be granted to any of the numerous Polish Jewish refugees in the USSR. Chobrutsky seemed eager to impress his visitor with the fact that he was able to be in contact with Jewish communities abroad and was pleased to show him a copy of the Palestine weekly *Palcor* (Palestine Correspondence).

On February 5, 1945, the JAC sent detailed lists of Jewish survivors[17] from Lublin, Polin, Vilna, Bialystok, Kovno, Riga, Dubno, and many lists from smaller towns such as Swir, Jezno, Olkeniki, and Meishegoly. The total number of Jewish survivors in many communities previously comprising hundreds of thousands of Jews was 3,122. The WJC urged the JAC to continue sending such lists, to help in the process of finding relatives and in documenting the scale of destruction.

On May 22, 1945, four cables[18] were received in the New York office of WJC from the JAC, hailing the victory over Nazism and Stalin's "decisive role in this greatest battle in history for freedom and happiness [of] mankind." The tragic Jewish losses are mourned, but the Jewish people, "though reduced in number . . . [are] full of hope and confidence that [a] new bright era is beginning for all nations." The message also notes that the "Jewish people have their own accounts to settle with Hitlerite Germany," that the war has consolidated the friendship of both countries and that "mutual understanding of Jews [in] all countries has grown," creating the basis for "close unity in [the] struggle for life . . . prosperity and culture [of] our people." But there is no reference to the WJC conference.

Apparently, the threads of negotiation regarding the conference had also been taken up by the WJC London office concurrently with the American section, or later. These discussions involved a Czech Jew, Yitzhak Rosenberg, who went to Moscow on an official mission in November 1944 as a member of a Czech government delegation. His assignment was twofold: to attend to all matters concerned with the welfare of Czech Jews in Soviet territory and to establish "the groundwork for formal relations between the World Jewish Congress and the JAC."[19] Rosenberg describes his first meeting with Shakhne Epshteyn and Feffer as "rather cool and formal," in contrast to the warmth of his meeting just a day before with Mikhoels, but all three men agreed that the visit of the JAC to London in the autumn of 1943 signaled, as Mikhoels himself had said, "the end of the isolation of Soviet Jewry."[20] Rosenberg referred to a resolution of the British Section of the WJC urging that Soviet Jewry be invited to join the WJC and spoke of an extensive exchange of publications as well as lists of surviving Jews and Jewish communities. His proposal was apparently accepted, for Epshteyn agreed to communicate the following agreement to the WJC in London through the Czech Embassy radio service:

> Had information talks [with] representatives Soviet Jewry Epshtein and Feffer. Agreed on cooperation, exchange of literature and news. Promised documents and material on atrocities against Czechoslovak Jews for Black Book. They agreed [to] attend conference of European Jewry. . . .[21]

Rosenberg considered this quick agreement to closer cooperation between the WJC and the JAC "as an indication of prior approval by the 'higher-ups' within the CPSU. Under the circumstances, it could not have been otherwise."[22] When Rosenberg was notified of plans to convene a WJC Emergency Conference of European Jewry, he suggested to Epshteyn that the JAC send a delegation and was told in a few days that the suggestion was accepted.

During the first week in January 1945, Epshteyn and Rosenberg had further talks about the coming conference, in which the JAC laid down three preconditions: First, the JAC had to participate in drafting and approving the conference agenda. Second, the number of JAC delegates had to be equal to the rest of world Jewry combined. Third, the JAC would have to have this same share on all WJC bodies such as the executive, the secretariat, and various committees—referred to later as the "fifty-fifty" condition.[23] These demands created serious difficulties in further negotiations because they would have necessitated a complete restructuring of the WJC. (Representation was based on the numerical strength of a particular Jewish national community). The full extent of Jewish losses in the Soviet Union was not yet known, but Feffer perhaps was still thinking of a kind of parity between American and Soviet Jewry. In New York during his visit, he had said: "The Jews in the Soviet Union and in the United States are the majority of the Jewish people. Together we are ten million Jews. Upon us lies the responsibility for the fate of the Jewish people." In fact, the matter of numerical equality was not debated, nor were ideological differences brought into the open. Rosenberg's impression was that Feffer was eager to keep the lines of communication open and that "some means would be found to overcome the difficulties raised."[24] He had suggested Prague as the site of the conference.

The decision of the JAC to affiliate with the WJC was made sometime during the first week in January 1945 and the news was communicated to Stephen S. Wise, the leader of the American Jewish Congress and one of the founding members of the WJC, and to the British Section of the WJC. Rosenberg urged a quick reply and specific instructions. However, the WJC failed to reply and the British Section replied too late to be of practical use. (In March 1946, when Rosenberg was in the United States, Wise convened a special meeting to hear a report of his mission to Moscow. Rosenberg was quoted as saying, "the WJC did not do what I and the Russian Jews asked them to do," at which point Wise interjected, "which we deeply regret.")[25]

Later there were continued efforts by mail, but Rosenberg believed "correspondence could not replace personal contact." These efforts are summarized in a WJC report:

> Both we in New York and our British Section tried to arrange a meeting with the leaders of the JAC in Prague or Paris or some other agreeable place. We did not succeed. We invited them to attend some of our international meetings. These invitations were politely received, but there was some other vague commitment which prevented acceptance. It was obvious in general that we were dealing with unseen factors, and my own view is that one or another of these invitations would have been accepted if the leaders of the JAC had been free to do so.[26]

The WJC did not respond to Rosenberg's request immediately; perhaps if it had, more light might have been shed on the "unseen factors." But the growing estrangement between the wartime Allies and the Soviet Union was very likely the main reason for the WJC delay. An era of distrust was beginning and would soon swell to the Cold War and Stalin's paranoia about security, spies, and "rootless cosmopolitans." By this time, of course, there was no longer any doubt that the numerical equality between Soviet Jewry and American Jewry did not exist, yet the importance of the formula apparently was still very important to Soviet officials. Rosenberg was of the opinion that it stemmed from "the desire to control the WJC and to use it to further Soviet interests."[27]

Were the men on the JAC already being pulled in opposite directions? Or was an unseen policy confusion moving toward a decision? Were official decisions being deliberately masked? The rejection of the *Black Book* project, the evasiveness in dealing with WJC invitations, the elimination of the Jewish identification of war heroes, and mounting anti-Semitism seemed to point to a new policy. Yet as late as 1947, the question of equality of representation in the WJC still rankled. At that time a member of the Swedish section of the WJC visited the office of the JAC and was told that "the representation of Soviet Jews for the proposed meeting of the General Assembly meeting of WJC in 1948 was inadequate."

Closer to home, many Jews who no longer had a place to live or who felt the postwar hostility of neighbors and employers hoped for a new beginning in the Crimea and looked to the JAC for help and leadership. It will be recalled that the Crimea was featured prominantly as an area of Jewish agricultural settlement in the 1920s, even after the Birobidzhan project was launched in 1928. Certain Jewish activists had even envisioned a Jewish republic in the Crimea and substantial settlements were created before and after Birobidzhan was officially proclaimed the favored area. Toward the end of the war, the JAC and certain Jewish writers began to think of the Crimea again as a possible answer to the hardships of Jews returning to their homes.

The region was liberated by the Red Army in April 1944, and the authorities began to deport large masses of Crimean Tatars from the area for collaboration with the Nazis and acts of sabotage during the war. The prewar Jewish settlements had been butchered and pillaged and the area was virtually empty of Jews. Many Jews believed the Soviet government would again look favorably at Jewish resettlement there and that, once more, world Jewry would help. One Polish Jewish writer living in the Soviet Union at the time had said that "at 10 Kropotkin Street [the address of the JAC] there at times prevailed that atmosphere of deliverance during 1944."[28] Rumors and hopes abounded, pivoting around the figure of the beloved Mikhoels. He was regarded as a man "who carried a great secret with him," but the exact nature of his knowledge was unknown. Many Polish Jews living in the Soviet Union at the time were themselves witness to this fever of excitement. Later it was rumored that Lazar Kaganovich had told someone that "there was a hope that Jews would get the Crimea."[29]

Joseph Rubinstein[30] has described the unusual air of enthusiasm that prevailed at a plenary meeting of the JAC in 1944. The hushed secret was the Crimea that "the Kremlin proposes to give us in compensation for our bereavement." Bergelson, Kvitko, and Kushnirov are described as excited. "All are enthralled by the sweet rumors . . . a dream is coming true. . . . Imaginations are fired." Ehrenburg, who was at the meeting, scoffed at the whole idea and said that Jews would return to their former homes. Epshteyn replied that "after such a terrible calamity," there would have to be "some sort of compensation." Yet according to the poet Sutzkever,[31] who recorded some of these events in his diary in July 1944, Litvinov, who was then Deputy Commissar for Foreign Affairs, had received a delegation of Soviet Jews, including Epshteyn. Epshteyn broached the idea of Jewish settlement in the Crimea, but Litvinov expressed the belief that Jews needed a territory of their own, preferably Palestine. According to Sutzkever, Ehrenburg was inclined to agree with him.

Rumors about the Crimea evidently reached as far as the prison camps of Uzbekistan and distant war fronts. When Hershel Vaynrauch, a Soviet Jewish writer, returned to Moscow from the front for a few days during this time, he attended a meeting of Jewish writers. In discussions of Jewish survivors and evacuees in Siberia and Central Asia, Nusinov, a Yiddish literary critic and member of the JAC, proposed that the writers request repatriation "not in the devastated cities and townships, but in some other place . . . say the Crimea."[32] Bergelson apparently shifted from enthusiasm to opposition when it became clear within a few months that there was no possibility of Jewish resettlement in the Crimea. The Jewish writers were told to stop talking about it. Birobidzhan soon re-emerged as the officially endorsed project (see Chapter 13) and was promoted in Jewish publications, including *Einikayt*, as early as 1944. Here, there was no allusion to the "neo-Crimean notion." In May 1944, on the tenth anniversary of the JAR in Birobidzhan, "*Einikayt* devoted several enthusiastic columns" to the event. Kalinin, the long-time loyal supporter of Jewish revival there, again lent his advocacy to Birobidzhan at the JAC meeting in Moscow.

Sometime in the summer of 1944 a memorandum on the Crimea was drafted by the JAC and submitted to Stalin, requesting that the area be transformed into a Jewish republic. It is not certain if this was conceived at the suggestion of Litvinov, Kaganovich, or Molotov, whose wife Paulina Zhemchuzhina was Jewish, or perhaps all three, but the existence of the memorandum is confirmed in several sources.[33] This action was to be fateful in the extreme. Throughout 1945, the JDC also urged Soviet officials to consider the Crimea for Jewish resettlement and *Einikayt* writers visited there and wrote about their impressions.[34] Markish was asked to sign the JAC memorandum, but refused on the grounds that the Tatars should have the Crimea.[35]

Years later, in an interview with a Paris journalist, Ehrenburg spoke of the Crimean idea as a "rash plan."[36] In the course of the talk he revealed several illuminating details: first, that the JAC had sent a memorandum dealing with the matter to Stalin, and second, that "Molotov was sympathetically disposed to the Crimea project and was consulted before the memorandum to Stalin was drawn up." This was the tissue of hope and interest out of which the accusation of a "Jewish conspiracy" to seize the Crimea was fabricated several years later (see Chapter 24), long after Jewish wishful thinking had been quenched and many Jewish lives had been wrecked or destroyed.

Boris Smolar, a Russian-born journalist who served as a correspondent for the *New York World* and visited the Soviet Union a number of times, was especially curious about the fate of Jewish settlers in the Crimea after the war and made many inquiries during his trip in 1968. He was told in Moscow that "there was nothing" for him to see, that the Nazis had killed about 90,000 Jews in the Crimea, that few if any Jews who had been evacuated from the Crimea had returned and that the farms were now occupied by Ukrainians. (In 1954 the Crimea was made part of the Ukrainian Soviet Republic.) Smolar confirmed the accounts of the enthusiasm of many Jews for Crimean settlement after the war and the existence of a JAC memorandum to Stalin. Based on his experience "in Jewish circles in Moscow" in 1968, he learned that the memorandum was signed by Mikhoels and Feffer.

When Stalin saw the project outlined in the Jewish memorandum, he took it as another confirmation of his suspicion that there existed a conspiracy of 'Jewish chauvinism' in the country in which even leading Jewish Communists participated. In his perverted mind, he saw in the Jewish memorandum an effort to strengthen this 'Jewish conspiracy.' In his eyes, the Jews in the Soviet Union were not only his personal enemies but also 'the internal enemy' of the country.[37]

Meanwhile, in 1946 work on the *Black Book* by the special literary commission was stopped and the entire project was turned over to the JAC. The commission was disbanded apparently on Stalin's orders, followed by an article in *Pravda* by G. Aleksandrov attacking Ehrenburg for "washing over differences between German fascists and German democrats." The book thus became a foil in postwar Soviet-German politik. East Germany was moving into the Soviet orbit, signifying a new policy toward Germans, and Stalin didn't want to emphasize Nazi outrages. During this period Stalin also ordered the dissolution of the

Extraordinary Commission to Ascertain and Investigate the War Crimes of the Fascist-German Invaders and Their Accomplices.[38] Thus, all cases which involved German crimes, including, of course, those against Jews were ordered closed. (These investigations were not resumed until the sixties.)

There is no doubt that, after the collapse of the literary commission, alterations in the text of the *Black Book* were made.[39] Copies of revised versions or excerpts of the book were sent to selected publishers and certain Jewish organizations in the United States, Romania, and Palestine, and books were published in the United States in 1946 and Romania in 1947.[40]

Ehrenburg tried to do everything possible to have the book published in Russian and believed it would be published by Der Emes Publishing House. It was finally ready for the printer and actually printed but never released for circulation. Late in 1948, after the JAC itself was liquidated, Stalin ordered the work suppressed.[41] The pages were burned and the type melted down. When the editor of *Morgen Freiheit*, Paul Novick, visited Ehrenburg in Moscow in 1959, he told him that Vasily Grossman had a copy of the book and added sadly, "whether it will appear in my lifetime I am not certain."[42]

The sudden decision by Stalin to stop publication of the book in the Soviet Union was undoubtedly part of the much larger assault against Soviet Jewry in 1948–49 (see Chapter 23), but, specifically, was aligned with a new policy line "to win the confidence of the beaten German people in preparation for the establishment of a Soviet satellite in East Germany."[43]

Meanwhile, the JAC continued to be busy, but uneasy and uncertain. Its activity was observed firsthand and described as a "big undertaking" by Ben Zion Goldberg, Yiddish correspondent and president of the American Committee of Jewish Writers, Artists, and Scientists, which had served as host during the visit of Mikhoels and Feffer to America in 1943 and had co-sponsored the American edition of the *Black Book*. Goldberg revisited the Soviet Union in January 1946 and was impressed by the scale of JAC work, reflected in its office headquarters in Moscow:

It occupied the entire ground floor of a sizable building and parts of the floor above. There was a considerable staff of workers—receptionists, stenographers, secretaries, messengers, researchers, writers, specialists, heads of departments. . . . On the one hand, the committee was geared to function on an international basis, like a miniature Vatican foreign office. . . . On the other hand, the committee operated like the civilian organ of the Soviet Jewish community. Soviet Jews had begun to regard the committee as their representative body, big brother, adviser, defender.[44]

After observing the activities of the JAC for a few days, Goldberg told Lozovsky that the committee seemed to be developing into a "sort of Soviet Jewish Congress, like the American Jewish Congress," but Lozovsky was pointedly silent.[45] (Ironically, one of the charges brought against him a few years later, which led to his execution in 1952, was that the JAC had, in fact, assumed the function of a general Jewish body.) Jews flocked to this center for a wide variety of individual and social problems. Goldberg was particularly distressed to hear of so many cases of Jews displaced from homes and positions who could not recover their rights for fear of inflaming Ukrainian anti-Semitism. Semi-autonomous Jewish groups such as the Association of Jewish Writers and Yiddish Theaters eagerly consulted with the JAC for guidance through the uncertain postwar period. Shimon Kipnis, a Soviet Jewish emigré to the United States, who knew Mikhoels and other members of the JAC well, himself saw shiploads of clothing and shoes, sent by American Jews, in JAC warehouses in Kiev, Odessa and Moscow where needy Jews and non-Jews clamored for supplies after the war. [46] Kipnis also confirmed the strong bonds that thousands of Soviet Jews forged with the JAC and their hope that it would remain the voice of Soviet Jewry.

Most of the JAC wartime staff of fifty writers were still on the job in early 1946. Some were genuinely interested in Jewish matters; others were obviously sent in by the party or needed jobs. Some were refugee writers hoping to return home. Feffer was planning a book called *Jewish Heroes in the Struggle against Fascism* to be issued jointly with Goldberg's American Committee, but Goldberg was skeptical after the failure of *The Black Book* project, and, indeed, although material was prepared in Moscow, this book, too, was never published.

For Goldberg, who was Sholem Aleikhem's son-in-law, the "greatest public cultural achievement of the JAC inside Russia, which turned out to be the last cultural event in the life of the Soviet Jewish community . . . was the thirtieth anniversary of the death of Sholom Aleichem."[47] The festive spirit during the commemoration was irresistible. The event was held in the imposing Hall of Columns near Red Square. Crowds jammed Gorky Street and the nearby subway station while mounted traffic police tried to clear a passage. Inside there was an exultant mood: "The audience responded with enthusiasm to the speeches and reading in Russian, but was literally in rapture during the reading in Yiddish" (see Photo 20.1).[48]

Goldberg then spent several months in the Soviet Union traveling about the country. The JAC arranged his trip and Feffer generally accompanied him.[49] Goldberg quickly noticed that he had to squeeze visits of Jewish interest between protracted courtesy calls on local party officials and directors of major enterprises. He was introduced in exaggerated phrases as an important American antifascist, instrumental in raising millions of dollars for Russian War Relief and now working for an antifascist peace and friendship with the Soviet people. He sensed an uneasy scrambling among Jews and non-Jews alike for signs of the emerging Soviet line. What were the new Soviet policies? Time and time again he heard the self-effacing expression, "I am only a little man," as if one were helpless to understand or change the drift of events.

Goldberg had the impression that Feffer was pleased after each meeting—he was always in good spirits, like a man who has done his job well: "He did not say it in so many words, but I could see that he

20.1 Participants in the Sholem Aleikhem Memorial Meeting in Moscow, May 13, 1946.

wanted the local official to know that Jews were influential in the United States and that they were interested in the fate of the Jews in the Soviet Union." Consciously or unconsciously, he seemed to feel that the interest of American Jewry gave Soviet Jews an element of security. Yet he once told Goldberg a fable about an old lion who made a hare the ruler of the forest. An unknowing tiger, seeing the hare on the lion's throne, stretched out his paw and picked up the hare and swallowed him. The other animals stood aghast, and then told the tiger that he had eaten the new king. "Woe is me," the tiger wailed, "I did not divine the latest switch of the lion's tail!"

All of Goldberg's meetings were officially arranged; there were no public meetings privately arranged. After a time Goldberg learned that some individuals who had visited him at his hotel were picked up by the police. In a revealing talk[50] he had with Ivan Polyansky, chairman of the Council for Religious Cults, Goldberg asked if Jews could avail themselves of his services in securing a yeshiva for training rabbis, prayer books, and a central religious body as other religious groups had. Polyansky said "yes" to everything and Goldberg cabled the news to his paper. He also met with Rabbi Solomon Shlieffer[51] of the Moscow Synagogue and other rabbis to tell them the good news. With the exception of Schlieffer, they were "shabbily dressed and miserably shod," and when they were introduced to Goldberg, they said absolutely nothing. Their silence was painful. Even when Goldberg began to recite a prayer about the children of Israel in captivity, the frightened rabbis "lowered their eyes—in shame or helplessness, or in fear of being called to account."

Yet there were signs of fragile but determined beginnings amid the uneasiness and war ruins: Jewish orphanages were being rebuilt; a musical called *Fraylekhs* (Rejoicing) was played at the Jewish State Theater in Moscow, and study sessions at the Yiddish dramatic school were resumed. There were ambitious plans to publish Purim plays and a Yiddish-Russian dictionary at the Office for Jewish Culture of the Ukrainian Academy of Science;[52] Der Emes Publishing House was planning to reprint old favorites and add hundreds of new works as part of a five-year plan, including a comprehensive history of Yiddish literature and extensive anthologies of biblical, talmudic, and midrashic literature.

Each time Goldberg seemed ready to leave, Mikhoels had a new suggestion for a trip, as if he couldn't bear to lose such a precious link. The JAC was hanging on to him, seeking to delay his departure as long as possible. When he finally asked why, Mikhoels replied confidentially, "We expect news from the Kremlin about Jews. A decision is about to be made, and I would like you to cable it first to the world. . . ."[53] Goldberg knew it was pointless to ask for what one is not told. Whatever the news might have been, it never arrived in the form Mikhoels had suggested.

Perhaps Goldberg's own frustrated attempts to get permission to visit Birobidzhan in 1946, precisely at a time when there was a sudden official campaign to revive Birobidzhan, signified more than it seemed. At the time it was believed that Molotov, who had to grant permission, was too busy with other things. In retrospect, Goldberg's request and other events of that time may have signalled internal political differences over the coming "Jewish line" or a deliberate, cunning camouflage of a subsequent brutal reversal which doomed Birobidzhan for Jews after enthusiastic official promotion in 1947–48 (see Chapter 22). But however ambiguous and vague the official signs or absence of them, some of the JAC members, Mikhoels included, considered Goldberg an important factor that might influence Soviet policy to continue Jewish cultural work after the war. He and the JAC agreed to work on a number of joint projects and the JAC, always mindful of its own propaganda function, told him "how important he was to Soviet aims abroad."[54]

It was those aims, not Jewish needs, that shifted the work of the JAC evermore toward fighting anti-Soviet criticism among American Jews, including the "Jewish fascists" of the socialist *Jewish Daily Forward*[55] and denouncing the United States. Pro-Soviet organizations such as Russian War Relief, the Jewish People's Fraternal Order, and YKUF (Yidisher Kultur Farband) were praised and expected to endorse and support Soviet policies. Jewish literature dealing with victimization during the war was quickly snuffed out. In 1946, it was *Einikayt* itself that provided "the clearest formulation of the party's warnings against devoting excessive attention to the Nazi extermination of the Jews." The trouble, according to *Einikayt*, was that in too many works "the German fascist crimes against the Jewish population are shown as isolated, and are not tied in with the Hitlerite murders of the Soviet people in general."[56]

The anti-American line, meanwhile, was being honed and refined by Andrei Zhdanov, who had succeeded Kirov as party head in Leningrad and was considered Stalin's heir apparent. Zhdanov was the architect of Stalin's domestic, cultural, and ideological policies after World War II, and it was Zhdanov whose name became virtually synonymous with the Cold War in the late 1940s. "Zhdanov's purpose was to wipe out the liberal and Westernizing tendencies that had been awakened in Russia by the wartime alliance with Britain and America."[57] His most prominent victims were at first not Jews, but his actions prefigured those of the "Black Years," during which Jews *were* the prime victims. As founder and boss of the Cominform, Zhdanov reversed the policy of cooperation with liberal and democratic elements that most of the Communist parties had carried over from the days of wartime underground resistance.

The end of the war, indeed, set the stage for a vast reappraisal of the Soviet foreign and domestic policy, a process that shook the wartime arrangements most profoundly and inevitably affected Soviet Jewry. Globally, the end of the war saw the eclipse of Nazi power in Europe and Japanese power in Asia, but left huge power vacuums, which only the Soviet Union and the United States could fill. After 1945, Soviet-American relations deteriorated rapidly and a Cold War atmosphere developed. When the whole range of Soviet-American conflict is scanned, the Jewish issue is a subissue in a superpower, global, geopolitical struggle, but this is the context in which the fate of Soviet Jewry has hung. Stalin's own xenophobia, insecurity, and imperial ambitions were intermixed with Soviet envy of American power and economic growth in contrast with Soviet postwar devastation and human losses. Thirty million Soviet people were killed in World War II. In the Near and Middle East after 1945, Soviet interests were most intense in Iran, Turkey, and Greece, but Soviet aims in all three places were thwarted. However, in Eastern Europe and certain areas of Asia, Soviet influence was very great.

Domestically, there was the massive task of reconstruction and social healing after the horrors of the war, and rededication to prewar ideological constraints. The war had brought with it a relative relaxation in the bitter struggle the government had been conducting against "nationalist deviations." But already by 1944, there were some signs of an impending reversion. In August 1944, for example, the Central Committee of the party decided on the need to "improve ideological activity" in the Tatar Autonomous Republic and to eliminate what was described as serious mistakes of a nationalist character made by historians and writers.[58] A similar criticism was leveled at the Bashkir Communists in January 1945.

Stalin had an intense mistrust of all Soviet ethnic minorities, whose loyalty to the Soviet state was tested and found largely wanting during the war. Moreover, many thousands of returning Soviet soldiers and civilians who had been outside Soviet territory during the war had had a taste of Europe and created problems for Stalin. Like Tsar Alexander I after the war with Napoleon, he turned to isolation and repression. Jews were particularly suspect because of Stalin's personal anti-Semitism and his suspicion that they were in dangerous contact with the West. The lightning speed of the invading German armies was made possible at least in part by the discontent of many non-Russian peoples who had forcibly been incorporated into the Soviet Union. The war, one historian has said, showed "the precariousness of this multinational structure . . . and stirred up nationalist feelings."[59] In the short term, Stalin had to make concessions to these sentiments; appeals to Communist values were clearly not enough.

The war had also proved to the central government that the borderlands were vulnerable, and that this vulnerability, in a tense international situation, might threaten the entire system with death. Also, Stalin had observed the weak response to appeals for international solidarity and decided it was necessary to replace them with an appeal for another kind of solidarity, one involving history, the nation, religion . . . [namely to] raise the Russian nation to the top rank, exalting its traditions and culture. The war provided him with an excellent pretext.[60]

Premonitory actions were taken in national territories from which the Germans had retreated. Between October 1943 and June 1944, the peoples of six small nations were accused of treason and deported to Central Asia or Siberia—the same fate that befell the Volga Germans in 1941. The six national groups were Chechens, Ingush, Karachays, Balkars, Kalmyks, and Crimean Tatars. In 1946, the national territories of the Chechens, Ingush, and Tatars were dissolved and for ten years they had no legal existence.

When he celebrated victory on May 24, 1945, Stalin toasted the *Russian*, not the Soviet, people. He declared that "Russia is the leading nation of the USSR," and that "in this war she had won the right to be recognized as the guide for the whole union."[61] Non-Russians were urged to recall from their national histories only these events which had brought them closer to Russia. "National cultures were suddenly denounced. . . . All the monuments of national cultures—sagas, ballads, legends—were subject to merciless attack and were banned. . . . Singing the praises of roses in imitation of the medieval Persian poet Saadi, even in a Soviet novel, became an intolerable display of nationalism."[62] A book called *A History of the Kazakh People*, which had been highly praised in 1943, was attacked for its nationalism in 1945.[63] Rapid Russification and the exaltation of all things Russian became the new Stalinist emendation of communism.

During the war, Alexander Fadeyev, the chairman of the Writers' Union and one of the chief expositors of the dangers of cosmopolitanism, wrote in a vein that must have strained the credibility of some readers: "The German invaders were deliberately encouraging rootless cosmopolitanism, which stems from the so-called idea that everybody is a 'citizen of the world.' "[64] Then in January 1945, a Soviet author stated that "communism and a consistent, active and altruistic love of one's homeland are one and the same thing," whereas "cosmopolitanism is an ideology alien to the workers. Communism has nothing in common with cosmopolitanism, . . . which is characteristic of . . . banking firms and international consortiums, great stock exchanges, speculators, and international suppliers of weapons and their agents."[65]

After World War II, when relations with the West began to deteriorate, patriotism, which came to be identified more and more with Russian nationalism, was frequently discussed in the mass media of the Soviet Union. "Cosmopolitanism" which in the 1920s had been identical with the term "internationalism," had slipped from favor in the 1930s and was soon to become a positive evil. In February 1946, Stalin warned that as long as capitalism existed there would be wars. Beginning in June 1946, a fierce campaign against bourgeois nationalism was aimed at the republics which had been liberated from German occupation, particularly the Ukraine. Idealization of the past and glorification of epochs of special significance to a particular nation were criticized, as were writers who did not sufficiently stress the bonds of friendship between Russians and non-Russians or emphasize the class war existing within all peoples.[66]

Inevitably, such an onslaught would strike Jews, too. One important signal for the start of a campaign against Jewish "nationalism" came in resolutions dealing with literature passed by the Central Committee of the party and in Zhdanov's speeches in August 1946. A member of the Politburo and leading spokesman on questions of doctrine, Zhdanov, who was regarded by Stalin as an expert on art and literature, condemned a group of Leningrad writers and the monthly journals *Leningrad* and *Zvezda* (The Star) in August 1946, causing disarray in literary circles. He attacked Western influence in the arts and scholarship, and the Writers' Union took this to mean a call to action against the freer wartime expression in art and literature.[67] Zhdanov's address "provided the basis for and justification for prolonged Soviet belligerence toward the West and strict Soviet control over all other Communist governments and parties." It was one of the first major policy statements to accuse the United States of having aggressive designs vis-à-vis the Soviet Union and "plans for the enslavement of Europe."[68] The hard-line Cold War policy was now in place.

The new repression that was ushered in became known as *Zhdanovshchina*, or the period of Zhdanov. Dynamic, energetic, and expressive, Zhdanov apparently believed with great passion that "the Soviet people had to be saved from the corruption of the West." Too many soldiers had been exposed to the material wealth in Europe, obvious even during the war, and had to be quarantined when they got back to the USSR. He also believed there would have to be a fight to the finish with the United States over Europe. Still young, well-educated, in accord with Stalin's core ideas, he "set the tone of the Soviet attitude towards the outer world from 1946 to 1948,"[69] while at home he took it upon himself to organize and prosecute the great purge of the arts, the struggle against "cosmopolitanism."

The party resolutions, which dealt with certain journals, the repertoire of the theater, and a film called "The Great Life," glorified the Soviet regime, stressed the superiority of the Russian people in all fields of science and culture, and expressed a hatred of the "decadent West," especially the United States.[70] They also attacked subservience to foreign culture and any individualism and pessimism in Soviet art and literature. The chief victims of the resolutions were the satirist Mikhail Zoshchenko, the composer Shostakovich, and the great poet Anna Akhmatova, all non-Jews, but there were many Jewish names (for example, Varshavsky, Khazin, Rybak) among those criticized. As yet, however, there was no explicit anti-Jewish tone, and a number of Jewish writers and critics, who were later to be among the chief victims of the anti-cosmopolitan campaign, came forward to support the new anti-

Western line. Many reviews that appeared in *Einikayt* in 1946 and 1947 after Zhdanov's speech reflected the new position. Ilya Ehrenburg, however, although he was very critical of the United States, drew the line at Shakespeare and Rembrandt. "It is impossible," he wrote, "to toady to Shakespeare or Rembrandt, because prostration before them cannot humiliate the worshipper."[71]

Zhdanov made Soviet artistic and intellectual productions effective weapons in the Cold War to counter the ideological threat from the West and prepare the Soviet people for sacrifices in the coming struggle. He attacked the ideological indifference and pessimism he found in many Soviet works and felt they would dangerously damage Soviet morale in any confrontation with the enemy camp.[72] Above all, literature had to inspire confidence in the Soviet future, to arouse the people's loyalty to the nation and its leaders. The pressure to strengthen Soviet patriotism and avoid the "bowing and scraping" to Western influences continued throughout 1946 and became more marked in 1947.[73] Some Soviet Jews began to feel apprehensive.

Yet, despite a sense of danger, many Yiddish writers boldly "set out to insure the continuation of their work by proving that there existed a demand for Yiddish books and that it was economically worthwhile."[74] There are repeated references in *Einikayt* to the great demand for Yiddish books and to the successful sales of such books throughout the USSR, and some evidence that Yiddish publishing and literature would have a future after the war. The Yiddish daily press was not re-established, but *Einikayt* was still coming out three times a week in Moscow and six issues of a literary almanac called *Heymland* appeared in 1947–48. (Number 7 was published but not circulated.)

Der Emes Publishing House in Moscow continued to be the main source of Soviet Yiddish publishing, but it did not announce its first postwar publishing plans until February 1947, and the number of books subsequently published was considerably less than that envisaged.[75] Much more material was prepared for publication than was actually published, obviously reflecting the new policy line following Zhdanov's speech in September 1946.[76] The prewar publishing houses in Kiev and Minsk were not re-established. In 1947, notices appeared about preparations for publishing books in Yiddish in Minsk, but no special department was established within the White Russian publishing structure. In that year the only Yiddish literary anthology, *Mit festn trot* (With a Firm Step) in the postwar period, was published before the final blow to Yiddish culture was struck in November 1948. Yiddish writers in Kiev made strenuous efforts to revive publishing there, but only seven issues of *Der shtern*, the literary almanac of Yiddish writers in the Ukraine, materialized;[77] the last one was not distributed.

Various articles and readers' letters in *Einikayt* indicated the demand for Yiddish books considerably surpassed the supply. There were also complaints about the lack of Yiddish books in the municipal libraries of Moscow and Leningrad.[78] Intensified Jewish consciousness had stimulated a taste for Yiddish books, which had been sold in large editions, amounting to one million roubles during the period 1941–43 alone. The war had influenced the demand for books on Jewish subjects, but by 1946 there were noticeable changes. The demand was still high, and Yiddish books worth 1,150,000 roubles were sold out quickly, but the editions were small—from 10 to 20,000 copies. Moreover, only eighteen books in Yiddish appeared in 1946, and many books that were officially advertised in *Einikayt* to appear in 1946–48 did not appear at all. Even so, in 1947, forty-nine Yiddish books and pamphlets were published, many with specifically Jewish content, especially in the field of belles-lettres, still reflecting the shock of the Holocaust and the softened nationality policy of the regime during the war.[79] Obviously, Yiddish writers found themselves in a difficult and uncertain time, wrestling with conflicting signals: the increases in Yiddish publication and promises of expansion as against Zhdanov's speech.

One negative sign was the refusal of the regime to re-open Yiddish schools, which foreclosed the possibility of new generations of Jews knowing very much about Jewish culture. Yet, there were other expressions that were permitted and were flourishing. Yiddish literary evenings were very popular in a number of cities, especially in the annexed areas in the cities of Chernovtsy and Vilnius,[80] and the Yiddish theater was enormously popular. Six Yiddish theaters were active after the war—the Moscow, Kiev, Odessa, Minsk, Birobidzhan, and Uzbek Yiddish Theaters. Their performances were warmly received, and the prestige of the theater in Moscow was much enhanced after Stalin prizes were awarded to its outstanding figures, Mikhoels, Zuskin and Tishler, in 1946. Yiddish drama and musical groups also performed in outlying towns and cities. In 1947, the "Mikhoels Office for the History of the Jewish Theater" which had emerged out of the "Chair for Jewish Theater" had publication plans, but they remained unrealized. A number of the Jewish scholars in Moscow had died in the war, but the demographer Zinger was able to publish the last of his socio-economic surveys, *Dos ufgerikhte folk* (A Re-awakened People) before all Jewish scholarly and cultural work was closed down. The Institute for Jewish Culture of the Ukrainian Academy, the last significant Jewish scholarly institution left, aroused much interest in the pro-Soviet Yiddish press abroad, but its publication plans, too, were aborted.[81]

In 1946 there were also several ominous attacks against Jewish writers. One of the first was a belated tirade against Isaac (Yitzhak) Nusinov's treatment of Pushkin in his book *Pushkin and World Literature.* Originally published in 1941, this was a small work by a man who had at one time been professor of European literature at Moscow University and was also a leading champion of Soviet Yiddish literature. Charges of attempting to "Europeanize" classical Russian literature were made against Nusinov in the summer of 1946 by the prominent Russian writer Nikolai Tikhonov in an article called "In Defense of Pushkin."[82] In it, Nusinov was referred to as a "vagabond without a passport," and "an Ivan who has forgotten his roots,"[83] a foreshadowing of the vehement campaign against "rootless cosmopolitans" that was soon to follow. Fadeyev denounced the "denationalization" of Pushkin by Nusinov, who, he said, had turned the Russian poet into "something universal, pan-European, all-embracing." Fadeyev charged that there wasn't "a single word to the effect that the national war of 1812 took place. . . . The fundamental idea of the book is that Pushkin's genius does not express the uniqueness of the historical development of the Russian nation, as a Marxist ought to have shown, but that Pushkin's greatness consisted of his being 'European' . . ."[84]

There was no allusion to Nusinov's Jewishness in this attack, but Fadeyev's choice could not have been accidental. Nusinov was one of the leading scholars of Jewish literature and was known as such among the Soviet intelligentsia. He answered the attack with an article, but the authorities refused to publish it. For a time, he held his ground, but at a closed meeting of the Writers' Union, he recanted, admitted his "errors," and promised to make amends.[85] Markish was present at the meeting and came home depressed and disheartened. "He didn't condemn Nusinov," his wife recalled; "he merely tried to analyze in good conscience what had happened. And he understood all too well where it was all leading."[86]

An article in *Einikayt* of September 24, 1946, reminded readers that the historic resolutions of the Central Committee were of direct concern to Jewish theater and literature. A number of important figures such as Halkin and Sutzkever were accused of producing works that were, from the Soviet point of view, apolitical, nationalist, and devoid of ideas. But Jewish national feeling could not be suppressed. An incident in 1946 involving Sutzkever, who had just returned from the Nuremburg War Crimes Trials,[87] revealed the strong, suppressed emotions toward Palestine among many Jews and some JAC members. Toward the end of his report to an overcrowded meeting, he said with great feeling: "Our greatest revenge would be realized if Jerusalem were to become ours." Sutzkever later wrote: "It seemed as if the audience froze for a moment . . . fear mixed with joy was apparent. . . . After a few seconds, however, thunderous applause followed. They applauded so fiercely that I myself became frightened."[88]

On October 10, 1946, *Einikayt* published a severe critique of S. Verite's book *When the Earth Burned*, in which the author was accused of being "too preoccupied with Jewish history" and of "slandering Soviet man and Soviet reality." Two days later the veteran literary critic Dobrushin appealed to Jewish writers not to confine themselves to a limited individualism but to describe general social processes and common interests of Soviet society generally.[89] During this time, Markish was demoted from his position as chairman of the Yiddish section of the Moscow branch of the Writers' Union and replaced by Leib Kvitko. His great epic poem *Di Milkhome* (The War) also came under harsh attack.

In 1947, the campaign was heated up. The Yiddish sections of the Writers' Union in Minsk and in Kiev were reorganized, and at meetings, the new directives were discussed. In Kiev, Feffer emphasized the lessons to be learned from the new policy. The national emphasis in Markish's drama "The Ghetto Uprising," was harshly criticized; he was told he should have stressed class conflict.[90]

In July and August 1947, a major campaign was conducted against Itzik Kipnis in the pages of the Yiddish and Ukrainian press and at writers' conventions, resulting in his expulsion from the Writers' Union and later arrest.[91] Kipnis' home was Kiev, the city of Babi Yar. In 1944, on the third anniversary of the mass slaughter, Kipnis had written a haunting piece about the agony of Babi Yar and of his sad return to the hollow city. But amid the lamentation, he evokes a consoling note: "A people half and three-quarters of which has been annihilated, is like a globule of mercury. Wrench half of it away, and the other half will become rounded and whole again." This search for Jewish wholeness was soon to become an incubus. The pretext for the official attack was a story that Kipnis wrote called "Without Giving It a Thought," which first appeared uncensored in Poland.[92] (It had been published in abridged form in *Einikayt* in July 1945 without certain "nationalistic" passages.) The story deals with a Ukrainian woman who saves two Jewish children during the war and raises them as part of her family. Kipnis is grateful, but wishes that they had been returned to their Jewish origins. He wrote:

I have become most jealous in the recent years. I am greatly concerned for what has remained whole. Whenever I see a Jewish student, a beautiful young girl, a bold and sturdy looking soldier, a learned old man, an academician and a plain, simple Jew, I yearn to hear them speak Yiddish to me. . . . "All Jews who now walk victoriously in the streets of Berlin should wear on their chests, next to their medals and decorations, also a little Star of David. He [Hitler] wanted to see the Jew tortured, abused, and spat upon. Now I wish all to see that I am a Jew, and that my Jewish pride and honor is not one bit less than that of all other freedom-loving citizens.[93]

Attacks on Kipnis were signalled in *Einikayt* of July 3rd, 1947, in a leading article entitled "Nationalism in the Guise of Friendship of Peoples." The critic alleged[94] that "Only a nationalist is capable of placing Soviet awards and medals, which symbolize the honor, greatness, and courage of Soviet people, side by side with . . . the Star of David. Jewish fighters would of course reject this award of Kipnis." Leib Kvitko joined in the attack, saying that Kipnis had ignored earlier warnings. In September the Ukrainian Writers' Union declared that "Kipnis slandered Soviet man . . . by wanting the Star of David, the Zionist symbol to be worn along the Soviet Star on the breast of the Soviet soldier." In October he was accused of "nationalist recidivism."

In September 1947, at the inaugural conference of the Cominform, Zhdanov's theme was the division of the world into two hostile camps and America's ambition of world domination. The regime was now poised for a new crackdown on "deviationism" that would mean near-catastrophe for many Jewish lives and for Jewish culture. But first Jews would be overjoyed—and deceived—by the regime's policy toward Jewish national aspirations in Palestine and toward the very idea of a Jewish state.

21

Soviet Policy toward the Jewish State and Hebrew Stirrings, 1946–49

I am glad and proud that I signed the appeal to the government of Israel and the Soviet Union to improve relations. Without good relations with the Soviet Union and with the great Russian people, our people will not survive the present moment. We must remember what happened during the war that preceded the formation of our state, and what an enormous role the Soviet Union played in granting help to our people. It is not a question of emotions or of some political situation; today, it is for us a question of life or death.

ROALD ZELICHENOK at his trial in 1985

A STRIKING contrast, indeed contradiction, existed between Soviet policy toward its own Jews and Soviet policy toward Jewish national aspirations in Palestine in the years 1946–48. Efforts have been made to analyze the nature of the relationship between these two developments, but full documentation is still unavailable and puzzling questions remain. More than most modern states, the Soviet Union is able to keep domestic policy clearly insulated from foreign policy and to make sudden shifts with cold contempt for consistency or steadiness. For Jews in the Soviet Union, the jolts were scarcely bearable. Hoping for some consideration after the terrible suffering and losses during the war, they found instead, a regime which expected them to be grateful, mounting anti-Semitism, and a swift, ruthless assault on Jewish cultural life which had just recently been officially fostered. The formal support for a Jewish state, converging as it did while Soviet Jewry was persecuted, and coming after a long history of Communist opposition to Zionism, further jolted Soviet Jews and confounded their grasp of affairs.

In the period from February 1945 to April 1947, there had been no official statement of Soviet policy on the Palestine question, apart from expressions of disapproval of British activity and Anglo-American co-operation: "On the one hand, Soviet communications media as well as Soviet diplomacy . . . tended to indicate a pro-Arab stand. On the other hand, the Soviets were quietly aiding the emigration of Jews from Eastern Europe, and particularly Poland, to western occupation zones of Germany and Austria, in the knowledge that these Jews intended to continue on to Palestine."[1] During that time, the USSR had been demanding that the Palestine question be discussed at the United Nations.

On May 1, 1947, Andrei Gromyko, Soviet deputy foreign minister and former ambassador to the United States, called for the termination of the British mandate, and at a special meeting of the General Assembly on the following day he insisted that any discussion of the Palestine question required the presence of Jews, specifically the Jews of Palestine, urging that the Jewish Agency be invited to present its case. The Polish delegate stressed the near-annihilation of Polish Jewry during the Holocaust and his country's commitment to the fate of the Jewish people as a whole and the Jewish refugees in particular. On May 8, in order to emphasize the importance of Soviet parity among the great powers and Soviet participation in the disposition of Palestine, Gromyko proposed that the five permanent members of the Security Council be included in the projected UN Special Committee on Palestine (UNSCOP). The Soviet interest in the Palestine question, he said, was "political," not "material," a distinction not altogether clear at the time. Then, in contrast with the Polish Jewish link to Palestine, Gromyko said, "The Soviet Union is not directly interested in the Palestine problem from the point of view . . . of the emigration of Jews to Palestine, since as far as I am aware, the Jewish population of the Soviet Union does not show any interest in emigration to Palestine."[2] However, he admitted that the "aspirations of a substantial portion of the Jewish people were bound up with the question of Palestine, and with the future structure of that country." Further, he declared that "there could be no justification for any attempts to deny the right . . . to the creation of their own state to those who had survived Nazi atrocities"—a complete about-face from the earlier demand for repatriation. Gromyko also made it clear that the "great powers" in the Security Council would fully participate in all deliberations and decisions—an unmistakable indication that the Soviet Union expected acknowledgment as a great power. (The Special Committee [UNSCOP] did not include the five permanent members of the Security Council, but two Soviet bloc countries, Czechoslovakia and Yugoslavia, were members.)

On May 14, Gromyko again addressed a plenary session of the General Assembly. After condemning Britain's failure to carry out the aims of the Mandate, Gromyko spoke with unusual feeling about Jewish suffering during the war:

> During the last war, the Jewish people underwent exceptional sorrow and suffering. Without any exaggeration, this sorrow and suffering are indescribable. It is difficult to express them in dry statistics. . . . The Jews in territories where the Hitlerites held sway were subjected to almost complete physical annihilation. The total number . . . who perished at the hands of the Nazi executioners is estimated at approximately six million. Only about a million and a half Jews in Western Europe survived the war. . . .
>
> Large numbers of the surviving Jews of Europe were deprived of their countries, their homes and their means of existence. Hundreds of thousands of Jews are wandering about in various countries of Europe in search of means of existence and in search of shelter. A large number of them are in camps . . . and are still continuing to undergo great privations . . .
>
> The fact that no western European State has been able to ensure the defense of the elementary rights of the Jewish people . . . explains the aspirations of the Jews to establish their own State. It would be unjust not to take this into consideration and to deny this right of the Jewish people. . . .[3]

An equitable solution, Gromyko continued, must provide for the "legitimate interests" of both Arabs and Jews in Palestine. If a single, independent state cannot be implemented, he proposed partition of Palestine into one Jewish and one Arab state. However, a binational state, in which protection of both Jewish and Arab peoples could be assured, according to Gromyko, was the preferred solution. Yet partition was mentioned, anticipating a later development and suggesting a course which would surely create much mischief for Britain.[4]

The Soviet Union thus projected itself as the one great power "willing to assume its responsibilities" in relation to the future of Palestine, while using the unresolved issue of Palestine to intensify its attacks against the United States and Britain. In this period of increased East-West tensions, the Soviet Union "was striving . . . to win support among Western public opinion, notably among . . . 'progressive' groupings,"[5] most especially American Jews. In this propaganda effort, Soviet Yiddish broadcasts to North America were increased from a quarter to a half-hour daily and Jewish masses were called on to unite with "progressive" forces and identify with the Soviet Union. Western anti-Semitism and "pogroms" contrasted with the Soviet "struggle against reaction and the remnants of Fascism" were recurring themes. Itzik Feffer in his broadcasts told Yiddish audiences that Jews could not maintain a neutral position. "Neutrality was merely a pseudonym for treason." In Palestine, he said, the Jewish people must achieve its aim by establishing ties with the "peace-loving peoples" and not by means of deals with "imperialist circles."[6]

The Jewish press in America reacted gratefully to Gromyko's remarks and was praised in the Soviet Union. Among others, an article "The Jewish Press in the U.S.A Welcomes A.A. Gromyko's Speech," in the May 20, 1947 issue of *Izvestiya* showed obvious pleasure in the enthusiasm Gromyko had evoked among Jews: "Gromyko's speech has the greatest historical significance not only for Zionists, but for the entire Jewish people."[7] *Tass* stressed the many congratulatory telegrams the Soviet deputy foreign minister had received.

For the next few months, however, the Soviet position on the future of Palestine was cautious and uncertain. At times it seemed to prefer a federated binational state, at other times, partition, but there were also warnings against thinking in terms of a Jewish state. Yet Moscow refused to help the British limit Jewish immigration to Palestine and continued to permit the outflow of Jews from Poland to Palestine.

Finally, apparently after Britain decided to give up its mandate (late in September) and leave Palestine, the USSR clarified its position. On October 13, the Soviet Union publicly declared its support for partition of Palestine "to give the right of self-determination of hundreds of thousands of Jews and Arabs living in Palestine." The Soviet delegate to the UN, Semen Tsarapkin, also referred to the great suffering of the Jewish people and said that "it would be unjust to deny [Jews] that right [to create a state of their own]."[8]

On November 29, 1947, the United Nations adopted a resolution to partition Palestine. The Soviet Union maintained full support for this decision against American reluctance and British opposition and opposed the efforts of the UN mediator Count Bernadotte to radically change the sense of the partition resolution.

Besides wanting to oust Britain and penetrate the Mediterranean area herself, the Soviet Union was apparently disappointed with the Arab national movement, which, during the war, had been pro-German, and was unable at the time to turn the Arab states into a progressive bloc. The decision to support Jewish statehood was based "on a cool evaluation of the factors that Moscow at the time believed would best further its power interests," regardless of past ideological objections to Zionism.[9] The Soviet interest in the Middle East generally can be gauged by a statement in *Pravda* just a day after Gromyko's speech to the UN on November 26, 1947, predicting "freedom" for the Iranian province of Azerbaidzan, "bordering the Soviet Union."

In addition to supporting the Partition Resolution, the Soviet Union gave military as well as political support to Palestine's Jewry in the form of Czechoslovakian arms.[10] According to Ben-Gurion, this arms aid, which continued after May 1948 until the Arab invasion was repelled, saved Israel from physical annihilation. Broadcasts over Radio Moscow in May 1948 compared the Jewish struggle to that of the Spanish Civil War.

Soviet motives were largely geopolitical: to dislodge Britain from the Middle East, and create a foothold there for the Soviet Union; to weaken the Western alliance by cooperating with the United States against Britain; to enhance the Soviet position at the UN and its international prestige; to promote Arab national movements and cause the collapse of conservative regimes that ruled the Arab world and were still tied in certain ways to Britain.[11] Some analysts have also suggested that the Soviet Union hoped to create a pro-Soviet position, even a base, in Israel, but this cannot be argued very convincingly. What was apparently not sufficiently comprehended in the Soviet pro-Israel position, brief though it was, was the great emotional response from Soviet Jewry to the struggle for Jewish statehood and then the reality of the Jewish state itself. (Interestingly, in the anti-Jewish campaign of 1948–49, the first attacks were on cosmopolitans; there were only, at first, rare references to Israel or Zionism.)[12]

On May 18, 1948, the Soviet Union granted *de jure* recognition of the State of Israel, four days after it was established, and during the war that followed took very pro-Israel positions on a number of issues. In August, the Soviet delegate to the UN Jacob Malik deplored British "great emphasis on the Arabs' so-called fear of Jewish immigration into Palestine . . . instead of helping to dissipate it." Later, during October, the Soviet Union supported Israel's conquest of the Negev and Galilee, and in the following month proposed a withdrawal of all foreign troops from Palestine. From the first day of its existence, it encouraged Israel to apply for UN membership and criticized the Arab invasion as well as British efforts to restrict Jewish immigration and arm the Arab armies.

Upon the official establishment of the State of Israel on May 14, telegrams of congratulations were sent to President Chaim Weizmann from the Jewish Antifascist Committee and Moscow's "Jewish community." Some Soviet Jews wanted to emigrate to Israel; others, including students and army officers, were eager to fight with the Israelis and went to the Soviet Foreign Ministry and OVIR (the passport office at the Ministry of Interior) to get permission to leave the country.[13] A few wrote directly to Stalin and later suffered. Others, at considerable risk, went to the Israeli legation, which, apparently at first, did not realize the dangers involved, especially after the passage of the State Secrets Act of June 9, 1947, which made virtually all contact with a foreigner an anti-Soviet activity.[14] A number of these were later arrested or disappeared. Contacts were also made with the JAC with suggestions to send aid, such as medical supplies to Israel, but Grigori Heifetz, who headed the JAC after Mikhoels' death, rejected the idea.[15]

Many Soviet Jews believed that their government's strong endorsement of a Jewish state loosened the constraints they might have otherwise felt. After many years during which it had been forbidden to mention Zionism and Palestine, it now was officially approved and supported. Jewish national consciousness was much heightened as Jews saw at first hand their own government's support of a Jewish state. Aside from personal feelings of joy and pride, there was the role model of their own government. They thus felt doubly propelled in their support and enthusiasm.

There were many signs of extreme interest and concern over Palestine Jewry's struggle for independence.[16] For example, during the Yiddish journalist Ben Zion Goldberg's visit to the Soviet Union in 1946, his references to that struggle met with intense feeling in a number of communities, and his remarks at the main synagogue in Moscow on Passover drew loud applause. Lozovsky, of the JAC expressed sympathy with the *bricha* movement (Palestine Jewry's efforts to move survivors out of the D.P. camps). After the declaration of Soviet support, *Einikayt* published information on developments in Palestine, especially on the fighting, and articles by well-known Jewish writers. David Bergelson wrote that the Soviet Union at the UN had revealed the links between the Jewish people and Palestine that had existed over a long period.[17] In the fall of 1948, Feffer said the new state of Israel was the concern of the entire Jewish people, and that the soldiers of Stalingrad and the workers of Leningrad contributed more to its creation than American Zionists.[18] Even Ehrenburg, who would soon take another position, during a visit to Poland in the winter of 1947–48, spoke warmly of Tsarapkin's and Gromyko's stands and said it was only natural that Soviet Jewry followed the course of the war with great interest. The shift to a sovereign and independent existence in Palestine, he said, would be of great value to the Jewish people.[19]

A manuscript written in Hebrew by a Soviet Jew between 1948 and 1953, which ultimately reached Israel, describes the atmosphere at the time: "The period immediately preceding the adoption of the UN Palestine Partition resolution . . . was a time of great agitation and ferment for the Jews of the Soviet Union. . . . We were overjoyed when we read the speeches of the Soviet representatives Gromyko and Tsarapkin. These speeches persuaded us (how sadly mistaken we were!) that the Soviet Government would not be opposed if some of its Jewish citizens wished to emigrate to Israel. . . ."[20]

The dramatic climax to this excitement was reached during the spontaneous demonstrations near the Moscow synagogue, on the High Holy Days in 1948, when Jews swarmed to greet Golda Meyerson (later Meir), the new envoy from Israel. The first hint that Mrs. Meyerson might be asked to serve as the first minister from Israel to the Soviet Union occurred a few days after May 14, 1948, when the establishment of the State of Israel was announced. Moshe Sharett (formerly Shertok), the new foreign minister, spoke to her about the problems of manning embassies and consulates and said he was especially worried about not having anyone for Moscow. "Well, thank God, you can't offer it to me," she replied. "My Russian is almost nonexistent." But, as it turned out, that didn't matter at all, and the first delegation from a Jewish state arrived in Moscow on September 3rd, with Mrs. Meyerson at its head.

The delegation[21] consisted of twenty-six people, including Mrs. Meyerson's daughter Sarah and Sarah's husband; an "indispensable" aide Eiga Shapiro, who knew Russian perfectly and could deal with practical matters, including the kinds of clothes Mrs. Meyerson would have to buy, and Lou Kaddar, a Paris-born Israeli, a woman who was to become a close companion. Mrs. Meyerson decided to set up the legation in the Israeli kibbutz style. The members would work together, eat together, get the same amount of pocket money, and take turns doing whatever chores had to be done. Their first residence was the old-fashioned Hotel Metropole, but the charges were so high for their modest budget that they decided to eat only one meal a day in the hotel dining room and cook their breakfasts and suppers on a hot plate. The trips to market early on frosty mornings were among the pleasantest experiences of all for Mrs. Meyerson, because of the "politeness, sincerity and warmth of the ordinary Russian," waiting patiently in the line or selling goods.

The legation hoped that Russians and especially Russian Jews would come to Mrs. Meyerson's open house every Friday evening, but none did. Newspapermen and representatives from other embassies and some visiting Jews came, but none of the people she wanted most to see. Some of the members of the delegation still had relatives in the Soviet Union, but they were afraid of making contact with them. After Mrs. Meyerson's credentials were read in the presence of the deputy president, she delivered a short speech in Hebrew, followed by a translation; a modest reception was then held in her honor. On the following Saturday, the delegation visited the Great Synagogue in Moscow, where they found only a hundred or so Jews, mostly old. Toward the end of the service, there was a blessing for the good health of the heads of state and one for Mrs. Meyerson who was sitting in the women's gallery. When her name was mentioned, the whole congregation turned to stare at her, but no one said anything. She introduced herself to Rabbi Schlieffer and they talked briefly and then parted. On her way back to the hotel, an elderly man brushed up against her and said in Yiddish, "Don't say anything. I'll walk on and you follow me." When they were near the hotel, he turned suddenly and standing there on the windy Moscow street, he recited the thanksgiving prayer *Shehekhiyanu* and then quickly slipped away. At Rosh Hashanah, the Jewish New Year, Mrs. Meir hoped there might be more Jews at the synagogue. Just a month before, Ehrenburg's article had appeared in *Pravda*, declaring that the State of Israel had nothing to do with the Jews of the Soviet Union, and that they had no need for a Jewish state (see p. 484).

Disregarding this obvious warning and the growing signs of repression, some 50,000 Jews crowded the street in front of the synagogue— Jews of all ages and persuasions, even Red Army officers (see Photo 21.1). Mrs. Meyerson was overwhelmed:

21.1 Golda Meyerson (Meir), Israel's first minister to the Soviet Union, enthusiastically greeted by crowds of Soviet Jews in Moscow, outside the main synagogue, October 16, 1948. Courtesy Anti-Defamation League.

For a minute I couldn't grasp what had happened—or even who they were. And then it dawned on me. They had come—those good, brave Jews—in order to be with us, to demonstrate their sense of kinship and to celebrate the establishment of the State of Israel. Within seconds they had surrounded me, almost lifting me bodily, almost crushing me, saying my name over and over again.[22]

When she was once again seated in the women's gallery, women would come over to touch her hand or stroke her dress, without words. Afterward, again in the street amid the surging crowd, unable to find words to match the power of this torrent of love, she said "clumsily, and in a voice that didn't even sound like my own, '*A dank eich vos ihr seit geblieben Yiden,*' (Thank you for having remained Jews), and I heard that miserable, inadequate sentence being passed on through the enormous crowd as though it were some prophetic saying."[23]

Twenty years later, Russian Jews brought to Israel yellowed prints of a photograph of that flooding moment, a crescendo of emotion for which Soviet Jews paid a heavy price.

There were huge crowds once more in the streets leading to the synagogue on Yom Kippur Eve, and inside the congregation refused to leave without her, although she had been told not to leave the synagogue after Kol Nidre until the crowds dispersed. There was another large demonstration on Yom Kippur Day and an immense, long-suppressed surge of feeling when the congregation recited the prayer, "Lashanah habah b'Yerushalayim" (Next Year in Jerusalem!) "The words shook the synagogue," Mrs. Meyerson said, "as they looked up at me. It was the most passionate Zionist speech I had ever heard."[24]

The struggle for a Jewish state also gave some Jewish poets in the Soviet Union a revived interest—sometimes obsessively—with the Hebrew language. In the mid-twenties, contact with the living language had been cut off, but in 1947–48, there were new stirrings. Yitzhak Cohen (Kahanov) wrote that he "clutched again at the Hebrew language, which I had abandoned for twenty-four long years."[25] With the help of a Bible and a Hebrew-Russian dictionary, he tried to refresh his knowledge while fighting off doubts. On September 12, 1948, nine days after Mrs. Meyerson's arrival in Moscow, he was arrested in Simferopol and brought in handcuffs to Moscow. Around the same time, two other Hebrew poets, Moshe Hyog and Zvi Preygerzon, were charged with sending a secret letter of encouragement to David Ben-Gurion and sending their Hebrew writings abroad by illegal methods.

While imprisoned, Cohen's tenacity to master and keep the Hebrew language within him is a remarkable human drama. He had no dictionary but decided to compose one in his head. For nine and a half months Cohen stored in his mind thousands of Hebrew words which he repeated to himself over and over again:

This internal preoccupation with the dictionary took place as I paced my cell and sat silent on my bed. . . . It was all done without moving my lips, without a sound. From time to time I would endeavor not only to recall the word and hold it in my memory, but also to imagine it written out in full, expressed and spoken, and framed in a sentence. . . . All this was done by intensive spiritual concentration. . . . I was totally imbued with Hebrew at all hours of the day and night. And I had no need of a dictionary or book from outside to aid me.[26]

The first surge of poetic inspiration struck him "like the wind, like waves beating against the shore." After sixteen months in prison, he was transferred to the Karaganda camp where he continued to "write" and memorize his poems. At interrogations, he was ordered to turn over his "book," and the names of a "Jewish nationalist organization" he was alleged to be a member of. In October 1953, Cohen was sentenced to death, but his sentence was commuted to twenty-five years and he was sent to camps in the far North. He was released two years later because of ill health, having stored 480 poems in his mind. All of his work ultimately reached Israel shortly before his emigration in 1976.

Cohen had been a friend of Hyog, who had translated Pasternak's *Safe Conduct* and some of Babel's stories into Hebrew. Hyog had met with several other Hebrew enthusiasts in Odessa in the early 1930s and made persistent, risky efforts to obtain Hebrew texts for his young son and Hebrew material for himself—even newspaper clippings. Mere luck, chance, and haphazard decisions by censors occasionally enabled him to receive a trickle. Toward the end of 1934, and for a year thereafter, he began to receive a steady stream from his friend Avraham Kariv, who had left the Soviet Union for Palestine. His own brother's preparation to leave Poland and go to Palestine apparently stirred Hyog deeply, but he could find no release for his yearnings.

After the war, sometime in January 1948, Hyog invited several other Hebrew enthusiasts—Zvi Preygerzon, Cohen, and Gregory Gordon—to his home. Gordon, also known as Sasha, was an agent provocateur, who pretended to be their friend and confidant. He suggested that the writers send their work to Palestine through an army physician who was about to leave for Bulgaria. He also suggested that they send a letter in invisible ink to Ben-Gurion to express Soviet Jewry's warm support for a Jewish state and give it to the doctor. Sasha also inspired petitions to the Soviet government urging a chair in Hebrew Studies at Moscow University. All of this data and detailed reports were immediately dispatched to the MGB. In September, Hyog was the first of a group of Hebrew writers to be arrested. Despite his great suffering in prison camps, Hyog's inner world was sustained by the balm of the Hebrew language: "among the waves of memory, and in the heart, in the brain," he hears the comforting verses from the Psalms and "the richest and most profound source of the language, from the Book of Books."

For Zvi Preygerzon[27] as well, Hebrew became an inner homeland, all the more astonishing inasmuch as he was a highly respected mining engineer and faculty member of Moscow University. Pained by the shattering of traditional Jewish life and the memory of "the patches of green in the alleyways of my youth," Preygerzon lived the split life of many other Soviet Jews, externally adjusted, internally grieving over what had vanished forever. With Preygerzon, too, the inner world was sustained by Hebrew. He first began writing stories in Hebrew in the thirties and his first novel *Bid'och Hamenora* (The Flickering Lamp)[28] during the war. In 1946, the informer "Sasha" [Gordon] who learned Hebrew from Preygerzon, urged him to send his work to Palestine through Polish citizens who began returning to Poland from the Soviet Union. Several of Preygerzon's notebooks, which he had showed to "Sasha" were turned over to the MGB.

Despite his long professional career and achievements in coal mining research, Preygerzon was taken from his apartment by MGB men on March 1, 1949 at 2 A.M. He was brought to the Lubyanka prison and interrogated in the customary Soviet manner: incessant grilling at midnight, accompanied by beatings, solitary confinement, threats against his family, a starvation diet, and relentless pressure to "confess." Preygerzon's interrogation lasted nine months, until he succumbed and signed a "confession" and 200 pages of a protocol admitting his guilt as a criminal under article 52, section 1 of the Criminal Code. His work in Hebrew had made him an "enemy of the people." He was removed to Butyrka prison, then to Karaganda in Siberia where he met many other Jews accused of Zionism, and finally to Vorkuta where the editors of *Emes* and *Einikayt* were also imprisoned.

Preygerzon's *Yoman HaZikhronot*[29] (Diary of Remembrance), is an important historical document not only for its details of conditions in Soviet camps and the behavior of the prisoners, but for Preygerzon's unfailing attachment to Hebrew. "Even when I was in prison," he later wrote, "I swore that I would not forsake the Hebrew language, and I have kept that [vow] until today . . . Until my very last breath, I will devote heart and soul to the Hebrew language." Wherever he was imprisoned, he sought the company of Jews who knew Hebrew or Hebrew songs, which he collected. One prisoner remembered that "in isolation, he would talk to himself in Hebrew in order not to forget it."[30]

In September 1951, he was required to live in a specially designated taiga area under the surveillance of the MGB. Finally, under the law of

September 3, 1955, permitting the release of invalids, he was released and rehabilitated and given back his former job at the mining academy.[31] He also continued lecturing at the university, resumed his literary work in Hebrew, took great delight in reading technical engineering and architectural journals in Hebrew at the Lenin Library, and maintained a correspondence in Hebrew with several authors in Israel. He died of a heart attack on March 15, 1969 and, in accordance with his last wishes, his ashes were brought to Israel and interred at Kibbutz Shfayim near Tel Aviv.

The popular Jewish reactions to Mrs. Meyerson in the fall of 1948 were unprecedented and apparently took Stalin and other Soviet authorities by surprise. The depth and passion of Jewish feeling was startling— and disquieting. After thirty years of Communist rule, "sovietization" of Soviet Jews, and rapid assimilation, these fires had not been quenched. Stalin also apparently began to fear and suspect Soviet Jewry's contacts with the West, their eager acceptance of the work of JAC, and the brief flowering of Yiddish culture. All of that would have to end and the standard bearers of that revival be reviled, exposed as dangerous, isolated, and removed from Soviet life. How much of this alleged threat Stalin himself believed and how much he exploited craftily for internal purposes is difficult to assess. Many observers have reported his growing paranoia and obsession with personal as well as national security, which reached a bizarre pitch of suspicion in the so-called doctors' plot of 1953 (see Chapter 24). He was also becoming obsessed with the alleged dangers of Soviet contamination by the West, with Jewish contacts in the West that took their minds out of rigid Soviet control. Moreover, he was giving more noticeable rein to a long-harbored dislike of Jews.

His daughter Svetlana has said that Stalin's feelings over the years changed "from political hatred to racial aversion for all Jews," and that his vehement anti-Semitism caused her divorce from her first husband Grigory Morozov, who was a Jew, and his deportation.[32] Stalin accused him of shirking military service. After their divorce, Stalin told her that "that first husband of yours was thrown your way by the Zionists," and that "the entire older generation is contaminated with Zionism and now they are teaching the young people too."[33] Svetlana as well as Khrushchev agreed that Stalin eventually regarded all Jews as "treacherous and dishonest" and came to view the members of the JAC as "agents of American Zionism."[34] Charles Bohlen, a former American ambassador to the Soviet Union, quoted Stalin as saying that "he did not know what to do" with the Jews: "I can't swallow them, I can't spit them out; they are the only group that is completely unassimilable."[35] Stalin had a number of Jews around him both officially and within his family but apparently never really liked them. The wife of his oldest son was Jewish, a situation that displeased him, and when his son was taken prisoner by the Nazis, Stalin's suspicions were aroused and he implicated his daughter-in-law.[36] The mixture of hope, anxiety, and then joyful relief among many Soviet Jews when the Jewish state was established unleashed these partially dissembled feelings and infuriated him.

The scenes in and around the Moscow Synagogue after Golda Meyerson's arrival and the visit of the Israelis to the Jewish Theater on September 16 were shocking enough for Soviet officials. But when Mrs. Meyerson raised the question of Jewish immigration with the Foreign Ministry's Middle East Department soon after her arrival, they stiffened harshly. Coming so soon after the establishment of diplomatic relations, this issue seemed a blunt challenge to a Communist state that had presumably solved its "Jewish problem." Ehrenburg's article in *Pravda* (September 21, 1948. See Chapter 22). was a clear retort to Jews both inside and outside the Soviet Union who might have had illusions about Soviet Jewish emigration and an emotional attachment to a Jewish homeland in Israel. In a reflex of stung pride and anger, the Soviet state punished its Jews for the reawakened zeal of some. The sudden, brutal liquidation of Jewish cultural life followed (see Chapter 20). Jews were warned not to slip out of the rigid corset of Soviet ideology. In grasping the signal the Soviet state itself was giving in supporting Israel, Jews found themselves utterly condemned and tainted. They had been expected to perform roles designed by the state and, instead, had surged out of control.

The first applications for emigration to Israel had reached the legation in Moscow on September 16, 1948.[37] One visitor to the Israeli legation was allowed to emigrate: a disabled war veteran from Firgana, Kazakhastan, was given his exit permit in April 1949, but thereafter other requests merely put their owners in great jeopardy. The Israeli legation, however, in view of Soviet diplomatic friendship, was unprepared for the severity of official Soviet reaction. In October, following the model of several other foreign missions, the legation had issued 150 copies of a stencilled information bulletin, including military and economic statistical material about Israel, and stressing Israel's relations with the USSR, about which Israel was very pleased. Very quickly, the cutting edge sharpened. Not only were there early indications of disapproval of Israel and its provisional government, but Soviet Jews were warned in Ehrenburg's article in *Pravda* against identifying with Israel. Feffer, like Ehrenburg, reiterated the anti-Zionist line that had been temporarily muted, and moderated his own recent enthusiasm for a Jewish state. In an article in *Einikayt* (October 19, 1948), he wrote: ". . . the sympathy of the Soviet Jews for the toiling masses of Israel does not mean that they (the Soviet Jews) consider Israel as their homeland."[38] Toward the end of 1948 a special pamphlet for party propagandists elaborated on the Zionist bourgeois nature of Israel's "ruling clique." On February 8, 1949, Deputy Foreign Minister Zorin summoned Mrs. Meyerson to discuss the legation's contact with Jews and the bulletin. He read a statement alleging that "the Israeli Legation is sending letters to Soviet citizens of Jewish nationality . . . encouraging them to leave the confines of the State, to relinquish their Soviet citizenship and to emigrate to Israel."[39] These activities, Zorin said, "are illegal and do not conform with the status of a diplomatic mission."[40]

Mrs. Meyerson vehemently denied these charges, saying that the legation "has never sought either in writing or orally to incite Soviet Jews to leave the USSR," that there had been a few isolated cases of Soviet Jews with relatives in Israel and Israelis with relatives in the Soviet Union who had requested entry permits."[41]

Molotov's wife, the Jewish Pauline Zhemchuzhina would later suffer exile because she had shown great warmth to Mrs. Meyerson personally and to the new State during a reception her husband gave in November, celebrating the Bolshevik Revolution: "May things go well with you. If all will be well with you, things will go well for Jews in the whole world."[42]

It has been suggested that Soviet disappointment with the shape of Israeli internal politics, namely the failure of a left-oriented state to form under the leadership of Mapam and/or Israeli Communists, may have caused a policy shift. Thus, the sharp anger over Israel's tilt to the United States, as expressed in an American loan. Soviet officials surely understood that Israel "depended in many ways on the United States and its Jews, particularly on the economic level,"[43] but hard-headed

Soviet policy makers are not known for their "understanding." After the first Israeli national elections in January 1949, any serious hopes that the left-wing parties would soften up Israel for Soviet penetration or influence were dashed.[44] The American loan of 100 million dollars offered a week before the elections was apparently a greater blow, although the Israeli government proposed that the USSR give Israel a similar loan, but the request, "while not refused, was indefinitely deferred." There was also an important Soviet foreign policy reappraisal in 1949 resulting in a tilt to the Arab world (see Chapter 23).

Underlying these events were two forces which made it unlikely that Israel would be considered apart from other entanglements: first, was the unfolding cooperation of the United States and Britain in international affairs; second, was the Jewish national awakening among Jews in the Soviet Union. They were interlocked with the growing Soviet attacks on Zionism and Israel in 1949, but one cannot know precisely how the forces interacted in the reshaping of Soviet policy. Professor Yaacov Ro'i has uncovered two Soviet treatises written in December 1948 which forsee Anglo-American cooperation, especially over "their common anti-Soviet policy."[45] One of the publications, Izrail Genin's *The Palestine Problem*, was highly critical of Israeli internal politics and looked to the Communist party, which has a "consistent and anti-imperialist stand" to "unify Israel's working class and progressive forces" and demonstrate "the danger of an agreement between Zionism and imperialism."[46]

The links between Israel and the West, the sudden interest of Soviet Jews in emigration, and official Soviet resentment began to converge at this time as well. Physical contact between Soviet Jews and the Israeli Legation in Moscow was forbidden, even at the synagogue. In January 1949, when the members of the legation visited the Moscow Yiddish Theater, they were accompanied by security men and no one was allowed to approach them. Synagogue officials were prevented from accepting a Jewish calendar from one of the diplomats.

However, Soviet internal repression was one matter; Soviet foreign policy quite another. Before Golda Meyerson left for a new post in April 1949, she assured Vyshinsky of Israel's intention to remain neutral vis-à-vis the two blocs and even suggested an expansion of economic relations between Israel and the Soviet Union.[47] With her successor, Mordecai Namir, there was again expression of the desire for continuation of friendly relations. Moshe Sharett, Israel's Foreign Minister, hoped to scotch all possible doubts by inviting Gromyko to Israel. The invitation did not come off, but Israel remained in good favor through all of 1949. There were occasional warnings not to work for "Anglo-American interests," and reminders of how much the Soviet Union had done for Israel, but the Soviet position on Israel's application for membership to the UN, the Arab refugee question, and the need for direct Arab-Israeli negotiations all chimed in with Israel's views.[48]

Meanwhile, Mrs. Meyerson remained in Moscow in chilling isolation for seven months. By the time she returned to Israel, she had seen at first hand the severity of the price Soviet Jews were paying for their expressions of solidarity. There were no longer any crowds at the synagogue. The Yiddish press and Jewish cultural institutions were closed down and a bitter darkness was descending. Soviet officials now momentarily dangled the appeal of a revived Birobidzhan to divert Jewish interest from Israel and recreate the notion of a Jewish homeland in the Soviet Union—a Soviet Zionism, as it were.

22

Birobidzhan Diversion and Onset of the Black Years, 1946–49

Everything has its special time. In our country policies change frequently. Our dialectical approach is dictated by life itself. What was correct yesterday may be incorrect—even criminal today."

SOVIET INVESTIGATOR

Cosmopolitanism is the gospel of so-called "world citizenship," the abandonment of allegiance to any nation whatsoever, the liquidation of the national traditions and culture of the peoples under the screen of creating a "world" culture. Cosmopolitanism is the denial of the historically evolved singularities in the development of the peoples, the denial of the national interest, national independence and state sovereignty of the peoples.

Pravda, April 7, 1949

The idea of a separate Jewish people, which is utterly untenable scientifically, is reactionary in its political implications. . . . The idea of a Jewish "nationality" is manifestly reactionary, not only when put forward by its consistent partisans (the Zionists), but also when put forward by those who try to make it agree with the ideas of social democracy (the Bundists). . . . [It] is in conflict with the interests of the Jewish proletariat, for . . . it engenders in its ranks a mood hostile to assimilation, a "ghetto" mood.

LENIN, *Iskra*, October 22, 1903

THE coming darkness was camouflaged by a seeming renewal of Birobidzhan in 1946–47, when a series of articles appeared in *Einikayt* calling once more for Jewish migration there. Correspondents of the paper were sent to Birobidzhan; the JAC sponsored meetings with potential settlers and set up a special committee to assist them.[1] The sudden revival of Birobidzhan aroused new hopes among some Jews but actually disguised a hardening Soviet Jewish policy.

During the war, there had been rumors that Jewish orphans had been evacuated to Birobidzhan. Toward the end of 1944, the government authorized the formation of *Ambijan* in the United States, to facilitate the transfer of Jewish orphans from Poland and Romania to Birobidzhan. A fund-raising campaign netted over one million roubles ($1,662,000), but only 95 orphans were brought to the area.[2] According to the Five Year Plan for 1938–42, 100,000 Jews were to have been resettled there,[3] but the war stopped all colonization and the area was declared a military zone. At the end of the war, there remained about 25,000 Jews out of a total population of 100,000. Jewish life had come to a standstill in Birobidzhan—even the *Birobidzhaner shtern* had stopped publishing.

The first sign of actual renewal after the war was a decree of the Soviet of Commissars of RSFSR of January 26, 1946 for the strengthening and development of the economy of the JAR.[4] The victory over Japan had removed the danger of the spread of war to the region, and colonization could be resumed. In March 1946, Shifra Kochina, a member of the Waldheim collective, reported that the number of Jews in collective farms and cities in Birobidzhan had decreased during the war, but that housing was now available for thousands of new settlers.[5] Between 1946 and 1948, numerous articles appeared in *Einikayt*, reporting the new settlement of Jews in Birobidzhan and their "contributions toward the creation and growth of Jewish self-government."[6] There were also long lists of decrees dealing with the establishment of trading enterprises and factories.

Various agencies adopted resolutions aimed at organizing the emigration of teachers, doctors, and construction workers to Birobidzhan, coinciding with the urgent needs of Jews who had returned to the Ukraine and Belorussia to find their homes and communities devastated. The new promotion of Birobidzhan spoke of "the consequences of this physical and spiritual destruction," and stressed that settlement would be a "free movement," that decisions would be based on "free will," even though it was well known that there was considerable pressure on Jews to migrate to Birobidzhan.[7]

In March 1946, the JAC organized special meetings in Moscow with Birobidzhan deputies, including Alexander Bakhmutsky, secretary of the Birobidzhan Regional Executive Committee of the party, and offered free passage to Jewish families, plus a per capita bonus of 300 roubles and a credit of 10,000 roubles.[8] A delegation of Birobidzhan Jews toured a number of towns and urged Jews to emigrate. By December 1946, special trains called "echelons" were taking hundreds of Jews on the long journey to Birobidzhan, the first from Vinnitsa, the second from the Crimea, and the next two from the Ukraine.[9] Each train contained forty-five to fifty cars. Many Jews were carried away by the new wave of propaganda and rushed to apply. Priority was given to "flashpoints of neo-anti-Semitism," such as Vinnitsa, Odessa, and Nikolaev; many meetings and visits were devoted to organizing and promoting emigration.[10]

These new settlers, despite their past suffering and the new rupture in their lives, adapted quickly. A large proportion went into collective and state farms and machine-tractor stations.[11] Many reports attest to the new hope for a secure Jewish future in Birobidzhan. Culturally, there was intense activity and solid—if short-lived planning. Der Nister, who was among the numerous well-known writers who went to Birobidzhan after the war, participated in these activities "with measured hope," he said, urging his colleagues to "exert themselves" and help "find a new birth of the Jewish people," as "birds feel spring tidings in their wings."[12] In the August 30, 1947 issue of *Einikayt*, he wrote that "the Soviet rulers were moved to reconsider the whole question of Birobidzhan, the question of Jewish statehood and the nationality policies of Lenin and Stalin."

Much basic work had to be redone and new projects started. Jewish education in the region, for example, had virtually disappeared. Only one Yiddish middle school was left with seventy children (as compared to 800 in 1936), housed in an old shabby house.[13] All of the others had been converted into Russian institutions. Some Yiddish was still being taught in the Yiddish Pedagogical Institute, but merely as a subject of study in a Russian milieu.[14] The Jewish writers and intellectuals kept raising the issue of Jewish education with Bakhmutsky and drew up a petition requesting elementary schools for their children.[15] Bakhmutsky was effusive and promised schools; he even promised to transfer plans for higher schools from Kiev to Birobidzhan. Kalinin's earlier fervor for Jewish national culture was recalled and his current support often mentioned.

Yiddish again appeared in administrative announcements and at meetings. An assembly hall in the town of Birobidzhan was built, seating 500 people. There were musical and literary evenings, and a festive Chanukkah celebration on December 30, 1946. Even before Yiddish journals in Moscow and Kiev were resumed, a new literary and political-economic *Almanac* was published in 1946 in Birobidzhan, to which all important writers and critics contributed. The *Birobidzhaner shtern* was revived and a Jewish publishing house started. The Yiddish and Judaica collection in the regional library was expanded. A Leningrad Jewish artist named Tshimerinoff founded a studio for art instruction and the Minsk composer Rabunsky came to reorganize the music school. Noted medical men left their posts to serve in the expanded Birobidzhan hospital. The Birobidzhan Jewish State Theater resumed and staged several new plays in 1947–48. There were ambitious plans for a Jewish university. Lively and interesting literary and musical events were presented. Jewish culture in Birobidzhan was pulsing with new life.[16] The future glowed with promise.

There was also renewed contact with Birobidzhan sponsors in the United States and American shipments of canned food, clothing, diesel motors, mechanical saws, and factory equipment were distributed enthusiastically.[17] In the city of Birobidzhan a new street was adorned with prefabricated houses bought in Holland by American contributors. In July 1948, Mikhail Levitin, chairman of the Provisional Executive of Birobidzhan, published an article in *Einikayt* which confidently summed up renewed immigration to the region.[18] The more Jewishly-oriented members of the JAC showed genuine enthusiasm for the Birobidzhan revival. Mikhoels, for example, gave Moshe Zilbershtain, the new and inexperienced chairman of the Regional Executive, fatherly advice on where to put the greatest weight: the elementary schools and top government offices.[19] The Yiddish journalist Ben Zion Goldberg had arranged with Feffer to make a trip there together to tour the region and make a film, but permission was not forthcoming although there was no formal refusal. After waiting for several weeks, Goldberg left the country confident that "if the current trend were only permitted to run another decade . . . there would be a real Jewish autonomous region, and probably a Jewish republic."[20]

Birobidzhan increasingly began to appear as a genuine refuge for Jews who wanted to live with other Jews and create a distinctive culture. The poet Israel Emiot said that "one felt at home here." During the two years of immigration, 1946–48, the rhythm of life, although not always smooth, was satisfactory.[21] Each successive contingent brought more arrivals from kolkhozes in the Ukraine and the Crimea who worked hard to create a sturdy economy.[22] Their hopes were based not only on a government-inspired promotion, but on a substantial reality.

In 1948, there were five special trains from the Ukraine and one from Samarkand. Bakhmutsky reported that the total number of newcomers was 20,000 (an exaggerated figure); another source mentions 1,770 families (about 6,100 people) in various occupational groups in the "echelons." Possibly another 500 families came on their own, making the Jewish postwar migration to Birobidzhan one of the most significant in the region's history.[23]

On October 9, 1948, a special echelon trainload, including many war veterans, arrived in Birobidzhan from Samarkand. A few days later, *Einikayt* reported that "at 8 o'clock in the morning, students and workers began assembling at the station, flowers in hand, nicely dressed, to greet the new arrivals. . . . At 9 o'clock, an orchestra began to play . . . and soon officials clustered around a podium to greet them."[24] But this was the last trainload; no more new settlers came to Birobidzhan. One month later, the bitter, bloody "cleansing" campaign against Jewish "nationalists" in Birobidzhan began (see Chapter 24).

Meanwhile, there were disquieting signs elsewhere that couldn't be clearly read at the time, but that later would be read as ominous. For example, official pressures and divisions within the JAC intensified during 1947, creating strains and widening personal hostilities. Some of these have been described by Markish's wife Esther.[25] Late in 1947, the Writers' Union secretary Alexander Fadeyev told Markish that he had been denounced before the Central Committee on charges of Zionism and Jewish bourgeois nationalism based apparently on a section in his poem "Milkhome" (War). Both Feffer and Shakhne Epshteyn had allegedly signed the denunciation. Fadeyev said the matter was extremely serious and was being referred back to the Writers' Union for recommendation to the Central Committee. The section of the poem involved dealt with the millions of Jews who had perished during the war and with the future of the Jewish people. Markish translated the material into Russian and gave it to Fadeyev who defended it before the Central Committee. (After Markish's rehabilitation in 1955, this material was censored out of the Russian edition of the work, but appears in the Yiddish.)

At the last meeting of the JAC that he attended, Markish learned that thousands of Jews who had survived the war were addressing letters to the JAC asking it to facilitate their emigration to Palestine. These letters were being forwarded to the Ministry of State Security, and according to Mrs. Markish, were "the last straw." Markish refused to have anything further to do with the Committee, and even refused to participate in the Sholem Aleikhem jubilee. For his part, Feffer played, or was given, the role of serving the regime.

In the lead article in *Einikayt* opening the year 1948,[26] Feffer put an optimistic face on Jewish as well as general affairs and looked forward to a bright future. The country had just celebrated the thirtieth anniversary of the Revolution and was at peak levels of building and development in all fields. The past year had been "a new phase in socialist democracy." Jewish workers have lived and worked hand in hand with all other workers, he declared. The upbuilding of Birobidzhan is going forward, and, although Yiddish literature and theater may not be up to earlier levels and must "raise themselves to meet new Soviet challenges," there have been admirable achievements. Feffer also hailed plans for a new Yiddish theater in Riga, a new auditorium in Birobidzhan, the broadening of work in the Cabinet of Jewish Culture under Eliahu Spivak, and ambitious plans of Der Emes Publishing House. At the same time, he emphasized the point that Soviet Jewish culture was and must remain an organic part of Soviet socialist culture. The "wise and mighty leadership" of Stalin was hailed in customarily effusive terms.

However, there were worrisome rumblings. Most shocking was the death of Shlomo Mikhoels on January 13, 1948, in a deliberately staged accident. Mikhoels and a theater critic V. Golubov-Potapov had gone to Minsk to judge some plays that were being considered for the Stalin Prize. Markish and his wife had planned to join them—in fact, they had already bought their train tickets, but at the last minute Markish received some page proofs which required immediate attention and they cancelled their trip.[27] On January 13, while Mrs. Markish was giving a French lesson in the studio of the Yiddish Theater in Moscow, she was told that "the old man is dead."[28] The following day, she and Markish went to the Belorussian Station to meet the train carrying Mikhoels' body. Two zinc caskets were removed—Golubov-Potapov, too, was killed, apparently to dispose of an embarrassing witness.

Mikhoels' corpse was taken to the Yiddish Theater, where Professor Zbarsky, who had embalmed Lenin, worked all day long trying to restore Mikhoels' crushed skull. Markish apparently had seen the effort and shouted to his wife, "Don't go up there! It's not the old man any more!" An official news bulletin said that Mikhoels had "lost his life in tragic circumstances."[29] But there was great uneasiness among Jews about those circumstances. The travesty of a magnificent state funeral and Zbarsky's skill could not allay spreading anxiety among many Soviet Jews. The death of Mikhoels was not investigated despite the suspicious circumstances under which he was killed. Beria's agents are generally implicated in the fatal accident,[30] but even if Stalin himself did not initiate the murder, he did not disapprove it. The absence of specific factual information gave rise to rumors and grave disquiet. An anonymous phone call was received at the Yiddish Theater in Moscow with the threatening message: "We have finished off your first Jew, and now comes the turn of all the rest of you."[31]

Whatever the exact facts, which may never be known, Mikhoels' death dealt a severe blow to Soviet Yiddish culture—"and that was apparently what was intended."[32] His murder was "obviously intended to do away with a public figure who had personified, since 1941, the trend toward organized Jewish communal life in the Soviet Union."[33] The loss of his wise counsel and leadership left a deep void in Soviet Jewish life and pervasive anxiety about the circumstances of his death and what it might portend.

The regime prepared a magnificent funeral in Moscow, which tens of thousands of mourners attended. There was also an outpouring of eulogies and poetic tributes, but nagging questions were not dispelled. At the time it was rumored that Mikhoels' apartment had been ransacked, and that a Jewish criminal investigator who attempted to investigate his death had "disappeared."[34] Broken threads eventually told a fuller story. Soon after his death, a Moscow-inspired story deliberately leaked to Jewish Communist circles abroad claimed that Mikhoels had been "silenced by American intelligence agents after the Soviet security services had uncovered an extensive spy ring in the USSR, operated by JDC and headed by Mikhoels"[35]—a role he allegedly assumed since his visit to America in 1943. (Later, in 1953, during the trial involving the so-called "doctors' plot," Mikhoels was posthumously charged with espionage.) Then toward the end of 1948, Benjamin Zuskin (who became director of the Jewish State Theater after Mikhoels' death) was arrested. As Ehrenburg wrote later, "everybody started wondering how Mikhoels had lost his life. . . . Now I realize that the commencement of certain events [the anti-Jewish Campaign] . . . is connected with Mikhoels' death."[36]

The elaborate funeral was an unconvincing effort to cover a deliberate official murder and may also have reflected an internal hesitancy over the future of Jewish policy, which in turn may have reflected a power struggle within the Kremlin (see Chapter 23).

Meanwhile, the anticosmopolitan campaign took on more and more an anti-Jewish tone. The avid interest Soviet Jews were exhibiting toward Israel was being watched suspiciously. During this period, too, there was a noticeable, continuous decline in the number of Jews in important party and government circles. In 1948 there were no Jews among ambassadors to key countries or among chief Soviet representatives to the UN and other international bodies.[37] They were being sent abroad mostly as technical advisers and Harrison Salisbury, the *New York Times* correspondent, noted that they were no longer being accepted for diplomatic training.

Attacks on "Jewish national exclusiveness" and "bourgeois nationalism" intensified in 1948. One particularly sharp article was by Chaim Loytsker, a Jewish literary critic in *Der shtern*, who called "For an Ideological Purification of Our Literature."[38] Loytsker denounced many Jewish authors, some for using Biblical associations such as the Burning Bush, Noah's Ark, references to the prophets, Hebraisms, "Jewish content" bordering on "bourgeois nationalism," and "narrow nationalism." For example, he attacked Hirsh Dobin for giving the hero of his story "On White Russian Soil" the name Chaim and for exaggerating his description of the courage of Jewish partisans. He also criticized the episode in which Chaim's non-Jewish friend falls in battle and Chaim asks a friend to repeat the Hebrew prayer *El Male Rakhamim* (O, God, full of compassion) after him. In the poem "In Ponary," Hirsh Osherovich is accused of placing Ezekiel on the heaps of bones at Babi Yar, Auschwitz, Maidanek, and Treblinka, and overemphasizing the "Jewishness" of his characters.

Besides these stepped-up literary attacks, there was a significant breakdown in April 1948 in Polish Jewish-JAC relations. One of the last outside contacts with the JAC may have been the one between Feffer and Hirsh Smoliar, editor of the Warsaw *Folkshtimme* at the time. In 1945–46, he and other Polish Jews had been involved in trying to win Polish government and party approval of a proposal to erect a monument commemorating the heroism and martyrdom of Polish Jewry during the Holocaust.[39] Party leaders did not oppose it but warned against the possible backlash of anti-Semitism. Thus, in 1948, Jewish leaders went ahead to prepare an international Jewish gathering for the unveiling of the monument which had been completed. Invitations were sent to Jewish communities and organizations all over the world. "Our attention," Smoliar wrote, "was focused on the Soviet Union, the country with the second-largest Jewish community. . . . All of us, whatever our party affiliations or views, hoped to see both the Jewish Antifascist Committee and Soviet Jewish combatants and partisans. . . ."

Smoliar kept in touch with the Soviet ambassador to Poland, Viktor Lebedev, to secure through him information about the members of the Soviet delegation and the date of their arrival. Smoliar was also in "constant touch by telephone with . . . Itzik Feffer, who kept on urging that we in Warsaw did everything in our power to make it possible for the delegation to come to the ceremony; all they could do in Moscow was to forward our invitation to the Central Committee of the Soviet Communist Party."

To all of Smoliar's inquiries, the Soviet ambassador had only one reply: "Be patient," promising to contact the Soviet Foreign Ministry when he learned that Communist parties from Western Europe were planning to send representatives. Finally, Smoliar was called to the Soviet embassy and told, "There will be no delegation from the Soviet Union." To Smoliar's pained questions, Lebedev hesitated and then replied: "I will tell you, but it must remain between ourselves. . . . Molotov is against the idea of sending a delegation. He thinks that a Jewish monument should not be erected before a Polish one."

Following this great disappointment, Smoliar recalled, "the mood that followed . . . was one of foreboding. We sensed that difficult times were ahead for the Jewish community in Poland too." After the commemoration, Smoliar was summoned to the party Central Committee and told of its displeasure because the inscription read that the monument had been erected by the Jewish people. What was all this about Jewishness? And where was the contribution of Poland, on whose soil the monument stood?

At this time Smoliar recalled a conversation he had had with the Belorussian Prime Minister Ponomarenko, in which he asked if Smoliar knew a man named Rapaport (this was Nathan Rapaport, who had executed the Warsaw Ghetto memorial). Smoliar replied that he was a sculptor. Ponomarenko looked at him so "intensely and triumphantly" that Smoliar warned Rapaport to leave and return to Poland as soon as possible.

No representative from the JAC had been able to go to the commemoration. Nor was a Soviet delegation permitted to attend the World Jewish Congress Assembly in August 1948 in Montreux.[40] Yet, at that very time, Feffer published an article in Einikayt[41] strongly defending Zionism and the State of Israel. In it, Feffer attacked the Congress "for not coming out more strongly in defence of the State of Israel when the War of Independence was still on"! He particularly singled out the delegations from Eastern Europe "for not pressing harder their opposition to the American and British delegations who appeared to be reluctant to condemn outright the American and British policies toward the new State of Israel." Obviously, the Soviet Union wanted to use this arena to condemn the Western "imperialists," but the irony of the situation in which old-time Communists from Eastern Europe are accusing long-time Western Zionists of being faint-hearted in their positions is certainly striking. "The State of Israel," Feffer wrote, "is no longer a monopoly of the World Jewish Congress or, for that matter, of the Zionist Organization; it is the concern of the Jewish people as a whole."[42] But that concern, in Soviet terms, would be defined and controlled by the Soviet Union. In its support for the Jewish state, it was aiming to win general as well as "progressive" Jewish support—except among Soviet Jews—and to channel its influence through the new state.[43]

The war and the immensity of Jewish suffering had turned Feffer's rejection of his Jewish past fully around. His penitence and intense feeling for the Jewish past seemed now to be turning once more toward acceptance of a Soviet opportunistic line. It is also significant that it was Feffer who had given the official account of Mikhoels' death, namely that he had been killed in an automobile accident, although later he seems to have understood that he was murdered.[44] It is not clear to what extent Feffer agreed with Einikayt's acting editor G. Zhits, who, as late as August 1948, was publishing articles which expressed the sympathy of the Soviet people and Soviet Jews for the struggling young State of Israel.[45] A month later the thunderbolt struck. Such sympathy suddenly became the equivalent of treason.

This message came in the form of an article by Ilya Ehrenburg, "On the Subject of One Letter," in Pravda, September 21, 1948.[46] Ehrenburg's article has been the subject of an ongoing controversy in which it has been alleged that he collaborated in Stalin's destruction of Jewish culture in 1948–49. The timing of the article as well as the substance have been hotly attacked by nationally minded Jews as treacherous and self-serving. But the views he expressed had already been crystallizing in the Soviet anticosmopolitan, antinationalist line and were, morever, Ehrenburg's own, and probably shared by certain other Soviet Jews as well. It should be recalled that the Jewish tragedy during the war had drawn his full-hearted sympathy. He had been working hard to publish *The Black Book* in the Soviet Union and was bitterly disappointed when publication was delayed and ultimately blocked. He had believed that Palestine must be thrown open to Jewish survivors after the war. But he was also a Soviet patriot who believed Soviet Jews had their homeland—in the Soviet Union. Many of them were being deflected from that attachment by the creation of the State of Israel, symbolized by Mrs. Meyerson's visit. The tumultuous response to her required a strong, unequivocal finishing stroke, and Ehrenburg was picked to do it.

The brief Soviet support of Jewish cultural activity and the Jewish state were no longer useful or necessary to the regime. A Jew was now required to condemn the momentary dispensation and express unequivocal loyalty to the new. Soviet Jewish feeling for the new Jewish state had passed beyond permissible limits. The earlier signs—Mikhoels' death, the harsh attacks on certain Yiddish writers, and the increasing anti-Semitism—now sharpened. Ilya Ehrenburg was selected to sound an unmistakable warning to Jews that the State insisted on a single loyalty.

According to his memoirs,[47] the editor of *Pravda* had asked him to write the article. The content does indeed clearly reject any possible "divided loyalty" on the part of Soviet Jews and reminds Soviet Jews that they are and must be loyal to Soviet Russia. The article also deals very vigorously with the anti-Semitism of the anticosmopolitan campaign and expresses the philosophy of an assimilated Jew who still has faith in Soviet communism. After describing "obscurantists" who for ages past have invented lies about Jews, claiming they were "eternally rootless" and bound together by mysterious ties, Ehrenburg writes bitterly of the isolated life of Jews in the ghettos, which had been forced upon them by "Catholic religious fanatics," and the "absorption of Jews into the common life of countries after the ghettos were thrown open." The tie among Jews, according to Ehrenburg, is the one forged by anti-Semitism: "The unspeakable atrocities committed by the German fascists, the mass murder of the Jewish population, the racial propaganda, beginning with humiliation and ending with the crematoria of Maidanek . . . created . . . the feeling of a strong common bond . . . the solidarity of the oppressed and outraged." As to Zionists, it was not they who drove Jews to Palestine, but "those anti-Semites who uprooted the Jews from their long-established homes . . ." He also recalls Lenin's attack against anti-Semitism and Stalin's pronouncement to a JTA correspondent in 1931 that anti-Semitism is a relic of cannibalism. The article deals further with the campaign of hatred against the so-called "cosmopolitans" which, "at the time, was a new form of Russian anti-Semitism." In conformity with the then current Soviet attitude toward Israel, Ehrenburg labeled it a bourgeois state and a tool of Anglo-American imperialism that was powerless to solve the Jewish problem.[48]

Against the subsequent assault on Jewish culture, there were persistent rumors that the few survivors among Jewish cultural figures who had escaped the terror, especially Ehrenburg, were suspect, that they might have been complicit in the persecution (see note 49 of present chapter). After all, it was said, they had escaped imprisonment and death. But there is no factual information whatsoever to confirm the charge; their survival was not necessarily subjectively desired by Stalin, but simply expedient.[49] Jews once more could do the nasty work of the regime, expounding a policy that would hurt many Jews and be unpopular and frightening to many others. Moreover, if the paranoid Stalin was anticipating the possibility of war with the United States,[50] where many Russian Jews had family connections, their loyalty would be divided. It is known that he was thinking of deporting Jews to Siberia at this time (see Chapter 24), but was apparently opposed in the Politburo. Then, as one seasoned journalist put it, he came to "a madman's decision: he would decapitate the leadership of the Jews—their poets, artists, scientists—and the great mass of frightened, bewildered Jews would thus be cowed. In preparation for the liquidation of the Jewish intelligentsia, a press campaign was launched on the theme that Jews were 'passportless vagabonds, cosmopolitans and gypsies without a fatherland.' "[51]

The whole truth of these wracking times may never be known, but it seems fairly certain that Ehrenburg was no Stalinist lackey. He did survive, and he was used by the regime to play a certain role, but he did not feel himself to be immune from the havoc all about him.[52]

Moreover, he seems to have been genuinely agitated by the waves of arrests and the vicious charges. He was also baffled by Stalin's sly, unpredictable contrariness,[53] which took people completely off guard and which has been described by others. Moreover, for a time beginning early in 1949, he himself was blocked from publishing. In any case, his article was an unmistakable warning to Jews in the Soviet Union that their enthusiasm for Israel was and would be highly suspect. But no one could have been prepared for the lightning strikes that soon followed.

Characteristically, the pace of the coming attacks was uneven. The last issue of *Heymland*, which had appeared regularly since the beginning of 1948, published its seventh issue in September, but it was suppressed. October passed without any dire actions, creating a false reassurance that the worst was over. Then, in the last two months of 1948, there came shattering physical assaults against Jewish culture and Jewish lives. The ambiguous signs of earlier months now became sledgehammer blows.

On November 20, the last issue of *Einikayt*, the organ of the Jewish Antifascist Committee, appeared, marking the end of the paper and of the Committee. A few weeks later, the Emes Publishing House was closed down. The staff had come to work as usual in the little old house on Ataropansky Lane and the presses were running, when, without warning, trucks filled with state security agents pulled up in front of the house, burst into the plant, and disconnected the machines.[54] The director Leib Strongin was ordered to close the operation. The December issue of the Kiev *Der shtern* was suppressed although the November issue solicited subscriptions for 1949. This journal was attacked for having been "severed from the Soviet people," from the "broad Jewish toiling masses," and for presuming to "draw a comparison between the Soviet Jew and the Jew abroad."[55]

In the last week of December, Feffer made an unexpected visit to the Yiddish Theater in Moscow. He was accompanied by Viktor Abakumov, the Minister of State Security and a loyal follower of Beria. Together they proceeded directly to Mikhoels' former office, which had temporarily been turned into a museum. They went through some papers and locked the door. A little later, young aspiring drama students who had been accepted in the theater studio school found the entrance barred.[56] On December 24, Feffer himself was arrested in his Moscow apartment. Later that evening security agents went to a hospital and siezed Zuskin, Mikhoels' successor. On January 23, 1949, David Bergelson and Leib Kvitko were arrested. Markish, who was being shadowed daily during this time, gave a briefcase of manuscripts to a relative and on the evening of January 27, seven agents came for him. When his wife Esther began to scream, one of them tried to calm her down. "Come now," he said, "no need to get excited. Our minister just wants to have a talk with your husband. Take it easy, get hold of yourself." Three hours later, four other agents holding a search warrant, barged into the apartment with an order for Markish's arrest, dated January 28. All of the shutters of the apartment were shut tight, all household items were searched, and books and papers were ripped apart.[57]

In the bathroom, one of the agents found a valise with old papers, including materials from the First Congress of Soviet Writers, a fragment of Markish's ode "To Mikhoels—Eternal Light" in Pasternak's translation, and a scenario for a film, all of which were confiscated. From time to time, one of the agents telephoned a superior saying that everything was in order. All visitors to the apartment were detained and their papers checked. In the evening, Mrs. Markish was told that three of the four rooms would be sealed up, and that if the seals were broken, she would go to prison for at least ten years. She and her son were confined to one room.

The following day rumors began to reach the family, sparked by the superintendent or caretaker's wife, reporting that Markish was an important American spy. A big sack of dollars and a radio transmitter had been found during the search, it was said. When Mrs. Markish began to make inquiries at Lefortovo prison, she found a long queue of similarly anxious relatives, including Masha, the sister of Chaim Weizmann, who had married a Russian who had been arrested for the sole reason that he was the brother-in-law of the president of Israel. Mrs. Markish was given permission to send some money to her husband in weekly installments—for which she was given receipts until February 1, 1953—five months after Markish was executed.[58] No longer able to work as a translater, Mrs. Markish began to earn some money by knitting hats, scarves, and sweaters under her maiden name and reading to the blind wife of a professor. One by one, old acquaintances drifted away.

Shortly after Markish's arrest, the Jewish Section of the Writers' Union was closed down. Alexander Bezymensky, the "Komsomol poet" summoned those Jewish writers still at large and told them that enemies of the people and traitors to the motherland had been unearthed in the Jewish Section. There followed a general meeting of the Moscow Section of the Writers' Union. Aaron Kushnirov, an officer during the war and poet whose "Mother Rachel" describing the slaughter at Babi Yar had deeply stirred Soviet Jews, was picked as the hatchet man. Yosef Kerler, a Soviet Yiddish writer who later emigrated to Israel, saw him at the time: "Kushnirov walks about like a shadow, an old broken man, no longer a military man. All of his friends have already been taken. Many younger than he have already been arrested."[59] On a chilly, rainy day, Kerler saw him near the Writers' House. "It's good to see a familiar face," he said wryly. "But why don't they come for me? I am the worst of all, and outcast." When he was called to the meeting to make charges against "enemies of the people" among the Yiddish writers, he was brought to the head table, a Communist and a Jew, and asked to tell about his close friends, the Jewish writers. He put his hand over his mouth, burst into tears, but could say nothing. The men in the room laughed loudly. Suddenly Kushnirov's body began to shake and he clutched his chest. Later that year, awaiting certain arrest, he died.[60]

During this time, Kerler himself was frequently stopped in the middle of a street and asked to show his documents. Deep inside, he said, "a mouse scraped around." He felt a great foreboding. While walking along Kropotkin Street, he came to the address of the JAC and was startled to see the doors closed. A uniformed guard surrounded the building and he was asked where he was from, where he was going, and whom he was planning to see. Did he have any direct contact with members of the JAC? Who had asked him to come? They took all of his identity papers and said that the JAC was liquidated "for the time being." When he asked about *Einikayt,* the answer was the same. "Liquidated for the time being."[61]

For months before their arrest, Markish and other writers and intellectuals had slept with bags of clothing, linens, and toilet articles near their beds, fearing and expecting the police at any moment. They scarcely dared go outside. Der Nister, who had returned from Birobidzhan, is described as sitting on a low bench, unable to read; his wife would try to comfort him with a glass of tea. One night in January, heavy ominous steps were heard. Der Nister blanched and muttered, "Thank the

Almighty. They're finally here for me."[62] Arrests also swept up Shmuel Halkin, David Hofshteyn, Yehezkel Dobrushin. Families of these writers, including small children and aged parents, were harassed, arrested, imprisoned, and exiled. Those who were not exiled were forced to live as social outcasts, without any means of support.

Sometime in June 1949, the great American singer Paul Robeson, who had lived in the Soviet Union for many years and had close friends among the Yiddish writers, revisited the country.[63] When he arrived, he was struck by the virulent campaign against "cosmopolitans" and Zionists. His son has described his visit with Feffer:

After he became politely but implacably insistent, his hosts finally arranged for . . . Feffer to come to see him. . . . He was unaccompanied and looked very well. . . . But [Robeson] quickly noticed that Feffer's comments were at variance with his gestures. . . . With the aid of a few handwritten words and phrases (later destroyed), Feffer 'told' him a terrible story in this surreptitious way. The room was bugged. Mikhoels had been murdered the year before on Stalin's personal order. Feffer was in serious trouble, and many of the most outstanding Jewish cultural figures had already been arrested. They would come for the rest of them soon. There was little hope for any of them, including Feffer (here Feffer drew his finger across his throat). And there had just been a massive purge of the Party in Leningrad[64]—like the awful days of 1937.

Both men embraced tearfully and then parted, Feffer to return to prison.

Soon afterward, Robeson performed at a concert in the largest hall in Leningrad and spoke of the enduring ties between American and Soviet Jews. As an encore he sang in Yiddish the famous songs of the Jewish partisans by Hirsh Glick, beginning "Zog nit keynmol . . ." ("Never say that you have reached the very end"). The ovation "swelled throughout the hall in waves—rising, falling, then rising again to an ever higher intensity," as if the audience were saying farewell at its end.

Throughout the summer of 1949, it was plain that the regime was bent on obliterating all signs and expressions of Jewish culture. The two Yiddish schools that had survived in Vilnius and Kaunas were closed down. All Jewish journals and papers except the nondescript two-page *Birobidzhaner shtern* were shut down. Manuscripts were confiscated or destroyed by the writers themselves in a reflex of dread. Jewish linotype machines were dismantled and Yiddish typeface destroyed. Bookshops were purged of all Jewish writing and Jewish libraries were liquidated. Jewish books disappeared, but some were withdrawn to special classified sections of public libraries to which Jews themselves had no access.[65] The historian Gilboa writes that so total was the extinguishing of Jewish culture that "Yiddish was denied even the right to continue praising Stalin, and the most patriotic works in this language were suppressed or banned."[66] Jewish phonograph records were likewise eliminated.

After Mikhoels' death an air of dread hung over the State Jewish Theater in Moscow and some of its personnel disappeared. The government subsidy was withdrawn and efforts to sell tickets were viewed with suspicion. The theater itself was closed down in November 1949, and many subscribers were subsequently arrested. Throughout 1949, all of the Jewish professional theaters which had resumed their activities after the war—in Kiev, Odessa, Kharkov, and Chernovtsy—were also shut down.

At meetings of party cells, at scientific and higher educational institutions, and at organizational gatherings of writers, artists and scientists, denunciations of Jews continued pouring out. Many were removed from the ranks of the Communist party, among whom were the theater and literary critics Yakovlev (Kholtsman), Altman, Kovarsky, Levin, Baskin, and Damin.[67] Arrests also claimed Itzik Kipnis, Chaim Loytsker, Elie Shekhtman, Hirsh Osherovich, and Nathan Zabara, and virtually the whole staff of the Ukrainian Academy's Institute for Jewish Culture.[68]

While the exact figure is not known, at least 430 Jewish writers, painters, actors, engineers, musicians, and public figures were arrested during the winter of 1948–49. Most of them perished in labor camps—as happened to Halkin and Der Nister. Special literary commissions were organized by the MGB in Kiev, Minsk, and Moscow, as well as Birobidzhan, which attacked Yiddish writers for their bourgeois nationalism, while "the MGB terrorized many writers into confessions, including Der Nister, who was said to have confessed sarcastically, 'Yes, I am the master Jewish nationalist.' "[69]

The waves of arrests and liquidations were accompanied by intensified anti-Semitic barrages, inspired or at least approved by the regime. By 1949, the campaign against "cosmopolitans" had taken on a pronounced anti-Jewish character. Cartoons began appearing showing figures with hooked noses identified as "cosmopolites without a fatherland." Newspaper articles pointed to the Jewish origin of persons charged with cosmopolitanism by adding the original Jewish names in brackets alongside their more common Russian names. Stebun became Katznelson; Martich, Finkelstein, and Volin, Katz.[70] Such practices gave sanction to popular anti-Jewish attitudes and inflamed readers to hate Jews without inhibitions. Especially virulent was a leading article in *Pravda* on January 28, 1949, which pointed to the existence of "an anti-patriotic group of theater critics" in headlines, and made the ominous suggestion of some sort of literary underground.[71] "This group," the article said, "hostile to Soviet culture, set itself the aim of vilifying the outstanding events of our literature and the best in Soviet dramaturgy."[72]

Most of the critics attacked in this group, including Abram Gurvich and Yu. (Iosif) Yuzovsky, were Jews. Ugly innuendos were directed at "the Gurviches and Yuzovskys." *Pravda* asked, "What notion could Gurvich possibly have of the national character of Soviet Russian man?" The Jewish critic Altman was denounced for hating all things Russian, the critic Levin for insulting the memory of the great poet-patriot Mayakovsky. The flood of venomous name-calling moved to the disclosure of pseudonyms to remove "the mask from the true faces" of the cosmopolitans,[73] an old and tested anti-Semitic tactic.

Some of the greatest writers, artists, and scholars of the Soviet Union were caught in the anticosmopolitan net. Akhmatova, one of Soviet Russia's great poets, had already suffered earlier punishment—she was not allowed to publish from 1922 to 1940—but had a few works published during the war. Then, after the war, when she returned to her beloved Leningrad from Tashkent, Zhdanov's fulminations against "laxity and liberalism" concentrated on her and Mikhail Zoshchenko. She was accused of being an enemy of the people and of writing in a mystical and erotic vein, and was expelled from the Writers' Union. Her colleagues treated her like a criminal and avoided her on the street. Zoshchenko was also singled out as a "cosmopolitan," "an enemy of the masses," and an example of "disintegration and decadence." All those who worked in comparative literature and studied foreign sources were condemned. The literary and artistic purges of the time punished many gifted men and women in the arts,[74] sciences, and social studies and led to absurd claims of Russian achievements and discoveries, including the notions of an obscure plant breeder T. D. Lysenko that new species could be created through changes in environment.

In this vast repression, Jewish losses were particularly heavy. The *New York Times* (May 12, 1949) conservatively estimated that 60 percent of all the intellectuals denounced were Jews. Later, a very detailed analysis of fifty-six Soviet newspapers and journals for 1948–53 puts the percentage at 90. In economics and sports, it was 80.

The sanctions against those attacked were removal from official, often prestigious, institutional posts and professional organizations, dismissals from jobs, and sudden arrests for the crime of "bourgeois nationalism," of which cosmopolitanism was a subcrime. Some Jews participated in this campaign, including the philosopher Mark Mitin, the journalist David Zaslavsky, and the orientalist Vladimir Lutsky, but as one scholar has concluded, "As it took on an ever plainer anti-Jewish character, their number declined."[75] Some attackers soon became victims themselves. Moreover, it soon became evident that the authorities wanted Jews *qua* Jews to be identified as enemies of the state.

The anti-Jewish character of the campaign was especially conspicuous in the Ukraine, Belorussia, and the Baltic republics. In the republics of Central Asia and the Caucasus, there was "little enthusiasm" and sometimes even "comparative silence" because of the relatively small number of Jews and the local concentration on the dangers of pan-Islamism, pan-Turkism, and pan-Iranism.[76] By contrast, in the other republics, especially in the Ukraine, since the anticosmopolitan campaign could not attack head-on the hated Russification, it could, with official support, attack cosmopolitans, that is, Jews, whose attitude toward Ukrainian and Belorussian culture was alleged to be "nihilistic and disparaging."[77] It was also easier to attack Jews rather than Russians and settle accounts with those Jews who still held envied positions. The atmosphere of the time was highly charged with incitement, distrust, and fear. Old grudges and personal hostilities which figured in the accusations were exploited to the full by the MGB and the courts.

And yet, could Stalin be thought of as originating, or contributing to anti-Semitism, in a society where this was considered a disease of capitalism and a criminal offense in Soviet Russia? The Soviet writer Alexander Fadeyev had told Ehrenburg at the beginning of 1949 that the campaign against "unpatriotic critics" had been launched on Stalin's instructions, but a few weeks later Stalin summoned the editors and said, "Comrades, the divulging of literary pseudonyms is inadmissible, it smells of anti-Semitism."[78] By the end of March, apparently, he had decided enough had been done and he wanted to seem to oppose the charge of anti-Semitism. Rumor ascribed the arbitrariness to those who did the persecution, while "Stalin came out of it as the one who had put a stop to it."[79] This technique of heavy camouflage and deceptiveness in Stalin's make-up has been remarked on by many writers and emigrés who have left the Soviet Union. Long after the horrors of the Black Years, many Russians, including some Jews, refused to believe that they had been due to Stalin's crimes—reactions similar to those during the purges of 1936–38. Khrushchev, too, has described Stalin's uncanny ability to disguise his own anti-Semitism, and officially rejecting it as shameful. He is described as often imitating "with an exaggerated accent the way Jews talk," possibly "a means of establishing some rapport with his Russian anti-Semitic subordinates." On the other hand, Khrushchev says that he, Stalin, "would have strangled anyone whose actions would have discredited his name, especially with something as indefensible and shameful as anti-Semitism."[80] He may have used Ehrenburg as proof against his own anti-Semitism, a token Jew who survived, whose survival would serve to counter condemnation of Soviet anti-Semitism, just as Birobidzhan, a smattering of Yiddish books, and a few touring dramatic groups have remained as tokens to refute the accusation of a culture erased.

Stalin may have disqualified himself from the taint of anti-Semitism, but the campaign rolled on. Toward the end of 1948, Jewish students began to be alarmed by the scores of expulsions from institutes. At the Faculty of Physics and Mechanics of the Polytechnical Institute in Leningrad, almost all first-year Jewish students were expelled without any explanation. "It soon became apparent," recalled one of the students, "that anti-Semitism was no longer considered to be a crime against 'communist morality.' "[81] The Komsomol dealt out mild reprimands to members who used anti-Jewish slurs.

A young student, becoming increasingly aware of anti-Semitism among his fellow students and in certain Russian writers, became absorbed and then obsessed with the question of Soviet anti-Semitism. In his "conversion" to Zionism in the late forties he learned the Hebrew alphabet but wanted a Hebrew textbook. He finally secured one published in 1880 from an elderly scholar, but as the anticosmopolitan campaign intensified, the man grew uneasy and wanted the book returned. On the phone, he did not mention the word "Hebrew" but asked for the "little book which I lent you." When they met, he said apologetically, "You understand, they're starting a campaign in the press against cosmopolitans. How will it end up? Many years ago a friend of mine said that the basic rule of life for a Jew is caution, caution."[82]

While Jewish life was being destroyed in the large Soviet centers in the West, Birobidzhan, which had experienced a brief reawakening after the war, and for which *Einikayt* held out bright prospects as late as the summer of 1948, was also struck by waves of arrests and liquidations. It will be recalled that the last echelon had left for Birobidzhan on October 9, 1948. Toward the end of the year and early 1949 waves of arrests and liquidations of institutions swept through the region. Among the resident Jewish writers arrested were Israel Emiot, Hershel Rabinkov, Buzi Miller, and Liuba Wasserman.

All Jewish institutions in Birobidzhan were closed down. The theater and several schools were given to the Communist Pioneer movement. The works of arrested writers were burned and many Yiddish books were thrown into cellars. Writers burned their manuscripts. Administrative forms and rubber stamps in Yiddish were destroyed; Yiddish typeface and typewriters were thrown into the streets. "For the second time," one survivor wrote, "Birobidzhan has become a terrible fire-trap, a target for anti-Jewish provocation. One would not wait for a third time. We began to run, run, run. . . ." Stalin's demons had to totally destroy every vestige of Jewish life. "The Jewish spirit had to disappear from the earth."[83]

Surviving schools and the Sholem Aleikhem Library, which had a rich collection of Jewish works in Yiddish and Hebrew, and the regional geographical museum were closed down. Many of the books were physically destroyed; the aged museum head Ber Slutsky, who was arrested, died in prison.[84] He and the others were charged with Jewish nationalist activity of one kind or another and conspiratorial espionage and sabotage in the service of the United States, even to the point of plotting to deliver the region into American hands, implicating the editor of the American pro-Communist paper *Morgen freiheit*, Paul Novick and the journalist Ben Zion Goldberg. Goldberg himself wrote of Birobidzhan:

The Jews there found themselves in a worse position than Jews elsewhere. They were more exposed—collected in small communities where everyone knew everyone else, and where many were involved in what could be called Jewish activity. . . . The official charge ran from artificially implanting Yiddish culture in order to impose it on the rest of the population, to treason and foreign espionage.

The Crimean plot charged against the leaders of the Jewish Anti-Fascist Committee was here turned into an indictment for seeking to detach Birobidzhan from the Soviet Union . . . and convert it into an international anti-Soviet base. . . . This was supposedly part of the treacherous plan Mikhoels brought back with him from his visit in the United States in 1943. . . .[85]

Jewish migration to Birobidzhan came to a halt, and after 1948 thousands of Jews fled, some settling in nearby Khabarovsk. It is estimated that between 1948 and 1959, the Jewish population dropped from 30,000 or so to about 14,000 (less than 9 percent of the total population).[86] Yiddish was no longer used as an administrative language and most Yiddish signs were removed. Yet the designation "Autonomous Jewish Province" remained in one of those curious Alice-in-Wonderland contradictions that was to serve Soviet propaganda interests later: the name could substitute for the reality and shout down the mounting criticism of the Soviet crushing of Jewish life. On maps and in the Soviet Constitution, there would be "proof" that Jews had full national rights. Soviet leaders were perhaps "apprehensive of some negative reactions abroad," fearing that a "drastic step could be construed as one more proof of their anti-Jewish bias."[87]

The fate of the political leadership was also sealed early in 1949, when Brakhin, in charge of propaganda in Birobidzhan, Alexander Bakhmutsky, secretary of the Regional Party Committee, and Mikhail Levitin, chairman of the Regional Executive Committee—were summoned to Moscow for a meeting of the Secretariat of the Communist party. The meeting was conducted by Georgy Malenkov, a new member of the Politburo and emerging challenger to Zhdanov, and Ponomarenko, Belorussian leader, ostensibly to hear a report from Bakhmutsky regarding the work of the party organization in the region.[88] Instead, he was harshly attacked for political failures of the region's party leadership, personally assailed, and warned to shape up. Then came the Birobidzhan regional conference, which was described as an "open anti-Semitism demonstration"[89] by an observer.

The conference[90] was held in the summer of 1949 in the Birobidzhan State Theater, which was surrounded by MGB agents in civilian clothes. Vile accusations were thrown at Bakhmutsky, Brakhin, Levitin, and Rutenberg, alleging that they had capitulated to American imperialism and had ties with the arrested Yiddish writers in Moscow and the "counterrevolutionary" JAC. (In 1952, they and four other loyal Jewish administrators of Communist policy were tried and charged with having organized a nest of spies and center for international reactionaries in Birobidzhan (see Chapter 24). After the conference, the four men had to leave Birobidzhan.[91] Gaglidze, head of the regional MGB and Beria's representative, had brought with him from Moscow to Khabarovsk a large retinue and a new party leadership. After that time, Russian was used in referring to the region (*Evreiskaya Avtonomnaya Oblast*). All posts were filled by "Russians," except for a few token posts that were filled by fully Russified or converted Jews. They knew no Yiddish and "ran from anyone who spoke Yiddish or touched a Yiddish paper."[92] Children instinctively learned to be "cautious" about their Jewish descent.[93] Jews in the region during this time (1949–50) were so terrified, they feared to touch even "approved" material. Circulation of the *Birobidzhaner shtern* fell from 4,000–5,000 to 50 or 60; toward the end of 1948 the *Birobidzhan Almanac*, with an authorized printing of 5,000 copies attracted only 40 takers; people were afraid to take copies gratis, and the *Almanac*, too, was closed down.[94]

The anticosmopolitan, anti-Jewish campaign spread through all Soviet mass media and penetrated the theater, cinema, scientific and popular culture, even wall notices at places of work. Stalin's personal interest was said to be acute.[95] Among the party and government leaders who took an active part in the campaign were Khrushchev in the Ukraine, Gusarev in Belorussia, Pelshe in Latvia, and the ministers Bolshakov and Shcherbina.[96] All areas of the arts and scholarship soon claimed their victims.[97] Today many Soviet intellectuals look back on this period—the end of 1946 to Stalin's death in March 1953—as the most arid in the entire history of the Soviet regime. For many non-Russian national figures, the purges and arrests were likewise devastating, but the national cultures they sprang from remained. For Jews, the assaults were a mortal blow. Jewish culture without a press, theater, schools, institutional center, creative artists, or culture-bearers could only be a shadow, a memory. From 1948 to 1959 not a single book in Yiddish was published in the Soviet Union.

The toll was grim: between 1936 and 1940, there had been approximately 800 Yiddish writers, journalists, critics, and editors.[98] Hundreds had perished or been imprisoned in 1948–49. About forty had fallen during the war. A number gave up writing except "for the drawer." In August 1961, when the new Yiddish magazine *Sovetish heymland* was officially permitted, 112 writers who would be contributors were listed, most of them not professional writers at all, but farmers, factory workers, and mechanics who happened to know Yiddish and were mobilized for the magazine (see Chapter 28).

Blacker years were still to follow, from 1949 to Stalin's death in 1953.

23

Power Struggles, the Cold War, Trials, and Purges, 1949–52

I weep for you with all the letters
   of the alphabet
that made your hopeful songs. I saw
   how reason spent
itself in vain for hope, how you
   strove against regret
and all the while your hearts were rent
to bits, like ragged prayer books. . . .

CHAIM GRADE,
"Elegy for the Soviet Yiddish Writers,"
translated by Cynthia Ozick

ALTHOUGH the Black Years of Soviet Jewry have generally been framed by the period 1948 to 1953, the fury of the anti-Semitic agitation and suffering were felt most sharply at the beginning and end of the period.

An understanding of the devastating onslaught against Jews and Jewish cultural life in 1948–49 can perhaps best be grasped if viewed through a dense, many-faceted prism. Not all of the lenses are clear, however, and some must be kept turning for a glimpse—intermittent at best—of the many complications crowding the field of vision. The dominant elements involve the vast changes in Soviet foreign and internal policy after the war: the emergence of the Soviet Union as a super-power in geopolitical conflict with the United States; the postwar ideological "rehabilitation" of the Soviet people, requiring a purging of "foreign influences" to which they had been subjected in various forms; the devaluation and punishment of non-Russian influences and minorities with the stigma of "bourgeois nationalism" and "cosmopolitanism"; Soviet obsession with security needs, fear of war, and revelation of "state secrets"; Stalin's personal xenophobia, anti-Semitism, imperial ambitions, and near-paranoid fear of "enemies," including Jews; a fixation on Israel as a source of divided loyalty in the consciousness of Soviet Jewry and on the perception of Jews as enemy agents with dangerous connections with the West, conjuring up images of an "international Jewish conspiracy" reminiscent of the myth of the Protocols of the Elders of Zion; and the disturbing and irksome continuation of Jewish group existence in the Soviet Union despite the massive assimilationist pressures to dissolve it.

Less clear are the specific consequences for Soviet Jews of the intricate internal power struggles and vicious political infighting among Soviet hierarchs from 1948 to Stalin's death in March 1953. However, some inferences can be drawn. Dissension and factional struggle go on behind the seeming monolithic character of Soviet totalitarianism, evident from the recurring purges, trials, and expulsions, and disappearances from public view of public figures. "The whole course of Soviet history, before, during, and since Stalin's supremacy, betrays the presence of internal strife"; the trials and purges "reflect, first and last, the presence of fierce political antagonism among the Soviet rulers."[1] Entangled in these murderous webs is the question of Stalin's own physical and mental soundness and the precise reach of his power in the last years of his life. The rivalry between Andrei Zhdanov and Georgy Malenkov was one such struggle, the outcome of which may have had the disastrous consequences we associate with the so-called "Black Years" of Soviet Jewish history (1948–53).

Zhdanov had been a member of the Politburo since 1939, a leading figure in the Leningrad and all-powerful Moscow party organizations, and, after the war, Stalin's chief lieutenant. He organized the Cominform in 1947 and masterminded the postwar ideological "rehabilitation" of Soviet citizens, including the assault on "bourgeois nationalism" and "cosmopolitanism." Zhdanov clearly wanted to "wipe out the liberal and Westernizing tendencies that had been awakened in the USSR by the wartime alliance with Britain and America." His founding of the Cominform was intended to "reverse the policy of cooperation with liberal and democratic elements"[2] that many Communist parties had carried over from the days of wartime underground resistance and create a new Communist international unity. In this, he needed the help of a number of Communist leaders in the Eastern European satellites, including Tito. For such a policy and leadership program, he "relied greatly on the support of leaders of Jewish origin" in the satellites, particularly in Czechoslovakia, where the putsch of February 1948 brought Rudolf Slansky to the position of party secretary-general—the same Slansky who was to become a purge victim in 1951–52. However, it is argued that this dependence could hardly have supported or entertained a slashing anti-Jewish campaign on the scale of the post-Zhdanov years[3] on "bourgeois nationalism" and "cosmopolitanism." In the past, Stalin had had all real and imagined opponents and potential rivals or threats to *his* power murdered. He, indeed, may have ordered the murder of Zhdanov, who died under mysterious circumstances on August 31, 1948, or he may have been murdered by agents of Malenkov.

After the purges of 1936, Malenkov emerged as a rising star in the Party Secretariat. During the war, he became known as a fiend for efficiency in charge of industrial and transport problems. In 1946 he became a member of the Politburo and emerged as Stalin's seeming choice to succeed him. But in that same year, Malenkov's leadership in the party's Central Committee was challenged. Zhdanov replaced him, only to be replaced, in turn, two years later. Thus, Zhdanov's death may have been caused by Malenkov.[4] The date of his death and subsequent events afflicting Soviet Jewry seem to reveal Malenkov as the real or chosen architect of the "Black Years." Zhdanov's death on August 31, 1948 occurred *before* the wholesale onslaught against Jewish culture and Jewish cultural leaders.[5]

After Zhdanov's death, the adjective "homeless," which had not been applied to "cosmopolitan" before 1949, was added—the kind of small verbal changes "that always have great importance in official Soviet pronouncements."[6] This left no doubt that Jews were meant. It is of significance, too, as well as considerable interest, that the period of strong support for Israel coincided with the brief period of Zhdanov's prominence. As to Mikhoels' death in January 1948, it has never been attributed to Zhdanov, but rather to Beria's agents, possibly without Stalin's knowledge.[7] His death dealt a severe blow to Jewish culture and is often interpreted as the beginning of the period of wholesale persecution. No one was punished for it and the suspicion grew that he was killed with official connivance. But which "official"? We may never know the full story, but it would appear that the guilty parties were anti-Jewish and anti-Israel, and that they were testing the political swirl to see if in *their* power struggle the murder could be used to unleash a more drastic policy. The general trend toward curtailment and shutdown of Jewish institutional life was certainly apparent at the time of Mikhoels' death, but the full power of the repressive state machinery was put to use only in the fall of 1948, after Zhdanov's death, and after Golda Meyerson's visit (see Chapter 21). It was only then that official anti-Semitic charges were expressed and promoted.[8] Malenkov was by then the central figure behind Stalin. His deep-dyed personal anti-Semitism now coincided with Stalin's magnified sense of the Jewish "danger," or exerted pressure in pushing the new line to excesses that resulted in mass, sudden arrests and a cyclone of purge trials and executions.

After Zhdanov's death, Malenkov immediately began purging the country of all Zhdanov's supporters and disciples, especially in Leningrad, and he and Beria soon emerged as the primary forces in the struggle to succeed Stalin, sometimes combining together, sometimes opposing each other.[9] It is also believed that Malenkov used anti-Semitism as a weapon to win support from important elements in the army, especially those who opposed the intrusion of secret police and political commissars in military affairs, a number of whom had been Jews. Since the days of the 1936 purge, "anti-Semitism in the army had grown fat on hatred of the NKVD. . . . A step against Jews by any party faction was therefore to be seen as a bid to the army's anti-Semites for support against the secret police."[10]

Antagonisms between the army and secret police have raged for many years in the Soviet Union and have played a significant role in the ongoing power struggles. Stalin had cunningly used non-Russian minority peoples (Letts, Poles, Jews, and then Caucasians) in his secret police forces to "narrow the risk of any spontaneous sympathy between them and the officers, who were mostly Russian."[11] (Marshal Alexander Shcherbakov, the first Russian to serve as political commissar of the army, died in 1945, and was very possibly murdered; his death was blamed on the "doctors' plot" of 1953, in which a number of Jewish doctors were implicated (see Chapter 24).

Malenkov, in contrast with older, cosmopolitan Bolsheviks who had lived for a time in Europe, worked closely with Stalin in the secretariat and saw the world almost entirely through the eyes of the Soviet espionage and party machines. He watched Stalin prepare the downfall of Trotsky, Bukharin, Zinoviev, and Kamenev and learned "how to use a campaign in favor of supposed ideological purity to crush an opponent."[12] He found a supposed heresy in dealing with Zhdanov and possibly hastened his death. In his struggle for power, Malenkov had to weaken Beria and extend his own support within the party machinery while neutralizing Soviet army opposition to the system of political commissars within the army.[13] Possibly Malenkov also had a hand in the assassination of Shcherbakov, who was head of this hated system.

Zhdanov has been described as a creative, dynamic, independent force in Stalin's inside circle, whereas Beria and Malenkov are described as "instruments" in his hands.[14] But was Stalin's tyranny complete and absolute, as it has generally been thought, after Malenkov became his heir apparent? A number of observers noticed his failing physical and mental powers and speculated on the dimensions of his power. For example, in 1948, Milovan Djilas, the well-known Yugoslavian dissident Communist, observed with astonishment the mental and physical decay in Stalin:

There was something both tragic and ugly in his senility . . . the ugly kept cropping up all the time. Though he had always enjoyed eating well, Stalin was now quite gluttonous, as though he feared that there would not be enough of the food he wanted. . . . His intellect was in even more apparent decline.[15]

Yet Djilas also noted that he was still "stubborn, sharp, suspicious whenever anyone disagreed with him. . . . Everyone paid court to him, avoiding any expression of opinion before he expressed his, and then hastening to agree with him."[16]

Another view was that in the last years of his life Stalin was

immured . . . in the Kremlin, refusing over the last twenty-five years of his life to have a look at a Soviet village; refusing to step down into a factory; refusing even to cast a glance at the Army of which he was the generalissimo; spending his life in a half-real and half-fictitious world of statistics and mendacious propaganda films . . . seeing enemies creeping at him from every nook and cranny . . . pulling the wires behind the great purge trials; personally checking and signing 383 black lists with the names of thousands of doomed Party members.[17]

He is also described as doodling wolves in red ink.

Malenkov knew apparently how to keep his hand on Stalin's pulse, and gauge how far he might go, but Stalin, despite mental lapses, kept *his* hand on the pulse of the struggle for succession, as it lurched ahead for the next four years, and blocked or destroyed any perceived threat to his power. He had not lost his cunning in tilting and pulling back complicated maneuvers. Adversaries and allies suddenly were juggled and their fates undone or saved as if by whim, sheer malice, or demonic cruelty. Against the manipulations and twists of these forces, Soviet Jews suffered as the particularly marked targets of state and party hatred, with the scene shifting from Soviet Russia itself to the satellites and then back.

The campaign against bourgeois nationalism that followed the rupture with Tito also erupted in the other Eastern European satellites and reflected Stalin's "deep suspicion of native Communist leaders and bureaucrats whose nationalist feelings or popularity . . . might cause them to follow Tito's lead."[18] These states—Czechoslovakia, Hungary, Bulgaria, Poland, and Romania—which had helped in the pro-Israel campaign, were steadily pressured to look upon Soviet socialism as the prototype for the entire Communist bloc, to reject "neutralism in foreign policy," and to adapt their economies to Soviet needs. In 1948 a number of high-ranking officials, including many Jews, were dismissed in Romania, Poland, and Hungary, and in 1949 a number of show trials began, directed against imperialist "spies" and Zionist "conspirators" and implicating leading Communists including Laszlo Rajk, Hungarian foreign minister; Traichko Kostov, veteran Bulgarian Communist leader; and Vladimir Clementis, Czech foreign minister.[19] A vehement anti-Zionist campaign caused waves of arrests among Jews who had never had any sympathy with Zionism or the state of Israel, as well as Zionists in Romania and Czechoslovakia, where Zionist activity and emigration to Israel had been quite legal.

At the beginning of 1951, a sensational "conspiracy" was uncovered, not in the government, but in the central secretariat of the party in Czechoslovakia, among the closest collaborators of the party secretary-general Rudolf Slansky, a Jew. The "conspirators" were conspicuously of Jewish origin: Otto Sling, Vitezslaw Fuchs, Hanus Lomsky-Lieben, Ruzena Dubova, and Bedrich Reycin. The accuser Vaclav Kopecky, the minister of information, had in 1947 referred to the Jewish refugees from Carpatho-Russia as "scum" and "bearded Solomons."[20] The accused were traitors and spies because they were "cosmopolitan" of "bourgeois origin." Slansky was now marked for having made the conspiracy possible, and in September 1951 he was removed from office and then arrested. On December 18, 1951, the Czech Premier Antonin Zapotocky announced that the Czech government "will tolerate no interference, be it from Washington, or London or Rome or Jerusalem." The press quickly picked up the theme and filled columns with alarms about "cosmopolitan elements" who had come from the ranks of the "Zionists" and had "no roots in the nation."[21]

These events were themselves rooted in a power struggle in the satellite countries, in which competing factions denounced each other to Stalin, and were, in turn, incited against each other by him. When the balancing act of splitting and restructuring power could no longer be played, persecution of scapegoats began, setting in motion a frenzy of accusation and reprisal. Under a familiar tempest of anti-Semitism, general discontent in the satellites and fractious Communist infighting could be swept away.

Overlapping these events were fundamental Soviet realignments in the world, including Israel and the Arab states in the Middle East. These shifts also gave impetus to the venomous attacks on Israel and Zionism which were central to the purges and trials of 1951–53. Behind these shifts an important Soviet foreign policy reappraisal took place in 1949, specifically related to the "national liberation struggle in the colonial and semi-colonial countries since the Second World War." At an important symposium held in June 1949 in Moscow, Professor Vladimir Lutsky expounded the new line, aimed at dislodging Arab dependence on Britain by providing a stimulus to Arab national movements that supported changes in the entrenched regimes and the expulsion of the British from their military position in the Arab world.[22] In Lutsky's interpretation, the value of Israel to the Soviet Union had already diminished: The United States has converted Zionist leaders into American agents and they have agreed to the "fettering conditions of an American loan," incompatible with state sovereignty.[23] Israelis were also accused of being ready to join the "aggressive Mediterranean bloc knocked together by the Anglo-American imperialists. . . . Thus, the U.N. resolution concerning the creation in Palestine of an independent, democratic Jewish state has in essence not been realized."[24] Lutsky goes on to say that whereas neither the Zionist nor Arab bourgeoisie are interested in abolishing colonial oppression in Palestine, "progressive workers in Palestine," under the leadership of the various

Communist organizations, will lead the way toward "fulfilling the fundamental tasks of the national-liberation movement."[25] By April 1950, the first official Arab voices called for closer relations with the Soviet Union.

A perceptible change came in 1950, the year of the Korean War, a time when the Soviet Union launched a wide-ranging peace offensive. It was also the year of the Tripartite Declaration by the United States, Britain, and France, which, among other matters, recognized the need of Israel and the Arab states to arm for self-defense and play a part in the defense of the area as a whole—a phrase which was interpreted by the Soviet Union to mean defense against a possible attack by her.[26] Israel could not denounce the declaration to please the Russians for she needed Western arms, but by welcoming it for her own security, "seeds of doubt—well nurtured by the Israeli Communist Party—now germinated."[27] Israel joined in the United Nations' condemnation of North Korean aggression, to Moscow's conspicuous anger and scorn. A change in relations resulted, but the new Soviet line was not openly anti-Israeli or pro-Arab. One historian has called it a policy of "passive neutrality" which lasted through 1950 and various crises in 1951,[28] including the plan to set up an Allied Middle East Command, which the Soviet Union also denounced. (Israel was never invited to join the command and the idea itself was stillborn.) Soviet reports about military bases in Israel continued. Israel's reassurances on every issue touching Soviet apprehensions did not appease them. But the Soviet Union did not take "an openly hostile attitude toward Israel."[29]

In 1952, the Soviet Union stepped up its attacks on the United States and Britain for alleged aggressive military objectives in the Middle East, but in a number of UN debates touching Israel directly, the Soviet Union was generally silent, abstaining. On February 2, Jacob Malik, the Soviet delegate to the UN, assured Abba Eban, the Israeli delegate, that the Soviet Union had not changed its policy of support for Israel. On October 20, on the thirty-fifth anniversary of the October Revolution, Ben-Gurion cabled Stalin, congratulating him and recalling with gratitude Soviet support. From time to time Israel would raise the question of Jewish emigration from the USSR. Turkey, meanwhile, had joined NATO and Iran signed a military and financial aid agreement with the United States.

At the Nineteenth Party Congress in October 1952, Stalin and Malenkov stressed the growing crisis of the capitalist and imperialist camp and the importance of newly independent countries in Asia and the Middle East. The stand of the Arab countries on a number of questions was praised. Meanwhile, the Soviet press continued to attack Israel's pro-West leanings and began to emphasize the pro-Soviet attitude of Arab countries in the UN.[30] Then, in November, the world was shocked by the show trial in Prague, with its explicitly anti-Jewish and anti-Israeli tone and substance.

Curiously, in the international areas, from 1949 to 1953, Moscow adopted a policy of strict neutrality toward Israel, but increasingly after the middle of 1951, it whipped up a vehement anti-Zionist and anti-Israel campaign internally, leading to the notorious Slansky Trial in Czechoslovakia, carefully organized by Moscow, and the so-called doctors' plot. In both cases, Israel was portrayed as an enemy of the Soviet Union and an instrument of reaction—again for domestic purposes. These incitements aroused an angry reaction in Israel. On February 9, a bomb was planted in the Soviet embassy in Tel Aviv; three days later Moscow broke off diplomatic relations with Israel.

Many observers at the time and subsequently have discerned a chilling similarity between Stalin's obsession and exploitation of the old "international Jewish conspiracy" with The Protocols of the Elders of Zion. Also, the pathological hostility and suspicion toward the United States and the bitter disappointment and sense of rejection at having been displaced in Middle East influence by the United States were reflected in countless ways. In 1951, for example, a correspondent named Khozov from the weekly *Novoye vremya* (published in many languages, including English) reported on the Israeli airline El Al. He wrote that all the crew members spoke English, that "Americans are the bosses of Israel's 'national' air line," that planned airports would not be built for internal use but would be a link in the chain of American military bases in the Mediterranean. American capitalistic investment is deplored, as is the "enslaving" 100 million dollar loan from the United States. The Tel Aviv-Haifa highway "leaves no doubt concerning its strategic character. The war planners of the Pentagon are planning to construct a strategic highway from Cairo to Constantinople." Khozov is encouraged by the existence of a Communist party and Mapam in Israel, but observes that "the ruling classes do the will of Washington and London and transform the land into a nest of imperialist intrigues."[31]

Arrests in the satellite countries began in November 1949 and various trials were started to prevent other states from taking the path of

Tito. One of the first of those arrested in Czechoslovakia was Dr. Eugene Loebl, deputy minister of foreign trade, interrogated by a Russian "adviser" in December 1949 and forced to testify against Slansky later. Dr. Loebl (who was released in 1955) described the interrogation:

> Two men were seated behind a desk; one . . . spoke Ukrainian, the other, Russian. At first, the Teachers tried to persuade me that sentence had already been passed on me. . . . They had plenty of effective means of making me talk, I was told. Then they delivered a long tirade against the Jews that would have done honor to any Gestapo man. . . .[32]

Thus, preparations for the Slansky Trial, which would catapult Israel and Zionism as the prime enemies of the Soviet Union, began in the wake of the anti-Jewish purges and liquidations in the Soviet Union itself.

In the satellite countries, emigration to Israel was drastically reduced by 1949 and subsequently completely discontinued. Soviet publications began accusing Israeli and Zionist organizations of stirring up the Jews of Eastern Europe and even of coercing them to emigrate.[33] Operations for purging the governments and party workers of Jews were energetically carried out, especially in 1951–52, sometimes by Jewish Communists themselves, like Matyas Rakosi of Hungary, in order to prove their absolute service to the new line.[34] Increasingly, Jews were becoming objects of suspicion and disloyalty because of their bourgeois origins, family ties with the West, sympathy with Israel, and similar charges. Arrests and "transfers" from "sensitive" cities to "safer" regions became commonplace. In various trials and purges, the "Zionist espionage" network was linked with American intelligence in anti-Soviet "conspiracies." It was openly hinted that Jews were apt to "spread subversive infections." Undoubtedly, the campaign served as a lightning rod to help deflect the intense dissatisfaction with sovietization in Eastern Europe, with a declining standard of living and widespread inefficiencies.[35] Scapegoats were needed for increasing exploitation and the excesses of terror. A frightening climax came during the trial of Rudolf Slansky and thirteen other defendants in Prague in November 1952. Eleven of the defendants were Jews, all having important official positions.

Rudolf Slansky, a Jew, was removed from his position as general-secretary of the Communist party of Czechoslovakia in September 1951 and arrested on charges of treason ten weeks later. The trial was accompanied by a steady drumbeat of anti-Zionist and anti-Jewish articles and editorials in the press and tirades on the radio.[36] Bearing a marked resemblance to the Moscow show trials of the thirties, there were repeated "confessions" of monstrous crimes, with defense attorneys and the court acting like prosecutors. Letters from families of the accused "demanded" punishment. All of the Jewish defendants were pointedly identified as being "from a family of merchants," the "son of a merchant and innkeeper," or "the son of a factory owner." Their "confessions" stressed their bourgeois origins and alienation from "toilers," giving the impression that there was a striking contrast between Jews, even those wrapped in Communist garb, and the true proletariat. Slansky was charged with shielding Zionist criminals, with heading a "Central Organization for Plotting Against the State," and with making contact with David Ben-Gurion, Henry Morgenthau, and other prominent Jews involved in an espionage chain which included Harry Truman, Dean Acheson, and others symbolizing American imperialism and the enslavement of Israel to the United States.

Zionism, at the trial, was attacked as "the loyal agency of American imperialism," threatening to undermine the foundations of the Czechoslovak People's Democracy. The "Central Plotters' Organization" helped Jews emigrate to Israel, involving the illegal export of large sums of money and important machinery which could have been used in the country's five year plans. Zionist sabotage, swindling, and plundering were described as the causes of low production and general economic decline. "It was clearly demonstrated," said the prosecutor, "that numerous difficulties which were often considered the side effects of our rapid reconstruction were the deliberate handiwork of these criminals. Like a thousand-armed octopus, they clove to the body of the state and sucked its blood and vitality."[37]

The day after the opening of the Slansky Trial, houses of Jews were smeared with expressions such as "Down with capitalist Jews!" The premises of the Israeli legation were pointed to as a center for espionage. A number of Jews committed suicide. Inside the courtroom, Slansky "confessed" to defending Zionism and exaggerating the danger of anti-Semitism. The court brushed aside any effort the defendants made to stress their own personal assimilation. Generally, indeed, they were known for their struggle against Zionism and Jewish national feeling.

Two Israeli citizens, Mordecai Oren and Shimon Orenstein, appeared as witnesses at the trial (later they stood trial themselves and received prison sentences) and after their release recounted the hair-raising details of their interrogation and imprisonment prior to the trial.[38] Oren "confessed" to his espionage for Britain and service as liaison between the Titoist "gang" and the traitors in Czechoslovakia. A Titoist-Jewish connection was thus established. When he was released and returned to Israel, although he was a member of the Mapam party, which had had a pro-Soviet orientation, he admitted that "anti-Semitism is possible in regimes aspiring to socialism" and that "anti-Semitism as a weapon" had not been uprooted "in the hands of the upper echelons of the country's leadership itself."[39]

During the thaw in Czechoslovakia in 1968, it was shown conclusively that the general concept of the trial in Prague had been planned in the Soviet Union and that Soviet "advisers" had prepared the materials for the prosecution. It would serve as a model for the case against the doctors, the so-called doctors' plot of early 1953 (see Chapter 24). A Czech historian K. Kaplan described the role of the Soviet advisers in the organization and staging of the trials:

The position of the Soviet advisers was quite extraordinary: Their proposals and opinions were accepted by the Minister (of Security) as well as by other officials of the Ministry, and their correctness was never questioned, while the leader of the advisers took part in conference with (President) Gottwald when security questions were involved.[40]

Interestingly enough, Kaplan believed that Stalin had advised against the trial of Slansky and that "an individual, a line, or a group of Soviet security organs, represented by Beria . . . worked on its own."[41] Or, it could conceivably have been the work of Malenkov-Beria, or Malenkov, in the throes of their struggle for power before Stalin's death.

In 1969, after the brief thaw in Czechoslovakia, in an important essay based on party archives and other documents, the author asks how it was possible to stage such trials, based on false accusations and involving innocent victims, in a country with democratic traditions. He confirms the "perfect staging of the [Slansky] trial," the "atmosphere of pogroms," and the use of "all communication media as well as psychological and police pressures to mould public opinion into complete consent with the trials."[42] The blurring of the term "Zionists" and "Jews" is also admitted:

While the terms cosmopolitanism or Zionism might have been too difficult or too general for some people, the term "of Jewish origin" used in the trials, was clear to everyone. . . .[43]

The author also acknowledges the exploitation of anti-Semitism in the trials to "divert the wrath of the workers from the Party" to Jews because of the economic unrest, including strikes in several important industrial plants.

At the end of the Prague trial, eleven of the defendants were sentenced to death, including Slansky and seven other Jews (they were executed on December 3, 1952); three were given life imprisonment. Besides Dr. Eugene Loebl and Dr. Vavro Hajdu, deputy minister of foreign affairs Artur London was spared—they were given life sentences, later commuted. London has left an important document in his book[44] which explains the process whereby wholly innocent men, committed to the Communist ideal, are forced to "confess" to fabricated crimes, after being subject to grueling, intolerable psychological and physical punishment. So contrived was the deception that for a time even London's wife believed the accusations and repudiated her husband. (London's own release came after the Hungarian and Polish parties had rehabilitated their victims, and partly in response to pressure from the French Communist party.)[45]

The meaning of the trial for the Soviet Union was described in the Moscow *New Times* of December 3, 1952:

At the trial in Prague it was incontrovertibly proved that the State of Israel has assumed the role of an international espionage center. In 1947 there was a secret conference in Washington that was attended by Truman, Acheson, David Ben-Gurion . . . and the former American Secretary of the Treasury Morgenthau. At this conference they came to an agreement . . . on the conditions on which America would support the State of Israel. One of the conditions was the espionage activity of that State in the service of the American imperialists. That is why Slansky placed Trotskyites, nationalists, and Zionists in the principal positions in the apparatus of the Central Committee of the party, the ministries of Foreign Affairs, Foreign Trade, Finance, and other departments.[46]

On January 19, 1953, in the Knesset, the Israel government declared its solidarity with Soviet Jews who

are cut off from the main body of their people, denied any contact with the State of Israel and other sections of Jewry, and are forced to bear their lot in isolation and solitude. . . . The denunciation of Zionism and the State of Israel which played so prominent a part in the Prague trial . . . and the slander . . . in Moscow . . . reveal a definite design. . . . Its purpose is to frighten the Jewish community of the Soviet Union and . . . in the States allied to it, and . . . to prepare the population of those countries for possible reprisals against the Jews.[47]

Meanwhile, inside the Soviet Union, sometime in 1952, plans were made to decimate the Jewish cultural leadership.